# Communications
# in Computer and Information Science   2576

Series Editors

Gang Li ⓘ, *School of Information Technology, Deakin University, Burwood, VIC, Australia*
Joaquim Filipe ⓘ, *Polytechnic Institute of Setúbal, Setúbal, Portugal*
Zhiwei Xu, *Chinese Academy of Sciences, Beijing, China*

**Rationale**
The CCIS series is devoted to the publication of proceedings of computer science conferences. Its aim is to efficiently disseminate original research results in informatics in printed and electronic form. While the focus is on publication of peer-reviewed full papers presenting mature work, inclusion of reviewed short papers reporting on work in progress is welcome, too. Besides globally relevant meetings with internationally representative program committees guaranteeing a strict peer-reviewing and paper selection process, conferences run by societies or of high regional or national relevance are also considered for publication.

**Topics**
The topical scope of CCIS spans the entire spectrum of informatics ranging from foundational topics in the theory of computing to information and communications science and technology and a broad variety of interdisciplinary application fields.

**Information for Volume Editors and Authors**
Publication in CCIS is free of charge. No royalties are paid, however, we offer registered conference participants temporary free access to the online version of the conference proceedings on SpringerLink (http://link.springer.com) by means of an http referrer from the conference website and/or a number of complimentary printed copies, as specified in the official acceptance email of the event.

CCIS proceedings can be published in time for distribution at conferences or as postproceedings, and delivered in the form of printed books and/or electronically as USBs and/or e-content licenses for accessing proceedings at SpringerLink. Furthermore, CCIS proceedings are included in the CCIS electronic book series hosted in the SpringerLink digital library at http://link.springer.com/bookseries/7899. Conferences publishing in CCIS are allowed to use Online Conference Service (OCS) for managing the whole proceedings lifecycle (from submission and reviewing to preparing for publication) free of charge.

**Publication process**
The language of publication is exclusively English. Authors publishing in CCIS have to sign the Springer CCIS copyright transfer form, however, they are free to use their material published in CCIS for substantially changed, more elaborate subsequent publications elsewhere. For the preparation of the camera-ready papers/files, authors have to strictly adhere to the Springer CCIS Authors' Instructions and are strongly encouraged to use the CCIS LaTeX style files or templates.

**Abstracting/Indexing**
CCIS is abstracted/indexed in DBLP, Google Scholar, EI-Compendex, Mathematical Reviews, SCImago, Scopus. CCIS volumes are also submitted for the inclusion in ISI Proceedings.

**How to start**
To start the evaluation of your proposal for inclusion in the CCIS series, please send an e-mail to ccis@springer.com.

Riccardo Guidotti · Ute Schmid · Luca Longo
Editors

# Explainable Artificial Intelligence

Third World Conference, xAI 2025
Istanbul, Turkey, July 9–11, 2025
Proceedings, Part I

*Editors*
Riccardo Guidotti
University of Pisa
Pisa, Italy

Ute Schmid
University of Bamberg
Bamberg, Germany

Luca Longo
Technological University Dublin
Dublin, Ireland

ISSN 1865-0929           ISSN 1865-0937 (electronic)
Communications in Computer and Information Science
ISBN 978-3-032-08316-6      ISBN 978-3-032-08317-3 (eBook)
https://doi.org/10.1007/978-3-032-08317-3

© The Editor(s) (if applicable) and The Author(s), under exclusive license
to Springer Nature Switzerland AG 2026. This book is an open access publication.

**Open Access** This book is licensed under the terms of the Creative Commons Attribution 4.0 International License (http://creativecommons.org/licenses/by/4.0/), which permits use, sharing, adaptation, distribution and reproduction in any medium or format, as long as you give appropriate credit to the original author(s) and the source, provide a link to the Creative Commons license and indicate if changes were made.
The images or other third party material in this book are included in the book's Creative Commons license, unless indicated otherwise in a credit line to the material. If material is not included in the book's Creative Commons license and your intended use is not permitted by statutory regulation or exceeds the permitted use, you will need to obtain permission directly from the copyright holder.
The use of general descriptive names, registered names, trademarks, service marks, etc. in this publication does not imply, even in the absence of a specific statement, that such names are exempt from the relevant protective laws and regulations and therefore free for general use.
The publisher, the authors and the editors are safe to assume that the advice and information in this book are believed to be true and accurate at the date of publication. Neither the publisher nor the authors or the editors give a warranty, expressed or implied, with respect to the material contained herein or for any errors or omissions that may have been made. The publisher remains neutral with regard to jurisdictional claims in published maps and institutional affiliations.

This Springer imprint is published by the registered company Springer Nature Switzerland AG
The registered company address is: Gewerbestrasse 11, 6330 Cham, Switzerland

If disposing of this product, please recycle the paper.

# Preface

Over the last decade, Explainable Artificial Intelligence (XAI) has developed into an ever-growing research field dedicated to approaches that make AI systems—especially those based on machine-learned black box models—more transparent, interpretable, and comprehensible to humans. The demand for XAI methods rises with the growing number of application areas for AI methods, from image-based medical diagnostics to personalised recommenders to scientific discovery. In the context of the European AI Act, requirements for trustworthy AI systems have been defined, including human agency and oversight, robustness, fairness, and transparency. Trustworthiness is crucial for critical application domains, such as healthcare, industrial production, and finance. XAI methods can help meet these requirements.

A growing variety of XAI methods has emerged over the last decade. Initially, a strong focus has been placed on feature relevance methods for classification models applied to images and tabular data. These methods are beneficial for model developers to assess the quality of learned models, particularly in addressing issues such as overfitting to training data or unwanted biases. Soon, the importance of non-expert users of AI systems was recognised, especially professionals in the respective application domain of an AI system and end-users who interact with AI systems in a private context. Consequently, the need for XAI methods that consider the specific information needs of these user groups has been recognised. This has resulted in a rich set of XAI methods, including counterfactual or contrastive explanations, prototype-based explanations, and concept-based explanations. Furthermore, it has been recognised that XAI must be an interdisciplinary endeavour to consider the cognitive demands of the explainees and design helpful human-AI interfaces.

While most XAI research has focused on local, post-hoc explanations for classifiers, XAI methods have expanded to unsupervised learning and generative AI approaches. Additionally, methods for explaining inherently interpretable AI models and providing global explanations are investigated. Methods of explanatory interactive learning broaden the scope of XAI research, shifting from explanation to understanding and revision. Over recent years, the need to systematically evaluate XAI methods has been recognised. To support understanding the output of a model, an explanation needs to be faithful concerning its inferential mechanisms.

To bring together the growing number of researchers dedicated to developing and evaluating XAI methods, the World Conference of Explainable Artificial Intelligence (xAI) was established in 2023. This conference aims to connect researchers from AI, computer science, cognitive science, human-computer interaction, social sciences, law, philosophy, and practitioners from all continents to share and discuss knowledge, new perspectives, experiences, and innovations in XAI. The Third World Conference on Explainable Artificial Intelligence (xAI 2025) took place in Istanbul, Turkey, from July 9 to 11, 2025. It attracted 224 submissions worldwide for the main track, as well as over

60 submissions for the late-breaking work and demo tracks. The conference also had a doctoral consortium, and 14 doctoral proposals were accepted.

Split over five volumes, the proceedings aggregate the best contributions received and presented at xAI 2025, describing recent approaches, methods, and techniques for explainability. The acceptance rate has been roughly 40 per cent, with 96 accepted papers for the main track. The accepted contributions were selected through a rigorous, single-blind peer-review process. Each article received at least three reviews, with an average of four reviews per paper, from more than 300 scholars in academia and industry. All accepted research contributions are included in these proceedings and their authors were invited to give oral presentations.

Several thematic sessions were organised, each proposed and chaired by various researchers. A parallel track was organised for work in progress, specifically preliminary novel research studies relevant to xAI, which were presented as posters during the event. A demo track was held, where researchers from academia and industry presented their software prototypes, focusing on explainability or real-world applications of explainable AI-based systems. A doctoral consortium was organised, with lecturers for PhD scholars who submitted their doctoral proposals on future research in XAI. Finally, two panel discussions were organised with renowned scholars in XAI, offering multidisciplinary views while inspiring the attendees with tangible recommendations to tackle challenges toward designing responsible, trustworthy AI-based technologies through explainable AI.

We would like to thank the volunteers who helped in the xAI 2025 organising committee, our local chair, Berrin Yanikoglu, and Pınar Karadayı Ataş. Thank you to the doctoral consortium chairs, Przemysław Biecek and Sławomir Nowarczyk, and the late-breaking work and demo chair Gitta Kutyniok. Also, a special thank you goes to Wojciech Samek, the keynote speaker for xAI 2025. A word of appreciation goes to the proposers of the special tracks and those who chaired them during the conference, and to all the senior chairs, including Charlie Abela, Christopher Anders, Omran Ayoub, Pietro Barbiero, Przemysław Biecek, Enrico Ferrari, Pascal Friederich, Francesco Giannini, Paolo Giudici, Julia Herbinger, Verena Klös, Tuwe Löfström, Gianmarco Mengaldo, Maurizio Mongelli, Anna Monreale, Grégoire Montavon, Francesca Naretto, Ann Nowe, Ruairi O'Reilly, Roberto Pellungrini, Alan Perotti, Salvatore Rinzivillo, Christin Seifert, Francesco Sovrano, Lenka Tětková, Giulia Vilone, Philipp Wintersberger, and Bartosz Zieliński. A word of appreciation goes to all the moderators and panellists of the two engaging sessions "Integrating XAI in industry processes challenges for responsible AI" and "From Explanations to Impact". Special thanks go to the researchers and practitioners who submitted their work, the various program committee members who provided valuable feedback during the peer-review process, and all who attended the event, making it a fantastic networking opportunity to share findings and learn from one another as a community.

July 2025

Riccardo Guidotti
Ute Schmid
Luca Longo

# Organization

## Programme Committee Chairs

Riccardo Guidotti — University of Pisa, Italy
Ute Schmid — University of Bamberg, Germany

## Doctoral Consortium Chairs

Przemysław Biecek — Warsaw University of Technology, Poland
Slawomir Nowarczyk — Halmstad University, Sweden

## Late-Breaking Work and Demo Chair

Gitta Kutyniok — LMU Munich, Germany

## Local Chairs

Berrin Yanikoglu — Sabancı University, Turkey
Pınar Karadayı Ataş — Istanbul Arel University, Turkey

## General Chair

Luca Longo — Technological University Dublin, Ireland

## Steering Committee

Sebastian Lapuschkin — Fraunhofer Heinrich Hertz Institute, Germany
Paolo Giudici — University of Pavia, Italy
Luca Longo — Technological University Dublin, Ireland
Christin Seifert — University of Marburg, Germany
Grégoire Montavon — Freie Universität Berlin, Germany

## Programme Committee

| | |
|---|---|
| Ad Feelders | Utrecht University, Netherlands |
| Adrian Byrne | CeADAR UCD/Idiro Analytics, Ireland |
| Alan Perotti | CENTAI Institute, Italy |
| Alberto Fernández | University of Granada, Spain |
| Alberto Freitas | University of Porto, Portugal |
| Alberto Tonda | INRAE, France |
| Alessandro Antonucci | IDSIA, Switzerland |
| Alessandro Renda | Università degli Studi di Firenze, Italy |
| Alex Freitas | University of Kent, UK |
| Alexander Schulz | Bielefeld University, Germany |
| Alexandros Doumanoglou | Information Technologies Institute, Greece |
| Amparo Alonso-Betanzos | University of A Coruña, Spain |
| André Artelt | Bielefeld University, Germany |
| André Panisson | CENTAI Institute, Italy |
| Andrea Apicella | University of Naples Federico II, Italy |
| Andrea Campagner | Università degli Studi di Milano-Bicocca, Italy |
| Andrea Passerini | University of Trento, Italy |
| Andrea Pazienza | NTT DATA Italia SpA & A3K Srl, Italy |
| Andrea Pugnana | University of Pisa, Italy |
| Andreas Holzinger | University of Natural Resources and Life Sciences, Vienna, Austria |
| Andreas Theissler | Aalen University of Applied Sciences, Germany |
| Andres Paez | Universidad de los Andes, Colombia |
| Andrew Lensen | Victoria University of Wellington, New Zealand |
| Angela Lombardi | Politecnico di Bari, Italy |
| Angelica Liguori | ICAR-CNR, Italy |
| Ann Nowe | Vrije Universiteit Brussel, Belgium |
| Anna Monreale | University of Pisa, Italy |
| Annalisa Appice | Università degli Studi di Bari Aldo Moro, Italy |
| Antonio Mastropietro | Università di Pisa, Italy |
| Antonio Moreno | Universitat Rovira i Virgili, Spain |
| Antonio Jesús Banegas-Luna | Universidad Católica de Murcia, Spain |
| Anurag Koul | Microsoft Research, USA |
| Arianna Agosto | University of Pavia, Italy |
| Aris Anagnostopoulos | Sapienza University of Rome, Italy |
| Astrid Rakow | German Aerospace Center (DLR) e.V., Germany |
| Athanasios Voulodimos | University of West Attica, Greece |
| Autilia Vitiello | University of Naples Federico II, Italy |
| Axel-Cyrille Ngonga Ngomo | Paderborn University, Germany |
| Barbara Hammer | Bielefeld University, Germany |

| | |
|---|---|
| Bartosz Zieliński | Jagiellonian University, Poland |
| Benoît Frénay | Université de Namur, Belgium |
| Bernard Zenko | Jožef Stefan Institute, Slovenia |
| Bettina Finzel | Otto-Friedrich-Universität Bamberg, Germany |
| Björn-Hergen Laabs | Universität zu Lübeck, Germany |
| Bruno Martins | INESC-ID - Instituto Superior Técnico, University of Lisbon, Portugal |
| Bruno Veloso | University of Porto & LIAAD - INESC TEC, Portugal |
| Carlo Metta | University of Florence, Italy |
| Carlos Soares | University of Porto, Portugal |
| Caroline Petitjean | Université de Rouen - LITIS EA 4108, France |
| Carsten Schulte | University of Paderborn, Germany |
| Caterina Senette | IIT-CNR, Italy |
| Cèsar Ferri | Universitat Politècnica de València, Spain |
| Charlie Abela | University of Malta, Malta |
| Chiara Renso | ISTI-CNR Pisa, Italy |
| Chirag Agarwal | University of Illinois Chicago, USA |
| Christian Lovis | University Hospitals of Geneva, Switzerland |
| Christin Seifert | University of Marburg, Germany |
| Christoph Schommer | University of Luxembourg, Luxembourg |
| Christophe Labreuche | Thales R&T, France |
| Christopher Anders | Technische Universität Berlin, Germany |
| Christos Dimitrakakis | University of Neuchâtel, Switzerland |
| Ciara Heavin | University College Cork, Ireland |
| Clemens Dubslaff | Eindhoven University of Technology, Netherlands |
| Corrado Mencar | Università degli Studi di Bari Aldo Moro, Italy |
| Damiano Verda | Rulex Innovation Labs Srl, Italy |
| Dariusz Brzezinski | Poznań University of Technology, Poland |
| Dave Braines | IBM United Kingdom Ltd., UK |
| David Leake | Indiana University, USA |
| David H. Glass | University of Ulster, UK |
| Diego Borro | CEIT and University of Navarra, Spain |
| Dino Ienco | IRSTEA, France |
| Domenico Talia | University of Calabria, Italy |
| Donato Malerba | Università degli Studi di Bari Aldo Moro, Italy |
| Duarte Folgado | Associação Fraunhofer Portugal Research, Portugal |
| Edel Garcia | CCG, Portugal |
| Eliana Pastor | Politecnico di Torino, Italy |
| Elio Masciari | University of Naples Federico II, Italy |
| Elvio Gilberto Amparore | Università di Torino, Italy |

| | |
|---|---|
| Emmanuel Müller | TU Dortmund University, Germany |
| Enea Parimbelli | University of Pavia, Italy |
| Enrico Ferrari | Rulex Innovation Labs Srl, Italy |
| Erasmo Purificato | Joint Research Centre, European Commission, Italy |
| Fabian Fumagalli | Bielefeld University, Germany |
| Fabio Fassetti | University of Calabria, Italy |
| Fabrizio Angiulli | University of Calabria, Italy |
| Fabrizio Marozzo | University of Calabria, Italy |
| Federico Cabitza | Università degli Studi di Milano-Bicocca, Italy |
| Florije Ismaili | South East European University, North Macedonia |
| Floris Bex | Utrecht University, Netherlands |
| Francesca Naretto | Scuola Normale Superiore, Italy |
| Francesco Flammini | University of Florence, Italy |
| Francesco Giannini | Scuola Normale Superiore, Italy |
| Francesco Guerra | Università di Modena e Reggio Emilia, Italy |
| Francesco Marcelloni | Università di Pisa, Italy |
| Francesco Sovrano | University of Zurich, Switzerland |
| Francesco Spinnato | University of Pisa, Italy |
| Françoise Fessant | Orange Labs, France |
| Frederic Jurie | University of Caen Normandie, France |
| Gabriella Casalino | Università degli Studi di Bari Aldo Moro, Italy |
| Ganna Grynova | University of Birmingham, UK |
| Georgiana Ifrim | University College Dublin, Ireland |
| Gesina Schwalbe | University of Lübeck, Germany |
| Gianmarco Mengaldo | National University of Singapore, Singapore |
| Giovanna Dimitri | University of Siena, Italy |
| Giovanni Ciatto | University of Bologna, Italy |
| Giulia Vilone | Technological University Dublin, Ireland |
| Giulio Rossetti | KDD Lab ISTI-CNR, Italy |
| Giuseppe Casalicchio | Ludwig-Maximilians-Universität München, Germany |
| Giuseppe Manco | ICAR-CNR, Italy |
| Giuseppe Marra | KU Leuven, Belgium |
| Gizem Gezici | Scuola Normale Superiore, Italy |
| Gjergji Kasneci | Technical University of Munich, Germany |
| Grégoire Montavon | Freie Universität Berlin, Germany |
| Grzegorz J. Nalepa | Jagiellonian University, Poland |
| Guido Bologna | University of Applied Sciences and Arts of Western Switzerland, Switzerland |
| Hamed Ayoobi | Imperial College London, UK |

| | |
|---|---|
| Heike Buhl | Paderborn University, Germany |
| Hendrik Baier | Eindhoven University of Technology, Netherlands |
| Henning Müller | HES-SO and University of Geneva, Switzerland |
| Henrik Boström | KTH Royal Institute of Technology, Sweden |
| Henrique Lopes Cardoso | University of Porto, Portugal |
| Heta Gandhi | Nurix Therapeutics, USA |
| Howard Hamilton | University of Regina, Canada |
| Ilir Jusufi | Blekinge Institute of Technology, Sweden |
| Iordanis Koutsopoulos | Athens University of Economics and Business, Greece |
| Isacco Beretta | Università di Pisa, Italy |
| Isel Grau | Eindhoven University of Technology, Netherlands |
| Jaesik Choi | Korea Advanced Institute of Science and Technology, South Korea |
| Jan Arne Telle | University of Bergen, Norway |
| Jane Courtney | Technological University Dublin, Ireland |
| Jaromir Savelka | Carnegie Mellon University, USA |
| Jasper S. van der Waa | TNO, Netherlands |
| Jaumin Ajdari | South East European University, North Macedonia |
| Jenny Benois-Pineau | LaBRI Université de Bordeaux, CNRS, France |
| Jérôme Guzzi | IDSIA, Switzerland |
| Jerzy Stefanowski | Poznań University of Technology, Poland |
| Jesús Alcalá-Fdez | University of Granada, Spain |
| João Gama | Porto University, Portugal |
| Jörg Hoffmann | Saarland University, Germany |
| Johannes Fürnkranz | Johannes Kepler University Linz, Austria |
| Johannes Langer | University of Bamberg, Germany |
| John Gilligan | Technological University Dublin, Ireland |
| John Lawrence | University of Dundee, UK |
| Jonathan Ben-Naim | Institut de Recherche en Informatique de Toulouse (IRIT-CNRS), France |
| Jonathan Dunne | IBM, Ireland |
| Jose Juarez | Universidad de Murcia, Spain |
| Jose M. Molina | Universidad Carlos III de Madrid, Spain |
| Jose Paulo Marques dos Santos | University of Maia, Portugal |
| Josep Domingo-Ferrer | Universitat Rovira i Virgili, Spain |
| Juan Corchado | University of Salamanca, Spain |
| Juan A. Recio-Garcia | Universidad Complutense de Madrid, Spain |
| Julia Herbinger | Ludwig-Maximilians-Universität München, Germany |
| Julien Delaunay | Université Rennes, France |

| | |
|---|---|
| Juri Belikov | Tallinn University of Technology, Estonia |
| Kary Främling | Umeå University, Sweden |
| Katharina Rohlfing | University of Paderborn, Germany |
| Katharina Weitz | Fraunhofer Heinrich Hertz Institute, Germany |
| Kirsten Thommes | Padeborn University, Germany |
| Konstantinos Makantasis | University of Malta, Malta |
| Kristoffer Wickstrøm | UiT The Arctic University of Norway, Norway |
| Larisa Soldatova | Goldsmiths, University of London, UK |
| Lars Kai Hansen | Technical University of Denmark, Denmark |
| Lenka Tětková | Technical University of Denmark, Denmark |
| Luca Ferragina | University of Calabria, Italy |
| Luca Oneto | University of Genoa, Italy |
| Lucas Rizzo | Technological University Dublin, Ireland |
| Lucie Charlotte Magister | University of Cambridge, UK |
| Luis Galárraga | Inria, France |
| Luis Macedo | University of Coimbra, Portugal |
| Luís Rosado | Fraunhofer Portugal AICOS, Portugal |
| Maguelonne Teisseire | Irstea - UMR Tetis, France |
| Malika Bendechache | University of Galway, Ireland |
| Manuel Mazzara | Innopolis University, Russia |
| Marcelo G. Manzato | University of São Paulo, Brazil |
| Marcilio De Souto | LIFO/University of Orléans, France |
| Marcin Luckner | Warsaw University of Technology, Poland |
| Marco Baioletti | Università degli Studi di Perugia, Italy |
| Marco Podda | University of Pisa, Italy |
| Marco Polignano | Università degli Studi di Bari Aldo Moro, Italy |
| Maria Kaselimi | National Technical University of Athens, Greece |
| Maria Riveiro | Jönköping University, Sweden |
| Marija Bezbradica | Dublin City University, Ireland |
| Mario Brcic | University of Zagreb, Croatia |
| Mario Giovanni C. A. Cimino | University of Pisa, Italy |
| Mark Hall | Airbus, UK |
| Markus Löcher | Berlin School of Economics and Law, Germany |
| Marta Marchiori Manerba | Università di Pisa, Italy |
| Martin Atzmueller | Osnabrück University, Germany |
| Martin Gjoreski | Università della Svizzera italiana, Switzerland |
| Martin Holeňa | Czech Academy of Sciences, Czechia |
| Martin Jullum | Norwegian Computing Center, Norway |
| Marvin Wright | Leibniz Institute for Prevention Research and Epidemiology - BIPS & University of Bremen, Germany |
| Massimo Guarascio | ICAR-CNR, Italy |

| | |
|---|---|
| Mathieu Roche | Cirad, TETIS, France |
| Mattia Cerrato | Johannes Gutenberg University Mainz, Germany |
| Mattia Setzu | University of Pisa, Italy |
| Maurizio Mongelli | CNR-IEIIT, Italy |
| Mauro Dragoni | Fondazione Bruno Kessler, Italy |
| Md Shajalal | University of Siegen, Germany |
| Megha Khosla | Delft University of Technology, Netherlands |
| Meiyi Ma | Vanderbilt University, USA |
| Melinda Gervasio | SRI International, USA |
| Mexhid Ferati | Linnaeus University, Sweden |
| Michail Mamalakis | University of Cambridge, UK |
| Michelangelo Ceci | Università degli Studi di Bari Aldo Moro, Italy |
| Miguel Couceiro | Inria, France |
| Miguel A. Gutiérrez-Naranjo | University of Seville, Spain |
| Miguel Angel Patricio | Universidad Carlos III de Madrid, Spain |
| Mirna Saad | Scuola Universitaria Professionale della Svizzera Italiana, Switzerland |
| Myra Spiliopoulou | Otto von Guericke University Magdeburg, Germany |
| Nick Bassiliades | Aristotle University of Thessaloniki, Greece |
| Nicolas Boutry | EPITA Research Laboratory (LRE), Le Kremlin-Bicêtre, France |
| Niki van Stein | Leiden University, Netherlands |
| Nikolay Tcholtchev | Fraunhofer FOKUS, Germany |
| Nikos Deligiannis | Vrije Universiteit Brussel, Netherlands |
| Nikos Karacapilidis | University of Patras, Greece |
| Nirmalie Wiratunga | Robert Gordon University, UK |
| Nuno Silva | INESC TEC & ISEP - IPP, Portugal |
| Oliver Eberle | Technische Universität Berlin, Germany |
| Oliver Ray | University of Bristol, UK |
| Omran Ayoub | Scuola Universitaria Professionale della Svizzera Italiana, Switzerland |
| Özgür Lütfü Özcep | University of Hamburg, Germany |
| Pance Panov | Jožef Stefan Institute, Slovenia |
| Paola Cerchiello | University of Pavia, Italy |
| Paolo Giudici | University of Pavia, Italy |
| Paolo Pagnottoni | University of Insubria, Italy |
| Paolo Soda | Umeå University, Sweden |
| Pascal Friederich | Karlsruhe Institute of Technology, Germany |
| Pascal Germain | Inria, France |
| Paulo Cortez | University of Minho, Portugal |
| Paulo Lisboa | Liverpool John Moores University, UK |

| | |
|---|---|
| Paulo Novais | University of Minho, Portugal |
| Pedro Sequeira | SRI International, USA |
| Peter Kieseberg | St. Pölten University of Applied Sciences, Austria |
| Peter Vamplew | Federation University Australia, Australia |
| Philipp Cimiano | Bielefeld University, Germany |
| Prasanna Balaprakash | Oak Ridge National Laboratory, USA |
| Przemysław Biecek | Polish Academy of Sciences, University of Wrocław, Poland |
| Renato De Leone | Università di Camerino, Italy |
| Ricardo Prudêncio | Universidade Federal de Pernambuco, Brazil |
| Riccardo Cantini | University of Calabria, Italy |
| Richard Jiang | Lancaster University, UK |
| Rita P. Ribeiro | University of Porto, Portugal |
| Rob Brennan | University College Dublin, Ireland |
| Roberta Calegari | Alma Mater Studiorum–Università di Bologna, Italy |
| Roberto Capobianco | Sapienza University of Rome, Italy |
| Roberto Interdonato | CIRAD - UMR TETIS, France |
| Roberto Pellungrini | University of Pisa, Italy |
| Roberto Prevete | University of Naples Federico II, Italy |
| Rocio Gonzalez-Diaz | University of Seville, Spain |
| Romain Bourqui | Université Bordeaux 1, Inria Bordeaux-Sud Ouest, France |
| Romain Giot | LaBRI Université de Bordeaux, CNRS, France |
| Rosa Lillo | Universidad Carlos III de Madrid, Spain |
| Rosa Meo | University of Turin, Italy |
| Rosina Weber | Drexel University, USA |
| Ruairi O'Reilly | Munster Technological University, Ireland |
| Ruben Laplaza | École Polytechnique Fédérale de Lausanne, Switzerland |
| Ruggero G. Pensa | University of Turin, Italy |
| Rui Mao | Nanyang Technological University, Singapore |
| Sabatina Criscuolo | University of Naples Federico II, Italy |
| Salvatore Greco | Politecnico di Torino, Italy |
| Salvatore Rinzivillo | ISTI-CNR Pisa, Italy |
| Salvatore Ruggieri | Università di Pisa, Italy |
| Sandra Mitrović | IDSIA, Switzerland |
| Sang Won Baae | Stevens Institute of Technology, USA |
| Santiago Quintana Amate | Airbus, UK |
| Sebastian Lapuschkin | Fraunhofer Heinrich Hertz Institute, Germany |
| Severin Kacianka | Technical University of Munich, Germany |
| Shahina Begum | Mälardalen University, Sweden |

| | |
|---|---|
| Shai Ben-David | University of Waterloo, Canada |
| Shujun Li | University of Kent, UK |
| Silvia Giordano | Scuola Universitaria Professionale della Svizzera Italiana, Switzerland |
| Simon See | Nvidia, Singapore |
| Simona Nisticò | University of Calabria, Italy |
| Simone Piaggesi | University of Bologna, Italy |
| Simone Stumpf | University of Glasgow, UK |
| Slawomir Nowaczyk | Halmstad University, Sweden |
| Sriraam Natarajan | University of Texas at Dallas, USA |
| Stefano Bistarelli | Università di Perugia, Italy |
| Stefano Mariani | Università di Modena e Reggio Emilia, Italy |
| Stefano Melacci | University of Siena, Italy |
| Stéphane Galland | Université de Technologie de Belfort-Montbéliard, France |
| Sylvio Barbon Junior | University of Trieste, Italy |
| Szymon Bobek | AGH University of Science and Technology, Poland |
| Takafumi Nakanishi | Musashino University, Japan |
| Tania Cerquitelli | Politecnico di Torino, Italy |
| Telmo Silva Filho | University of Bristol, UK |
| Teodor Chiaburu | Berliner Hochschule für Technik, Germany |
| Thach Le Nguyen | University College Dublin, Ireland |
| Thomas Guyet | Inria, France |
| Thomas Lukasiewicz | University of Oxford, UK |
| Tiago Pinto | Universidade de Trás-os-Montes e Alto Douro/INESC-TEC, Portugal |
| Tjitze Rienstra | Maastricht University, Netherlands |
| Tomáš Kliegr | Prague University of Economics and Business, Czechia |
| Tommaso Turchi | University of Pisa, Italy |
| Tran Cao Son | New Mexico State University, USA |
| Tuan Pham | Queen Mary University of London, UK |
| Tuwe Löfström | Jönköping University, Sweden |
| Udo Schlegel | University of Konstanz, Germany |
| Ulf Johansson | Jönköping University, Sweden |
| Vân Anh Huynh-Thu | University of Liège, Belgium |
| Vedran Sabol | Know-Center GmbH, Austria |
| Verena Klös | Carl von Ossietzky Universität Oldenburg, Germany |
| Vincent Andrearczyk | HES-SO, Switzerland |
| Vincenzo Moscato | University of Naples, Italy |

Vincenzo Pasquadibisceglie  Università degli Studi di Bari Aldo Moro, Italy
Weiru Liu  University of Bristol, UK
Werner Bailer  JOANNEUM Research, Austria
Wojciech Samek  Technical University of Berlin, Germany
Yazan Mualla  Université de Technologie de
 Belfort-Montbéliard, France
Zahraa S. Abdallah  University of Bristol, UK

# Contents – Part I

**Concept-Based Explainable AI**

Global Properties from Local Explanations with Concept Explanation Clusters .................................................................. 3
   *Elena Haedecke, Maram Akila, and Laura von Rueden*

From Colors to Classes: Emergence of Concepts in Vision Transformers ...... 28
   *Teresa Dorszewski, Lenka Tětková, Robert Jenssen, Lars Kai Hansen, and Kristoffer Knutsen Wickstrøm*

V-CEM: Bridging Performance and Intervenability in Concept-Based Models ........................................................................ 48
   *Francesco De Santis, Gabriele Ciravegna, Philippe Bich, Danilo Giordano, and Tania Cerquitelli*

Post-hoc Concept Disentanglement: From Correlated to Isolated Concept Representations .................................................... 68
   *Eren Erogullari, Sebastian Lapuschkin, Wojciech Samek, and Frederik Pahde*

Concept Extraction for Time Series with ECLAD-ts ....................... 90
   *Antonia Holzapfel, Andres Felipe Posada Moreno, and Sebastian Trimpe*

**Human-Centered Explainability**

A Nexus of Explainability and Anthropomorphism in AI-Chatbots ........... 115
   *Kudzai Sauka, Youssef Saou, Frederik B. I. Situmeang, and Monika Kackovic*

Comparative Explanations: Explanation Guided Decision Making for Human-in-the-Loop Preference Selection ........................... 139
   *Tanmay Chakraborty, Christian Wirth, and Christin Seifert*

Generating Rationales Based on Human Explanations for Constrained Optimization ........................................................ 162
   *Inga Ibs and Constantin A. Rothkopf*

Algorithmic Knowability: A Unified Approach to Explanations in the AI Act ................................................................. 185
   *Salvatore Sapienza and Monica Palmirani*

Predicting Satisfaction of Counterfactual Explanations from Human
Ratings of Explanatory Qualities .......................................... 210
   *Marharyta Domnich, Rasmus Moorits Veski, Julius Välja, Kadi Tulver, and Raul Vicente*

**Explainability, Privacy, and Fairness in Trustworthy AI**

Too Sure for Trust. The Paradoxical Effect of Calibrated Confidence
in Case of Uncalibrated Trust in Hybrid Decision Making ................... 233
   *Federico Cabitza, Caterina Fregosi, and Lucia Vicente*

The Impact of Concept Explanations and Interventions on Human-Machine
Collaboration ............................................................. 255
   *Jack Furby, Dan Cunnington, Dave Braines, and Alun Preece*

Leaking LoRa: An Evaluation of Password Leaks and Knowledge Storage
in Large Language Models .................................................. 281
   *Ryan Marinelli and Magnus Eckhoff*

Exploring Explainability in Federated Learning: A Comparative Study
on Brain Age Prediction ................................................... 295
   *Giuseppe Fasano, Angela Lombardi, Antonio Ferrara, Eugenio Di Sciascio, and Tommaso Di Noia*

The Dynamics of Trust in XAI: Assessing Perceived and Demonstrated
Trust Across Interaction Modes and Risk Treatments ........................ 316
   *Mohsen Abbaspour Onari, Gregor Baer, Chao Zhang, Isel Grau, Marco S. Nobile, and Yingqian Zhang*

**XAI in Healthcare**

Systematic Benchmarking of Local and Global Explainable AI Methods
for Tabular Healthcare Data ............................................... 337
   *Gizem Karagoz, Tanir Ozcelebi, and Nirvana Meratnia*

A Combination of Integrated Gradients and SRFAMap for Explaining
Neural Networks Trained with High-Order Statistical Radiomic Features ..... 359
   *Oleksandr Davydko, Vladimir Pavlov, and Luca Longo*

FAIR-MED: Bias Detection and Fairness Evaluation in Healthcare
Focused XAI .............................................................. 380
   *Katsiaryna Bahamazava and Ruairi O'Reilly*

Weakly Supervised Pixel-Level Annotation with Visual Interpretability ....... 402
 *Basma Nasir, Tehseen Zia, Muhammad Nawaz, and Catarina Moreira*

Assessing the Value of Explainable Artificial Intelligence for Magnetic
Resonance Imaging .................................................. 423
 *Giada Frasson, Matteo Rizzo, Marco Salvatore Nobile, Amalia Lupi,
 and Emilio Quaia*

**Author Index** ....................................................... 449

# Concept-Based Explainable AI

# Global Properties from Local Explanations with Concept Explanation Clusters

Elena Haedecke[1,2]( ), Maram Akila[2,3], and Laura von Rueden[2,4]

[1] University of Bonn, Bonn, Germany
elena.haedecke@fraunhofer.iais.de
[2] Fraunhofer IAIS, Sankt Augustin, Germany
[3] Lamarr Institute, Sankt Augustin, Germany
[4] Hochschule für Technik Stuttgart, Stuttgart, Germany

**Abstract.** The complexity of AI systems raises concerns about their trustworthiness. This strongly motivates effective AI assessments to appropriately evaluate and manage potential risks; yet this evaluation process is complicated by the black-box nature of these models. In particular, current explainable AI methods provide local and global insights into model behavior, but face limitations: local methods often lack context, leading to misinterpretation, while global methods oversimplify, sacrificing critical detail. To bridge this gap, we propose the Concept Explanation Clusters (CEC) method. Our methodology connects local explanations to a broader understanding of model behavior by identifying regional clusters of similar cases, where similarities are based on patterns of significant features and input data. This approach allows efficient recognition of such patterns or sub-concepts across the entire dataset. CEC thereby derives global explanations, in terms of human-understandable feature combinations, from the individual local explanations. In this paper, we present our methodology and experimental results by demonstrating the application of CEC to tabular and textual data. We show that CEC enables efficient identification of both frequent and rare decision patterns and thus enables a deeper understanding of model behavior.

**Keywords:** Trustworthy AI · Explainability · AI Assessment · Human-Centered AI

## 1 Introduction

Although AI systems offer significant benefits, often outperforming traditional methods, their complexity poses a challenge for evaluating their trustworthiness and requires detailed risk assessments to adequately manage the associated risks. Consequently, regulations like the EU AI Act [8] have been established to enforce certain practices and conformity assessments [33–35,42]. Transparency and understanding of the model are crucial, as experts and auditors need to evaluate and address the inherent AI risks across various trustworthiness dimensions.

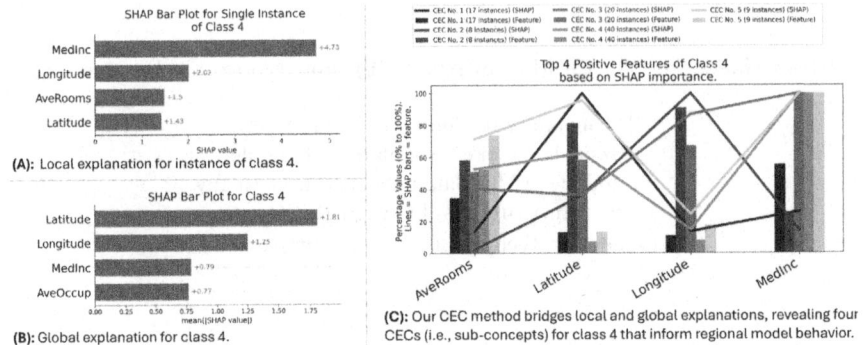

**Fig. 1. Linking local and global explanations with our Concept Explanation Clusters (CEC) method.** (A) shows a typical local explanation, where 'MedInc' is the most important feature. (B) shows the global explanation for the whole class, where other features, namely 'Latitude' and 'Longitude', are the most important. In (C) we show the five CECs identified by our method. It can be seen that the model uses five different sub-concepts for predicting class 4, which differ finely in feature values (represented by bars) and feature importance (represented by lines). The feature concept of the local explanation of (A) is reflected in the green-colored CEC, while the global explanations of (B) are rather reflected in the other CECs in (C). This example shows how CEC enables the understanding of regional model behavior. (Color figure online)

However, such assessments remain largely manual since not all parts can be automated. It is therefore crucial for human assessors to understand model behavior in various scenarios. While intrinsically interpretable models are designed to be understandable, many applications require complex, non-transparent deep neural networks (DNNs). Thus, the field of explainable AI (XAI) [3,6,12,29] has emerged to help understand the inner workings of these black box models.

Most XAI methods can be categorized into two types: (a) local methods, which provide explanations for a model's predictions for specific inputs, and (b) global methods, which describe the model's behavior across all inputs. However, each category has its own limitations: (a) local XAI methods may be misinterpreted because they lack context, and they can overwhelm human analysts with impractical explanations for each individual case [32], while (b) global XAI methods tend to offer less explanatory power due to their aggregated approach.

For example, let $X$ be the data with features $f_1, ..., f_n$ and S an explanation method that identifies $f_1$ and $f_5$ as important for prediction $p_1$ of data instance $i_1 \in X$. Without information about the actual values of $f_1$ and $f_5$, it is unclear which characteristics of the input data influenced the model's decision [1]. Additionally, one local explanation gives no information about the occurrence of this importance pattern, i.e., whether the raw data values of $i_1$ are unique or whether it is a concept that can also be found in other instances. The exact opposite is true for global explanations, where the aggregation over the entire data makes it clear which concepts occur more frequently overall and are therefore important for the model. However, this eliminates precisely those rarely occurring cases such as outliers or corner cases, the detection and investigation of which are particularly important in the context of a safety argument or risk assessment. We illustrate this exemplarily for a dataset with the task of classifying house prices (from low to high) in Fig. 1, (A) and (B).

Essentially, there is currently a lack of a human-centered connection between local and global explanations that enables auditors to conduct efficient, in-depth, and comprehensible evaluations of models. To address this gap, local explanations, that already provide in-depth information on model behavior, need to be enhanced with global properties. Promising solutions to this challenge are emerging from the field of concept-based explanations, which involve human-understandable combinations of features that illustrate model prediction strategies. However, most of these approaches rely on latent space concepts.

Therefore, we propose our method *Concept Explanation Clusters (CEC)*[1], identifying concepts by integrating local explanations with input space features. We use the local explanations as a weighting factor for the pairwise distances in the input feature space to identify regional clusters of similar cases. Each cluster contains concepts in the form of significant feature patterns that provide clues for the regional model behavior, as shown in Fig. 1(C).

Our method combines aspects of three research areas, namely (1) XAI (via local explainability), (2) data similarity (inspired by case-based reasoning), and (3) human-centered evaluation (inspired by visual analytics).

Building up on our interim results [13], this work deepens the methodology, especially in the area of human-centered evaluation, and demonstrates the applicability of CEC across diverse data domains. To this end, we present detailed results of our experiments on tabular and textual data. Furthermore, we experimentally explore the possible integration of LLMs to make the interpretation of CECs even more human-understandable and efficient.

Our paper is structured as follows: We first present a comprehensive review of related work in Sect. 2. We then describe the methodology of CEC in Sect. 3 and present the results of our experiments in Sect. 4. Lastly, we conclude in Sect. 5 with a discussion of results and an outlook to future work.

## 2 Related Work

In the following, we present related work from the three research areas that inspired us, see Fig. 2. It is interesting to note that the goals of the research

---

[1] Code is available at https://gitlab.com/pycake/concept-explanation-clusters-cec.

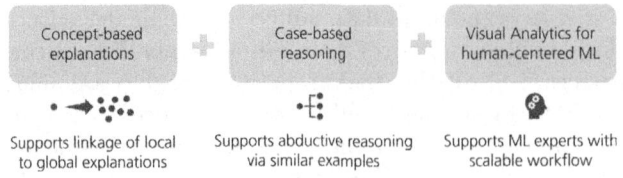

**Fig. 2.** Our CEC method combines the main aspects of the three research areas *concept-based explanations*, *case-based reasoning* and *visual analytics*.

areas "concept-based explanations" and "case-based reasoning" overlap to a large extent in that both aim to generate human-understandable explanations for the predictions of (deep) neural networks by identifying crucial feature concepts. Nevertheless, the two fields seem to have developed separately, as their respective publications seem to contain little to no references to the other field. We take advantage of this thematic overlap, and add in particular the aspects of human-centeredness and scalability from the research field of visual analytics. Finally, we briefly point out certain aspects of the human mental model regarding explanations that we considered when developing our CEC method.

### 2.1 Concept-Based Explanation

Concept-based explanation methods [7,9,20,31] aim to provide users with understandable concepts that bridge local and global views of a model's behavior. These concepts aggregate similar local explanations, offering regional context for the model's predictions. While humans and models often use the same input features for a prediction, the model can also use 'non-human' strategies to predict outcomes. Additionally, traditional explainability methods can suffer from imprecision, so concept-based approaches seek to mitigate both issues by presenting abstractions and prototypes alongside detailed local explanations.

For instance, Nauta et al. [31] recognize that the similarity perceived by humans may differ from the resemblance learned by the model. To this end, they quantify the importance of visual characteristics of ProtoPNet predictions and enhance the image-based prototypes with quantitative textual information. TCAV [20] uses the model's internal concept activation vectors (CAV) and quantifies their importance w.r.t. user-defined concepts. The combination with integrated gradients (IG) [40] additionally provides local explanations to TCAV's global quantification. ACE [11] clusters image concepts based on their distance in the activation space and uses TCAV to score their importances. ICE [44] and CRAFT [10] discover concepts with Non-Negative Matrix Factorization (NMF). Fel et al. [9] distill both methods into two fundamental steps: concept extraction and concept importance scoring and present their strategic cluster graph as visual representation of the model strategies. The approaches SpRAy [24], CRP [1] and PCX [7] leverage the explanation method layer-wise relevance propagation (LRP) to identify concepts relevant for the model's decision. As explanation, SpRAy presents clusters of the relevance maps, CRP visualizes the important areas of input images corresponding to identified concepts, and PCX identifies prototypes corresponding to prediction strategies.

These approaches primarily utilize latent space features to identify concepts based on the neural network's internal interpretations, typically using the model's last layers. However, for latent representations, two effects are possible: similar concepts may be mapped to different representations, or various input data might be viewed as similar and mapped to the same latent concept. To maintain input data reference, methods that operate directly on input data present a viable alternative, though they complicate concept aggregation. With the CEC method presented in this paper and our previous work, we aim to address precisely this research gap.

## 2.2 Case-Based Reasoning

The aim of case-based reasoning (CBR) methods [4, 18, 25] is to explain individual predictions by showing the user a similar case or a small number of similar cases as an explanation. For this purpose, a distance metric is applied to the training set, which then identifies similar cases for the so-called query case, e.g., in the simplest case using k-nearest neighbor methods. Therefore, no model is learned [4] here and accordingly CBR methods are considered naturally transparent and human-centered, as the reasoning process is very similar to that of humans [25]. In case of neural network explanations, the distance metric must be developed in relation to the model to create explanation-by-examples for the model predictions. Recent approaches employ CBR methods in a "twin-system" fashion to explain neural networks (NN), where both NN and CBR system use the same case-base [19]. To explain a single NN prediction, the CBR system searches for the most similar cases based on the learned feature weights of the NN. Similarly, [18] explain single predictions in the image domain by searching the training data for image regions with the closest match to important image regions of the input and presenting these as similar cases.

## 2.3 Visual Analytics

Visual analytics (VA) supports humans in analytical reasoning through interactive visual interfaces [5, 16], emphasizing the use of human expertise and tacit knowledge in the analysis workflow. This workflow is tailored to specific use cases and user groups, enabling users to formulate and verify hypotheses effectively. A recent focus is on VA for human-centered ML [2], integrating the human into the analysis of complex deep neural networks while ensuring both, efficiency and detail. For instance, the interactive interface ScrutinAI [14] helps model developers identify weaknesses using semantic understanding, featuring interactive plots, visualizations, and data filtering options. It includes a similarity-based image search function to explore features not captured in structured data. This so called "query by example" technique [23] is very similar to the principles of case-based reasoning and can be seen as an explorative version.

Various tools have emerged to enhance model understanding across different user groups. CheXplain [43] assists doctors in interpreting AI predictions for chest X-ray diseases by presenting similar patient cases. explAIner [41] allows users to view local and global explanations for AI model refinement. Summit [15] employs feature visualization and summarization techniques for scalable understanding of learned features. Lastly, La Rosa et al. [21] highlight the benefits of using VA and visualization techniques for model understanding and point out research gaps.

### 2.4 Human Mental Model

Presenting explanations that align with human reasoning is vital for understanding model behavior and relates to the human mental model. Explanations should utilize a comprehensible feature space and be embedded in an environment that offers supplementary information, especially for local explanations where users primarily rely on the explanation and their own knowledge [28]. AI model strategies may not always align with human considerations [22,26], risking biased hypotheses and incorrect conclusions. Common attribution methods only explain correlations without clarifying the importance of certain features, leaving users to contextualize explanations with their own knowledge [30,39]. Qi et al. [36] highlight that humans need substantial relevant information for comprehensibility and often use an exploratory attention strategy. However, it is essential to balance the quantity of information and explanation complexity to manage cognitive load, with Ramaswamy et al. [37] suggesting that explanations should use 32 concepts or fewer.

## 3 Methodology

We first introduce our general approach and subsequently, in Sect. 3.2, provide details on our two experimental setups.

### 3.1 Enhancing Local Explanations with Global Properties

Our methodology seeks to connect local explanations to a more comprehensive and efficient understanding of global models. Local explanations alone do not enable abstraction from specific feature importances to the overarching input feature concepts relevant in a broader context, cp. Fig. 1(A) and (B). Therefore, our approach provides context by identifying regional clusters of similar cases, where similarities are based on significant features and input data patterns, cp. Fig. 1(C). This allows for efficient recognition and understanding of the patterns or sub-concepts that the model utilizes for its decisions within these clusters. The method consists of three steps, as illustrated in Fig. 3:

1. Generate model predictions and local explanations regarding their predicted classes for each dataset instance.

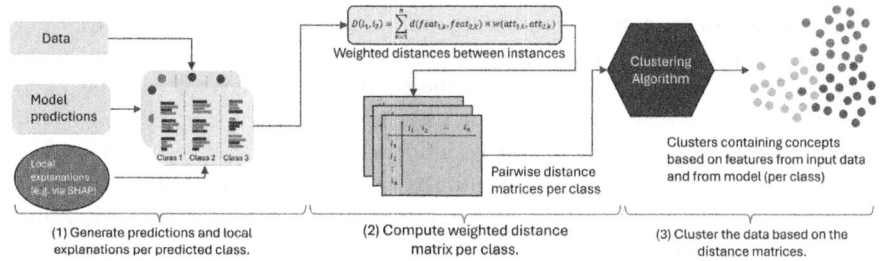

**Fig. 3. Overview of our methodology.** The process starts with generating predictions and local explanations for each class, followed by calculating pairwise distances, which are weighted based on the values and differences in feature importances. Using these distance matrices, a clustering algorithm identifies the semantic Concept Explanation Clusters (CECs). This methodology allows for the adaptation of the model, data domain, explanation method, and clustering algorithm to the specific use case.

2. Compute a weighted distance matrix for each class.
3. Cluster the data based on the distance matrix for each class.

In the **first step**, we start by constructing a comprehensive set that encompasses the input data elements, the model predictions for each element, and the local explanations linked to each prediction, e.g., local SHAP explanations. This structured representation facilitates the analysis of the relationship between input features and model predictions. By organizing the data by predicted classes, we can later identify distinct clusters and sub-concepts for each class. This classification is essential as it allows for a focused examination of the model's behavior, providing insights into how it interprets and utilizes features in the data, and sets the stage for effective analyses in the subsequent steps of the methodology.

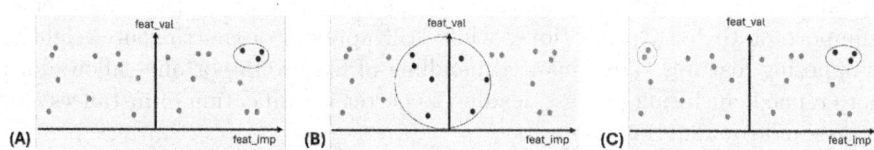

**Fig. 4. Desiderata for weighting distances.** The plots illustrate instances with different combinations of input feature values (y-axis 'feat_val') and feature importance values (x-axis 'feat_imp') and how they should be grouped into clusters. Case (A): Higher similarity for instances, that share same feature values AND have high feature importance values, i.e., slightly de-weighing the similarity of feature values. Case (B): Higher similarity for instances, that have low feature importance values, i.e., largely de-weighing the similarity of feature values. Case (C): Lower similarity for instances with opposite feature importance values (= positive vs. negative importance), i.e., slightly de-weighing similarity of feature values.

In the **second step**, we integrate information from input feature values (rather than latent space features) and their corresponding feature importances as derived from local explanation methods. A crucial part of calculating the distance matrix involves weighting the pairwise distances between input feature values of two instances. This weighting influences which instances are more likely to cluster together based on their similarity, while also accounting for dissimilar instances. The key idea is that input feature values should significantly impact distance calculations only when they hold high local importance for the model decision. Instances are considered close if the important features have similar values, i.e., small distances, even if they differ in less important features. Additionally, distances should be increased when feature importance values are oppositional i.e., high positive vs. high negative, despite similar input values. These desiderata are illustrated in Fig. 4. The weighted distance $D(i_1, i_2)$ between two instances $i_1, i_2$ is defined as:

$$D(i_1, i_2) = \sum_{k=1}^{n} d(\text{feat}_{1,k}, \text{feat}_{2,k}) \times w(\text{attr}_{1,k}, \text{attr}_{2,k}), \tag{1}$$

where $d$ is a (per-feature) distance function (e.g., manhattan distance), $\text{feat}_{1,k}$, $\text{attr}_{1,k}$ are the $k$-th input feature and feature attribution values (of the $n$ total features) of $i_1$ and $i_2$, respectively, and $w$ is a weighting function explained below.

We introduce two distinct weighting functions, $w_1$ and $w_2$, designed to effectively manage the influence of feature importances on the distance calculations between instances, as shown in the heatmaps in Fig. 5. The function $w_1$ is particularly focused on emphasizing opposing attributions, allowing it to highlight instances with contrasting feature importances while disregarding features that are neutral or non-contributory. This approach ensures that only the most significant features, which play a crucial role in the model's decision-making process, have a substantial impact on the calculated distances. On the other hand, $w_2$ takes a slightly different approach by neglecting features that are deemed unimportant to both predictions, while still applying less stringent weighting to opposing features. This nuanced handling of feature importance allows for a more refined clustering process, leading to better identification of instances that share similar underlying concepts.

In the **third step**, we employ a clustering algorithm that utilizes the distance matrices generated for each class to uncover the predominant sub-concepts, i.e., the CECs, present within the data. This algorithm systematically groups instances based on their weighted distances, facilitating the identification of meaningful clusters that reflect the semantic relationships among the data points. Once the clustering is complete, the resulting CECs for each class are visualized in a manner that enables users to quickly and intuitively recognize patterns related to the input values, feature importances, and the corresponding model predictions. This visualization not only enhances understanding of the model's behavior but also allows for a deeper analysis of the underlying concepts driv-

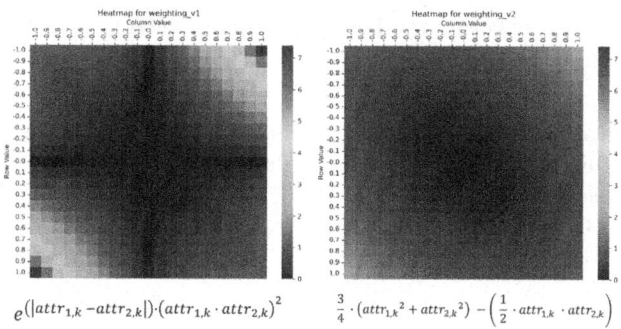

**Fig. 5. Weighting functions $w_1$ and $w_2$.** The heatmaps illustrate the different weighting strategies for the pairwise feature distances that are intended with the two functions. In comparison, $w_1$ stronger weights opposing attributions, while $w_2$ follows a less stringent weighting.

ing the clustering, thereby providing valuable insights into the decision-making process of the model.

### 3.2 Experimental Setup

We experimentally evaluate our approach on two classification datasets, a structured tabular one and an unstructured textual dataset.

**Classification on Tabular Data.** The California Housing dataset [17] focuses on predicting house prices based on eight features, including median income, average number of rooms, and median house median age. To facilitate the identification of dedicated (sub)concepts for each class, we perform equal-width binning, dividing the data into five classes (0 to 4) based on ascending price ranges. We train an XGBoost classifier using a 5-fold cross-validation on 95% of the data, selecting the best-performing model to generate predictions on the 5% hold-out test set.

**Classification on Textual Data.** Additionally, we evaluate the flexibility of our approach by conducting experiments on another data domain: textual data. For this, we utilize the 20 Newsgroups dataset [38], which comprises approximately 20,000 newsgroup documents, organized into 20 different newsgroups. From the 20 classes, we select two subgroups of classes for our experiments: on the one hand, we select the five classes that correspond to the top-level category "computer", on the other hand, we randomly select six diverse classes. This selection allows us to analyze the applicability of the CEC both for classes that have very similar content, making it more difficult for the model to distinguish between them, and for classes that are fundamentally more thematically different. We vectorize the data using the TF-IDF method and train a Stochastic Gradient Descent (SGD) logistic regression classifier using a 5-fold cross-validation on 60% of the data, selecting the best-performing model to generate predictions on the 40% hold-out test set.

**Local Explanations.** For local explanations, we utilize the widely used SHAP [27], which provides valuable insights into both the positive and negative importance of features affecting the local model predictions. We compute SHAP feature importances for each test data set and point. Since our weighting function is defined for values between $-1$ and $1$, we scale the SHAP values accordingly.

**Clustering.** Based on the model predictions, we organize the input data and explanations into sets for each of the corresponding classes. We scale and normalize the input data and compute the weighted distance matrices using Eq. 1. Since we particularly want to investigate the influence of opposing important features on cluster formation for our purpose, we only use weighting function $w_1$ for the experiments in this paper. For the textual data, we then reduce the number of features to only the relevant features per data subset per class. Therefore, feature columns containing absolute SHAP values below a threshold of 0.01 are filtered out. The distance matrix data subsets then consist only of feature columns with at least one value above the defined threshold and form the basis for hierarchical clustering.

We initially evaluated clustering performance based on several clustering metrics (e.g., the Calinski-Harabasz score) to determine an optimized set of hyperparameters (e.g., threshold and linkage criterion) in our earlier work [13]. However, given that the distances among data instances within a class are typically small, standard cluster quality metrics often fail to detect fine patterns, which are nevertheless recognizable in the visual analysis of a cluster map. Consequently, we adopted a visual analytics approach, allowing for a more intuitive identification of the clusters by visualizing the cluster map and the corresponding dendrogram. The cluster map represents a heatmap of the distances between the instances, with lighter colored areas indicating stronger similarity of the corresponding instances. The tree structure of the dendrogram visualizes the different hierarchy levels and thus makes it clear at which points the instances can be combined into a larger cluster due to their similarity. This shift enabled us to leverage human expertise in discerning subtle patterns within the data, enhancing the overall effectiveness of our methodology.

**CEC Identification.** As explanation concepts that describe the behavioral pattern of the model within an identified cluster, we provide the top predominant features to obtain concepts that are visually compact. Typically, the feature space of the data sets is large, leading to numerous features that influence the model decisions. Therefore, to distill these into the explanation concepts, we utilize two steps filtering the features according to the following questions: (i) Does the model utilize the feature for its predictions?, and, (ii) Is the feature important?

**Visualization of CECs.** For the visualization of the CECs, it is important that both feature importance values and the input data values of the features are displayed together. This allows the important features to be visually mapped to the characteristics of the concepts in the input data space. In our previous work, we used a table format with colored cells to display attribute values along with their importances. However, this approach is unfeasible for larger and more complex datasets as used here. Therefore, to obtain a compact representation that can be adapted to different datasets and data domains, we regionally aggregate the feature and importance values per feature for each CEC in this paper.

We use two dedicated subplots to distinguish concepts with positive feature importance from those with negative importance. To highlight the differences among CECs within a class, the plot is generated for all CECs of a class, whereby feature values are represented as bars and SHAP importance values as lines. For a better visual comparison, the values are scaled to percentages ranging from 0% to 100% for the positive SHAP and feature values, and with a range from 0% to −100% for negative SHAP values. This is done by first identifying the mean for each respective feature and corresponding SHAP values in a cluster and normalizing on the maximum of these means. In order to take into account positive and negative influences of a feature on the basis of its SHAP scores, positive and negative SHAP values are considered separately for each feature and the absolute maximum is determined in each case. These maximum values are defined as a 100% reference point (or −100% reference point in the case of negative values) and the lower values are then scaled accordingly. To focus the analysis on the predominant and statistically more relevant concepts, outlier clusters with very few members are filtered out using a user-definable threshold. However, for a later detailed analysis of these outliers that might inherit interesting corner-cases or misclassifications, the indices, prediction, ground truth, and cluster labels for misclassified instances are stored in a dictionary. We describe the analysis of misclassifications for the textual data in the corresponding subsection of Sect. 4.2.

## 4 Results

In the following, we focus on step 3 of our method, recall Fig. 3. We describe the procedure of identifying the Concept Explanation Clusters (CECs), as well as their interpretation for the tabular and textual datasets. We exemplarily give a detailed description of the resulting CECs for selected classes.

### 4.1 Tabular Data

Based on the computed distance matrices, we perform hierarchical clustering for each class to identify the CECs within the data. According to our visual analytics inspired approach, we visualize the full clustermap and dendrogram for different linkage criteria. We evaluate the resulting clustermaps for visually identifiable clusters and define the cutoff accordingly. For example, in Fig. 6, three larger clusters can be recognized by the light blue, contiguous square areas along the diagonal. Thus, the dendrogram is cut at the point where these three clusters are formed. The resulting clusters form our three CECs, which are numbered consecutively and added to the input data as a label column for the later analysis and visualization.

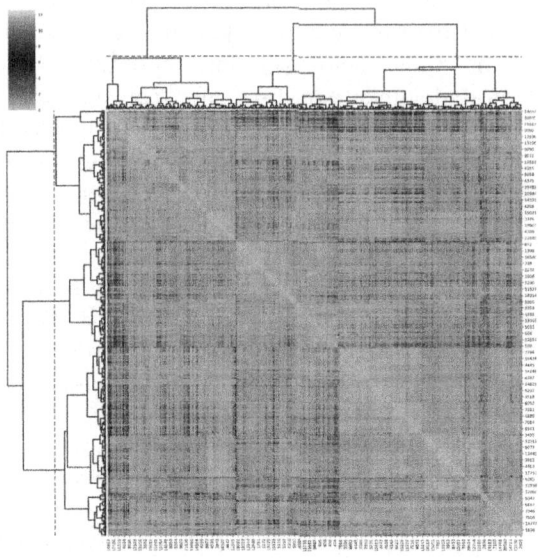

**Fig. 6. Clustermap for class 1 (lower-priced houses) of California Housing dataset.** We visually evaluate the identified clusters and cut the dendrogram at a suitable point. Here, for example, the formation of three clusters, indicated by the square lighter colored areas along the diagonal, can be easily recognized. The corresponding dendrogram cutting point is illustrated by the red dotted line, resulting in three CECs. (Color figure online)

**Interpretation of California Housing CECs.** For the interpretation of the identified CECs, we have created a visualization that shows both the features and feature importances of the individual CECs, and thus helps to understand regional model behavior. In the following, we describe the interpretation of the three identified CECs for class 1, the lower-priced houses (see Fig. 7).

As expected, the three CECs of class 1 show differences in the positive and negative feature importances, as indicated by the lines in the upper and lower plot of Fig. 7(a). In addition, some large differences in the values of the features themselves are recognizable, as shown by the bars in the respective subplots. More specifically, the line peaks reveal that longitude stands out as the most important positive feature in CEC 1 (■ lightblue) and CEC 3 (■ **pink**), while latitude is the most important feature in CEC 2 (■ green). The CECs reveal also distinct concepts in terms of the feature importance ranking. For CEC 1 ■, the most important features are longitude and latitude. For CEC 3 ■ the ranking is longitude, but then AveOccup. The corresponding feature bar, which shows the maximum value, indicates the high importance of the high average number of household members. For CEC 2 ■, on the other hand, the most important is latitude followed by the median income MedInc.

Looking at the geographical location of the instances, see Fig. 7(b), helps to further understand, and also verifies, how the CECs explain the model behavior. The data points belonging to CEC 1 ■ are primarily distributed across the urban areas of Los Angeles (LA) and San Diego (SD). This location is mainly determined by the feature longitude, whose absolute value is on average in the lower range, as can be seen from the bar in Fig. 7(a). Isolated instances are also located on the coast or in the hinterland of San Francisco (SF). The instances from CEC 3 ■ behave similarly, but overall they are less scattered around the cities of LA and SD, which is also reflected in the lowest mean of the absolute feature values, i.e., the lowest bars, for both geographical features. In contrast, the instances of CEC 2 ■ tend to be located at high latitude values around the coast and the hinterland of SF. This geographical location is primarily determined by a high latitude value, which is the case for CEC 2 ■, as can be seen from the highest bar. Overall, the map clearly shows why the feature longitude has the highest positive importance for CEC 1 ■ and 3 ■, while this is the case for latitude in CEC 2 ■. For all three CECs, the negative significance of the other geographical feature is due to the fact that variations in the most important positive geographical feature lead to a change in geographical location, while variations in the other feature have less of an impact. Additionally, within each CEC further fine substructures are present, as visible in the clustermap in Fig. 6, which explain the wider dispersion of instances beyond geographical cluster centers. These sub-concepts then contain, for example, houses with slightly different feature rankings or feature characteristics.

Considering the other important features and their values, the following concepts emerge: CEC 1 ■ includes the oldest houses with the highest number of rooms for class 1, primarily located in medium income neighborhoods around LA and SD. CEC 2 ■ describes older houses around SF with medium incomes. The middle-aged houses from CEC 3 ■ are primarily located in the centers of LA and SD, i.e., highest population value of the class, and have the highest occupancy.

Results for the class 4, the most expensive houses, can be found in Fig. 1. The most expensive houses in California are typically located along the coast line and in the three city centers, with a few exceptions in the hinterland. Thus, it is not surprising that geographic features of latitude and longitude have the highest importance when considering purely global SHAP explanations, recall Fig. 1(B). However, the analysis of CECs per class shows that the model does not exclusively use these two features to predict the different classes. Rather, different sub-strategies can be identified per class, each based on different combinations of features, represented by the five CECs (see Fig. 1(C)).

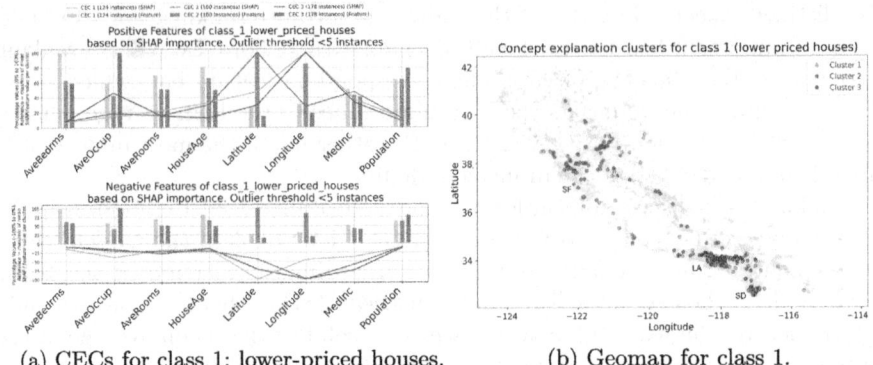

(a) CECs for class 1: lower-priced houses.  (b) Geomap for class 1.

**Fig. 7.** CEC visualization as bar/line plots and geographical map for California Housing class 1. Lines represent mean SHAP values and bars represent mean feature values, both scaled to percentage values. The upper plot shows the most positive influential features (i.e., with the highest positive SHAP values), and the lower plot the most negative influential features (i.e., with the lowest negative SHAP values) of all three identified CECs, respectively. The differences in the CECs of (a) can be further analyzed with reference to the geographical location of the instances in (b). (Color figure online)

For detailed analysis and description of the CECs for class 4, we refer to our proof-of-concept in [13]. Compared to that prior work, the current paper offers a more compact visualization with the bar and line plots, which enables a more immediate recognition and interpretation of the CECs of a class. Moreover, the current paper has further developed the methodology itself, such as the dendrogram cluster identification and the linkage criteria, which leads to slight differences in the composition of the CECs. All in all, while the results in this paper are consistent with the proof-of-concept they allow for easier recognition and transfer to more complex data, as shown next.

### 4.2 Textual Data

Analogous to the tabular data, we identify the CECs for the textual data for each class by hierarchical clustering. Following, we present the procedure and our results, see Figs. 9 and 10, as well as Table 1, exemplarily for the class "comp.sys.mac.hardware".

During the clustering process, the resulting dendrogram is cut at the visually identified most suitable point. For example, the dendrogram of class "comp.sys.mac.hardware", see Fig. 8, is cut at the point where three larger clusters are formed.

Figure 9 illustrates the identified concepts of the CECs in terms of their features and feature importances through the bar-and-line plot. The top-$N$ (in our case $N = 15$) positive and negative words per cluster are subsequently identified for each class, based on an ordered list of mean values, which is calculated

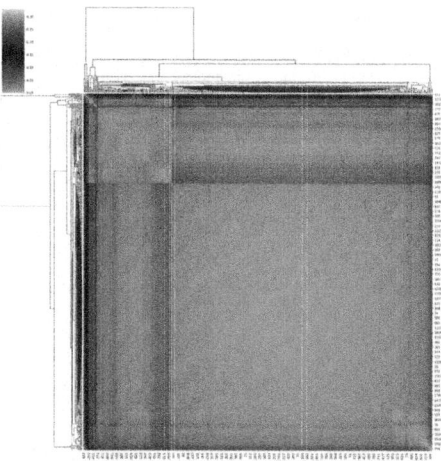

**Fig. 8. Clustermap for class 3 "comp.sys.mac.hardware".** The three large clusters are easily recognizable. Cutting the dendrogram at this point results in several outliers, i.e., single instances and smaller clusters.

separately for all positive and all negative values of the features. The selection of the top words has been done, because a visual representation of all words in the text corpus would be too extensive and is not necessary.

The selection is based on an ordered list of mean values computed separately for all positive and for all negative values of the features. A summarized list of all occurring top words and without duplicates is created from the individual top words of each cluster. This means that the global top list can consist of more than the specified number of "top-$N$ words", as different clusters usually have a different selection of most important words.

**Interpretation of Newsgroups CECs.** We exemplarily show the results of the CECs for the class 'comp.sys.mac.hardware' as one of the five classes that are part of the top-level category "computer". Based on a threshold of 10 instances, below which clusters are filtered out as outliers, three CEC have been identified. The resulting global "positive top words" list consists of 27 words and the "negative top words" list consists of 37 words. By visualizing the SHAP values as lines and the feature values as bars, it is easy to see that the clusters have fundamental differences in the composition of their concepts, see Fig. 9. While some words have a similar positive or even negative importance for all three clusters (i.e., the SHAP lines show a similar height), there are also words for which the importance differs greatly. From the combined plotting of SHAP and feature values it can also be observed that high feature values (i.e., high mean TF-IDF values) do not automatically correspond to high SHAP importances.

To facilitate a focused concept interpretation, we also create bar charts that show the absolute importance of the words (based on the SHAP values) sorted by

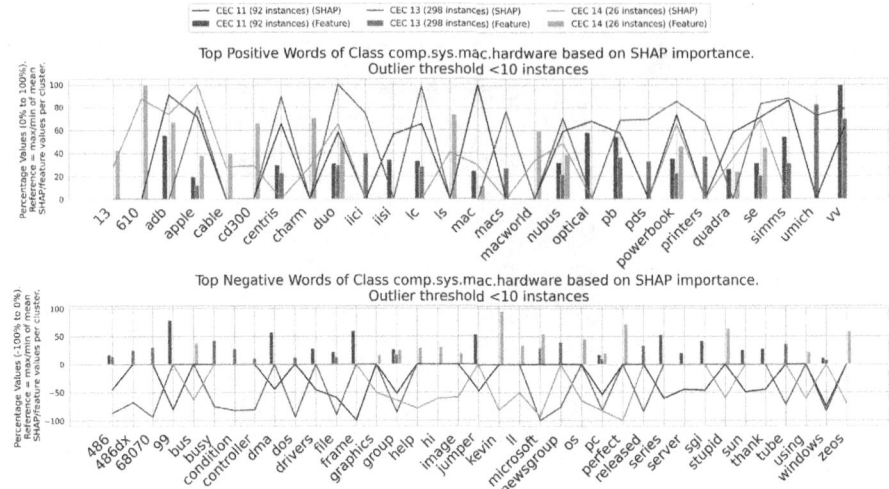

**Fig. 9.** Most influential words per CEC for class "comp.sys.mac.hardware". The class primarily centers on Mac products and hardware, though the sub-concepts within the three clusters vary in detail. Notably, negatively associated words also exhibit distinct sub-concepts. CEC 11 ■ mainly addresses Powerbook and SE models along with their peripherals, while CEC 13 ■ covers a wider range of models. In contrast, CEC 14 ■ focuses specifically on Apple peripherals. Feature values can only have positive values or are zero, i.e., the word does not appear in the cluster.

clusters in descending order, see Fig. 10(a) to (c). The threshold for the importance can be user-specified; here, we chose 70%. The combination of both types of plots makes it possible to understand the concepts and their differences and thus draw conclusions about the model behavior. The exemplary analysis performed in this way is described in Table 1.

Overall, the focus within the class is naturally on Mac products and Mac hardware, although the sub-concepts of the three clusters differ in fine details. It is also interesting to note that the negatively associated words also show dedicated sub-concepts. While CEC 11 ■ focuses primarily on Powerbook and SE models and their peripherals and features, a broader range of models is discussed in CEC 13 ■. Apple-specific peripherals, on the other hand, are a primary focus of CEC 14 ■.

As can be seen in the clustermap in Fig. 8, the three CECs themselves still contain fine substructures. This may indicate that these substructures themselves still represent finer subconcepts. In case it is necessary to examine these structures as part of a rigorous model evaluation, the cutoff for the dendrogram can be selected in such a way that these substructures are also identified as individual CECs. In CEC 11 ■, for example, this could reveal a separation into the two Apple models 'powerbook' and 'se', or in peripherals and other hardware.

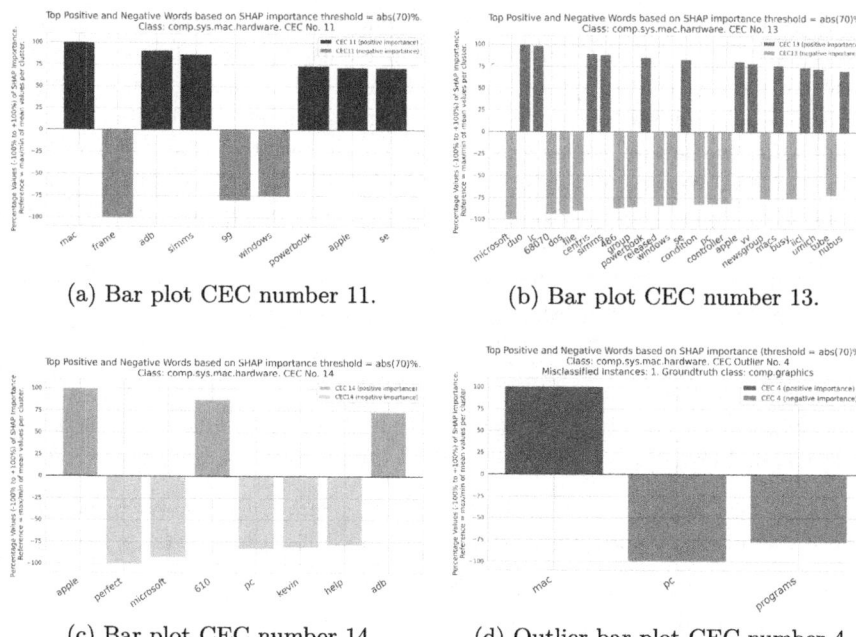

**Fig. 10. Bar plots for the top words of class "comp.sys.mac.hardware".** Figures (a) to (c) show the top words of the three identified CECs. Figure (d) shows the top words of outlier CEC 4. Refer to the subsections of Sect. 4.2 for a detailed description.

**Table 1.** Interpretation of CEC concepts based on Figs. 9 and 10.

|  |  | Top positive words | Top negative words | Interpretation of concept |
|---|---|---|---|---|
| CEC | 11 | mac, adb, simms, powerbook, apple, se | frame, 99, windows | Discussion focus lies on 'mac'/'apple' hardware ('simms' for RAM module and 'adb' for peripherals), specifically related to 'powerbook' and 'se' models. While 'windows' and 'frame' indicate discussion on comparisons or graphics aspects and have higher feature values, the model does not concentrate on these. |
| CEC | 13 | lc, duo, centris, simms, se, apple, vv, macs, powerbook, iici, umich, nubus | microsoft, 68070, dos, file, 486, group, released, windows, condition, pc, controller, newsgroup, busy, tube | Discussion is about specific apple models (macintosh series 'lc', 'se', 'centris', 'icii', 'duo' and 'powerbook'). Components ('simms') are also discussed, but the corresponding feature value is lower compared to CE 11. 'umich' likely corresponds to University of Michigan and has a high feature value. The apple products are contrasted to windows hardware and models ('microsoft', 'dos', '68070', '486', etc.), which all have feature values below 50%. |
| CEC | 14 | apple, abd, 610 | perfect, microsoft, pc, kevin, help | Discussion focuses on apple-specific hardware products with high feature values for peripherals ('adb' and '610'). Competitor products ('microsoft', 'pc') have negative impact and lower feature values. |

**Analysis of Outliers and Misclassifications.** As described above, based on a defined threshold value for instances per cluster, those clusters that were below this number (in this case <10) were filtered out. To examine the 14 outlier clusters, we also create both types of plots using the stored dictionary, which contains information on the indices, prediction, ground truth, and cluster labels for misclassified instances. The majority of the outlier CECs contain one or two instances. As an example, Fig. 10(d) shows the bar plot for outlier CEC 4 ■. It consists of an isolated, misclassified instance, whose ground truth makes it clear that the instance actually belongs to class 'comp.graphics'. Using the dictionary with the stored instance indices, we can retrieve the index of this misclassified instance to analyze the corresponding original text data:

> "I am interested in finding 3D animation programs for the Mac. I am especially interested in any programs that don't exist in a PC port and are so good that they would make me go buy a Mac. Do any such exist?"

Analyzing the original text reveals why this instance was likely misclassified: while it includes the word 'mac', the main focus appears to be on graphics.

### 4.3 LLM Description for CECs

To make analyzing the CECs based on the two types of plots even more human-friendly and efficient, we experimentally utilize a large language model (LLM) for concept description of the 20 Newsgroup dataset. The used model is GPT 4o mini. Since some of the data contains domain-specific abbreviations, the LLM should help to understand these special words in the context of the respective clusters. The following information is passed to the LLM for this purpose: The information that the task is an evaluation of a model for classifying newsgroup discussions; the class to which the cluster belongs; the positive and negative top words belonging to the cluster; the data instances (i.e., the original texts) associated with the present class and the present cluster based on the model prediction. In the prompt we define 3 tasks for the LLM: (i) Describe how the top positive words are linked to the actual raw text data. Include one exemplary excerpt from the raw textual data for each word concept. (ii) Describe how the top negative words link to the actual raw data. What conclusions can be drawn when contrasting them with the positive classification concepts from (i)? Include one exemplary excerpt from the raw textual data for each word concept. (iii) Give an overall conclusion on the concepts that are relevant to the model's decision.

We exemplarily show the results for the top positive words of CEC 11 ■ of the class 'comp.sys.mac.hardware' in Table 2. Analogously, the LLM produced a table for the top negative words. The overall conclusion of the LLM is the following:

> ***Positive concepts:*** *The positive words such as "mac", "adb", and "powerbook" highlight key components and features associated with Macintosh systems. These*

**Table 2.** The LLM's description of the concepts related to the positive words in CEC number 11 ■.

| Positive word | Concept description | Exemplary excerpt |
|---|---|---|
| mac | Refers to Macintosh computers and their ecosystem. | "It is a data acquisition board for the Mac II series." |
| adb | Refers to Apple Desktop Bus, a connection for peripherals. | "I would like to find out about the ADB connector on the back of the macintosh powerbooks." |
| simms | Refers to Single Inline Memory Modules, used for memory expansion. | "However, I can't get it to boot after I install the 2 extra SIMMs." |
| powerbook | Refers to Apple's line of portable computers. | "I have a question (or two) about the serial ports for the powerbooks (specifically the 145 with system 7.0.1)." |
| apple | Refers to Apple Inc., the company that produces Macs and associated hardware. | "It is true that Apple has lower their pricing on the low end models." |
| se | Refers to Macintosh SE, a model in the Mac line. | "I have a Mac IIsi and SE30 as primary home computers, and Quadra and IIci at work in the lab" |

terms reflect discussions about specific Mac models, their capabilities, and peripheral connections. The recurring references to hardware, such as "simms", emphasize the focus on upgrading and enhancing Mac systems, which is prevalent in user discussions about compatibility, performance, and configuration.

**Negative concepts:** Conversely, the negative words like "windows" and "frame" indicate concepts that are typically associated with non-Mac systems or broader computing environments. Their presence suggests that while there are mentions of PC compatibility or issues, they are less relevant to the core discussions about Mac hardware. The classifier seems to associate these negative terms with different classes, reinforcing the notion that the texts primarily concentrate on Macintosh-specific topics rather than cross-platform comparisons or issues.

**In summary**, the classifier demonstrates a strong ability to focus on relevant Macintosh hardware discussions while effectively filtering out concepts more closely associated with non-Mac environments, thus reinforcing its classification accuracy for the "comp.sys.mac.hardware" group.

The LLM's descriptions and its summary are consistent with our own manual analyses. The use of an LLM can therefore help to understand the identified concepts and the interplay between positively and negatively associated features in the context of the predicted class. For a more in-depth analysis, it is still useful to consult the plots, but the LLM descriptions provide a good initial overview of the concepts found, thus increasing efficiency for a subsequent more in-depth analyses. Textual data sets, due to their nature, are particularly suitable for this approach; at the same time, it is also conceivable to use this approach for the language-based concept description of structured data sets.

### 4.4 Ablation

We perform ablation experiments on the more complex text dataset 20 Newsgroups to evaluate the effectiveness of our approach compared to using SHAP values or feature values alone. Using the same preparation steps, we compute distance matrices for SHAP values and for feature values separately, i.e., without any weighting based on a combination of both as in our CEC approach. The distance matrices are analogously used to generate clustermaps. For class "comp.sys.mac.hardware", these clustermaps are shown in Fig. 11(a) and (b). It can be observed that without the specific CEC weighting, which combines SHAP and feature values, such fine structures - and thus also dedicated clusters for subconcepts within a class - cannot be identified (cp. Fig. 8). This further means, human-understandable concepts, that describe the model behavior, would be harder to derive.

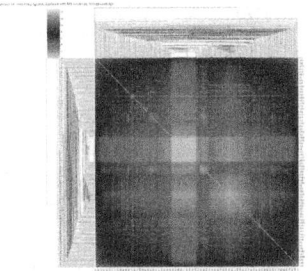

(a) Clustermap for Class 3 based only on SHAP values.

(b) Clustermap for Class 3 based only on feature values.

**Fig. 11. Clustermaps of ablation experiments.** Both the heatmaps and the dendrograms for class "comp.sys.mac.hardware" of the 20 Newsgroups dataset show that clustering based solely on SHAP or feature values leads to many isolated instances and few coherent groups, which would otherwise be shown by large bright areas. In comparison, our method identifies fine-grained structures, cf. Figs. 6 and 8

## 5 Conclusion and Discussion

The Concept Explanation Clusters (CEC) method enables efficient identification of regional concepts, representing sub-strategies used by the model for its predictions. Within a class, but also in distinction to other classes, the regional concepts provide important context that promotes the understanding of the model behavior. In this way, the CEC method provides a link between local and global explanations, providing both sufficient detail for regionally occurring feature patterns and an appropriate level of abstraction to infer global model behavior. In addition to the identification of dominant concepts, we have also shown that the analysis of outlier CECs and misclassifications can provide valuable insights into the weaknesses of a model. This is especially important in the context of an AI trustworthiness assessment.

The ablation experiments have shown that the sole use of SHAP or feature values for cluster identification cannot identify comparable contiguous groups of instances. For the considered data, only the hybridization of our approach, which uses local explanations as weights for the pairwise distances in the input space, enables the identification of fine-grained coherent structures in the data.

Due to the complexity of data, most methods utilize the latent space to identify concepts, as seen in [7,10]. However, our CEC approach highlights the benefits of using input features instead of latent space concepts, thereby maintaining a direct link to the original data. This enhances its compatibility with existing visual analytics frameworks. Furthermore, the exploratory nature of our method and its associated visualizations are inherently suitable for this integration. This would enable an even more human-centered and focused analysis of the CECs. For instance, individual CECs could be emphasized for examination while others are faded out to minimize cognitive overload, particularly when many dominant CECs are present. Additionally, when combined with other visualizations like the presented bar plots or geomaps, linked brushing can aid in identifying broader contexts. However, we defer the integration into a corresponding VA framework, e.g., ScrutinAI [14], to future work.

Our method was originally designed for tabular data, necessitating other data types to be organized into a structured format. In this paper, we have introduced an approach for textual data and intend to broaden the applicability of CEC to other models and data types, including unstructured data like images, in the future. To this end, the CEC method has been designed to allow its application to different types of models and data. This is emphasized by the method's openness to other local XAI variants, distance measures or clustering methods, which can be selected to suit the use case and data at hand.

The aggregation of the concepts at regional level has already increased the efficiency of the analysis and interpretation of the CECs compared to our first work [13]. In the future, we want to develop this approach even further in the direction of prototype formulation, e.g., through a stronger integration of large language models (LLM). Our first experimental application on text data in this work has shown that summarizing the concepts in natural language and explaining domain-specific features can further support interpretation.

To summarize, our CEC method not only bridges the gap between local and global explanations, but also enhances the transparency of AI models by providing human-centered insights into regional model behavior. CEC provides a more nuanced understanding of model predictions, facilitating effective trustworthiness assessments in AI systems.

**Acknowledgments.** The research leading to this publication was supported by the Ministry of Economic Affairs, Industry, Climate Action and Energy of the State of North Rhine-Westphalia (Grant number [005-2011-0048]) as part of the flagship project ZERTIFIZIERTE KI.

**Disclosure of Interests.** The authors have no competing interests to declare that are relevant to the content of this article.

# References

1. Achtibat, R., et al.: From attribution maps to human-understandable explanations through Concept Relevance Propagation. Nat. Mach. Intell. **5**(9), 1006–1019 (2023). https://doi.org/10.1038/s42256-023-00711-8
2. Andrienko, N., Andrienko, G., Adilova, L., Wrobel, S.: Visual analytics for human-centered machine learning. IEEE Comput. Graphics Appl. **42**(1), 123–133 (2022). https://doi.org/10.1109/MCG.2021.3130314
3. Buhrmester, V., Münch, D., Arens, M.: Analysis of explainers of black box deep neural networks for computer vision: a survey. Mach. Learn. Knowl. Extr. **3**(4), 966–989 (2021). https://doi.org/10.3390/make3040048
4. Caruana, R., Kangarloo, H., Dionisio, J.D.N., Sinha, U.S., Johnson, D.B.: Case-based explanation of non-case-based learning methods. In: Proceedings AMIA Symposium, pp. 212–5 (1999). https://pmc.ncbi.nlm.nih.gov/articles/PMC2232607/
5. Cook, K.A., Thomas, J.J.: Illuminating the path: the research and development agenda for visual analytics. Technical report, Pacific Northwest National Lab. (PNNL), Richland, WA (United States) (2005). https://www.osti.gov/biblio/912515
6. Doshi-Velez, F., Kim, B.: Towards a rigorous science of interpretable machine learning. arXiv: Machine Learning (2017). https://arxiv.org/abs/1702.08608
7. Dreyer, M., Achtibat, R., Samek, W., Lapuschkin, S.: Understanding the (extra-)ordinary: validating deep model decisions with prototypical concept-based explanations. In: Proceedings of the IEEE/CVF Conference on Computer Vision and Pattern Recognition (CVPR) Workshops, pp. 3491–3501 (2024). https://doi.org/10.1109/CVPRW63382.2024.00353
8. European Union, The European Parliament, The Council: Regulation of the European parliament and of the council laying down harmonised rules on artificial intelligence and amending
9. Fel, T., et al.: A holistic approach to unifying automatic concept extraction and concept importance estimation. In: Proceedings of the 37th NeurIPS, NIPS 2023, vol. 37. Curran Associates Inc., Red Hook (2024)
10. Fel, T., et al.: Craft: concept recursive activation factorization for explainability. In: 2023 IEEE/CVF Conference on Computer Vision and Pattern Recognition (CVPR), pp. 2711–2721 (2023). https://doi.org/10.1109/CVPR52729.2023.00266
11. Ghorbani, A., Wexler, J., Zou, J., Kim, B.: Towards Automatic Concept-based Explanations, pp. 9277–9286. Curran Associates Inc., Red Hook (2019)
12. Gilpin, L.H., Bau, D., Yuan, B.Z., Bajwa, A., Specter, M.A., Kagal, L.: Explaining explanations: an overview of interpretability of machine learning. In: 2018 IEEE 5th International Conference on Data Science and Advanced Analytics (DSAA), pp. 80–89 (2018). https://doi.org/10.1109/DSAA.2018.00018

13. Haedecke, E., Akila, M., von Rueden, L.: Towards linking local and global explanations for AI assessments with concept explanation clusters. In: Proceedings of the AAAI Symposium Series, vol. 4, no. 1, pp. 106–109 (2024). https://doi.org/10.1609/aaaiss.v4i1.31779
14. Haedecke, E., Mock, M., Akila, M.: ScrutinAI: a visual analytics tool supporting semantic assessments of object detection models. Comput. Graph. **114**, 265–275 (2023). https://doi.org/10.1016/j.cag.2023.06.010
15. Hohman, F., Park, H., Robinson, C., Polo Chau, D.H.: Summit: scaling deep learning interpretability by visualizing activation and attribution summarizations. IEEE Trans. Visual Comput. Graphics **26**(1), 1096–1106 (2020). https://doi.org/10.1109/TVCG.2019.2934659
16. Keim, D., Andrienko, G., Fekete, J.D., Görg, C., Kohlhammer, J., Melançon, G.: Visual Analytics: Definition, Process, and Challenges, pp. 154–175. Springern, Heidelberg (2008). https://doi.org/10.1007/978-3-540-70956-5_7
17. Kelley Pace, R., Barry, R.: Sparse spatial autoregressions. Stat. Probab. Lett. **33**(3) (1997). https://doi.org/10.1016/S0167-7152(96)00140-X
18. Kenny, E.M., Delaney, E., Keane, M.T.: Advancing post-hoc case-based explanation with feature highlighting. In: Proceedings of the Thirty-Second International Joint Conference on Artificial Intelligence, Macao, P.R. China, IJCAI 2023 (2023). https://doi.org/10.24963/ijcai.2023/48
19. Kenny, E.M., Keane, M.T.: Twin-systems to explain artificial neural networks using case-based reasoning: comparative tests of feature-weighting methods in ANN-CBR twins for XAI. In: Proceedings of the Twenty-Eighth International Joint Conference on Artificial Intelligence, IJCAI-19, pp. 2708–2715 (2019). https://doi.org/10.24963/ijcai.2019/376
20. Kim, B., et al.: Interpretability beyond feature attribution: quantitative testing with concept activation vectors (TCAV). In: Dy, J., Krause, A. (eds.) Proceedings of the 35th International Conference on Machine Learning. Proceedings of Machine Learning Research, vol. 80, pp. 2668–2677 (2018). https://proceedings.mlr.press/v80/kim18d.html
21. Rosa, B., et al.: State of the art of visual analytics for explainable deep learning. Comput. Graph. Forum **42**(1), 319–355 (2023). https://doi.org/10.1111/cgf.14733
22. Lai, Q., Khan, S., Nie, Y., Sun, H., Shen, J., Shao, L.: Understanding more about human and machine attention in deep neural networks. IEEE Trans. Multimedia **23**, 2086–2099 (2021). https://doi.org/10.1109/TMM.2020.3007321
23. von Landesberger, T., Schreck, T., Fellner, D.W., Kohlhammer, J.: Visual Search and Analysis in Complex Information Spaces—Approaches and Research Challenges, pp. 45–67. Springer, London (2012). https://doi.org/10.1007/978-1-4471-2804-5_4
24. Lapuschkin, S., Wäldchen, S., Binder, A., Montavon, G., Samek, W., Müller, K.R.: Unmasking Clever Hans predictors and assessing what machines really learn. Nat. Commun. **10**(1), 1096 (2019). https://doi.org/10.1038/s41467-019-08987-4
25. Leake, D.: Case-based explanation: making the implicit explicit. In: CCBR XCBR 2022: 4th Workshop on XCBR: Case-based Reasoning for the Explanation of Intelligent Systems at ICCBR-2022 (2022)
26. Liu, G., Zhang, J., Chan, A.B., Hsiao, J.H.: Human attention guided explainable artificial intelligence for computer vision models. Neural Netw. **177**, 106392 (2024). https://doi.org/10.1016/j.neunet.2024.106392
27. Lundberg, S.M., Lee, S.I.: A unified approach to interpreting model predictions. In: NeurIPS, vol. 30 (2017). http://papers.nips.cc/paper/7062-a-unified-approach-to-interpreting-model-predictions.pdf

28. Miller, T.: Explanation in artificial intelligence: insights from the social sciences. Artif. Intell. **267**, 1–38 (2019). https://doi.org/10.1016/j.artint.2018.07.007
29. Molnar, C.: Interpretable Machine Learning, 2 edn. Leanpub (2022). https://christophm.github.io/interpretable-ml-book
30. Molnar, C., et al.: General Pitfalls of Model-Agnostic Interpretation Methods for Machine Learning Models, pp. 39–68. Springer, Cham (2022). https://doi.org/10.1007/978-3-031-04083-2_4
31. Nauta, M., Jutte, A., Provoost, J., Seifert, C.: This looks like that, because ... explaining prototypes for interpretable image recognition. In: Kamp, M., et al. (eds.) Machine Learning and Principles and Practice of Knowledge Discovery in Databases, pp. 441–456. Springer, Cham (2021). https://doi.org/10.1007/978-3-030-93736-2_34
32. Nguyen, G., Kim, D., Nguyen, A.: The effectiveness of feature attribution methods and its correlation with automatic evaluation scores. In: Ranzato, M., Beygelzimer, A., Dauphin, Y., Liang, P., Vaughan, J.W. (eds.) Advances in Neural Information Processing Systems, vol. 34, pp. 26422–26436. Curran Associates, Inc., (2021). https://proceedings.neurips.cc/paper_files/paper/2021/file/de043a5e421240eb846da8effe472ff1-Paper.pdf
33. Peylo, C., Slama, D., Hallensleben, S., Hauschke, A., Hildebrandt, S.: VCIO based description of systems for AI trustworthiness characterisation. VDE SPEC 90012 V1.0 (en) (2022). https://www.vde.com/resource/blob/2177870/a24b13db01773747e6b7bba4ce20ea60/vde-spec-90012-v1-0--en--data.pdf
34. Poretschkin, M., Mock, M., Wrobel, S.: Zur Systematischen Bewertung der Vertrauenswürdigkeit von KI-Systemen. In: Zimmer, D. (ed.) Regulierung für Algorithmen und Künstliche Intelligenz, 1 edn., pp. 175–202. Nomos Verlagsgesellschaft mbH & Co. KG, Baden-Baden (2021). https://doi.org/10.5771/9783748927990-175
35. Poretschkin, M., et al.: Guideline for trustworthy artificial intelligence – AI assessment catalog (2023). https://arxiv.org/abs/2307.03681
36. Qi, R., Zheng, Y., Yang, Y., Cao, C.C., Hsiao, J.H.: Explanation strategies in humans versus current explainable artificial intelligence: insights from image classification. Br. J. Psychol. (2024). https://doi.org/10.1111/bjop.12714
37. Ramaswamy, V.V., Kim, S.S.Y., Fong, R., Russakovsky, O.: Overlooked factors in concept-based explanations: dataset choice, concept learnability, and human capability. In: 2023 IEEE/CVF Conference on Computer Vision and Pattern Recognition (CVPR), pp. 10932–10941 (2023). https://doi.org/10.1109/CVPR52729.2023.01052
38. Rennie, J.: The 20 newsgroups dataset. http://qwone.com/~jason/20Newsgroups/
39. Roscher, R., Bohn, B., Duarte, M.F., Garcke, J.: Explainable machine learning for scientific insights and discoveries. IEEE Access **8**, 42200–42216 (2020). https://doi.org/10.1109/ACCESS.2020.2976199
40. Schrouff, J., et al.: Best of both worlds: local and global explanations with human-understandable concepts (2022). https://arxiv.org/abs/2106.08641
41. Spinner, T., Schlegel, U., Schäfer, H., El-Assady, M.: Explainer: a visual analytics framework for interactive and explainable machine learning. IEEE Trans. Visual Comput. Graphics **26**(1), 1064–1074 (2020). https://doi.org/10.1109/TVCG.2019.2934629
42. Tabassi, E.: Artificial intelligence risk management framework (AI RMF 1.0). Technical report. NIST AI 100-1, National Institute of Standards and Technology (U.S.), Gaithersburg, MD (2023). https://doi.org/10.6028/NIST.AI.100-1

43. Xie, Y., Chen, M., Kao, D., Gao, G., Chen, X.A.: CheXplain: enabling physicians to explore and understand data-driven, AI-enabled medical imaging analysis. In: Proceedings of the 2020 CHI Conference on Human Factors in Computing Systems, CHI 2020, pp. 1–13. Association for Computing Machinery, New York (2020). https://doi.org/10.1145/3313831.3376807
44. Zhang, R., Madumal, P., Miller, T., Ehinger, K.A., Rubinstein, B.I.P.: Invertible concept-based explanations for CNN models with non-negative concept activation vectors. In: Proceedings of the AAAI Conference on Artificial Intelligence, vol. 35, pp. 11682–11690 (2021). https://doi.org/10.1609/aaai.v35i13.17389

**Open Access** This chapter is licensed under the terms of the Creative Commons Attribution 4.0 International License (http://creativecommons.org/licenses/by/4.0/), which permits use, sharing, adaptation, distribution and reproduction in any medium or format, as long as you give appropriate credit to the original author(s) and the source, provide a link to the Creative Commons license and indicate if changes were made.

The images or other third party material in this chapter are included in the chapter's Creative Commons license, unless indicated otherwise in a credit line to the material. If material is not included in the chapter's Creative Commons license and your intended use is not permitted by statutory regulation or exceeds the permitted use, you will need to obtain permission directly from the copyright holder.

# From Colors to Classes: Emergence of Concepts in Vision Transformers

Teresa Dorszewski[1](✉)[iD], Lenka Tětková[1][iD], Robert Jenssen[2,3,4][iD],
Lars Kai Hansen[1][iD], and Kristoffer Knutsen Wickstrøm[2][iD]

[1] Department of Applied Mathematics and Computer Science, Technical University of Denmark, Kongens Lyngby, Denmark
{tksc,lenhy,lkai}@dtu.dk
[2] Department of Physics and Technology, UiT The Arctic University of Norway, Tromsø, Norway
{robert.jenssen,kristoffer.k.wickstrom}@uit.no
[3] Pioneer Centre for AI, University of Copenhagen, Copenhagen, Denmark
[4] Norwegian Computing Center, Oslo, Norway

**Abstract.** Vision Transformers (ViTs) are increasingly utilized in various computer vision tasks due to their powerful representation capabilities. However, it remains understudied how ViTs process information layer by layer. Numerous studies have shown that convolutional neural networks (CNNs) extract features of increasing complexity throughout their layers, which is crucial for tasks like domain adaptation and transfer learning. ViTs, lacking the same inductive biases as CNNs, can potentially learn global dependencies from the first layers due to their attention mechanisms. Given the increasing importance of ViTs in computer vision, there is a need to improve the layer-wise understanding of ViTs. In this work, we present a novel, layer-wise analysis of concepts encoded in state-of-the-art ViTs using neuron labeling. Our findings reveal that ViTs encode concepts with increasing complexity throughout the network. Early layers primarily encode basic features such as colors and textures, while later layers represent more specific classes, including objects and animals. As the complexity of encoded concepts increases, the number of concepts represented in each layer also rises, reflecting a more diverse and specific set of features. Additionally, different pretraining strategies influence the quantity and category of encoded concepts, with finetuning to specific downstream tasks generally reducing the number of encoded concepts and shifting the concepts to more relevant categories.

**Keywords:** Concepts · Vision Transformers · Explainability

# 1 Introduction

Vision Transformers (ViTs) [5] are becoming increasingly important in the field of computer vision [9], but the understanding of their feature extraction process is still in its infancy. This understanding is crucial, as the myriad of learned features form the basis of the network's decision process and can reveal biases [8] and shortcuts [13], providing a deeper understanding of the learning process as a whole [22]. One path towards improving this understanding is to investigate where semantic concepts are learned throughout the network. Several such studies exist for convolutional neural networks (CNNs) (e.g. [2,3,36]), but very few studies exist for ViTs (e.g. [30]) or are mainly focused on the output layer and do not analyze what concepts are learned in intermediate layers (e.g. [3,20]). In CNNs, a hierarchical way of processing information is given by the architecture and the constrained receptive fields, which leads to early layers being focused on colors, patterns, and edges while only later layers are able to process complex information like objects and scenes [3]. In ViTs, however, this hierarchical information processing is not given by the architectural constraints, as the self-attention layers act globally and can attend to the full image from layer one [5]. ViTs could therefore in principle learn complex features already in early layers. While it has been shown that ViTs process information differently and develop more uniform representations compared to CNNs [26], it has not been investigated where ViTs start processing complex information and if they focus on colors and patterns in earlier layers just as CNNs do. Therefore, there is a need for a deeper analysis to understand the layer-wise learning process of ViTs and we propose using concept-based explainability to gain these insights.

In this work, we propose a comprehensive analysis of the layer-wise learning process in ViTs using neuron labeling [20]. We aim to identify and understand the semantic concepts learned at different layers of the network, providing insights into the hierarchical feature extraction process. We use the CLIP-dissect method introduced by Oikarinen and Weng [20], which provides a fast and reliable method for neuron labeling, due to its flexibility, computational speed, and high quality labels (e.g. shown in a recent quantitative study [16]).

Most of these methods showcase neuron labeling in CNNs, such as ResNets [11], and have only limited or no experiments on transformer-based models, which are becoming increasingly popular in the computer vision domain [10,24]. The previous works also lack a thorough quantitative analysis of how the concepts develop across layers, and where what kind of information is processed. In this paper, we aim to close this gap by providing a deep analysis of encoded concepts through neuron labeling in ViTs. We find that, despite not being locally constrained, ViTs tend to learn simpler concepts like colors and patterns early on and more complex concepts like objects and natural elements in late layers. Figure 1 shows how different concept categories develop across layers in ViTs.

Our study highlights the hierarchical feature extraction in ViTs and provides the first comprehensive layer-wise concept analysis of ViTs. Our main findings include:

- ViTs encode more universal concepts, like colors and textures, in early layers and more specialized concepts, like objects and natural elements, and a greater amount of different concepts in later layers.

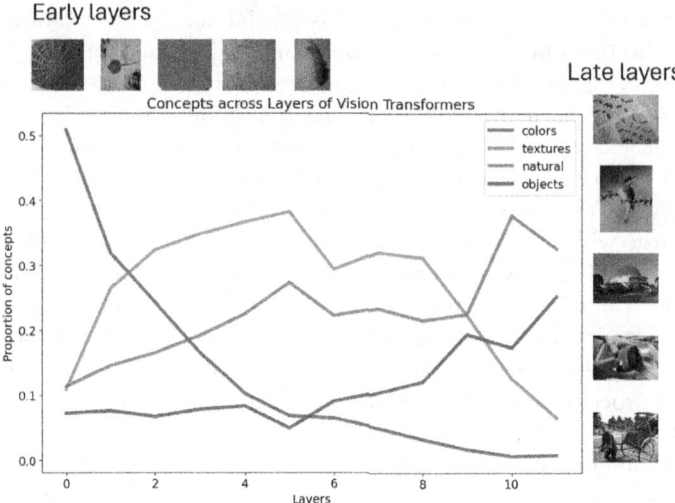

**Fig. 1.** We analyze how different concepts develop across the layers of vision transformers. Early layers tend to process simpler concepts and images while late layers focus on more complex and diverse concepts.

- Neurons in early layers mostly activate on *simpler* images while neurons in late layers react on more *complex* images.
- Finetuning to specific downstream tasks reduces the number of encoded concepts and can lead to a concept shift to task-relevant concepts while forgetting irrelevant concepts.

## 2 Related Work

Here, we present an overview of investigations from prior works that align the most closely to our work.

*Layer-Wise Concept Analysis in CNNs.* Numerous studies have investigated the complexity of concepts learned in different layers of the network. An early work by Yosinski et al. [35] demonstrated empirically that earlier layers learn to extract more general and low-level features while later layers extract more complex and task-specific features. A later work by Bau et al. [3] modeled concepts explicitly through the Network Dissection framework and found that earlier layers extract concepts related to color and textures while later layers extract concepts related to objects. A recent study by Fel et al. [28] used information-theoretic estimators to quantify the complexity of concepts learned throughout the layers of CNNs, which also found that CNNs encode *simple* concepts in early layers and build more *complex* concepts in late layers, with *simple* concepts flowing through residual connection to stay available throughout the network.

*Layer-Wise Concept Analysis in ViTs.* To the best of our knowledge, very little work has been conducted in layer-wise concept analysis in ViTs. Recently, Vielhaben et al. [30] looked into concept-based alignment in ViTs and revealed that early and middle layers encode fewer concepts, that are not well aligned with WordNet categories, while the last layer encodes more concepts than can be semantically organized by WordNet classes (i.e. objects and organisms). Visual inspection revealed that early layers mainly encode colors and structures, however, no quantitative analysis was done. Another notable study by Raghu et al. [26] investigated the representations of ViTs in comparison with CNNs, which found striking differences in terms of how the similarity of representations are distributed between layers. However, they only looked at the similarity of representations and not into what concepts are encoded in each layer. Two other studies found ViTs to be more consistent with human decision- and error-making and exhibiting less of a texture bias than CNNs, suggesting that ViTs rely on higher-level and more general features and concepts [19,29].

*Neuron Labeling in Computer Vision.* The analysis in this work is based on the CLIP-Dissect method, due to its high flexibility, high computational speed, and good performance in recent quantitative studies [16]. However, several neuron labeling techniques have been proposed recently, and could provide additional perspectives in future studies. The Network Dissection framework [3] was one of the earliest general framework for labeling neurons, The MILAN technique allowed neuron labeling beyond predefined labels and to an open-vocabulary setting [12]. INVERT took a compositional concept approach, which eliminated the need for segmentation masks that prior methods relied on [4]. A recent study did a quantitative evaluation of the quality of the labels [16], which found that CLIP-Dissect generally has strong performance.

## 3   Theoretical Framework for Neuron Labeling

In this section, the CLIP-Dissect method will be described as introduced by Oikarinen and Weng [20]. For all experiments, we use the original implementation[1], with only minor changes to support models from the Hugging Face framework [33]. This is meant to give an overall understanding of how the method works, for more details please refer to the original publication [20].

The CLIP-Dissect algorithm requires a neural network to be analyzed, in our case different ViTs, a set of probing images ($D_{probe}$) which can be any dataset without the need for concept labels, and a set of concepts ($C$), which is provided as a list of words. The output of CLIP-Dissect is a set of neuron labels that identify the concept associated with each individual neuron.

---

[1] https://github.com/Trustworthy-ML-Lab/CLIP-dissect.

The algorithm consists of three main steps:

1. Compute concept-activation matrix $\mathbf{P}$ by computing the $M$ text embeddings $\mathbf{t}_j$ and $N$ image embeddings $\mathbf{i}_i$ of the concepts $c_j$ in the concept set $C$ and the images $\mathbf{D}_i \in \mathbb{R}^{C \times H \times W}$ in the probing set $D_{probe}$ using the text and image encoder of the CLIP model [25]. $\mathbf{P} \in \mathbb{R}^{N \times M}$ is a matrix where the inner product of the embeddings gives the $(i, j)$-th element: $\mathbf{P}_{i,j} = \mathbf{i}_i \cdot \mathbf{t}_j$
2. Record activation of neurons for every image $\mathbf{D}_i \in D_{probe}$
3. Determine neuron label of neuron $k$ by finding the most similar concept $c_m$ (based on mutual information) given the set of highest activating images $B_k$ as activation vector $\mathbf{q}_k$. The label is then given by $\arg\max_m \text{sim}(c_m, \mathbf{q}_k; \mathbf{P})$. The similarity function is the softWPMI, which is defined as:

$$\text{sim}(c_m, \mathbf{q}_k; \mathbf{P}) \triangleq \text{soft\_wpmi}(c_m, \mathbf{q}_k) = \log \mathbb{E}\left[p(c_m \mid B_k)\right] - \lambda \log p(c_m), \quad (1)$$

where $\log \mathbb{E}\left[p(c_m \mid B_k)\right] = \log \left( \prod_{\mathbf{D} \in \mathcal{D}_{\text{probe}}} \left[1 + p(\mathbf{D} \in B_k)(p(c_m \mid \mathbf{D}) - 1)\right] \right)$.

The algorithm outputs a label and a similarity score for each neuron of the model. Since we can not expect every neuron to have a clear label, we propose to add adaptive thresholding to the similarity scores to analyze only neurons that have an accurate and trustworthy label. The procedure for this is described in the next section.

## 4 Layer-Wise Concept Analysis in Vision Transformers

The code for all experiments and results of the neuron labeling are available at https://github.com/teresa-sc/concepts_in_ViTs.

### 4.1 Analysis of Concepts

The analysis of concepts is based on the CLIP-dissect method [20], which is described in detail in Sect. 3. It outputs a description ("concept") and similarity score for each neuron in analyzed layers. We analyze the final MLP layer in each transformer block of the ViT models (a total of 12 layers with 768 neurons each) and the last convolutional layer in each residual block in the ResNet50 (a total of 5 layers, with 64, 156, 512, 1024, and 2048 neurons respectively). The exact models are described in Subsect. 4.3.

To analyze only reliably labeled neurons, we propose to threshold the neurons by the similarity score and analyze only the descriptions of the neurons that have a high similarity score, i.e. a reliable label. According to a user study performed by Oikarinen and Weng [20], around 55–80% of the descriptions are fitting and around 20–30% of the neurons do not have a simple label, i.e. are uninterpretable. They suggest using an interpretability cutoff of $\tau = 0.16$ [20].

However, the similarity score depends on the concepts and probing dataset. Therefore, we decided to introduce a mean thresholding that can directly be

**Table 1.** Mean threshold $\tau$ across layers for each analyzed model and the number of neurons with similarity scores above $\tau$ (average for all vision transformer models, exact number for all layers of ResNet).

| model | threshold $\tau$ | # of labeled neurons |
|---|---|---|
| ViT | $0.17 \pm 0.01$ | $317 \pm 13$ |
| DINOv2 | $0.21 \pm 0.04$ | $323 \pm 11$ |
| CLIP | $0.17 \pm 0.03$ | $309 \pm 13$ |
| MAE | $0.17 \pm 0.02$ | $331 \pm 17$ |
| ResNet50 | $0.21 \pm 0.05$ | $32, 92, 209, 423, 893$ |

applied to new models and changed datasets. We threshold the descriptions of each layer by the mean of the similarity scores in that layer, which results in slightly different thresholds $\tau$ in each layer of each model, but a comparable amount of labeled neurons so the following quantitative and qualitative analysis is comparable across models and datasets. The exact thresholds and number of neurons with an analyzed description are detailed in Table 1.

We analyze how many different concepts are encoded in each layer and which categories these concepts belong to. The number of concepts is determined by simply counting the unique descriptions after thresholding. Each concept is part of a category, as described in Subsect. 4.3, and we analyze the percentage of labeled neurons that belong to which category. Here we do not only count unique concepts but all neurons that have a concept related to each category, so for example if 10 neurons have the label *blue*, it would count as one concept for counting the amount of different concepts but as 10 *color* neurons. This also ensures that the categories are comparable, even if the amount of different concepts in each category varies.

### 4.2 Complexity of Concepts

We measure the perceived image complexity of the 5 top activating images for each neuron. We estimate the complexity of each image using ICNet [7], which was trained to predict the image complexity scores based on a human-annotated dataset of 9600 diverse images. For each image, we take the mean of the complexity map (a mask with per-pixel complexity scores). The resulting complexity score is a number between 0 and 1, with higher values indicating more complexity. We average these scores across all neurons in each layer.

### 4.3 Models and Data Selection for Concept Analysis

We analyze four commonly used pretrained ViT models, namely the classical supervised Vision Transformer (sup-ViT) [5], DINOv2 [24], Masked Autoencoder (MAE) [10] and Contrastive Language-Image Pretraining (CLIP) with a ViT backbone [25]. All models were obtained in their pretrained form from Hugging

**Table 2.** Learning rate (lr) and test accuracy (acc) in % for all models trained on CUB and bloodMNIST.

| model | CUB | | bloodMNIST | |
|---|---|---|---|---|
| | lr | acc | lr | acc |
| sup-ViT | $1e^{-4}$ | 0.84 | $1e^{-4}$ | 0.99 |
| DINOv2 | $1e^{-5}$ | 0.87 | $1e^{-5}$ | 0.99 |
| CLIP | $1e^{-5}$ | 0.80 | $1e^{-5}$ | 0.98 |
| ResNet50 | $1e^{-4}$ | 0.76 | $1e^{-4}$ | 0.98 |

Face [33]. The models all share the same architecture of 12 transformer blocks with an embedding size of 768 in each block and take images of the size 224 × 224 as input. They only differ in their pretraining strategy. Sup-ViT is pretrained in a supervised fashion on ImageNet-21k [5]. DINOv2 uses self-supervised learning based on a self-distillation method with pseudo labels. The model is pretrained on a dataset of 142 million images without labels, focusing on producing robust visual features [24]. MAE is pretrained using a self-supervised approach where parts of the input image are masked, and the model learns to reconstruct the missing parts, which helps in learning meaningful representations [10]. CLIP is pretrained on a variety of image-text pairs from the internet, learning to predict the most relevant text snippet for a given image, enabling zero-shot capabilities [25]. We also run the same analysis on ResNet50 [11] trained on ImageNet-1k for a comparison of ViTs with a CNN.

To investigate the effect of finetuning, we also analyze sup-ViT, DINOv2, CLIP and ResNet50 finetuned to Caltech-UCSD Birds-200-2011 Dataset (CUB) [32] and a dataset of the MedMNIST collection [34], the bloodMNIST dataset [1]. The CUB dataset consists of 200 different bird species, which are close to animal and bird images in the pretraining datasets. However, to solve this task, a greater focus on details and parts of the birds is necessary, so it is interesting to investigate how the models and concepts adapt to such fine-grained classification tasks. The bloodMNIST dataset, on the other hand, consists of 8 classes of microscopic peripheral blood cell images, which are very different from the images in the pretraining datasets. This analysis can give insights into how the models and their concepts adapt to new domains.

The trained models are available on https://huggingface.co/teresas. All models were trained with a batch size of 32, a scheduler and early stopping for a maximum of 10000 steps, the learning rate was optimized using a validation set. The exact learning rates and final test accuracies can be seen in Table 2.

We label the 768 output neurons of each transformer's block final MLP layer using CLIP-dissect [20]. For this, we use the ImageNet validation set [27] and Broden [3] as probing dataset (total of 50000 + 63305 = 113305 images) and a list of 20k most common words in English as concept set, as it was defined and used in the original method.

Out of the 20k concepts, only 1450 different words are used as neuron labels after thresholding the labels across all models. We divide these words into semantic categories, namely colors, textures and materials, objects and machines, places and buildings, natural elements and organisms, activities, names, abstract, and unknown. Each word belongs to exactly one category (see Table 3 for the number of words in each category). This categorization was done by Microsoft Copilot [18] and ChatGPT [23] with manual supervision and adjustments. In case of words fitting to multiple categories, we chose the one subjectively most appropriate. The final list of categories is available at https://github.com/teresa-sc/concepts_in_ViTs/tree/main/data.

**Table 3.** Frequency of words in our semi-manual categorization.

| Category | Number of words | Examples |
| --- | --- | --- |
| Colors | 45 | green, orange, turquoise |
| Textures and materials | 74 | tiles, dotted, woven |
| Objects and machines | 449 | furniture, violin, telescope |
| Places and buildings | 270 | library, Scotland, cabin |
| Natural elements and organisms | 254 | elephant, mushroom, plant |
| Activities | 154 | golf, fishing, cooking |
| Abstract | 127 | itinerary, habit, adorable |
| Names | 43 | fujifilm, firefox, merlin |
| Unknown | 34 | aaa, scooby, slashdot |

## 5 Results

Here, we present the main results of our analysis. First, we present a layer-wise analysis of numerous state-of-the-art ViTs using the procedure outlined in Sect. 4. Then, we compare the behaviour of ViTs and CNNs, before we investigate the effect of finetuning on the concepts found in different layers.

### 5.1 Layer-Wise Analysis of Concepts

We labeled and analyzed the neurons of four different ViTs using CLIP-dissect [20] and found many similarities between the models and a few distinct differences. The full list of labeled neurons for each model is available at https://github.com/teresa-sc/concepts_in_ViTs/tree/main/results.

When looking at the overall similarity scores for the description of each neuron all transformer models follow a very similar distribution, as can be seen in Fig. 2, with only the DINOv2 model showing overall slightly higher similarity scores. When analyzing the number of different concepts encoded in each layer

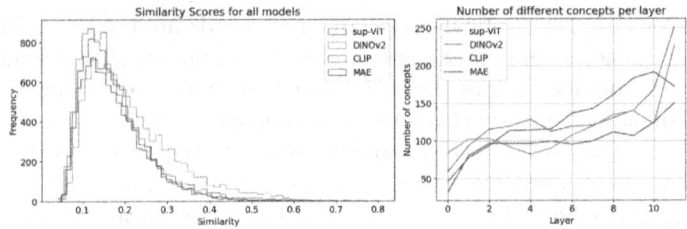

**Fig. 2.** Similarity scores for concepts and number of different concepts encoded in each layer.

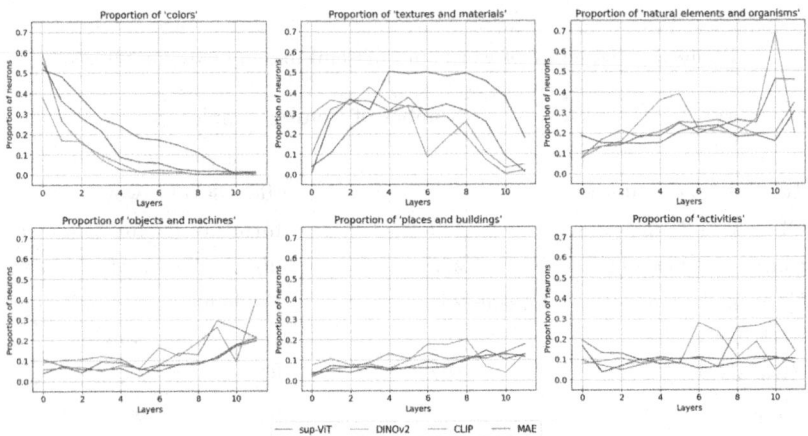

**Fig. 3.** Categories of concepts compared across models. Early layers focus mostly on *colors* while middle layers have a large proportion of neurons assigned to *textures and materials* while *objects* and *natural elements* appear in later layers. The overall trend is similar for all models but small differences can be observed, e.g. CLIP has a higher amount of neurons assigned to activities in late layers.

(after thresholding), a similar trend across models can be observed. At early layers, the models encode fewer concepts (<100) and the number of concepts increases steadily to around double the amount in late layers, the sup-ViT tends to have the most different concepts while the MAE has the least. The DINOv2 follows a slightly different trend with a small decrease of concepts across early layers and a sharp increase in the last layer.

The smaller amount of concepts is not due to less reliable labels, all layers have a comparable amount of labeled neurons after thresholding (around 310–330), but due to many neurons encoding the same concepts. For example, in the first layer some concepts appear 10–20 times (e.g. "green" appears 19 times in sup-ViT layer 1), while in later layers concepts usually only appear once or twice.

We break down the concepts into different categories and analyze how they develop across the layers in Fig. 3, where most concept categories develop similarly across modes. All models start with *colors* as the main concept category present in the first layer, which continually disappears and is almost non-existent in the last layer. *Textures and materials* is also mainly present in early and middle layers and loses importance in late layers but does not disappear completely. Other, more specific categories like *objects and machines* and *natural elements and organisms* start with a small part in early layers and become dominant in late layers. In these categories, we also see some differences between the models. The CLIP model has the highest proportion of *objects and machines* in most layers, but in the last layer, DINOv2 shows a steep increase in this category. All models show a relatively high proportion of *natural elements and organisms*, with DINOv2 and sup-ViT having a very high percentage of neurons belonging to this category in late layers. The DINOv2 model shows a peak in middle layers for the category *places and buildings* and *activities* which other models do not express, they rather show a mostly stable proportion across layers, except for the CLIP model, which has a high proportion (∼25%) of neurons dedicated to *activities* in late layers. This could be explained by the training strategy of the CLIP model, which is trained by image-caption pairs that might include many activity descriptions. The MAE model seems to have a higher focus on *textures and materials* than other models; it attributes almost half of its neurons in the middle layers to this category.

Overall, we see a similar pattern of early layers focusing on *simple* concepts like colors, patterns and textures, and late layers specializing to more *complex* concepts like specific objects and natural elements. We excluded the categories *abstract, names* and *unknown* from the detailed analysis and figures as they all have a very small proportion (<5%) for all layers and models and show no interesting patterns.

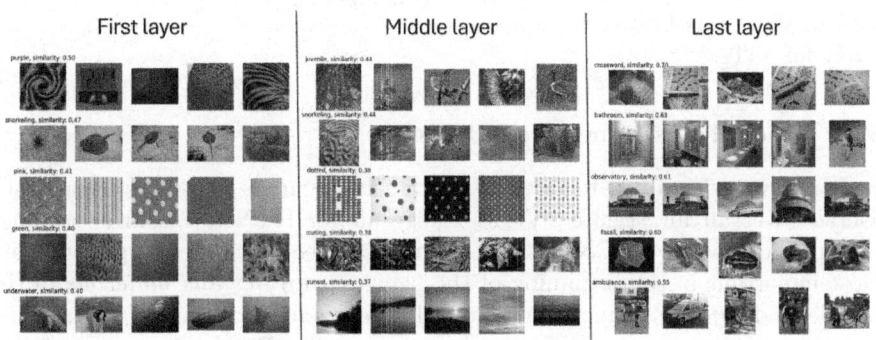

**Fig. 4.** Examples of the highest activating images for five neurons after the first, the sixth and the last transformer block in the sup-ViT model. While this only shows a small subset, the images are representative of most highest activating images, also across models, and show how the models react mainly to simple images in early layers and more complex images in later layers. Similar plots for other models can be found in the Appendix Fig. 9.

## 5.2 Complexity of Concepts

When looking at the top-activating images for each neuron (Fig. 4), it already becomes apparent that early layers mostly activate on *simple* images of mainly colors and patterns while neurons in the last layer mostly activate on more *complex* images of objects and places. Middle layers react on a mix of both with still some *simpler* images mainly driven by color schemes but also on more *complex* images like animals and nature.

To not only rely on a subjective interpretation on the complexity of images, we also quantify the image complexity using ICNet [7] scoring of the five top-activating images for all neurons and average over each layer (see Fig. 5). We can observe a constant increase in complexity for all models except for DINOv2 which peaks in middle layers and decreases a little before increasing again in the last layer.

Overall, this analysis in combination with analysis of concept categories shows how ViTs process images in a hierarchical way where early layers focus on basic concepts, like colors and patterns, and late layers specialize on complex and individual concepts. While this has been observed in CNNs as well, where this is enforced by design, ViTs could, in theory, learn complex features from the start, but still seem to build up their information processing in a similar way. We belive our analysis is the first to show this behaviour conclusively for ViTs.

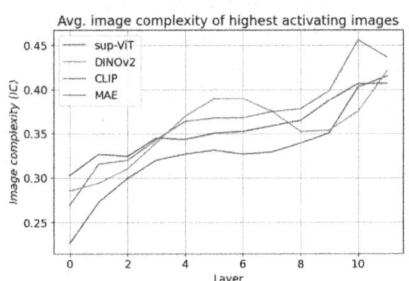

**Fig. 5.** Complexity of the five highest activating images for each neuron averaged across layers measured by ICNet [7]. All models show an increase in image complexity across layers.

## 5.3 Vision Transformers vs. CNNs

In Fig. 6, we compare categories of the labeled neurons in ResNet50 and the average over all investigated ViTs. The result for ResNet50 is in accordance with previous works for CNNs [3,28]. Namely, we see that concepts of *colors* are most important in the beginning of the network, *textures and materials* in the middle, and *objects* and more complicated concepts towards the end, progressing from simple concepts to more complicated ones. The ResNet50 seems to put a higher focus on textures and patterns while the ViTs focus more on objects and natural elements in middle layers. However, the general trend is very similar for both architectures, even though the transformer architecture does not have any inductive bias enforcing this way of processing visual concepts.

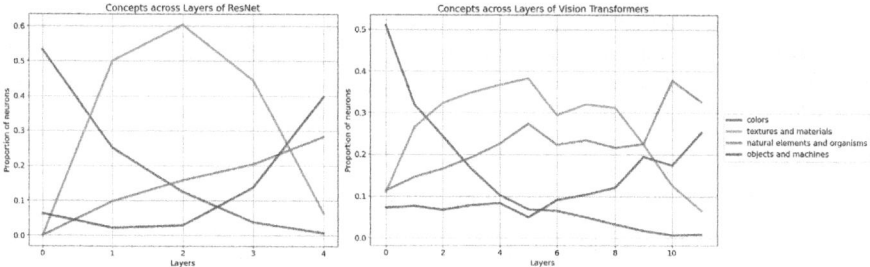

**Fig. 6.** Categories of labeled neurons throughout the models - a comparison of CNN (ResNet50, left) and the average over four ViTs (Vision Transformer, right) architectures. We see that the general trend is very similar for both architectures.

### 5.4 Change in Concepts After Finetuning

How do concepts change when a model is finetuned to a specific downstream task? To investigate this, we analyze three ViTs finetuned for two different classification tasks, on the CUB dataset [32], which contains 200 bird species, and the bloodMNIST dataset [1], which comprises of 8 different blood cells. For the classification of birds, it seems obvious that birds and nature elements are important but also colors and patterns could be useful for the classification. For the blood cells, mainly color and shape are relevant. So when finetuning the models to these classification tasks, we might expect more concepts belonging to these relevant categories to appear while other, not so important concepts might be forgotten and disappear.

Indeed, we observe the expected changes. The number of encoded concepts decreases (see Fig. 7), and the concepts shift to more relevant categories, as seen in Fig. 8. For models finetuned to bloodMNIST, the category *colors* and *textures and patterns* increase, while *natural elements and organisms*, *objects and machines*, and *activities* decrease. For models finetuned for the CUB dataset, we can also see an increase in the *colors* concepts, but surprisingly only a small increase in *natural elements and organisms*, where any *bird* and *nature* concepts would fall under. The category *textures and materials* 

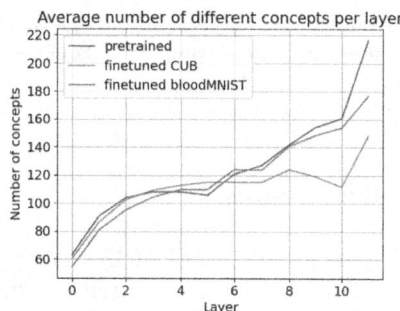

**Fig. 7.** Number of different concepts averaged over three Vision Transformer models in their pretrained and finetuned versions. Finetuning generally decreases the number of different concepts in late layers.

seems relatively unchanged while all other categories show a decrease in proportion, as they are not as relevant for the task. Interestingly, when looking at the individual models (see Appendix Fig. 10), we observe that the CLIP model has a very high increase in the *natural elements and organisms* category in late layers while DINOv2 and sup-ViT are almost unchanged. This might be due to these models already being relatively good at distinguishing animals and birds while the CLIP model needs to adapt its weights more to solve this task.

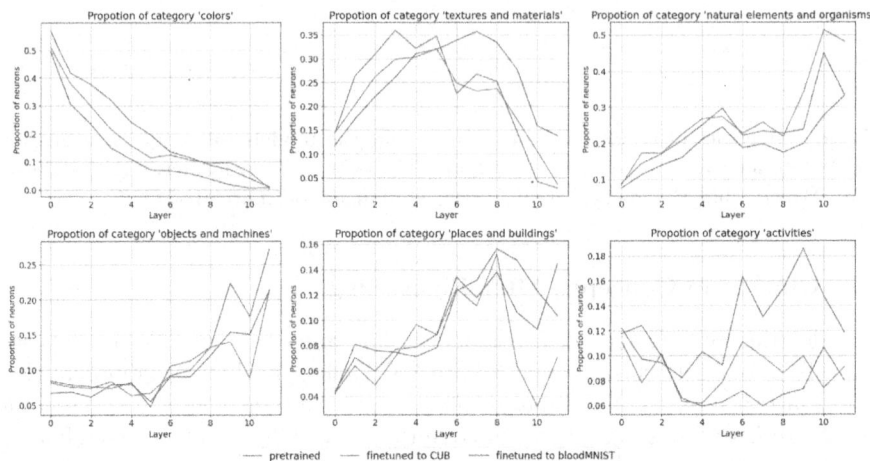

**Fig. 8.** Change in concepts after finetuning averaged over three different Vision Transformer models. The models are finetuned to the CUB dataset and the bloodMNIST dataset and adapt their concepts by putting more focus on relevant categories and "forgetting" irrelevant concepts.Change in concepts after finetuning averaged over three different Vision Transformer models. The models are finetuned to the CUB dataset and the bloodMNIST dataset and adapt their concepts by putting more focus on relevant categories and "forgetting" irrelevant concepts.

## 6 Discussion

In this study, we conducted a comprehensive layer-wise analysis of concepts encoded in ViTs using neuron labeling techniques. Our findings provide new insights into the hierarchical feature extraction process of ViTs, revealing how concepts evolve from basic features in the early layers to more complex and specific classes in the later layers, even with the global attention mechanisms that theoretically allow ViTs to learn complex concepts and relations in early layers. We discuss some implications of our findings and highlight future research directions, and also address some limitations of our approach.

*On the Emergence of Distributed Representations in ViTs.* CNNs are designed to learn simpler features and progressively compose them into more complex features, primarily due to the limited receptive field in their early layers. This hierarchical feature extraction process is well-documented, with early layers capturing basic visual elements such as edges and textures and deeper layers encoding more complex structures and objects [3,28]. In contrast, ViTs can model long-range dependencies from the very first layer, thanks to their self-attention mechanism, which allows them to capture global context across the entire image. Despite this capability, we find that ViTs still tend to learn basic concepts in the initial layers, similar to CNNs. This phenomenon suggests that even with the ability to process global information, the hierarchical nature of feature extraction remains beneficial, and nonlinearities that come with layer-depth might be needed to encode complex concepts.

We observe that different ViTs learn similar concepts, especially in early layers, where the models learn more general concepts. In later layers, the concepts become more specialized and diverge in some models based on their pretraining strategy. This convergent training on universal concepts has also been observed in CNNs [17].

*On the Effects of Finetuning.* After finetuning we observe a shift in concepts as the model adapts to its new task. This shift to more relevant concepts also results in some concepts being forgotten, which could be linked to the challenge of catastrophic forgetting [15]. We observe some differences between the models; while DINOv2 and sup-ViT only change marginally when finetuned to CUB, CLIP shows a large shift towards *natural organisms and elements* in the last layers, but still performs worse on the task than the other models. This can be explained by the different pretraining strategies and training datasets and highlights how choosing a model already prepared for the downstreaming task can be beneficial. When finetuning to a more out-of-distribution dataset, e.g. medical images, we observe a larger shift in concepts across all models, which shows how the models can adapt well to new image types, however they most likely lose a greater part of their generalization capabilities during this adaptation. Future work should look deeper into this process and build a greater understanding of catastrophic forgetting using concept-based analysis.

*On the Differences of DINOv2.* While all ViTs we investigated show very similar trends, DINOv2 stands out multiple times with slightly different observations. The neuron descriptions have higher similarity scores than the descriptions for other models, which can be interpreted as the highest activating images having a clearer common description and the neurons potentially being more monosemantic or specialized. The DINOv2 model also has a higher proportion of neurons reacting to *natural elements and organisms* than other models and a higher complexity of concepts in middle layers. During finetuning, the concept categories change the least for DINOv2, especially for the CUB dataset, where we see almost no change at all, despite the model performing the best on both tasks compared to the other models. This points to the model already being well-prepared for the downstream tasks and able to generalize to these new datasets without much need for adjusting its weights and encoded concepts. DINOv2 has been shown to outperform many other models and generalize quite well [24], however, the internal structures that make this possible remain unstudied. A deeper look into how the model processes information and forms concepts can help understand its capabilities, pave the way to even more powerful models, and is a promising direction for future research.

## 6.1 Limitations

*Thresholding Procedure.* We chose to employ a mean-thresholding separately on each layer, which leads to a comparable amount of labeled neurons and a higher chance of all investigated neurons having reliable and trustworthy labels, however it also suppresses the chance that some layers and models have more interpretable neurons than others. While for sup-ViT, MAE and CLIP the threshold was $\sim 0.17$, which is close to the interpretability cut-off (0.16) determined by a user study [20], the mean similarity score for DINOv2 was higher at $\sim 0.21$. If we employed a fixed threshold, DINOv2 would stand out with a higher number of concepts, however, the category and finetuning analysis remain unchanged even with a fixed threshold.

*Categorization.* We categorized the concepts with a mix of large language models and manual work, the categories were inspired by previous works and computer vision tasks, however, in the end, subjectively chosen. While we did quality check the categorization, we cannot guarantee there are no mistakes, or others would categorize some concept slightly differently. Therefore, the analysis could look slightly different based on a different categorization. But we are confident, that even with a different categorization or concept set, the main conclusions would not change and the insights gained in our study hold regardless. Future work could include drafting an even more reliable concept set and categorization that would benefit concept-based analysis and explainability in general by providing comparable concept sets across many studies.

*Definition of Concepts.* Many other studies in concept-based explainability define concepts differently then we assume here. Often, concepts are seen as direction in latent space [14], specific subspaces [31] or overcomplete dictionaries with which features can be decomposed into concepts [6]. We view concepts as concrete labels for neurons, which requires at least some degree of monosematicity of neurons. This has been shown to not be the case for many neurons and models typically encode many more concepts than they have neurons [21]. However, in our analysis, we observe that many neurons do react to a specific type of image, which can be described by common features, i.e. concepts. With our thresholding, we ensure that neurons that are non-interpretable on their own are not included in our analysis. Therefore, we cannot guarantee that we cover all encoded concepts but we can be sure that the concepts we analyze are actually learned by the models and our findings are representative of what neurons react on in each layer and model. Potential future work could include layer-wise analysis using other methods of concept discovery, but many methods are not as easily applied in an automatic and fast way or would need to be adapted to even work on intermediate representations.

## 7 Conclusion

In this study, we conducted a comprehensive layer-wise analysis of concepts encoded in ViTs using neuron labeling techniques. Our findings provide new insights into the hierarchical feature extraction process of ViTs, revealing how concepts evolve from basic features in the early layers to more complex and specific classes in the later layers. Despite the global attention mechanisms that theoretically allow ViTs to learn complex concepts and relations in early layers, our results show that ViTs still tend to learn basic concepts initially, similar to CNNs. This hierarchical nature of feature extraction in ViTs, even without architectural constraints, suggests that such a hierarchical processing remains beneficial for visual processing and several layers seem to be needed to encode complex concepts.

We observed that different pretraining strategies can influence the category of encoded concepts, and finetuning to specific downstream tasks generally reduces the number of encoded concepts and shifts the concepts to more relevant categories. Especially finetuning to out-of-distribution tasks can cause large concept shifts.

Overall, our study enhances the understanding of the layer-wise learning process in ViTs and highlights the critical need for future research to focus on concept-based explainability in these models. Future research could further explore the internal structures that enable models like DINOv2 to generalize well and investigate other methods of concept discovery to enhance our understanding of neural representations in ViTs.

**Acknowledgments.** This work was supported by the Pioneer Centre for AI, DNRF grant number P1, by the Novo Nordisk Foundation grant NNF22OC0076907 "Cognitive spaces - Next generation explainability", and by Visual Intelligence, a Centre for Research-based Innovation funded by the Research Council of Norway, grants 309439 and 303514.

**Disclosure of Interests.** The authors have no competing interests to declare that are relevant to the content of this article.

# Appendix

In Fig. 9, we show some examples of the highest activating images for five neurons after layers 0, 6, and 11. Some differences between models become apparent, e.g. DINOv2 already has more complex images in the middle layers while MAE still has some *simple* textures in the last layer.

**Fig. 9.** Examples of the highest activating images for DINOv2, CLIP and MAE after layer 0, 6 and 11. Examples for sup-ViT can be seen in Fig. 4.

In Fig. 10, the change in every model during finetuning for the two downstream tasks can be seen. When finetuning to CUB, concepts in DINOv2 change only marginally while CLIP changes a lot for *natural elements and organisms*. For finetuning to bloodMNIST, the overall change is larger, especially DINOv2 changes a lot towards colors and textures.

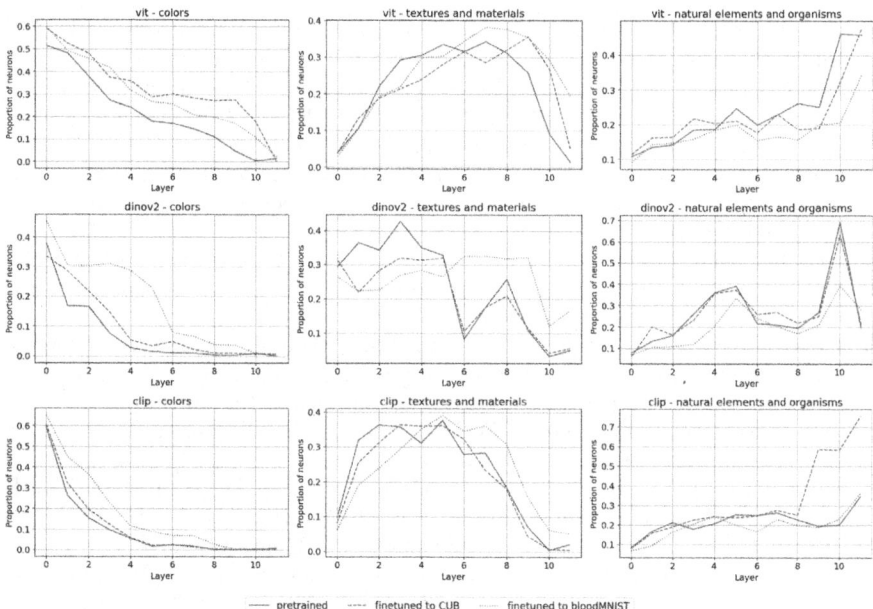

**Fig. 10.** Change during finetuning to the CUB dataset and the bloodMNIST dataset for each model.

## References

1. Acevedo, A., Merino, A., Alférez, S., Molina, Á., Boldú, L., Rodellar, J.: A dataset of microscopic peripheral blood cell images for development of automatic recognition systems. Data Brief **30**, 105474 (2020). https://doi.org/10.1016/j.dib.2020.105474
2. Alain, G., Bengio, Y.: Understanding intermediate layers using linear classifier probes. arXiv preprint arXiv:1610.01644 (2016). https://doi.org/10.48550/arXiv.1610.01644
3. Bau, D., Zhou, B., Khosla, A., Oliva, A., Torralba, A.: Network dissection: quantifying interpretability of deep visual representations. In: Proceedings of the IEEE Conference on Computer Vision and Pattern Recognition, pp. 6541–6549 (2017)
4. Bykov, K., Kopf, L., Nakajima, S., Kloft, M., Höhne, M.: Labeling neural representations with inverse recognition. Adv. Neural Inf. Process. Syst. **36** (2024)
5. Dosovitskiy, A., et al.: An image is worth 16x16 words: transformers for image recognition at scale. In: International Conference on Learning Representations (ICLR) (2021)
6. Fel, T., et al.: Craft: concept recursive activation factorization for explainability. In: Proceedings of the IEEE/CVF Conference on Computer Vision and Pattern Recognition, pp. 2711–2721 (2023)
7. Feng, T., et al.: IC9600: a benchmark dataset for automatic image complexity assessment. IEEE Trans. Pattern Anal. Mach. Intell. **01**, 1–17 (2023). https://doi.org/10.1109/TPAMI.2022.3232328
8. Geirhos, R., et al.: Shortcut learning in deep neural networks. Nat. Mach. Intell. **2**(11), 665–673 (2020). https://doi.org/10.1038/s42256-020-00257-z

9. Han, K., et al.: A survey on vision transformer. IEEE Trans. Pattern Anal. Mach. Intell. **45**(1), 87–110 (2022). https://doi.org/10.1109/TPAMI.2022.3152247
10. He, K., Chen, X., Xie, S., Li, Y., Dollár, P., Girshick, R.: Masked autoencoders are scalable vision learners. In: Proceedings of the IEEE/CVF Conference on Computer Vision and Pattern Recognition, pp. 16000–16009 (2022)
11. He, K., Zhang, X., Ren, S., Sun, J.: Deep residual learning for image recognition. In: Proceedings of the IEEE Conference on Computer Vision and Pattern Recognition, pp. 770–778 (2016)
12. Hernandez, E., Schwettmann, S., Bau, D., Bagashvili, T., Torralba, A., Andreas, J.: Natural language descriptions of deep visual features. In: International Conference on Learning Representations (2021)
13. Ilyas, A., Santurkar, S., Tsipras, D., Engstrom, L., Tran, B., Madry, A.: Adversarial examples are not bugs, they are features. Adv. Neural Inf. Process. Syst. **32** (2019)
14. Kim, B., et al.: Interpretability beyond feature attribution: quantitative testing with concept activation vectors (TCAV). In: International Conference on Machine Learning, pp. 2668–2677. PMLR (2018)
15. Kirkpatrick, J., et al.: Overcoming catastrophic forgetting in neural networks. Proc. Natl. Acad. Sci. **114**(13), 3521–3526 (2017). https://doi.org/10.1073/pnas.1611835114. https://www.pnas.org/doi/abs/10.1073/pnas.1611835114
16. Kopf, L., Bommer, P.L., Hedström, A., Lapuschkin, S., Höhne, M., Bykov, K.: CoSy: evaluating textual explanations of neurons. Adv. Neural. Inf. Process. Syst. **37**, 34656–34685 (2024)
17. Li, Y., Yosinski, J., Clune, J., Lipson, H., Hopcroft, J.: Convergent learning: do different neural networks learn the same representations? arXiv preprint arXiv:1511.07543 (2015). https://doi.org/10.48550/arXiv.1511.07543
18. Microsoft: Microsoft copilot. Generated using https://copilot.microsoft.com. Accessed 13 Feb 2025
19. Naseer, M.M., Ranasinghe, K., Khan, S.H., Hayat, M., Shahbaz Khan, F., Yang, M.H.: Intriguing properties of vision transformers. Adv. Neural. Inf. Process. Syst. **34**, 23296–23308 (2021)
20. Oikarinen, T., Weng, T.W.: Clip-dissect: automatic description of neuron representations in deep vision networks. In: The Eleventh International Conference on Learning Representations (2023)
21. Olah, C., Cammarata, N., Schubert, L., Goh, G., Petrov, M., Carter, S.: Zoom in: an introduction to circuits. Distill (2020). https://doi.org/10.23915/distill.00024.001. https://distill.pub/2020/circuits/zoom-in
22. Olah, C., et al.: The building blocks of interpretability. Distill **3**(3), e10 (2018). https://doi.org/10.23915/distill.00010
23. OpenAI: ChatGPT, model GPT-4O (2023). https://chat.openai.com. Accessed 13 Feb 2025
24. Oquab, M., et al.: DINOv2: learning robust visual features without supervision. arXiv preprint arXiv:2304.07193 (2023https://doi.org/10.48550/arXiv.2304.07193
25. Radford, A., et al.: Learning transferable visual models from natural language supervision. In: International Conference on Machine Learning, pp. 8748–8763. PMLR (2021)
26. Raghu, M., Unterthiner, T., Kornblith, S., Zhang, C., Dosovitskiy, A.: Do vision transformers see like convolutional neural networks? Adv. Neural. Inf. Process. Syst. **34**, 12116–12128 (2021)
27. Russakovsky, O., et al.: ImageNet large scale visual recognition challenge. Int. J. Comput. Vis. (IJCV) **115**(3), 211–252 (2015). https://doi.org/10.1007/s11263-015-0816-y

28. Thomas, F., Béthune, L., Lampinen, A.K., Serre, T., Hermann, K.: Understanding visual feature reliance through the lens of complexity. In: The Thirty-eighth Annual Conference on Neural Information Processing Systems (2024)
29. Tuli, S., Dasgupta, I., Grant, E., Griffiths, T.L.: Are convolutional neural networks or transformers more like human vision? arXiv preprint arXiv:2105.07197 (2021). https://doi.org/10.48550/arXiv.2105.07197
30. Vielhaben, J., Bareeva, D., Berend, J., Samek, W., Strodthoff, N.: Beyond scalars: concept-based alignment analysis in vision transformers. arXiv preprint arXiv:2412.06639 (2024). https://doi.org/10.48550/arXiv.2412.06639
31. Vielhaben, J., Bluecher, S., Strodthoff, N.: Multi-dimensional concept discovery (MCD): a unifying framework with completeness guarantees. Trans. Mach. Learn. Res. (2023)
32. Wah, C., Branson, S., Welinder, P., Perona, P., Belongie, S.: The caltech-UCSD birds-200-2011 dataset (2011). https://authors.library.caltech.edu/27452/?utm_campaign=The%20Batch&utm_source=hs_email&utm_medium=email&_hsenc=p2ANqtz--Sx1nvaahZe38-PWjKtUaD7qc__1GepLnIdt39_cou747ve6R6_mI2mgUTn45sU0V089Fp
33. Wolf, T., et al.: Transformers: state-of-the-art natural language processing. In: Proceedings of the 2020 Conference on Empirical Methods in Natural Language Processing: System Demonstrations, pp. 38–45. Association for Computational Linguistics, Online (2020). https://doi.org/10.18653/v1/2020.emnlp-demos.6. https://www.aclweb.org/anthology/2020.emnlp-demos.6
34. Yang, J., et al.: MedMNIST v2 - a large-scale lightweight benchmark for 2D and 3D biomedical image classification. Sci. Data **10**(1), 1–10 (2023). https://doi.org/10.1038/s41597-022-01721-8. https://www.nature.com/articles/s41597-022-01721-8
35. Yosinski, J., Clune, J., Bengio, Y., Lipson, H.: How transferable are features in deep neural networks? In: Proceedings of the 28th International Conference on Neural Information Processing Systems, NIPS 2014, vol. 2, pp. 3320–3328 (2014)
36. Zeiler, M.D., Fergus, R.: Visualizing and understanding convolutional networks. In: Fleet, D., Pajdla, T., Schiele, B., Tuytelaars, T. (eds.) ECCV 2014, Part I. LNCS, vol. 8689, pp. 818–833. Springer, Cham (2014). https://doi.org/10.1007/978-3-319-10590-1_53

**Open Access** This chapter is licensed under the terms of the Creative Commons Attribution 4.0 International License (http://creativecommons.org/licenses/by/4.0/), which permits use, sharing, adaptation, distribution and reproduction in any medium or format, as long as you give appropriate credit to the original author(s) and the source, provide a link to the Creative Commons license and indicate if changes were made.

The images or other third party material in this chapter are included in the chapter's Creative Commons license, unless indicated otherwise in a credit line to the material. If material is not included in the chapter's Creative Commons license and your intended use is not permitted by statutory regulation or exceeds the permitted use, you will need to obtain permission directly from the copyright holder.

# V-CEM: Bridging Performance and Intervenability in Concept-Based Models

Francesco De Santis[1(✉)], Gabriele Ciravegna[1,2], Philippe Bich[1], Danilo Giordano[1], and Tania Cerquitelli[1]

[1] Politecnico di Torino, 10129 Turin, Italy
{Francesco.DeSantis,Gabriele.Ciravegna,Philippe.Bich,
Danilo.Giordano,Tania.Cerquitelli}@polito.it
[2] Centai Institute, 10138 Turin, Italy

**Abstract.** Concept-based eXplainable AI (C-XAI) is a rapidly growing research field that enhances AI model interpretability by leveraging intermediate, human-understandable concepts. This approach not only enhances model transparency but also enables human intervention, allowing users to interact with these concepts to refine and improve the model's performance. Concept Bottleneck Models (CBMs) explicitly predict concepts before making final decisions, enabling interventions to correct misclassified concepts. While CBMs remain effective in Out-Of-Distribution (OOD) settings with intervention, they struggle to match the performance of black-box models. Concept Embedding Models (CEMs) address this by learning concept embeddings from both concept predictions and input data, enhancing In-Distribution (ID) accuracy but reducing the effectiveness of interventions, especially in OOD scenarios. In this work, we propose the Variational Concept Embedding Model (V-CEM), which leverages variational inference to improve intervention responsiveness in CEMs. We evaluated our model on various textual and visual datasets in terms of ID performance, intervention responsiveness in both ID and OOD settings, and Concept Representation Cohesiveness (CRC), a metric we propose to assess the quality of the concept embedding representations. The results demonstrate that V-CEM retains CEM-level ID performance while achieving intervention effectiveness similar to CBM in OOD settings, effectively reducing the gap between interpretability (intervention) and generalization (performance).

**Keywords:** XAI · C-XAI · Interpretable-AI

## 1 Introduction

Concept-Bottleneck Models (CBMs) [13] have emerged as a promising approach to interpretable machine learning by making task predictions through intermediate, human-understandable concepts. This architecture enhances model transparency by providing insight into the decision-making process through an interpretable mapping between concepts and outputs. Additionally, CBMs offer a distinctive advantage: the ability for human users to *intervene* on the intermediate concept predictions. This allows users both to rectify misclassified concepts, improving model performance, and to gain a deeper understanding of the relationships between concepts and task labels.

However, CBMs struggle with generalization, exhibiting limited performance. Their performance is constrained by the intermediate bottleneck, which restricts their ability to match the predictive accuracy of black-box models that directly map inputs to outputs. To address this issue, Concept Embedding Models [11,25] (CEMs) have been introduced. CEMs generate dedicated embedding representations for each concept, thus alleviating the constrained representational capacity of the concept bottleneck. This approach improves model performance achieving black-box accuracy, while preserving a degree of intervenability (i.e., the level of efficacy of intervention) and interpretability. Besides testing model intervenability in In-Distribution (ID) settings, in this paper we propose testing model intervenability in Out-of Distribution scenarios (OOD). Our experiments show that the CBM architecture remains responsive to interventions on concept representations in both ID and OOD settings. In contrast, CEM exhibits very limited intervenability in OOD scenarios. Theoretically, this is due to CBM relying exclusively on predicted concepts for final decisions, whereas CEMs predictions are based on concept embeddings, which integrate both concept predictions and raw input data. This entanglement negatively impacts CEM's intervenability in OOD settings. To address this challenge, we propose the Variational Concept Embedding Model (V-CEM), which utilizes variational inference to achieve black-box-level accuracy on ID tasks, while maintaining high intervention responsiveness in both ID and OOD scenarios.

In summary, this work makes the following key contributions: i) We demonstrate that while CEMs can achieve higher ID accuracy compared to CBMs, their ability to support interventions in OOD scenarios is significantly limited; ii) We introduce V-CEM, a model that achieves black-box generalization performance under ID conditions, comparable to CEMs; iii) We show that V-CEM retains responsiveness to interventions in both ID and OOD scenarios, similar to CBMs.

The manuscript is structured as follows. In Sect. 2, we provide the foundational concepts necessary to understand this work. Section 3 introduces V-CEM, while Sect. 4 outlines the metrics used to evaluate concept representations. In Sect. 5, we present the results of our experimental campaign. Finally, in Sect. 6, we review related works, and Sect. 7 offers concluding remarks. Code is publicly available[1].

## 2 Background

**Concept Bottleneck Models (CBMs).** Let $x \in X \subset \mathbb{R}^d$ be an input realization, $c \in C \subset [0,1]^k$ represent interpretable concepts, and $y \in Y \subset \{0,\ldots,N\}$ denote the task label. CBMs assume a generative process where $x$ determines $c$,

---
[1] GitHub Repo.

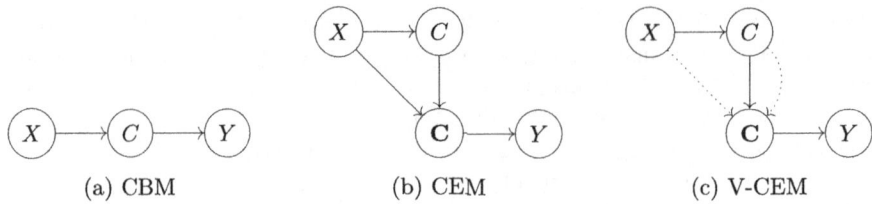

**Fig. 1.** Probabilistic Graphical Models of a) CBMs, b) the CEMs, and c) the proposed V-CEM architecture. Solid lines represent the data generation process, while dotted lines represent inference.

which in turn influences $y$. A CBM consists of a concept encoder $p(c \mid x)$ and a task classifier $p(y \mid c)$, trained end-to-end to approximate $p(y, c \mid x) = p(y \mid c)p(c \mid x)$. The corresponding Probabilistic Graphical Model (PGM) is shown in Fig. 1a. Modifying a concept $c_j$ removes its reliance on $x$. This characteristic is especially crucial in OOD scenarios, as it enables to completely replace the concept representation generated by the concept encoder for a given concept. However, the bottleneck on $c$, while enhancing interpretability, limits performance in ID settings, resulting in a trade-off between interpretability and accuracy.

**Concept Embedding Models (CEMs).** CEM alleviates the usual conflict between interpretability and performance by introducing a rich concept representation, the concept embedding $\mathbf{c} \in \mathbf{C} \subset \mathbb{R}^{k \times m}$, as shown in CEM PGM in Fig. 1b. Unlike the CBM architecture, CEM defines a new conditional distribution $p(\mathbf{c} \mid c, x)$ that integrates both the input $x$ and the concept $c$, enabling the generation of concept embeddings that capture concept-specific information enriched by the input instance $x$. These embeddings are then used to model the distribution $p(y \mid \mathbf{c})$, which predicts task labels. Similarly to CBMs, CEM is trained to approximate $p(y, c \mid x)$. Despite utilizing embeddings, CEM maintains the ability to support concept interventions: modifying a concept influences the conditional distribution $p(\mathbf{c} \mid x, c)$, thereby altering the generated embeddings. The dependence on $x$, which contributes to high ID performance, still remains after human intervention. The reliance on $x$, which contributes to strong ID performance, persists even after human intervention. As a result, CEM becomes less responsive to interventions in OOD scenarios, as the concept embedding generated in these cases may contain poor-quality information that cannot be overridden by human input.

**Intervention.** Interventions in Concept based Models enable humans to correct model errors and gain insights into the relationship between concepts and tasks. This capability is crucial for developing interpretable models by improving transparency, trust, and control over decision-making. For instance, in a classification task where the objective is to categorize birds based on a set of concepts representing their features, if the concept *Red Breast* of an image depicting a

*Red Breasted Parrot* is misclassified, the model might assign an incorrect bird label to the image. A human can adjust the concept prediction, which in turn may alter the final task prediction of the model. Different approaches enable various types of interventions: concept intervention [13,25], where the predicted concept is directly replaced, and concept embedding intervention [11], where the concept's embedding is adjusted. Formally, in concept intervention, the concept $c_j \sim p(c_j \mid x)$ is replaced with $c_j := c'_j$, where $c'_j$ is the concept assigned by the human. In a similar manner, in concept embedding intervention, $\mathbf{c}_j \sim p(\mathbf{c}_j \mid x)$ is substituted with $\mathbf{c}_j := \mathbf{c}'_j$, where $\mathbf{c}'_j$ is the embedding representing concept $j$ that the human uses to correct the misclassified concept.

## 3 Variational CEM

We propose Variational CEM, a methodology to maintain CEM performance in ID settings by leveraging the rich, sample-specific information of the concept embeddings while ensuring their dependence primarily on the underlying concepts. At the same time, V-CEM enables targeted interventions on the concept embeddings that completely override their dependency on the input, ensuring high intervenability also in OOD scenarios. In Sect. 3.1 we describe V-CEM architecture, while in Sect. 3.2 we describe its training.

### 3.1 V-CEM Architecture

As shown in Fig. 2, V-CEM is composed first of a concept encoder $p(c|x)$, mapping the input data $x$ to an intermediate, interpretable concept layer $c$. Concept embeddings, $\mathbf{c}$, are generated from $q(\mathbf{c} \mid x, c)$ using both concept predictions and input features. The classification head $p(y|\mathbf{c})$ works on the concept embeddings to produce the final class prediction $y$.

However, from a probabilistic point of view, we assume a generative process where the concept embeddings $\mathbf{c}$ are only influenced by the interpretable concepts $c$ and not by the input $x$, which is only used to derive the concept $c$. Similarly to CEM, the task label $y$ is generated from a distribution conditioned on the concept embeddings. The PGM corresponding to this formulation is depicted by the solid lines in Fig. 1c. This generative framework leads to the following factorization:

$$p(x, c, \mathbf{c}, y) = p(x)p(c|x)p(\mathbf{c}|c)p(y|\mathbf{c}) \tag{1}$$

With respect to the CEM architecture, we introduce a prior $p(\mathbf{c} \mid c)$, which we will discuss in detail later. Also, notice how the concept embedding probability is only conditioned by the concept predictions $p(\mathbf{c}|c)$. Similarly to CBM and CEM, our objective is to approximate the joint distribution $p(y, c \mid x)$. Since $\mathbf{C}$ is unobservable, we account for its effect on the relationships between $X$, $C$, and $Y$ by marginalizing over all possible values of $\mathbf{C}$:

$$p(c, y|x) = \int_{\mathbf{C}} \frac{p(x, c, \mathbf{c}, y)}{p(x)} d\mathbf{c} \tag{2}$$

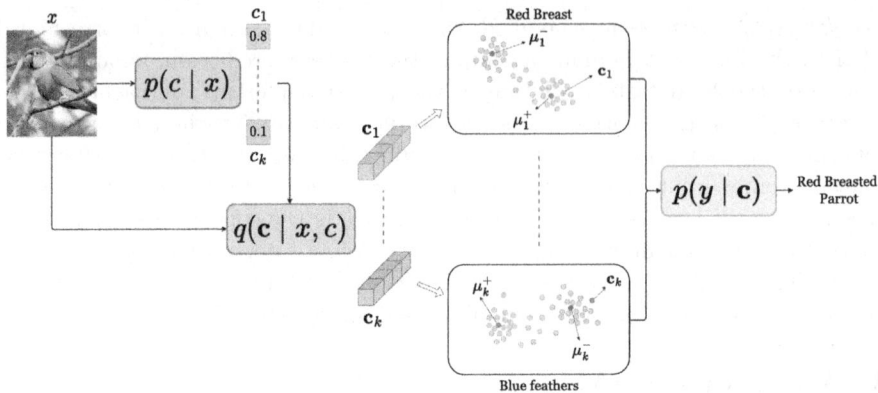

**Fig. 2.** Illustration of the V-CEM architecture. Given an image of a parrot with a red breast, V-CEM concept encoder $p(c|x)$ assigns a high probability to the "Red Breast" concept and a low probability to "Blue Feathers", which is absent. The approximate posterior $q(c|x,c)$ maps concept prediction to concept embeddings clustered around $\mu^+_{\text{Red Breast}}$ and $\mu^-_{\text{Blue Feathers}}$, respectively. These embeddings are then employed to condition $p(y \mid \mathbf{c})$ and enable a correct label prediction ("Red Breasted Parrot"). (Color figure online)

**Loss Derivation.** Using a variational inference approach, we define an approximate posterior distribution, $q(\mathbf{c} \mid x, c)$, which, like CEM, generates concept embeddings by conditioning on both the input and the concept (as illustrated by the dotted lines in Fig. 1c). This allows for amortized inference, as the true posterior $p(\mathbf{c} \mid x, c)$ is intractable. This approach leads to the derivation of the following Evidence Lower Bound (ELBO) for the log-likelihood of the conditional distribution $p(c, y \mid x)$:

$$\log p(c,y|x) \geq \underbrace{- E_q \left[ \log \frac{q(\mathbf{c}|x,c)}{p(\mathbf{c}|c)} \right]}_{\text{Pior Matching}} + \underbrace{\log p(c|x)}_{\text{Concept Loss}} + \underbrace{E_q [\log p(y|\mathbf{c})]}_{\text{Task Loss}} \quad (3)$$

A comprehensive derivation of the loss function is provided in Appendix A. The first term in the ELBO is the Kullback-Leibler (KL) divergence between the approximate posterior $q(\mathbf{c} \mid x, c)$ and the prior $p(\mathbf{c} \mid c)$, ensuring their alignment. We refer to this term as *Prior Matching*. This alignment is crucial, as it encourages the approximate posterior $q(\mathbf{c} \mid x, c)$—which depends on both the input $x$ and concept predictions $c$—to resemble the prior $p(\mathbf{c} \mid c)$, which is independent of $x$. Maximizing the second and third terms of the ELBO (Concept and Task loss) optimizes both concept and task accuracy. Since the third term involves averaging over concept embeddings sampled from the approximate posterior $q$, we approximate this by using the Monte Carlo method. Specifically, as described in [12,17], we employ a large batch size and draw a single sample of $\mathbf{c}$ per data point using the reparameterization trick. All the distributions in the ELBO, besides the prior distribution $p(\mathbf{c} \mid c)$, are parameterized by neural networks.

**Concept Embedding Encoder.** We assume that each concept $c_j$ is independent of the others. Consequently, we define each concept embedding $\mathbf{c}_j$ as independent of the other concept embeddings and model it as a mixture of two multivariate normal distributions:

$$p(\mathbf{c}_j|c_j) = \delta(c_j)\mathcal{N}(\mathbf{c}_j; \mu_j^+, I) + (1 - \delta(c_j))\mathcal{N}(\mathbf{c}_j; \mu_j^-, I),$$

where $\mu_j^+, \mu_j^- \in \mathbb{R}^m$ are learnable embeddings, $I$ is the identity matrix, and $\delta(\cdot)$ represents the Dirac delta function, which evaluates to 1 if $c_j = 1$ and 0 otherwise. Here, $\mu_j^+$ corresponds to the expected embedding when the concept is active ($c_j = 1$), while $\mu_j^-$ represents the expected embedding when the concept is inactive ($c_j = 0$). For the sake of simplicity, we define the approximate posterior as a multivariate normal distribution:

$$q(\mathbf{c}_j|x, c_j) = \mathcal{N}(\mathbf{c}_j; \hat{\mu}_j(x, c_j), \text{diag}(\sigma_j(x, c_j)))$$

where $\hat{\mu}_j(x, c_j), \sigma_j(x, c_j) \in \mathbb{R}^m$.

Given this definition for the prior and the approximate posterior, the *Prior Matching* term can be expressed in a closed-form solution. A detailed derivation of this formulation is presented in Appendix B. During training, the *Prior Matching* term encourages the approximate posterior $q$ to position the multivariate normal distribution near $\mu_j^+$ when $c_j = 1$ and near $\mu_j^-$ otherwise. This regularization promotes the formation of dense clusters for each concept state, ensuring that each state is represented by a distinct concept embedding: $\mu_j^+$ for $c_j = 1$ and $\mu_j^-$ for $c_j = 0$. By exploiting this property of V-CEM, we can perform concept embedding intervention, thereby decoupling the concept embedding from the raw input data.

### 3.2 V-CEM Training

The model is trained to optimize the ELBO by minimizing its negative counterpart. Assuming each concept $c_j$ follows a Bernoulli distribution, the second term in the ELBO reduces to a sum of binary cross-entropy losses, denoted as $L_c$. Similarly, if the task variable $y$ follows a categorical distribution, the third term in ELBO corresponds to the expected cross-entropy loss over $y$, referred to as $L_t$.

Following standard practices in concept bottleneck models [25], we introduce a weighting parameter $\lambda_t \in [0, 1]$ to balance the task loss $L_t$, allowing for trade-offs between concept learning and task performance. Additionally, a scaling factor $\lambda_p \in [0, \infty)$ is applied to the *Prior Matching* term $L_p$, influencing the model's regularization. Increasing $\lambda_p$ progressively aligns V-CEM with a CBM, while setting $\lambda_p = 0$ removes constraints on concept embeddings, making the model function like CEM.

V-CEM is trained by minimizing the following objective function:

$$L = \frac{1}{k}L_c + \lambda_t L_t + \lambda_p L_p \tag{4}$$

where $L_c$ is normalized by the number of concepts $k$. In this work, we set $\lambda_t = 0.1$ and $\lambda_p = 0.05$. An ablation study exploring the effect of varying $\lambda_p$ on V-CEM's performance is provided in Appendix D.

To enhance the responsiveness of V-CEM to ID interventions, the *RandInt* regularization strategy [11,25] is employed during the training phase, performing random concept embedding interventions with a predefined probability. Additional details about the specific settings of the proposed methodology and the baseline methods are provided in Appendix E.2.

## 4 Evaluating Concept Representations

In order to properly evaluate the model's intervenability in OOD settings, particularly when dealing with concept embeddings, concept accuracy might not be sufficient. In this section, we describe two further metrics that we use for this scope: OOD intervenability and *Concept Representation Cohesiveness (CRC)*.

**OOD Intervenability.** Concept interventions are generally used to assess the intervenability of a model [13], i.e., whether a model's predictions change when concept predictions are modified while keeping other factors constant. Model intervenability is normally evaluated ID by replacing concept predictions with concept labels. However, ID concept predictions are often already correct, thus the possibility to obtain a counterfactual prediction is low. Furthermore, for models relying on concept embeddings, this phenomenon is even more evident as part of the task prediction depends on $x$ rather than $c$. Thus, in this paper we evaluate model intervenability OOD. More specifically, we propose to analyze responsiveness to interventions under varying conditions by progressively adding random noise $\epsilon \sim N(0, I)$ to the input $x$. The perturbed input is thus defined as:

$$\tilde{x} = (1 - \theta) \cdot x + \theta \cdot \epsilon, \quad \theta \in [0, 1]$$

where $\theta$ controls the noise intensity. Interventions are applied randomly on misclassified concepts, with an increasing probability $p_{int} \in [0, 1]$.

**Concept Representation Cohesiveness.** Concept embeddings allow concept-based models to avoid the performance trade-off due to the CBM concept-bottleneck layer, as they enrich concept representation with sample-based information. Still, it is fundamental that this information represents the concept and not other input features; otherwise we may incur in the so-called "concept leakage" issue [19,20], where the concepts encode spurious information related to other concepts. In other words, we would like each point in the concept embedding space **C** to represent a different instantiation of an active or inactive concept. As training a decoder for each concept is non-trivial, in this paper we propose to assess this characteristic through an evaluation of the cohesiveness of the clusters associated with active and inactive concepts. More precisely, we compute $CRC$ by splitting all concept embeddings into two clusters according to their concept predictions, and we compute the corresponding silhouette score as follows:

$$CRC = \frac{1}{|C|} \sum_{i=0}^{|C|} s_i(\mathbf{c}_i, c_i) \tag{5}$$

where $|C|$ represents the number of concepts and $s_i(\mathbf{c}_i, c_i)$ represents the silhouette coefficient computed for the $i$th concept over concept embedding representation $\mathbf{c}_i$ and considering as clustering labels the concept prediction $c_i$. For further detail on the computation of $s_i$ we refer the reader to Appendix C. A higher silhouette score indicates a denser and tighter concept embedding space. This, in turn, indicates a model more responsive to OOD concept embedding intervention, as it samples from a denser representation.

## 5 Experimental Evaluation

To evaluate V-CEM, we seek to address several key research questions that guide our investigation. Specifically, we aim to answer the following:

(1) Does V-CEM exhibit comparable task performance to Black-box and CEM in ID settings?
(2) Is V-CEM more responsive than concept embedding-based approaches (CEM and Prob-CBM) in OOD scenarios?
(3) How does V-CEM concept representation compare to CBM representation, despite its reliance on concept embeddings?

### 5.1 Experimental Setting

In this section, we outline the experimental setup used to evaluate the performance of V-CEM. Specifically, we present the datasets, the baseline models and the training details.

**Datasets.** We conduct experiments on a diverse set of vision and NLP datasets. For vision, we use MNIST Even/Odd and MNIST Addition, which are derived from the MNIST dataset [14] and involve binary classification and digit-sum prediction tasks, respectively. For these two datasets digits are used as concepts. We conduct experiments also on CelebA [16], a large-scale facial attribute dataset, where selected attributes serve as concepts and others as prediction targets. For NLP, we experiment with CEBaB [1], a dataset designed to study causal effects of concepts in sentiment analysis, and IMDB [18], where movie reviews are classified as positive or negative using interpretable aspects. More details on dataset preprocessing and structure are provided in Appendix E.

**Baselines.** To assess the effectiveness of the proposed methodology, we compare it against several baseline models. For vision tasks, we extract embeddings using a frozen ResNet-34 [8], while for NLP tasks, we use *all-distilroberta-v1*[2]. Both

---
[2] We use the pretrained model available at https://huggingface.co/sentence-transformers.

**Table 1.** The average task accuracy and corresponding standard deviation in ID settings obtained by the various methodologies across different datasets. V-CEM performance are the highest on average when considering concept-based models, surpassing also Black-box performance on three datasets.

|  | MNIST E/O | MNIST+ | CelebA | CEBaB | IMDB |
|---|---|---|---|---|---|
| Black-box | 98.56 ±0.01 | 67.59 ±0.57 | **64.66** ±0.07 | **80.20** ±0.25 | 86.98 ±0.48 |
| CBM+Linear | 98.82 ±0.04 | 44.19 ±1.86 | 49.75 ±0.18 | 63.66 ±3.48 | 87.30 ±0.58 |
| CBM+MLP | 98.82 ±0.13 | 68.63 ±0.72 | 51.01 ±0.51 | 72.51 ±5.88 | 86.48 ±1.88 |
| CEM | 98.75 ±0.07 | 69.84 ±0.91 | 64.49 ±0.08 | 80.12 ±0.14 | 86.79 ±0.77 |
| Prob-CBM | 97.38 ±0.61 | 27.31 ±3.92 | 51.64 ±7.12 | 77.86 ±0.95 | 85.90 ±0.38 |
| V-CEM | **98.91** ±0.05 | **73.12** ±0.35 | 64.49 ±0.15 | 79.62 ±1.29 | **87.94** ±0.86 |

backbones are used without fine-tuning to extract embeddings from the input data. All baselines operate on these precomputed embeddings. The compared models include: (1) a standard Black-box model, implemented using two consecutive linear layers, (2) two variations of CBMs [13]: the first employing a single linear layer to map concepts to the task (CBM+Linear), and the second utilizing two consecutive linear layers (CBM+MLP), (3) Prob-CBM [11], (4) CEM [25]. Training details for all models are reported in Appendix E.

### 5.2 Results

The results highlight three key findings: (1) V-CEM outperforms CBMs and Prob-CBM while remaining comparable to CEM and Black-box models in ID settings, (2) it exhibits high responsiveness to interventions in OOD scenarios compared to CEMs and Prob-CBM, and (3) its concept embedding space **C** is more cohesive than that of concept embedding-based models.

**In-Distribution Performance.** In Table 1, we present the task accuracy results for the various models evaluated across different datasets in ID settings. The results clearly demonstrate that **V-CEM consistently outperforms traditional CBMs and Prob-CBM** in average ID performance. This trend is consistent across all datasets and this is particularly evident in MNIST Addition, where V-CEM achieves over 40% higher task accuracy compared to Prob-CBM and outperforms CBM+Linear by nearly 30%. Overall, V-CEM achieves ID performance comparable to CEM and the Black-box model while also attaining the highest average accuracy for MNIST E/O, MNIST+, and IMDB. This is achieved while maintaining similar concept accuracy across all models, as reported in Appendix F.

**Intervention Responsiveness.** Figure 3 illustrates the task accuracy of various models when human intervention is used to correct misclassified concept

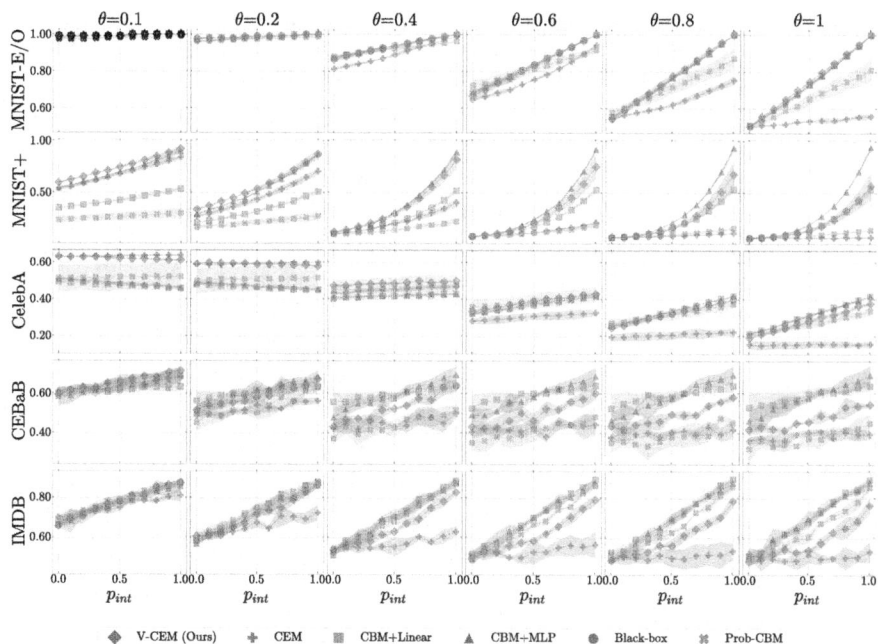

**Fig. 3.** The solid lines represent the mean task accuracy under random interventions at probability $p_{int}$, while the shaded areas indicate the standard deviation of each method. Results are reported across different models and datasets, under varying levels of input noise $\theta \in [0, 1]$. The Black-box model is not shown since it does not allow human interventions.

predictions under varying levels of input noise $\theta \in [0, 1]$, revealing several key insights. As anticipated, CEM shows minimal responsiveness to interventions, underscoring a key limitation: its strong dependence on input, which makes it less effective in the presence of distributional shifts. In contrast, **V-CEM consistently shows greater responsiveness to interventions in OOD settings**, outperforming Prob-CBM, which only surpasses V-CEM in responsiveness for the IMDB dataset. This suggests that V-CEM retains intervention efficacy by more effectively utilizing concept embeddings. Overall, V-CEM demonstrates responsiveness similar to CBMs while achieving superior performance in the ID scenario.

**Concept Embedding Space Evaluation.** As outlined in Sect. 5, to further investigate why V-CEM outperforms CEMs in terms of intervention responsiveness while maintaining performance comparable to CBMs in OOD settings, we propose to analyze the cohesiveness of the concept embedding space.

Ideally, each point in the concept embedding space should correspond to a distinct instance of an active or inactive concept. Specifically, for each concept, we here identify two clusters and compute the $CRC$ score across all concepts for each

**Table 2.** The average *CRC* values and their respective standard deviations in ID settings evaluated for all methodologies and datasets. The higher the better. V-CEM values are close to CBMs and always higher than both CEM and Prob-CBM.

|  | MNIST E/O | MNIST+ | CelebA | CEBaB | IMDB |
|---|---|---|---|---|---|
| CBM+Linear | 0.99 ± ≤0.01 | 0.92 ±0.01 | 0.73 ±0.01 | 0.70 ±0.01 | 0.73 ±0.01 |
| CBM+MLP | 0.99 ± ≤0.01 | 0.91 ±0.01 | 0.72 ±0.01 | 0.71 ±0.01 | 0.74 ±0.01 |
| CEM | 0.65 ±0.01 | 0.65 ±0.02 | 0.32 ±0.02 | 0.33 ±0.03 | 0.45 ±0.04 |
| Prob-CBM | 0.73 ±0.01 | 0.59 ±0.02 | 0.31 ±0.03 | 0.41 ±0.05 | 0.50 ±0.02 |
| V-CEM | 0.98 ±0.01 | 0.85 ±0.02 | 0.41 ±0.03 | 0.59 ±0.02 | 0.67 ±0.02 |

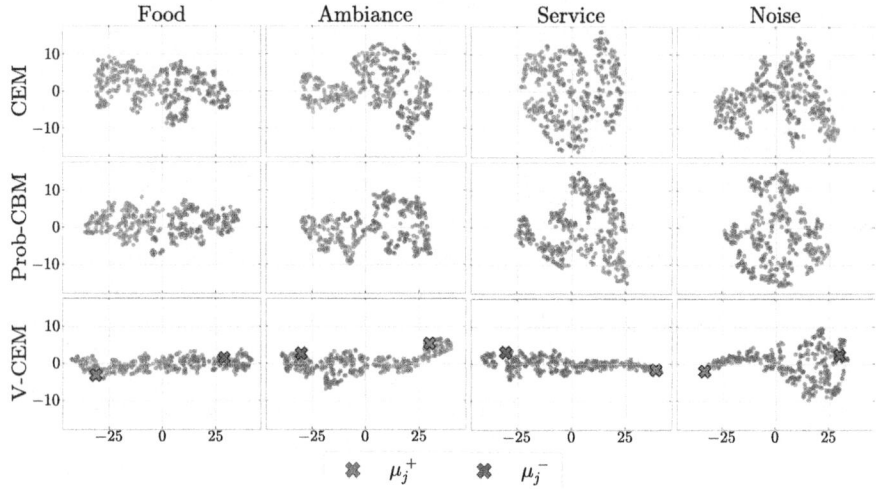

**Fig. 4.** 2D t-SNE visualization of the concept embedding space **c** for the CEBaB dataset, comparing V-CEM, Prob-CBM and CEM. V-CEM concept representation is much denser than the ones of CEM and Prob-CEM.

model and dataset. Table 2 presents the results, showing that **V-CEM's concept embedding space is more cohesive than that of concept embedding based models** (CEM and PRob-CBM) while remaining comparable to CBMs. Additionally, Fig. 4 provides a 2D t-SNE visualization comparing the concept embedding spaces of CEM, Prob-CBM and V-CEM for different concepts in the CEBaB dataset, further illustrating this effect.

## 6 Related Works

C-XAI [21] has gained prominence as a solution to the growing demand for machine learning models that provide explanations in human-understandable terms [22]. Unlike traditional feature-based approaches, C-XAI emphasizes associating a model's behavior with human-interpretable concepts, offering a more intuitive and accessible way to understand model decisions.

A foundational approach in this domain is Testing with Concept Activation Vectors (T-CAVs), introduced in [10], which leverages directions in the latent space to measure, post-hoc, a model's sensitivity to predefined human-understandable concepts. In contrast, explainable-by-design models incorporate interpretability directly into their architecture. A prominent example is CBM [2,4,13], which integrates supervised concepts as intermediate representations within the prediction pipeline, enabling more transparent and controllable decision-making. This integration facilitates direct intervention and correction of errors, thus enabling a more interactive approach to model understanding.

Additionally, Concept Embedding Models (CEMs) [25] push the boundaries of the interpretability-performance trade-off by incorporating concept embeddings into the learning process, enabling richer representations while maintaining concept-based explanations. Building on this approach, Prob-CBM [11] employs concept embeddings to capture uncertainty in concept predictions, offering explanations that incorporate both the concept and its associated uncertainty.

However, a critical challenge remains: ensuring robustness in OOD scenarios. OOD generalization is essential in machine learning, as it determines a model's ability to maintain reliable performance when encountering data that deviates from the training distribution.

Methodologies such as Outlier Exposure [9] and ODIN [15] aim to enhance the detection and management of OOD samples during inference. Additionally, studies like [7] underscore the necessity of benchmarking OOD performance through meticulously designed experimental protocols. More recently, other works [3,24] have demonstrated that the decline in the performance of deep learning models following deployment in real-world applications can be mitigated by incorporating human assistance to support OOD generalization. Motivated by this approach, we seek to investigate the potential of leveraging the interveneability characteristic of concept-based models to enable human interventions under OOD conditions. The interplay between OOD generalization and concept-based explainability remains a relatively unexplored yet promising research direction. Integrating these domains could pave the way for more resilient and interpretable models that provide actionable explanations, even in challenging and unforeseen scenarios.

## 7 Conclusion

We introduced V-CEM, a model that achieves ID performance comparable to Black-box and CEM while maintaining strong responsiveness to interventions in both ID and OOD settings. We have shown that its improved performance compared to other concept embedding based models originates from the cohesiveness of its concept embedding space which is ensured by the generative process that is conditioned on the concept prediction only.

Although V-CEM demonstrates strong responsiveness in OOD scenarios, it lacks an inherent mechanism for identifying OOD samples. Implementing such a mechanism would be beneficial, as it could assist human intervention by highlighting concepts associated with samples that deviate from those the model encountered during training. This could improve the model's ability to flag and address potential OOD instances, enhancing its overall reliability and reducing the risk of misclassification. Moreover, V-CEM was evaluated exclusively on OOD scenarios generated by introducing random noise into the input. Additional experiments are required to assess its performance on other types of distributional shifts.

**Future Works.** Future research directions include extending V-CEM to handle multimodal inputs, allowing the model to integrate and process information from multiple data sources effectively, thereby creating shared and aligned concept embeddings across modalities. Another promising avenue is the incorporation of generative models as decoders for concepts, leveraging their capabilities to create concept visualizations from V-CEM cohesive concept embedding space. Finally, V-CEM models concepts independently from each other. In scenarios where the presence of a concept significantly affects other concepts, it may be opportune to explicitly model this dependency. Merging V-CEM with the strategy suggested in [5,6] might offer a method for accomplishing this.

**Acknowledgement.** The research leading to these results has been funded by the Italian Ministry of University as part of the 2022 PRIN Project ACRE (AI-Based Causality and Reasoning for Deceptive Assets - 2022EP2L7H).

# Appendix

## A  Loss Derivation

This appendix provides the complete derivation of the loss function that V-CEM is trained to approximate:

$$\log p(c, y|x) = \log \int_\mathbf{C} \frac{p(x, c, \mathbf{c}, y)}{p(x)} d\mathbf{c} \tag{6}$$

$$= \log \int_\mathbf{C} p(c|x) p(\mathbf{c}|c) p(y|\mathbf{c}) d\mathbf{c} \tag{7}$$

$$= \log \int_\mathbf{C} \frac{q(\mathbf{c}|x, c)}{q(\mathbf{c}|x, c)} p(c|x) p(\mathbf{c}|c) p(y|\mathbf{c}) d\mathbf{c} \tag{8}$$

$$= \log E_q \left[ \frac{p(c|x) p(\mathbf{c}|c) p(y|\mathbf{c})}{q(\mathbf{c}|x, c)} \right] \tag{9}$$

$$\geq E_q \left[ \log \frac{p(c|x) p(\mathbf{c}|c) p(y|\mathbf{c})}{q(\mathbf{c}|x, c)} \right] \tag{10}$$

$$= -E_q \left[ \log \frac{q(\mathbf{c}|x, c)}{p(\mathbf{c}|c)} \right] + \log p(c|x) + E_q \left[ \log p(y|\mathbf{c}) \right] \tag{11}$$

We begin by re-expressing the target conditional probability $p(x, y \mid \mathbf{c})$ through marginalization over $\mathbf{C}$ and factorizing the joint distribution $p(x, c, \mathbf{c}, y)$ according to the generative process illustrated in Fig. 1c. Next, to amortize inference we introduce an approximate posterior distribution $q(\mathbf{c}|x, c)$ (Eq. 8). By applying Jensen's inequality, we obtain a lower bound on the log-likelihood, known as the ELBO, as shown in Eq. 10. Finally, Eq. 11 expands the ELBO into three terms: the first term is the negative KL divergence between $q(\mathbf{c}|x, c)$ and $p(\mathbf{c}|c)$, which measures the difference between the approximate posterior and the true prior; the second term is the log-likelihood of $c$, and the third term is the expected log-likelihood of $y$.

## B  Prior Matching Formulation

An important assumption we make, which is a standard assumption for concept based methodologies, is that the different concepts, and therefore the different concepts embeddings, are independent one another. Therefore, $q(\mathbf{c}|x,c) = \prod_{j=1}^{k} q(\mathbf{c}_j|x, c_j)$ and $p(\mathbf{c}|c) = \prod_{j=1}^{k} p(\mathbf{c}_j|c_j)$. This allows to rewrite the *Prior Matching* term as the sum of KL divergences between the approximate posterior and the true prior of each concept:

$$E_q \left[ \log \frac{q(\mathbf{c}|x,c)}{p(\mathbf{c}|c)} \right] = \int_{\mathbf{C}} q(\mathbf{c}|x,c) \log \frac{q(\mathbf{c}|x,c)}{p(\mathbf{c}|c)} d\mathbf{c} \tag{12}$$

$$= \sum_{j=1}^{k} \int_{\mathbf{C}} \prod_{i=1}^{k} q(\mathbf{c}_i|x, c_i) \log \frac{q(\mathbf{c}_j \mid x, c_j)}{p(\mathbf{c}_j \mid c_j)} d\mathbf{c} \tag{13}$$

$$= \sum_{j=1}^{k} \int_{\mathbf{C}} q(\mathbf{c}_j|x, c_j) \log \frac{q(\mathbf{c}_j \mid x, c_j)}{p(\mathbf{c}_j \mid c_j)} d\mathbf{c} \tag{14}$$

$$= \sum_{j=1}^{k} E_q \left[ \log \frac{q(\mathbf{c}_j|x,c_j)}{p(\mathbf{c}_j|c_j)} \right] \tag{15}$$

The prior is modeled as a mixture, governed by the function $\delta(\cdot)$, which selects the appropriate normal distribution based on the value of $c_j$. As a result, the KL divergence is computed differently depending on whether $c_j$ is active or inactive. When $c_j = 1$, it quantifies the divergence between the approximate posterior and the corresponding normal distribution in the prior for $c_j = 1$. Similarly, when $c_j = 0$, it measures the divergence between the approximate posterior and the prior distribution associated with $c_j = 0$. Defining

$$\mu_j = \begin{cases} \mu_j^+ & \text{if } c_j = 1, \\ \mu_j^- & \text{if } c_j = 0 \end{cases}$$

allows to rewrite the *Prior Matching* term as:

$$E_q\left[\log\frac{q(\mathbf{c}|x,c)}{p(\mathbf{c}|c)}\right] = \frac{1}{2}\sum_{j=1}^{k}\left[||\hat{\mu}_j(x,c) - \mu_j||^2 + \sum_{z=1}^{m}\sigma_{jz}^2(x,c) - m - \sum_{z=1}^{m}\log\sigma_{jz}^2(x,c)\right]$$

where $\sigma_{jz}^2(x,c)$ denotes the variance of the concept embedding $j$ for the latent dimension $z$.

## C  Concept Representation Cohesiveness

In our manuscript we introduce a novel metric to compute the Concept Representation Cohesiveness, a metric to comprehend how spread the representation are in the concept space which is particularly useful to assess how prone a model is to concept leakage and in turn how likely we can correctly perform concept intervention also OOD. Recalling from Sect. 4, Eq. 5, we defined CRC as:

$$CRC = \frac{1}{|C|}\sum_{i=0}^{|C|} s_i(\mathbf{c}_i, c_i)$$

More specifically, we now define how to compute $s_i$ (here and in the following we drop the dependency from $\mathbf{c}_i$, $c_i$):

$$s_i = \frac{1}{2}\left(\frac{b_i^+ - a_i^+}{\max(b_i^+, a_i^+)} + \frac{b_i^- - a_i^-}{\max(b_i^-, a_i^-)}\right),$$

$$a_i^+ = \frac{1}{|\mathcal{C}_i^+|}\sum_{j\in\mathcal{C}_i^+}\frac{1}{|\mathcal{C}_i^+ - 1|}\sum_{k\in\mathcal{C}_i^+, k\neq j}||\mathbf{c}_{ij} - \mathbf{c}_{ik}||_1$$

$$b_i^+ = \frac{1}{|\mathcal{C}^+ - 1|}\sum_{j\in\mathcal{C}_i^+}\frac{1}{|\mathcal{C}^-|}\sum_{k\in\mathcal{C}_i^-}||\mathbf{c}_{ij} - \mathbf{c}_{ik}||_1$$

and where $\mathcal{C}_i^+ \mathcal{C}_i^-$ are the set of sample indexes associated to positive and negative concept prediction for concept $i$ and are thus computed as: $\mathcal{C}_i^+ = \mathbb{1}_{c_i > 0.5}$ and $\mathcal{C}_i^- = \mathbb{1}_{c_i \leq 0.5}$.

## D  Ablation on $\lambda_p$ Variation

In our manuscript we introduce a scaling factor $\lambda_p \in [0,\infty)$ to regulate the *Prior Matching* term, allowing fine-grained control over the model's behavior. Increasing $\lambda_p$ progressively aligns V-CEM with a standard CBM, whereas setting $\lambda_p = 0$ eliminates constraints on concept embedding generation, making the model function similarly to a CEM. In this appendix we show how modifying $\lambda_p$ modifies the model performance.

In Fig. 5, we report the ID performance of V-CEM on CEBaB and IMDB as an example of performance datasets when modifying $\lambda_p$. The observed transition aligns with expectations: for $\lambda_p = 0$, the model achieves good performance

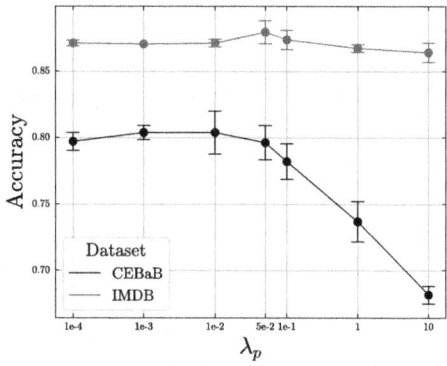

**Fig. 5.** Variation in V-CEM's ID accuracy across different values of $\lambda_p$ on the CEBaB and CelebA datasets.

similar to CEM, while increasing $\lambda_p$ leads to performance degradation, making it more similar to that of CBMs.

Similar results can be observed in Fig. 6, where for low values of $\lambda_p$, responsiveness to interventions is weaker—a characteristic typical of CEM—while it improves as $\lambda_p$ increases, approaching the responsiveness of CBMs. To balance both in-distribution performance and responsiveness to interventions, we set $\lambda_p = 0.05$ in this manuscript.

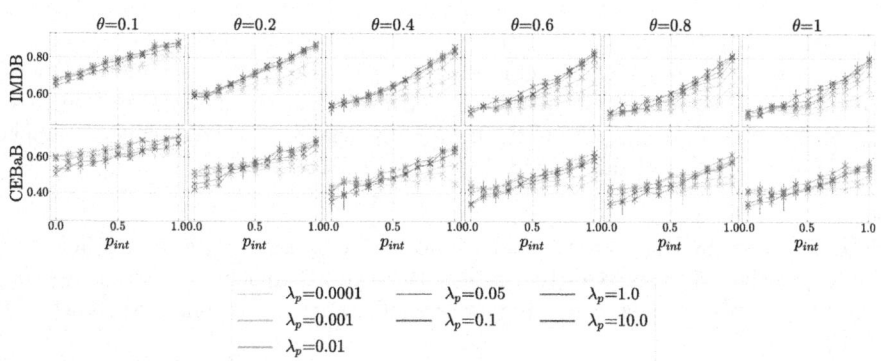

**Fig. 6.** Impact of interventions on V-CEM's OOD accuracy across different $\lambda_p$ values.

## E    Dataset Details

In this appendix, we provide additional details on the datasets used to evaluate the performance of the tested models, followed by a description of the training procedure.

### E.1 Datasets

**MNIST Even/Odd.** MNIST Even/Odd is a binary classification dataset derived from MNIST, where digits, used as concept labels, are categorized as either even or odd. It consists of 60 000 training images and 10 000 test images, each of size $28 \times 28$ and in grayscale. All images were converted to a three-channel format and rescaled to $224 \times 224$.

**MNIST Addition.** MNIST Addition is constructed by pairing two MNIST digits (used as concepts) and assigning a label equal to the sum of their individual values. The dataset retains the original MNIST structure, containing 60 000 training samples and 10 000 test samples. Each input is a grayscale image formed by concatenating two MNIST digits side by side. Alslo in this case, images were converted to a three-channel format and rescaled to $224 \times 224$.

**CelebA.** CelebA is a large-scale facial attribute dataset containing over 2 00 000 images of celebrities, each of size $178 \times 218$. The dataset is divided into training, validation, and test sets. We use the following attributes as concepts: No Beard, Young, Attractive, Mouth Slightly Open, Smiling, Wearing Lipstick, and High Cheekbones, as they are the most balanced attributes in the dataset. The task is a multi-class classification problem, where the goal is to predict the attributes Wavy Hair, Black Hair, and Male. All images are already in RGB format and are rescaled to $224 \times 224$.

**CEBaB.** CEBaB is a dataset designed to study the causal effects of real-world concepts on NLP models. It includes short restaurant reviews annotated with sentiment ratings at both the overall review level (positive, neutral, and negative reviews) and for four dining experience aspects, which are used as concept labels: Good Food, Good Ambiance, Good Service, and Good Noise.

**IMDB.** The IMDB dataset consists of 50 000 movie reviews labeled as either positive or negative. To predict the overall review sentiment, we use four interpretable concepts: Acting, Cinematography, Emotional arousal, and Storyline.

For datasets that do not provide a validation set, we randomly removed 10% of the training data to create a validation set.

### E.2 Training Details

All models were trained up to 500 epochs, employing an early stopping criterion with a patience of 20 epochs. The Adam optimizer was used along with a learning rate scheduler that reduced the learning rate by a factor of 0.1 every 100 epochs. The initial learning rate was dataset-specific: $2e-3$ for MNIST

Even/Odd and MNIST Addition, $1e-4$ for CelebA, $5e-4$ for CEBaB, and $1e-2$ for IMDB. All baseline models were trained with default hyperparameters. Both Prob-CBM and CEM were trained following the *RandInt* technique proposed in [25], setting it to 0.25 for CEM and to 0.5 for Prob-CBM, as suggested in the respective papers. To ensure a fair comparison across different methodologies, we applied the *RandInt* technique during the training of CBM+MLP, CBM+Linear, and V-CEM. Specifically, we set the intervention probability to 0.25 for these approaches. For V-CEM, random interventions were introduced starting from the 20th epoch for the CelebA dataset (given the larger size of the training-set), while for all other datasets, they were applied from the 3rd epoch onward.

For the V-CEM model, the *Prior Matching* term was scaled using a factor of $\lambda = 0.05$. As for Prob-CBM and CEM, we used a concept embedding dimension of 16. Each model was trained using three different random seeds.

## F Concept Accuracy

In this appendix, we report the concept accuracy values for all models and datasets. The results reported in Table 3 confirm that, in terms of concept accuracy, the performance of all models is comparable, with V-CEM being on average the best (despite overlapping standard deviations).

**Table 3.** Concept accuracy comparison across different datasets in ID settings.

|            | MNIST E/O | MNIST+ | CelebA | CEBaB | IMDB |
|---|---|---|---|---|---|
| CBM+Linear | 99.44 ±0.01 | 95.24 ±0.00 | 83.02 ±0.03 | 80.33 ±0.74 | 84.41 ±0.05 |
| CBM+MLP    | 99.46 ±0.01 | 95.08 ±0.04 | 82.91 ±0.05 | 80.81 ±0.79 | 84.49 ±0.12 |
| CEM        | 99.35 ±0.03 | 94.91 ±0.05 | 82.77 ±0.04 | 79.51 ±0.17 | 83.30 ±0.18 |
| Prob-CBM   | 99.18 ±0.07 | 95.08 ±0.09 | 82.93 ±0.03 | 80.70 ±0.66 | 83.48 ±0.41 |
| V-CEM      | 99.49 ±0.00 | 95.22 ±0.09 | 83.04 ±0.01 | 80.37 ±0.52 | 84.16 ±0.19 |

## G ID Interventions

In addition to demonstrating strong responsiveness to interventions in OOD settings, V-CEM maintains high accuracy even when interventions occur in ID settings. As shown in Fig. 7, the performance of the various models remains stable across different datasets. This stability is primarily attributed to the high concept accuracy (Table 3) achieved by these models, which limits the potential for further improvement following interventions. Notably, in MNIST+, accuracy increases linearly with the intervention probability ($p_{int}$) for all the methodologies. Conversely, for CBM+MLP and CBM+Linear on the CEBaB and CelebA datasets, performance slightly declines post-intervention, likely due to the lower concept accuracy in these datasets (approximately 80%). This observation highlights the greater robustness of concept embedding methodologies to interventions in such scenarios.

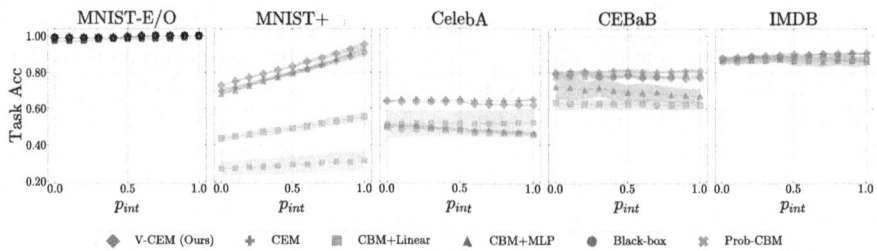

**Fig. 7.** Mean and standard deviation of task accuracy with random interventions at probability $p_{int}$ across different models and datasets without noise (ID settings).

## References

1. Abraham, E.D., et al.: Cebab: estimating the causal effects of real-world concepts on nlp model behavior. Adv. Neural. Inf. Process. Syst. **35**, 17582–17596 (2022)
2. Alvarez Melis, D., Jaakkola, T.: Towards robust interpretability with self-explaining neural networks. In: Advances in Neural Information Processing Systems, vol. 31 (2018)
3. Bai, H., Zhang, J., Nowak, R.: Aha: Human-assisted out-of-distribution generalization and detection. arXiv preprint arXiv:2410.08000 (2024)
4. Ciravegna, G., et al.: Logic explained networks. Artif. Intell. **314**, 103822 (2023)
5. De Felice, G., et al.: Causally reliable concept bottleneck models. arXiv preprint arXiv:2503.04363 (2025)
6. Dominici, G., et al.: Causal concept graph models: beyond causal opacity in deep learning. arXiv preprint arXiv:2405.16507 (2024)
7. Gulrajani, I., Lopez-Paz, D.: In search of lost domain generalization. arXiv preprint arXiv:2007.01434 (2020)
8. He, K., Zhang, X., Ren, S., Sun, J.: Deep residual learning for image recognition. In: Proceedings of the IEEE Conference on Computer Vision and Pattern Recognition, pp. 770–778 (2016)
9. Hendrycks, D., Mazeika, M., Dietterich, T.: Deep anomaly detection with outlier exposure. arXiv preprint arXiv:1812.04606 (2018)
10. Kim, B., Wattenberg, M., Gilmer, J., Cai, C., Wexler, J., Viegas, F., et al.: Interpretability beyond feature attribution: quantitative testing with concept activation vectors (tcav). In: International Conference on Machine Learning, pp. 2668–2677. PMLR (2018)
11. Kim, E., Jung, D., Park, S., Kim, S., Yoon, S.: Probabilistic concept bottleneck models. In: International Conference on Machine Learning, pp. 16521–16540 (2023)
12. Kingma, D.P.: Auto-encoding variational bayes. arXiv preprint arXiv:1312.6114 (2013)
13. Koh, P.W., et al.: Concept bottleneck models. In: International Conference on Machine Learning, pp. 5338–5348. PMLR (2020)
14. Lecun, Y., Bottou, L., Bengio, Y., Haffner, P.: Gradient-based learning applied to document recognition. Proc. IEEE **86**(11), 2278–2324 (1998). https://doi.org/10.1109/5.726791
15. Liang, S., Li, Y.: Enhancing the reliability of out-of-distribution image detection in neural networks. arXiv preprint arXiv:1706.02690 (2017)

16. Liu, Z., Luo, P., Wang, X., Tang, X.: Deep learning face attributes in the wild. In: Proceedings of International Conference on Computer Vision (ICCV), December 2015
17. Louizos, C., Welling, M., Kingma, D.P.: Learning sparse neural networks through $l\_0$ regularization. arXiv preprint arXiv:1712.01312 (2017)
18. Maas, A.L., Daly, R.E., Pham, P.T., Huang, D., Ng, A.Y., Potts, C.: Learning word vectors for sentiment analysis. In: Lin, D., Matsumoto, Y., Mihalcea, R. (eds.) Proceedings of the 49th Annual Meeting of the Association for Computational Linguistics: Human Language Technologies, pp. 142–150. ACL, Portland, Oregon, USA, June 2011, https://aclanthology.org/P11-1015/
19. Mahinpei, A., Clark, J., Lage, I., Doshi-Velez, F., Pan, W.: Promises and pitfalls of black-box concept learning models. arXiv preprint arXiv:2106.13314 (2021)
20. Marconato, E., Passerini, A., Teso, S.: Glancenets: interpretable, leak-proof concept-based models. Adv. Neural. Inf. Process. Syst. **35**, 21212–21227 (2022)
21. Poeta, E., Ciravegna, G., Pastor, E., Cerquitelli, T., Baralis, E.: Concept-based explainable artificial intelligence: a survey. arXiv preprint arXiv:2312.12936 (2023)
22. Rudin, C.: Stop explaining black box machine learning models for high stakes decisions and use interpretable models instead. Nat. Mach. Intell. **1**(5), 206–215 (2019)
23. Sanh, V.: Distilbert, a distilled version of bert: smaller, faster, cheaper and lighter. arXiv preprint arXiv:1910.01108 (2019)
24. Vishwakarma, H., Lin, H., Vinayak, R.: Human-in-the-loop out-of-distribution detection with false positive rate control. In: NeurIPS Workshop on Adaptive Experimental Design and Active Learning in the Real World (2023)
25. Zarlenga, M.E., et al.: Concept embedding models. In: NeurIPS 2022-36th Conference on Neural Information Processing Systems (2022)

**Open Access** This chapter is licensed under the terms of the Creative Commons Attribution 4.0 International License (http://creativecommons.org/licenses/by/4.0/), which permits use, sharing, adaptation, distribution and reproduction in any medium or format, as long as you give appropriate credit to the original author(s) and the source, provide a link to the Creative Commons license and indicate if changes were made.

The images or other third party material in this chapter are included in the chapter's Creative Commons license, unless indicated otherwise in a credit line to the material. If material is not included in the chapter's Creative Commons license and your intended use is not permitted by statutory regulation or exceeds the permitted use, you will need to obtain permission directly from the copyright holder.

# Post-hoc Concept Disentanglement: From Correlated to Isolated Concept Representations

Eren Erogullari[1], Sebastian Lapuschkin[1,2(✉)], Wojciech Samek[1,3,4(✉)], and Frederik Pahde[1(✉)]

[1] Department of Artificial Intelligence, Fraunhofer Heinrich Hertz Institute, Berlin, Germany
{sebastian.lapuschkin,wojciech.samek,frederik.pahde}@hhi.fraunhofer.de
[2] Centre of eXplainable Artificial Intelligence, Technological University Dublin, Dublin, Ireland
[3] Department of Electrical Engineering and Computer Science, Technische Universität Berlin, Berlin, Germany
[4] BIFOLD – Berlin Institute for the Foundations of Learning and Data, Berlin, Germany

**Abstract.** Concept Activation Vectors (CAVs) are widely used to model human-understandable concepts as directions within the latent space of neural networks. They are trained by identifying directions from the activations of concept samples to those of non-concept samples. However, this method often produces similar, non-orthogonal directions for correlated concepts, such as "beard" and "necktie" within the CelebA dataset, which frequently co-occur in images of men. This entanglement complicates the interpretation of concepts in isolation and can lead to undesired effects in CAV applications, such as activation steering. To address this issue, we introduce a post-hoc concept disentanglement method that employs a non-orthogonality loss, facilitating the identification of orthogonal concept directions while preserving directional correctness. We evaluate our approach with real-world and controlled correlated concepts in CelebA and a synthetic FunnyBirds dataset with VGG16 and ResNet18 architectures. We further demonstrate the superiority of orthogonalized concept representations in activation steering tasks, allowing (1) the *insertion* of isolated concepts into input images through generative models and (2) the *removal* of concepts for effective shortcut suppression with reduced impact on correlated concepts in comparison to baseline CAVs. (Code is available at https://github.com/erenerogullari/cav-disentanglement.)

## 1 Introduction

With the growing reliance on deep learning in critical domains, such as applications in medicine [8] or criminal justice [47,51], the need for eXplainable Artificial Intelligence (XAI) has become more relevant to ensure transparency and trust in model's decision-making processes. XAI methods can be broadly categorized into local approaches, explaining individual predictions by attributing importance scores to input features (*e.g.*, [4,27,40]), and global approaches, aiming to uncover broader decision-making patterns learned by a model (*e.g.*, [1,14,23]). As such, concept-based explanations seek to represent abstract, human-understandable concepts in the model's latent space, offering insights into how these concepts influence predictions. Specifically, Concept Activation Vectors (CAVs) allow interpreting Deep Neural Networks (DNNs) by modeling high-level concepts as directions in latent space [23]. They are typically learned using linear classifiers, *e.g.*, linear Support Vector Machines (SVMs), to separate activations corresponding to the presence vs absence of a concept, represented by the normal to the decision hyperplane of the classifier. However, while this approach optimizes the directional correctness of *individual* concepts, it may fail to isolate a concept's direction from others when multiple correlated concepts are trained simultaneously. This is caused by highly entangled neural representations [13], *i.e.*, multiple concepts being encoded along overlapping directions due to correlations present in the dataset. This entanglement manifests in latent space as non-orthogonal concept directions [30], making it challenging to isolate individual concepts and leading to ambiguity and less interpretability in CAV-based explanations. For example, CAV-based steering applications, attempting to add [36] or remove [2] specific concepts, may unintentionally modify other entangled concepts, as illustrated in Fig. 1 (*top right*).

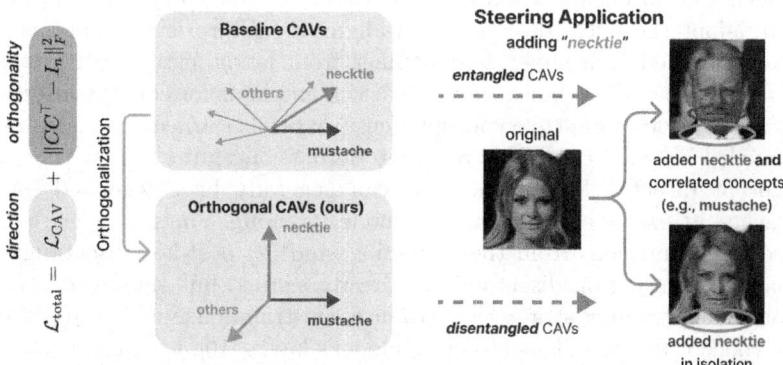

**Fig. 1.** *Left:* Our novel CAV objective encourages the orthogonalization of multiple concept directions trained simultaneously. *Right:* The resulting disentangled CAVs are beneficial for various CAV applications, as concepts can be targeted in isolation. For example, when inserting the "necktie" concept to an input image in a steering task, the usage of *entangled* baseline CAVs might add correlated concepts as well (*e.g.*, "mustache"), while *disentangled* CAVs add the targeted concept in isolation.

To tackle this issue holistically, we propose a novel CAV training objective penalizing non-orthogonality between concept directions trained simultaneously, thereby encouraging disentangled representations in latent space (Fig. 1, *left*). Our proposed loss term can be utilized in conjunction with any objective targeting directional correctness in a weighted manner to balance the trade-off between both optimization goals. We further introduce targeted orthogonalization, allowing to selectively enforce separation between specific concept pairs.

We evaluate our post-hoc concept orthogonalization approach through both controlled and real-world experiments using the CelebA and FunnyBirds datasets with VGG16 and ResNet18 architectures. Furthermore, we demonstrate the effectiveness of reduced concept entanglement in activation steering applications. This includes (1) the insertion of isolated concepts in latent encodings of contemporary Diffusion models as shown in Fig. 1 (*bottom right*) and (2) the precise concept removal for shortcut suppression with minimal impact on correlated concepts. We compare orthogonalized CAVs to baseline CAVs trained in isolation and provide both qualitative and quantitative results.

## 2 Related Work

Existing works either interpret concepts as individual neurons [1,31], higher-dimensional subspaces [48], geometric structures, such as convex sets [16], cones [32], or boxes [22], or linear directions within the latent space [9,23,28,34]. The latter provides a flexible way to capture representations by interpreting them as superpositions of multiple neurons [13]. Matrix factorization methods, such as non-negative matrix factorization, can be utilized to extract meaningful basis components in an unsupervised manner that act as interpretable concepts [14, 52]. We adopt the linear-directions paradigm and interpret concepts as linear directions learned in a supervised manner from latent model activations. As many concept-based methods, such as steering methods for concept insertion or suppression, scale to multiple concepts, ensuring that learned directions remain disentangled becomes crucial to avoid interfering concepts.

Concept disentanglement methods can generally be categorized into (1) approaches utilized before or during model training, aiming to learn disentangled representations from the beginning, and (2) post-hoc disentanglement approaches, focusing on disentangling already learned but entangled concepts. Pre- or during-training strategies introduce constraints like whitening layers to ensure concept disentanglement across model's layers [10], leverage metadata to separate relevant features from biases [38], or focus on learning disentangled representations of the underlying concepts in the data [49], either in a supervised [7,46] or in an unsupervised manner [20,24,42]. Post-hoc methods, on the other hand, typically extend classic dimensionality-reduction techniques like Principal Component Analysis (PCA) or Independent Component Analysis (ICA) [11] to uncover disentangled directions from pretrained models without altering their original training pipelines. In contrast to other methods, we introduce a *supervised post-hoc* concept disentanglement approach by extending CAVs [23,34] to enforce orthogonal concept directions within the latent space.

## 3 Post-hoc Concept Orthogonalization

**Notation.** Given a neural network $f : \mathcal{X} \to \mathcal{Y}$ that maps input samples $\mathbf{x} \in \mathcal{X}$ to target labels $y \in \mathcal{Y}$, we can decompose the network into two functions $f = h \circ g$, with feature extractor $g : \mathcal{X} \to \mathcal{Z}$ with $\mathcal{Z} \subseteq \mathbb{R}^m$ mapping input samples to hidden layer activations $\mathbf{z} \in \mathcal{Z}$ at a given layer with $m$ neurons, and classifier $h : \mathcal{Z} \to \mathcal{Y}$ mapping hidden layer activations to target labels $y$. Furthermore, given $n \in \mathbb{N}$ concepts with binary concept labels $\mathbf{t}^{(i)} \in \{-1, 1\}^n$ for each sample $\mathbf{x}^{(i)} \in \mathcal{X}$, the set of latent activations $\mathcal{Z}$ of samples can be partitioned into two sets for each concept $c$ with $\mathcal{Z} = \mathcal{Z}_c^+ \cup \mathcal{Z}_c^-$, where $\mathcal{Z}_c^+ := \{g(\mathbf{x}^{(i)}) \,|\, \mathbf{x}^{(i)} \in \mathcal{X}$ and $t_c^{(i)} = 1\}$ is the set of activations with the target concept c, and $\mathcal{Z}_c^- := \{g(\mathbf{x}^{(i)}) \,|\, \mathbf{x}^{(i)} \in \mathcal{X}$ and $t_c^{(i)} = -1\}$ is the set of activations without the target concept. Whereas the choice of layer is problem-specific, in practice, commonly the penultimate layer is used, as research suggests that later layers have higher receptive fields and capture more complex and abstract concepts [6,31,37].

### 3.1 Concept Modeling via Concept Activation Vectors

The CAV associated with a concept $c$ is defined as the direction in latent space pointing from activations of samples *without* the target concept $\mathcal{Z}_c^-$ to activations of samples *with* the target concept $\mathcal{Z}_c^+$ [23]. Most commonly, it is obtained from the weight vector $\mathbf{w} \in \mathbb{R}^m$ of a linear classifier [17,50], *i.e.*, the hyperplane separating latent activations of these sample sets, some of which are linear SVMs minimizing the hinge loss with L2 regularization [12] and logistic, or ridge regression models minimizing the squared error loss with L2 regularization [21]. By finding the optimal classification boundary, linear classifiers aim to achieve the directional correctness of concepts.

Given $k = |\mathcal{X}| \in \mathbb{N}$ samples, a concept $c$, and a simple linear model $f_{\text{lin}}(\mathbf{z}) = \mathbf{w}^T \mathbf{z} + b$ with weight vector $\mathbf{w} \in \mathbb{R}^m$ and bias $b \in \mathbb{R}$ as the classifier along with a ridge regression term, we typically obtain the objective function

$$\arg\min_{\mathbf{w},b} \mathcal{L}(Z \,;\, \mathbf{w}, b) = \arg\min_{\mathbf{w},b} \|\mathbf{t} - Z\mathbf{w} - \mathbf{b}\|_2^2 + \|\mathbf{w}\|_2^2 \qquad (1)$$

with $\mathbf{t} \in \{-1, 1\}^k$ representing the label vector with concept label $t_c^{(i)}$ as the $i^{th}$ element, $\mathbf{b} \in \mathbb{R}^k$ as an $n$-wise repetition of $b$, and $Z \in \mathbb{R}^{k \times m}$ as the input matrix with latent activations $\mathbf{z}^{(i)} \in \mathbb{R}^m$ on its rows.

Equation (1) aims to find a weight that maximizes class-separability, which is prone to capturing distractor components that arise from noise and unrelated features in the data [17]. To address this, Pahde et al. [34] introduce Pattern-CAVs, assuming a linear dependency between the activations and the concept labels and aiming to find a pattern that explains $Z$ w.r.t concept labels $\mathbf{t}$, where the objective becomes

$$\arg\min_{\mathbf{w},b} \mathcal{L}_{\text{CAV}}(Z \,;\, \mathbf{w}, \mathbf{b}) = \arg\min_{\mathbf{w},b} \|Z - \mathbf{t}\mathbf{w}^T - \mathbf{b}\|_2^2 \qquad (2)$$

leading to a solution invariant under feature scaling and more robust to noise.

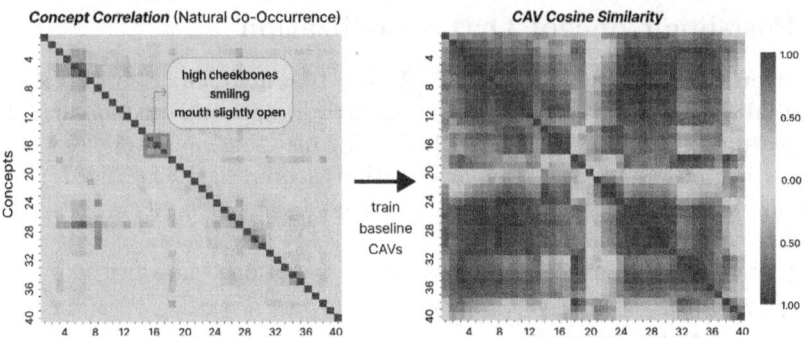

**Fig. 2.** *Left:* Correlations of known concepts based on their co-occurrence in CelebA. *Right:* Pair-wise cosine similarities between concept representations via CAVs trained in isolation. Concepts frequently co-occurring in the training data (*e.g.*, "high cheekbones", "smiling", and "mouth slightly open") result in highly similar and entangled CAVs.

However, both perspectives optimize CAVs in isolation and independent of other concepts, such that concept directions have no impact on other CAVs. This can result in solutions where CAVs share similar orientations and become entangled due to existing correlations in the training data. Throughout this paper, we will utilize Pattern-CAVs, as defined in Eq. (2), as the *baseline* CAVs.

### 3.2 Measuring Concept Entanglement

Concept entanglement in DNNs is caused by (1) the concept hierarchy, as sub- and super-concepts may share similar orientations, such as "goatee" and "beard", and (2) world-induced co-occurrence statistics of concepts present in the data, *i.e.*, concepts that frequently appear together, such as "beard" and "necktie", or those that do not, such as "mustache" and "makeup". Both forms of entanglement cause concepts to have similarly oriented latent representations by the DNN and thus we consider concepts as entangled if their representations share similar orientations within the latent space of the DNN. We further consider concepts to be disentangled, or independent, if their latent representations lie orthogonal to each other and thus capture linearly independent directions within the latent space. The entanglement of concepts can thus be analyzed empirically by their cosine similarity matrix. The cosine similarity between two vectors measures their angular similarity and, given two CAVs $c_i$ and $c_j$, is defined as

$$\cos(\mathbf{c}_i, \mathbf{c}_j) = \frac{\mathbf{c}_i \cdot \mathbf{c}_j}{\|\mathbf{c}_i\| \|\mathbf{c}_j\|} \qquad (3)$$

where values near 1 indicate high alignment, *i.e.*, entanglement, between the concepts, values near -1 indicate a strong inverse correlation or opposing directions in the feature space, and values near 0 suggest orthogonality and independence. The resulting matrix $C = (C_{ij}) = (\cos(\mathbf{c}_i, \mathbf{c}_j))$ provides insight into concept entanglement, where highly similar concepts may occupy overlapping regions in latent space. To quantify the orthogonality of a given concept to all others, we use the average cosine similarity, effectively describing the orthogonality of a concept in terms of a single metric, defined in Eq. (4).

An example for highly entangled concepts is shown in Fig. 2, where we show the CAVs trained on the CelebA dataset [26], consisting of images of celebrity faces with concept level annotations, such as "beard", "mustache", and "makeup". The resulting cosine similarity matrix of CAVs contains naturally emerging entanglement blocks, where different sets of concepts point in similar or opposite directions.

**Orthogonality Metric.** Given a finite set $\mathcal{C}$ of concepts with $|\mathcal{C}| > 1$, we define the *orthogonality* $O_i$ of a concept $\mathbf{c}_i \in \mathcal{C}$ as:

$$O_i = 1 - \frac{1}{|\mathcal{C}| - 1} \sum_{\tilde{\mathbf{c}} \in \mathcal{C} \setminus \{\mathbf{c}_i\}} |\cos(\mathbf{c}_i, \tilde{\mathbf{c}})| \qquad (4)$$

where $|\cdot|$ is the absolute value function. Consequently, the value of $O_i$ ranges between 0 and 1, where 1 represents perfect disentanglement and orthogonality of the given concept, and 0 represents complete entanglement and alignment with other concepts, sharing the same orientation in the latent space. We further define *average orthogonality* $\bar{O}$ as the average of all concepts' orthogonality values and use it as an indicator of overall disentanglement of concepts. Average orthogonality of a set of vectors effectively measures the linear independency of the vectors in terms of a scalar.

## 3.3 Orthogonalization of CAVs

Given a hidden layer with $m \in \mathbb{N}$ neurons and a finite set of concepts $\mathcal{C}$ present in the dataset with $n = |\mathcal{C}|$ concepts, and further assuming a setting where the dimensionality of the latent space is significantly higher than the number of concepts, *i.e.*, when $m \gg n$, there is sufficient room for CAVs to be orthogonal to one another. Therefore, to disentangle concept representations, we propose an additional loss term, encouraging orthogonality between CAVs in latent space. Specifically, we define the orthogonality loss $\mathcal{L}_{\text{orth}}$ as

$$\mathcal{L}_{\text{orth}} = \|CC^\top - I_n\|_F^2 \qquad (5)$$

where $C \in \mathbb{R}^{n \times m}$ is the matrix of $n$ CAVs with each row corresponding to a normalized CAV, $I_n$ is the $n$-dimensional identity matrix and $\|\cdot\|_F^2$ denotes the squared Frobenius norm. This loss term penalizes the deviation of the pair-wise cosine similarity matrix $CC^\top$ from the identity matrix $I_n$, effectively encouraging the CAVs to be orthogonal. The orthogonality loss $\mathcal{L}_\text{orth}$ can be combined with the original loss term $\mathcal{L}_\text{CAV}$ (e.g., in Eq. (2)) in a weighted manner as:

$$\mathcal{L} = \mathcal{L}_\text{CAV} + \alpha\,\mathcal{L}_\text{orth} \tag{6}$$

yielding the minimization objective with weighting parameter $\alpha > 0$ balancing the trade-off between the potentially competing goals to (1) maximize directional correctness with $\mathcal{L}_\text{CAV}$ and (2) orthogonalize the CAVs with $\mathcal{L}_\text{orth}$. With $\alpha = 0$ the optimization objective becomes the original objective, which does not penalize the concept entanglement, whereas with $\alpha \to \infty$ the orthogonality term will dominate the loss and the optimization will most likely yield random orthogonal concept directions that fail at directional correctness.

In practice, our novel training objective can either be employed to optimize CAVs from random initialization or to disentangle pre-trained CAVs in a fine-tuning step. While the former can balance the directional correctness objective and the orthogonality constraint from the beginning, it may require more iterations for convergence. The latter approach can lead to faster convergence, however, the magnitude of $\alpha$ must be chosen carefully to prevent over-correction by the orthogonality term. Finally, the average orthogonality $\bar{O}$ can be used as a global metric to measure overall orthogonality of CAVs during optimization.

### 3.4 Targeted Orthogonalization with Weighted Penalization

While orthogonalization of all CAVs is beneficial, not all concepts require the same level of adjustment. For example, already disentangled concepts, *i.e.*, minimally correlated concepts, should remain largely unaffected, while entangled concepts should be prioritized. To achieve this, we introduce a symmetric weighting matrix $W_\beta \in \mathbb{R}^{n \times n}$ to adjust the weighting of concept pairs, resulting in the $\beta$-weighted orthogonalization loss $\mathcal{L}^\beta_\text{orth}$ defined as:

$$\mathcal{L}^\beta_\text{orth} = \|W_\beta \odot (CC^\top - I_n)\|^2_F \tag{7}$$

where

$$(W_\beta)_{ij} = (W_\beta)_{ji} = \begin{cases} \beta & \text{if } (i,j) \text{ is a targeted pair,} \\ 1 & \text{otherwise.} \end{cases} \tag{8}$$

where $\beta \in \mathbb{R}$ with $\beta > 0$ describing the relative importance of target pairs over non-target pairs and $\odot$ denoting the Hadamard (element-wise) product. Having $\beta > 1$ will enforce a stricter disentanglement on the target pairs, while having $0 < \beta < 1$ will effectively relax the orthogonality constraint. Plugging the new $\mathcal{L}^\beta_\text{orth}$ loss in to Eq. (6) yields a new optimization objective, penalizing non-orthogonality of selected pairs of concepts over the others. This formulation allows selective penalization, focusing on disentangling specific pairs of highly entangled concepts while leaving already disentangled pairs largely unaffected. Note, that this formulation can easily be extended to individual weights for each pair, i.e. different values for each entry in $W_\beta$, while keeping $W_\beta$ symmetric. In practice, target pairs can be defined as a list of most entangled pairs with high correlations or high cosine similarities.

### 3.5 Practical Implications: Directional Correctness and Orthogonality Trade-Off

In order to maximize concept orthogonality while maintaining directional correctness, we monitor the macro-averaged Area Under Receiver Operating Curve (AUROC)[1], as a proxy metric for directional correctness, together with average orthogonality. Monitoring AUROC allows to ensure that the optimization does not compromise the primary goal of CAVs. We can further use AUROC to define an early-exit criteria, e.g., thresholds based on the average AUROC, average-drop of AUROC, or max-drop of AUROC. This ensures that the concept disentanglement preserves the directional correctness by preventing over-optimization at the expense of predictive performance, ensuring the CAVs remain useful for their intended purpose.

## 4 Experiments

We empirically evaluate our *post-hoc* concept disentanglement methods in a *supervised* setting using real-world concepts in CelebA and controlled concepts in the synthetic FunnyBirds dataset. Specifically, our experiments investigate whether our approach can successfully disentangle CAV-based concept representations for given concept labels while preserving the directional correctness measured via their AUROC as a proxy metric.

### 4.1 Experiment Details

We conduct experiments with the real-world CelebA dataset [26] and the synthetic FunnyBirds dataset [19]. The former consists of images of faces along with binary concept labels for 40 attributes (see Appendix A for details). We consider the task of classifying samples with and without "blond hair". Figure 2 (*left*) presents the correlation matrix between these attributes, revealing two distinct blocks that reflect natural groupings of concepts associated with male and female attributes. Moreover, we utilize a synthetic dataset with generated images of 50 bird classes with part-level annotations for 5 body parts (beak, eye, foot, tail, and wing), which are transformed into binary concept labels (see Appendix B for details). We inject controlled correlations between "beak" and "tail" concepts, such that 70% of samples with a given beak type have a specific corresponding tail type. For example, beak type "beak01.glb" has a 70% probability of being paired with tail type "tail01.glb", while the remaining 30% is split

---

[1] Note, that although our CAVs are *not* computed as predictors, their dot products with latent activations can be used to measure the concept separability.

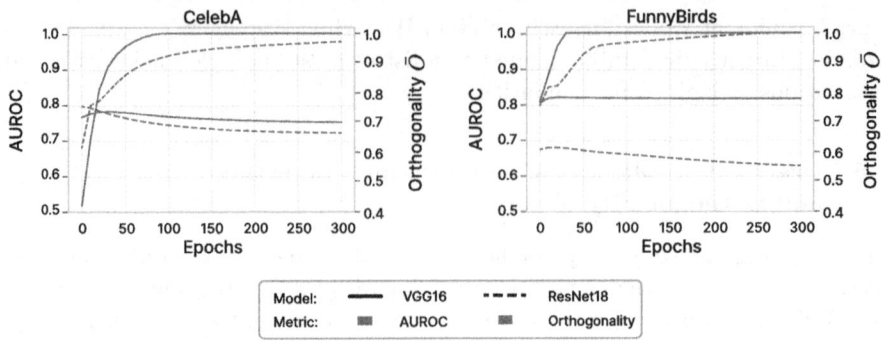

**Fig. 3.** Evolution of AUROC (*blue*) and average orthogonality $\bar{O}$ (*red*) during CAV optimization for ResNet18 and VGG16 models trained on CelebA (*left*) and FunnyBirds (*right*). Our approach achieves near-perfect orthogonalization, while preserving directional correctness as measured via AUROC. (Color figure online)

equally between the other tail types. This pattern is similarly applied to other beak types, resulting in controlled correlations between these concept attributes. Here, we consider the task of classifying the 50 bird classes for training the models. For both datasets, we train VGG16 [41] and ResNet18 [18] models and train CAVs using activations from the last convolutional layers of both models.

### 4.2 Concept Disentanglement

To measure the orthogonality of CAVs and directional correctness during the proposed optimization procedure, we (1) monitor the per-concept orthogonality $O_i$, average orthogonality $\bar{O}$, as well as per-concept and macro-averaged AUROC during optimization and (2) compare the cosine similarity matrices between CAVs before and after optimization. In both experimental settings we optimize CAVs starting from both random and pre-trained initializations, *i.e.*, the solution for Eq. (2), and apply orthogonalization, as defined in Eq. (6).

**Orthogonalization and Directional Correctness.** First, we evaluate our proposed optimization objective on all datasets using both models. We finetune pre-trained CAVs for 300 epochs (see Appendix C for details). The results are shown in Fig. 3. Across all experiments, we observe a drastic increase in orthogonality, with CAVs achieving either near-perfect or complete orthogonalization within 300 epochs. This strong shift towards orthogonality indicates that our method effectively promotes concept disentanglement, ensuring that learned representations become more independent.

We further observe that, while enforcing orthogonality, directional correctness – measured via AUROC as a proxy metric – remains largely preserved. This indicates that the orthogonalization of CAVs only minimally harms their primary objective. Notably, in most experiments AUROC exhibits an initial increase at

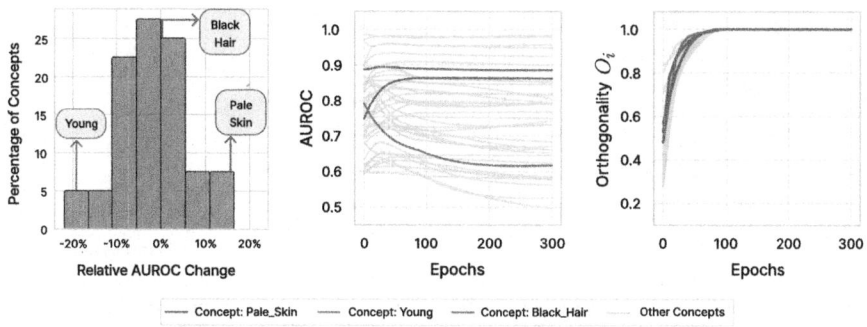

**Fig. 4.** *Left*: Distribution of relative AUROC change before and after CAV optimization for the VGG16 model for CelebA. *Middle and Right*: Evolution of per-concept metrics orthogonality $O_i$ and AUROC. We highlight concepts with the highest increase (*green*), the highest decrease (*red*), and the smallest change in AUROC (*blue*).

the beginning of optimization before undergoing a gradual decay and finally stabilizing at a slightly lower level. The initial increase in AUROC is likely due to the orthogonality constraint, which provides the optimization with a term that helps CAVs to be optimized jointly, as opposed to the baseline objective where each CAV is optimized separately. This encourages a better use of latent space via a more structured adjustment of CAVs. Overall, our results demonstrate that concept disentanglement can be effectively achieved without compromising directional correctness, making this approach robust across various settings.

**Concept Dynamics Under Orthogonalization.** As certain concepts are initially more entangled than others, different CAVs undergo different directional changes in the latent space. In order to get an insight into how individual directional changes happen, and how these changes affect the performance of individual concepts, we provide an in-depth analysis of the orthogonality and AUROC metrics of individual concepts during CAV optimization. Here, we finetune CAVs trained on the VGG16 model for the CelebA dataset.

Figure 4 illustrates the changes in AUROC and orthogonality of each CAV during optimization. Out of all concepts present in the CelebA dataset, we highlight three, namely the concept with the highest increase ("Pale Skin"), highest decrease ("Young"), and least change in AUROC ("Black Hair"). We observe that while all concepts increase in orthogonality during optimization, some experience an improvement, while others suffer from a decline in their classification performance. Furthermore, although some concepts maintain a relatively stable AUROC performance, e.g. concept with blue line on Fig. 4, they still experience an increase in orthogonality, either due to the fact that they change their direction without losing their classification performance, or that other entangled concepts move away from the concept, such that it becomes more orthogonal to them.

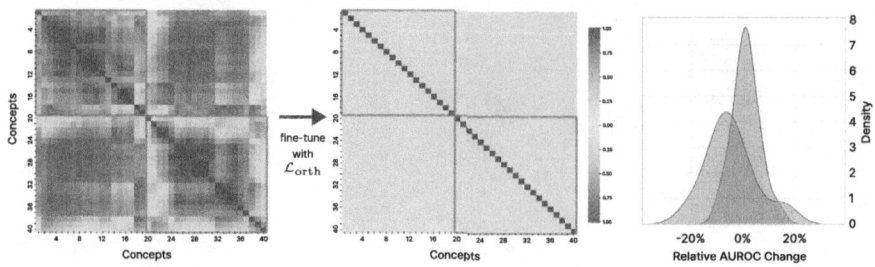

**Fig. 5.** *Left and Middle*: Cosine similarity matrices of CAVs, trained on VGG16 model on CelebA dataset, before and after the fine-tuning. *Right*: Kernel Density Estimation of relative AUROC changes of individual concepts in two entangled blocks of female- (*red*) and male-associated (*blue*) concepts.

The dynamics of entangled concepts during optimization is further highlighted in Fig. 5, where we show the AUROC change distribution of two different sets of entangled concepts before and after the optimization on the CelebA dataset starting from an optimal state for CAVs. The sets are chosen from the initial cosine similarity matrix of CAVs that are optimized without any orthogonalization, where we observe naturally emergent blocks due to correlations in dataset associated with female- and male-related concepts. The resulting AUROC change distribution shows that in each entanglement block, there are concepts that experience an increase in AUROC, concepts that suffer from a decrease in AUROC, and concepts that are relatively stable in terms of AUROC, which is a clear indication that CAVs undergo a redistribution of representational importance. Some concepts sacrifice their distinctiveness or classification ability to reduce redundancy and entanglement, while others gain clarity and improved directional correctness as a result of orthogonalization. Figure 5 further depicts a global image of concept orthogonalization in latent space, where we consider the cosine similarity matrices of CAVs before and after the optimization. The resulting cosine similarity matrix after orthogonalization illustrates the achievement of the secondary goal of optimization, *i.e.*, concept disentanglement, as it resembles the identity matrix, which was the desired root point of $\mathcal{L}_{\text{orth}}$ defined in Sect. 3.3. Similar results are obtained for the FunnyBirds dataset, as shown in Appendix B.

**Impact of Weighting Parameter $\alpha$:** We measure the orthogonality and AUROC of CAVs after optimization with our disentanglement loss introduced in Eq. (6) with various weightings $\alpha \in [10^{-10}, 10^{-9}, ..., 10^{10}]$. We run the optimization for randomly initialized CAVs for the VGG16 model for CelebA with a learning rate of 0.1 and 500 epochs. The results are shown in Fig. 6, where the AUROC and orthogonality metrics are displayed for each value of the weighting parameter $\alpha$. The results indicate that higher $\alpha$ values expectedly lead to a better level of orthogonalization and plateau when perfect orthogonalization is achieved. Interestingly, we observe that for small weighting parameters, the average AUROC slightly *increases* compared to the baseline CAVs without orthogonality

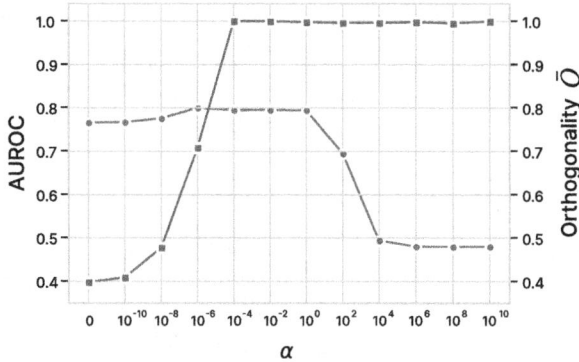

**Fig. 6.** The average orthogonality $\bar{O}$ and AUROC after CAV training on the last convolutional layer of VGG16 for CelebA. The x-axis represents the magnitude of $\alpha$, while AUROC (blue) and orthogonality (red) are shown on the y1- and y2-axis, respectively.

constraint ($\alpha = 0$). This reflects the findings discussed in Sect. 4.2, *i.e.*, the joint optimization of *all* concept directions simultaneously can positively impact the directional correctness. However, with larger $\alpha$ values we observe a drastic drop in AUROC, indicating that the orthogonalization constraint outweighs the directional correctness objective. These results demonstrate the role of $\alpha$ to balance the trade-off between directional correctness, measured via AUROC, and the level of orthogonalization. Our results further indicate that optimal $\alpha$ values, where both AUROC and $\bar{O}$ are maximized (here: values between $10^{-4}$ and $10^{0}$), can (1) achieve perfect concept orthogonalization, and (2) refine directional correctness and achieve higher AUROC scores.

### 4.3 Disentanglement of Concept Heatmaps

Although evaluating concept disentanglement through metrics like orthogonality and AUROC offer valuable insight into the quantitative performance of our method, they come short in providing a qualitative understanding of the underlying representational changes of concepts. To address this, we utilize Layer-wise Relevance Propagation (LRP) [4] to generate heatmaps for entangled concept pairs before and after orthogonalizing the CAVs using the zennit library [3]. More specifically, we compute the inner product between the activation of a sample and the CAV of interest, and then backpropagate the resulting relevances back to the input space [2,33,35]. Similarly, other attribution methods such as Guided Backpropagation [44], SmoothGrad [43], and Integrated Gradients [45] can be used to obtain such local explanations [9]. The heatmaps obtained from the VGG16 model, trained on the CelebA dataset, are illustrated in Fig. 7. The baseline CAVs successfully identify the regions associated with each concept; however, they show limitations in isolating the concepts entirely. Specifically, due to inherent correlations in the dataset, such as the high negative correlation observed between "blond hair" and "necktie" attributes, the heatmaps display

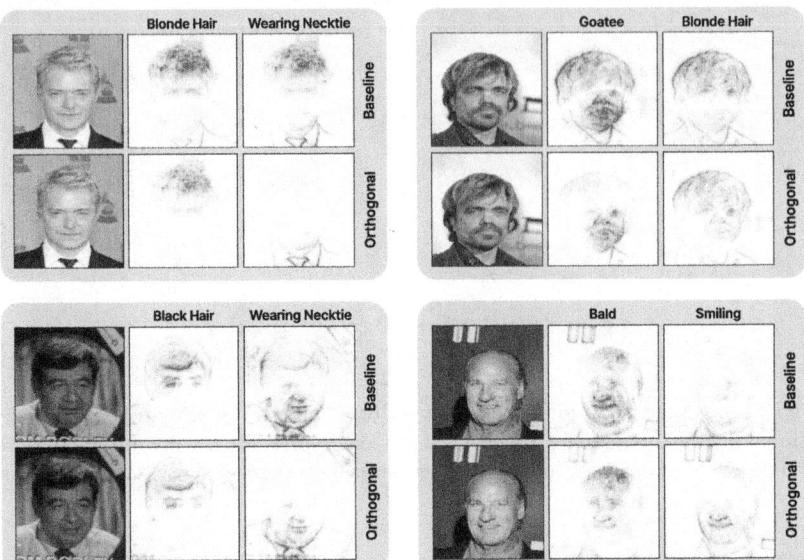

**Fig. 7.** Concept heatmaps for 4 entangled pairs of concepts obtained using LRP on the VGG16 model for CelebA. For each pair, the three columns represent the original image (*left*) and the heatmaps corresponding to first (*middle*) and second (*right*) concept, respectively, whereas the rows represent the heatmaps obtained before and after CAV orthogonalization. Red and blue regions indicate positive and negative relevance.

negative relevance in each others regions that are unrelated to the original concept. In other words, the model tends to rely on the presence of one concept to indicate the absence of the other, or vice versa. Conversely, following the orthogonalization of the CAVs, the heatmaps continue to accurately highlight the relevant regions, thereby demonstrating directional correctness, while substantially reducing the negative correlations and improving the isolation of individual concepts. This outcome indicates that CAVs obtained by our method not only effectively capture the relevant spatial regions within the input space but also achieve superior performance in disentangling and isolating the concepts.

## 5 CAV-Based Activation Steering Applications

To evaluate the benefits of orthogonalized CAVs, we compare the results for CAV-based steering tasks using baseline CAVs without non-orthogonality penalization and orthogonalized CAVs. Specifically, we use CAVs to model concept directions in the latent space to either *insert* isolated concepts into input samples using generative models in qualitative experiments (Sect. 5.1), or to *remove* targeted concepts during inference time for shortcut suppression in a controlled scenario with both quantitative and qualitative results (Sect. 5.2).

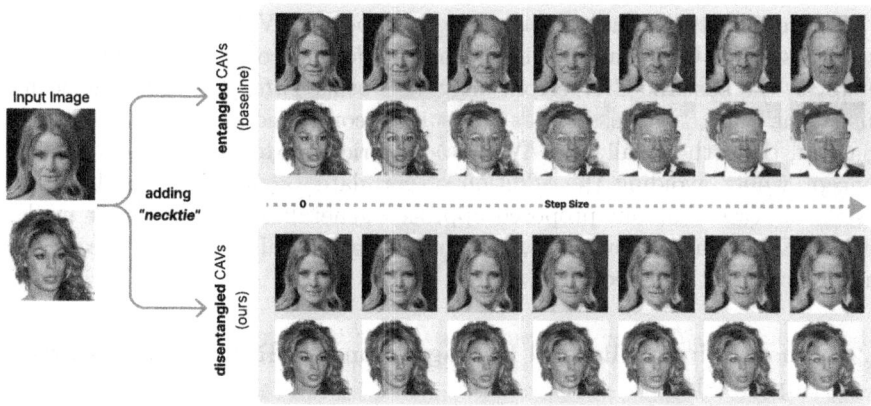

**Fig. 8.** Given input images (*left*), we utilize a Diffusion Autoencoder to reconstruct manipulated latent encodings obtained at the bottleneck layer of the Diffusion Autoencoder. Specifically, we add activations with different step sizes into the concept direction for "necktie", as modeled via baseline (*top*) and orthogonalized (*bottom*) CAVs. Whereas entangled baseline CAVs add correlated concepts in addition to the target concept, the disentangled CAV is capable of adding the "necktie" in isolation with minimized impact on other concepts.

### 5.1 Concept Insertion with Generative Models

As a first steering task, we consider the insertion of concepts by adding activations into the CAV direction. Intuitively, if precisely modeled, this corresponds to adding the concept to the input image. However, if concept representations are entangled, such as "wearing necktie" and "mustache" concepts in CelebA, adding activations along the CAV directions might lead to undesired effects. To investigate this qualitatively, we utilize a Diffusion Autoencoder [36] trained on CelebA dataset. Diffusion Autoencoders are a class of generative models that learn structured latent representations by combining a learnable encoder with a diffusion-based decoder. Unlike traditional autoencoders, Diffusion Autoencoders separate the latent space into two components: a semantic subcode, which encodes high-level, structured information, and a stochastic subcode, which models low-level stochastic variations. This separation allows Diffusion Autoencoders to achieve both meaningful representation learning and high-level reconstruction capabilities, making them well-suited for activation steering applications. This allows the generation of images representing the manipulated encoding with added activations, *i.e.*, inserted concepts.

We train both *baseline* and *orthogonalized* CAVs on the bottleneck layer of the Diffusion Autoencoder, using the pretrained model weights provided by the authors of [36]. Subsequently, we utilize the learned CAV for the concept "wearing necktie" to insert the target concept by adding activations along its direction with different step sizes. Lastly, we decode the manipulated encoding to obtain the corresponding images.

**Acknowledgements.** This work was supported by the Federal Ministry of Education and Research (BMBF) as grant BIFOLD (01IS18025A, 01IS18037II); the European Union's Horizon Europe research and innovation programme (EU Horizon Europe) as grants [ACHILLES (101189689), TEMA (101093003)]; and the German Research Foundation (DFG) as research unit DeSBi [KI-FOR 5363] (459422098).

## A CelebA Details

In this section we provide additional details on the CelebA dataset. Figure 10 presents the correlation and cosine similarity matrices for concepts extracted from the last convolutional layer of a VGG16 model trained on CelebA. The highlighted blocks in both matrices reveal two natural concept groups associated with female (*red*) and male (*blue*) attributes. The concept labels of these groups are listed in Table 1 using the same color coding for both entanglement blocks.

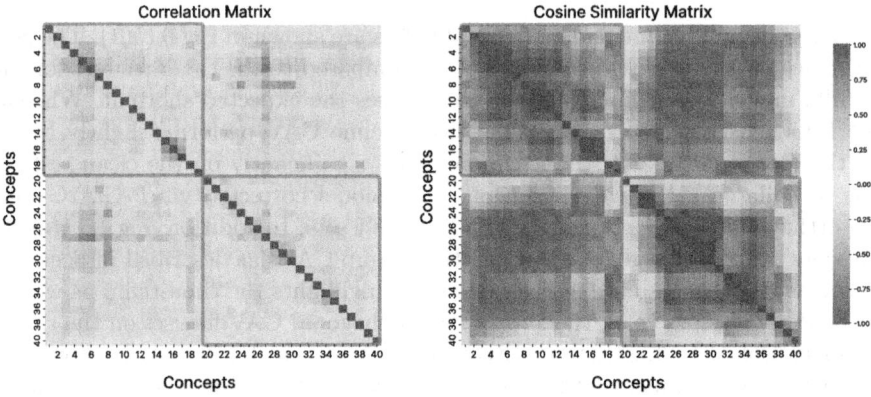

**Fig. 10.** *Left*: Correlation matrix of all concepts in CelebA. *Right*: Cosine similarity matrix of concepts fitted on the last convolution layer of VGG16 trained on CelebA dataset. The two highlighted blocks on both matrices indicate the two natural groups of female (*red*) and male (*blue*) associated concepts.

## B FunnyBirds Details

We provide details about the synthetic FunnyBirds dataset we generated for our experiments. In Table 2 we list the probabilities we used for the co-occurrence of concepts during the dataset generation to enforce correlations in the dataset, namely between *beak* and *tail* concepts. The resultant correlations, as well as the cosine similarity matrices before and after the CAV fine-tuning are illustrated in Fig. 12, where we fine-tune CAVs on the ResNet18 model trained on the FunnyBirds dataset (see Appendix C for more details). Finally, in Fig. 11 we display some example samples for the first 4 classes out of 50 total classes.

**Table 1.** Concept labels present in the CelebA dataset, ordered and highlighted as in the correlation and cosine similarity matrices (best seen in color).

| Index | Concept | Index | Concept | Index | Concept |
|---|---|---|---|---|---|
| 1 | Pale Skin | 15 | High Cheekbones | 29 | Goatee |
| 2 | Oval Face | 16 | Smiling | 30 | Sideburns |
| 3 | Attractive | 17 | Mouth Slightly Open | 31 | Wearing Necktie |
| 4 | Arched Eyebrows | 18 | Young | 32 | Receding Hairline |
| 5 | Heavy Makeup | 19 | Big Lips | 33 | Bald |
| 6 | Wearing Lipstick | 20 | Brown Hair | 34 | Double Chin |
| 7 | Wavy Hair | 21 | Straight Hair | 35 | Chubby |
| 8 | No Beard | 22 | Black Hair | 36 | Eyeglasses |
| 9 | Wearing Necklace | 23 | Bushy Eyebrows | 37 | Wearing Hat |
| 10 | Pointy Nose | 24 | 5 o'Clock Shadow | 38 | Gray Hair |
| 11 | Rosy Cheeks | 25 | Bags Under Eyes | 39 | Blurry |
| 12 | Wearing Earrings | 26 | Big Nose | 40 | Narrow Eyes |
| 13 | Bangs | 27 | Male | | |
| 14 | Blond Hair | 28 | Mustache | | |

**Table 2.** Correlations between beak models and tail models based on enforced probabilities during dataset generation.

| Beak Model | tail01.glb | tail02.glb | tail03.glb |
|---|---|---|---|
| beak01.glb | 0.7 | 0.15 | 0.15 |
| beak02.glb | 0.15 | 0.7 | 0.15 |
| beak03.glb | 0.15 | 0.15 | 0.7 |
| beak04.glb | 0.15 | 0.15 | 0.7 |

## C  CAV Training Details

In this section, we provide the hyperparameters used for training CAVs. Table 3 lists the learning rate, weighting parameter $\alpha$ and number of epochs used for fine-tuning CAVs for each dataset-model combination.

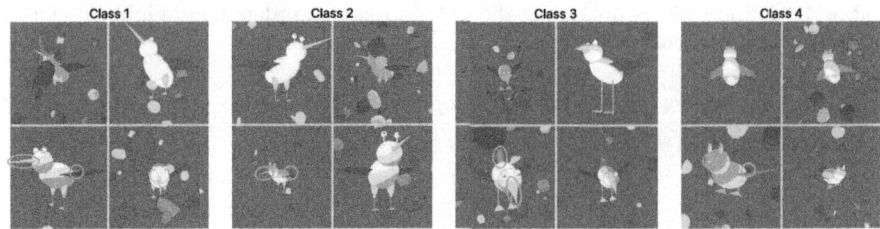

**Fig. 11.** Example samples generated in the first 4 classes of the FunnyBirds dataset. Some examples of concepts with enforced correlations are highlighted.

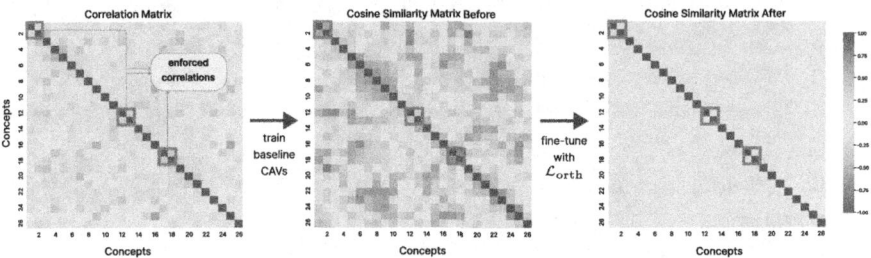

**Fig. 12.** *Left*: Correlations of known concepts based on their co-occurrence in FunnyBirds dataset. *Middle and Right*: Cosine similarity matrices of CAVs, trained on ResNet18 model on the FunnyBirds dataset, before and after the fine-tuning. The highlighted blocks indicate the concept pairs with enforced correlations.

**Table 3.** Hyperparameters used for CAV fine-tuning. $\alpha$ denotes the weighting parameter used in Eq. (5).

| Dataset | Model | LR | $\alpha$ | Epochs |
|---|---|---|---|---|
| CelebA | VGG16 | 0.001 | 0.01 | 300 |
| | ResNet18 | 0.001 | 0.01 | 300 |
| FunnyBirds | VGG16 | 0.001 | 0.1 | 300 |
| | ResNet18 | 0.001 | 0.01 | 300 |

# References

1. Achtibat, R., et al.: From attribution maps to human-understandable explanations through concept relevance propagation. Nat. Mach. Intell. **5**(9), 1006–1019 (2023)
2. Anders, C.J., Weber, L., Neumann, D., Samek, W., Müller, K.R., Lapuschkin, S.: Finding and removing clever hans: using explanation methods to debug and improve deep models. Inf. Fusion **77**, 261–295 (2022)
3. Anders, C.J., Neumann, D., Samek, W., Müller, K.-R., Lapuschkin, S.: Software for dataset-wide xai: from local explanations to global insights with zennit, corelay, and virelay. arXiv preprint arXiv:2106.13200 (2021)

4. Bach, S., Binder, A., Montavon, G., Klauschen, F., Müller, K.R., Samek, W.: On pixel-wise explanations for non-linear classifier decisions by layer-wise relevance propagation. PloS one **10**(7), (2015)
5. Bareeva, D., Dreyer, M., Pahde, F., Samek, W., Lapuschkin, S.: Reactive model correction: mitigating harm to task-relevant features via conditional bias suppression. In: Proceedings of the IEEE/CVF Conference on Computer Vision and Pattern Recognition, pp. 3532–3541 (2024)
6. Bau, D., Zhu, J.-Y., Strobelt, H., Lapedriza, A., Zhou, B., Torralba, A.: Understanding the role of individual units in a deep neural network. Proc. Natl. Acad. Sci. **117**(48), 30071–30078 (2020)
7. Bouchacourt, D., Tomioka, R., Nowozin, S.: Multi-level variational autoencoder: learning disentangled representations from grouped observations. In: Proceedings of the AAAI Conference on Artificial Intelligence, vol. 32 (2018)
8. Brinker, T.J., et al. Deep learning outperformed 136 of 157 dermatologists in a head-to-head dermoscopic melanoma image classification task. Eur. J. Can. **113**, 47–54 (2019)
9. Brocki, L., Chung, N.C.: Concept saliency maps to visualize relevant features in deep generative models. In: 2019 18th IEEE International Conference on Machine Learning and Applications (ICMLA), pp. 1771–1778. IEEE (2019)
10. Chen, Z., Bei, Y., Rudin, C.: Concept whitening for interpretable image recognition. Nat. Mach. Intell. **2**(12), 772–782 (2020)
11. Chormai, P., Herrmann, J., Müller, K.R., Montavon, G.: Disentangled explanations of neural network predictions by finding relevant subspaces. IEEE Trans. Pattern Anal. Mach. Intell. (2024)
12. Cortes, C., Vapnik, V.: Support-vector networks. Mach. Learn. **20**, 273–297 (1995)
13. Nelson Elhage, Tristan Hume, Catherine Olsson, Nicholas Schiefer, Tom Henighan, Shauna Kravec, et al. Toy models of superposition. arXiv preprint arXiv:2209.10652 (2022)
14. Fel, T., et al.: Craft: concept recursive activation factorization for explainability. In: CVPR, pp. 2711–2721 (2023)
15. Geirhos, R., Jacobsen, J.-H., Michaelis, C., Zemel, R., Brendel, W., et al.: Shortcut learning in deep neural networks. Nat Mach Intell **2**(11), 665–673 (2020)
16. Gutierrez Basulto, V., Schockaert, S.: From knowledge graph embedding to ontology embedding? an analysis of the compatibility between vector space representations and rules (2018)
17. Haufe, S., et al.: On the interpretation of weight vectors of linear models in multivariate neuroimaging. NeuroImage **87**, 96–110 (2014)
18. He, K., Zhang, X., Ren, S., Sun, J.: Deep residual learning for image recognition. In: CVPR pp. 770–778 (2016)
19. Hesse, R., Schaub-Meyer, S., Roth, S.: Funnybirds: a synthetic vision dataset for a part-based analysis of explainable ai methods. In: Proceedings of the IEEE/CVF International Conference on Computer Vision, pp. 3981–3991 (2023)
20. Hjelm, R.D., et al.: Learning deep representations by mutual information estimation and maximization. In: Proceedings of the International Conference on Learning Representations (ICLR) (2019)
21. Hoerl, A.E., Kennard, R.W.: Ridge regression: biased estimation for nonorthogonal problems. Technometrics **42**(1), 80–86 (2000)
22. Jackermeier, M., Chen, J., Horrocks, I.: Dual box embeddings for the description logic el++. Proc. ACM Web Conf. **2024**, 2250–2258 (2024)

23. Kim, B., Wattenberg, M., Gilmer, J., Cai, C., Wexler, J., Viegas, F., et al.: Interpretability beyond feature attribution: quantitative testing with concept activation vectors (tcav). In: ICML, pp. 2668–2677. PMLR (2018)
24. Kim, H., Mnih, A.: Disentangling by factorising. In: ICML, pp. 2649–2658. PMLR (2018)
25. Kumar, A., Tan, C., Sharma, A.: Probing classifiers are unreliable for concept removal and detection. Adv. Neural. Inf. Process. Syst. **35**, 17994–18008 (2022)
26. Liu, Z., Luo, P., Wang, X., Tang, X.: Deep learning face attributes in the wild. In: Proceedings of International Conference on Computer Vision (ICCV), December 2015
27. Lundberg, S.M., Lee, S.-I.: A unified approach to interpreting model predictions. In: NeurIPS, vol. 30 (2017)
28. Nanda, N., Lee, A., Wattenberg, M.: Emergent linear representations in world models of self-supervised sequence models. In: Proceedings of the 6th BlackboxNLP Workshop: Analyzing and Interpreting Neural Networks for NLP, pp. 16–30 (2023)
29. Neuhaus, Y., Augustin, M., Boreiko, V., Hein, M.: Spurious features everywhere-large-scale detection of harmful spurious features in imagenet. In: ICCV (2023)
30. Nicolson, A., Schut, L., Noble, J.A., Gal, Y.: Understanding concept activation vectors. In: TMLR, Explaining explainability (2025)
31. Olah, C., Mordvintsev, A., Schubert, L.: Feature visualization. Distill **2**(11) (2017)
32. Özcep, Ö.L., Leemhuis, M., Wolter, D.: Embedding ontologies in the description logic alc by axis-aligned cones. J. Artif. Intell. Res. **78**, 217–267 (2023)
33. Pahde, F., Wiegand, T., Lapuschkin, S., Samek, W.: Ensuring medical ai safety: explainable ai-driven detection and mitigation of spurious model behavior and associated data. arXiv preprint arXiv:2501.13818 (2025)
34. Pahde, F., et al.: Navigating neural space: revisiting concept activation vectors to overcome directional divergence. arXiv preprint arXiv:2202.03482 (2022)
35. Pahde, F., Dreyer, M., Samek, W., Lapuschkin, S.: Reveal to revise: an explainable ai life cycle for iterative bias correction of deep models. In: MICCAI, pp. 596–606. Springer (2023)
36. Preechakul, K., Chatthee, N., Wizadwongsa, S., Suwajanakorn, S.: Diffusion autoencoders: toward a meaningful and decodable representation. In: CVPR, pp. 10619–10629 (2022)
37. Radford, A., Jozefowicz, R., Sutskever, I.: Learning to generate reviews and discovering sentiment. arXiv preprint arXiv:1704.01444 (2017)
38. Rakowski, A., Monti, R., Huryn, V., Lemanczyk, M., Ohler, U., Lippert, C.: Metadata-guided feature disentanglement for functional genomics. Bioinformatics **40** (2024)
39. Ravfogel, S., Elazar, Y., Gonen, H., Twiton, M., Goldberg, Y.: Null it out: guarding protected attributes by iterative nullspace projection. In: Jurafsky, D., Chai, J., Schluter, N., Tetreault, J. (eds.) ACL, pp. 7237–7256, July 2020
40. Selvaraju, R.R., Cogswell, M., Das, A., Vedantam, R., Parikh, D., Batra, D.: Grad-cam: visual explanations from deep networks via gradient-based localization. In: ICCV, pp. 618–626 (2017)
41. Simonyan, K., Zisserman, A.: Very deep convolutional networks for large-scale image recognition. In: Bengio, Y., LeCun, Y., (eds.) ICLR 2015 (2015)
42. Singh, K.K., Ojha, U., Lee, Y.J.: Finegan: unsupervised hierarchical disentanglement for fine-grained object generation and discovery. In: CVPR, pp. 6490–6499 (2019)
43. Smilkov, D., Thorat, N., Kim, B., Viégas, F., Wattenberg, M.: Smoothgrad: removing noise by adding noise. arXiv preprint arXiv:1706.03825 (2017)

44. Springenberg, J.T., Dosovitskiy, A., Brox, T., Riedmiller, M.: Striving for simplicity: the all convolutional net. arxiv 2014. In: Workshop Track at International Conference on Learning Representations (2014)
45. Sundararajan, M., Taly, A., Yan, Q.: Axiomatic attribution for deep networks. In: ICML (2017)
46. Träuble, F., et al.: On disentangled representations learned from correlated data. In: ICML, pp. 10401–10412. PMLR (2021)
47. Travaini, G.V., Pacchioni, F., Bellumore, S., Bosia, M., De Micco, F.: Machine learning and criminal justice: a systematic review of advanced methodology for recidivism risk prediction. Int. J. Environ. Res. Public Health **19**(17), 10594 (2022)
48. Vielhaben, J., Bluecher, S., Strodthoff, N.: A unifying framework with completeness guarantees. TMLR, Multi-dimensional concept discovery (mcd) (2023)
49. Wang, X., Chen, H., Wu, Z., Zhu, W., et al.: Disentangled representation learning. IEEE Trans. Pattern Anal. Mach. Intell. (2024)
50. Yuksekgonul, M., Wang, M., Zou, J.: Post-hoc concept bottleneck models. In: ICLR Workshops (2022)
51. Završnik, A.: Algorithmic justice: algorithms and big data in criminal justice settings. Eur. J. Criminol. **18**(5) (2021)
52. Zhang, R., Madumal, P., Miller, T., Ehinger, K.A., Rubinstein, B.I.: Invertible concept-based explanations for cnn models with non-negative concept activation vectors. In: Proceedings of the AAAI Conference on Artificial Intelligence, vol. 35, pp. 11682–11690 (2021)

**Open Access** This chapter is licensed under the terms of the Creative Commons Attribution 4.0 International License (http://creativecommons.org/licenses/by/4.0/), which permits use, sharing, adaptation, distribution and reproduction in any medium or format, as long as you give appropriate credit to the original author(s) and the source, provide a link to the Creative Commons license and indicate if changes were made.

The images or other third party material in this chapter are included in the chapter's Creative Commons license, unless indicated otherwise in a credit line to the material. If material is not included in the chapter's Creative Commons license and your intended use is not permitted by statutory regulation or exceeds the permitted use, you will need to obtain permission directly from the copyright holder.

# Concept Extraction for Time Series with ECLAD-ts

Antonia Holzapfel, Andres Felipe Posada Moreno[✉], and Sebastian Trimpe

Institute for Data Science in Mechanical Engineering (DSME), RWTH Aachen University, Theaterstraße 35-39, 52062 Aachen, Germany
holzapfel@dsme.rwth-aachen.de, andres.posada@rwth-aachen.de

**Abstract.** Convolutional neural networks (CNNs) for time series classification (TSC) are being increasingly used in applications ranging from quality prediction to medical diagnosis. The black box nature of these models makes understanding their prediction process difficult. This issue is crucial because CNNs are prone to learning shortcuts and biases, compromising their robustness and alignment with human expectations. To assess whether such mechanisms are being used and the associated risk, it is essential to provide model explanations that reflect the inner workings of the model. Concept Extraction (CE) methods offer such explanations, but have mostly been developed for the image domain so far, leaving a gap in the time series domain. In this work, we present a CE and localization method tailored to the time series domain, based on the ideas of CE methods for images. We propose the novel method ECLAD-ts, which provides post-hoc global explanations based on how the models encode subsets of the input at different levels of abstraction. For this, concepts are produced by clustering timestep-wise aggregations of CNN activation maps, and their importance is computed based on their impact on the prediction process. We evaluate our method on synthetic and natural datasets. Furthermore, we assess the advantages and limitations of CE in time series through empirical results. Our results show that ECLAD-ts effectively explains models by leveraging their internal representations, providing useful insights about their prediction process.

**Keywords:** Concept Extraction · Interpretability · Time Series

## 1 Introduction

Convolutional neural networks (CNNs) for time series classification (TSC) are currently being used in the industry, e.g., for quality prediction [27], as well as in more safety critical domains, like medical diagnosis [13]. These models are powerful, but they are also black boxes. Therefore, explanations are necessary to allow developers, users, and stakeholders to understand the operations of models and whether they are aligned with human expectations. With such knowledge, the involved agents can improve models, or choose the 'correct' models, upon which they can build an adequate level of trust. A 'correct' model is a model that uses information that is relevant for its task, in accordance with human know-how, and avoids the use of harmful biases or spurious correlations present in the data. A priori, there is no guarantee that a model will learn to use the desired information. Conveniently, Concept Extraction (CE) methods provide such insights, which would make them useful for time series models.

In the time series domain, global model explanations exist in the form of prototypes [4]. However, these explanations do not directly reflect how the model encodes information, which can be problematic for detecting shortcut learning and other biases. Concept testing methods for global explanations have also been applied in time series, e.g., to EEG [19] and bearing fault classification models [17]. These methods require the labeling of concepts to test whether the model can distinguish their presence and importance in the inputs, which implies manual effort and expertise in the field of application. Additionally, it induces biases with respect to which concepts are tested—the concepts being used by the model do not necessarily coincide with the labeled concepts. Similarly, MultiVISION, a Concept Extraction method for time series, has been proposed by [26]. This method extracts concepts by clustering subsamples corresponding to the receptive field of highly active neurons. However, MultiVISION's reliance on the receptive field of a network makes it unusable for some deep architectures. For example, the receptive field of an InceptionTime network with 10 inception blocks is 343. This means that for a network with an input size smaller than 343, the concept patches can be as big as the input, turning the 'concept clustering' into input clustering. On the other hand, methods for automatic concept extraction exist in the image domain [14,15,23] and they have shown promising results, but have not been applied to time series yet. A transfer to the time series domain requires considering domain-specific characteristics, such as the dimensionality and channel-specific information.

In this work, we propose ECLAD-ts, an algorithm that produces post-hoc global explanations through automatic concept extraction and localization. Our method is based on ECLAD [22,23] from the image domain, because it provides granular explanations by taking into account the equivariance property of CNNs, which enables not only extraction, but also localization of concepts. We introduce mechanisms that make ECLAD suitable for time series. ECLAD-ts produces concepts by clustering Local Aggregated Descriptors (LADs), which are timestep-wise aggregations of CNN activation maps. Additionally, ECLAD-ts computes an importance score for each concept based on its impact on the model predictions according to the model gradients. We test the method on synthetic and natural datasets, and compare it to other CE methods from the time series and the image domain, like vanilla ECLAD, ConceptShap, and MultiVISION. Furthermore, we explore the benefits and limitations of such methods in time series.

We show that time series models encode patterns in their latent space distinctively and thus, concepts can be extracted with ECLAD-ts using the inner representations of the model. The extracted concepts provide useful insights on the prediction process of the model.

To summarize, the main contributions in this work are:

1. ECLAD-ts, a novel algorithm for CE and localization in the time series domain, which captures temporal and channel-wise information.
2. An importance scoring mechanism that quantitatively assesses the relevance of a concept considering channel-wise gradient information.
3. Experiments in both synthetic and natural time series, with empirical results that compare several CE methods in time series and highlight their advantages and limitations of CE methods.

## 2 Related Work

The goal of this paper is to enhance the interpretability of deep TSC models through post-hoc explanation, allowing for a better understanding of their alignment with human expectations. This research falls under the domain of explainable artificial intelligence (XAI), specifically, post-hoc explainability methods [1,3]. Post-hoc methods analyse an existing model after training and provide insights either on single predictions (local) or on the model's general prediction process (global). Examples of local explanation methods include saliency maps such as SHAP [18] and Grad-CAM [24], which provide sensitivity scores to quantify the influence of each feature of a datapoint on the prediction. In comparison, global explanation methods such as concept extraction [8,14,22,23] and prototypes [4] analyse a model within the context of a complete dataset, providing explanations about its overall decision-making process. This is, the insights of global explanations can be extrapolated to new predictions, providing a general rationale of what a model considers in its prediction process.

Our work is related to Concept Extraction methods, which are post-hoc global explanations. Concept-based methods explain the decision-making process of a model through the patterns it learns to identify. These patterns, referred to as concepts, represent human-understandable features that the model has learned to distinguish [15]. Earlier works tested whether a specific concept is present in the model's internal representations by comparing how sets of manually labeled instances are encoded within the latent space of models. Representative concept testing approaches include TCAV [15] and CAR [2]. In contrast, Concept Extraction focuses on automatically identifying and isolating these concepts. Methods such as ACE [8], ConceptShap [25], PACE [14], SPACE [21], and ECLAD [22,23] have been primarily proposed for the image domain, providing significant insights, but have not been transferred to the time series domain yet. The main reason being the particularities of time series data, such as the dimensionality, or channels having disentangled information, which results challenging for current CE methods. In this context, we propose extending and transferring the CE method ECLAD for analysing CNNs used in TSC.

In the domain of time series, five concept-based approaches have been proposed. The first two approaches perform concept testing with TCAV [15] for concepts in EEG [19] and bearing fault classification [6]. In these approaches, sets of samples are manually annotated or modified to contain specific concepts, to test whether the model can distinguish their presence in an input. Similarly, the third approach relates concepts to the presence of specific frequencies by creating negative samples through handcrafted filters applied to the time series [17]. The fourth approach relies on preprocessing data through an autoencoder and analysing the impact of the autoencoder's latent dimensions on the classification of the reconstructed signal [20]. Lastly, the fifth approach performs concept extraction by clustering slices of the inputs that correspond to the receptive field of highly active neurons. The current approaches either (1) rely on manual annotation, and creation of concept samples, (2) are directly unrelated to the latent space of models, or (3) rely on the receptive field of NN layers for the extraction of concepts. The first case requires significant human involvement for manual annotation. The second case ties concepts to features directly extracted from the data, which are not necessarily the features learned by models, especially in cases of shortcut learning [7], defeating the purpose of these explanations. The third case is not usable for deep models, since their receptive field can become too large to produce meaningful concepts. For example, a 1D DenseNet121 has a large enough receptive field such that clustering is performed over the whole input. In our work, we propose a CE method to automatically extract concepts based on how models encode time spans of the input through different levels of abstraction, without relying on human annotations nor on the receptive field of the NN. Our approach provides concept extraction and localization capabilities directly related to how the model encodes input information and uses it for its prediction process.

## 3 Methods

In this section, we explain the ECLAD-ts algorithm and our experimental setup. This includes the validation of our method using synthetic datasets and implementation details.

### 3.1 ECLAD-ts

In this work, we use ECLAD [22,23] from the image domain as a base framework to develop our method for performing CE in TSC models. ECLAD is an algorithm that provides explanations based on three key steps: The encoding of the latent space of neural networks, the mining of patterns and the assessment of how relevant they are for the prediction process of the model. ECLAD-ts has two main differences with respect to ECLAD:

1. The latent space representation is modified to be compatible with time series data.
2. The importance score is modified to account for the importance of channel-specific information and for concepts that affect all classes similarly, which are pervasive in time series models.

Below, we describe in detail each step of ECLAD-ts.

**Encoding of the Latent Space.** In the first step, ECLAD-ts uses the notion of **Local Aggregated Descriptors (LADs)**, which are timestep-wise descriptors of how models encode a region at different levels of abstraction. These are obtained by aggregating the activation maps of multiple layers $l$ of a CNN model.

In the case of TSC with $n_k$ classes, a typical CNN maps the inputs of the model $x_i \in \mathbb{R}^{w \times d}$, to an output $y \in \mathbb{R}^{n_k}$ with a function $f : x \mapsto y$, where $w$, and ch are the length and channels of the input. The function $f$ is a composition of multiple functions ordered in layers, where the model encodes the information of the input into the latent spaces of each layer. An activation map $a_l = f_l(x)$ belonging to the latent space $\mathbb{R}^{\text{ch}_l, w_l}$ of layer $l$ is computed by a partial evaluation of the model until said layer. The dimensions of $a_l$ depend on the type of layer evaluated.

We aggregate the activation maps of a predefined set of $n_l$ layers $L = \{l_1, \ldots, l_{n_l}\}$, upscaled with linear interpolation ($f_U$) to the dimensions of $x_i$. This produces a descriptor $d_{x_i} = [f_U(f_{l_1}(x_i)) \ldots f_U(f_{l_{n_l}}(x_i))] \in \mathbb{R}^{w \times \text{ch}^*}$, where ch* is the sum of the number of units in all layers in $L$. A LAD refers to each timestep $d_{x_i}(b) \in \mathbb{R}^{1 \times \text{ch}^*}$ of $d_{x_i}$, where $b$ denotes its position along the width of $d_{x_i}$. LADs contain information about the model encoding of timesteps at different levels of abstraction. Here, we effectively reduced the dimensionality of the LADs introduced in ECLAD.

**Mining of Patterns and Visualization.** In the second step of ECLAD-ts, we separate the latent space of the model into clusters of different patterns using LADs. For this, we apply a **mini-batch k-means algorithm** to the LADS extracted from a set of inputs and obtain a set $\Gamma = \{\gamma_{c_1}, \ldots, \gamma_{c_{n_c}}\}$ of centroids $\gamma_{c_j} \in \mathbb{R}^{1 \times \text{ch}^*}$ defining the **concepts**. The centroids represent similarly encoded time subsequences.

For a human-understandable visualization, the concepts $c_j$ can be located in an input $x_i$ by creating a **mask** $m_{x_i}^{c_j} \in \mathbb{R}^{w \times 1}$ that analyses the LAD at each timestep, and assesses whether they belong to a cluster $\gamma_{c_j}$ as in

$$m_{x_i}^{c_j}(b) = \begin{cases} 1 & \arg\min_{c_q}(||d_{x_i}(b) - \gamma_{c_q}||_2) = c_j \\ 0 & \text{otherwise.} \end{cases} \quad (1)$$

Each of these masks has only one channel. For both visualization and importance score computation, the masks are expanded to have the same number of channels than the input. This produces ch expanded masks for each concept, each containing zeros at all channels except the $p$-th, $p \in \{1, \ldots, \text{ch}\}$, which contains the original mask $m_{x_i}^{c_j}$.

**Relevance Computation.** A key contribution of our work is the way we calculate the relevance of each concept. For the last step of ECLAD-ts, the **importance score (IS)** of a concept is determined, which quantifies the relevance of its related visual cues towards the prediction of the analysed model. Building on

ECLAD's, we propose a new metric that is compatible with multilabel classification and can discriminate the importance of a concept over multiple channels for multivariate timeseries. The reason for this is that, unlike images, timeseries often have channels encoding different types of information (e.g., channels that correspond to different kinds of sensor) and thus contain information that can vary in importance for the same timestep. Therefore, it can be necessary to know which channel is important for a concept explanation.

To determine the IS, we first compute the instance-wise sensitivity $R_{x_i}^{c_j}$ of the timeseries regions belonging to a concept,

$$R_{x_i}^{c_j} = \nabla_x g(f(x_i)) \odot m_{x_i}^{c_j}, \quad R_{x_i}^{c_j} \in \mathbb{R}^{\text{ch} \times w}, \tag{2}$$

where $\odot$ denotes the element-wise product between matrices and $g(y)$ is a wrapper of the model $f$. The wrapper $g(y)$ is defined as

$$g(y) = \|y \cdot \mathbf{1}^T - \mathbf{1} \cdot y^T\|_2,$$

for multiclass classification, where $y \in \mathbb{R}^{n_k}$ is the output of $f$, $n_k$ is the number of classes, and $\mathbf{1}$ is the vector of ones of the same size as $y$.

The timestep-wise sensitivity for a channel $\text{ch}_p$ is computed as

$$r_{x_i, \text{ch}_p}^{c_j} = \sum_{b \in w} R_{x_i, \text{ch}_p}^{c_j}(b) \tag{3}$$

where $R_{x_i, \text{ch}_p}^{c_j}(b) \in \mathbb{R}^{1 \times 1}$ refers to each timestep of $R_{x_i}^{c_j}$ at channel $\text{ch}_p$.

This step is modified from the metric used in ECLAD by replacing the 1-norm in Eq. 4 of [22] by the sum over the timesteps. The rationale behind this is that concepts having a negative gradient in Eq. 2 are concepts that reduce the distance between the logits. This means that they are concepts that make the model 'less sure' about its output, which is the opposite of what concepts with a positive gradient do. Thus, it is important to retain the sign of the gradient for computing the importance score, which is achieved by our modification in Eq. 3. While this characteristic of the importance score might not have been noticeable in the image domain, it has a visible effect in the time series domain.

Using our IS metric, a concept with an importance score close to 1 is a concept that is useful for distinguishing between the classes, while a concept with an importance score close to $-1$ is a concept that puts in question the predicted class and, in a way, represents the features that make the model unsure of its output. Consequently, a concept with a score close to 0 is 'unimportant'

The IS computation ends by aggregating $r_{x_i}^{c_j}$ over the timeseries in the dataset $E$ and scaling the mean relevance of each concept to obtain the final IS per channel

$$I_{c_j}^{\text{ch}_p} = \frac{r^{\hat{c}_j}}{\max_{c_j} |r^{\hat{c}_j}|}, \quad \text{where} \quad r^{\hat{c}_j} = \frac{1}{n_{c_j}} \sum_{x_i \in E} r_{x_i}^{c_j} \tag{4}$$

and $n_{c_j}$ is the number of datapoints containing a concept. The resulting $I_{c_j}^{\text{ch}_p}$ is the importance of a concept $c_j$ in channel $\text{ch}_p$.

With these three steps, ECLAD-ts can extract patterns that are meaningful for the model and can be represented in human-understandable visualizations. These patterns leverage the equivariance properties of the models.

## 3.2 Validating CE

Testing CE methods is challenging, because we do not have access to the 'ground truth' of the patterns learnt by a CNN. To validate CE methods, we can instead generate synthetic datasets using primitive concepts (e.g., a local structure) that are important for the labels by design. We understand primitives to be patterns that have associated annotations as binary masks, denoting their position.

If the synthetic dataset is designed correctly, a good model must use at least a subset of the patterns in the primitives for its task. Thus, in an ideal case, the concepts related to primitives would have high importance scores, and the concepts unrelated to them would have low importance scores. Considering this, the primitives can serve as a surrogate for the ground truth of an accurate model. It is important to note that the primitives cannot be considered equivalent to a ground truth. Due to shortcut learning, models can learn a sufficient subset of features and still achieve perfect accuracy. This means that for some primitives, the importance score is not going to be close to 1, even though they are designed to be important. Nevertheless, it stands to reason that for a model with $N$ primitives and $N$ classes, at least $N - 1$ concepts related to the primitives are needed for proper classification. Given this, the primitives remain useful to test a model's concepts.

For the objective validation of CE methods, we consider particular aspects. First, given that the primitives serve as a proxy ground truth, the extracted concepts should be temporally consistent with these ground truth primitives—i.e., their localization masks must align closely with those of the primitives. Second, the importance assigned to each concept should reflect its association with critical primitives; concepts closely associated to important primitives should receive high importance scores, whereas those with weaker associations should be deemed less important. This dual criterion ensures that the concepts not only mirror the ground truth in their temporal location but also capture the intended relevance of the underlying features.

To quantify the precision of a CE method, as in [23], we compute the two-way distance $\text{DST}_{p_0, c_j}$ to compare the masks of concepts learned by the model with those of the primitives. We associate each concept to its closest primitives, respecting a minimum threshold (here, 20% of the maximum possible distance between concept masks and primitives). As a result, we clarify which concept represents which primitive from the ground truth, labeling as aligned concepts if they are closely related to important primitives. Furthermore, we apply the Representation Correctness (RC) and Importance Correctness (IC) metrics form [23] to quantify the alignment of the extracted concepts with the visual cues and intended importance of the features of the dataset. *Representation correctness* is defined as the average of the negative association distance $\text{DST}_{p_0, c_j}$ of all aligned concepts extracted from the examined models. Whenever no concept alignments are found, the Representation correctness score is set to 40% of the maximum penalty for visualization purposes. *Importance correctness* is the mean importance of all aligned concepts, minus the mean importance of all unaligned concepts, normalized by the maximum importance of all concepts. The idea behind these metrics is that aligned concepts should be well represented (RC close to zero) and scored as important (high IC), whereas unaligned concepts should be scored as unimportant.

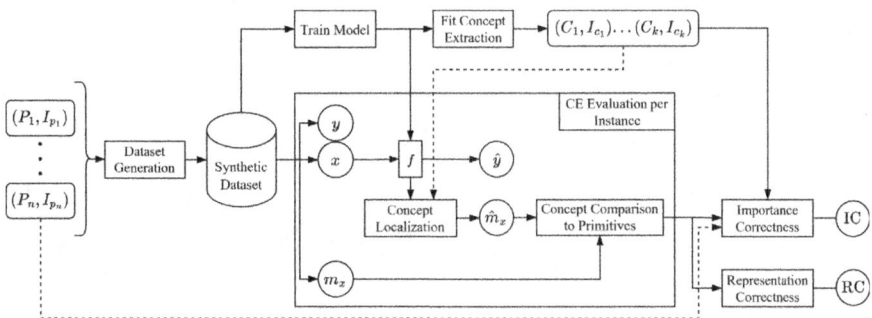

**Fig. 1.** Validation Pipeline for Concept Extraction. (1) Primitives definition. (2) Synthetic dataset generation. (3) Models are trained on the synthetic dataset and concept extraction is performed. (4) Extracted concepts are localized and compared with the ground truth primitives to establish associations. (5) Evaluation metrics for representation and importance correctness are computed.

The validation pipeline CE methods is illustrated in Fig. 1, the step by step process is: (1) Define a set of primitive concepts along with their associated importance scores. (2) Generate a synthetic dataset using these primitives, where each data point is a tuple $(x, y, m_x)$—with $x$ as the input, $y$ as the output, and $m_x$ as the primitives mask. (3) Train several models $f$ on the synthetic dataset, then fit a concept extraction method to obtain a set of concepts and their importance scores. (4) For each instance, localize each concept and obtain their masks to associate each concept with its closest primitive. (5) Finally, compute the evaluation metrics—Representation Correctness (RC) and Importance Correctness (IC)—to assess how well the extracted concepts capture the intended visual cues and importance of the primitives.

For the purpose of this work, we generated three synthetic datasets. The syntheticL2 and syntheticL4 datasets each have local features as primitives and a single channel. The syntheticLm dataset also has local features as primitives, but two channels. The purpose is to test if CE methods can extract meaningful concepts that are close to the primitives in position and importance. By 'meaningful concept' we refer to patterns in the latent space that translate to recognizable patterns in the input space. During our validation, we evaluate both objectively (through the introduced metrics), as well as qualitatively, if the concepts provide further insights in the models' prediction processes.

**syntheticL2 and syntheticL4.** The syntheticL2 and syntheticL4 datasets have two classes that are generated using primitives. SyntheticL2 is generated using primitive $p_0$ in class 0, and no 'no $p_0$' in class 1. Both classes have a background consisting of square wave and white noise. Uninterrupted background is considered to be a second primitive ($p_1$), as it can be used by the model instead of $p_0$. SyntheticL4 is generated using two primitives, $p_0$ being in class 0 and $p_1$ being in class 1. All primitives for these datasets are designed to be important and will thus make close concepts eligible for the alignment criterion in the RC and IC scores. Both classes have a background consisting of a sine wave and Gaussian noise. The classes are balanced for both synthetic datasets. Examples of these datasets are depicted in Fig. 2.

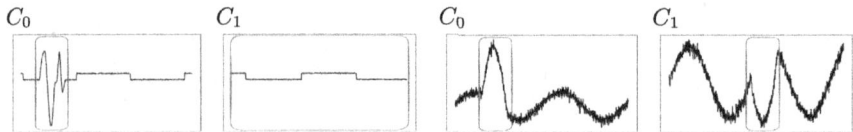

$C_0$ $\qquad\qquad$ $C_1$ $\qquad\qquad$ $C_0$ $\qquad\qquad$ $C_1$

**Fig. 2.** Left: Examples of class 0 and 1 of syntheticL2 dataset. Right: Examples of class 0 and 1 of syntheticL4 dataset. The red boxes signalize the primitives used for generating the samples of each class. (Color figure online)

**syntheticLm.** The syntheticLm dataset has three classes, generated from two primitives. Class 0 has $p_0$ at channel 0, while class 1 has $p_1$ present at channel 1, and class 3 has no primitives present. Each case happens with 33% probability, and random noise is added to all samples. Additionally, as background, channel 0 has a sine wave and channel 1 has a random polynomial of degree up to 5. Examples of each of the classes can be seen in Fig. 3.

$C_0$ $\qquad\qquad\qquad$ $C_1$ $\qquad\qquad\qquad$ $C_2$

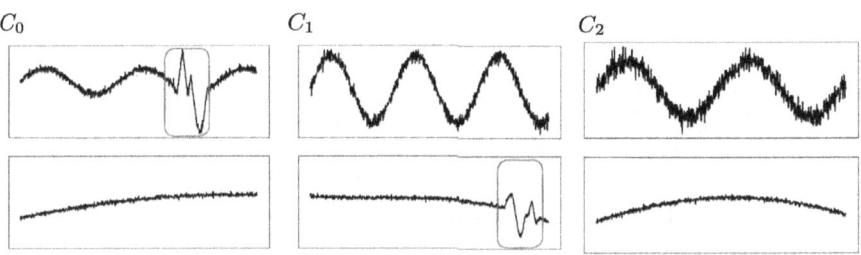

**Fig. 3.** Examples of classes 0, 1, and 2 of syntheticLm dataset. The red boxes signalize the primitives used for generating the samples of each class. (Color figure online)

## 3.3 Implementation Details

In this work, an experimental run consisted of training a model with a dataset and a specific random seed, and then applying CE as described below. Our implementation will be made publicly available upon publication of this work.

**Data.** The datasets used in this paper are the syntheticL$n_{DS}$, syntheticLm, the GunPoint dataset from the UCR archive [5] and the Production Press Sensor Data (P2S) dataset from [16]. All datasets are used for multiclass classification. Several data augmentations including resizing, time warping and Gaussian noise were applied to the data. These datasets were chosen for a general validation of the CE methods: the three synthetic datasets enable an objective validation of the CE methods in controlled scenarios with multiple ground truth primitives, GunPoint provides a straightforward test in a different real-world domain, and P2S presents a more complex industrial use case where the conditions for classification and the related more challenging features.

**Models.** To evaluate the robustness and generalization capability of our concept extraction methods, we trained three different 1D CNN architectures. The CNN architectures were InceptionTime [12] with 10 inception blocks, resnet18 [9] and DenseNet121 [11]. Furthermore, we repeated the experiments with 10 random seeds (seeds 0 to 9), allowing us to account for the stochastic nature of both model training and the explanation (concept extraction) process. Each model was trained until convergence, using early stopping with a patience of 15 epochs. The training was performed using the Adam optimizer with weight decay set to 0.01 and an initial learning rate of $1e^{-5}$. We used a ReduceLROnPlateau scheduler with a factor of 0.1 based on the NLL of the models. The data was split into 0.8 for training and 0.2 for validation. The same split was used for extracting the concepts with ECLAD-ts and visualizing them.

**Concept Extraction.** All CE methods were implemented using Pytorch. At least 2560 samples were used for CE for each model, and the same seed was used as for the model training. We tested a range of hyperparameter values for the number of concepts, namely $\{3, 5, 10, 15, 20\}$, and the final number of concepts shown in the reports was chosen via visual inspection to ensure they are representative of the overall results. The layers used for each CE method can be found in Table 1. They were chosen at regular intervals for ECLAD and ECLAD-ts. For ConceptShap and MultiVISION, they were chosen at bottlenecks to avoid examining possibly skipped blocks due to residual connections Table 1.

Additionally, for ConceptShap, Shapley values were computed using a Monte Carlo approximation as described in the original implementation. Specifically, we performed 20 iterations of Monte Carlo estimation with hyperparameters set to $\lambda_{CS,1} = 0.0001$, $\lambda_{CS,2} = 0.1$, and $\beta_{CS} = 0.2$. The $\lambda$ terms were modified for convergence, while $\beta_{CS}$ followed the original recommendation of the method.

**Table 1.** Layers for CE with each method and model

| CE methods | ECLAD and ECLAD-ts |
|---|---|
| InceptionTime10 | 'model.inception_block.inception_layers.$n_b$.bottleneck', $n_b \in \{6, 7, 8, 9\}$ |
| ResNet18 | 'model.layers.$n_b$.1.relu', $n_b \in \{0, 1, 2, 3\}$ |
| DenseNet121 | 'model.features.transition$n_b$.conv', $n_b \in \{0, 1, 2, 3\}$ |
|  | 'model.features.denseblock4.block.15.conv2' |
| CE methods | ConceptShap and MultiVISION |
| InceptionTime10 | 'model.inception_block.inception_layers.9.bottleneck' |
| ResNet18 | 'model.layers.2.1.relu' |
| DenseNet121 | 'model.features.transition3.conv' |

For MultiVISION, we set the threshold for neuron activation extraction to the 0.99 quantile of the examined layer. K-means clustering was employed for grouping activations, leveraging its partial fit capability for scalability and to enhance the stability of the resulting clusters. Additionally, we adapted the representativeness metric as an importance score, defined as the frequency of a concept per class, where the maximum frequency across classes is normalized by the overall maximum frequency.

## 4 Results

In this section, we show the results of CE with ECLAD-ts and the three compared benchmarks (ECLAD, ConceptShap, and MultiVISION) on three CNN model architectures trained on synthetic and natural datasets, performed as described in the methods section. We must highlight that the concept mining of ECLAD-ts is identical to that of ECLAD (which was adapted from the original image ECLAD directly to time series), but it uses our modified channel-wise visualization and our modified IS. Thus, the RC of ECLAD and ECLAD-ts should be very similar for univariate datasets. We first analyze synthetic datasets—where ground truth primitives are known—to demonstrate how ECLAD-ts accurately localizes and scores key features. We then validate these findings on natural datasets, highlighting our method's ability to adapt to real-world data. In each case, we show a representative example for CE and describe the obtained insights. The key takeaways of this result section are that:

1. Useful patterns are encoded distinctively within the latent space of models.
2. For synthetic datasets, concepts are closely related to primitives and a subset of them are scored with the intended importance. This demonstrates that ECLAD-ts works as intended.
3. ECLAD-ts allows for understanding the prediction process and detecting shortcut learning in models.
4. ECLAD-ts is able to localize concepts not only in time, but also channel-wise.

5. ECLAD-ts outperforms the benchmarks in terms of representation and importance correctness.

**Evaluation on Synthetic Datasets.** Experiments on synthetic datasets were conducted because the underlying primitives are predefined and easily interpretable, allowing for controlled and simplified experiments where models learn these primitives as proxy ground truth of concepts. Visualization of the extracted concepts provides a crucial sanity check for the concept extraction methods. Moreover, the controlled environment of synthetic data enables the computation of objective metrics—namely, representation correctness and importance correctness—that quantitatively evaluate the alignment between extracted concepts and the underlying primitives in terms of localization and relevance.

The **syntheticL2** dataset has one channel and a single primitive $p_0$ which is present in half of the instances. 'Uninterrupted background' is also considered to be a primitive $p_1$, since a model can also discriminate between the classes by (exclusively) detecting the lack of background interruptions. Figure 4 shows a representative example of the CE results for the syntheticL2 dataset. This figure shows the concepts extracted from a ResNet18 model trained on the syntheticL2 dataset, as well as their importance scores. We observe that the first and most important concept for all models seems to be related to the background ($p_1$). Concepts 2 and 3 for both ECLAD-based methods are also distinctively related to primitive $p_0$, but are less important. For ConceptShap, they also seem to relate to a broad area that can be interpreted as the background, and for MultiVISION, they are empty for the observed samples, but otherwise relate similarly to the background.

In all cases, the CE methods show that the CNN is using the background as a primary classification cue. Nonetheless, the difference between the background and actual features is not present in the concept representation of ConceptShap or MultiVISION. In contrast, ECLAD-ts and ECLAD are able to extract concepts relating to both the background and to the primitive $p_0$ of the dataset. This is, the LADs show that the models encode these features differently, which provides valuable information for understanding the model's behavior. Furthermore, according to ECLAD-ts concepts and scores, the CNN is performing shortcut learning in the sense that it does not rely directly on $p_0$ to make a prediction, but is mostly detecting whether a "background uninterrupted by a structure (like $p_0$)" is present.

The representation and importance correctness metrics for all CE methods on the syntheticL2 dataset are shown in Fig. 5. In terms of representation correctness, ECLAD-ts and ECLAD are, as expected, very similar. In addition, they consistently outperform the other methods, showing a better alignment between the extracted concepts and the underlying primitives. Notably, due to the network's large receptive fields, MultiVISION is unable to localize any concepts beyond the background. Although ConceptShap localizes important concepts when used with InceptionTime, its performance is inconsistent across other models. Its high performance in that particular case is due to its masks often

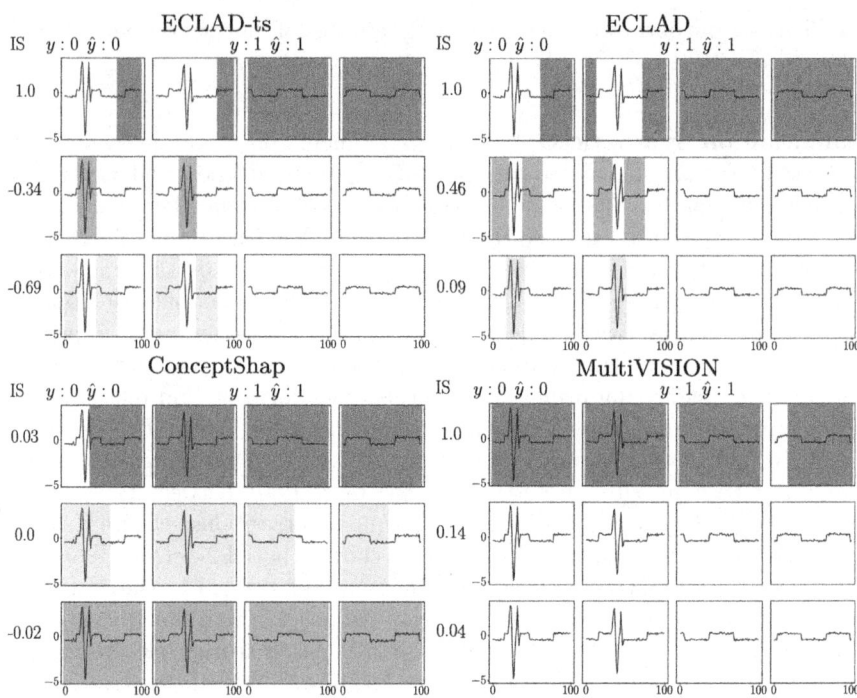

**Fig. 4.** Concept extraction from ResNet18 on the syntheticL2 dataset is illustrated for four methods. The dataset consists of one channel with a primary primitive $p_0$ and an uninterrupted background $p_1$, both serving as discriminative cues. The model (seed = 1) achieved a validation accuracy of 100%. In each panel, rows denote individual concepts and columns represent instances (with headers showing actual/predicted labels: the first two for class 0 and the latter two for class 1), highlighted regions indicate where concepts appear, and left labels report their importance scores. Notably, ECLAD-ts and ECLAD extract $p_0$-related concepts in $c_1$ and $c_2$, respectively, while ConceptShap and MultiVISION capture background cues.

showing complete instances with one class, which can perfectly overlap with prmitive $p_1$ (uninterrupted background). Regarding importance correctness, the overall mean performance is similar across models; however, ECLAD-ts achieves the highest importance correctness compared to ECLAD, ConceptShap, and MultiVISION. This shows that the modification to the IS in ECLAD-ts indeed improves its correctness. It is worth mentioning here that regardless of parameter tuning, ConceptShap failed to converge to coherent importance scores for several seeds and concept numbers. This is partly due to the nature of ConceptShap's evaluation scheme, its Monte Carlo approximation, and the task at hand. The simple tasks in these datasets require only one meaningful concept for the model to succeed. ConceptShap always takes one concept out and re-trains its surrogate model, making the importance a function of the final accuracy difference. However, if the concepts are all redundant, a perfect accuracy is possible after taking each of the concepts out.

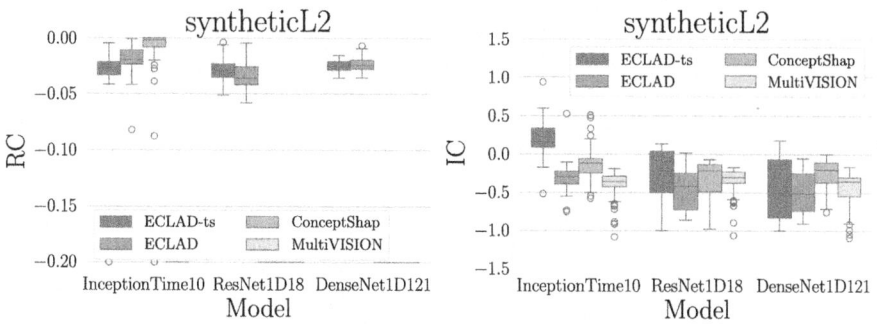

**Fig. 5.** Boxplots of (left) representation correctness and (right) importance correctness for CE methods on the syntheticL2 dataset. The box plots aggregate the data across all random seeds and the concept numbers chosen as a hyperparameter. All models achieved a validation accuracy of 100%. In both plots higher is better, as it means that the extracted concepts are more aligned with the ideal results of a concept extraction method. The plots that are collapsed at $-0.200$ are methods that exclusively obtained the maximum penalty by failing to identify alignment. ECLAD-based methods consistently achieve higher representation correctness, while ECLAD-ts attains the best importance correctness overall, highlighting its ability to extract concepts which are aligned with the underlying primitives.

The **SyntheticL4** dataset has a sinusoidal background and two primitives: a bump upwards $p_0$ for class 0 and a bump downwards $p_1$ for class 1. Figure 6 presents the concepts extracted by each method from an InceptionTime model trained on this dataset. The concepts show that the model learns to recognize the backgrounds lacking $p_1$. The latent representations in ECLAD-ts and ECLAD do differentiate the bump down, as we can see in the other concepts. However, according to ECLAD-ts' importance scores, this is also a case of shortcut-learning, where $p_1$ is primarily relied on for predictions. The distinction between background and features from the primitives is depicted by both ECLAD and ECLAD-ts, but not by ConceptShap and MultiVISION. Both ConceptShap and MultiVISION fail to extract coherent features from the model.

The metrics in Fig. 7 show, similar as before, that the representation correctness of the ECLAD-based methods is better than for the other methods. ConceptShap and MultiVISION always get a representation correctness score of $-0.2$, which corresponds to the 40% of the maximum penalty given when no alignment is detected, indicating that they are not able to localize the features in the primitives. In the case of the importance correctness, we still see increased performance from ECLAD-ts w.r.t. the other methods.

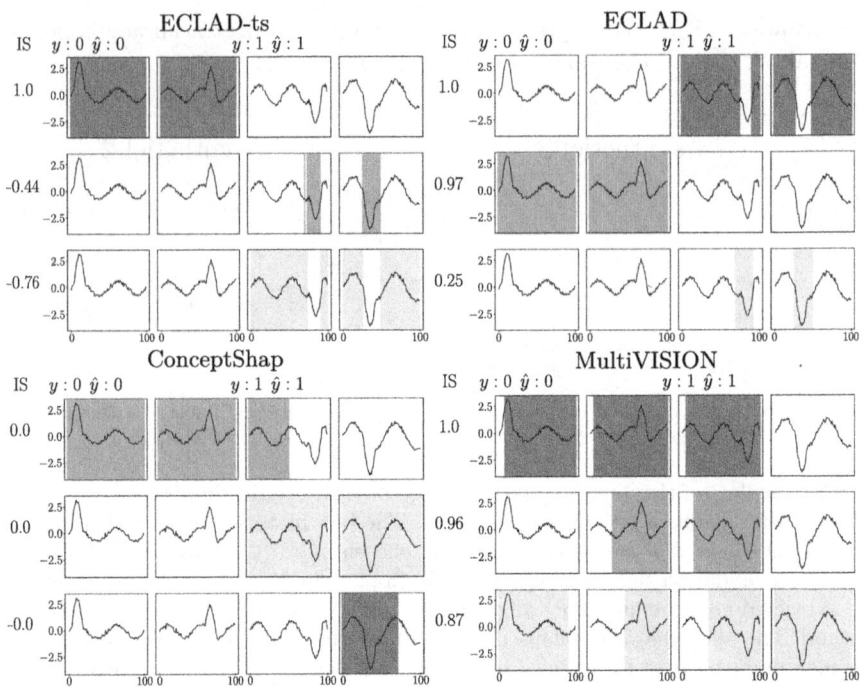

**Fig. 6.** Concept extraction from InceptionTime on the SyntheticL4 dataset. The dataset is composed of a sinusoidal background with two primitives: an upward bump $p_0$ for class 0 and a downward bump $p_1$ for class 1. The model (seed = 1) achieved a validation accuracy of 100%. In each panel, rows denote individual concepts and columns represent instances (with headers showing actual/predicted labels); highlighted regions indicate the presence of concepts, while left-hand labels report their importance scores. ECLAD-ts and ECLAD differentiate the $p_1$ feature from the background, whereas ConceptShap and MultiVISION fail to capture coherent primitive-related features.

The third synthetic dataset, **syntheticLm**, contains two channels and two primitives. Primitive $p_0$ is located in the first channel and $p_1$ in the second channel. The presence of $p_0$ determines class 0, the presence of $p_1$ determines class 1, and class 2 occurs when neither primitive is present; they never co-occur. This dataset highlights a key challenge in explaining time series: features can be distinctly encoded across channels, making channel-wise localization critical. Thus, an ideal CE method should be capable of isolating and localizing such features.

In Fig. 8, the concepts extracted by each of the methods are shown consecutively. For ECLAD-ts, we can see that concepts 0 and 3 correspond clearly to primitives $p_1$ and $p_0$, respectively. ECLAD is able to localize the same concepts through time, but not able to differentiate them through channels. In contrast, it is unclear what the extracted concepts from ConceptShap and MultiVISION refer to. The particularity of time series containing different information in each channel is not taken into account by ECLAD, ConceptShap or MultiVISION.

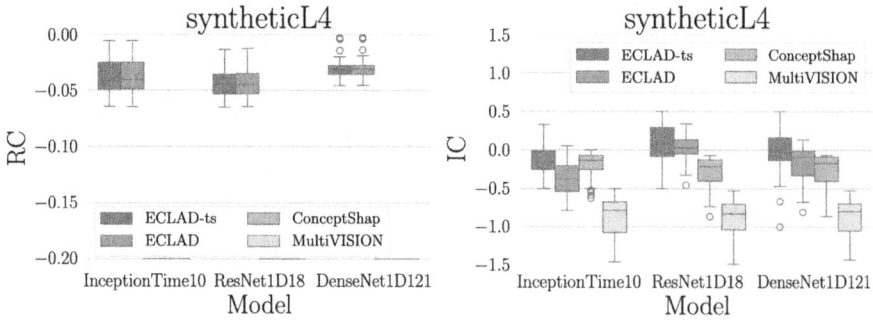

**Fig. 7.** Boxplots of (left) representation correctness and (right) importance correctness for CE methods on the SyntheticL4 dataset. The box plots aggregate the data across all random seeds and the concept numbers. All models achieved a validation accuracy of 100%. Higher scores indicate better alignment of extracted concepts with the underlying primitives. The plots that are collapsed at −0.200 are methods that exclusively obtained the maximum penalty by failing to identify alignment. ECLAD-based methods consistently outperform ConceptShap and MultiVISION, with the latter methods scoring −0.2 in representation correctness—highlighting their inability to localize primitive features—while ECLAD-ts achieves the best importance correctness overall.

With the extracted concepts of the ECLAD-based methods, we can analyze the inputs in the columns of Fig. 6 and understand how they are classified according to the concepts present in them. For example, for the sample in the first column, using ECLAD-ts: InceptionTime classifies it as class 0 because it detects $p_0$, and gives little importance to the background.

The capability of ECLAD-ts to localize features channel-wise is translated into the representation and importance correctness metrics, as shown in Fig. 9. We observe that ECLAD-ts is the only method that achieves concept alignment, and that it has a better mean importance correctness than all other methods. This shows that the proposed method is able to recognize channel-wise features encoded differently and score their importance accordingly, better than other methods.

CE with synthetic datasets demonstrates that models **encode input patterns into latent space patterns**, and that these patterns and their importance for the prediction process can be identified using ECLAD-ts. Additionally, we confirm that **ECLAD-ts performs as desired**: The concepts directly highlight the primitives, localizing them in time and channel-wise, the distance between concepts and their primitives is small, and the importance correctness achieved is higher than for the compared methods. We also show that **extracted concepts provide insights on the model**, like the most important features for the model or the presence of shortcut learning. These insights allow us to assess the alignment of the model with human expectations and make informed decisions with respect to the model to avoid unnecessary risks.

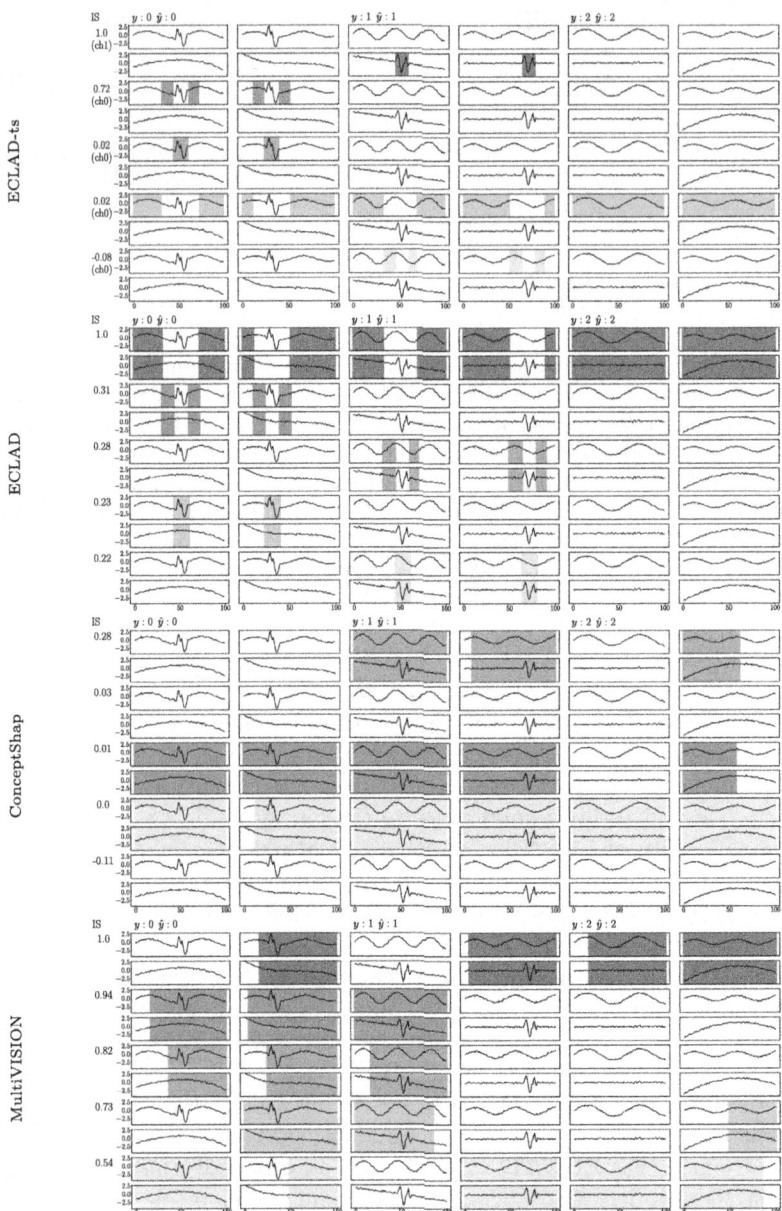

**Fig. 8.** Concept extraction from a DenseNet121 (seed = 1) with 100% validation accuracy trained on the syntheticLm dataset. In each panel, a pair of rows (channels) represents a concept and each column a sample, with headers showing ground truth/predicted labels and left labels indicating the importance scores. For concepts sharing a centroid in ECLAD-ts, only the most important concept is shown, and its channel index is indicated as 'ch'. Notably, ECLAD-ts localizes $p_1$ in concept 0 and $p_0$ in concept 3, whereas ECLAD fails to differentiate channels and both ConceptShap and MultiVISION yield ambiguous results.

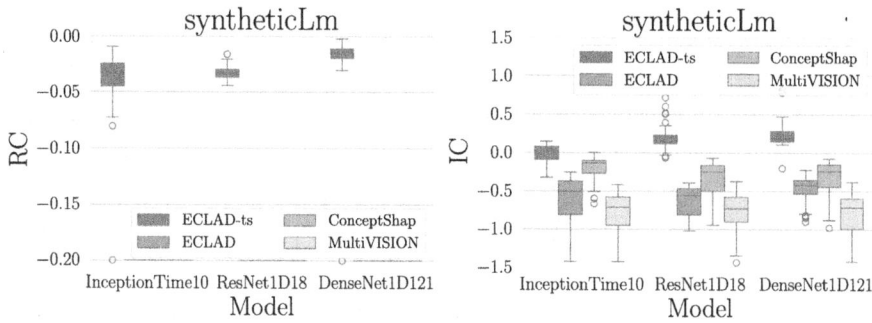

**Fig. 9.** Boxplots of (left) representation correctness and (right) importance correctness for CE methods on the syntheticLm dataset. The box plots aggregate the data across all random seeds and the concept numbers chosen as a hyperparameter. All models achieved a validation accuracy of 100%. Higher scores indicate better alignment of extracted concepts with the underlying channel-specific primitives. The plots that are collapsed at −0.200 are methods that exclusively obtained the maximum penalty by failing to identify alignment. ECLAD-ts is the only method that achieves representation alignment and obtains the highest mean importance correctness.

**Evaluation on Natural Datasets.** We now examine the results of CE with InceptionTime models trained on the **GunPoint** dataset, shown in Fig. 10. The dataset has position sensor data for the hand movement of actors holding a prop gun (class 0) or not (class 1) while making the motions of drawing, pointing and then lowering the prop. The dataset is included due to it having real world sensor data where it is known which specific features are important for the prediction [10]. These correspond to the 'overshoot' motion when lowering the arm in class 1 and the 'extra lifting' movement in class 0 (or the lack of such features in the opposite class).

For the InceptionTime model, we observe that the ECLAD-based methods both observe the important concepts corresponding to the 'overshoot' and 'extra lifting' motions. These insights allow us to asses the model alignment with human expectations. In contrast to this, ConceptShap and MultiVISION produce very broad concept masks that are inconclusive w.r.t. the important features.

Finally, we test the CE methods using the **P2S** dataset, which shows their performance in an industrial setting. The Production Press Sensor Data (P2S) dataset consists of sensor recordings from a sheet metal production process involving stamping, deep drawing, and bending operations. Each sample is a time series capturing internal forces, with the goal of classifying production runs as normal or faulty.

CE on the P2S dataset in Fig. 11 offers similar insights as those in the GunPoint dataset. The datasets' most important features are located on the slopes before the concavity in the middle. ECLAD-ts and ECLAD both produce concepts that distinguish between the background, slopes of one type, and the concavity. Furthermore, ECLAD-ts assigns a very high importance to the slopes of class 1. We can additionally examine the missclassified sample on the right of

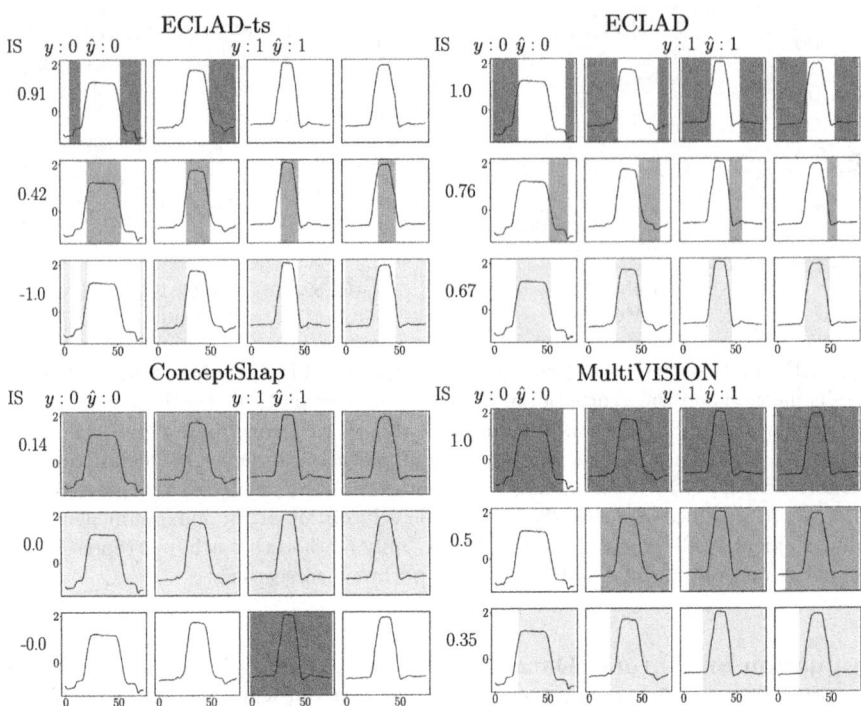

**Fig. 10.** Concept extraction from InceptionTime on the GunPoint dataset is depicted for four methods. The model (seed = 1) achieves a 96.6% validation accuracy. The dataset contains sensor data on hand movement for actors holding a prop gun or not. Two parts of the input are known to be the most significant: the 'extra lifting' movement before the higher position and the 'overshoot' motion when arriving at the lower position [10]. In each panel, rows denote individual concepts and columns represent instances (with headers showing actual/predicted labels: the first two for class 0 and the latter two for class 1), highlighted regions indicate where concepts appear, and left labels report their importance scores. ECLAD-ts and ECLAD extract concepts related to the specified features ('overshoot' and 'extra lifting' motions), while ConceptShap and MultiVISION capture background cues.

Fig. 11. It shows us that the model has mistaken the slope of a class 0 sample with the one of class 1. Observing the concepts present in missclassified samples (and e.g., further examining the confounding slope) can be a good insight for practitioners, and help improve the models.

From the CE on natural datasets GunPoint and P2S models, we see that ECLAD-ts is capable of producing **explanations for models trained on real datasets** with relevant local structures, **revealing biases and shortcut learning**. The obtained insights allow humans to understand which patterns the model is using **generally and for single instances**, why a model makes a particular prediction and which risks exist in the prediction process.

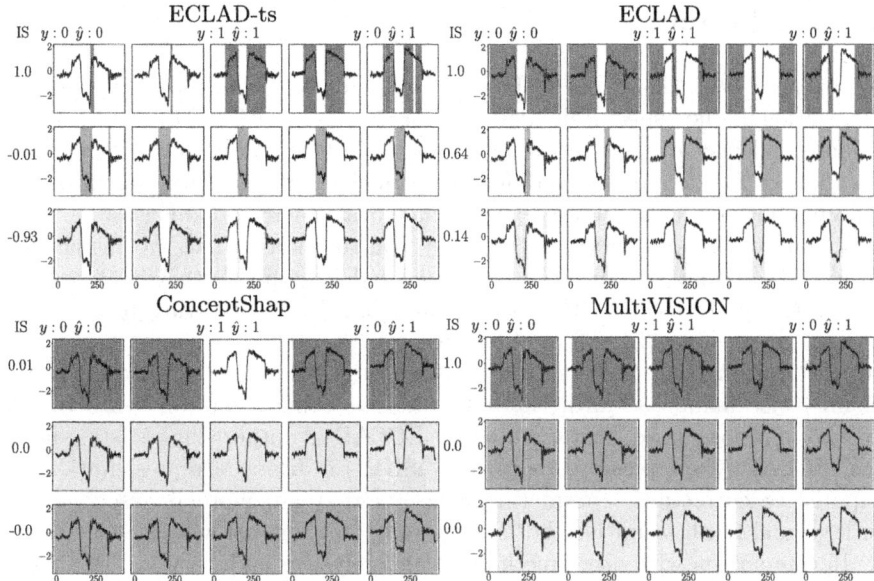

**Fig. 11.** Concept extraction from InceptionTime on the P2S dataset is illustrated for four methods. The model has seed 0 and achieved a validation accuracy of 99.7%. The dataset consists of sensor recordings of a part production process at different speeds, with either normal or faulty outcomes. The most significant part of the input according to experts is the area are the beginning and end of the slopes before the concavity in the middle. In each panel, rows denote individual concepts and columns represent instances (with headers showing actual/predicted labels: the first two for class 0, the latter two for class 1), and the final column referring to misclassified instances. Highlighted regions indicate where concepts appear, and left labels report their importance scores. ECLAD-ts and ECLAD extract concepts related to the aforementioned features, while ConceptShap and MultiVISION capture background cues.

Overall, our results demonstrate that CNNs encode meaningful latent patterns which can be effectively extracted using our concept extraction approach. The experiments on both synthetic and natural datasets showed that ECLAD-based methods have a robust capability for localizing relevant features. In particular, ECLAD-ts can do this in the channel dimension, which is crucial for explaining time series models. Additionally, ECLAD-ts consistently outperforms other concept extraction methods (ECLAD, ConceptShap, and MultiVISION) across both synthetic and natural datasets, in the granularity of the obtained masks, and in the representation and importance correctness metrics. Given this, CE with ECLAD-ts provides significant insights into model behavior for e.g., detecting shortcut learning and understanding the most important factors for a prediction.

## 5 Conclusion

We propose ECLAD-ts as the first global automatic concept extraction and localization method specifically designed for time series. ECLAD-ts addresses the unique challenges of time series data—particularly its high dimensionality and the distinct functionalities of different channels—by extracting and localizing concepts not only along the temporal axis but also across channels.

In our work, we introduce three key contributions. First, we introduce a novel method that leverages Local Aggregated Descriptors (LADs) to extract meaningful patterns from the latent space of CNNs, capturing both temporal and channel-specific information. Second, we develop an importance scoring mechanism that quantitatively assesses the relevance of a concept in a channel-wise manner. Third, through extensive experiments on synthetic and real-world datasets, we demonstrate that ECLAD-ts outperforms existing methods (ECLAD, ConceptShap, and MultiVISION) in terms of representation and importance correctness—extracting concepts that are more precisely aligned with ground truth primitives both temporally and channel-wise.

In comparison with other methods, which rely on shapley values, ECLAD-ts is more efficient and can be easily integrated for explaining CNNs, making it scalable and suitable for large-scale, real-world applications. While our experiments focus on synthetic data and industrial classification, the underlying framework is broadly applicable to any field involving multivariate time series, such as predictive maintenance, financial forecasting, environmental monitoring, and sensor data analysis.

In our current work, multiple challenges were observed. In particular, the visualization of complex features in the time series domain can be problematic. Similarly, all considered concept extraction methods exhibit sensitivity to hyperparameter settings, especially to the number of concepts, which highlights the importance of developing more adaptive techniques. Moreover, concept compositionality and correlation, which is a common phenomenon in time series, can also be explored in the context of CE. Future work will focus on refining these aspects and exploring the integration of concept extraction into real-time model training.

Here, we have focused on porposing ECLAD-ts, yet it is still an open question whether other methods like ConceptShap and MultiVISION can be modified to work properly in the time series domain. For these two methods, this could be achieved, e.g., by producing visualizations based on a meaningful subset of the receptive field.

In summary, ECLAD-ts represents a step toward better understanding the decision-making processes of convolutional neural networks for time series classifiers, enhancing model transparency, which can improve trust across diverse application domains.

**Acknowledgments.** We would like to thank Alexander Gräfe for his support in the upscaling of the experiments in this work. In addition, model training and experiments were partially performed with computing resources granted by RWTH Aachen University, under project p0022034.

**Disclosure of Interests.** This work is partially funded by the Deutsche Forschungsgemeinschaft (DFG) within the Priority Program SPP 2422 (TR 1433/3-1) and Germany's Excellence Strategy–EXC-2023 Internet of Production – 390621612.

# References

1. Burkart, N., Huber, M.F.: A survey on the explainability of supervised machine learning. JAIR (2021)
2. Crabbé, J., van der Schaar, M.: Concept activation regions: a generalized framework for concept-based explanations. In: NeurIPS, vol. 35, pp. 2590–2607 (2022)
3. Das, A., Rad, P.: Opportunities and challenges in explainable artificial intelligence (XAI): a survey. arXiv preprint arXiv:2006.11371 (2020)
4. Das, S., Xu, P., Dai, Z., Endert, A., Ren, L.: Interpreting deep neural networks through prototype factorization. In: International Conference on Data Mining Workshops (ICDMW), pp. 448–457. IEEE (2020)
5. Dau, H.A., et al.: The UCR time series classification archive (2018)
6. Decker, T., Lebacher, M., Tresp, V.: Explaining deep neural networks for bearing fault detection with vibration concepts. In: INDIN, pp. 1–6 (2023). https://doi.org/10.1109/INDIN51400.2023.10218170
7. Geirhos, R., et al.: Shortcut learning in deep neural networks. Nat. Mach. Intell. **2**(11), 665–673 (2020). https://doi.org/10.1038/s42256-020-00257-z
8. Ghorbani, A., Wexler, J., Zou, J.Y., Kim, B.: Towards automatic concept-based explanations. In: NeurIPS. vol. 32. Curran Associates, Inc. (2019)
9. He, K., Zhang, X., Ren, S., Sun, J.: Deep residual learning for image recognition. In: CVPR, pp. 770–778 (2016)
10. Hills, J., Lines, J., Baranauskas, E., Mapp, J., Bagnall, A.: Classification of time series by shapelet transformation. Data Mining and Knowledge Discovery (2014)
11. Huang, G., Liu, Z., Van Der Maaten, L., Weinberger, K.Q.: Densely connected convolutional networks. In: CVPR, pp. 4700–4708 (2017)
12. Ismail Fawaz, H., et al.: Inceptiontime: finding alexnet for time series classification. Data Min. Knowl. Disc. **34**(6), 1936–1962 (2020)
13. Jiang, X., Hu, Z., Wang, S., Zhang, Y.: Deep learning for medical image-based cancer diagnosis. Cancers **15**(14) (2023)
14. Kamakshi, V., Gupta, U., Krishnan, N.C.: PACE: posthoc architecture-agnostic concept extractor for explaining CNNs. In: IJCNN, pp. 1–8 (2021). https://doi.org/10.1109/IJCNN52387.2021.9534369
15. Kim, B., et al.: Interpretability Beyond Feature Attribution: Quantitative Testing with Concept Activation Vectors (TCAV). In: ICML, pp. 2668–2677. PMLR (2018)
16. Kraus, M., Steinmann, D., Wüst, A., Kokozinski, A., Kersting, K.: Right on time: revising time series models by constraining their explanations. arXiv preprint arXiv:2402.12921 (2024)
17. Küsters, F., Schichtel, P., Ahmed, S., Dengel, A.: Conceptual explanations of neural network prediction for time series. In: IJCNN, pp. 1–6 (2020). https://doi.org/10.1109/IJCNN48605.2020.9207341
18. Lundberg, S.M., Lee, S.I.: A unified approach to interpreting model predictions. In: NeurIPS, pp. 4768–4777. NIPS, Curran Associates Inc. (2017)

19. Madsen, A.G., Lehn-Schiøler, W.T., Jónsdóttir, Á., Arnardóttir, B., Hansen, L.K.: Concept-based explainability for an EEG transformer model. In: MLSP, pp. 1–6. IEEE (2023)
20. Obermair, C., Fuchs, A., Pernkopf, F., Felsberger, L., Apollonio, A., Wollmann, D.: Example or Prototype? Learning Concept-Based Explanations in Time-Series. In: ACML, pp. 816–831. PMLR (2023)
21. Posada-Moreno, A.F., Kreisköther, L., Glander, T., Trimpe, S.: Scale-preserving automatic concept extraction (SPACE). Mach. Learn. **112**(11), 4495–4525 (2023). https://doi.org/10.1007/s10994-023-06373-2
22. Posada-Moreno, A.F., Müller, K., Brillowski, F., Solowjow, F., Gries, T., Trimpe, S.: Scalable Concept Extraction in Industry 4.0. In: Longo, L. (ed.) xAI 2023. CCIS, vol. 1903, pp. 512–535. Springer, Cham (2023)
23. Posada-Moreno, A.F., Surya, N., Trimpe, S.: ECLAD: extracting concepts with local aggregated descriptors. Pattern Recogn. **147**, 110146 (2023)
24. Selvaraju, R.R., Cogswell, M., Das, A., Vedantam, R., Parikh, D., Batra, D.: Gradcam: visual explanations from deep networks via gradient-based localization. In: ICCV, pp. 618–626 (2017)
25. Yeh, C.K., Kim, B., Arik, S., Li, C.L., Pfister, T., Ravikumar, P.: On completeness-aware concept-based explanations in deep neural networks. In: NeurIPS, vol. 33, pp. 20554–20565 (2020)
26. Younis, R., Zerr, S., Ahmadi, Z.: Multivariate time series analysis: an interpretable CNN-based model. In: International Conference on Data Science and Advanced Analytics (DSAA), pp. 1–10. IEEE (2022)
27. Yuan, X., et al.: Quality prediction modeling for industrial processes using multi-scale attention-based convolutional neural network. IEEE Trans. Cybern. (2024)

**Open Access** This chapter is licensed under the terms of the Creative Commons Attribution 4.0 International License (http://creativecommons.org/licenses/by/4.0/), which permits use, sharing, adaptation, distribution and reproduction in any medium or format, as long as you give appropriate credit to the original author(s) and the source, provide a link to the Creative Commons license and indicate if changes were made.

The images or other third party material in this chapter are included in the chapter's Creative Commons license, unless indicated otherwise in a credit line to the material. If material is not included in the chapter's Creative Commons license and your intended use is not permitted by statutory regulation or exceeds the permitted use, you will need to obtain permission directly from the copyright holder.

# Human-Centered Explainability

# A Nexus of Explainability and Anthropomorphism in AI-Chatbots

Kudzai Sauka[1,2]($\boxtimes$)[iD], Youssef Saou[1], Frederik B. I. Situmeang[1,2][iD], and Monika Kackovic[2][iD]

[1] Faculty of Economics and Business, Amsterdam University of Applied Sciences, Amsterdam, The Netherlands
k.sauka@hva.nl
[2] Faculty of Economics and Business, University of Amsterdam, Amsterdam, The Netherlands

**Abstract.** AI chatbots are transforming customer service, yet their black-box nature often undermines consumer trust and hinders adoption. Drawing on Explainable AI (XAI), Computers as Social Actors (CASA), and Trust in Automation (TiA) frameworks, this study examines how explainability and anthropomorphism shape consumer trust in AI chatbots and influence adoption across high-stakes (Finance) and low-stakes (Retail) industries. Our findings reveal that explainability strengthens consumer trust, which drives adoption, reinforcing its role in building consumer confidence. Additionally, chatbots that are both explainable and anthropomorphic generate stronger consumer trust, though the influence of anthropomorphism differs by industry. In high-stakes industries, where transparency and reliability are critical, chatbot design should emphasise clear, structured explanations while ensuring that anthropomorphic cues support rather than overshadow trust-building. Conversely, in low-stakes industries, where engagement and interaction quality may take precedence over transparency, anthropomorphic cues play a more significant role in trust formation. Despite these differences, consumer trust remains the strongest predictor of AI chatbot adoption across both industries, highlighting its fundamental role in AI acceptance. This study provides a theoretical framework and practical recommendations for designing AI chatbots that effectively balance explainability and anthropomorphism to enhance consumer trust and adoption in different industry contexts.

**Keywords:** Explainable AI (XAI) · Anthropomorphism · Consumer Trust · AI-Chatbot · Trust in Automation

## 1 Introduction

Artificial intelligence (AI) has transformed multiple industries, driving efficiency, automation, and enhanced decision-making capabilities [47,53]. As AI evolves, businesses increasingly integrate AI-powered chatbots (AI chatbots) into customer service operations to improve user experience, personalize interactions, and streamline workflows [5]. AI chatbots use natural language processing (NLP) and machine learning to simulate human-like conversations. This technology enables businesses to provide 24/7 assistance, respond instantly to inquiries, and lower operational costs [36,52].

Fierce competition has emerged across industries as companies strive to position themselves at the forefront of the fourth and fifth industrial revolutions, leveraging AI to enhance their competitive advantage [7]. This has led to the widespread adoption of AI chatbots in banking, finance, and retail [10,12]. Kushwaha et al. [36] emphasize that chatbots help businesses tackle scalability challenges and improve efficiency, a view echoed by Chen et al. [11]. However, despite these advantages, trust concerns hinder widespread adoption [10,11]. Users often hesitate to rely on AI chatbots due to concerns about transparency, interpretability, privacy, and reliability [10,11]. The black-box nature of AI further exacerbates scepticism and mistrust, as many users struggle to comprehend how AI-driven decisions are made, particularly in high-stakes industries such as finance and healthcare [49]. Addressing these concerns is crucial for fostering consumer confidence and ensuring AI-driven customer service solutions are both effective and trustworthy.

Trust in AI chatbots and AI, in general, is widely debated, lacking a universal definition [33]. In this study, we adopt Lee and See's [37] definition, which describes trust as an attitude that an agent will assist in achieving individual goals in the midst of uncertainty. To measure trust, we utilize the Trust in Automation (TiA) framework, a dominant methodology in automation and human-machine interaction research. TiA builds on Mayer's [41] model of interpersonal and organizational trust, defining trustworthiness by ability, integrity, and benevolence. Lee and See [37] adapted these dimensions for automation into performance-based trust (system reliability), process-based trust (transparency and algorithm integrity), and purpose-based trust (user perception of AI goals) [33]. While these dimensions are theoretically distinct, in this study, we combined them into a single composite score for analysis, aligning with prior research on AI trust and adoption [13,55].

Choi and Ji [13] emphasise the importance of trust in adopting AI, especially in industries that handle sensitive data. Their research shows that trust acts as a mediator between technological capabilities and user acceptance. Similarly, Gunning et al. [23] stress that transparency is vital to establishing trust in AI systems. Without transparent decision-making processes, scepticism can obstruct user adoption. Recent studies identify two main factors influencing user trust in AI chatbots: explainability and anthropomorphism [14,24,60]. In the context of chatbots, explainability refers to a chatbot's ability to clarify its reasoning and actions to users [23]. Meanwhile, anthropomorphism refers to the extent to which non-human entities display human-like attributes—plays a key role in this process [56]. Explainability contributes to cognitive trust by enhancing perceptions of competence and integrity, helping users better understand the chatbot's reasoning process [19]. Anthropomorphism, on the other hand, promotes trust by evoking familiarity and social presence through human-like cues [52,56]. Angelov [3] observes that clear explanations can build trust by addressing AI's black-box nature. Hamm et al. [24] further asserts that explainability reduces scepticism and enhances confidence in AI interactions. Additionally, explainability is linked to ethical compliance, particularly in sectors like finance and healthcare, where accountability is paramount [3,27]. In finance, for instance, AI must justify its decisions to ensure fairness, especially regarding loan approvals and investment advice [57]. Failure in the AI system in this type of industry can lead to a higher severity of consequences both to the customer and the company. On the other hand, anthropomorphism plays a significant role in enhancing trust by making chatbot interactions more relatable and engaging [32,50]. This approach helps create natural, emotionally appealing interactions [4,51]. Research indicates that personalised, human-like chatbot interactions can improve trust through increased social presence and rapport [36,59]. However, balancing explainability and anthropomorphism presents a challenge; overemphasising human-like traits without adequate justification can undermine credibility, leading to user scepticism [16].

Research on the relationship between explainability and anthropomorphism in AI-powered chatbots is limited, even though these factors play a crucial role in building trust. Previous studies have primarily examined these components separately: explainability enhances cognitive trust by increasing transparency (e.g., [24]), while anthropomorphism fosters social trust through perceived human likeness (e.g. [52]). However, to our knowledge, no research has investigated how these two elements collectively shape consumer trust and adoption intention, particularly in industries with varying user risk perceptions. This study aims to fill that gap by exploring the combined effects of AI explainability and anthropomorphism on trust and chatbot adoption. We analyse their contributions to trust, how their interaction strengthens trust formation, and whether trust mediates the relationship between explainability and adoption. Furthermore, we introduce industry as a moderator, demonstrating that the importance of explainability and anthropomorphism differs between high-stakes (Finance) and low-stakes (Retail) sectors. Additionally, we test a sequential mediation model showing that explainability influences adoption directly and indirectly through trust, with anthropomorphism playing a distinct role across industries.

By integrating concepts from Explainable AI (XAI) [1,40], Computer as Social Actor (CASA) [44,45], and Trust in Automation (TiA) [26,37], this study contributes new empirical evidence to these frameworks. Our findings provide a more comprehensive model for understanding chatbot trust formation and offer industry-specific design recommendations beyond previous research focusing solely on explainability and anthropomorphism.

## 2 Theoretical Framework and Hypothesis Development

### 2.1 Explainability in AI Chatbots

Explainable AI (XAI) aims to make AI systems' decision-making processes transparent and understandable to users [40]. Effective explainability enhances trust by providing clear justifications for chatbot responses, reducing uncertainty, and increasing confidence in AI-driven interactions [1,29,57]. The XAI framework suggests that structured explanations improve perceptions of competence, integrity, and transparency, fostering greater user trust and engagement with AI systems [6,19,42].

Bauer et al. [8] highlight the role of explainability in reshaping users' mental models of AI systems. Their study, grounded in Mental Model Theory (MMT) (see [28]), shows that explanations improve decision-making accuracy, enhance adoption intent, and increase user satisfaction. When users understand how AI-generated recommendations are derived, they develop more accurate mental representations of the system, reinforcing trust and reliance on AI-driven decision support [8,29]. However, overly complex explanations can overload users cognitively, reducing usability and trust [8,29,39]. This underscores the need for balance—ensuring explanations are transparent yet cognitively manageable.

The significance of explainability varies by industry. In high-stakes sectors such as finance, users demand greater transparency and interpretability to make informed decisions, reinforcing the role of explainability in trust formation [3,57]. In contrast, consumer-facing applications such as e-commerce may prioritize engagement and usability over extensive explanations [59]. This suggests that while explainability remains crucial, its implementation should align with user expectations across different domains.

Consequently, explainability is expected to play a central role in AI adoption by enhancing user trust, reducing cognitive uncertainty, and improving confidence in chatbot-generated recommendations. Hence, we propose the following hypothesis:

$H1$: Explainability in AI chatbots positively influences user adoption intention.

### 2.2 Computer as Social Actor (CASA)

The Computers as Social Actors (CASA) framework suggests that users apply human social norms to AI systems, treating chatbots as social actors rather than mere automation [44,45]. This phenomenon occurs despite users' awareness that AI chatbots are not human, indicating that human likeness (anthropomorphism) in chatbot design can significantly shape user perceptions and behaviours.

AI chatbots can exhibit anthropomorphic traits through three primary social cues: visual cues (e.g., human-like avatars), identity cues (e.g., human-associated names), and conversational cues (e.g., natural language, emotional expressions) [22]. Research shows that strategically incorporating these cues can enhance user engagement, build social rapport, and reduce psychological distance, making interactions feel more natural and intuitive [17,48,52,58]. When chatbots appear more human-like, users are more likely to ascribe trustworthiness, competence, and social presence, fostering higher acceptance and engagement [9,34,35].

However, the effectiveness of anthropomorphism is context-dependent. While moderate anthropomorphism enhances trust, excessive human-like design without substantive explanations can create uncanny valley effects, leading to discomfort and scepticism [43,54]. Overly anthropomorphic chatbots may also trigger concerns about social judgment, reducing users' willingness to disclose information, particularly in sensitive interactions [25,31]. Furthermore, research suggests that perceived anthropomorphism strengthens the relationship between interaction quality and trust, meaning users who perceive a chatbot as both human-like and capable are more likely to forgive minor errors in interaction quality [10,32].

Given that both explainability and anthropomorphism contribute to trust formation, their interaction warrants further examination. Explainability enhances trust by clarifying competence and process-based transparency, while anthropomorphism fosters purpose-based trust by making the chatbot socially engaging and relatable. However, the degree to which anthropomorphism amplifies or moderates the effect of explainability on trust remains unclear. Thus, we propose:

$H2a$: Higher explainability in AI chatbots enhances consumer trust in AI chatbots.

$H2b$: The effect of explainability on consumer trust in AI chatbots is mediated by anthropomorphism.

### 2.3 Trust in Automation (TiA)

Trust plays a key role in technology acceptance, especially in AI-driven systems where users must rely on automated decisions [10,30,33]. While researchers widely recognise its importance, trust remains a contested construct, often defined as a willingness to accept vulnerability based on positive expectations [41]. The Trust in Automation (TiA) framework extends Mayer's [41] model, adapting performance-based trust, process-based trust and purpose-based trust to automation systems [37]. TiA acknowledges that trust in automation depends not only on human-like attributes but also on system functionality [26,37]. Explainability supports performance- and process-based trust in AI chatbot interactions by clarifying AI decision-making processes, overcoming AI black box problems, reducing uncertainty, and ensuring transparency [26]. While anthropomorphism fosters purpose-based trust by making AI chatbots feel more socially present, relatable, and engaging [52,56]. By defining trust as a first-order construct, we integrate performance, process, and purpose-based trust into a single measurement approach, providing insights into how explainability and anthropomorphism influence trust formation and chatbot adoption. Thus, we propose:

$H3$: Explainability positively influences adoption intention through the mediating effect of anthropomorphism and consumer trust in AI chatbots.

## 2.4 The Role of Industry as a Moderator

Consumer trust in AI varies across industries due to differing consumer expectations and perceived risks. Glikson et al. [21] found that trust in AI fluctuates based on industry-specific risks; however, research directly comparing how explainability and anthropomorphism influence trust across sectors remains limited. Frank [20] further demonstrated that decision stakes significantly impact AI adoption, with higher stakes heightening self-threat and diminishing trust in AI-powered agents. In finance, studies such as [38] suggest that accuracy, reliability, and fairness are critical factors in establishing trust, making explainability a vital consideration. Consumers in this sector frequently seek clear, justifiable reasoning, particularly regarding loan approvals and investment decisions [2,3]. In contrast, retail research indicates that consumers tend to prioritise engagement, personalisation, and emotional connection, rendering anthropomorphism more influential [4,46,51,54]. However, excessive anthropomorphism has been linked to the uncanny valley effect, which may cause discomfort among users [16,54]. These findings underscore the need for further research to explore how explainability and anthropomorphism interact in AI adoption across industries, particularly in contexts where decision stakes and consumer risk perceptions influence trust dynamics. Thus, we propose:

$H4$: Industry moderates the relationship between explainability and anthropomorphism.

$H5a$: Industry moderates the relationship between explainability and adoption intention through anthropomorphism.

$H5b$: Industry moderates the relationship between explainability and adoption intention through trust.

$H5c$: Industry moderates the indirect effect of explainability on adoption intention through anthropomorphism and trust

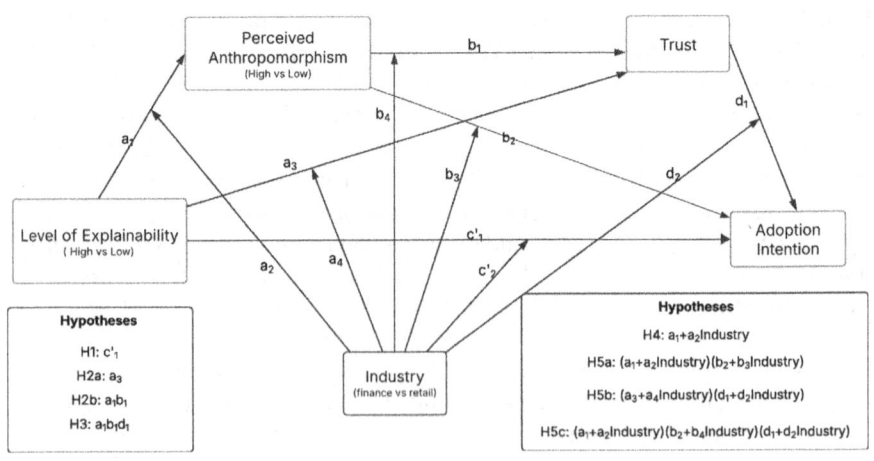

Fig. 1. A conceptual model of all hypotheses.

**Table 1.** Summary of Hypotheses

| Hypothesis | Details |
|---|---|
| H1 | Explainability in AI chatbots positively influences user adoption intention. |
| H2 | Higher explainability in AI chatbots enhances consumer trust in AI chatbots. |
| H2b | The effect of explainability on consumer trust in AI chatbots is mediated by anthropomorphism. |
| H3 | Explainability positively influences adoption intention through the mediating effect of anthropomorphism and consumer trust in AI chatbots. |
| H4 | Industry moderates the relationship between explainability and anthropomorphism. |
| H5a | Industry moderates the relationship between explainability and adoption intention through anthropomorphism. |
| H5b | Industry moderates the relationship between explainability and adoption intention through trust. |
| H5c | Industry moderates the indirect effect of explainability on adoption intention through anthropomorphism and trust. |

Figure 1 presents the conceptual model of the proposed hypotheses. Table 1 provides a detailed summary of all hypotheses tested in this study.

## 3 Methodology

### 3.1 Study Design

Two hundred thirty-nine participants were recruited from Prolific to take part in an online between-subjects experiment. An a priori power analysis using G*Power [18] was conducted to determine the required sample size. Results indicated a minimum of 119 participants to detect medium effect sizes at 95% power ($\alpha = .05$). Our final sample exceeds this threshold, supporting the robustness of the results. All participants were over 18 years of age and provided informed

**Table 2.** Experimental Conditions

| Condition | Description |
|---|---|
| Condition 1 | High Explainability_High Anthropomorphism (Retail) |
| Condition 2 | High Explainability_Low Anthropomorphism (Retail) |
| Condition 3 | Low Explainability_High Anthropomorphism (Retail) |
| Condition 4 | Low Explainability_Low Anthropomorphism (Retail) |
| Condition 5 | High Explainability_High Anthropomorphism (Finance) |
| Condition 6 | High Explainability_Low Anthropomorphism (Finance) |
| Condition 7 | Low Explainability_High Anthropomorphism (Finance) |
| Condition 8 | Low Explainability_Low Anthropomorphism (Finance) |

consent before participation. Participants were randomly assigned to one of eight experimental conditions, each representing a different combination of high/low explainability and high/low anthropomorphism across two industries (Retail and Finance). Each condition was carefully designed to manipulate the chatbot's behavior (see Appendix B for stimuli, Table 2).

In the high-explainability conditions, the chatbot clarified its decision-making process, referring to specific algorithmic factors that influenced its recommendation. In contrast, low-explainability conditions offered vague or generic justifications without referencing decision logic. High-anthropomorphism chatbots displayed human-like characteristics—such as natural language, polite tone, and a human name—whereas low-anthropomorphism chatbots used a more mechanical tone and lacked social presence.

Following the interaction, participants evaluated the chatbot's perceived explainability, anthropomorphism, trustworthiness, and their intention to adopt its recommendations. This study assessed explainability from the user's perspective rather than treating it as a static feature of the system, consistent with the user-centred approach proposed by Hamm et al. [24].

### 3.2 Measures

Reliability testing used Cronbach's Alpha for key variables to ensure construct validity (see **Appendix A**). Perceived explainability was measured on a multi-item scale $\alpha = 0.947$, focusing on chatbot transparency and clarity. Perceived anthropomorphism was assessed via a Likert scale $\alpha = 0.923$, evaluating human-like traits like conversational style and emotional expressiveness. Trust was gauged using a seven-item scale $\alpha = 0.964$, covering competence, benevolence, and integrity. Adoption intention reflected users' willingness to continue using the chatbot $\alpha = 0.940$. Lastly, the Industry Context was classified into Finance and Retail to explore trust formation and adoption differences across sectors. The Cronbach's Alpha values demonstrated high internal consistency for all constructs, confirming the reliability of the measurements. These validated measures ensured accurate capture of participants' perceptions regarding chatbot explainability, anthropomorphism, trust, and adoption intention.

### 3.3 Correlation Analysis

The Pearson correlation analysis in Table 3 demonstrates strong positive relationships among explainability, anthropomorphism, trust, and adoption intention. Explainability is correlated with trust ($r = 0.805, p < 0.001$) and adoption intention ($r = 0.765, p < 0.001$), indicating that transparent chatbot responses enhance both trust and adoption. Anthropomorphism also shows a positive correlation with trust ($r = 0.657, p < 0.001$) and adoption intention ($r = 0.677, p < 0.001$), suggesting that human-like features improve user engagement and trust. Trust exhibits the strongest correlation with adoption intention ($r = 0.880, p < 0.001$), underscoring its role as a mediator between chatbot design features and user adoption. Furthermore, explainability and anthropomorphism are significantly correlated ($r = 0.552, p < 0.001$), indicating an interactive effect on trust. These findings support the hypothesised relationships and necessitate further mediation and moderation analyses.

**Table 3.** Overall Correlations

|  | Expl | Anthro | Trust |
|---|---|---|---|
| Explainability | - | - | - |
| Anthropomorphism | 0.552** | - | - |
| Trust | 0.805** | 0.657** | - |
| Adoption Intention | 0.765** | 0.677** | 0.880** |

**Note:** *Significant correlation at the 0.01 level (2-tailed) is denoted with \*\*.*

### 3.4 Data Analysis

Our empirical testing follows a structured approach to examine the mechanisms underlying trust formation and adoption of AI chatbots. First, we use ANOVA to investigate the direct and interaction effects of explainability and anthropomorphism on trust. Next, we apply PROCESS Model 6 to assess whether anthropomorphism and trust sequentially mediate the relationship between explainability and adoption intention. To explore industry-specific variations, we employ PROCESS Model 59 to test whether the industry moderates the mediation process in the explainability → anthropomorphism → adoption and explainability → trust → adoption pathways. Finally, we extend this analysis using PROCESS Model 92, which allows us to determine whether the sequential mediation of explainability through anthropomorphism and trust on adoption is moderated by industry. By incorporating these analytical techniques, we aim to provide a comprehensive understanding of how explainability influences chatbot adoption through anthropomorphism and user trust in AI chatbots.

## 4 Results

A one-way ANOVA was conducted to test $H1$, examining whether explainability significantly influences adoption intention (see Table 4). The results showed a significant main effect, $F(1, 237) = 33.448, p < .001$, indicating that higher explainability leads to increased adoption. Participants in the high-explainability condition reported more outstanding adoption intention ($M = 4.745, SD = 1.266$) than those in the low-explainability condition ($M = 3.623, SD = 1.626$). A regression analysis using PROCESS Model 6 further confirmed the direct effect of explainability on adoption ($b = 0.147, SE = 0.049, t = 3.01, p = .003, 95\%$ CI $[0.051, 0.244]$), supporting $H1$.

**Table 4.** Hypothesis 1: One-Way ANOVA and Descriptive Statistics

| ANOVA Results | | | | |
| --- | --- | --- | --- | --- |
| Path | Test | Test Statistic | Effect Size | p-value |
| Explainability Adoption | One-Way ANOVA | $F(1, 237) = 33.448$ | $\eta^2 = .124$ | $< .001$ |

| Adoption intent by explainability level | | |
| --- | --- | --- |
| Variable | Mean (M) | SD |
| Adoption intention (High Explainability) | 4.745 | 1.266 |
| Adoption intention (Low Explainability) | 3.623 | 1.626 |

**Table 5.** Hypothesis 2a: One-Way ANOVA (Direct Effect Model)

| Path | Test | Test Statistic | Effect Size | p-value |
| --- | --- | --- | --- | --- |
| Explainability Trust | One-Way ANOVA | $F(1, 237) = 41.462$ | $\eta^2 = .149$ | $p < .001$ |

| Descriptive Statistics for Trust by Explainability Level | | |
| --- | --- | --- |
| Explainability | M | SD |
| Trust (High Explainability) | 5.288 | 1.255 |
| Trust (Low Explainability) | 4.099 | 1.518 |

*H2a: Explainability → Trust.* A one-way ANOVA was conducted to examine whether explainability directly influences trust. The results in Table 5 revealed a significant effect of explainability on trust ($F(1, 237) = 41.462, p < .001, \eta^2 = .149$), indicating that higher chatbot explainability leads to greater consumer trust. Users in the high-explainability condition reported significantly higher trust ($M = 5.288, SD = 1.255$) than those in the low-explainability condition ($M = 4.099, SD = 1.518$). The effect size ($\eta^2 = .149$) suggests that explainability accounts for 14.9% of the trust variance. This finding supports $H2a$, reinforcing that explainability in AI chatbots enhances user trust.

*H2b: Explainability → Anthropomorphism → Trust (Mediation).* We conducted a mediation analysis using PROCESS Model 4 (Hayes, 2022) to determine whether anthropomorphism mediates the relationship between explainability and trust (see Table 6. Explainability significantly positively affected anthropomorphism ($b = 0.559, SE = 0.055, t = 10.193, p < .001$), suggesting that explainability in AI chatbots enhances the chatbot's perceived anthropomorphism. The indirect effect of explainability on trust through anthropomorphism was significant. ($b = 0.162, BootSE = 0.035$, 95% CI $[0.096, 0.234]$). Since the direct effect of explainability on trust remained significant ($b = 0.610, p < .001$), this indicates partial mediation, supporting $H2b$. This result suggests that when users perceive a chatbot as more explainable, they see it as more human-like, further enhancing trust. However, since the direct path from explainability to trust remained significant, this mediation effect is partial rather than complete.

**Table 6.** Hypothesis 2b: Mediation Analysis (PROCESS Model 4)

| Path | Effect (b) | SE | 95% CI (LL, UL) |
|---|---|---|---|
| Direct Effect (Explainability → Trust) | 0.610 | 0.040 | [0.531, 0.689] |
| Indirect Effect (Explainability → Anthropomorphism → Trust) | 0.162 | 0.035 | [0.096, 0.234] |

Note: All confidence intervals are 95% CI; Number of bootstrap samples = 5000.

*H3: Explainability → Anthropomorphism → Trust → Adoption (Mediation).* A sequential mediation analysis using PROCESS Model 6 (Hayes, 2022) tested whether anthropomorphism and trust mediate the relationship between explainability and adoption intention ($H3$). The total indirect effect was significant ($b = 0.612, SE = 0.050$, 95% CI $[0.517, 0.711]$), confirming strong mediation. Explainability influenced adoption behavior through anthropomorphism ($b = 0.0918, SE = 0.025$, 95% CI $[0.047, 0.145]$, partial mediation) and trust ($b = 0.411, SE = 0.053$, 95% CI $[0.308, 0.517]$, strong mediation). The sequential pathway (explainability → anthropomorphism → trust → adoption) was also significant ($b = 0.109, SE = 0.025$, 95% CI $[0.064, 0.159]$), indicating that both factors contribute in sequence. Since the direct effect remained significant ($b = 0.147, SE = 0.049, t = 3.01, p = .003$, 95% CI $[0.051, 0.244]$), mediation was partial, supporting $H3$ (see Table 7).

**Table 7.** Hypothesis 3: Sequential Mediation Analysis (PROCESS Model 6)

| Path | Effect (b) | BootSE | 95% CI (LL, UL) |
|---|---|---|---|
| **Total Indirect Effect** | 0.611 | 0.050 | [0.517, 0.711] |
| Explainability → Anthropomorphism → Adoption | 0.092 | 0.025 | [0.047, 0.145] |
| Explainability → Trust → Adoption | 0.411 | 0.053 | [0.308, 0.517] |
| Explainability → Anthropomorphism → Trust → Adoption | 0.109 | 0.025 | [0.064, 0.159] |
| **Direct Effect of Explainability on Adoption** | 0.147 | 0.049 | [0.051, 0.244] |

Note: All confidence intervals are 95% CI; Number of bootstrap samples = 5000.

A moderated mediation analysis using PROCESS Model 59 (Hayes, 2022) examined whether industry (Finance vs. Retail) moderates the relationships between explainability, anthropomorphism, trust, and adoption intention in AI-powered customer service chatbots.

*H4: Moderation Effects on Anthropomorphism (Explainability → Anthropomorphism).*

Explainability alone did not significantly predict perceived anthropomorphism ($b = 0.157, SE = 0.175, t = 0.895, p = 0.372$, 95% CI $[-0.188, 0.501]$), suggesting that greater transparency does not necessarily enhance perceptions of human-like attributes in AI chatbots. However, industry significantly moderated this relationship ($b = 0.264, SE = 0.109, t = 2.419, p = 0.016$, 95% CI

[0.049, 0.478]), indicating that the effect of explainability on anthropomorphism varies across sectors. As shown in Table 8, conditional effects analysis revealed that in finance, explainability had a moderate impact on anthropomorphism ($b = 0.420, SE = 0.079, t = 5.319, p < .001$, 95% CI [0.265, 0.576]). In contrast, in retail, this effect was more substantial ($b = 0.684, SE = 0.075, t = 9.106, p < .001$, 95% CI [0.536, 0.831]). This suggests that while explainability enhances perceptions of human likeness in both industries, its influence is more pronounced in retail, supporting $H4$.

**Table 8.** Hypothesis 4: Model 59 (Industry Moderation on Explainability → Anthropomorphism)

| Path | Effect (b) | SE | p-value | 95% CI |
|---|---|---|---|---|
| Explainability → Anthropomorphism | 0.157 | 0.175 | .372 | [−0.188, 0.501] |
| Industry Moderation Effect | 0.264 | 0.109 | .016 | [0.049, 0.478] |
| **Conditional Effects** | **Effect (b)** | **SE** | **p-value** | **95% CI** |
| Finance | 0.420 | 0.079 | < .001 | [0.265, 0.576] |
| Retail | 0.684 | 0.075 | < .001 | [0.536, 0.832] |

**Note:** *All confidence intervals are 95% CI; Number of bootstrap samples = 5000.*

*Conditional Indirect Effects of Explainability on Adoption (H5 a&b)*. We examined whether explainability indirectly influences adoption intention through anthropomorphism and trust and whether these effects differ by industry. For H5a (Industry moderates explainability → Anthropomorphism → Adoption) (see Table 9), the results indicate that in finance, explainability significantly enhances anthropomorphism, which in turn drives adoption ($b = 0.100, SE = 0.041$, 95% CI [0.036, 0.197], significant). However, in retail, this pathway was weaker and not significant ($b = 0.066, SE = 0.035$, 95% CI [−0.000, 0.138], not significant). This indicates that financial sector users may consider explainability a key driver of anthropomorphism, which in turn fosters trust and influences chatbot adoption. In contrast, retail consumers might prioritize other chatbot features. Since this effect was significant in finance but not retail, the industry moderates the pathway but not consistently across both sectors, providing partial support for H5a.

For H5b (Industry moderates explainability → trust → adoption), trust remained a consistent mediator in both industries (see Table 9). In finance, trust significantly mediated the relationship between explainability and adoption intention ($b = 0.484, SE = 0.081$, 95% CI [0.320, 0.648], significant), and in retail, the effect was similarly strong ($b = 0.443, SE = 0.072$, 95% CI [0.394, 0.681], significant). Unlike anthropomorphism, trust plays a consistent role as a mediator between explainability and adoption intention across sectors. This indicates that users, regardless of industry, rely on trust when adopting AI chatbots. Since the effect was significant in both industries and the difference

**Table 9.** Hypothesis 5a & b: Moderated Mediation Analysis (PROCESS Model 59)

| Hypothesis 5a | | | |
|---|---|---|---|
| Industry Moderation of Explainability Anthropomorphism Adoption | | | |
| Industry | Effect (b) | BootSE | 95% CI (LL, UL) |
| Finance | 0.100 | 0.041 | [0.036, 0.197] |
| Retail | 0.066 | 0.035 | [−0.000, 0.138] |

| Hypothesis 5b | | | |
|---|---|---|---|
| Industry Moderation of Explainability Trust Adoption | | | |
| Industry | Effect (b) | BootSE | 95% CI (LL, UL) |
| Finance | 0.484 | 0.081 | [0.320, 0.648] |
| Retail | 0.443 | 0.072 | [0.394, 0.681] |

Note: *All confidence intervals are 95% CI; Number of bootstrap samples = 5000.*

between the coefficients was not statistically significant, the industry did not moderate this pathway, leading to the rejection of H5b. These findings highlight trust as the primary mediating mechanism through which explainability influences adoption, whereas anthropomorphism exhibits a sector-specific effect, particularly in finance, where explainability-driven anthropomorphism enhances adoption.

**Table 10.** Hypothesis 5c: Moderated Mediation Analysis (PROCESS Model 92)

| Explainability → Anthropomorphism → Trust → Adoption | | | |
|---|---|---|---|
| Industry | Effect (b) | BootSE | 95% CI (LL, UL) |
| Finance | 0.097 | 0.030 | [0.041, 0.156] |
| Retail | 0.097 | 0.032 | [0.039, 0.166] |
| **Index of Moderated Mediation** | 0.001 | 0.044 | [−0.084, 0.091] |

Note: *All confidence intervals are 95% CI; Number of bootstrap samples = 5000.*

*Moderated Mediation Analysis (Explainability → Anthropomorphism → Trust → Adoption, Moderated by Industry.* We tested whether industry moderates the indirect effect of explainability on adoption through anthropomorphism and trust ($H5c$) (see Table 10). The conditional indirect effect of explainability on adoption through anthropomorphism and trust was significant in both finance ($b = 0.097, BootSE = 0.030$, 95% CI [0.041, 0.156]) and retail ($b = 0.097, BootSE = 0.032$, 95% CI [0.039, 0.166]). However, the index of moderated mediation was not significant ($b = 0.001, BootSE = 0.044$, 95% CI [−0.084, 0.091]), indicating that the indirect effect did not differ significantly between industries. These findings suggest that explainability enhances anthropomorphism, which in turn strengthens trust, ultimately leading to increased adoption. However, the moderated mediation effect was not supported, meaning that while these relationships are significant across both industries, industry does not meaningfully moderate the overall indirect pathway. Thus, H5c is not supported.

## 5 Discussion

### 5.1 Theoretical Contributions

This study advances research in eXplainable AI (XAI), Computers as Social Actors (CASA), and Trust in Automation (TiA) by demonstrating that explainability and anthropomorphism jointly shape consumer trust in AI-driven interactions. While previous studies have examined these factors separately, our findings highlight the importance of balancing both elements to maximise trust. Additionally, by introducing industry as a Moderator in chatbot trust formation, this study contributes to TiA theory by showing how the impact of explainability and anthropomorphism differs across service domains. This industry-specific perspective offers a deeper understanding of trust-building mechanisms in AI adoption.

### 5.2 Practical Implications

By bridging the gap between theoretical research and real-world application, this study equips AI developers and business stakeholders with insights to design more effective, trustworthy AI chatbots, ensuring that customer interactions are transparent and engaging across diverse industries.

The findings highlight that industry context influences the trust adoption pathway and the relative importance of explainability and anthropomorphism in chatbot design aligning with [20,21]. While explainability alone does not significantly predict adoption, its effects manifest indirectly through different pathways in Finance and Retail. In finance, trust and explainability play key roles in adoption, whereas in retail, trust is the dominant mechanism, and the explainability-driven anthropomorphism effect is unreliable. This suggests that AI chatbot strategies should be industry-specific: In finance, where users prioritise transparency and human-like characteristics, chatbot designs should enhance explainability and anthropomorphism to build trust and drive adoption, as also shown by [3,24]. In retail, where explainability does not significantly mediate the adoption process, chatbot strategies should instead focus on strengthening trust through user engagement, personalisation, and conversational style rather than anthropomorphism alone.

### 5.3 Limitations and Future Research

Future research can build on these findings in several ways. First, longitudinal studies could explore how explainability and anthropomorphism influence consumer trust over time, offering insights into sustained engagement and AI adoption. Second, while this study manipulated industry context, participants were recruited from a general population sample on Prolific rather than domain-specific workers (e.g., finance or retail). This may limit the practical generalizability of findings, especially for real-world applications. Future studies should consider recruiting industry practitioners to capture contextual nuances in high-stakes sectors better.

Third, Prolific, though suitable for behavioral experiments, poses limitations regarding ecological validity and applicability to real-world environments. This should be considered when interpreting practical implications. Fourth, while explainability and anthropomorphism were shown to impact trust and adoption positively, there is a potential risk of overtrust or miscalibrated trust in AI systems. Excessive human likeness may trigger psychological discomfort—the Uncanny Valley phenomenon. Future research should investigate this boundary, exploring when and why anthropomorphic cues shift from engaging to unsettling and cautioning users' reliance on explainable AI. Fifth, expanding the study to industries like healthcare or education could uncover sector-specific trust dynamics. In healthcare, explainability is critical for ethical compliance and informed decision-making, while in education, anthropomorphism may enhance engagement and learning outcomes. Lastly, incorporating live chatbot interactions would allow researchers to capture real-time user responses and trust-building mechanisms, improving the ecological validity of chatbot trust research. Future work should also consider moderating factors such as cultural background, personality traits, and prior AI experience to better understand individual-level variation in chatbot acceptance.

## 6 Conclusion

This study offers a comprehensive framework for understanding how explainability and anthropomorphism shape consumer trust and the adoption of AI-powered customer service chatbots. By integrating insights from Explainable AI (XAI), Computers as Social Actors (CASA), and trust in Automation (TiA) and empirically testing these relationships, we provide a deeper understanding of trust formation in AI-driven interactions. The findings emphasise that a balanced approach, tailored to industry-specific expectations, is essential for fostering chatbot trust and adoption. Chatbots in finance, a high-risk sector, should prioritise explainability to reinforce perceptions of competence and reliability. In contrast, in retail, a lower-risk sector, anthropomorphic design elements should be leveraged to enhance user engagement and ease of interaction. This study contributes theoretically and practically, offering AI developers, businesses, and researchers an evidence-based framework for designing AI-driven customer service systems that build trust and encourage adoption. Future research should explore additional contextual factors, such as personalisation, long-term user engagement, and regulatory considerations, to refine chatbot trust-building strategies further.

**Acknowledgements.** This publication is part of the project LESSEN with project number NWA.1389.20.183 of the research program NWA ORC 2020/21, which is (partly) financed by the Dutch Research Council (NWO).

**Disclosure of Interests.** The authors have no competing interests to declare that are relevant to the content of this article.

## Appendix A  Measurement Items and Reliability Analysis

| Measurement/Items | Item-Total Correlation | Cronbach's Alpha |
|---|---|---|
| **Perceived Explainability [24,57]** | | .947 |
| The chatbot made its reasoning process clear to me | .860 | |
| I could understand why the chatbot recommends the products to me | .807 | |
| The explanations provided by the chatbot were detailed and informative | .869 | |
| The chatbot's explanations helped me understand how the recommendations were made | .864 | |
| The transparency of the chatbot's reasoning process increased my confidence in its recommendations | .889 | |
| **Trust [12,13]** | | .964 |
| Overall, I trust this chatbot in product recommendations | .897 | |
| The chatbot is reliable for making product recommendations | .904 | |
| I felt the chatbot's behaviour and response could meet my expectations | .906 | |
| I feel confident in the chatbot's ability to address my issues | .903 | |
| The chatbot instils confidence in its recommendations | .874 | |
| **Perceived Anthropomorphism [24,57]** | | .923 |
| The chatbot seemed to have human-like characteristics (name, avatar, conversational style) | .815 | |
| I felt like I was interacting with a human when using the chatbot | .874 | |
| The chatbot used language that felt natural and human-like | .797 | |
| The chatbot's responses were emotionally engaging | .818 | |
| **Adoption Intention [13,14]** | | .940 |
| I intend to use this chatbot for product recommendations again | .883 | |
| I expect to use this chatbot over seeking advice from a human | .730 | |
| I plan to rely on the recommendations from this chatbot | .851 | |
| I find the chatbot helpful in making purchase decisions | .877 | |
| Using this chatbot enhances my efficiency in finding suitable products | .852 | |

## Appendix B  Manipulation Stimuli

*This appendix presents a subset of the manipulation stimuli materials; for illustration. Profile pictures of the agents were generated using Dezgo - Stable Diffusion [15] (Figs. 2, 3, 4 and 5). The selected examples include:*

- High Explainability - High Anthropomorphism (Retail)
- Low Explainability - Low Anthropomorphism (Retail)
- High Explainability - High Anthropomorphism (Finance)
- Low Explainability - Low Anthropomorphism (Finance)

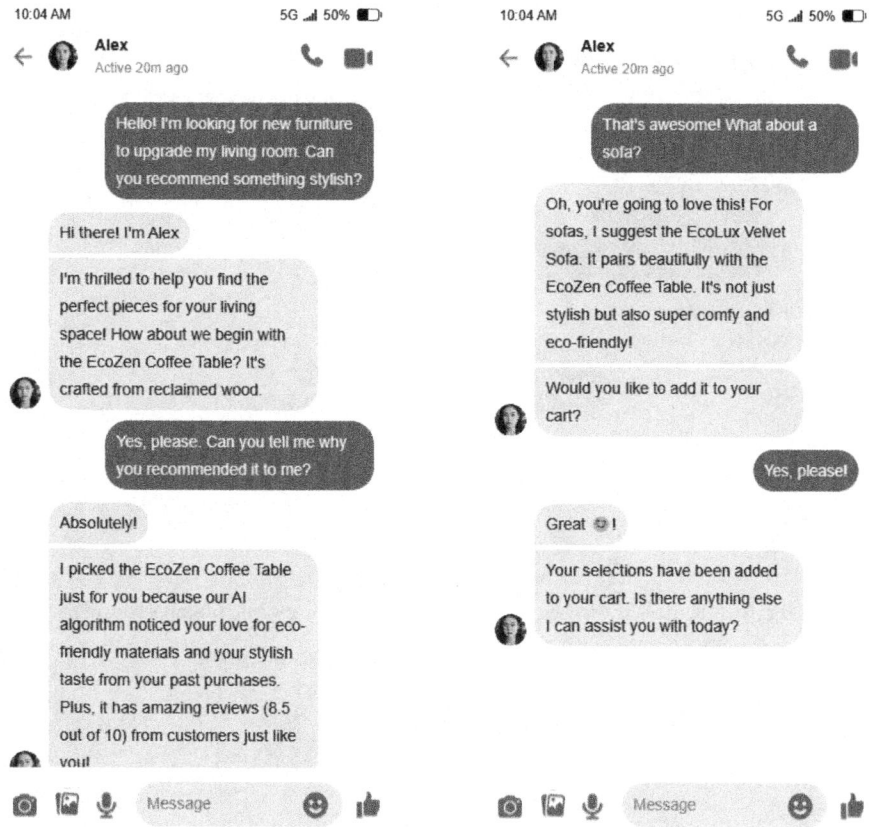

**Fig. 2.** Group 1: High Explainability-High Anthropomorphism (Retail)

## Appendix B: Manipulation Stimuli

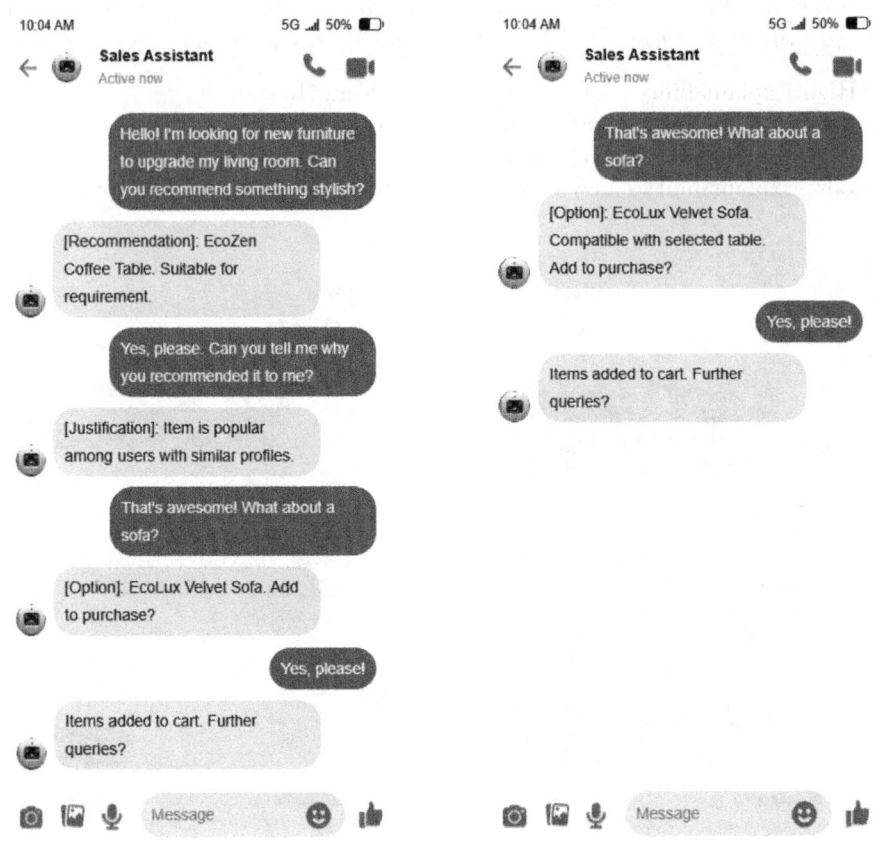

**Fig. 3.** Group 4: Low Explainability-Low Anthropomorphism (Retail)

# Appendix B: Manipulation Stimuli

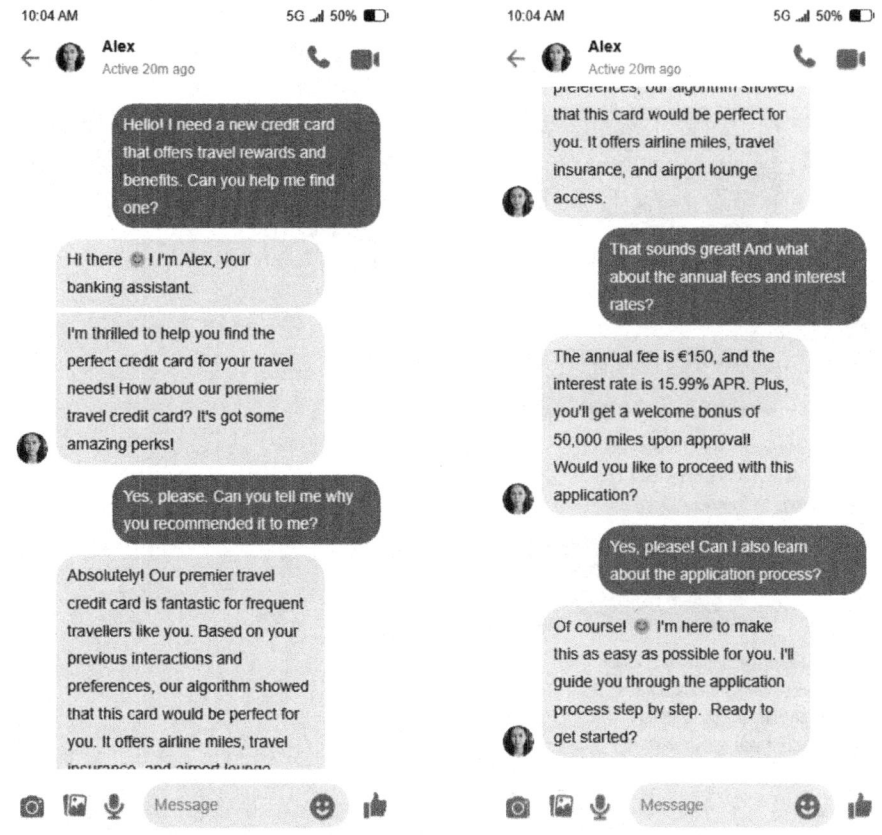

**Fig. 4.** Group 5: High Explainability-High Anthropomorphism (Finance)

## Appendix B: Manipulation Stimuli

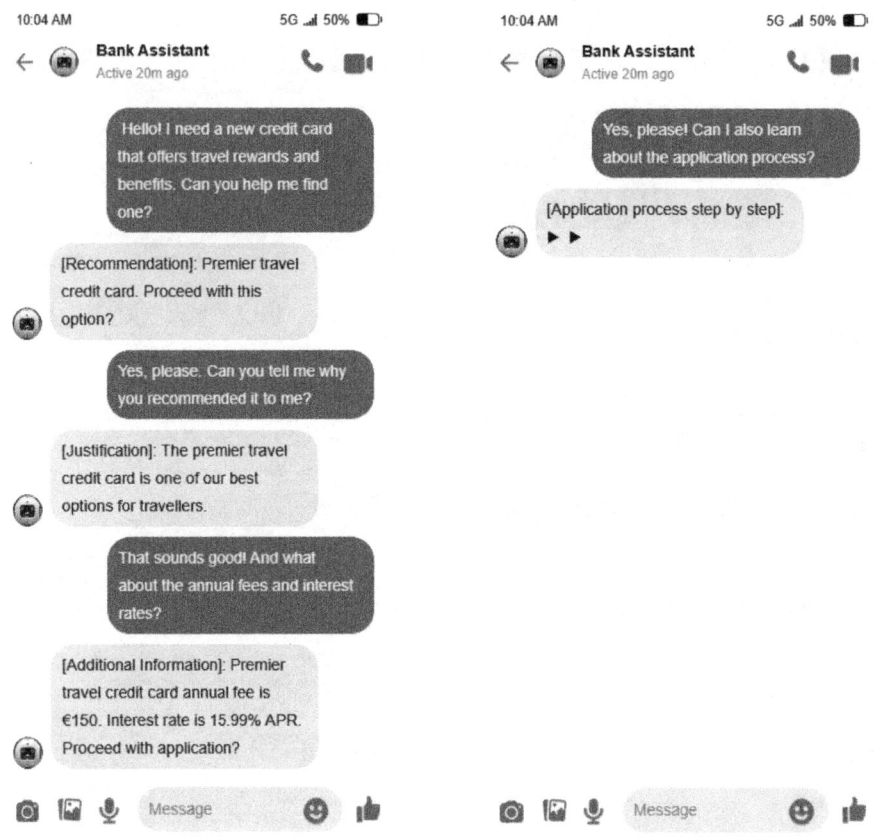

**Fig. 5.** Group 8: Low Explainability-Low Anthropomorphism (Finance)

## References

1. Adadi, A., Berrada, M.: Peeking inside the black-box: a survey on explainable artificial intelligence (XAI). IEEE Access **6**, 52138–52160 (2018). https://doi.org/10.1109/ACCESS.2018.2870052
2. Ahmad Bhatti, A.: Exploring the adoption of artificial intelligence in the finance industry: the case of Chatbots in the Kenyan Finance Industry (2019). https://doi.org/10.2139/ssrn.3493340
3. Angelov, P.P., Soares, E.A., Jiang, R., Arnold, N.I., Atkinson, P.M.: Explainable artificial intelligence: an analytical review. WIREs Data Min. Knowl. Discovery **11**(5), e1424 (2021). https://onlinelibrary.wiley.com/doi/pdf/10.1002/widm.1424

4. Araujo, T.: Living up to the chatbot hype: the influence of anthropomorphic design cues and communicative agency framing on conversational agent and company perceptions. Comput. Hum. Behav. **85**, 183–189 (2018). https://doi.org/10.1016/j.chb.2018.03.051
5. Arora, P., Narula, S.: Linkages between service quality, customer satisfaction and customer loyalty: a literature review. IUP J. Mark. Manag. **17**(4), 30 (2018)
6. Baker, S., Xiang, W.: Explainable AI is responsible AI: how explainability creates trustworthy and socially responsible artificial intelligence. arXiv preprint arXiv:2312.01555 (2023)
7. Bal, H.C., Erkan, C.: Industry 4.0 and competitiveness. Procedia Comput. Sci. **158**, 625–631 (2019). https://doi.org/10.1016/j.procs.2019.09.096
8. Bauer, K., Zahn, M., Hinz, O.: Expl (AI) ned: the impact of explainable artificial intelligence on users' information processing. Inf. Syst. Res. **34**(4), 1582–1602 (2023)
9. Blut, M., Wang, C., Wünderlich, N.V., Brock, C.: Understanding anthropomorphism in service provision: a meta-analysis of physical robots, chatbots, and other AI. J. Acad. Mark. Sci. **49**, 632–658 (2021)
10. Chakraborty, D., Kumar Kar, A., Patre, S., Gupta, S.: Enhancing trust in online grocery shopping through generative AI chatbots. J. Bus. Res. **180**, 114737 (2024). https://doi.org/10.1016/j.jbusres.2024.114737
11. Chen, Q., Gong, Y., Lu, Y., Tang, J.: Classifying and measuring the service quality of AI chatbot in frontline service. J. Bus. Res. **145**, 552–568 (2022). https://doi.org/10.1016/j.jbusres.2022.02.088
12. Cheng, X., Zhang, X., Cohen, J., Mou, J.: Human vs. AI: understanding the impact of anthropomorphism on consumer response to chatbots from the perspective of trust and relationship norms. Inf. Process. Manag. **59**(3), 102940 (2022). https://doi.org/10.1016/j.ipm.2022.102940
13. Choi, J.K., Ji, Y.G.: Investigating the importance of trust on adopting an autonomous vehicle. Int. J. Hum.-Comput. Interact. **31**(10), 692–702 (2015). https://doi.org/10.1080/10447318.2015.1070549
14. Cui, T., Peng, X., Wang, X.: Understanding the effect of anthropomorphic design: towards more persuasive conversational agents. In: Proceedings of the 2020 International Conference on Information Systems (ICIS) (2020)
15. DezgoSAS: Dezgo - stable diffusion (2022). https://dezgo.com/text2image/sdxl
16. Dubiel, M., Daronnat, S., Leiva, L.A.: Conversational agents trust calibration: a user-centred perspective to design. In: Proceedings of the 4th Conference on Conversational User Interfaces, pp. 1–6. CUI '22, Association for Computing Machinery, New York, NY, USA (2022). https://doi.org/10.1145/3543829.3544518
17. Epley, N., Waytz, A., Cacioppo, J.T.: On seeing human: a three-factor theory of anthropomorphism. Psychol. Rev. **114**(4), 864–886 (2007). https://doi.org/10.1037/0033-295X.114.4.864
18. Faul, F., Erdfelder, E., Buchner, A., Lang, A.G.: Statistical power analyses using g* power 3.1: tests for correlation and regression analyses. Behav. Res. Methods **41**(4), 1149–1160 (2009)
19. Ferrario, A., Loi, M.: How explainability contributes to trust in AI. In: 2022 ACM Conference on Fairness, Accountability, and Transparency, pp. 1457–1466. ACM, Seoul Republic of Korea (2022). https://doi.org/10.1145/3531146.3533202
20. Frank, D.A., Chrysochou, P., Mitkidis, P., Otterbring, T., Ariely, D.: Navigating uncertainty: exploring consumer acceptance of artificial intelligence under self-threats and high-stakes decisions. Technol. Soc. **79**, 102732 (2024). https://doi.org/10.1016/j.techsoc.2024.102732

21. Glikson, E., Woolley, A.W.: Human trust in artificial intelligence: review of empirical research. Acad. Manag. Ann. **14**(2), 627–660 (2020)
22. Go, E., Sundar, S.S.: Humanizing chatbots: the effects of visual, identity and conversational cues on humanness perceptions. Comput. Hum. Behav. **97**, 304–316 (2019)
23. Gunning, D., Stefik, M., Choi, J., Miller, T., Stumpf, S., Yang, G.Z.: XAI—explainable artificial intelligence. Sci. Rob. **4**(37), eaay7120 (2019). https://doi.org/10.1126/scirobotics.aay7120
24. Hamm, P., Klesel, M., Coberger, P., Wittmann, H.F.: Explanation matters: an experimental study on explainable AI. Electron. Mark. **33**(1), 17 (2023). https://doi.org/10.1007/s12525-023-00640-9
25. Han, B., Deng, X., Fan, H.: Partners or opponents? How mindset shapes consumers' attitude toward anthropomorphic artificial intelligence service robots. J. Serv. Res. **26**(3), 441–458 (2023)
26. Hoff, K.A., Bashir, M.: Trust in automation: integrating empirical evidence on factors that influence trust. Hum. Factors **57**(3), 407–434 (2015). https://doi.org/10.1177/0018720814547570
27. Holzinger, A., Biemann, C., Pattichis, C.S., Kell, D.B.: What do we need to build explainable AI systems for the medical domain? arXiv preprint arXiv:1712.09923 (2017)
28. Jones, N.A., Ross, H., Lynam, T., Perez, P., Leitch, A.: Mental models: an interdisciplinary synthesis of theory and methods. Ecol. Soc. **16**(1) (2011)
29. Joshi, R., Graefe, J., Kraus, M., Bengler, K.: Exploring the impact of explainability on trust and acceptance of conversational agents – a wizard of Oz study. In: Degen, H., Ntoa, S. (eds.) Artificial Intelligence in HCI, pp. 199–218. Springer, Cham (2024). https://doi.org/10.1007/978-3-031-60606-9_12
30. Kim, D.J., Ferrin, D.L., Rao, H.R.: A trust-based consumer decision-making model in electronic commerce: the role of trust, perceived risk, and their antecedents. Decis. Support Syst. **44**(2), 544–564 (2008). https://doi.org/10.1016/j.dss.2007.07.001
31. Kim, H., So, K.K.F., Wirtz, J.: Service robots: applying social exchange theory to better understand human-robot interactions. Tour. Manage. **92**, 104537 (2022). https://doi.org/10.1016/j.tourman.2022.104537
32. Klein, K., Martinez, L.F.: The impact of anthropomorphism on customer satisfaction in chatbot commerce: an experimental study in the food sector. Electron. Commer. Res. **23**(4), 2789–2825 (2023). https://doi.org/10.1007/s10660-022-09562-8
33. Kohn, S.C., de Visser, E.J., Wiese, E., Lee, Y.C., Shaw, T.H.: Measurement of trust in automation: a narrative review and reference guide. Front. Psychol. **12** (2021). https://doi.org/10.3389/fpsyg.2021.604977
34. Konya-Baumbach, E., Biller, M., Janda, S.: Someone out there? A study on the social presence of anthropomorphized chatbots. Comput. Hum. Behav. **139**, 107513 (2023)
35. Kull, A.J., Romero, M., Monahan, L.: How may I help you? Driving brand engagement through the warmth of an initial chatbot message. J. Bus. Res. **135**, 840–850 (2021)
36. Kushwaha, A.K., Kumar, P., Kar, A.K.: What impacts customer experience for B2B enterprises on using AI-enabled chatbots? Insights from Big data analytics. Ind. Mark. Manage. **98**, 207–221 (2021). https://doi.org/10.1016/j.indmarman.2021.08.011
37. Lee, J.D., See, K.A.: Trust in automation: designing for appropriate reliance. Hum. Factors **46**(1), 50–80 (2004). https://doi.org/10.1518/hfes.46.1.50_30392

38. Leichtmann, B., Humer, C., Hinterreiter, A., Streit, M., Mara, M.: Effects of explainable artificial intelligence on trust and human behavior in a high-risk decision task. Comput. Hum. Behav. **139**, 107539 (2023). https://doi.org/10.1016/j.chb.2022.107539
39. Liao, Q.V., Varshney, K.R.: Human-centered explainable AI (XAI): from algorithms to user experiences. arXiv preprint arXiv:2110.10790 (2021)
40. Lipton, Z.C.: The mythos of model interpretability: in machine learning, the concept of interpretability is both important and slippery. Queue **16**(3), 31–57 (2018). https://doi.org/10.1145/3236386.3241340
41. Mayer, R.C., Davis, J.H., Schoorman, F.D.: An integrative model of organizational trust. Acad. Manag. Rev. **20**(3), 709–734 (1995). https://doi.org/10.2307/258792
42. Miller, T.: Explanation in artificial intelligence: insights from the social sciences. Artif. Intell. **267**, 1–38 (2019). https://doi.org/10.1016/j.artint.2018.07.007
43. Mori, M., MacDorman, K.F., Kageki, N.: The uncanny valley [from the field]. IEEE Robot. Autom. Mag. **19**(2), 98–100 (2012)
44. Nass, C., Moon, Y.: Machines and mindlessness: social responses to computers. J. Soc. Issues **56**(1), 81–103 (2000). https://doi.org/10.1111/0022-4537.00153
45. Nass, C., Steuer, J., Tauber, E.R.: Computers are social actors. In: Proceedings of the SIGCHI Conference on Human Factors in Computing Systems, pp. 72–78. ACM, Boston Massachusetts USA (1994). https://doi.org/10.1145/191666.191703
46. Nguyen, M., Casper Ferm, L.E., Quach, S., Pontes, N., Thaichon, P.: Chatbots in frontline services and customer experience: an anthropomorphism perspective. Psychol. Mark. **40**(11), 2201–2225 (2023). https://onlinelibrary.wiley.com/doi/pdf/10.1002/mar.21882
47. Obrenovic, B., Gu, X., Wang, G., Godinic, D., Jakhongirov, I.: Generative AI and human–robot interaction: implications and future agenda for business, society and ethics. In: AI & SOCIETY, pp. 1–14 (2024)
48. Pfeuffer, N., Benlian, A., Gimpel, H., Hinz, O.: Anthropomorphic information systems. Bus. Inf. Syst. Eng. **61**(4), 523–533 (2019). https://doi.org/10.1007/s12599-019-00599-y
49. Rane, N., Choudhary, S., Rane, J.: Explainable artificial intelligence (XAI) approaches for transparency and accountability in financial decision-making (2023). https://doi.org/10.2139/ssrn.4640316
50. Rao Hill, S., Troshani, I.: Chatbot anthropomorphism, social presence, uncanniness and brand attitude effects. J. Comput. Inf. Syst., 1–17 (2024). https://doi.org/10.1080/08874417.2024.2423187
51. Salimi, P.: Addressing trust and mutability issues in XAI utilising case based reasoning. In: Proceedings of the 30th Doctoral Consortium of the International Conference on Case-Based Reasoning (ICCBR-DC 2022). CEUR Workshop Proceedings (2022)
52. Seeger, A.M., Heinzl, A.: Chatbots often fail! Can anthropomorphic design mitigate trust loss in conversational agents for customer service? In: ECIS2021 (2021)
53. Shepherd, D.A., Majchrzak, A.: Machines augmenting entrepreneurs: opportunities (and threats) at the nexus of artificial intelligence and entrepreneurship. J. Bus. Ventur. **37**(4), 106227 (2022)
54. Song, M., Zhu, Y., Xing, X., Du, J.: The double-edged sword effect of chatbot anthropomorphism on customer acceptance intention: the mediating roles of perceived competence and privacy concerns. Behav. Inf. Technol., 1–23 (2024). https://doi.org/10.1080/0144929X.2023.2285943

55. Srivastava, B., Lakkaraju, K., Koppel, T., Narayanan, V., Kundu, A., Joshi, S.: Evaluating chatbots to promote users' trust – practices and open problems. arXiv preprint arXiv:2309.05680 (2023)
56. Visser, E.J., et al.: Almost human: anthropomorphism increases trust resilience in cognitive agents. J. Exp. Psychol. Appl. **22**(3), 331–349 (2016). https://doi.org/10.1037/xap0000092
57. Wang, W., Benbasat, I.: Empirical assessment of alternative designs for enhancing different types of trusting beliefs in online recommendation agents. J. Manag. Inf. Syst. **33**(3), 744–775 (2016). https://doi.org/10.1080/07421222.2016.1243949
58. Waytz, A., Cacioppo, J., Epley, N.: Who sees human? The stability and importance of individual differences in anthropomorphism. Perspect. Psychol. Sci. **5**(3), 219–232 (2010). https://doi.org/10.1177/1745691610369336
59. Wirtz, J., et al.: Brave new world: service robots in the frontline. J. Serv. Manag. **29**(5), 907–931 (2018). https://doi.org/10.1108/JOSM-04-2018-0119
60. Zhang, Z., Tsiakas, K., Schneegass, C.: Explaining the wait: how justifying Chatbot response delays impact user trust. In: ACM Conversational User Interfaces 2024, pp. 1–16. ACM, Luxembourg, Luxembourg (2024). https://doi.org/10.1145/3640794.3665550

**Open Access** This chapter is licensed under the terms of the Creative Commons Attribution 4.0 International License (http://creativecommons.org/licenses/by/4.0/), which permits use, sharing, adaptation, distribution and reproduction in any medium or format, as long as you give appropriate credit to the original author(s) and the source, provide a link to the Creative Commons license and indicate if changes were made.

The images or other third party material in this chapter are included in the chapter's Creative Commons license, unless indicated otherwise in a credit line to the material. If material is not included in the chapter's Creative Commons license and your intended use is not permitted by statutory regulation or exceeds the permitted use, you will need to obtain permission directly from the copyright holder.

# Comparative Explanations: Explanation Guided Decision Making for Human-in-the-Loop Preference Selection

Tanmay Chakraborty[1,3](✉), Christian Wirth[2], and Christin Seifert[3]

[1] Continental Automotive Technologies GmbH, AI Lab Berlin, Berlin, Germany
tanmay.chakraborty@continental-corporation.com
[2] Continental Automotive Technologies GmbH, Frankfurt, Germany
christian.2.wirth@continental-corporation.com
[3] Marburg University, Marburg, Germany
christin.seifert@uni-marburg.de

**Abstract.** This paper introduces Multi-Output LOcal Narrative Explanation (MOLONE), a novel comparative explanation method designed to enhance preference selection in human-in-the-loop Preference Bayesian optimization (PBO). The preference elicitation in PBO is a non-trivial task because it involves navigating implicit trade-offs between vector-valued outcomes, subjective priorities of decision-makers, and decision-makers' uncertainty in preference selection. Existing explainable AI (XAI) methods for BO primarily focus on input feature importance, neglecting the crucial role of outputs (objectives) in human preference elicitation. MOLONE addresses this gap by providing explanations that highlight both input and output importance, enabling decision-makers to understand the trade-offs between competing objectives and make more informed preference selections. MOLONE focuses on local explanations, comparing the importance of input features and outcomes across candidate samples within a local neighborhood of the search space, thus capturing nuanced differences relevant to preference-based decision-making. We evaluate MOLONE within a PBO framework using benchmark multi-objective optimization functions, demonstrating its effectiveness in improving convergence compared to noisy preference selections. Furthermore, a user study confirms that MOLONE significantly accelerates convergence in human-in-the-loop scenarios by facilitating more efficient identification of preferred options.

**Keywords:** Explainable Bayesian optimization · Preferential Bayesian optimization · Explainable Artificial Intelligence · Comparative Explanations

## 1 Introduction

Bayesian Optimization (BO) is a model-based sequential optimization framework for efficiently solving global optimization problems where function evaluations are costly [32]. It is widely used in multi-output applications such as material design [11,21,34], A/B testing [3], battery design [1], and simulation-based optimization [16,36]. In these domains, decision-makers often lack explicit objective functions, necessitating methods that incorporate human insights for optimizing unknown objectives.

Human-in-the-loop BO enables decision-makers to guide the optimization process by iteratively incorporating human knowledge through interactive feedback, such as in A/B testing scenarios. When the true objective function is unknown but can be inferred from human preferences, Preferential Bayesian Optimization (PBO) models latent preferences within the design space, enabling efficient convergence to optimal solutions [15,24]. By leveraging preference data rather than direct function evaluations, PBO provides a practical approach for optimizing complex black-box systems where explicit numerical feedback is impractical or unavailable.

PBO assumes that human decision-makers can reliably express preferences in a multi-output setting where solutions are generated by a black-box model (Fig. 1). However, selecting between samples is challenging without additional information, as trade-offs require balancing competing objectives that may not be explicitly defined. Decision-makers' priorities vary based on subjective preferences, expertise, and context as well. Additionally, uncertainty, incomplete, or correlated information further complicate decision-making [23,33]. These limitations highlight the need for strategies that improve interpretability and support informed preference selection.

Recent advancements in Explainable Artificial Intelligence (XAI) for BO, such as CoExBo [1] and ShapleyBO [30], aim to enhance decision-making by providing input feature importance explanations for algorithm-suggested samples. However, these methods primarily focus on explaining the importance of input variables (i.e., features or design parameters), overlooking the importance of output variables that directly influence human preferences.

For decision-makers to make informed selections, explanations must extend beyond input feature importance to include output importance, clarifying how trade-offs align with their objectives. For instance, in A/B testing, if usability is the priority, they need to know which option better supports that goal. Existing solutions focus only on input-level factors, such as image placement or recommendation accuracy, without addressing the core question: *Why choose Sample A rather than Sample B?* [22].

To address this limitation, we introduce Multi-Output LOcal Narrative Explanation (MOLONE), a comparative explanation method that provides both input feature and outcome importance to support preference-based decision-making. Unlike existing methods, MOLONE compares importance values across two samples, attributing higher values as reasons *for* selection and lower values as reasons *against*. This structured comparison helps decision-makers understand trade-offs, effectively answering: "Why choose Sample A rather than Sample B?" By highlighting both strengths and weaknesses,

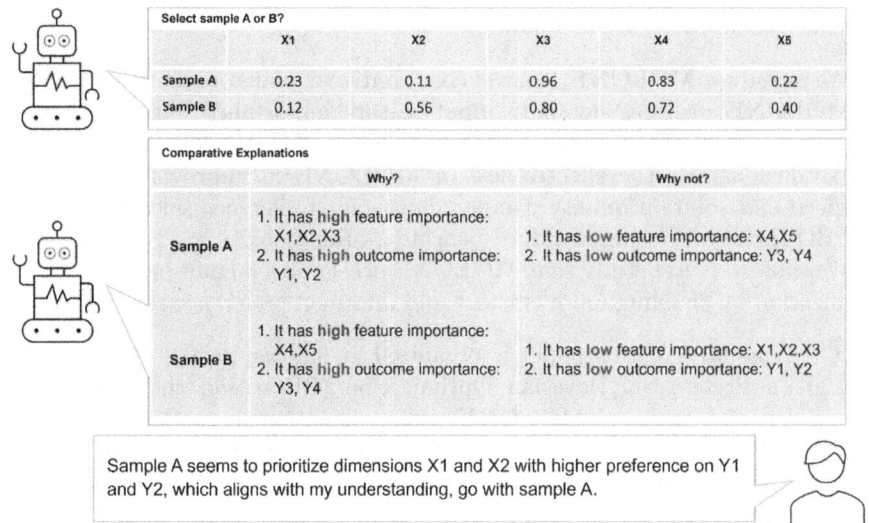

**Fig. 1.** Comparative explanations for preference selection in PBO. It shows why the DM should select one sample and why the DM should not select a sample.

MOLONE aligns with Evaluative XAI [5,27], ensuring that decisions remain human-centered while AI provides the necessary explanatory support.

MOLONE is a local explanation method for PBO where preference selections are made between a limited set of candidate samples. These samples exist within a vast optimization landscape, making it crucial to analyze their input feature and outcome importance in their local distribution. Since neighboring samples share similar characteristics, comparing them provides a more meaningful basis for preference selection. Thus, MOLONE effectively contrasts two local distributions rather than isolated points thus aligning with the local geometry.

We evaluate MOLONE on standard optimization benchmarks from the literature (DTLZ2, DTLZ4, and ZDT1) [9,38], each with five input dimensions and multiple outputs. Our results show that explanation-informed preference feedback achieves higher utility than preference selection with simulated human errors, which account for decision-maker uncertainty. This confirms MOLONE's high fidelity in generating meaningful explanations.

We evaluate MOLONE in a human-in-the-loop setting, and we investigated whether explanations improve decision-making efficiency. Using the common multi-objective optimization dataset DTLZ2, we conducted a between-group experiment where five expert users performed 10 preference selections under two conditions: with and without explanations. Our results show that users with explanations converged faster, demonstrating that MOLONE effectively aids decision-making by helping users identify better options more efficiently.

Our contributions are as follows:

1. We introduce MOLONE, a novel comparative explanation method for PBO. MOLONE provides not only input feature importance but also outcome importance, enabling decision-makers to make efficient preference selections.
2. We demonstrate the effectiveness of MOLONE in improving convergence speed and solution quality compared to noisy preference selection within a PBO framework using standard benchmark functions.
3. We show in a user study that MOLONE accelerates human-in-the-loop optimization by enabling more efficient and informed preference selections.

The remainder of this paper is organized as follows: Sect. 2 provides background on Preferential Bayesian Optimization (PBO) and the problem setting. Section 3 introduces MOLONE, our explanation methodology. Section 4 describes the experimental setup, Sect. 5 presents the results of our evaluations. Section 6 reviews related work, and Sect. 7 summarizes our findings and future research directions.

## 2 Background

This section provides a background on Bayesian Optimization (BO) and Preferential Bayesian Optimization (PBO). We then describe the preference selection problem in PBO.

### 2.1 Bayesian Optimization

Bayesian Optimization (BO) is a sequential, model-based technique for minimizing a black-box function:

$$\mathbf{x}^* = \arg\min_{\mathbf{x} \in \mathcal{X}} f_{true}(\mathbf{x}), \qquad (1)$$

where $f_{true} : \mathbb{R}^d \to \mathbb{R}$ is an unknown function. BO is effective when function evaluations are costly and lack a closed-form expression. It operates iteratively using a **Gaussian Process (GP)** surrogate model to approximate $f_{true}$ based on previously sampled points $\mathcal{D}_i = \{(\mathbf{x}_j, \mathbf{y}_j)\}_{j=1}^{n}$ and a mathematical objective function $g_{true}$, where $\mathbf{x}_j \in \mathcal{X}$ is drawn from a predefined search space, and $\mathbf{y}_j = f_{true}(\mathbf{x}_j)$.

Each iteration consists of three steps: (1) **Selecting a query point** using an acquisition function [13], (2) **Evaluating the objective function** at the chosen point, and (3) **Updating the GP model** with the new data. This process repeats until a stopping criterion is met, such as a predefined number of iterations or sufficient optimization progress [29].

## 2.2 Preferential Bayesian Optimization

In standard BO, evaluations of $f_{true}$ provide numerical feedback on the objective function. However, in many real-world scenarios, the true objective is unobservable, and only *human preferences* over outcome pairs are available. Preferential Bayesian Optimization (PBO) extends BO to leverage preference-based feedback, optimizing the latent objective. The optimization problem is formulated as:

$$\mathbf{x}^* = \arg\min_{\mathbf{x} \in \mathcal{X}} g_{true}(f_{true}(\mathbf{x})), \tag{2}$$

where:

- $f_{true} : \mathbb{R}^d \to \mathbb{R}^k$ represents an black-box function that generates **multi-output outcomes** based on input $\mathbf{x}$.
- $g_{true} : \mathbb{R}^k \to \mathbb{R}$ is an **unknown objective function** that maps these $k$-dimensional outcomes to a single scalar value, reflecting the decision-maker's implicit preferences.
- The composite function $g_{true}(f_{true}(\mathbf{x}))$ is **not directly available**, making explicit optimization infeasible.

Since $g_{true}$ is unknown and cannot be evaluated directly, it is inferred through preference-based feedback. Instead of numerical evaluations, the decision-maker selects a preferred option between two candidates $f_{true}(\mathbf{x})$ and $f_{true}(\mathbf{x}')$, implicitly conveying information about the objective. PBO modifies BO by adapting the acquisition function to select two candidate points $(\mathbf{x}, \mathbf{x}')$. The decision-maker compares them and selects the preferred option:

$g_{true}(f_{true}(\mathbf{x})) \geq g_{true}(f_{true}(\mathbf{x}'))$ ? $f_{true}(\mathbf{x}) : f_{true}(\mathbf{x}')$.

This feedback serves as an indirect observation of $g_{true}$, refining the optimization of $g_{true}(f_{true}(\mathbf{x}))$. The process iterates, using accumulated preference data to guide the search toward $\mathbf{x}^*$, enabling optimization through human expertise rather than explicit function evaluations.

## 2.3 Problem Setting

In PBO, the goal is to select between two candidates (Fig. 1), $f_{true}(\mathbf{x})$ and $f_{true}(\mathbf{x}')$, whose outcomes are generated by an unknown black-box function $f_{true} : \mathbb{R}^d \to \mathbb{R}^k$. Since the objective function $g_{true}$ is unobservable, optimization relies on preference feedback rather than explicit function evaluations.

The black-box function $f_{true}$ is modeled by a GP surrogate $\mathcal{M}$, while the decision-maker's unknown utility function, $g_{true}$, is approximated by a second GP model, $\mathcal{M}_{pref}$. These models provide predictive distributions over outcomes and inferred preferences, forming the basis for preference selection.

The core selection challenge in PBO is non-trivial because (1) the vector-valued outcomes $f_{true}(\mathbf{x})$ and $f_{true}(\mathbf{x}')$ may conflict or be correlated, requiring trade-offs that are not explicitly defined [23,33]; (2) decision-makers may prioritize different features or outcomes based on subjective preferences, making informed selections difficult without additional information; and (3) $g_{true}$ is unknown and only approximated by $\mathcal{M}_{pref}$, introducing uncertainty in aligning selections with user preferences.

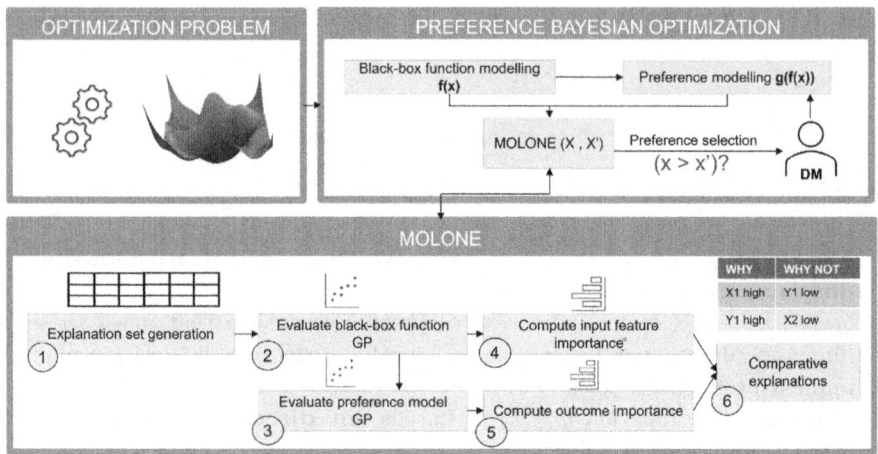

**Fig. 2.** In MOLONE, (1) we generate local explanation data by applying Latin Hypercube Sampling (LHS) within a sphere around each input $x$ and $x'$. (2) The GP model $\mathcal{M}$ evaluates sampled points, returning mean predictions and uncertainty. (3) The preference GP model $\mathcal{M}_{pref}$ computes utility scores based on these predictions. (4–5) Input feature importance based on $\mathcal{M}$ and outcome importance based on $\mathcal{M}_{pref}$ are then derived by analyzing the sensitivity of two GP models. (5) Importance values are then compared against each other and a comparative matrix integrates these insights.

## 3  Multi-output LOcal Narrative Explanation (*MOLONE*)

This section details our approach to the preference selection problem in PBO and then presents our comparative explanation generation method MOLONE.[1]

### 3.1  Approach

Our goal is to provide explanations that help decision-makers make a selection between two candidate inputs (Fig. 1), $f_{true}(\mathbf{x})$ and $f_{true}(\mathbf{x}')$, whose outcomes are generated by an unknown black-box function. Our approach involves solving the optimization problem using PBO and addressing the preference selection problem using XAI techniques.

---

[1] loss landscape image attributed to https://github.com/tomgoldstein/loss-landscape.

In the PBO loop for each preference query, we generate comparative explanations to support the decision-maker in the selection task between two candidate samples.

We assume access to the background GP models of PBO and focus on two explanation components extracted from the GP models. The first is **local input feature importance**, which analyzes how each feature in $\mathbf{x}$ and $\mathbf{x}'$ contributes to the predicted outcomes of $f_{true}$ modeled by GP $\mathcal{M}$. This helps the decision-maker understand the influence of different input variables in the local optimization landscape. The second is **outcome importance**, which evaluates how each dimension of $f_{true}(\mathbf{x}) = \mathbf{y}$ and $f_{true}(\mathbf{x}') = \mathbf{y}'$ contributes to the inferred utility model $g_{true}$ as modeled by preference GP $\mathcal{M}_{pref}$. This allows the decision-maker to assess which aspects of $\mathbf{y}$ and $\mathbf{y}'$ are most relevant for preference selection.

We structure the explanations extracted from $\mathcal{M}$ and $\mathcal{M}_{pref}$ into two sets by comparing the importance scores of features and outcomes between the two samples. The High Importance set ($\mathcal{H}$) aggregates features and outcomes that have higher importance in sample $A$ compared to sample $B$, explaining *why $A$ should be chosen*. Conversely, the Low Importance set ($\mathcal{L}$) includes features and outcomes with lower importance in $A$ relative to $B$, explaining *why $A$ should not be chosen*.

---

**Algorithm 1.** Explanation Generation Algorithm

---
**Require:** Two points: $\mathcal{X} = \{\mathbf{x}, \mathbf{x}'\}$,
1: Number of samples: $N$,
2: GP model for $f_{true}$: $\mathcal{M}$,
3: Preference GP model for $g_{true}$: $\mathcal{M}_{pref}$
4: **procedure** MOLONE ($\mathcal{X}, N, \mathcal{M}, \mathcal{M}_{pref}, r$)
5:     **for** each $\mathbf{x} \in \mathcal{X}$ **do**
6:         $\mathcal{X}_{\text{lhs}} \leftarrow \{\mathbf{x}'_1, \ldots, \mathbf{x}'_N\} \sim \text{LHS}(\mathbf{x}, \text{radius} = r)$     ▷ Generate explanation set
7:         $\mu_f(\mathbf{x}_s), \sigma_f(\mathbf{x}_s) \leftarrow \mathcal{M}(\mathbf{x}_s), \quad \forall \mathbf{x}_s \in \mathcal{X}_{\text{lhs}}$     ▷ $\text{GP}_f$ model evaluation
8:         $\mu_g(\mu_f(\mathbf{x}_s)), \sigma_g(\mu_f(\mathbf{x}_s)) \leftarrow \mathcal{M}_{pref}(\mathcal{M}(\mathbf{x}_s)), \quad \forall \mathbf{x}_s \in \mathcal{X}_{\text{lhs}}$   ▷ $\text{GP}_g$ model evaluation
9:         $\phi_x \leftarrow \text{InputFeatureImportance}(\mathcal{M}, \mathcal{X}_{\text{lhs}})$     ▷ Input feature importance
10:        $\phi_y \leftarrow \text{OutcomeImportance}(\mathcal{M}_{pref}, \mu_f(\mathbf{x}_s))$     ▷ Outcome importance
11:     **end for**
12:     $\mathcal{H} \leftarrow \{\text{High}(\phi_x), \text{High}(\phi_y)\}$     ▷ Why explanations
13:     $\mathcal{L} \leftarrow \{\text{Low}(\phi_x), \text{Low}(\phi_y)\}$     ▷ Why not explanations
14:     $\text{CompMatrix} \leftarrow \text{Combine}(\mathcal{H}_{WhyExp}, \mathcal{L}_{WhyNotExp})$     ▷ Comparative matrix
15:     **return** CompMatrix
16: **end procedure**

---

### 3.2 Comparative Explanations

Our method for generating comparative explanations for the preference exploration stage of PBO is MOLONE (Multi-Output LOcal Narrative Explanation)

(Fig. 2). MOLONE consists of six steps (Alg. 1). First, given two input samples, MOLONE begins by generating a local explanation set by using *Latin Hypercube Sampling (LHS)* within a sphere centered at each input point. Second, the GP model $\mathcal{M}$ for $f_{true}$ evaluates each sampled point, returning the mean and uncertainty of the predictions. And the preference GP model $\mathcal{M}_{pref}$ for $g_{true}$ is then evaluated using the outcomes generating utility scores based on the mean predictions from $\mathcal{M}$. Third, input feature importance is computed based on the sensitivity of $\mathcal{M}$ predictions to the input dimensions, and outcome importance is calculated similarly based on the preference model $\mathcal{M}_{pref}$. Fourth, these importance values are used to compare the two input samples, identifying high and low contributions for both the input features and vector outcomes. Fifth, using these comparisons, 'why' explanations are generated by combining the high contributions, and 'why not' explanations by combining the low contributions. Finally, a $2 \times 2$ comparative matrix integrates these explanations, providing decision support for preference-based optimization.

**Explanation Set Generation.** In PBO, data points are iteratively sampled from a defined search space and evaluated by a GP model. Unlike standard XAI settings in machine learning, PBO lacks a predefined training or testing dataset, leading to the absence of an explanation dataset [6,7]. To address this, we align with the PBO principle by sampling new points from the search space to generate the necessary explanation data. We chose Latin Hypercube Sampling (LHS), a method that divides the input hypercube into smaller grids and ensures a fair distribution of sampled points, providing a representative set for the underlying space [19].

Given a sample $f_{true}(\mathbf{x})$ that requires explanation, we need to explore the space around $\mathbf{x}$ to generate local explanations. Initially, one could consider using only LHS in a hypercube centered around $\mathbf{x}$. However, this approach requires defining explicit bounds for each dimension, which can be arbitrary and may not properly capture the local neighborhood around the point. On the other hand, using only *spherical sampling* results in points concentrated on the surface of the sphere, failing to explore the full volume around the point, which would limit the representativeness of the explanation set [12].

To overcome these limitations, we combine both approaches by first constraining the sampling to a small radius sphere centered around $\mathbf{x}$ and then applying LHS within this sphere. This allows us to sample points uniformly within a spherical neighborhood, ensuring that all regions within the sphere are covered. By generating $N$ samples from this constrained spherical region, we form our explanation set: $\mathcal{X}_{\exp} = \{\mathbf{x}'_1, \ldots, \mathbf{x}'_N\}$, where each sample is within the sphere and respects the local geometry of the search space around $\mathbf{x}$.

Mathematically, this approach can be described as follows: LHS generates $N$ points $\mathbf{u}_i$ uniformly within a unit cube $[0,1]^d$. These points are then transformed into a spherical region by first normalizing them to lie on the surface of a sphere and then scaling them by a radius $r \sim U(0,1)^{1/d}$, ensuring uniform sampling within the volume of the sphere. Finally, the points are translated to be centered at **x**: $\mathbf{x}'_i = \mathbf{x} + r\frac{\mathbf{u}_i}{\|\mathbf{u}_i\|}$, where $\mathbf{u}_i$ is the LHS-sampled point, $r$ is the radius, and $\|\mathbf{u}_i\|$ is the Euclidean norm of $\mathbf{u}_i$.

To adaptively determine the sampling radius $r$ around a given point **x**, we first generate an initial exploratory set of $N$ points $\mathbf{x}_i\}_{i=1}^N$ within a default radius $r_0$. The Euclidean distances of these points from **x** are computed as $d_i = \|\mathbf{x}_i - \mathbf{x}\|_2$. The final sampling radius is then defined as $r = \sigma_d$, which is the standard deviation of the distances $d_i$. This ensures that the neighborhood size dynamically adjusts to the local data distribution, preventing the selection of an arbitrary fixed radius that may not accurately capture the characteristics of the black-box function. A visual example of the sampling is given in Appendix A.

**GP Models Evaluation.** To assess the behavior of the GP models $\mathcal{M}$ and $\mathcal{M}_{pref}$ within the identified hyperlocal space, we evaluate them using the samples in $\mathcal{X}_{\text{exp}}$.

First, we apply the GP model for the true function $f_{true}$: $\mathcal{M}$, to each sample $\mathbf{x}_s \in \mathcal{X}_{\text{exp}}$. The GP model's posterior distribution provides both the mean prediction $\mu_f(\mathbf{x}_s)$ and the associated predictive uncertainty $\sigma_f(\mathbf{x}_s)$. These are used to summarize the behavior of $\mathcal{M}$ in the local region around the point of interest. Next, we evaluate the preference GP model for $g_{true}$, denoted as $\mathcal{M}_{pref}$, using the outcomes of $\mathcal{M}$. Specifically, we feed the vector-valued mean predictions $\mu_f(\mathbf{x}_s)$ from $\mathcal{M}$ into $\mathcal{M}_{pref}$, obtaining the preference mean $\mu_g(\mu_f(\mathbf{x}_s))$ and the corresponding uncertainty $\sigma_g(\mu_f(\mathbf{x}_s))$.

**Input Feature and Outcome Importance Calculation.** In GPs, the kernel function can be marginalized to compute a feature importance score $\phi$ by measuring the sensitivity of the model's output to changes in specific input features. This method evaluates how sensitive the GP kernel is to individual features, particularly within the local region defined by $\mathcal{X}_{\text{exp}}$. We compute input feature importance by determining the maximum sensitivity of each feature in this local space. The intuition is that features causing the greatest variation in the GP's output are the most influential in this area. In PBO, the output is a vector in case of $\mathcal{M}$. We aggregate the sensitivity into a single value based on maximum change over all the individual output dimensions for ease of importance computation. The resulting importance scores form a vector $\phi_x$ of size $|\mathbf{x}|$, representing the feature importance for the input space [35].

In addition to computing feature importance from the GP model for $\mathcal{M}$, we also compute outcome importance based on the preference model $\mathcal{M}_{pref}$. The preference model evaluates the outcomes of $\mathcal{M}$, and the sensitivity of $\mathcal{M}_{pref}$ to changes in these outcomes provides a measure of the importance of these outcomes in determining preferences. Since the output of $\mathcal{M}_{pref}$ is single-dimensional, aggregation is unnecessary here. For each sample $\mathbf{x}_s \in \mathcal{X}_{\text{exp}}$, we compute how the preference scores $\mu_g(\mu_f(\mathbf{x}_s))$ vary with respect to changes in the input features of $\mathcal{M}$. This results in an outcome importance vector $\phi_y$, which reflects how much influence each input feature has on the preference outcome in this local space.

Together, the input feature importance vector $\phi_x$ (from $\mathcal{M}$) and the outcome feature importance vector $\phi_y$ (from $\mathcal{M}_{pref}$) provide a comprehensive understanding of how input features impact both the underlying model's predictions and the resulting preferences in the local region around **x**. These vectors are used in subsequent steps to generate explanations by comparing them against each other.

**Importance Comparison.** The input and outcome importances of the two samples are compared against each other to identify their differences.

First, we compare the input feature importance vectors, $\phi_x$, for both samples **x** and **x**′. These vectors represent the sensitivity of the GP model $\mathcal{M}$ to variations in each input dimension, capturing how strongly each feature influences the model's predictions in the local space. By directly comparing $\phi_x$ for **x** and **x**′ against each other, we classify each feature's importance as either high or low, identifying which features contribute more to the utility in one sample relative to the other.

Next, we compare the outcome importance vectors, $\phi_y$, for $f_{true}(\mathbf{x})$ and $f_{true}(\mathbf{x}')$. These vectors quantify how input features influence the preference model $\mathcal{M}_{pref}$, which is the utility. By directly comparing $\phi_y$ between the two samples, we determine which outcome dimensions affect utility $\mathcal{M}_{pref}$. This comparison allows us to classify outcome importance as high or low, attributing importance to outcomes that influence utility between the two samples.

Together, these two comparisons–input feature importance and outcome importance–provide a comprehensive understanding of the differences between the two samples. This comparative view allows us to generate detailed explanations, distinguishing which features and outcomes are important in terms of their influence on the utility.

**Generating 'Why' and 'Why Not' Explanations.** To generate 'Why' explanations $\mathcal{H}$, we aggregate the high input feature importance, and high outcome importance. For 'Why Not' explanations $\mathcal{L}$, we aggregate low input feature importance, and low outcome importance.

**Comparative Matrix Generation.** Guided by the principles of Evaluative XAI, which emphasize providing evidence both *for* and *against* a hypothesis, we developed a decision matrix that integrates the 'why' and 'why not' to support informed decision-making [27]. A decision matrix, commonly used in business, systematically identifies relationships between important factors by organizing them into rows and columns [28]. The point selection problem in PBO shares characteristics with decision-making challenges in business, making this structure particularly relevant. In our matrix, the rows represent the samples, while the columns capture the 'why' and 'why not' reasons for selecting or rejecting each option.

In line with Evaluative XAI principles, we intentionally do not provide a direct recommendation, as our goal is to keep decision-makers cognitively engaged in weighing the pros and cons of each sample. The matrix structure (Fig. 3) allows decision-makers to efficiently analyze both sides of the argument, facilitating a more informed and balanced decision.

|  | Why? | Why not? |
|---|---|---|
| Sample A | 1. high feature importance on these input dimensions X1,X3,X4<br>2. high outcome importance: Y1, Y2, Y3 | 1. low feature importance on these input dimensions X2,X5<br>2. low outcome importance: Y4 |
| Sample B | 1. high feature importance on these input dimensions X2,X5<br>2. high outcome importance: Y4 | 1. low feature importance on these input dimensions X1,X3,X4<br>2. low outcome importance: Y1,Y2 |

**Fig. 3.** Example of comparative explanations provided to the decision-maker.

## 4 Experimental Setup

We evaluate MOLONE's fidelity and usefulness within the PBO framework through preference selection tasks using both automated preference selection proxy agents and evaluations with humans.

*We hypothesize that explanations provided by MOLONE lead to more informed decisions, resulting in faster convergence toward optimal solutions compared to preference selection without explanatory support.*

### 4.1 Optimization Benchmark Functions/Dataset

For our evaluation, we employ widely used benchmark functions from the optimization literature: **DTLZ2**, **DTLZ4**, and **ZDT1**. These functions are applied in multi-objective optimization contexts [9,38], and their Pareto fronts are visualized in Fig. 4. To use these benchmarks in a single-objective setting, required for PBO, we adjust their objectives to prioritize specific output dimensions. This simulates real-world decision-making where certain outcomes have more importance than others.

The **DTLZ2 problem** is a $d$-dimensional function with 5 decision variables (inputs) and 4 outputs, evaluated over the domain $[0,1]^d$ [9]. We adapt this problem for PBO by modifying its objective to maximize the sum of the first three outputs, reflecting decision-making scenarios where certain dimensions hold greater importance.

The **DTLZ4 problem** is a variation of DTLZ2, introducing an exponent $\alpha = 100$ on the first decision variable, which skews the distribution of solutions toward the edges of the objective space [9]. This effect is visible in the solution clustering near the boundaries in Fig. 4. Similar to DTLZ2, we modify its objective by maximizing the sum of the first three outputs to align with the PBO framework.

The **ZDT1 problem** involves 5 decision variables and 2 objectives, evaluated over the domain $[0,1]^d$. This function tests the algorithm's ability to handle

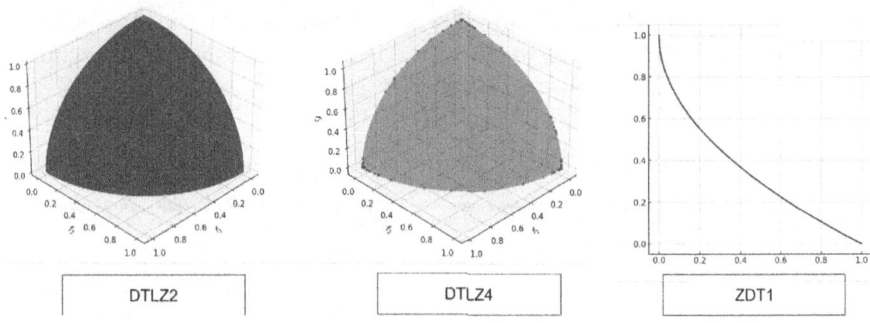

**Fig. 4.** Example illustration of optimization benchmarks and their solution spaces in a multi-objective setting with three output dimensions for visualization purposes in DTLZs (we use four output dimensions in our work). Although the Pareto fronts for DTLZ2 and DTLZ4 appear similar, their solution distributions differ. In DTLZ2, solutions are evenly spread across the Pareto front, whereas in DTLZ4, they are concentrated near the edges, as indicated by the red points. (Color figure online)

trade-offs between a linearly scaled objective and a non-linear function that depends on the remaining variables [38]. We adapt ZDT1 to the PBO framework by modifying the objective to maximize the sum of its two outputs.

By modifying these benchmark functions, we create a framework tailored for PBO where decision-makers prioritize specific outputs.

### 4.2 PBO Settings

For our experiments, we employed the BoTorch framework to implement Bayesian Optimization with Preference Exploration (BOPE) [4]. To ensure consistency and reproducibility, we adhered to the default parameters for the GP model as specified in the BoTorch documentation[2].

Each benchmark function was evaluated across 40 independent runs, each initialized with a distinct random seed to account for variability. Each run consisted of two main phases: a preference exploration stage and an experimentation stage. During the preference exploration stage, an acquisition function (i.e., a preference exploration strategy) was used to adaptively generate pairs of samples. For evaluating MOLONE, comparative explanations were generated and provided for the two samples as well. The decision-maker (or a simulated preference model) was asked to express their preference between two options in each pair. This process refined the model of the unknown utility function by collecting feedback that captured subjective evaluations of trade-offs.

In the experimentation stage, we employed a batch version of the Noisy Expected Improvement acquisition function with integrated uncertainty over the utility function, referred to as qNEIUU [37]. This strategy efficiently selected

---

[2] https://botorch.org/tutorials/bope.

candidates for evaluation while accounting for the uncertainty in the preference model and the black-box function.

Each run consisted of four preference exploration stages followed by eight rounds of BO, resulting in 32 pairwise comparisons per run (4 stages × 8 rounds = 32). To initialize the optimization process, 20 quasi-random points were sampled from the defined search space using Sobol sequences, ensuring diverse coverage of the input space. These initial samples established a foundation for modeling the surrogate function $f_{true}$.

Following the initialization, four random pairwise comparisons were generated between the sampled points to provide a baseline for training the preference model $\mathcal{M}_{pref}$.

### 4.3 Evaluation Metrics

To evaluate the fidelity and usefulness of MOLONE, we conduct a series of experiments to determine whether explanation-driven preference selection improves the efficiency of preference exploration in BOPE.

We measure convergence performance by tracking the mean utility value achieved by each preference selection strategy across runs. A higher mean value indicates better convergence toward the global optimum. This metric reflects the optimization algorithm's ability to efficiently navigate the search space and identify high-utility regions based on the decision-maker's preferences.

By comparing runs with and without explanations, we assess the fidelity of MOLONE, i.e., how accurately the explanations reflect the underlying model behavior and its usefulness in guiding decision-makers toward better outcomes during the optimization process.

### 4.4 Evaluation with Automated Preference Selection Proxy

To test our hypothesis, we simulate three types of decision-making agents, each representing different levels of decision-making capability across pairwise comparisons:

The **Ideal Selection Agent** represents an ideal decision-maker with perfect knowledge of the utility function. This agent always selects the option with the higher objective value, providing a strong performance baseline. While this scenario is impractical in real-world settings, it is a useful benchmark for comparison. However, due to the inherent randomness in the PBO algorithm, this does not represent a strict upper bound for performance.

The **Noisy Selection Agent** simulates a more realistic scenario where the decision-maker has general knowledge of the objective but faces uncertainty, occasionally making wrong choices. We simulate human mistakes by introducing noise. Our noisy selection agents make incorrect selections at varying rates: approximately 31% (10 wrong selections), 25% (8 wrong selections), and 18% (6 wrong selections) across 32 total pairwise comparisons. These settings are designed to reflect real-world variability, where both the complexity of the problem and the inherent error rates influence decision-making accuracy. **Note:**

The error rates and number of comparisons needed to achieve convergence are problem-specific and can vary greatly from one use case to another.

The **MOLONE Guided Selection Agent** uses explanations generated by MOLONE to guide preference selection. Instead of relying directly on objective function values, this agent selects the candidate with the highest aggregated outcome importance based on MOLONE's explanation scores. For DTLZ benchmarks, the selection is based on the importance of the first three output dimensions, while for ZDT1, it considers two dimensions. This approach allows us to assess how well explanation-driven decision-making can facilitate convergence compared to direct or noisy selections.

For all agents, pairwise selection decisions are based on predefined rules. The ideal and noisy agents compare the sum of specific output dimensions, while the MOLONE guided agent bases its choices on the sum of the importance of those dimensions, simulating that the decision maker knows the first three dimensions are important. This setup allows us to systematically compare the effectiveness of explanation-supported selection against conventional and noisy preference exploration strategies.

### 4.5 Evaluation with Humans

We conduct a human-in-the-loop experiment to evaluate the usefulness of explanations in decision-making within the PBO framework. We hypothesize that participants with access to explanations would make more effective decisions, leading to better convergence than those without explanations.

To ensure that our evaluation is focused purely on decision-making performance rather than background knowledge or domain expertise, we used the DTLZ2 problem, which is artificial data with non-interpretable features. The DTLZ2 problem provides a well-defined multi-output optimization benchmark where feature relationships are not intuitive. This allowed us to isolate the effect of explanations, ensuring that participants relied solely on the provided information during optimization rather than prior knowledge.

Participants were tasked with making pairwise preference selections to maximize the first three output dimensions of the objective function. They completed two sequential tasks: in the first, they made preference selections without any explanatory support (baseline), relying only on the provided input and output vectors from PBO; in the second, they were aided by comparative explanations from MOLONE for preference selection (experimental condition).

Before starting, participants were briefed on the significance of the first three output dimensions for achieving convergence. For each condition, they performed ten pairwise comparisons, selecting the candidate they believed would maximize utility. For the explanation-supported condition, participants used a comparative explanation matrix to guide their selections.

To analyze the impact of explanations, we recorded the mean utility achieved in both conditions and compared the results against an ideal automated baseline from previous experiments. This between-group comparison allowed us to assess how effectively human decision-makers leverage explanations and how their performance differs from fully automated agents and non-assisted decision-making.

We recruited five participants, all with a background in computer science and holding a Master's degree. Each participant was also an active researcher in Artificial Intelligence, giving them expertise in algorithmic problem-solving and decision-making tasks relevant to this evaluation. (**Note:** Authors were not part of the study).

In accordance with local law and the policy of the senior (last) author's institution, this study did not require pre-registration with an institutional review board (IRB). It does not involve deception and is of low physical risk, i.e., no risks other than those associated with everyday life. It does not contain harmful content, address potentially triggering issues, or involve the collection of sensitive or identifiable information. In addition, all participants gave informed consent to take part.

## 5 Results

This section presents some qualitative results as well as the quantitative results from our evaluations with the automated preference selection proxy and evaluations with humans.

### 5.1 Qualitative Results

MOLONE provides an explanation in a matrix format listing both the pros and cons of individual samples by comparing the importances of samples against each other. Some qualitative results for DTLZ2 and DTLZ4 are given in Fig. 5. Each user is presented with two vector-valued samples, $A$ and $B$, alongside a comparative explanation. Reasons supporting a selection are color-coded in green to indicate "for," while opposing reasons are marked in red to signify "against." To minimize cognitive load, we conveyed through concise, list format sentences the difference in input feature importance and outcome importance in the explanation matrix. The arrangement does not provide a recommendation but serves as an decision-making aid, ensuring users retain full control over their selections.

### 5.2 Evaluation with Automated Preference Selection Proxy

Our results (Fig. 6) show that the explanation-guided agent performs comparably to the ideal selection agent on average, demonstrating the high-fidelity of MOLONE's explanations in capturing the behavior of the black-box function as modeled by BO. The performance of the explanation agent improved as the number of comparisons increased, suggesting that the explanations became more effective as the underlying GP model gathered more information about the optimization landscape.

In contrast, the noisy selection agents consistently underperformed relative to the explanation-guided and ideal selection agents. An exception was observed

### (a) DTLZ2

| | X1 | X2 | X3 | X4 | X5 |
|---|---|---|---|---|---|
| Sample A | 0.08 | 0.28 | 0.74 | 0.86 | 0.43 |
| Sample B | 0.85 | 0.30 | 0.57 | 0.79 | 0.53 |

| | Why? | Why not? |
|---|---|---|
| Sample A | 1. high feature importance on these input dimensions X2,X3<br>2. high outcome importance: Y1 | 1. low feature importance on these input dimensions X1,X4,X5<br>2. low outcome importance: Y2,Y3,Y4 |
| Sample B | 1. high feature importance on these input dimensions X1,X4,X5<br>2. high outcome importance: Y2,Y3,Y4 | 1. low feature importance on these input dimensions X2,X3<br>2. low outcome importance: Y1 |

### (b) DTLZ4

| | X1 | X2 | X3 | X4 | X5 |
|---|---|---|---|---|---|
| Sample A | 0.33 | 0.93 | 0.67 | 0.48 | 0.62 |
| Sample B | 0.07 | 0.16 | 0.53 | 0.15 | 0.47 |

| | Why? | Why not? |
|---|---|---|
| Sample A | 1. high feature importance on these input dimensions X1,X2,X3, X4<br>2. high outcome importance: Y1, Y2 | 1. low feature importance on these input dimensions X5<br>2. low outcome importance: Y3,Y4 |
| Sample B | 1. high feature importance on these input dimensions X5<br>2. high outcome importance: Y3,Y4 | 1. low feature importance on these input dimensions X1,X2,X3,X4<br>2. low outcome importance: Y1,Y2 |

**Fig. 5.** Qualitative results of comparative explanation generated by MOLONE for different optimization problems.

in the DTLZ2 benchmark, where the noisy selection agent with an 18% error rate (6 incorrect selections across 32 pairwise comparisons) performed on par with the explanation-guided agent. This result could be attributed to the well-distributed solution space of DTLZ2, which may be more forgiving of occasional selection errors than other benchmarks.

We also notice a lot of outliers in the results for noisy selection agents; this is due to the randomness introduced by the selection mistakes, causing the algorithm to not converge for certain runs.

Our findings also highlight the detrimental impact of incorrect selections in PBO. Uncertainty or inconsistency in choosing candidates can lead to suboptimal optimization outcomes, emphasizing the importance of accurate and informed preference selections for effective convergence.

### 5.3 Evaluation with Humans

To assess the impact of explanations on decision-making, we compared the mean utility achieved across three conditions (between-group): (1) the **experimental condition** (users with explanations), (2) the **baseline condition** (users without explanations), and (3) the **ideal condition** (ideal selection agent).

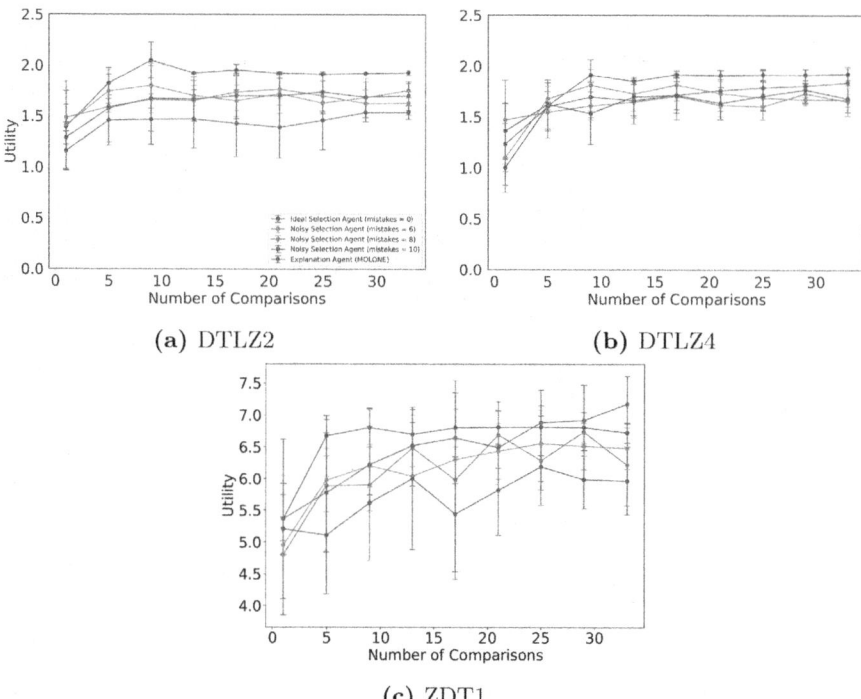

**Fig. 6.** Mean performance comparison (number of pairwise comparisons vs. mean utility reached) of automated preference selection proxy agents shows that explanation-based preference selection not only outperforms noisy preference selection but also matches the performance of ideal preference selection.

A Shapiro-Wilk test confirmed that the distributions of mean utility were non-normal for all groups: ideal agent ($W = 0.9, p < 0.01$), users without explanations ($W = 0.8, p < 0.01$), and users with explanations ($W = 0.8, p < 0.01$). The results (Fig. 7) indicate that users with explanations performed on par with the ideal selection agent, achieving a mean utility of $M = 1.83$ (ideal agent: ±0.075, users with explanations: ±0.070). In contrast, users without explanations had a lower mean utility of $M = 1.69 \pm 0.036$, suggesting that the absence of explanations negatively impacted decision quality. A Kruskal-Wallis test confirmed that this difference was statistically significant ($X^2(2, N = 5) = 18.87, p < 0.01$).

Post-hoc Dunn's tests further confirmed our findings. No significant difference was found between the ideal agent and users with explanations ($p > 0.05$). As expected, the ideal agent outperformed users without explanations ($p < 0.01$). Similarly, users with explanations improved performance compared to not having explanations ($p < 0.01$).

Based on our statistical analysis, we confirm our hypothesis that providing explanations improves decision-making in PBO. Users with explanations achieved significantly higher mean utility than those without, and their performance was statistically indistinguishable from the ideal selection agent. This demonstrates that explanatory support enables human decision-makers to make more effective and accurate preference selections.

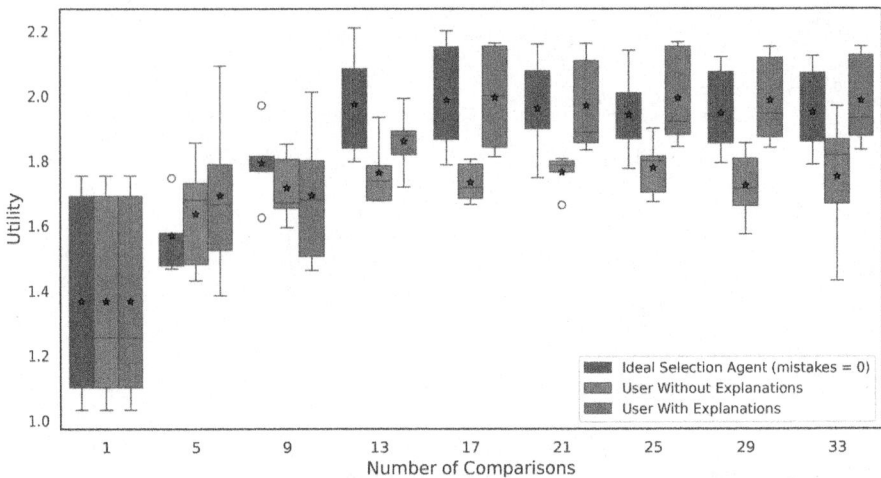

**Fig. 7.** The mean utility of five users with corresponding error bars illustrating variance. Results indicate that users with explanations consistently outperform those without. Notably, users assisted by explanations achieve performance levels comparable to an ideal selection agent who does not make mistakes.

### 5.4 Result Summary

To summarize our results, MOLONE provided high-fidelity explanations, which helped users in preference selection compared to not having explanations.

Our user study confirms that explanations significantly enhance human-AI collaboration, aligning with findings from related research [1,30,31]. This validation extends to the effectiveness of the Evaluative XAI framework employed by MOLONE, which facilitated easy decision-making [27].

Despite the ongoing debate about the intrinsic value of explanations in AI systems [2,10], our empirical results provide clear evidence of their utility, demonstrating a significant boost in performance within PBO contexts. This substantiates the role of well-designed explanations in improving system usability and effectiveness, highlighting their critical importance in complex AI applications.

## 6 Related Work

**Explainable Bayesian Optimization** methods can be broadly categorized into post-hoc methods and online local explainability methods. Post-hoc methods are global approaches that aim to explain the full problem space as approximated by a learned surrogate model. For example, RX-BO [7] and TNTRules [6] are rule-based post-hoc methods designed for single-outcome BO, effectively highlighting multiple local minima within the optimization space. Another method, GPShap, provides Shapley explanations that highlight global input feature importances of the backbone GP of BO [8].

In contrast, online local explainability methods CoExBo and ShapleyBO generate Shapley-based explanations tailored to individual candidates in PBO [1, 30]. While these methods aim to help decision-makers by highlighting feature importance, they have two key limitations. First, Shapley values provide feature importance targeting single outcomes [25], falling short of offering joint assessments across multiple outputs in a multi-outcome model where different outcomes may be correlated. Second, expert decision-making often demands a comparative evaluation of the strengths and weaknesses of different samples [14, 18], a task that input feature importance alone cannot adequately support as it lacks a comprehensive view of the objective space. Thus both CoExBo, and ShapleyBO are not directly comparable with our method as MOLONE explicitly compares inputs as well as outputs to illustrate the influence of inputs on user-defined objectives, whereas CoExBo and ShapleyBO focus solely on input feature importance, without accounting for the relationship between inputs and outputs in the decision-making process.

While MOLONE shares some similarities with **contrastive explanation** models, it differs in several key ways. Traditional non-common effects analysis [22] explains human decision-making by identifying the unique consequences of actions, assuming that distinct effects drive choices. In contrast, MOLONE does not infer intent or focus on outcome differences. Instead, it explains selections by analyzing the intrinsic characteristics of the samples and the underlying BO model. MOLONE also stands apart from **counterfactual explanations** [20, 26], which modify variables to explore hypothetical outcomes [17]. In MOLONE, both Sample A and Sample B represent real, viable choices rather than hypothetical alternatives. While counterfactuals alter inputs to see how outputs change, MOLONE examines the chosen samples as they are, providing insight into why the BO algorithm selected them rather than speculating on what might have happened under different conditions.

## 7 Conclusion

In this paper, we introduced MOLONE, a novel comparative explanation framework that shifts from traditional causal explanations to direct comparisons for interpretability. Within the PBO framework, MOLONE enhances decision-making by providing localized comparative explanations of candidate options. Integrated into an Evaluative XAI framework, these explanations systematically highlight each candidate's strengths and weaknesses, enabling users to make more informed and confident decisions. Our empirical results demonstrate that providing explanations significantly improves preference selection, leading to better optimization outcomes than strategies without explanatory support. These findings show the crucial role of explanations in enhancing decision-making by making trade-offs between samples more transparent and interpretable.

This work opens several promising avenues for future research. While synthetic benchmarks such as DTLZ and ZDT provided a controlled testing environment, applying MOLONE to real-world scenarios would further validate its effectiveness across diverse domains and assess its potential for practical deployment in complex decision-making tasks.

Expanding human-in-the-loop evaluations is another key direction. Larger-scale user studies would provide stronger statistical power and deeper insights into how comparative explanations influence decision-making. Additionally, exploring the long-term effects of explanations on user learning, decision speed, and confidence could reveal valuable educational and usability benefits, improving their effectiveness in real-world applications.

Future research could also explore the role of comparative explanations in domains such as preference learning, personalization systems, and recommendation engines. Extending the MOLONE framework to these areas can deliver more robust and interpretable decision-making, enabling systems to better align with user preferences and domain-specific objectives.

In conclusion, our findings show the potential of comparative explanations for enhancing human decision-making within PBO. MOLONE provides a strong foundation for further research, offering both theoretical and practical contributions toward more transparent, interpretable, and human-centric optimization frameworks. This work paves the way for integrating comparative explanations into various decision-support applications.

**Acknowledgments.** This study was supported by BMBF Project hKI-Chemie: humancentric AI for the chemical industry, FKZ 01—S21023D, FKZ 01—S21023G and Continental AG.

## A  Local Area Sampling

We use a Latin Hyper Cube sampling inside a volume of a sphere. Figure 8 shows in green the area we sample from.

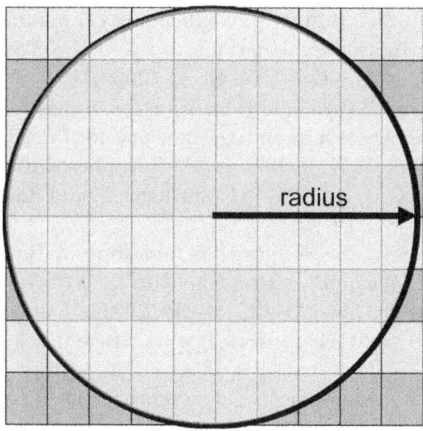

**Fig. 8.** Visual representation of the sampling inside the volume of a sphere.

# References

1. Adachi, M., et al.: Looping in the human: collaborative and explainable Bayesian optimization. In: AISTATS (2024)
2. Arora, S., Pruthi, D., Sadeh, N., Cohen, W.W., Lipton, Z.C., Neubig, G.: Explain, edit, and understand: rethinking user study design for evaluating model explanations. In: Proceedings of the AAAI Conference on Artificial Intelligence, vol. 36, pp. 5277–5285 (2022)
3. Bakshy, E., et al.: Ae: a domain-agnostic platform for adaptive experimentation. In: Conference on Neural Information Processing Systems, pp. 1–8 (2018)
4. Balandat, M., et al.: Botorch: a framework for efficient monte-carlo bayesian optimization. In: Larochelle, H., Ranzato, M., Hadsell, R., Balcan, M., Lin, H. (eds.) Advances in Neural Information Processing Systems. vol. 33, pp. 21524–21538. Curran Associates, Inc. (2020). https://proceedings.neurips.cc/paper_files/paper/2020/file/f5b1b89d98b7286673128a5fb112cb9a-Paper.pdf
5. Cabitza, F., Natali, C., Famiglini, L., Campagner, A., Caccavella, V., Gallazzi, E.: Never tell me the odds: Investigating pro-hoc explanations in medical decision making. Artif. Intell. Med. **150**, 102819 (2024)
6. Chakraborty, T., Seifert, C., Wirth, C.: Explainable Bayesian optimization. arXiv preprint arXiv:2401.13334 (2024)
7. Chakraborty, T., Wirth, C., Seifert, C.: Post-hoc rule based explanations for black box Bayesian optimization. In: Nowaczyk, S., et al. (eds.) European Conference on Artificial Intelligence, pp. 320–337. Springer, Cham (2023). https://doi.org/10.1007/978-3-031-50396-2_18
8. Chau, S.L., Muandet, K., Sejdinovic, D.: Explaining the uncertain: Stochastic shapley values for gaussian process models. In: Advances in Neural Information Processing Systems, vol. 36 (2024)
9. Deb, K., Gupta, H.: Searching for robust pareto-optimal solutions in multi-objective optimization. In: Coello Coello, C.A., Hernández Aguirre, A., Zitzler, E. (eds.) EMO 2005. LNCS, vol. 3410, pp. 150–164. Springer, Heidelberg (2005). https://doi.org/10.1007/978-3-540-31880-4_11

10. Dinu, J., Bigham, J., Zico Kolter, J.: Challenging common interpretability assumptions in feature attribution explanations. In: NeurIPS Workshop: ML Retrospectives, Surveys & Meta-Analyses (ML-RSA) (2020)
11. Frazier, P.I., Wang, J.: Bayesian optimization for materials design. In: Information Science for Materials Discovery and Design, pp. 45–75 (2016)
12. Freeden, W., Nashed, M.Z., Schreiner, M.: Applicabilities and applications. In: Spherical Sampling. GM, pp. 525–531. Springer, Cham (2018). https://doi.org/10.1007/978-3-319-71458-5_19
13. Gan, W., Ji, Z., Liang, Y.: Acquisition functions in Bayesian optimization. In: 2021 2nd International Conference on Big Data & Artificial Intelligence & Software Engineering (ICBASE), pp. 129–135. IEEE (2021)
14. Gary, A.K.: Sources of Power: How People Make Decisions. Mass, Cambridge (1999)
15. González, J., Dai, Z., Damianou, A., Lawrence, N.D.: Preferential Bayesian optimization. In: International Conference on Machine Learning, pp. 1282–1291. PMLR (2017)
16. Gordon, D.F., McGreavy, C., Christou, A., Vijayakumar, S.: Human-in-the-loop optimization of exoskeleton assistance via online simulation of metabolic cost. IEEE Trans. Rob. **38**(3), 1410–1429 (2022)
17. Halpern, J.Y., Pearl, J.: Causes and explanations: a structural-model approach. Part I: causes. Br. J. Philos. Sci. **56**(4), 843–887 (2005). http://www.jstor.org/stable/3541870
18. Hoffman, R.R., Yates, J.F.: Decision making [human-centered computing]. IEEE Intell. Syst. **20**(4), 76–83 (2005)
19. Iman, R.L.: Latin Hypercube Sampling. John Wiley and Sons, Ltd. (2014). https://doi.org/10.1002/9781118445112.stat03803, https://onlinelibrary.wiley.com/doi/abs/10.1002/9781118445112.stat03803
20. Jacovi, A., Swayamdipta, S., Ravfogel, S., Elazar, Y., Choi, Y., Goldberg, Y.: Contrastive explanations for model interpretability (2021). https://arxiv.org/abs/2103.01378
21. Jin, Y., Kumar, P.V.: Bayesian optimisation for efficient material discovery: a mini review. Nanoscale **15**(26), 10975–10984 (2023)
22. Jones, E.E., Davis, K.E.: From acts to dispositions the attribution process in person perception1. Adv. Exp. Soc. Psychol. **2**, 219–266 (1965). https://api.semanticscholar.org/CorpusID:144754193
23. Keeney, R.L., Raiffa, H., Rajala, D.W.: Decisions with multiple objectives: preferences and value trade-offs. IEEE Trans. Syst. Man Cybern. **9**(7), 403–403 (1979). https://doi.org/10.1109/TSMC.1979.4310245
24. Lin, Z.J., Astudillo, R., Frazier, P., Bakshy, E.: Preference exploration for efficient bayesian optimization with multiple outcomes. In: International Conference on Artificial Intelligence and Statistics, pp. 4235–4258. PMLR (2022)
25. Lundberg, S.M., Lee, S.I.: A unified approach to interpreting model predictions. In: Advances in Neural Information Processing Systems, vol. 30 (2017)
26. Miller, T.: Contrastive explanation: a structural-model approach. Knowl. Eng. Rev. **36**, e14 (2021)
27. Miller, T.: Explainable AI is dead, long live explainable AI! Hypothesis-driven decision support using evaluative AI. In: Proceedings of the 2023 ACM Conference on Fairness, Accountability, and Transparency, pp. 333–342 (2023)
28. Nicholls, J.: The mcc decision matrix: a tool for applying strategic logic toeveryday activity. Manag. Decis. **33**(6), 4–10 (1995)

29. Rasmussen, C.E., Williams, C.K.: Gaussian Processes for Machine Learning, ser. Adaptive Computation and Machine Learning, vol. 38, pp. 715–719. MIT Press, Cambridge (2006)
30. Rodemann, J., et al.: Explaining Bayesian optimization by Shapley values facilitates human-AI collaboration. arXiv preprint arXiv:2403.04629 (2024)
31. Senoner, J., Schallmoser, S., Kratzwald, B., Feuerriegel, S., Netland, T.: Explainable AI improves task performance in human-AI collaboration. Sci. Rep. **14**(1), 31150 (2024)
32. Shahriari, B., Swersky, K., Wang, Z., Adams, R.P., Freitas, N.: Taking the human out of the loop: a review of Bayesian optimization. Proc. IEEE **104**(1), 148–175 (2015)
33. Slovic, P.: The construction of preference. Am. Psychol. **50**(5), 364 (1995)
34. Wang, K., Dowling, A.W.: Bayesian optimization for chemical products and functional materials. Curr. Opin. Chem. Eng. **36**, 100728 (2022)
35. Xu, C., Gertner, G.Z.: Uncertainty and sensitivity analysis for models with correlated parameters. Reliab. Eng. Syst. Saf. **93**(10), 1563–1573 (2008)
36. Zhao, Z., et al.: Optimization of spinal cord stimulation using Bayesian preference learning and its validation. IEEE Trans. Neural Syst. Rehabil. Eng. **29**, 1987–1997 (2021)
37. Zhou, H., Ma, X., Blaschko, M.B.: A corrected expected improvement acquisition function under noisy observations. In: Yanıkoğlu, B., Buntine, W. (eds.) Proceedings of the 15th Asian Conference on Machine Learning. Proceedings of Machine Learning Research, vol. 222, pp. 1747–1762. PMLR (2024)
38. Zitzler, E., Deb, K., Thiele, L.: Comparison of multiobjective evolutionary algorithms: empirical results. Evol. Comput. **8**(2), 173–195 (2000). https://doi.org/10.1162/106365600568202

**Open Access** This chapter is licensed under the terms of the Creative Commons Attribution 4.0 International License (http://creativecommons.org/licenses/by/4.0/), which permits use, sharing, adaptation, distribution and reproduction in any medium or format, as long as you give appropriate credit to the original author(s) and the source, provide a link to the Creative Commons license and indicate if changes were made.

The images or other third party material in this chapter are included in the chapter's Creative Commons license, unless indicated otherwise in a credit line to the material. If material is not included in the chapter's Creative Commons license and your intended use is not permitted by statutory regulation or exceeds the permitted use, you will need to obtain permission directly from the copyright holder.

# Generating Rationales Based on Human Explanations for Constrained Optimization

Inga Ibs[1,2]() and Constantin A. Rothkopf[1,2,3]

[1] Centre for Cognitive Science, TU Darmstadt, Darmstadt, Germany
inga.ibs@tu-darmstadt.de
[2] Institute of Psychology, TU Darmstadt, Darmstadt, Germany
[3] Hessian Center for AI (hessian.AI), Darmstadt, Germany

**Abstract.** Many constrained optimization problems, including those relevant to infrastructure planning, e.g., energy systems or logistics, can be effectively solved using white-box solvers based on linear programming. While these algorithms are well understood by the experts who developed them, explanations of the solutions they find are still necessary to communicate their implications to laypeople. However, it is unclear what such explanations should look like since the linear program solvers' high-dimensional and abstract representations of the problem likely do not match human representations. Here, we propose an algorithm for finding rationales that align with human representations of constrained optimization problems. The proposed algorithm incorporates key insights from prior research on the structure, complexity, and representations of human explanations for constrained optimization. Specifically, we introduce a grammar of predicates derived directly from participants' explanations and behavioral data from our previous studies on human optimization strategies. With a prior that regularizes rule complexity, this grammar forms the foundation of a rational rules model, which we use to generate rationales modeled after human explanations. Given that human explanations for constrained optimization problems reflect a sequential decision process, our approach searches the space of sequential solution representations within a Markov Decision Process to identify the most interpretable sequence and corresponding rationale. We evaluate our algorithm on human solutions and demonstrate that the generated rationales have a high dataset description score and complexity similar to human explanations, suggesting that the rationales capture human decision processes well and, therefore, align with the representations and structure of human explanations.

**Keywords:** Human explanation · Rule-based XAI · Constrained Optimization

# 1 Introduction

Computational solutions for constrained optimization problems shape the modern world we live in. Constrained optimization methods are widely applied to optimizing our infrastructure, from planning the integration of renewable energy into our energy system [5] to resource allocation and treatment plans in health care [6]. Many of the systems solving constrained optimization problems like linear programs are well understood by experts and are guaranteed to find the optimal solution. Furthermore, explanation techniques that support engineers while they build the systems exist [4,9,11,22]. These explanation techniques engage with the theoretical foundations of the systems but do not generate explanations for the solutions accessible to laypeople. These could include policymakers deciding on the proposals obtained with these systems or citizens affected by the policies. However, research on human approaches to constrained optimization problems suggests that people do not consider the full solution space, as solvers like the Simplex method [7] or Branch and Bound methods [10] do. Instead, people rely on sequential, local actions, or heuristics, that focus on the system's current state, iteratively adding elements to their solution [13,16]. Moreover, they explain their solutions in terms of their decision heuristics [13]. Therefore, a gap exists between the solver's and people's representation, translating to a gap in the representations featured in explanations.

This gap is especially problematic in domains where infrastructure plans have to be realized and regulated by decision-makers who are not the engineers of the systems, like in energy system design [12]. Suppose a government uses a system for constrained optimization to identify the best integration of renewable energy sources while minimizing costs and ensuring supply stability. The solver operates in an abstract mathematical space, searching for the optimal solution within the polytope of feasible solutions. While, depending on the solution approach, the solution is guaranteed to be optimal, the explanation of the solution in terms of the systems approach: "We have to build fifty wind turbines because this corresponds to the best vertex on the polytope of feasible solutions." is not accessible to laypeople. Interpretability methods like sensitivity analyses of input-output dependencies help systems engineers to interpret optimization systems' outputs. However, explanations obtained with these methods are not straightforward to interpret without extensive theoretical knowledge. Individual inputs often change the complete solution, making explanations based on these relations unintuitive [12]. For example, the explanation "With 90 % of the assumed energy demand, the best plan would be to build two coal plants and ten solar power plants instead." does little to help laypeople understand or trust the system, even though its decisions may directly impact them. Policymakers and citizens require explanations in terms of their priorities [2,12] –how the proposed energy mix relates to electricity prices and carbon emissions that match their representation of the problem. One way to close the representational gap is to use insights from cognitive science on human explanations and representations of problems to generate explanations based on concepts that are intuitive for the explainee [18,21].

In this paper, we propose a method for generating human-inspired rationales for constrained optimization solutions. We focus on constrained optimization problems where objectives and constraints are defined using linear relationships. This widely used formulation of linear constrained optimization problems allows us to build on research on how people understand these types of problems. We use an interdisciplinary approach by integrating findings from cognitive science on how people solve and explain these types of problems to generate rationales that align with human explanations. We refer to the generated expressions as rationales because rather than referring to the mathematical solvers reasoning, they rationalize the solution with rules based on human representations of the solution process. For our approach, we model solutions as sequences within a Markov Decision Process (MDP). We define rationales as combinations of programs from a probabilistic context-free grammar, which we derive from human heuristic strategies for constrained optimization. This grammar, along with a prior over program compositions, form the basis of our rationale generation method. A heuristic search algorithm explores sequences of actions from the MDP for which we match rationales with probabilistic program induction. We select the most probable rule-based rationale that best aligns with one of the sequences. Our evaluation shows that the generated rationales align with human decision-making patterns, mirror the complexity properties of human explanations, and generalize across different problem instances.

The paper is structured as follows. We start by discussing related work on interpretability methods for constrained optimization and human-inspired explainable artificial intelligence (XAI) methods in Sect. 2. Next, in Sect. 3, we will summarize insights we obtained in a prior study [13] on structure, complexity, and form of human explanations for resource allocation problems, a subclass of constrained optimization problems. These insights fundamentally shape the development of our rationale generation algorithm. Our method for the rationale generation is detailed in Sect. 4. In Sect. 5, we illustrate our method by first discussing a rationale for one example problem in detail. We then evaluate the rationale generation method on human-generated solutions to linear constrained optimization problems, which shows that the rationales capture human decision-making patterns. Furthermore, we test our algorithm on randomly generated problems and demonstrate that the algorithm generalizes across problems. Finally, we discuss the implication of the rationales and address limitations of this approach in Sect. 6.

## 2 Related Work

Since solvers for many optimization problems are theoretically well understood and, in many cases, guaranteed to be optimal, methods explaining the solvers' output focus mainly on the interpretability of the input-output relationship rather than explaining the solution in terms of the solution process.

Sensitivity analysis methods are a widely used tool by engineers to gain insights into the system's sensitivity to changes in the problem's input [9]. While these methods are helpful for system engineers who know which parameters and which changes are important, the high dimensionality of sensitivity results makes the output inaccessible to laypeople. Attribution methods, adopted from the domain of explainable AI for neural networks like LIME [23] and gradient-based attribution methods, aim to provide more focused relevance scores of a system's input to the output [4,11]. While these methods produce more accessible explanations, they depend highly on the right choice of independent interpretable parameters and additional translations of the meaning of the changes to laypeople. The tool SimplifEx [22] aims to support systems engineers in understanding a solution for linear programs by using a mixture of preprocessing methods, dominance relations, and heuristics that are similar to human strategies to explain the structure of a solution. While parts of the output from the tool are possibly accessible for laypeople since they are modelled after human strategies, the other outputs presuppose theoretical knowledge about linear programs.

One way to make explanations more accessible to laypeople is to integrate insights from social sciences. Particularly in cases where it is unclear what an intuitive explanation consists of, empirical studies and theories on how people conceptualize problems and how mental representations shape the structure of their explanations can guide the explanation generation process [21].

In the domain of decision support systems, recommendations based on human strategies are shown to improve human problem-solving. Rule-based procedural instructions, derived from human strategies for solving information acquisition tasks, have been shown to enhance participant performance [3,25]. For spatial constrained optimization problems, recommendations based on human strategies also improved the performance of participants solving these tasks [15]. Another approach to generating human-inspired explanations is to use human explanations as training data for an XAI method. Ehsan et al. [8] train a neural translation model directly on explanations from humans playing Frogger to automatically produce rationales that match the language and the features used by humans. In user evaluation studies, they demonstrate that the rationales align with human intuitions and representations of the task context. While these results are promising in that users perceive recommendations and rationales based on human representations as helpful, our objective here is different. Firstly, we aim to provide rationales for solutions for complex constrained optimization problems for which we have to rely on computers to calculate the optimal solution. Secondly, while automatic rationale generation from a corpus of human explanations can enable direct communication between AI agents and users, they do not allow to test and validate the automatically generated rationales. Our goal here is to obtain rationales that can act as a policy, meaning that following the rationales leads to the solution they are rationalizing. This approach allows the validation of rationales and provides the basis for analyzing the structure of the rationales and their transferability.

In order to model the rationales after human explanation, we build directly on insights we obtained in a previous study on human explanations for linear constrained optimization problems [13]. In this previous study, we elicited

**Immediate Profit**

"First, you look at what currently brings in the most profit (usually either bookcases or beds) and then focus on that. Then you pay attention to the extent to which this production brings your materials into imbalance and then produce either tables or chairs accordingly, which require a lot of one of the materials." **Balancing**

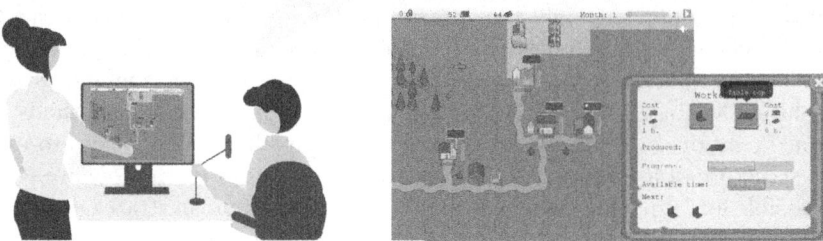

**Fig. 1.** Post-hoc explanation given by a participant for the Furniture Factory. The explanation is a composite of two heuristic strategies, *immediate profit* and *balancing*, marked by different text colors. The interface of the Furniture Factory game used in [13] for the elicitation of post-hoc explanations is shown in the bottom right corner.

explanations from people solving constrained optimization problems. From these explanations, heuristic strategies were derived and matched to behavior. The results of this study are summarized in Sect. 3.1. In this work, we use the heuristic strategies as a basis for the rationales for constrained optimization problems. We generalize and extend the formal versions of the strategies from our previous study [13] and introduce compositional versions to enable the generation of rationales for various linear constrained optimization problems. Furthermore, the results from the analysis of the structure and complexity of human explanations from our previous work [13] inform the rationale generation here. Since peoples' explanations refer to a sequential decision-making process, we implement this structure in the rationale generation by expressing the solution as sequences from an MDP. This problem formulation, usually used to define the problem space for reinforcement learning, allows us here to describe human decision-making processes. By performing a probabilistic search on candidate sequences based on a prior that regularizes complexity, we generate rationales that refer, like human explanations, to a sequential decision-making process without being excessively complex.

## 3 Features of Human Rationales

To generate human-like rationales for solutions to constrained optimization problems, it is first necessary to understand how people explain these solutions and how these explanations relate to their problem representation. In previous work [13], we collected a dataset of explanations from people while they solved problems from a constrained optimization task instantiated in two different versions as computer games, the *Furniture Factory*. This section summarizes the experiment, analyses, and results from the previous study [13], which serve as the foundation for the method proposed in this paper.

### 3.1 The Furniture Factory Game

In the games (one variant shown in Fig. 1), participants were asked to solve instances of the *Furniture Factory*, a resource allocation problem. The goal of the task was to maximize the factory's profit by determining the optimal set of furniture items while adhering to the resource constraints. The decision variables of the problem corresponded to the different types of furniture: bookcases, beds, tables, and chairs. Each item had different associated profits and used different amounts of wood, metal, and workshop hours from four workshops.

The Furniture Factory was posed in two variants in two separate experiments to obtain different types of explanations from participants. One variant was used to elicit concurrent explanations, which are explanations for each action while solving the problem, and the other, shown in Fig. 1, was used to elicit post-hoc explanations, i.e. explanations provided for the solution after solving the problem In each experiment, participants had to solve multiple problem instances, characterized by various amounts of resources available and profits associated with the furniture items.

In the following, we will summarize the main insights about the form and content of the rationales obtained from this study, which are relevant to the automatic generation of rationales.

### 3.2 Form of Human Explanations

The explanations given by the participants for their solution process were composites of decision heuristics. We identified and formalized four main heuristics: *immediate profit*, *balancing* of material or workshop hours, *gap reduction*, and *cost-benefit* (see [13] for further details on the formalization process). Figure 1 shows one of the post-hoc explanations given by the participants to answer the question *'What should I do to find the best possible solution?'* posed by a fictional coworker. In this example, two of these main heuristics are assembled into one explanation. First, the participant recommended building the items with the immediate maximum profit, which corresponds to the *immediate profit* strategy. Then, they described a version of the *balancing* strategy. The heuristic strategies relate to individual decisions in the process of arriving at a solution. This decision process differs from an automatic solver's process of finding a solution in that the heuristic strategies relate to a representation of the state of a problem in terms of the available resources rather than the solution space. Importantly, not all heuristic strategies featured in explanations incorporate the complete representation of the constrained optimization problem. Many strategies referred to a subset of the information that was available, which we quantified with a complexity score calculated over the compared attributes in each strategy (we refer the reader to [13] for details on this complexity score). Furthermore, each post-hoc explanation the participants gave featured only a subset of the four heuristics.

The formal heuristic strategies derived from participants' verbal protocols were validated by analyzing their alignment with individual decision steps from a separate validation dataset [13]. Data from 167 participants was collected via Prolific, and strategy decisions were compared to actual participant choices to assess the similarity of the strategies' decisions to the participants. The similarity of the strategy decisions with the participant's decisions was defined as the proportion of steps in a trajectory where the participant's choice aligned with at least one strategy in the set. This score was 0.87 (SD: 0.18) for a validation dataset (we refer the reader to [13] for further details on this analysis). The results revealed that combinations of these strategies effectively captured participants' decision-making behavior. While we do not claim that the general versions of the strategies fully capture the participants' cognitive decision process, the ability to match the behavior shows that they are promising as building blocks for explanations.

## 4 Search for Human-Inspired Rationales for Constrained Optimization Solutions

The post-hoc explanations we elicited in our previous study [13] are composites of heuristic strategies that refer to an sequential decision-making process. Furthermore, the explanations show a preference for the reuse of the building blocks. Rather than explaining each step individually, strategies are reused to explain multiple steps. Also, the strategies refer to reduced representations of the underlying information. To align the rationales with human explanations, we propose a method for automatic rationale generation for solutions to constrained optimization problems that incorporate human preferences[1].

In Fig. 2, we show a graphical representation of our approach. We model constrained optimization problems as Markov Decision Processes to represent solutions as sequences of state-action pairs. By leveraging a domain-specific language grounded in human heuristic strategies, we formalize rationales as logical expressions that provide structured, compositional descriptions for these sequences. For the efficient search of solution sequences and matching rationales, sequences are iteratively expanded with generated states and actions from the solution set. Using logical program policies, a probabilistic program induction algorithm by Silver et al. [24], combinations of programs from the grammar are identified that fit the current sequence. Sequences yielding a non-zero likelihood rationale are further expanded into child sequences using the most promising actions. The most promising rationales from each leaf of this search tree with the highest likelihood are compared, and the rationale with the highest prior is chosen as the final rationale for the solution.

---

[1] The code can be found at the Open Science Framework (https://osf.io/zw4da).

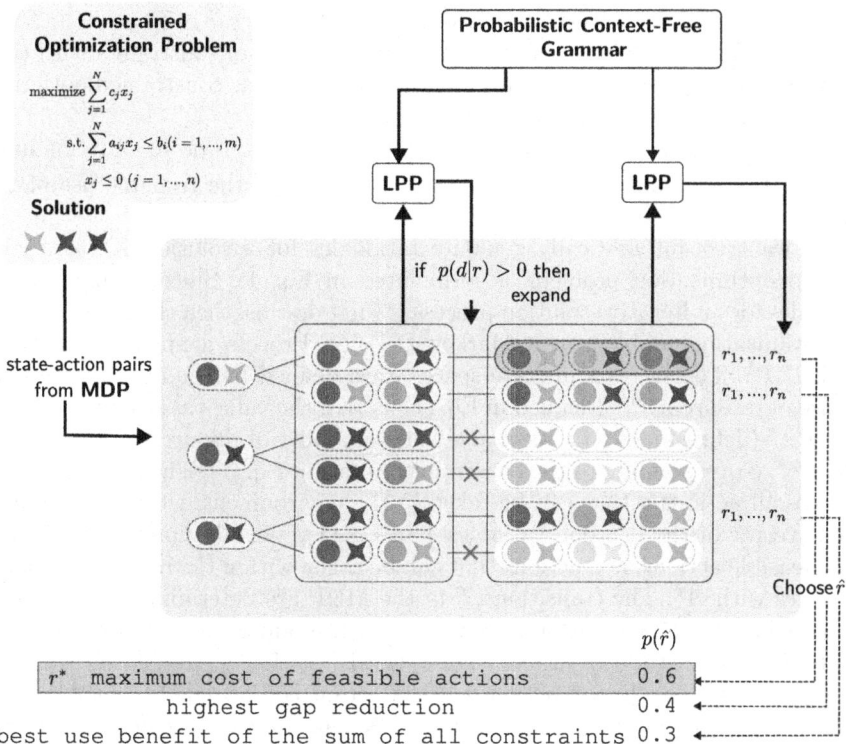

**Fig. 2.** Visualization of the rationale-generation algorithm.

This section introduces our approach in detail. We first formalize the problem setup and structure of rationales before defining a context-free grammar that captures human strategies. We then describe our probabilistic search method for discovering rationales and sequences.

### 4.1 Constrained Optimization Problems as Markov Decision Processes

Constrained optimization problems are problems for which an optimal solution has to be found under consideration of constraints. A common class of these problems are linear constrained optimization problems or linear programs, where the restrictions of the solution space are expressed as a list of linear inequalities, and the objective is also of linear form:

$$\begin{aligned} \underset{\mathbf{x} \in \mathbb{Z}^n}{\text{maximize}} \quad & c^T x \\ \text{s.t.} \quad & Wx \leq b \\ & x \geq 0 \end{aligned} \quad (1)$$

Here, $x$ corresponds to the vector of decision-variables, $b \in \mathbb{Z}^n$ and $c \in \mathbb{Z}^n$ to vectors and $W \in \mathbb{Z}^{m \times n}$ to a matrix. We denote the set of constraints with $U$.

We focus on one type of specific subproblems of linear constrained optimization problems, *Resource Allocation Problems*.

In resource allocation problems $c \in \mathbb{R}^n_{\geq 0}$ describes the profit of items in $x$, $b \in \mathbb{R}^n_{\geq 0}$ the availability of resources and $W \in \mathbb{R}^{m \times n}_{\geq 0}$ the resource use of the items in $x$.

We want to automatically generate rationales for a solution $\mathbf{X}^*$ to a constrained optimization problem as formulated in Eq. (1). Since people provide rationales for an iterative solution process ("First do this, then this"), we express the optimization problem as a Markov Decision Process defined by the tuple $(\mathcal{S}, A, \mathcal{T}, \mathcal{R})$. The states $s$ in state space $\mathcal{S}$ are defined by the information over the use of resources $s^{\text{use}}$ (defined in Eq. (1) as $W$), the values associated with the costs $s^{\text{cost}}$ (defined in Eq. (1) as $c$) and the availability of resources in the current state $s^{\text{res}}$, corresponding to the constraint limits $b$ in Eq. (1). The action space $A$ includes all actions $a$ that can be taken in the environment, which corresponds to the vector of the decision variables $x$ in Eq. (1). We additionally denote the set of feasible actions, i.e., actions that can be taken within the range of available resources with $A^f$. The transitions $\mathcal{T}$ in the MDP are deterministic. Taking an action $a$ in state $s'$ leads to a new state $s$, corresponding to the previous state minus the resource use from $s^{\text{use}}$. The reward function $\mathcal{R}$ assigns the value of the cost function $c_a$ for an action $a$ if the action is selected. We want to find a sequential representation of the solution $\mathbf{X}^*$, in form of a sequence of state-action pairs $d = ((s_0, a_0), ..., (s_{|\mathbf{X}^*|}, (a_{|\mathbf{X}^*|}))$ with states $s \in \mathcal{S}$ and actions from the solution set $a \in \mathbf{X}^*$ for which we can find a rationale $r$ which maps onto the sequence.

### 4.2 Structure of Rationales

Participants' post-hoc explanations for their solution process in the Furniture Factory task were compositions of the different strategies they used to solve the problem. For example, "First you build the item with the highest profit, then you build the item that balances the resources best" can be composed of the *immediate profit* and the *balancing* strategy. For the automatic generation of rationales, we build on this compositionality. We generate rationales for a solution to a constrained optimization problem in the form of logical concatenations of programs $q$ from a probabilistic context-free grammar that captures human strategies. The rationales can be represented in disjunctive normal form (DNF):

$$r \propto h(s,a) \triangleq \bigvee_{i=1...K} ( \bigwedge_{j=1...L_i} q_{i,j}(s,a)^{\beta_{i,j}} (1 - (q_{i,j}(s,a))^{1-\beta_{i,j}})) \qquad (2)$$

with $K$ as the number of *or* concatenations of a number $L_i$ *and* concatenations of programs from the grammar. The negation of programs is implemented with the binarized parameter $\beta$. If the rationale is evaluated as true ($r \propto h(s,a) = 1$) for a state-action pair $(s,a)$ the action $a$ is in alignment with the rationale, else ($r \propto h(s,a) = 0$) it violates the rationale.

## 4.3 A Probabilistic Context-Free Grammar for Constrained Optimization

To specify a domain-specific language that captures human representations, we derive a probabilistic context-free grammar [19] from the heuristic strategies we identified with human studies in [13]. The programs $q$ that can be generated from this grammar form the rationales (see Eq. (2)).

The formal strategies we defined in our previous work [13] serve as exemplars of the heuristics mentioned by participants. While these specific formalizations matched many of the participants' decisions, other implementations of the heuristics are possible. For example, the *cost-benefit* strategy can be expressed through various functions that balance the cost (the benefit) of an item against resource use. These functions might consider, for example, the aggregate use of all resources or focus exclusively on the use of a single resource. The explanations elicited from the participants in [13] allow different interpretations of the form of implementation. To use the flexibility of these strategies in automated rationale generation, we propose the probabilistic context-free grammar, shown in Table 1. This framework provides a structured way to define a broader range of strategies that capture the concepts featured in peoples' explanations.

The grammar consists of five conditions C that evaluate state-action pairs. Depending on the type, these conditions can take different forms and consider different functions F on the constraints and action sets A. The functions F operate either on all constraints or specific constraint sets specified by their input CS. The different evaluation criteria specified by the conditions are described in detail in the appendix (see Sect. A). The five different types of conditions, max_cost, min_use, best_use_benefit, most_equal_use and highest_gap_reduction, are designed to capture peoples heuristic strategies.

The condition max_cost implements the *immediate profit* strategy of the participants since in resource allocation problems with a maximization objective, the cost function can be conceptualized as profits. This condition is true if the action in question is associated with the highest cost of all actions in an action set A. The condition min_use is true if the action in the state-action pair that is evaluated has the minimum value with regard to some function on the use attributes of actions. These functions, represented by F, include the sum over the use of resources of an action, the average use of resources, and the normalized sum or average use of resources. The condition best_use_benefit evaluates a state-action pair as true if the ratio of the cost of the action to the use of resources is the highest compared to all other actions in A. Again, the use of resources is calculated via a function F. Max_cost, min_use, best_use_benefit can be state-independent if the input function F does not include a normalization term and the action set A consists of all available actions. The state independence ensures that strong preferences mentioned in participants' reasoning [13], such as "First build the item with the highest profit," are captured. However, the action set can also represent the set of all feasible actions.

The condition most_equal_use captures the *balancing* strategy of the participants, which chooses the action with the most balanced use of resources. Bal-

**Table 1.** Probabilistic context-free grammar derived from human heuristic strategies

| Production rule | Probability |
|---|---|
| **CONDITION** | |
| C → min_use( F, A ) | 1/5 |
| C → max_cost( A ) | 1/5 |
| C → best_use_benefit( F, A ) | 1/5 |
| C → most_equal_use( CS ) | 1/5 |
| C → highest_gap_reduction( CS ) | 1/5 |
| **FUNCTION** | |
| F → mean_use( CS ) | 1/4 |
| F → mean_normalized_use( CS ) | 1/4 |
| F → sum_use( CS ) | 1/4 |
| F → sum_normalized_use( CS ) | 1/4 |
| **CONSTRAINT SET** | |
| CS → all_constraints | 1/7 |
| CS → most_critical_constraint | 1/7 |
| CS → most_critical_shared_constraint | 1/7 |
| CS → least_critical_constraint | 1/7 |
| CS → least_critical_shared_constraint | 1/7 |
| CS → most_shared_constraints | 1/7 |
| CS → most_shared_constraints_feasible | 1/7 |
| **ACTION SET** | |
| A → all_actions | 1/2 |
| A → feasible_actions | 1/2 |

ancing the use of resources allows multiple constraints to be taken into account. The condition most_equal_use assigns a truth value to a state-action pair if its use ratio is the most similar to the available resource ratio compared to all other feasible actions. At last, the condition highest_gap_reduction considers constraints with the highest and lowest availability of resources and chooses the action with the highest use ratio of both. The constraint sets CF include the set of all resource constraints, the set of the most shared resource constraints, the maximum available resource, and the minimal available resource.

### 4.4 Probabilistic Search over Rationales with Logical Program Policies

To search for rationales on a sequence of decisions, $D$, we use Logical program policies (LPP) originally proposed by Silver et al. [24], an imitation learning method that allows us to probabilistically search a space of policies that match the sequence of decisions best. The LPP algorithm takes as input a sequence, a context-free grammar and a prior over the programs from the grammar and searches for policies whose behaviors match the sequence. The policies are represented as DNFs comprised of programs from the probabilistic context-free grammar, and assign boolean values to each state-action pair in the sequence. By constructing positive (the action associated with the state) and negative examples (all other actions possible) from the input sequence, the LPP algorithm performs standard induction of the decision tree with features based on the set of programs in the grammar that classify the examples in the dataset correctly. The algorithm returns a posterior over programmatic policies. The programmatic policies provide the basis for the rationales.

**Complexity Regularized Prior.** For the inference of the rationales, we use the same prior as defined by Silver et al. [24] as a prior over rationales which favors rationales with simpler and fewer programs:

$$p(r) \propto \prod_{i=1}^{K} \prod_{j=1}^{L_i} p(q_{i,j}) \tag{3}$$

Here, p(r) reflects the probability of independently generating the probabilistic programs $q$ in a DNF from a probabilistic context-free grammar. To address the improper prior, we follow the procedure from Silver et al. [24] and impose a uniform prior over $\sum_i^K L_i$ from 1 to a large value $\alpha$, which results in the factor $1/\alpha$ which is independent of the rationale and can be absorbed into a proportionality constant for the calculation of the posterior.

**Likelihood.** For the likelihood of a sequence of state-action pairs we account for unmatched state-action pairs in the sequence by introducing a noise parameter $\epsilon$. The likelihood captures the assumption that an action in the sequence can be explained by the rationale with probability $(1 - \epsilon)$ or consists of an unexplained random action with probability $\epsilon$. We additionally introduce a threshold $\gamma$ to limit cases where too many steps in the trajectory are unexplained by the rationale. The resulting likelihood corresponds to

$$p(d|r) \propto \begin{cases} \prod_i^N (1-\epsilon) r(a_i|s_i) + \frac{\epsilon}{|A|} & \text{if } \frac{1}{N} \cdot \sum_i^N r(a_i|s_i) \geq (1-\gamma) \\ 0 & \text{else} \end{cases} \tag{4}$$

We reduce the search space and complexity of rationales by considering only those with a prior greater than a small threshold $\delta$. To approximate the posterior over all rationales, we estimate the normalizing constant using the likelihood and priors from this set: $p(d) \propto \sum_{r^{p(r)>\delta}} p(d|r)p(r)$. The approximated posterior over rationales corresponds accordingly to

$$p(r|d) \propto \frac{p(r)p(d|r)}{p(d)}. \tag{5}$$

The maximum a posteriori estimate for the rationale which captures the sequence best is then defined as $\hat{r} = argmax\ p(r|d)$.

## 4.5 Heuristic Search over Sequences

For many constrained optimization problems, solutions do not have an intrinsic order. However, since our rationales impose a specific sequence of actions, identifying the best rationale for a solution requires matching valid action sequences. The challenge arises from the sheer size of the possible sequence space, which combinatorially explodes with the number of actions. We use a heuristic search to extend sequences iteratively that are most promising for matching rationales.

The search procedure is visualized in Fig. 2. A search tree is initialized for each action type in the solution set $\mathbf{X}^*$, starting with a single node representing the state-action pair of the initial state and the action of the corresponding action type. Each search tree is then incrementally expanded by adding child nodes. Each child node consists of the parent's state-action pairs and a new tuple formed by the state resulting from the last action in the parent's sequence and a new drawn action from the solution set. In this structure, each node represents a (partial) candidate sequence for the solution set. To keep the search efficient, we apply two heuristics to search only among the most promising sequences. First, we only further extend sequences for which we can find a rationale with a non-zero likelihood using the LPP approach. Second, we introduce the parameter $\eta$, which limits the number of child nodes per parent node to the top $\eta$-actions – those that yield the highest number of programs evaluated as true within the program set. The tree leaves represent the candidate sequences from the solution set for which we induce a distribution of rationales. Note that a suitable candidate sequence can be found. From the leaves of all search trees, we identify those for which the number of steps matched by a rationale is highest. We extract each sequence's maximum posterior rationale $\hat{r}$. Finally, we return the rationale with the highest prior $r^* = argmax_{\hat{r}}\, p(\hat{r})$ and the corresponding sequence $d^*$.

## 4.6 Pruning Rationales

By running the algorithm on a solution, we obtain a rationale in disjunctive normal form. In this form, the rationale functions as a policy, i.e., to evaluate different state-action pairs, allowing us to validate the rationale and transfer it to other problems. However, it is not guaranteed to be optimal for any other problem. The composition of rules ensures that the right action is taken in every state of the sequence it matches and, therefore, minimizes the probability of taking the wrong action. Though this property is necessary for using the rationale as a policy, a lower complexity can be advantageous when we want to translate the rationales into text for a specific solution. To reduce complexity, we evaluate the DNF formula on each state-action pair in the associated sequence and search for the minimal set of programs that unambiguously determine the action in question within the relevant conjunction (see Fig. 3 for an example). As a result, we obtain a mapping of conjunctions of programs for each state, which we can translate into a procedural text.

## 5 Experiments and Results

In this section, we evaluate the proposed algorithm on optimal as well as human solutions for constrained optimization problems. We start by discussing one generated rationale in detail in Sect. 5.1. Next, in Sect. 5.2, we evaluate our algorithm on a dataset of human solutions for the Furniture Factory optimization problem to investigate how well we can describe human decisions with the rationales and how similar the rationales are to human explanations. Finally, we discuss the results of the rationale generation on randomly sampled problems and investigate the validity of the sequence search (see Sect. 5.3).

### 5.1 Detailed Example

We begin by examining a rationale for a problem from the Furniture Factory (see Sect. 3.1 for a description of the problem structure). In Fig. 3 A, we show the problem description, including the cost function and six constraints related to resources – wood, metal, and workshop hours across four workshops (A to D). The optimal solution obtained using an integer program solver consists of one bed, four bookcases, two tables, and one chair (highlighted in blue).

Applying the algorithm to this solution produces a rationale expressed as a DNF formula, illustrated in Fig. 3 B. This formula consists of four distinct program rules derived from a probabilistic context-free grammar: one condition addressing maximum cost, one focusing on minimal resource use under specific constraints, and two variants related to the highest gap reduction condition. In this form, the rationale functions as a policy. By evaluating state-action pairs and selecting actions where the rule holds, the rationale can be validated and even applied to different problems. Note that the complete rule is necessary for executing the rationale as a policy since the additional programs ensure that the correct conjunction determines the action in each state. The pruning of components, however, makes the rationale more interpretable when used as a descriptive explanation. We can identify the minimal set of programs that describe the state-action relation by evaluating each program in the true conjunction of the formula separately for one state-action pair. By retaining only this minimal set, we can reduce the complexity of the description. Figure 3 C illustrates this process for the candidate sequence associated with the rationale. In this case, two programs are sufficient to describe the sequence. Figure 3 D shows an example of such a procedural description in text form. The example demonstrates how the rationale we generate provides a context and an intuition for the solution.

### 5.2 Matching Human Solutions

As a next step, we aim to validate our rationale generation method using a dataset of human solutions. Evaluating how well the generated rationales align with human solutions helps assess their ability to capture and explain human approaches to constrained optimization. If we can find reasonable rationales for human solutions, it suggests that the domain-specific language on which the

**A** Constrained Optimization Problem

$$\text{maximize} \quad 3x_0 + 6x_1 + 4x_2 + 2x_3$$
$$\text{s.t.} \quad 4x_0 + 5x_1 + 2x_2 + 4x_3 \leq 40 \quad \text{wood}$$
$$3x_0 + 7x_1 + 5x_2 + 1x_3 \leq 44 \quad \text{metal}$$
$$4x_2 + 4x_3 \leq 26 \quad \text{workshop A}$$
$$6x_2 + 1x_3 \leq 30 \quad \text{workshop B}$$
$$3x_0 + 5x_1 \leq 23 \quad \text{workshop C}$$
$$4x_0 + 3x_1 \leq 26 \quad \text{workshop D}$$

$x_0$ = Bed
$x_1$ = Bookcase
$x_2$ = Table
$x_3$ = Chair

Optimal Solution
$X^* = \{1x_0, 4x_1, 2x_2, 3x_3\}$

**B**
$$r^* \propto h(s,a) = \mathtt{f}_1 \wedge \neg \mathtt{f}_2 \vee \neg \mathtt{f}_1 \wedge \mathtt{f}_3 \wedge \mathtt{f}_4$$

$\mathtt{f}_1$ = max_cost(feasible_items)
$\mathtt{f}_2$ = min_use(mean_use(least_critical_shared_constraint),all_items)
$\mathtt{f}_3$ = highest_gap_reduction(most_shared_constraints_feasible)
$\mathtt{f}_4$ = highest_gap_reduction(all_constraints)

**C**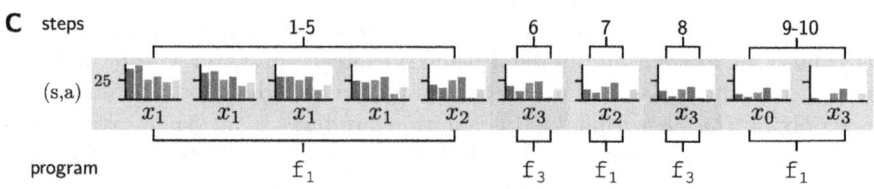

**D** The solution consists of 4 bookcases and one table which have the highest profit among the feasible items, then one chair, which reduces the gap between the most and least available of the shared resources, then one table which has the highest profit among the feasible items, then one chair which reduces the gap between the most and least available of the shared resources, and one bed and one chair which have the highest profit among the feasible items.

**Fig. 3.** Translation of rationales to text. **A** Constrained optimization problem with the optimal solution set. **B** Rationale in disjunctive normal form obtained using sequence and rationale search for the optimal solution. **C** Mapping of programs to the state-action pairs in the sequence. Steps correspond to the steps in the sequence. The bar-diagrams indicate the resource distribution in the state. **D** Translation of the rationale to a natural language description. (Color figure online)

rationales are based captures human intuition. Furthermore, evaluating the algorithm on human solutions allows us to assess whether the rationales accurately explain solutions obtained with diverse strategies by different individuals.

We ran our algorithm on human solutions in the validation dataset, which we recorded in our previous study [13]. This dataset comprises 1,001 solutions submitted by 167 participants, each solving six problems of the Furniture Factory optimization task. The study in which the dataset was obtained was approved by the local ethics committee. To characterize the description quality of the rationales, we calculated the *proportion of described actions* by dividing the

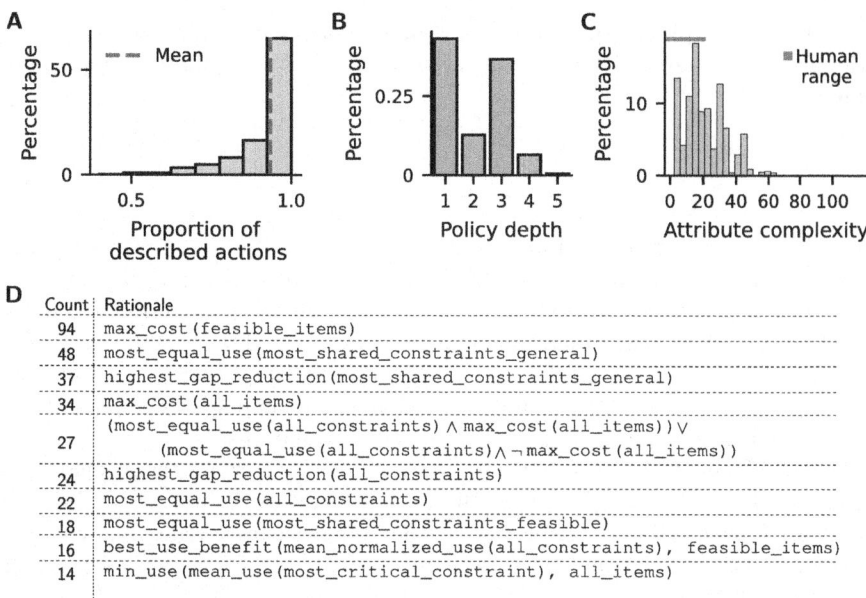

**Fig. 4.** Results for the rationale generation for the human solutions. **A** Distribution of the proportions of actions described by the best rationale found for each solution. **B** Distribution of policy depth values. **C** Distribution of attribute-complexity values. **D** Ten most common rationales that were matched to the solutions.

number of actions in the candidate sequence $d^*$ that are described unambiguously by the rationale by the length of the sequence. We applied the algorithm with a search budget $\eta = 4$. Figure 4 A shows the distribution of the proportion of described actions for the participants' solution. On average, the rationales found by our algorithm can describe 0.93 (SD: 0.04) of the items in the participants' solutions. The high description score shows that our algorithm can find sequences and rationales that capture the participants' solution process.

Next, we investigated the complexity of the generated rationales. In principle, the rationales could be comprised of distinct conjunctions of programs for each solution part, resulting in high complexity. Rationales of too high complexity are difficult to understand and quite dissimilar to human explanations, which have limited complexity in both the representation of the problems and the number of strategies mentioned in the explanation. We evaluated the complexity of the rationales with respect to rationale depth and attribute complexity. Rationale depth refers to the maximum number of programs in one conjunction of the DNF. Deeper rationales correspond to more programs that have to be checked. Figure 4 B shows the distribution of the rationale depth. Generally, the rationale depth for all rationales is below 5, and almost 43% of rationales consist of only one program. In comparison, the participants' post-hoc explanations usually consisted of one to three heuristic strategies.

Attribute complexity quantifies the number of attributes featured in a pruned rationale when matched to a sequence of actions. We calculate the attribute complexity with

$$\sum_{\text{unique conjunctions for } d^*} |A| \cdot |s_{\text{CS}}^{\text{action}}| + |s_{\text{CS}}^{\text{res}}|$$

with $s_{\text{CS}}^{\text{action}}$ referring to attributes such as the cost of resource use associated with an item and $s_{\text{CS}}^{\text{res}}$ to state attributes representing resource availability. The number of attributes in each set varies depending on the program and is determined by operations and constraint sets given as input. This calculation follows the same formula used to determine the attribute complexity of participants' post-hoc explanations. As a result, we can directly compare the complexity of the matched rationales with the participants' explanations.

Figure 4 C shows the distribution of attribute complexity for the pruned rationales. The attribute complexity of the participants' explanations lay between 2 and 22. The attribute complexity of the generated rationales has a higher variability and higher values than human explanations. However, 56 % of the rationales fall in the same interval as that of the participants, and 95 % of the values are below 44. Note that the complexity of the participants' post-hoc explanations can be viewed as a lower bound for the complexity of their decision-making since participants did not exhaustively explain every decision step. However, the rationales that we match to the solutions aim to describe all the parts of the solution, which can lead to a higher complexity. Figure 4 D gives an overview of the most common rationales that matched the data. Notably, almost all the most common rationales consist of only one program. The most common rationales agree well with the heuristic strategies mentioned by the participants. For example, the most common rationale `max_cost(feasible_items)` corresponds to the *immediate profit* strategy. The second most common rationale `most_equal_use(most_shared_constraints_general)` corresponds to the heuristic strategy *balance material*, since wood and metal are the most shared resources in this task. In summary, we observe a high description score for the generated rationales for the human solutions in the dataset. While some rationales have a higher complexity than human explanations in general, most of the rationales fall into the same complexity range observed in human explanations. Furthermore, even though the programs in our grammar include more general and variable versions of the human heuristic strategies, the most commonly matched rationales correspond to the specific versions of strategies mentioned by participants, demonstrating that the algorithm can recover human intuitions.

## 5.3 Generalization to Other Problems

Finally, we test our algorithm on a set of randomly generated integer resource allocation problems to evaluate if the grammar that is derived from human explanations for the Furniture Factory can express solutions for other problems. As a benchmark, we generate 100 problems by randomly sampling the number of

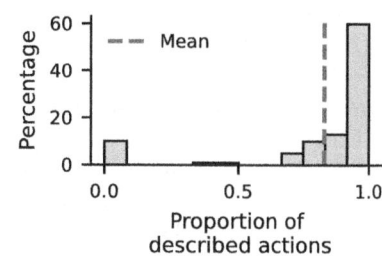

|      | constraints | items | items in solution |
|------|-------------|-------|-------------------|
| mean | 16.9        | 11.4  | 12.24             |
| std  | 7.6         | 5.3   | 5.7               |
| min  | 30          | 2     | 25                |
| max  | 2           | 20    | 2                 |

**Fig. 5.** Description of Benchmark dataset and results. **A** shows the parameters of the problems in the dataset. **B** Description score of the generated rationales.

constraints from $[0, 200]$, the number of actions from $[2, 20]$, costs from $[10, 1000]$, resource use from $[0, 200]$, and constraint limits from $[500, 5000]$. The generated problems are solved, and only instances with an optimal solution containing at most 25 selected actions are retained to ensure a feasible runtime. Figure 5 A shows the general description of the dataset. We evaluated the algorithm with a budget of $\eta = 3$ and a lower limit for the program prior of $log(\delta) = -30$, which limits the complexity to a total number of 12 distinct programs in any given rationale. Figure 5 B shows the description quality of the generated rationales for the benchmark dataset. For 53 problems, a rationale describing the full solution was found (proportion of described actions equals 1); for 37 problems, a rationale that partially described the solution was found. The mean description score is 0.83. For 10 problems no rationale consisting of at most 12 programs could be found. Notably, these problems have a higher number of actions ($> 10$) in the action set.

One reason for the unsuccessful search on these problems could be that for a higher number of actions, the ranking between actions with programs could be more ambiguous, for example, if two actions have the same cost value. In that case, more programs might be needed to describe the actions unambiguously. By setting the lower limit for the rationales $\delta$ to a lower value, more complex rationales could be generated. Another reason for the unsuccessful search could be that the grammar is not expressive enough or that the algorithm did not search within the right sequences. While these caveats exist, the high proportion of solutions described in the benchmark suggests that the algorithm is generally applicable.

## 6 Discussion

Solutions to complex, constrained optimization problems shape the world we live in. While mathematical optimization techniques provide reliable solutions, explanations for these solutions for non-experts must be presented in a way that aligns with their intuitions. In this work, we introduce a novel approach for generating rationales that reflect human representations of constrained optimization problems.

Insights from cognitive science on how people solve and explain constrained optimization problems shape our algorithm in multiple ways. We propose a probabilistic context-free grammar derived from human heuristic strategies for constrained optimization. We define a model for the structure of the rationales, which consists of logical compositions of programs from this grammar, and add a complexity regularizing prior to aid our search for simpler rationales. Since human heuristic strategies relate to a sequential solution approach, the rationales inspired by them describe sequences of decisions. By formulating constrained optimization problems as MDPs and leveraging heuristic search techniques and probabilistic program induction methods, we simultaneously search for sequences generated from the solution and rationales for these sequences. As a result, we obtain rationales that can be used as a policy. This allows us to validate the rationales by comparing the behavior they induce with the solution. Furthermore, programs from the rationales that are not necessary to describe a specific sequence can be pruned, which enables the translation of the rationales to a natural language description.

We evaluated the algorithm on human-generated solutions obtained in a prior problem-solving study and observe a high dataset description score, suggesting that the rationales capture human decision processes. The analysis of the complexity of the rationales demonstrates that a large part of the automatically generated rationales have a complexity comparable to human explanations. Finally, tests on randomly generated problems confirm that the algorithm can generate rationales for a broader range of constrained optimization problems beyond those used in human behavioral studies.

The human-inspired rationales we propose here provide a way to communicate solutions for complex constrained optimization problems to people not well versed in mathematical optimization. These rationales serve as post-hoc local explanations because they provide insights specific to individual problems rather than detailing the global behavior of the solver [26]. The underlying rule-based model acts as a surrogate, explaining the solver's reasoning results through a different, more intuitive form of logic over heuristics. One important concern is that, even though such explanations might be plausible to the user, they are not faithful to the actual reasoning process of the solver [14,20]. The constrained optimization solvers we regard here are often white-box solvers, i.e., theoretically well-understood and guaranteed to be optimal, reducing the ethical problems associated with surrogate models. However, our model can also be applied to solutions obtained with black-box solvers. The rationales obtained here do not aim to equip the user to debug or check the model, a responsibility that should be up to the engineers. Instead, they provide a way to increase the plausibility of the solutions to laypeople affected by them. This can increase the trust and acceptance of the solutions, which is not necessarily problematic in the case of well-tested models. To this end, empirical studies are needed to determine whether the generated rationales provide meaningful information and to identify the most effective ways to present them to people who have to interpret solutions in complex domains.

While the constrained optimization problems we regard in this study are limited to resource allocation problems with a linear cost maximization objective and linear constraints, there is in principle nothing that precludes applying this methodology to other constrained optimization problems. A natural next step to account for more problems is to extend the grammar with programs that apply to satisfaction problems and problems to minimize the cost function, which are often used to describe energy systems planning [1,17]. This can be implemented by adapting operators in conditions and distinguishing between satisfaction and use constraints. While we focus here on solutions from linear programming solvers, this approach to rationale generation is solver-agnostic and could be applied to solutions obtained with other solvers like reinforcement learning agents or neural networks. The grammar, however, captures heuristic strategies people use for problems with linear objectives and linear constraints. An open question is how differently people conceptualize nonlinear optimization problems, and how much the grammar for the rationales would have to be adapted to account for this difference.

One current limitation is the scalability of the approach. The search on sequences and the repeated calculation of the likelihood of the rationales are computationally expensive. To apply the method to larger problems, a more targeted search on sequences or the chunking of solution items is needed. With a better model of when people use which heuristic, a prior over sequences could enable a more targeted search for sequences. However, more research in the field of cognitive science is needed to expand the theoretical understanding of how people solve and perceive constrained optimization problems.

**Acknowledgments.** We would like to thank Dominik Straub, Claire Ott and Thea Behrens for their valuable comments on this manuscript. This work was funded by the German Federal Ministry of Education and Research (Bundesministerium für Bildung und Forschung, BMBF) in the project 'PlexPlain: Erklärende KI für komplexe Lineare Programme am Beispiel intelligenter Energiesysteme' [grant number 01IS19081] and by the Hessian Ministry of Higher Education, Research, Science and the Arts (Hessisches Ministerium für Wissenschaft und Kunst) and its LOEWE research priority program 'WhiteBox' [grant number LOEWE/ 2/13/519/03/06.001(0010)/77].

**Disclosure of Interests.** The authors have no competing interests to declare that are relevant to the content of this article.

# A  Appendix

In the following we describe the components of the probabilistic context-free grammar from Table 1. Table 2 provides a description for the operations in the conditions C, Table 3 describes the functions F and Tables 4 and 5 describe the constraint sets CS and action sets A respectively.

**Table 2.** Descriptions of conditions C.

| Condition | Description |
|---|---|
| min_use(s, a', F, A) | $F_{a'} \leq F_a \,\forall a \in \mathbf{A}$ |
| max_cost(s, a', A) | $s^{\text{cost}}_{a'} \geq s^{\text{cost}}_a \,\forall a \in \mathbf{A}$ |
| best_use_benefit(s, a', F, A) | $\frac{s^{\text{cost}}_{a'}}{F_{a'}} \geq \frac{s^{\text{cost}}_a}{F_a} \,\forall a \in \mathbf{A}$ |
| most_equal_use(s, a', CS) | $\frac{s^{\text{res}}\mid_{\text{CS}} \cdot s^{\text{use}}_{:a'}\mid_{\text{CS}}}{\|s^{\text{res}}\mid_{\text{CS}}\| \|s^{\text{use}}_{:a'}\mid_{\text{CS}}\|} \geq \frac{s^{\text{res}}\mid_{\text{CS}} \cdot s^{\text{use}}_{:a}\mid_{\text{CS}}}{\|s^{\text{res}}\mid_{\text{CS}}\| \|s^{\text{use}}_{:a}\mid_{\text{CS}}\|} \,\forall a \in \mathbf{A}$ |
| highest_gap_reduction(s, a', CS) | $g'_a \geq g_a \,\forall a \in \mathbf{A}$ <br> $g_a := \begin{cases} s^{\text{use}}_{\max,a}, & \text{if } a \in A^f \text{ and } s^{\text{use}}_{\min,a} = 0, \\ \frac{s^{\text{use}}_{\max,a}}{s^{\text{use}}_{\min,a}}, & \text{if } a \in A^f \text{ and } s^{\text{use}}_{\min,a} > 0, \\ 0, & \text{otherwise.} \end{cases}$ <br> $min = \mathrm{argmin}(s^{\text{res}}\mid_{\text{CS}}),$ <br> $max = \mathrm{argmax}(s^{\text{res}}\mid_{\text{CS}})$ |

**Table 3.** Description of functions F.

| Functions (F) | Description |
|---|---|
| sum_use | $\sum_{u \in \text{CS}} a_{u,a}$ |
| mean_use | $\frac{1}{|\text{CS}|} \sum_{u \in \text{CS}} a_{u,a}$ |
| sum_normalized_sum | $\sum_{u \in \text{CS}} \frac{a_{u,a}}{b^s_u}$ |
| mean_normalized_use | $\frac{1}{|\text{CS}|} \sum_{u \in \text{CS}} \frac{a_{u,a}}{b^s_u}$ |

**Table 4.** Description of constraint sets CS.

| Constraint Sets (CS) | Description |
|---|---|
| all_constraints | $U$ |
| most_shared | $\bigcap_{a_i \in A} \{u \mid a_{u,a} \neq 0, u \in U\}$ |
| most_shared_feasible | $\bigcap_{a_i \in A^f} \{u \mid a_{u,a} \neq 0, u \in U\}$ |
| most_critical_constraint | $\mathrm{argmin}_{u \in U} \sum_{a \in A^f} \frac{b^s_u}{a_{u,a}}$ |
| most_critical_shared_constraint | $\mathrm{argmin}_{u \in \text{most\_shared}} \sum_{a \in A^f} \frac{b^s_u}{a_{u,a}}$ |
| least_critical_constraint | $\mathrm{argmax}_{u \in U} \sum_{a \in A^f} \frac{b^s_u}{a_{u,a}}$ |
| least_critical_shared_constraint | $\mathrm{argmax}_{u \in \text{most\_shared}} \sum_{a \in A^f} \frac{b^s_u}{a_{u,a}}$ |

**Table 5.** Description of action sets A.

| Action Sets (A) | Description |
|---|---|
| all_actions | $A$ |
| all_feasible_actions | $A^f$ |

# References

1. Barbosa, J., Ripp, C., Steinke, F.: Accessible modeling of the German energy transition: an open, compact, and validated model. Energies **14**(23), 8084 (2021)
2. Barredo Arrieta, A., et al.: Explainable artificial intelligence (XAI): concepts, taxonomies, opportunities and challenges toward responsible AI. Inf. Fusion **58**, 82–115 (2020)
3. Becker, F., Skirzyński, J., van Opheusden, B., Lieder, F.: Boosting human decision-making with AI-generated decision aids. Comput. Brain Behav. **5**(4), 467–490 (2022)
4. Busch, F.P., Zečević, M., Kersting, K., Dhami, D.S.: Elucidating linear programs by neural encodings. Authorea Preprints (2023)
5. Connolly, D., Lund, H., Mathiesen, B.V., Leahy, M.: A review of computer tools for analysing the integration of renewable energy into various energy systems. Appl. Energy **87**(4), 1059–1082 (2010)
6. Crown, W., et al.: Constrained optimization methods in health services research–an introduction: report 1 of the ISPOR optimization methods emerging good practices task force. Value Health **20**(3), 310–319 (2017)
7. Dantzig, G.B.: Linear programming and extensions. In: Linear Programming and Extensions. Princeton University Press (2016)
8. Ehsan, U., Tambwekar, P., Chan, L., Harrison, B., Riedl, M.O.: Automated rationale generation: a technique for explainable AI and its effects on human perceptions. In: Proceedings of the 24th International Conference on Intelligent User Interfaces, pp. 263–274 (2019)
9. Greenberg, H.: A functional description of ANALYZE: A computer-assisted analysis system for linear programming models. ACM Trans. Math. Software **9**(1), 18–56 (1983)
10. Huang, L., et al.: Branch and bound in mixed integer linear programming problems: a survey of techniques and trends. arXiv preprint arXiv:2111.06257 (2021)
11. Hülsmann, J., Barbosa, J., Steinke, F.: Local interpretable explanations of energy system designs. Energies **16**(5), 2161 (2023)
12. Hülsmann, J., Steinke, F.: Explaining complex energy systems: A challenge. In: Proceedings of the 34th Conference on Neural Information Processing Systems (NeurIPS 2020), Virtual Conference, pp. 6–12 (2020)
13. Ibs, I., Ott, C., Jäkel, F., Rothkopf, C.A.: From human explanations to explainable AI: insights from constrained optimization. Cogn. Syst. Res. **88**, 101297 (2024)
14. Jacovi, A., Goldberg, Y.: Towards faithfully interpretable NLP systems: How should we define and evaluate faithfulness? In: Proceedings of the 58th Annual Meeting of the Association for Computational Linguistics, pp. 4198–4205 (2020)
15. Kefalidou, G.: When immediate interactive feedback boosts optimization problem solving: a "human-in-the-loop' approach for solving capacitated vehicle routing problems". Comput. Hum. Behav. **73**, 110–124 (2017)
16. Kefalidou, G., Ormerod, T.C.: The fast and the not-so-frugal: human heuristics for optimization problem solving. In: Proceedings of the Annual Meeting of the Cognitive Science Society, vol. 36 (2014)
17. Lauinger, D., Caliandro, P., Kuhn, D., et al.: A linear programming approach to the optimization of residential energy systems. J. Energy Storage **7**, 24–37 (2016)
18. Longo, L., et al.: Explainable artificial intelligence (XAI) 2.0: a manifesto of open challenges and interdisciplinary research directions. Inf. Fusion **106**, 102301 (2024)

19. Manning, C., Schutze, H.: Foundations of Statistical Natural Language Processing. MIT Press (1999)
20. Mariotti, E., Sivaprasad, A., Moral, J.M.A.: Beyond prediction similarity: ShapGAP for evaluating faithful surrogate models in XAI. In: Longo, L. (ed.) World Conference on Explainable Artificial intelligence, vol. 1901, pp. 160–173. Springer, Cham (2023). https://doi.org/10.1007/978-3-031-44064-9_10
21. Miller, T.: Explanation in artificial intelligence: insights from the social sciences. Artif. Intell. **267**, 1–38 (2019)
22. Ott, C., Jäkel, F.: Simplifex: simplifying and explaining linear programs. Cogn. Syst. Res. **88** (2024)
23. Ribeiro, M.T., Singh, S., Guestrin, C.: "Why should i trust you?" explaining the predictions of any classifier. In: Proceedings of the 22nd ACM SIGKDD International Conference on Knowledge Discovery and Data Mining, pp. 1135–1144 (2016)
24. Silver, T., Allen, K.R., Lew, A.K., Kaelbling, L.P., Tenenbaum, J.: Few-shot Bayesian imitation learning with logical program policies. In: Proceedings of the AAAI Conference on Artificial Intelligence, vol. 34, pp. 10251–10258 (2020)
25. Skirzyński, J., Becker, F., Lieder, F.: Automatic discovery of interpretable planning strategies. Mach. Learn. **110**(9), 2641–2683 (2021). https://doi.org/10.1007/s10994-021-05963-2
26. Speith, T.: A review of taxonomies of explainable artificial intelligence (XAI) methods. In: Proceedings of the 2022 ACM Conference on Fairness, Accountability, and Transparency, pp. 2239–2250 (2022)

**Open Access** This chapter is licensed under the terms of the Creative Commons Attribution 4.0 International License (http://creativecommons.org/licenses/by/4.0/), which permits use, sharing, adaptation, distribution and reproduction in any medium or format, as long as you give appropriate credit to the original author(s) and the source, provide a link to the Creative Commons license and indicate if changes were made.

The images or other third party material in this chapter are included in the chapter's Creative Commons license, unless indicated otherwise in a credit line to the material. If material is not included in the chapter's Creative Commons license and your intended use is not permitted by statutory regulation or exceeds the permitted use, you will need to obtain permission directly from the copyright holder.

# Algorithmic Knowability: A Unified Approach to Explanations in the AI Act

Salvatore Sapienza and Monica Palmirani

CIRSFID-ALMA AI, Department of Legal Studies, University of Bologna, Bologna, Italy
{salvatore.sapienza,monica.palmirani}@unibo.it

**Abstract.** The European Union's AI Act introduces a complex framework for algorithmic transparency and explainability. This paper examines the AI Act's explainability requirements through the lens of legal informatics. First, it provides a framework for explainability provisions in the EU digital regulation by discussing the GDPR, Digital Services Act (DSA), Digital Markets Act (DMA), and the withdrawn AI Liability Directive. Then, it identifies four interpretative dimensions of explainability under the AI Act: *deployer-oriented* (ensuring system transparency for appropriate use), *compliance-oriented* (documentation for regulatory adherence), *individual-empowering* (rights to contest AI-supported decisions), and *oversight-oriented* (tools enabling meaningful human control). These dimensions collectively form a framework of *Algorithmic Knowability*, which bases upon the necessity of contextual explanations tailored to diverse stakeholders: providers, deployers, regulators, and affected individuals. The study then evaluates the Knowability approach in the light of ongoing current standardization initiatives and XAI research. The paper concludes that the AI Act's explainability provisions necessitate a shift from one-size-fits-all explanations to context-dependent approaches.

**Keywords:** Algorithmic Transparency · Explainability · EU AI Act · Meaningful Human Control · Standardization

## 1 Introduction and Method

"Explainability" of Machine Learning (ML) algorithms has become an established research area over the past few years. Several disciplines - including epistemology, computer science, design, and many others - have attempted to tackle the issues related to the intrinsic opaqueness of advanced algorithmic models, also known as "Black Box" [33]. Legal studies are not exempted from this trend as they have contributed to the discussion in multiple ways, including by proposing ethical approaches [2] or discussing norms and regulations [20,51].

The recent entry into force of the European Union (EU) Artificial Intelligence Act[1] is a crucial turning point in the discourse related to explainability, which is reinvigorated from the new provisions. While many early commentators have claimed that the entry into force of specific provisions on explainability shall be welcomed as the first clear example of norms directly tackling this issue, the AI Act seems to be placed in a continuum with other legislations rather than as a true normative revolution. However, the Act introduces notable elements of novelty, and new relevant questions arise along these lines. This paper proposes an original contribution to this topic by investigating three crucial questions strictly derived from the entry into force of the Act:

- **RQ1**: How should explainability provisions in the AI Act be interpreted in the light of the applicable EU legal landscape?
- **RQ2**: How should explainability provisions in the AI Act be interpreted to ensure a consistent understanding and application within the Act?
- **RQ3**: Are current standardisation initiatives in the EU aligned with this direction?

The paper adopts the interdisciplinary method of legal informatics, which keeps into account the twofold relationship between legal disciplines and emerging technologies. Legal informatics also encompasses contextual issues regarding the influence of technology on the nature of law, such as the emergence of new legal domains or shifts in legal interpretation and application scope [41]. This entails analysing how integrating algorithms into different sectors of our information society, such as healthcare and finance, gives rise to new legal and ethical challenges, including privacy, transparency, accountability, and fairness concerns [22,23], in the light of the EU legal framework [6].

This paper is divided into six sections. Following this introduction, Sect. 2 discusses related work in the field of explainability and the AI Act. Then, Sect. 3 identifies explainability provisions in the EU digital law by discussing the most prominent regulations applicable today that mention algorithmic transparency. Section 4 critically evaluates the provisions enshrined in the AI Act and proposes a 4-dimension interpretation of explainability provisions enclosed in a unified Knowability framework, whereas Sect. 5 discusses the current state of standardisation initiatives jointly with the XAI research community efforts. Section 6 proposes some final remarks and possible avenues for future research.

## 2 Related Work

In recent years, the academic literature has produced several studies on the topic of algorithmic transparency and explainability from technical and legal perspec-

---

[1] Regulation (EU) 2024/1689 of the European Parliament and of the Council of 13 June 2024 laying down harmonised rules on artificial intelligence and amending Regulations (EC) No 300/2008, (EU) No 167/2013, (EU) No 168/2013, (EU) 2018/858, (EU) 2018/1139 and (EU) 2019/2144 and Directives 2014/90/EU, (EU) 2016/797 and (EU) 2020/1828.

tives. Surveys by Adadi and Berrada [1] and Guidotti et al. [12] have systematically reviewed methods for understanding the inner workings of black-box models, while Lipton [19] has offered a critical discussion on the inherent challenges and conceptual ambiguities surrounding models' interpretability. Ribeiro et al. [35] introduced model-agnostic techniques such as LIME, which have been discussed in the field of local explanations for classifier predictions. Complementary perspectives are presented by Montavon et al. [24] and Samek et al. [38], who focus on visualization and decomposition approaches tailored for deep neural networks.

Beyond technical contributions, there is a growing corpus of scholarly work addressing regulatory and governance issues in AI. First, the discussion on ethical standards, as exemplified by Jobin et al. [14], underlines the importance of establishing common ethical and technical guidelines to foster trust and reliability in AI systems. Collectively, these academic contributions offer a comprehensive foundation that bridges methodological advances in explainable AI with emerging legal and ethical frameworks. Then, with the discussion on the AI Act being finalised, analyses of the regulation have highlighted its potential to shape transparency and accountability in automated systems [3,34]. In parallel, the notion of meaningful human control - especially in safety-critical and autonomous systems - has that robust human oversight is essential for ensuring ethical and responsible AI deployment [44]. The discussion on operationalising transparency has been framed within a broader reflection on EU digital policy [8,27].

However, while some papers have discussed explainability provisions in the AI Act's Proposal [46], few studies have focused on the final version of the Act, mainly due to its novelty. Therefore, this study proposes an original contribution discussing the adopted version of the AI Act currently in force by relying on the direction set by previous works.

## 3 Explainability and Algorithmic Transparency as a Cornerstone of the EU Digital Law

While certainly innovative, the legal innovations brought by the AI Act concerning explainability and algorithmic transparency are not entirely a complete "revolution". When read alongside other provisions of the EU Digital Strategy, the Act's provisions show a high degree of continuity. This can be observed when discussing the diverse pieces of legislation that constitute the EU Digital Strategy. First, the 2021 Communication "2030 Digital Compass: the European way for the Digital Decade" stresses the centrality of "Ethical principles for human centric algorithms"[2] among which explainability is undoubtedly placed since its first introduction [2,13,25]. The legal landscape of algorithmic transparency covers key legal texts such as the General Data Protection Regulation (GDPR), the

---

[2] Available at https://eur-lex.europa.eu/legal-content/EN/TXT/HTML/?uri=CELEX:52021DC0118.

**Table 1.** The Legal Landscape of EU Algorithmic Transparency

| Directive/Regulation | Topic | Articles | Recital |
|---|---|---|---|
| General Data Protection Regulation | Automated Decision-Making | Art.13(2)(f), 14(2)(g), 15(1)(h) | [60] |
| | | Art.22 | [71] |
| AI Liability Directive (Withdrawn Proposal) | Accessibility to evidence in trials regarding AI products/systems | Art.3(1) | [16-21] |
| | | Art.4 | [22-30] |
| Digital Services Act | Online Platforms transparency including Algorithms | Art.27(1),(2) | [68] |
| | | Art.40(3) | [141] |
| | | Art.69(2)(d),(5) | [146] |
| | | Art.72 | [93, 141] |
| Digital Markets Act | On request by the Commission, access to explanations regarding recommendation systems | Art.21(1),(2) | [81] |
| | | Art.23(2)(d),(4) | [83] |
| Artificial Intelligence Act | AI system transparency | Art.11 + All. IV | [9, 53, 107] |
| | | Art.13 | [27] |
| | | Art.52 | [119] |
| | | Art.86 | [93] |

AI Liability Directive (Withdrawn Proposal), the Digital Services Act (DSA), the Digital Markets Act (DMA) and the AI Act. Table 1 below summarises the key relevant legal provisions.

### 3.1 "Meaningful Information" About the Automated Decision-Making Process in the GDPR

The GDPR has been the object of massive scrutiny in the literature and case law. The controversial existence of a "right to explanation" for algorithmic decision-making has culminated in the *SHUFA*[3] case. In summary, the debate revolved around the lack of an explicit reference for a right to "obtain an explanation" of the automated decision in Art. 22 - contrary to the corresponding non-binding Recital 71 - specifically addressing the consequences of automated processing.

---

[3] Case C-634/21 OQ v Land Hesse [2023] ECLI:EU:C:2023:220.

Instead, the data subject's right to obtain "meaningful information about the logic involved" in an automated decision in the case of algorithmic decision-making, including profiling, is enshrined in Art. 13(2)(f), Art. 14(2)(g) and Art. 15(1)(h) of the GDPR, which cover the *ex ante* right to information (both when the data is provided by the data subject or obtained elsewhere) and the *ex post* right to access. [4, 5, 7, 10, 16, 20, 28, 42, 51]

While the *SHUFA* case has significantly clarified - and noteworthily expanded - the scope of "automated decision-making" and "profiling" in the GDPR, it is also worth noticing that it did not directly tackle the interpretation of a) whether a right to explanation exists in the GDPR, b) what constitutes "meaningful information" for the purposes of the other articles and c) to what extent such "meaningful information" include the logic of the algorithms used in the automated decision. These questions were referred to the Court of Justice in the pending *CK v Dun & Bradstreet Austria case*[4]. In September 2024, the Advocate General's opinion suggested that although Article 15(1)(h) GDPR grants data subjects access to "meaningful information", this necessarily implies the existence of a corresponding "right to an explanation"[5]. Information that is unclear or lacks context cannot be considered "meaningful" from the data subject's perspective or in light of the provision's intent, which is allowing the data subject to verify "consistency and causal link between, on the one hand, the method and criteria used, and on the other hand, the result arrived at by the automated decision"[6]. However, AG de la Tour clarified that Article 15(1)(h) GDPR does not require the disclosure of the algorithm itself. Given the likely complexity of the algorithm, it may be incomprehensible to individuals without specialized technical knowledge[7].

The decision on *Dun & Bradstreet* was delivered on 27 February 2025. Several points deserve attention. First, the Court clarified that the meaning of Art. 15(1)(h) "must be understood as a right to an explanation of the procedure and principles actually applied in order to use, by automated means, the personal data of the data subject with a view to obtaining a specific result [...]. In order to enable the data subject effectively to exercise the rights conferred on him or her by the GDPR and, in particular, Article 22(3) thereof, that explanation must be provided by means of relevant information and in a concise, transparent, intelligible and easily accessible form. Those requirements cannot be satisfied

---

[4] Case C-203/22 CK v Dun & Bradstreet Austria GmbH and Magistrat der Stadt Wien [2024] ECLI:EU:C:2024:745.
[5] Para 67.
[6] Para 68.
[7] Para 72. This is consistent with the interpretation provided in the *SHUFA* case by the Advocate General, para 57, "In my view, those requirements exclude any obligation to disclose the algorithm, given its complexity. The benefit of communicating a particularly complex formula without providing the necessary explanations for it would be questionable. Regard should be had in this connection to recital 58 of the GDPR, according to which compliance with the aforementioned requirements is of particular relevance 'in situations where ... the technological complexity of practice [makes] it difficult for the data subject to know and understand whether, by whom and for what purpose personal data relating to him or her are being collected'.".

either by the mere communication of a complex mathematical formula, such as an algorithm, or by the detailed description of all the steps in automated decision-making, since none of those would constitute a sufficiently concise and intelligible explanation."[8]. Therefore, "the controller should find simple ways to tell the data subject about the rationale behind, or the criteria relied on in reaching the automated decision [...]. The GDPR requires the controller to provide meaningful information about the logic involved in that decision, but 'not necessarily a complex explanation of the algorithms used or disclosure of the full algorithm'."[9]. Moreover, in the Court's view, the right to explanation is not absolute. It needs to be balanced against other rights and freedoms, such as the protection of third-party data and trade secrets. Where providing full information would infringe on these rights, controllers may need to provide the information to a supervisory authority or to a court, which will then determine the extent to which the data subject can access the data[10].

## 3.2 The Withdrawn AI Liability Directive Proposal and Transparency of AI Systems in Trials

A different perspective is the one provided by the formerly known AI Liability Directive Proposal. Two of its provisions are particularly relevant. On the one hand, according to Article 3(1), EU Member States must empower national courts to order the disclosure of relevant evidence concerning a specific high-risk AI system suspected of causing damage. This applies when a potential claimant has previously requested such evidence from a provider, a person subject to the provider's obligations under Article 24 or Article 28(1) of the AI Act, or a user, and that request was refused. As with the "meaningful information" under the GDPR, the scope of "relevant evidence" is yet to be defined. On the other hand, according to Article 4, national courts shall presume a causal link between a defendant's fault and damage caused by an AI system if certain conditions are met. These conditions include, for claims against providers of high-risk AI systems, that they claimant must prove that the provider failed to meet specific requirements the ones on transparency enshrined in Article 13 of the AI Act discussed below. The presumption is deemed necessary to restore the informational imbalance between the claimant and the provider in reconstructing the causal link between the AI's output and the damage suffered[11]. In February 2025, the

---

[8] Para 58-59.
[9] Para 60.
[10] Paras 68, 76.
[11] See Recital 28: "The presumption of causality could also apply to AI systems that are not high-risk AI systems because there could be excessive difficulties of proof for the claimant. For example, such difficulties could be assessed in light of the characteristics of certain AI systems, such as autonomy and opacity, which render the explanation of the inner functioning of the AI system very difficult in practice, negatively affecting the ability of the claimant to prove the causal link between the fault of the defendant and the AI output.".

Commission announced in its *2025 Work Programme* that it will withdraw the Proposal due to the lack of foreseeable agreement[12]

### 3.3 Digital Services Act and Online Platforms Explanations Requirements

The Digital Services Act (DSA)[13] is aimed at supporting the effective operation of the EU internal market for digital intermediary services by establishing harmonised rules that create a safe, predictable, and trusted online environment, fostering innovation while ensuring the protection of fundamental rights and consumer protection. The DSA contains specific obligations for very large online platforms (VLOPs) and very large online search engines (VLOSE), which are online platforms meeting higher user numbers criteria.

With regards to algorithmic transparency, it has to be noted that according to Art. 27, providers using recommender systems must clearly explain the main parameters of these systems and how users can modify or influence them. The parameters should explain why certain information is suggested and include details on the key criteria and their relative importance, with an option for users to choose and modify their preferred option directly within the relevant section of the platform[14]. According to Art. 40(3), VLOPs or VLOSE providers shall, at the request of national authorities or the Commission, explain the design, the logic, the functioning and the testing of their algorithmic systems, including their recommender systems. Conversely, under Art. 69(2)(d), the Commission can also require that VLOPs and VLOSE providers to provide access to and explanations on its organisation, functioning, IT system, algorithms, data-handling and business practices and to record or document the explanations given. Similar actions can be pursued by the Commission in its compliance monitoring power under Art. 72.

### 3.4 The Digital Markets Act and Recommender Systems

The Digital Markets Act (DMA)[15] aims to improve the functioning of the EU digital internal market by regulating businesses and gatekeepers, i.e., large online platforms that control access to digital markets, significantly influencing the flow of information and services between businesses and consumers. These platforms

---

[12] Available at https://commission.europa.eu/document/download/7617998c-86e6-4a74-b33c-249e8a7938cd_en?filename=COM_2025_45_1_annexes_EN.pdf p. 26.

[13] Regulation (EU) 2022/2065 of the European Parliament and of the Council of 19 October 2022 on a Single Market For Digital Services and amending Directive 2000/31/EC.

[14] Noteworthly, micro and small enterprises are excluded from this provisions (Art. 19), whereas VLOSE providers are required to include an option for recommender systems which is not based on profiling (Art. 38).

[15] Regulation (EU) 2022/1925 of the European Parliament and of the Council of 14 September 2022 on contestable and fair markets in the digital sector and amending Directives (EU) 2019/1937 and (EU) 2020/1828.

often have substantial market power, making it challenging for other companies to reach users without their involvement. To address this, the DMA imposes specific obligations on gatekeepers to promote fair competition and protect consumers. In September 2023, the European Commission designated six companies as gatekeepers under the DMA: Alphabet (Google), Amazon, Apple, Booking, ByteDance (TikTok), Meta (Facebook), and Microsoft. The provisions are meant to increase the benefit of consumers. Similarly to the DSA, the European Commission holds the authority to request information from companies and their associations to fulfill its responsibilities under the DMA under Art. 21. This includes the power to access data, algorithms, and testing information, as well as to seek explanations regarding these elements. Moreover, the Commission may require the undertaking to provide access to and explanations on its organisation during inspections. Such explanations can also include information on IT system and algorithms.

## 3.5 Common Traits in the EU Digital Landscape on Algorithmic Transparency: A Balance Between Complexity and Comprehensibility

The examination of the various regulatory instruments reveals some common elements and traits that highlight the peculiarities of the EU's approach. First, across the GDPR, the DSA, and the DMA, a primary goal is to ensure that individuals and authorities are provided with "meaningful information" about automated decision-making. The provided information shall serve a specific purpose ("meaningfulness") depending on the explainee [46–48]. Therefore, every time "meaningful information" is mentioned, it is meant to empower the explainee scrutinise decisions made by these systems.

Second, all the legislative instruments acknowledge the inherent complexity of modern algorithms. They strive to strike a balance between technical detail and user comprehension by mandating that explanations be tailored to be accessible to the explainee [18,43,46]. This can be observed in the case law related to the GDPR, which insists on providing "meaningful information", but carefully avoids the full disclosure of information that might stating that it might overwhelm data subjects.

At the heart of these legislative measures is the protection of individual rights. Whether through the GDPR's rights to information and access or the proactive regulatory oversight mechanisms under the DSA and DMA, the EU consistently reaffirms the need to safeguard citizens from opaque decision-making processes. However, this reading might not be consistent with the policy goals of some of these instruments, in particular the market-oriented ones like the DSA or the DMA. The GDPR is fundamentally designed to protect individual data subjects by granting them the right to obtain "meaningful information" on automated decisions. In contrast, the DSA and DMA are primarily focused on the regulation large online platforms and gatekeepers.

Another notable difference consists on the enforcement methods and, in particular, on the competent authorities. The GDPR empowers individuals and relies on the judicial interpretation to define the boundaries of the rights provided by the Regulation. The same would have happened with the now-withdrawn AI Liability Directive Conversely, the DSA and DMA grant national authorities and the Commission proactive powers to demand technical explanations and comprehensive documentation, thus partly preventing the judicial intervention.

## 4 Four Interpretations of Explainability and Algorithmic Transparency in the AI Act: Entities, Roles, Processes

The level of complexity of explainability provisions in the AI Act is significantly higher than the other provisions in the EU legal framework. This is due to several reasons. In fact the AI Act:

1. Explicitly covers AI systems by giving a broad definition[16], thus increasing the range of possible applications that fall within the scope of application;
2. Provides rigorous definitions for the entities involved in the AI systems' life-cycle, thus increasing the range of entities subject to the regulation;
3. Mandates that compliance requirements are operationalised, this raising the necessity of providing concrete design measures for AI system [39].

Provisions on explainability apply to high risk systems[17] and sub-categories like "General Purpose AI Systems"[18] and "General Purpose AI systems with systemic risk"[19], if such systems fall within the category of high risk systems[20].

The AI Act contains four sets of explainability obligations, namely a) *Deployer-oriented*, b) *Compliance-oriented*, c) *Individual-empowering*, and d) *Oversight-oriented*.

---

[16] See the 2025 "Guidelines on the definition of an artificial intelligence system established by AI Act" by the EU Commission, available at https://digital-strategy.ec.europa.eu/en/library/commission-publishes-guidelines-ai-system-definition-facilitate-first-ai-acts-rules-application.

[17] According to Art. 6, High-risk AI systems include those used as safety components or stand-alone products requiring third-party assessment under EU laws, such as AI in medical devices or autonomous vehicles. Moreover, AI systems listed in Annex III, which include biometric identification, critical infrastructure management, and law enforcement applications, are also classified as high-risk due to their potential impact on health, safety, and fundamental rights. The European Commission will provide further guidelines by February 2026 and may adjust classifications based on emerging evidence while ensuring regulatory protection.

[18] Art. 3(66): "general-purpose AI system" means an AI system which is based on a general-purpose AI model and which has the capability to serve a variety of purposes, both for direct use as well as for integration in other AI systems.

[19] Art. 3(65): "systemic risk" means a risk that is specific to the high-impact capabilities of general-purpose AI models, having a significant impact on the Union market due to their reach, or due to actual or reasonably foreseeable negative effects on public health, safety, public security, fundamental rights, or the society as a whole, that can be propagated at scale across the value chain.

[20] See Recital. 84.

## 4.1 Deployer-Oriented Explainability

The first part of Art. 13(1) mandates that "High-risk AI systems shall be designed and developed in such a way as to ensure that their operation is sufficiently transparent to enable deployers to interpret a system's output and use it appropriately".

A literal interpretation of the provisions suggests some important elements. The core of the provisions consists of ensuring that AI system providers make the system - by design (*"design and developed"*) - *sufficiently transparent* to the deployers in a way that they can a) *interpret* the system's output and b) use it *appropriately*. This wording creates a *cascade* procedure, according to which the system should be transparent enough to allow the interpretation by the deployer and the proper use of the system. However, critically:

1. the wording of the requirement goes beyond a simple *understanding* and calls for the possibility of an *interpretation* by the deployer, thus implying some degree of active intelligibility of the system's output;
2. the appropriateness of the use is also unclear, especially on whether such quality use should be intended formally, i.e., in the sense of a procedural correctness, or substantially, i.e., in the sense of guaranteeing fair outputs. In practice, the interpretation has relevant consequences. For instance, one system could simply be designed to allow the interpretation of the output in a formal sense by allowing a general scrutiny of the correct functioning of the system. Alternatively, the system could be designed to provide guidelines on understanding whether the output was substantially fair or not.

To answer to this questions, it is necessary to evaluate the requirements of deployer-oriented explainability further specified in Art. 13(2), according to which "High-risk AI systems shall be accompanied by instructions for use in an appropriate digital format or otherwise that include concise, complete, correct, and clear information that is relevant, accessible and comprehensible to deployers". The requirements of conciseness, completeness, correctness, and clarity are not different from similar design provisions (e.g., Art. 13 GDPR). However, information provided to the deployer has to be:

- **Relevant**, i.e., non-redundant and appropriate for a correct use. The relevance of the information depends on the (yet unclear) meaning of proper use. If the proper use extends to substantially fair deployment, then instructions should also provide guidance on how to achieve non-harmful results other than a procedurally correct use.
- **Accessible**, i.e., able to be reached. While this requirement may seem a restatement of the conciseness, completeness, correctness, and clarity, it may create some practical limitations with regards of Intellectual Property Rights protection when some information is kept hidden from the deployer for reasons linked to copyright, patents or trade secrets.
- **Comprehensible**, i.e., easily understandable. This requirement suggests to take into account the target user-persona, which should ideally correspond

to ideal deployers. Identifying such entities might be complex in high-risk systems with multiple kinds of deployers.

Art. 13(3) lists the element that should be included in the instructions. With regards to explainability, some of these elements are particularly relevant *inter alia*:

1. The characteristics, capabilities, and performance limitations of the high-risk AI system, including the intended purpose, the level of accuracy, known or foreseeable risks to health, safety, or fundamental rights due to intended use or foreseeable misuse, technical capabilities to explain the AI system's output, performance regarding specific persons or groups targeted by the system, input data specifications and relevant details on training, validation, and testing datasets, where applicable, information enabling deployers to interpret and use the system's output appropriately.
2. Human oversight measures, including technical measures for deployers to interpret outputs.
3. Where relevant, mechanisms for deployers to collect, store, and interpret logs[21]

Given these elements, it may be argued that the interpretation of the system's output shall be guaranteed by transparency on its capabilities as emerge from elements which go beyond the output's logic and the embrace a larger context. In deployer-oriented explainability provisions, transparency about datasets, practices, limitations, risks, potential misuses provide guidance on how to interpret the output alongside technical measures. Therefore, the "appropriate use" that such provisions aim to guarantee shall be interpreted to be not only procedurally correct, but also substantially fair. While this finding seems aligned with the risk-based approach of the EU AI Act [29], it places significant burdens on the AI system provider. However, some criticalities remain, in particular in the balance between the relationship between explainability, IPRs, and personal data used for training when information has to be made available to AI systems deployers (Fig. 1).

### 4.2 Compliance-Oriented Explainability

The second part of Art. 13(1) provides that "An appropriate type and degree of transparency shall be ensured with a view to achieving compliance with the relevant obligations of the provider and deployer set out in Sect. 3."

This second goal of algorithmic transparency is clearly *compliance-oriented* and it aims at easing the process of making systems adequate to the AI Act and, in turn, minimise risks for fundamental rights and freedoms. This provision has to be read in conjunction with Art. 11 on Technical Documentation for High-Risk AI systems and Annex IV, which contains the minimum requirements to be included in the documentation.

---

[21] See also Art. 12 with regards to logging requirements.

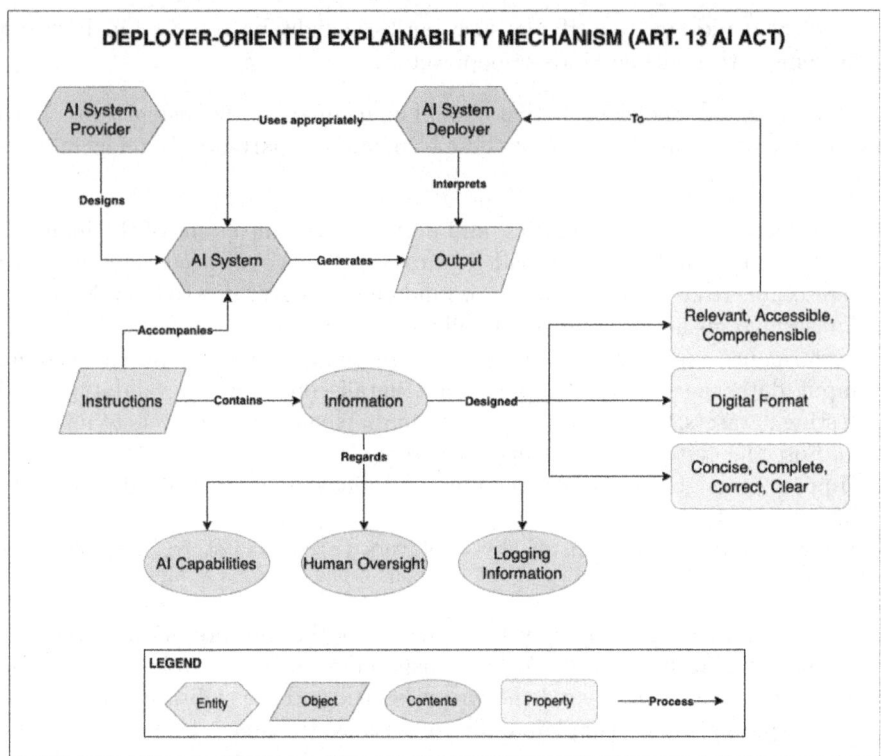

**Fig. 1.** Deployer-oriented explainability provisions under Art. 13 AI Act.

With regards to algorithmic explainability, some elements of the technical documentation are worth mentioning, including:

- the design specifications of the system, namely the general logic of the AI system and of the algorithms;
- the key design choices including the rationale and assumptions made, including with regard to persons or groups of persons in respect of who, the system is intended to be used;
- the main classification choices; what the system is designed to optimise for, and the relevance of the different parameters;
- the description of the expected output and output quality of the system;
- the decisions about any possible trade-off made regarding the technical solutions adopted to comply with the requirements for high risk-systems

The first paragraph stands out as the closest to the concept of a global explanation ("general logic") [9,13,31], but with reference to the system and the algorithms rather than their output. The remaining provisions provide with some context to the first requirement, in particular with regards to arbitrary choices made by the provider in the design of the system. The instructions for use for the deployer under Art. 13 shall also be included in the documentation.

## 4.3 Individual-Empowering Explainability

Finally, Art. 86 ("Right to explanation of individual decision-making") states that "Any affected person subject to a decision which is taken by the deployer on the basis of the output from a high-risk AI system [...] and which produces legal effects or similarly significantly affects that person in a way that they consider to have an adverse impact on their health, safety or fundamental rights shall have the right to obtain from the deployer clear" and meaningful explanations of the role of the AI system in the decision-making procedure and the main elements of the decision taken.

However, this provisions "shall not apply to the use of AI systems for which exceptions from, or restrictions to, the obligation under that paragraph follow from Union or national law in compliance with Union law" and it shall apply only if the right to explanation is not otherwise provided for under Union law.

This provision can be considered a form of *Individual-empowering Explainability* due to its close connection to its role in supporting claims against the automated decisions. The conditions from the right to apply consists of cumulative elements:

(a) A decision is taken by the deployer. If interpreted consistently with the *SHUFA* case, the concept of decision "implies an 'opinion' or 'position' on a certain situation. It must also have 'binding character' in order to distinguish it from mere recommendations', which in principle have no legal or factual consequences."[22].
(b) The decision is based on the output of an AI system. this goes beyond the remit of GDPR's automated decision-making and includes algorithmic-mediated decisions, i.e., those in which the AI system is used as a support tool for a human decision-maker [40]. Crucially, the wording "on the basis" is relatively unclear, especially when the deployer decides to take a decision rejecting the proposed output. Whether or not such decision is taken "on the basis" of an AI system's output is unclear;
(c) Such system is a classified as a high-risk according to the parameters set in Art. 6, which reference Annex III containing the list of presumed high-risks systems. However, it is crucial to note that if the system is "not materially influencing the outcome of decision making", it shall not be considered to fall in the high risk category. More specifically, such non-influence occurs any time AI system performs a narrow procedural task, improve the results of a human activity, does not replace the human assessment, or it is intended to perform a preparatory task for the purposes of an AI system listed in Annex III[23].
(d) The decision produces legal effects or similarly significantly affects an affected person. Importantly, the concept of "affected person" broadens the

---

[22] *SHUFA* case para 36.
[23] This last point seems also inconsistent with the *SHUFA* case, which has include the preparatory credit assessment - listed as a High-risk AI system in Annex III para 5(b) - in the remit of an automated-decision making.

scope of the right to obtain a meaningful explanation provided by the GDPR and discussed above. In fact, the AI Act right to explanation is not granted to the "data subject" by to "any affected person". While the same entity can play the same role in practice, nothing prevents a person to be affected by an AI-decision as a result of the processing of non-personal data.
(e) The person considers to have an adverse impact. The concept of "adverse impact" in the context of the right to explanation is not defined. The only plausible anchoring seems to be Recital 29, which clarifies that such adverse impacts can occur on "physical, psychological health or financial interests" when AI systems are used to "materially distorting human behaviour" by impairing "autonomy, decision-making and free choices".
(f) Such adverse impact is on health, safety or fundamental rights. Notably, the concept of "fundamental right" can be prone to different interpretations depending on the jurisdiction of the affected person. However, given the context of the AI Act, it is safe to assume that the scope of fundamental rights encompasses at least the ones enshrined in the European Charter of Fundamental Rights[24]. Recital 48 of the AI Act clarifies that "Art. 24 of the Charter and in the United Nations Convention on the Rights of the Child, further developed in the UNCRC General Comment No 25 as regards the digital environment" mandate specific rights for children, which are applicable in the context of AI-supported decisions[25] and "require consideration of the children's vulnerabilities and provision of such protection and care as necessary for their well-being"

The explanation should be "clear and meaningful". Following the reasoning of *SHUFA*, the meaningfulness should be related to the ability to challenge the decision with the remedies provided by the AI Act, in particular the Right to lodge a complaint with a market surveillance authority under Art. 85. As with similar provisions (e.g., Art. 13 of the GDPR), it is hard to identify an ideal explainee for creating template explanations. The explanation should comprise a) the role of the AI system in the decision-making procedure, and b) the main elements of the decision taken. Notably, none of these aspects comprises the logic of the algorithm, thus raising concerns regarding the effectiveness of the right to explanation.

Despite the broader subjective scope in comparison to the GDPR, the several exceptions and limitations of the objective scope of Art. 86 AI Act make the right to explanations and, consequently, the Individual-empowering explainability, applicable to a very limited amount of decision-making process. Crucially, the mechanisms that prevent the classification of high-risk systems for their procedural, non-invasive and non-decisive role in the decision-making process might give rise to controversies in practical applications like credit scoring.

---

[24] Noteworthly, Recital 48 AI Act stresses the relevance of the right to a high level of environmental protection.

[25] However, this seems also inconsistent with Recital 71 of the GDPR, which prohibits automated decision-making on minors, thus indirectly reinforcing the broader scope of Art. 86 AI Act in comparison to Art. 22 GDPR.

## 4.4 Oversight-Oriented Explainability

As noted by the AI Act when defining the adverse impacts, human autonomy comes into direct contact with the functional autonomy of ML algorithms deployed in decision-making processes, Annex IV(3) further specifies that the documentation should include "the human oversight measures needed in accordance with Article 14, including the technical measures put in place to facilitate the interpretation of the outputs of AI systems by the deployers".

Annex IV contains the technical documentation to be submitted to the authorities for compliance purposes. This is clarified by Article 11(1), according to which it "shall be drawn up in such a way as to demonstrate that the high-risk AI system complies with the requirements [...] and to provide national competent authorities [...] with the necessary information in a clear and comprehensive form to assess the compliance of the AI system with those requirements".

However, Article 13 clarifies that, among the information to be transmitted to the deployer, "human oversight measures [...], including the technical measures put in place to facilitate the interpretation of the outputs of the high-risk AI systems by the deployers" shall be included.

While these two documentation requirements fall within the *compliance-oriented* and the *deployer-oriented* explainability requirements, they also constitute a relevant specification that is required to "facilitate the interpretation" by the deployer and upon which there is a specific scrutiny by the competent authorities.

This additional form of explainability mentioned among documentation requirements shall be treated as an in-between category. Given its specific scope, it can be referred to as an *Oversight-oriented* form of an explainability.

The High Level Expert Group on AI was the first to articulate three models of human intervention on AI systems. It is interesting to note how the HLEG differentiates between human control [13, para 64] and human oversight [13, para 65]. While human control refers to human authority and responsibility over the AI system as a whole, whereas human oversight concerns human involvement in monitoring and supervising the system's operation.

Human control can occur through governance mechanisms that allow for a human-in-the-loop (HITL), human-on-the-loop (HOTL), or human-in-command (HIC) approach. The HITL approach envisions the possibility of human intervention in every decision-making cycle of the system, which in many cases, according to the HLEG, is neither feasible nor desirable due to the time and resource constraints that would be required for such constant and pervasive supervision. The HOTL approach, on the other hand, involves human intervention during the system's design cycle and monitoring of its operation, allowing for greater understanding and control of the AI system in use. Finally, the HIC approach goes beyond supervision and implies complete control over the AI system's activity as a whole. This includes monitoring and evaluating its overall effects at the economic, social, legal, and ethical levels, as well as the ability to make informed decisions about the system's use in specific situations.

Conceptual differences must therefore be identified between *functional* or *process* control and *substantive* or *product* control. While the former evaluates whether the system or product meets predefined requirements and specifications, the latter focuses on the quality and effectiveness of the system in achieving the desired objectives, not only from a strictly technical perspective but also from economic, social, and ethical standpoints.

Article 14 of the AI Act titled "Human Oversight" is applicable only to high-risk systems and requires the provider of the system to implement appropriate measures for effective supervision by natural persons during the system's use (para. 1). The provision specifically refers to human-machine interfaces, thus attributing a central role to the system's interactivity with the user [18]. These measures must enable two types of actions (para. 4): on the one hand, those aimed at understanding the capabilities, functioning, and limitations of the algorithm (letter a), and correctly interpreting the system's output (letter c); on the other hand, those for monitoring the algorithm's operation, i.e., deciding not to use the system (letter d) and intervening to stop its execution (letter e). The two groups of actions –control and oversight – converge in the goal of preventing excessive reliance on the AI system, also known as automation bias (letter b).

Considering these provisions, the HITL model seems only partially included, as there is no reference to "positive" intervention in every decision-making cycle (e.g., activation of the cycle), but the possibility of a "negative" intervention to stop the system during execution is preserved. The HIC model also seems to be set aside, at least in the text of this regulatory provision. Instead, the HOTL model seems applicable to the second set of actions assigned to the person responsible for oversight, i.e., the possibility to reject the output or interrupt execution. However, this possibility necessarily and ontologically requires that measures be in place to evaluate the system's capabilities, operational limits, and outputs. Otherwise, it would be impossible for the person responsible for oversight to consciously decide not to use the system or to interrupt its execution. According to this interpretation of the HOTL model, it is possible to see an extension of the model from the *operational-functional* level to the *epistemic-hermeneutic* level, in particular due to the wording such as "properly understand the relevant capacities and limitations of the high-risk AI system" (Art. 14(4)(a)) and "correctly interpret the high-risk AI system's output, taking into account, for example, the interpretation tools and methods available" (Art. 14(4)(c)).

Explainability provisions discussed earlier - *deployer-oriented, compliance-oriented, individual-empowering* - are directed, respectively, to deployers, competent authorities, and individuals subject to AI-supported decisions. An additional form of explainability is the one mandated by human-oversight provisions which are functional to "prevent or minimise the risks to health, safety or fundamental rights that may emerge when a high-risk AI system is used in accordance with its intended purpose or under conditions of reasonably foreseeable misuse" and target the natural persons using the system. They should be able to effectively monitor the functioning of the system and intervene in case risks to fundamental rights and freedoms become evident. Therefore, an *oversight-oriented* explainability emerges as the requirement needed to ensure a meaningful human control over the functioning of the system.

## 5 Algorithmic Knowability and the Explainability Cascade

Given this 4-way interpretation to explainability provisions, an unified theoretical framework seems necessary to discuss them from a higher level of abstraction, in particular to identify common traits and differences.

Therefore, in our interpretation of the AI Act:

- **Knowability** refers to the holistic framework encompassing different forms of explainability frameworks
- **Explainability** refers to disclosure of elements referred to the inner elements of the algorithms used in the AI system

The issue of algorithms and Knowability is not new to legal-informatics doctrine [31,32,36]. Starting from the issue of algorithmic explainability in the context of automated decisions and the GDPR [30], knowability redefines its contours by reiterating that other elements beyond the explainability of the systems are needed to explain the outputs of ML algorithms [36]. According to the proposed knowability approach, it is necessary to provide adequate information on the data processed, the computational approaches used, the logic employed by the algorithms, the derived and inferred data. To achieve full knowability, it is necessary to provide information on the system's representation of knowledge, in particular about intensional, extensional, and semantic structures - such as computational ontologies - to ensure reliability, authenticity, and adherence to human's representation of reality.

When considering explanations in the AI Act holistically according to the lens of Knowability, the framework is composed by the aforementioned obligations to share details regarding the algorithms used, occasionally with reference to the logic used in the generation of the output. Eventually, even the policy goals of promoting algorithmic explainability shall be considered holistically. When displayed together (Fig. 2), such policy goals become clear.

The overall goal of the Knowability framework appearing from the juxtaposition of each of explainability is to ensure the monitoring on the functioning of the algorithms from two sides: on the one hand, by allowing competent authorities to verify *ex ante* the level of compliance and scrutinise the functioning of the AI system; on the other hand, this allows competent authorities to provide redress to individuals who have suffered detriment and harm from the use of AI systems through the right to lodge a complain.

Logically, the provider is the main source of information with regards to explainability and the main target for the provisions. Its role is the core of the Knowability framework and its level of compliance is crucial in ensuring the "cascade" effect to the deployer, the user of the system, and the individuals subject to AI-assisted decisions.

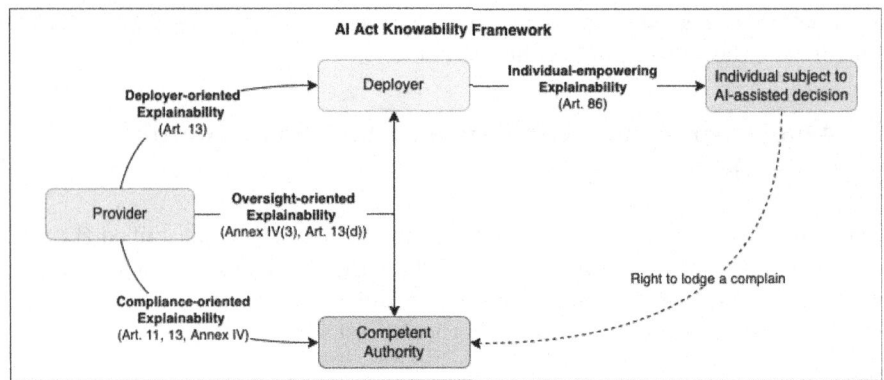

**Fig. 2.** Knowability Framework in the AI Act.

Knowability should encompass three levels of explainability. First, the explainability intended for the deployer and, conversely, the person responsible for human control and aimed guaranteeing human oversight; second, the explainability necessary for the institutions responsible for verifying the level of compliance of the high-risk system with the Act; third, the explainability of the role played by the machine in the decision-making process, the parameters, and the data used, functional to the individual subject to the algorithmic decision, aimed at the possibility of acting against it.

These three levels and the purposes associated to each of them present a crucial disadvantage for the Provider to calibrate the explanation according to the different types of recipients of the explanation[26]. The most immediate consequence of this threefold approach to explainability is the need to develop methodologies and criteria adequate to evaluate the quality and information that the system is able to provide, for example through measurements[27]. Naturally, the theoretical assumption of these criteria and methods is the measurability of the level of adequacy to ethical principles. Although this premise is not exempt from criticism[28], it can be seen as a "necessary evil" to make the measures pro-

---

[26] Not all theories of explanation, in fact, assume the recipient of the explanation as the centre of interest. See, on this point, the reflections of [46], p. 129 and Table 1, regarding the epistemic premises of explanation theories. The authors observe that "Ordinary Language Philosophy, Cognitive Science and Scientific Realism do not constrain explanations to causality, studying the Act of explaining as an iterative process involving broader forms of question answering. Cognitive Science and Scientific Realism are more focused on the effects that an explanation has on the explainee (the recipient of the explanation)".

[27] For instance, some studies on explainability metrics [43,46,52] and fairness [17].

[28] See the observations in [26], which notes "The basic idea across this strain of research is to make concrete progress in improving AI by breaking the often nebulous concept of 'ethics' down into measurable metrics and discrete goals".

vided for by the AI Act concretely applicable with regard to the explanation of algorithmically mediated decisions.

The direction traced by this interpretation supports the necessity of *contextual* explanations, i.e., appropriate to the complexity of the concrete situation in which the explanation takes place. In this sense, the regulatory direction seems to favour an evolution of the traditional distinction between *local* explanation, referring to the single decision-instance, and *global* explanation, referring to the entire functioning of the algorithm. The updated version of this bipartition could go in the direction of an explanation that is, depending on the case:

- **Enabling Explanation**, i.e., aimed at making the supervisor and, hopefully, the system user capable of choosing whether or not to use the system for their decision;
- **Certifying Explanation** or **Confirming Explanation**, i.e., aimed at verifying and, if necessary, aligning the algorithm with regulatory or judicial dictates, the state of the art, or industry standards; or
- **Actionable Explanation**, i.e., useful to the individual subject to the decision to act in defence of their rights or interests.

The consequence of the tripartition of the explanation and the respective recipients - the deployer and the person responsible for human control, the institutions responsible for compliance verification, or the individual subject to the AI-assisted decision - implies that a *one-size-fits-all* explanation is not legally compliant.

In fact, each recipient must be put in a position to know the algorithm differently from the others, as their epistemic purpose, i.e., the *ratio* underlying the explanation, is different from that of the other actors.

## 6 Implementing Knowability Through Standards and XAI Research

When an AI system adheres to established harmonized standards, it is automatically presumed to meet the corresponding requirements set forth in the AI Act (Art. 40(1). Despite its critiques [50], this presumption simplifies the conformity assessment process and it meant to reduce the administrative burden on providers and facilitating smoother market access [49]. Article 40 outlines the procedure for developing harmonized standards to ensure AI systems comply with the Act's requirements. The European Commission is tasked with issuing standardization requests to European standardization organizations, specifying that these standards must be clear, consistent, and aligned with existing sector-specific standards. In preparing these requests, the Commission consults the European Artificial Intelligence Board and relevant stakeholders, including an advisory forum, to ensure a comprehensive and inclusive standardization process.

This process must adhere to Regulation (EU) No 1025/2012, which governs European standardization. This regulation outlines the roles and responsibilities of the European Commission and European Standardization Organizations

(ESOs) in developing harmonized standards. The Commission issues standardization requests to ESOs, which then draft the required standards through a collaborative process involving various stakeholders. Once these standards are established, products or services conforming to them are presumed to comply with the corresponding EU legislation, facilitating market access and ensuring a high level of safety and performance across the Union.

The ISO/IEC JTC 1/SC 42 technical committee on Artificial Intelligence is currently working on developing several standards addressing various aspects of AI systems, including:

- SO/IEC 5259-1: Data quality for analytics and machine learning (ML) – Part 1: Overview, terminology, and examples.
- ISO/IEC 12792: Transparency taxonomy of AI systems.
- ISO/IEC 5392: Reference architecture of knowledge engineering.
- ISO/IEC 5469: Functional safety and AI systems.
- ISO/IEC TS 6254: Objectives and approaches for explainability of ML models and AI systems.

However, most of them remain undisclosed to the general public, hence limiting access to the operationalisation processes of the Act [50]. Moreover, as noted in a study supported by the JRC [45], the tools listed in ISO/IEC TS 6254 are not mandatory to ensure human oversight as described in Article 14 of the EU AI Act. The AI Act does not explicitly require specific solutions for explainability or interpretable/transparent-by-design models. Additionally, many of these technical solutions currently face limitations, including issues with reliability, robustness, lack of standardized evaluation frameworks, and an under-explored relationship between AI explanations and automation bias. Therefore, harmonized standards should be comprehensive and consider alternative, well-established, and effective solutions.

Room for implementation is certainly available to the XAI research community. Recent studies [21] discuss how emerging techniques also focus on documentation and transparency methods (such as [11,15], which are an essential pillar of the AI Act, may enhance trust, facilitate validation, and help users interpret model predictions. However, challenges arise with complex models and large datasets, as incomplete or outdated documentation can hinder understanding and lead to misinterpretation. Authors note that visualization [37] (e.g., in oversight-oriented and local individual-empowering explanations) enhances accessibility and transparency by simplifying complex information and revealing patterns, trends, and anomalies in a decision-making process. However, poorly designed or misleading visuals can lead to misinterpretation, as insights may vary depending on the viewer's perspective. Other scholars [47] support the view that one-size-fits-all explanations are not truly explanatory and propose alternative frameworks, such as Explanatory Artificial Intelligence (YAI) also discussing some empirical results. These findings should set a common ground for explainability standards. In fact, they point to the same direction of the proposed Knowability framework and align with the provisions in the AI Act.

However, its validation is highly dependent on the implementation of the AI Act. Importantly, metrics [46] will play a fundamental role in understanding to what extent AI models can be explained to different categories of explainees. If a Knowability approach would be used in the evaluation of an AI system (e.g., by a judge), a possible use could be the one of comparing the model under scrutiny with one deemed explainable.

## 7 Final Remarks

The intricate framework of explainability under the EU AI Act reflects a significant effort to balance technical feasibility, accountability, and ethical principles. By delineating four distinct (yet, interconnected) forms of explainability – Deployer-oriented, Compliance-oriented, Individual-empowering, and Oversight-oriented - the Act seeks to address the risks posed by high-risk AI systems in a multi-layered approach. This stratified approach brings the necessity of providing contextualised explanations depending on the needs and roles of a wide range of heterogeneous explainees: stakeholders, providers, deployers, regulators and affected individuals. The proposed concept of algorithmic Knowability emerges as the unifying lens capable of capturing the connections between different forms of explanations and ensure consistent understanding and application. Thanks to this approach, the interplay between these provisions reveals tensions and ambiguities that raise critical questions in the practical implementation, yet to be resolved in the standardisation stages.

A primary limitation lies in the operationalisation of abstract legal requirements into concrete technical and organizational practices. For instance, the requirement for "sufficient transparency" to enable deployers to appropriately interpret outputs remains unclear, thus leaving room for possible divergent interpretations. The tension between transparency obligations and IPRs further complicates this landscape, as providers may resist disclosing proprietary information critical for meaningful explanations. Similarly, the individual-empowering right to explanation under Art. 86 is constrained by exceptions and limitations that risk narrowing its applicability, also in the light of the recent jurisprudence of the European Court of Justice.

Further research is needed to address these gaps and refine the conceptual underpinnings of explainability. One avenue involves developing robust methodologies to evaluate the quality and adequacy of explanations across different stakeholder groups. For example, studies could explore how deployers interpret technical documentation or how affected individuals utilize explanations to challenge decisions, shedding light on the practical efficacy of Art. 86. Another critical area is the harmonization of standards for explainability metrics, particularly in light of ongoing ISO/IEC initiatives, to ensure alignment with the AI Act's risk-based approach. This area remains largely covered given the ongoing closed-door discussions in standardisation entities.

XAI research could also focus on creating explainability tools that reconcile transparency with IPR protection. Interdisciplinary studies examining the interplay between human oversight mechanisms and automation bias could inform the design of more effective Oversight-oriented explainability frameworks. These two often areas appear separated and interconnected research seems unavoidable in the light of the necessity to implement the Act.

**Acknowledgments.** This project is conducted with the support of the European Commission funds within ERC HyperModeLex. Grant agreement ID: 101055185.

# References

1. Adadi, A., Berrada, M.: Peeking inside the black-box: a survey on explainable artificial intelligence (XAI). IEEE Access **6**, 52138–52160 (2018)
2. AI4People: AI4People — Atomium (2018). https://www.eismd.eu/ai4people/
3. Boch, A., Hohma, E., Trauth, R.: Towards an accountability framework for AI: ethical and legal considerations. Institute for Ethics in AI, Technical University of Munich, Munich, Germany (2022)
4. Brkan, M.: Do algorithms rule the world? Algorithmic decision-making and data protection in the framework of the GDPR and beyond. Int. J. Law Inf. Technol. **27**(2), 91–121 (2019)
5. Cabral, T.: AI and the right to explanation: three legal bases under the GDPR. In: Hallinan, D., Leenes, R., De Hert, P. (eds.) Data Protection and Privacy: Data Protection and Artificial Intelligence, pp. 29–56. Hart Publishing (2021)
6. Corea, F., Fossa, F., Loreggia, A., Quintarelli, S., Sapienza, S.: A principle-based approach to AI: the case for European union and Italy. AI & Society **38**(2), 521–535 (2023)
7. Custers, B., Heijne, A.S.: The right of access in automated decision-making: the scope of article 15(1)(h) GDPR in theory and practice. Comput. Law Secur. Rev. **46** (2022)
8. Cuypers, A., Nisevic, M., De Bruyne, J.: Explainable AI: can the ai act and the GDPR go out for a date? Available at SSRN 5014179 (2024)
9. Doshi-Velez, F., Kim, B.: Towards a rigorous science of interpretable machine learning. arXiv preprint arXiv:1702.08608 (2017)
10. Edwards, L., Veale, M.: Slave to the algorithm? Why a 'right to an explanation' is probably not the remedy you are looking for. Duke Law Technol. Rev. **16**, 18–84 (2017)
11. Felzmann, H., Fosch-Villaronga, E., Lutz, C., Tamò-Larrieux, A.: Towards transparency by design for artificial intelligence. Sci. Eng. Ethics **26**(6), 3333–3361 (2020)
12. Guidotti, R., Monreale, A., Ruggieri, S., Turini, F., Giannotti, F., Pedreschi, D.: A survey of methods for explaining black box models. ACM Comput. Surv. **51**(5), 93:1–93:42 (2018)
13. HLEG, A.: Ethics guidelines for trustworthy AI. Ethics Guidelines for Trustworthy AI (2019)
14. Jobin, A., Ienca, M., Vayena, E.: The global landscape of ai ethics guidelines. Nat. Mach. Intell. **1**, 389–399 (2019)
15. Kale, A., Nguyen, T., Harris, F.C., Li, C., Zhang, J., Ma, X.: Provenance documentation to enable explainable and trustworthy AI: a literature review. Data Intell. **5**(1), 139–162 (2023)

16. Kaminski, M., Malgieri, G.: Algorithmic impact assessments under the GDPR: producing multi-layered explanations. Int. Data Priv. Law **11**(2), 125–144 (2021)
17. Koumeri, L.K., Legast, M., Yousefi, Y., Vanhoof, K., Legay, A., Schommer, C.: Compatibility of fairness metrics with EU non-discrimination laws: Demographic parity & conditional demographic disparity. arXiv preprint arXiv:2306.08394 (2023)
18. Liao, Q.V., Gruen, D., Miller, S.: Questioning the AI: informing design practices for explainable AI user experiences. In: Proceedings of the 2020 CHI Conference on Human Factors in Computing Systems, pp. 1–15 (2020)
19. Lipton, Z.C.: The mythos of model interpretability. arXiv preprint arXiv:1606.03490 (2016)
20. Malgieri, G., Comandé, G.: Why a right to legibility of automated decision-making exists in the general data protection regulation. Int. Data Priv. Law **7**(4), 243–265 (2017)
21. Mathew, D.E., Ebem, D.U., Ikegwu, A.C., Ukeoma, P.E., Dibiaezue, N.F.: Recent emerging techniques in explainable artificial intelligence to enhance the interpretable and understanding of ai models for human. Neural Process. Lett. **57**(1), 16 (2025)
22. Mittelstadt, B., Allo, P., Taddeo, M., Wachter, S., Floridi, L.: The ethics of algorithms: Mapping the debate. Big Data Soc. **3**(2), 2053951716679679 (2016)
23. Mittelstadt, B., Floridi, L.: The ethics of big data: current and foreseeable issues in biomedical contexts. Sci. Eng. Ethics **22**(2), 303–341 (2016)
24. Montavon, G., Samek, W., Müller, K.R.: Methods for interpreting and understanding deep neural networks. arXiv preprint arXiv:1806.10758 (2018)
25. Morley, J., Floridi, L., Kinsey, L., Elhalal, A.: From what to how: an initial review of publicly available ai ethics tools, methods and research to translate principles into practices. Sci. Eng. Ethics, 1–28 (2019)
26. Munn, L.: The uselessness of ai ethics. AI Ethics **3**(3), 869–877 (2023)
27. Nannini, L., Alonso-Moral, J.M., Catalá, A., Lama, M., Barro, S.: Operationalizing explainable ai in the EU regulatory ecosystem. IEEE Intell. Syst. (2024)
28. Naudts, L., Dewitte, P., Ausloos, J.: Meaningful transparency through data rights: a multidimensional analysis. In: Research Handbook on EU Data Protection Law, pp. 530–571. Elgar (2022)
29. Orwat, C., Bareis, J., Folberth, A., Jahnel, J., Wadephul, C.: Normative challenges of risk regulation of artificial intelligence. NanoEthics **18**(2), 11 (2024)
30. Pagallo, U.: Algoritmi e conoscibilità. Rivista di filosofia del diritto **9**(1), 93–106 (2020)
31. Palmirani, M.: Big data e conoscenza. Rivista di filosofia del diritto **9**(1), 73–92 (2020)
32. Palmirani, M., Sapienza, S.: Big data, explanations and knowability. Ragion Pratica **2**, 349–364 (2021)
33. Pasquale, F.: The Black Box Society. Harvard University Press (2015)
34. Pavlidis, G.: Unlocking the black box: analysing the EU artificial intelligence act's framework for explainability in AI. Law Innov. Technol. **16**(1), 293–308 (2024)
35. Ribeiro, M.T., Singh, S., Guestrin, C.: "why should i trust you?" Explaining the predictions of any classifier. In: Proceedings of the 22nd ACM SIGKDD International Conference on Knowledge Discovery and Data Mining, pp. 1135–1144. ACM (2016)

36. Rodríguez-Doncel, V., Palmirani, M., Araszkiewicz, M., Casanovas, P., Pagallo, U., Sartor, G.: Introduction: a hybrid regulatory framework and technical architecture for a human-centered and explainable AI. In: International Workshop on AI Approaches to the Complexity of Legal Systems, pp. 1–11. Springer (2018)
37. Samek, W., Wiegand, T., Müller, K.R.: Explainable artificial intelligence: understanding, visualizing and interpreting deep learning models. arXiv preprint arXiv:1708.08296 (2017)
38. Samek, W., Wiegand, T., Müller, K.R.: Explainable artificial intelligence: understanding, visualizing and interpreting deep learning models. arXiv preprint arXiv:1708.08296 (2017)
39. Sapienza, S., et al.: La regolazione dell'ia generativa e il ruolo preventivo delle norme e del design. PARADOXA **17**(4), 109–123 (2023)
40. Sapienza, S., et al.: Decisioni Algoritmiche e Diritto. Giuffré (2024)
41. Sartor, G.: L'informatica giuridica e le tecnologie dell'informazione: Corso di informatica giuridica, vol. 2. G Giappichelli Editore (2016)
42. Selbst, A., Powles, J.: "meaningful information" and the right to explanation. In: Conference on Fairness, Accountability and Transparency, pp. 48–48. PMLR (2018)
43. Seth, P., Sankarapu, V.K.: Bridging the gap in XAI-why reliable metrics matter for explainability and compliance. arXiv preprint arXiv:2502.04695 (2025)
44. Santoni de Sio, F., Van den Hoven, J.: Meaningful human control over autonomous systems: a philosophical account. Front. Rob. AI **5**, 15 (2018)
45. Soler Garrido, J., et al.: Analysis of the preliminary ai standardisation work plan in support of the ai act. Publications Office of the European Union, Luxembourg (2023)
46. Sovrano, F., Sapienza, S., Palmirani, M., Vitali, F.: Metrics, explainability and the european ai act proposal. Journal **5**(1), 126–138 (2022)
47. Sovrano, F., Vitali, F.: Explanatory artificial intelligence (YAI): human-centered explanations of explainable AI and complex data. Data Min. Knowl. Disc. **38**(5), 3141–3168 (2024)
48. Sovrano, F., Vitali, F., Palmirani, M.: Making things explainable vs explaining: requirements and challenges under the GDPR. In: International Workshop on AI Approaches to the Complexity of Legal Systems, pp. 169–182. Springer (2018)
49. Tartaro, A.: Regulating by standards: current progress and main challenges in the standardisation of artificial intelligence in support of the ai act. Eur. J. Privacy L. Tech., 147 (2023)
50. Veale, M., Zuiderveen Borgesius, F.: Demystifying the draft EU artificial intelligence act—analysing the good, the bad, and the unclear elements of the proposed approach. Comput. Law Rev. Int. **22**(4), 97–112 (2021)
51. Wachter, S., Mittelstadt, B., Floridi, L.: Why a right to explanation of automated decision-making does not exist in the general data protection regulation. Int. Data Priv. Law **7**(2), 76–99 (2017)
52. Zhou, J., Gandomi, A.H., Chen, F., Holzinger, A.: Evaluating the quality of machine learning explanations: a survey on methods and metrics. Electronics **10**(5), 593 (2021)

**Open Access** This chapter is licensed under the terms of the Creative Commons Attribution 4.0 International License (http://creativecommons.org/licenses/by/4.0/), which permits use, sharing, adaptation, distribution and reproduction in any medium or format, as long as you give appropriate credit to the original author(s) and the source, provide a link to the Creative Commons license and indicate if changes were made.

The images or other third party material in this chapter are included in the chapter's Creative Commons license, unless indicated otherwise in a credit line to the material. If material is not included in the chapter's Creative Commons license and your intended use is not permitted by statutory regulation or exceeds the permitted use, you will need to obtain permission directly from the copyright holder.

# Predicting Satisfaction of Counterfactual Explanations from Human Ratings of Explanatory Qualities

Marharyta Domnich[1](✉)[iD], Rasmus Moorits Veski[1,2], Julius Välja[1], Kadi Tulver[1][iD], and Raul Vicente[1][iD]

[1] Institute of Computer Science, University of Tartu, Tartu, Estonia
marharyta.domnich@ut.ee
[2] École Polytechnique Fédérale de Lausanne, Lausanne, Switzerland

**Abstract.** Counterfactual explanations are a widely used approach in Explainable AI, offering actionable insights into decision-making by illustrating how small changes to input data can lead to different outcomes. Despite their importance, evaluating the quality of counterfactual explanations remains an open problem. Traditional quantitative metrics, such as sparsity or proximity, fail to fully account for human preferences in explanations, while user studies are insightful but not scalable. Moreover, relying only on a single overall satisfaction rating does not lead to a nuanced understanding of why certain explanations are effective or not. To address this, we analyze a dataset of counterfactual explanations that were evaluated by 206 human participants, who rated not only overall satisfaction but also seven explanatory criteria: feasibility, coherence, complexity, understandability, completeness, fairness, and trust. Modeling overall satisfaction as a function of these criteria, we find that feasibility (the actionability of suggested changes) and trust (the belief that the changes would lead to the desired outcome) consistently stand out as the strongest predictors of user satisfaction, though completeness also emerges as a meaningful contributor. Crucially, even excluding feasibility and trust, other metrics explain 58% of the variance, highlighting the importance of additional explanatory qualities. Complexity appears independent, suggesting more detailed explanations do not necessarily reduce satisfaction. Strong metric correlations imply a latent structure in how users judge quality, and demographic background (e.g., medical or ML expertise) significantly affects ranking patterns, highlighting the need for context-specific designs. These insights directly inform the development of improved counterfactual algorithms, highlighting the need to tailor explanatory qualities (completeness, consistency, fairness, complexity) to diverse user expertise and specific domain contexts.

**Keywords:** Counterfactual Explanations · Explainable AI · Human-Centric Evaluation · Explanatory Virtues

## 1 Introduction

The increasing scale and complexity of AI models has spurred development of post-hoc explainability techniques in Explainable AI (XAI). Among these, counterfactual explanations have rapidly emerged as a practical method to show how minimal alterations to an input can change the model's output [22]. For instance, Keane's famous example [16] illustrates an automated paper review system stating, "if your paper had more novelty, it would have been accepted to this conference". Such explanations are inherently contrastive and actionable, guiding users towards potential modifications to achieve a desired result. Furthermore, they align closely with human reasoning, where counterfactual alternatives are naturally considered [17].

Despite the promise of counterfactual explanations, evaluating their effectiveness for users remains an open challenge. Traditional XAI evaluations have relied heavily on proxy metrics and intuition rather than direct user feedback [16]. Automated metrics, such as validity (whether the counterfactual flips the model's prediction), proximity (the degree of change from the original input), sparsity (the number of altered features), plausibility or data fidelity (the realism of the counterfactual), and diversity (the availability of distinct alternatives) [14,15], are useful for algorithmic comparisons but "often fall short in capturing the human perspective" [7]. An explanation that scores well on proximity and sparsity, for example, might still confuse a user or leave out information the user considers important as "excellent computational explanations may not be good psychological explanations." [16].

User studies, which are considered the gold standard for evaluating explanation quality, remain surprisingly scarce in the XAI literature. Keane (2021) reported that only about 21% of 100 counterfactual explanation studies incorporated human evaluations, and Adadi and Berrada (2018) stated that the "neglect of user studies is the original sin" of the field [1].

Direct user feedback can reveal qualities like clarity or usefulness that automated metrics overlook. However, user studies are costly and difficult to scale: recruiting a large number of participants (often domain experts) for evaluating explanations is time-consuming and expensive. Additionally, when user studies are conducted, their findings are difficult to generalize, as user preferences and mental models vary widely and what counts as a "good" explanation can differ from person to person. Recently, researchers have begun exploring large language models (LLMs) to mimic human evaluations as a way to scale these studies [6,7]. Although offering valuable complementary insights, LLM-based assessments cannot yet fully capture the nuanced sentiment provided by direct human feedback.

However, simply asking users to provide an overall satisfaction score makes it difficult to pinpoint which underlying factors drive that satisfaction, where *understanding what contributes to users' overall satisfaction and how to model it through other measurable explanatory qualities is the main direction of this paper.* In our prior study, we developed a benchmark dataset of 30 diverse counterfactual scenarios (spanning different domains and qualities), each evaluated by

206 human participants on eight evaluation metrics [9]. These metrics included Overall Satisfaction as a summary measure, alongside specific explanatory qualities such as Feasibility, Consistency, Completeness, Trust, Fairness, Complexity, and Understandability. In this study, we extend that line of research by shifting the focus to modeling overall user satisfaction based on the underlying explanatory metrics. Our goal is to understand and predict how satisfied a user will be with a counterfactual explanation given its scores on various quality dimensions. We explicitly investigate the relationship between the individual metric ratings and the overall satisfaction judgment. To guide this investigation, we pose the following research questions:

- Can overall satisfaction be accurately predicted using these seven evaluation metrics (Feasibility, Trust, Consistency, Completeness, etc.)?
- Among the chosen metrics, which ones are truly essential for predicting overall satisfaction, and to what extent can we simplify (i.e., omit certain metrics) while retaining high predictive accuracy?

## 2 Related Works

Counterfactual explanations resonate with natural human cognitive processes, as individuals often engage in "what if" scenarios to understand events around them. Cognitive science research indicates that people often consider alternatives to reality to understand causal relationships or to learn from past actions. Byrne's studies, for example, highlight that humans process counterfactual conditionals differently from direct causal statements, which can lead to unique inferences and sometimes suppress certain logical outcomes [5]. While counterfactual explanations align with natural human reasoning patterns, making them intuitively appealing, they can also introduce cognitive complexities that may not align with the designers' intentions. In later works, Byrne argues that the interpretation of causal versus counterfactual explanations can lead to fundamentally different mental models of the same situation, sometimes enhancing understanding but not necessarily increasing satisfaction [4]. For example, Warren et al. observed that while counterfactual explanations provided users with a richer mental model of decision-making processes in AI systems, they were not always preferred over simpler explanations [24]. *This discrepancy highlights a critical gap between what enhances performance or understanding and what users find most satisfying or intuitive.*

Recent studies further report mixed effects: while counterfactual explanations can enhance objective comprehension, they do not always boost subjective satisfaction [21]

For example, Van der Waa et al. observed that although counterfactual explanations led to higher satisfaction and trust, they did not significantly improve prediction accuracy compared to simpler approaches [20]. The opposite effect is demonstrated in Wang and Yin's user study, where counterfactual explanations improved users' factual comprehension of AI decisions (measured by prediction accuracy on test cases), but did not reliably increase users' subjective confidence or trust in the model [23]. This reflects a gap between performance and preference: an explanation type that best supports accuracy of understanding may not be the one that users find most satisfying or intuitive.

Another insight from cognitive science is that humans do not always favor the simplest explanation. While Occam's razor holds in science, people sometimes equate a "good" explanation with a more comprehensive account of causes. Zemla et al., for instance, found that for everyday phenomena, people preferred an explanation that combined multiple contributing factors (e.g. policy, demographics, and behavior in explaining a social trend) over an explanation that cites a single cause [25]. Participants tended to feel that an event was not fully explained until all salient causes were mentioned, even if the added causes were not actually factual. This suggests that a minimal counterfactual (changing just one factor) might appear to users as too shallow. The effect is more evident in specialized domains like medicine, where medical doctors preferred explanations with the biggest number of causes [3]. In contrast, XAI algorithmic approaches often prioritize sparsity (altering only one or few features) to generate counterfactuals [8,18]. *Therefore, explanations that make sense to humans may require going beyond algorithmic intuition, ensuring that the format and the content of counterfactual explanations truly support human decisions.*

Supporting this perspective, VanNostrand noted that while users appreciated understanding the decision-making process, their overall satisfaction was heavily influenced by the explanation's alignment with an intuitive sense of fairness and their perceived ability to act on the provided information [21]. Similarly, Förster et al. reported that coherent counterfactual explanations were associated with higher overall satisfaction [11]. *This highlights that user overall satisfaction of explanation is more complex than mere comprehension of the model's operation.* In our prior work [7], we compiled a list of cognitive biases informed by the literature and observed a positive correlation with satisfaction for seven evaluation metrics: feasibility, consistency, completeness, trust, understandability, fairness, and complexity. Building on these insights, our current work aims to analyze how Overall Satisfaction can be predicted from these underlying explanatory qualities. Notably, we have not identified any studies that analyze the intercomparison of these metrics in predicting overall satisfaction, which highlights a gap in the existing literature.

## 3 Human Evaluation of Counterfactual Explanations

We base our study on the CounterEval dataset [9], a recent human evaluation benchmark for counterfactual explanation evaluation. This dataset consists of 30 diverse counterfactual scenarios evaluated by 206 human respondents across 8 key metrics: Overall Satisfaction, Feasibility, Consistency, Completeness, Trust, Fairness, Complexity, and Understandability [9], resulting in a total of 6180 individual ratings. Each participant rated each scenario on these metrics, providing a data cube of scores (participants × scenarios × metrics). All metrics are measured on a Likert-type scale (from 1 to 6 for all metrics, except Complexity which is measured from -2 to 2), allowing comparative quantitative analysis. The scenarios are based on actual outputs from counterfactual frameworks on tabular datasets like Adult and the Pima Indian Diabetes, commonly used in counterfactual explanation algorithms evaluations [19]. In some cases, the outputs were modified to intentionally span a wider range in explanatory quality metrics, while in others, features were tailored to improve clarity for human evaluators after pilot study (more details in [9]). Based on exclusion criteria, 10 participants were removed who failed on three or more of these criteria: attention check, response time, average understandability score, response clustering and three indicator questions.

### 3.1 Exploratory Analysis

Using this dataset, our methodology combines statistical analysis and machine learning to identify which explanation metrics drive overall satisfaction and to build predictive models of satisfaction.

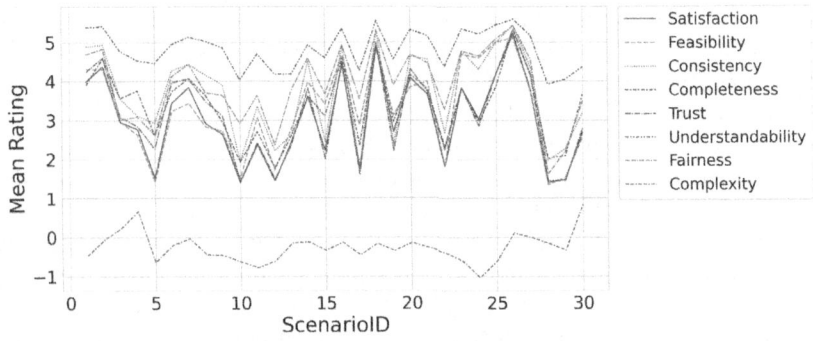

**Fig. 1.** Mean ratings of each metric (Overall Satisfaction, Feasibility, Consistency, Completeness, Trust, Understandability, Fairness, and Complexity) across all 30 scenarios. The y-axis shows the average participant rating per scenario, with Complexity on a -2 to +2 scale (0 = ideal complexity) and the other metrics on a 16 scale.

Previous work [7] reported strong correlations for all metrics. To investigate this further, the line plot (Fig. 1) shows the average rating of each metric for each of the 30 scenarios. Most metrics track relatively close together, indicating that scenarios viewed favorably (or unfavorably) on one metric often receive similar evaluations on others. Complexity (gray dashed line) follows a separate -2 to +2 range, showing that some scenarios were considered slightly "too simple" or "too complex", while many scenarios clustered near the "desired" complexity level 0.

Figure 2 shows how each metric distribution corresponds to three Overall Satisfaction categories (Low: 12, Medium: 34, High: 56). *Feasibility, Consistency, Completeness,* and *Trust* (all on a 16 scale) exhibit clear alignment with

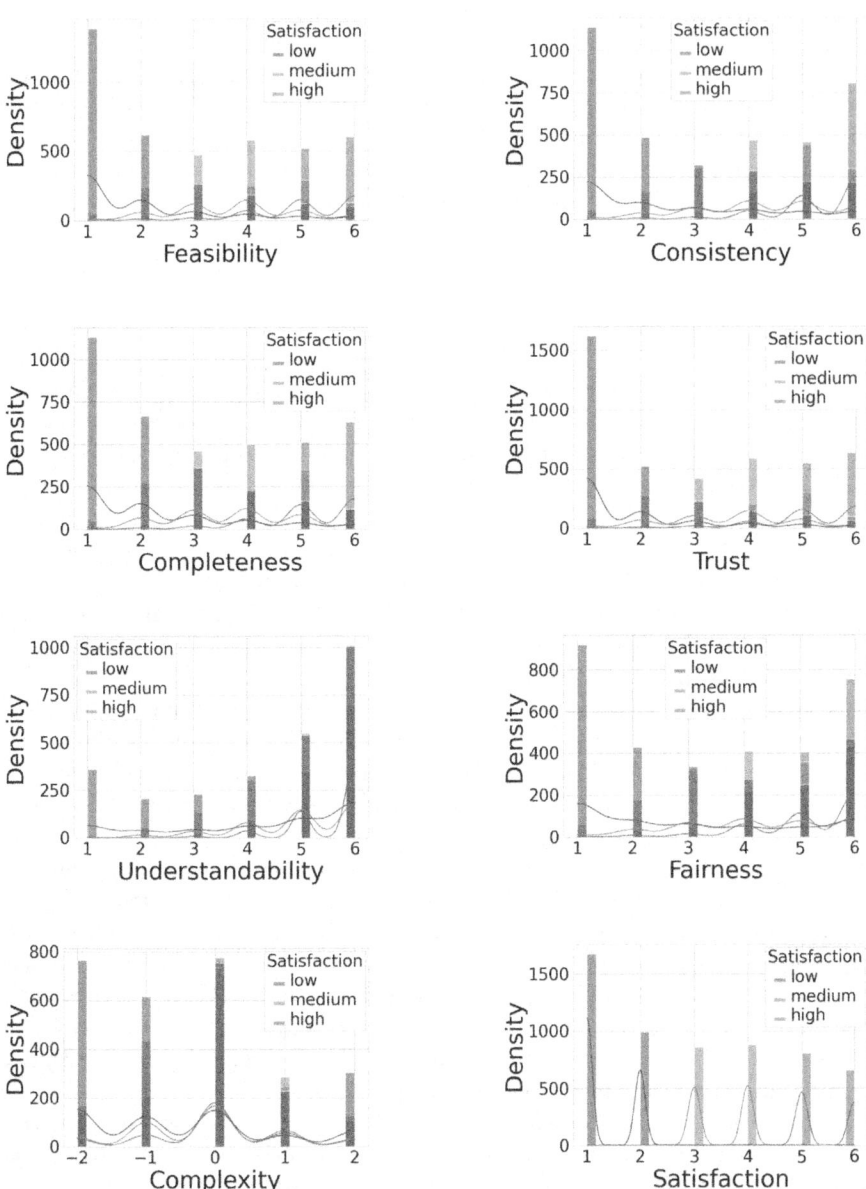

**Fig. 2. Per-metric distributions grouped by Satisfaction level (low, medium, high).** Each histogram is color-coded by the participant's Satisfaction category, illustrating how Feasibility, Consistency, Fairness, Completeness, Trust, Understandability, and Complexity vary for each class. The final subplot depicts the overall Satisfaction distribution itself.

satisfaction categories: low satisfaction aligns with ratings of 12, high satisfaction with 56, and medium levels in between. *Fairness* follows a similar pattern, though it exhibits a few cases of disagreement. For Complexity (−2 to +2, with $0 = desired$), high-satisfaction scenarios cluster near 0, whereas low-satisfaction scenarios are more frequent at the extremes (−2 = "too simple" or +2 = "too complex"). Understandability was defined as "I feel like I understood the phrasing of the explanation well," and was primarily meant to filter out poor English comprehension. While most participants rated Understandability relatively high, there is still some spread possibly reflecting different interpretations of "understandable".

## 3.2 Bi-clustering Analysis

To further explore latent patterns of agreement among participants and scenarios, we performed a bi-clustering (simultaneously clustering of rows = participants, and columns = scenarios) using each metric's rating matrix (Fig. 3). We applied Spectral Co-clustering to identify clear and distinct groups of participants (who systematically differ in their evaluation patterns) and explanatory metrics (rated similarly by certain groups of participants). We varied the number of clusters from 2 to 6, choosing the best $k$ to minimize the Frobenius norm (reconstruction error). Several metrics, such as Feasibility, Completeness, and Fairness, favor a 5-cluster, while others (e.g., Consistency, Trust, Complexity, Satisfaction) align better with 4.

Vertically, distinct scenario clusters emerge, indicating groups of scenarios that receive systematically higher or lower scores for a given metric. In the *Satisfaction* subplot, for instance, some columns (scenarios) are predominantly blue, indicating many participants deem them highly satisfactory, while others lean more red, reflecting lower satisfaction across most evaluators. *Feasibility* and *Trust* similarly show strong column-based patterns, suggesting consensus among participants on which scenarios appear feasible or trustworthy.

Horizontally, we see participant clusters signifying "generally high raters", "generally low raters", or more moderate profiles. *Complexity*, in particular, exhibits horizontal stripes, implying that participants differ in perceiving an explanation's complexity, some appear to rate nearly all scenarios as highly complex, while others rate them as simpler. We further refine this intuition by checking evaluators' background data.

For *Consistency* and *Completeness*, the presence of red columns suggests that when a scenario is perceived as incomplete or inconsistent, most participants converge on low scores, while for other scenarios some graders remain more conservative, with only a few having clear vertical blue line. A similar dynamic arises for *Fairness*: highly biased scenarios provoke universal low ratings, while more ambiguous cases show greater disagreement. Meanwhile, *Understandability* ratings are high, indicating that participants typically grasp the definition of "understandable", yet a few row deviate, suggesting different interpretation.

It is worth noting that all scenarios were presented in random order, so these vertical clusters do not reflect any intended sequence or grouping in the survey.

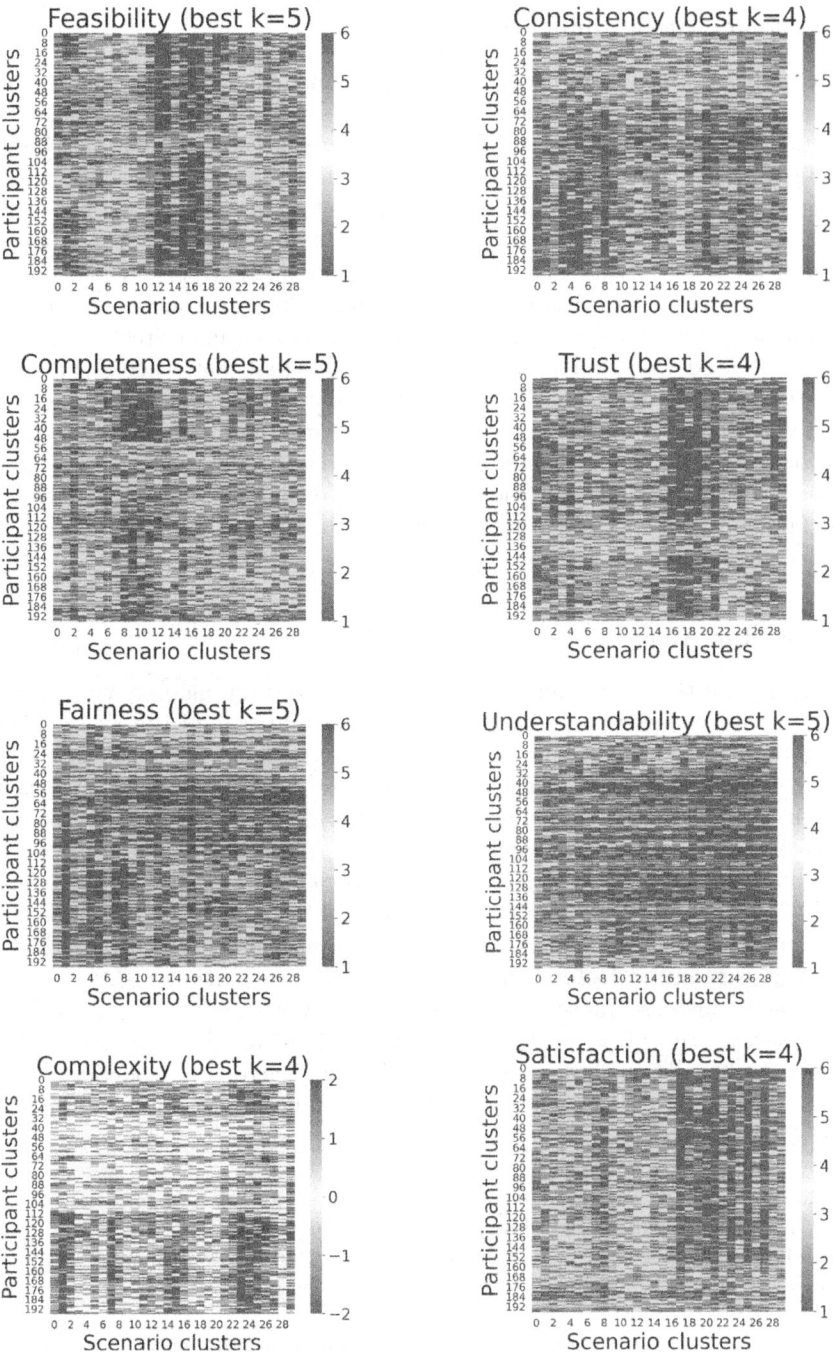

**Fig. 3. Bi-clustering results for all metrics.** Each heatmap shows participants (rows) and scenarios (columns) reordered into $k$ co-clusters, where $k$ is selected by minimizing the reconstruction error.

## 3.3 Demographic Influences

To see whether respondent backgrounds explained these cluster memberships, we analyzed demographic and experience-related data (e.g., age, education, ML experience). As shown in Fig. 4, **Machine Learning Experience** and **Medical Background** emerged as the most relevant demographic factors, both showing statistically significant differences across the clusters ($p = 0.0299$ and $p = 0.0162$, respectively). This indicates that domain experts often require more thorough justification before trusting computational outputs [2], particularly in healthcare context [12]. It is also evident that people with Machine Learning knowledge tend to evaluate model reasoning more critically, displaying under-reliance [10]. On the other hand, Age, Education did not differ significantly across bi-clusters ($p > 0.05$). Likewise, Metric Understanding showed no major effect, suggesting that while participants' perceived familiarity with the metrics varied (indicating confidence in their understanding), their overall ranking behavior remained aligned. Lastly, no sufficient evidence emerged to link Counterfactual Explanation familiarity to specific rating patterns, likely due to the small proportion of participants reporting such experience.

## 3.4 Factor Analysis

To investigate the underlying structure among the seven metrics, we concluded an exploratory factor analysis. We used Bartlett's test and the Kaiser-Meyer-Olkin (KMO) measure of sampling adequacy to verify if factor analysis is appropriate. The Bartlett test was highly significant ($\chi^2 = 28150.28$, $p < 0.001$), indicating that the correlation matrix is not an identity matrix, while the KMO value of 0.893 indicating sampling adequacy. A scree plot of the eigenvalues suggested three factors, as there was a clear "elbow" after the third component. Table 1 shows the rotated (varimax) factor loadings for the three-factor solution. The first factor alone accounts for approximately 40.5% of the total variance, the second factor brings the cumulative variance to 56.9%, and the third factor increases it to 65.9%. Evidently, several metrics (e.g., Feasibility, Consistency, Trust) load strongly on the first factor, whereas Understandability loads most heavily on the second factor. The third factor has moderate loadings (up to 0.5719), indicating a separate, though smaller, source of variance among the items.

**Table 1.** Varimax-rotated loadings of the first three extracted factors from a factor analysis on the seven metrics (Feasibility, Consistency, Completeness, Trust, Understandability, Fairness, and Complexity). The final column shows the cumulative percentage of variance explained by the corresponding factor.

| Factor | Feasib. | Consist. | Complet. | Trust  | Understand. | Fairness | Complex. | Cumul. var. |
|--------|---------|----------|----------|--------|-------------|----------|----------|-------------|
| 0      | 0.7805  | 0.7697   | 0.6273   | 0.7896 | 0.3721      | 0.6884   | 0.0319   | 40.5%       |
| 1      | 0.1543  | 0.2696   | 0.2820   | 0.1846 | 0.9200      | 0.2965   | −0.0612  | 56.9%       |
| 2      | 0.1018  | 0.1628   | 0.5719   | 0.3332 | −0.1031     | −0.0688  | 0.3778   | 65.9%       |

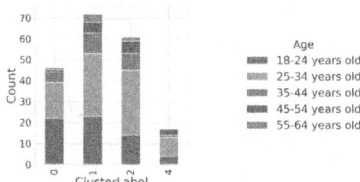

(a) **Age vs. ClusterLabel.** *Chi-square=14.005, p=0.3004, dof=12. Age distribution does not differ significantly across clusters.*

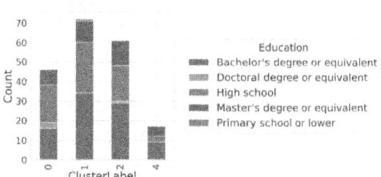

(b) **Education vs. ClusterLabel.** *Chi-square=13.860, p=0.3098, dof=12. No significant difference in education across clusters.*

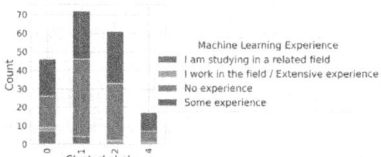

(c) **MLExperience vs. ClusterLabel.** *Chi-square=18.490, p=0.0299, dof=9. Significant difference in ML experience across clusters.*

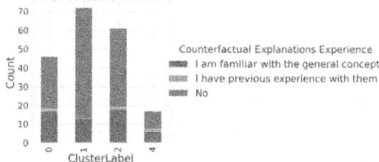

(d) **CFEExperience vs. ClusterLabel.** *Chi-square=9.899, p=0.1290, dof=6. Not significant for counterfactual frameworks experience.*

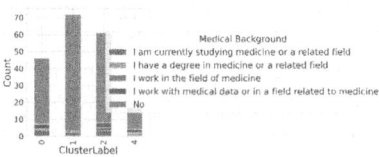

(e) **MedicalBackground vs. ClusterLabel.** *Chi-square=24.728, p=0.0162, dof=12. Significantly different across clusters.*

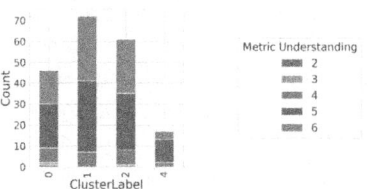

(f) **MetricUnderstanding vs. ClusterLabel.** *Chi-square=8.700, p=0.7283, dof=12. No significant difference in how well participants understood metrics.*

**Fig. 4.** Distribution of evaluators' background (Age, Education, Machine Learning Experience, etc.) within the four discovered clusters. Chi-square tests (with p-values and degrees of freedom) assess whether the distributions differ significantly among clusters. We find that Machine Learning Experience ($p=0.0299$) and Medical Background ($p=0.0162$) differ significantly across clusters, whereas Age, Education, Counterfactual Explanations Experience, and Metric Understanding do not show significant differences.

## 4 Predicting Overall Satisfaction with Machine Learning Methods

We employed a series of supervised machine learning methods to model overall satisfaction. Satisfaction was modeled as both regression (treating it as continuous outcome) and classification (categorizing it into low, medium, high). The dataset cube consists of 30 scenarios and 196 evaluators, each providing ratings on seven explanatory metrics plus an overall satisfaction score, resulting in 5,880 total instances. Notably, demographic variables were not used as predictive features. We then applied two data-splitting strategies:

1. *Random Split*: We randomly partitioned the 5,880 instances into 80% training set and a 20% test set, then performed 5-fold cross-validation on the training subset.
2. *Scenario-Based Split*: We assigned entire scenarios to either training or test sets, with 24 scenarios (24×196 = 4,704 instances) for training and 6 scenarios (6×196 = 1,176 instances) for testing. This ensures the model is evaluated on completely unseen scenarios.

### 4.1 Predicting Overall Satisfaction as Regression Problem

**Estimating Coefficients with OLS Regression.** We then used ordinary least squares (OLS) regression to model Overall Satisfaction directly. Table 2 presents the estimated coefficients, standard errors, and confidence intervals. The intercept is small but significant (0.1766), forming a baseline for Satisfaction when all metrics are zero. Overall, the OLS model achieves a high $R^2 = 0.757 \pm 0.008$, meaning these metrics collectively explain a substantial portion of participants' Satisfaction ratings variation. *Feasibility* ($\beta \approx 0.358$) and *Trust* ($\beta \approx 0.362$) bring the largest positive effects: a 1-point increase in either metric (while holding all other metrics constant) corresponds to approximately a 0.36-point increase in Satisfaction. *Completeness* also shows a substantial positive coefficient ($\beta = 0.170; p < 0.001$), while *Consistency* ($\beta = 0.067$) and *Complexity* ($\beta = 0.080$) have somewhat smaller (but still significant) positive effects.

By contrast, *Understandability* ($\beta \approx -0.069$) exhibits a negative sign, suggesting that when other metrics are accounted for, higher Understandability ratings slightly reduce predicted Satisfaction. Given the correlated nature of these metrics, the coefficient reflects the complex overlaps between Understandability and the other factors. Finally, *Fairness* is borderline significant ($p \approx 0.056$, $\beta = 0.017$), with a 95% CI that narrowly includes zero, suggesting it adds limited explanatory power once Feasibility, Trust, and the other predictors are included.

**Omitting Feasibility and Trust.** To assess the relative importance of *Feasibility* and *Trust*, we reran the training after removing them from the predictor set. This reduced model's performance dropped to $R^2 = 0.580 \pm 0.081$, underscoring Feasibility and Trust's critical role in explaining Satisfaction. In the reduced specification, *Completeness* ($\beta \approx 0.413$) becomes the strongest driver, followed

**Table 2.** OLS regression results modeling Overall Satisfaction. Reported are the coefficient estimates, standard errors, t-values, p-values, and 95% confidence intervals for each predictor.

| Predictor | Coefficient | Std. Error | t-value | p-value | 95% CI |
|---|---|---|---|---|---|
| Intercept | 0.1766 | 0.040 | 4.410 | 0.000 | [0.098, 0.255] |
| Feasibility | **0.3581** | 0.010 | 36.563 | 0.000 | [0.339, 0.377] |
| Consistency | 0.0665 | 0.010 | 6.347 | 0.000 | [0.046, 0.087] |
| Completeness | 0.1702 | 0.011 | 16.144 | 0.000 | [0.150, 0.191] |
| Trust | **0.3618** | 0.011 | 31.796 | 0.000 | [0.340, 0.384] |
| Understandability | −0.0690 | 0.010 | −7.036 | 0.000 | [−0.088, −0.050] |
| Fairness | 0.0170 | 0.009 | 1.908 | 0.056 | [−0.000, 0.034] |
| Complexity | 0.0802 | 0.010 | 7.658 | 0.000 | [0.060, 0.101] |

by *Consistency* ($\beta \approx 0.322$), *Fairness* ($\beta \approx 0.182$), *Complexity* ($\beta \approx 0.096$), and *Understandability* remains negative ($\beta \approx -0.082$) with all coefficients being significant. Nonetheless, even without Feasibility and Trust the model still captures around 58% of Satisfaction's variance, meaning that other factors (especially Completeness) also play a notable part. In practical terms, while enhancing Feasibility and building Trust in such explanations are the most important for maximizing user satisfaction, addressing Completeness, Consistency, and Complexity can further refine users' overall satisfaction.

**Comparing Regression Models.** We next compared Linear Regression (OLS), Decision Tree Regressor, and Random Forest Regressor under both data-splitting strategies using 5-fold cross-validation. Table 3 shows that *Linear Regression* achieved RMSE $\approx 0.890 \pm 0.017$ (random split) and $0.891 \pm 0.071$ (scenario-based), with $R^2 \approx 0.73$. Decision Tree slightly improves upon OLS in the random split (RMSE $\approx 0.859 \pm 0.030, R^2 \approx 0.755 \pm 0.016$) but performs worse in the scenario-based split (RMSE $\approx 1.128, R^2 \approx 0.549$). This indicates that the Decision Tree may overfit specific scenarios. *Random Forest* achieves similar results to Linear Regression on both splits.

**Table 3.** Comparison of regression model performances in predicting satisfaction using 5-fold cross-validation for two data-splitting strategies: random split and scenario-based split. Reported metrics are RMSE and $R^2$, presented as mean ± standard deviation.

| Model | Random Split | | Scenario-Based Split | |
|---|---|---|---|---|
| | RMSE | $R^2$ | RMSE | $R^2$ |
| Linear Regression | 0.890 ± 0.017 | 0.737 ± 0.013 | 0.891 ± 0.071 | 0.721 ± 0.070 |
| Decision Tree | 0.859 ± 0.030 | 0.755 ± 0.016 | 1.128 ± 0.104 | 0.549 ± 0.131 |
| Random Forest | 0.888 ± 0.020 | 0.738 ± 0.015 | 0.890 ± 0.069 | 0.721 ± 0.071 |

These results suggest that Trust and Feasibility stand out as the main predictors of Satisfaction in all models. The Decision Tree may capture slight non-linearities and interaction effects, achieving marginally better RMSE and $R^2$ than Linear Regression, while the Random Forest performance is comparable to linear regression on average, it lacks inherent interpretability. To clarify feature contributions in the Random Forest model, we applied SHAP (SHapley Additive exPlanations) analysis. SHAP values quantify the contribution of each feature to the predicted outcome. Figure 5apresents the global SHAP summary plot, confirming that Feasibility and Trust show the highest average impacts on predicted satisfaction, reinforcing findings from previous analyses.

To illustrate how specific explanatory metrics influence individual predictions, we examined an instance (Scenario 1): *"You are a 31-year-old divorced woman with high-school education, working 20 h per week, earning below average salary. To earn above average, you must increase your education from high-school to Bachelor's degree."* Fig. 5bprovides the SHAP waterfall plot for this scenario.

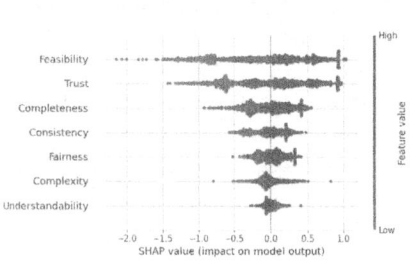
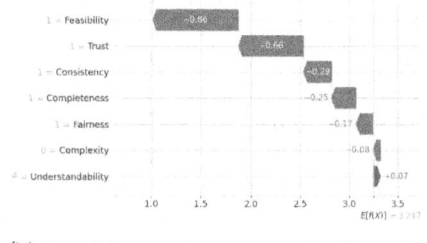

(a) Global feature importance. Features are ranked by their mean absolute SHAP values, indicating their average impact on the predicted satisfaction.

(b) Local feature importance for Scenario 1. Red bars represent positive contributions increasing the predicted satisfaction, while blue bars indicate negative contributions.

**Fig. 5.** SHAP analysis illustrating global and local feature importances for the Random Forest Regression model.

### 4.2 Predicting Overall Satisfaction as a Classification Problem

To investigate discrete satisfaction levels, we converted Overall Satisfaction into three classes: Low (1–2), Medium (3–4), High (5–6) with (2666, 1747, and 1467 instances, respectively). This led to a multi-class classification task. We applied Logistic Regression, Decision Tree, and Random Forest and similarly evaluated with 5-fold cross-validation under both random and scenario-based splits. To balance class distribution we used SMOTE-TOMEK resampling. Figure 6 shows the confusion matrices for each classifier. Logistic Regression (Fig. 6a) tends to misclassify borderline cases of Medium vs. High, though it shows relatively fewer errors distinguishing Low from Medium. Decision Tree (Fig. 6b) overall has more correct classifications on the diagonal, particularly in distinguishing High from Medium, reflecting its higher accuracy in Table 4. However, it can still confuse Medium with Low in certain scenarios. Random Forest (Fig. 6c) exhibits a pattern similar to Logistic Regression, with Medium and High sometimes misclassified. Importantly, the Decision Tree allows for a transparent visualization of how metrics form top-level splits when predicting satisfaction (Apendix A. Figure 8). The tree classifies user satisfaction (low, medium, high) by first splitting on *Trust* and *Feasibility*, with deeper nodes considering metrics like *Completeness* or *Complexity*.

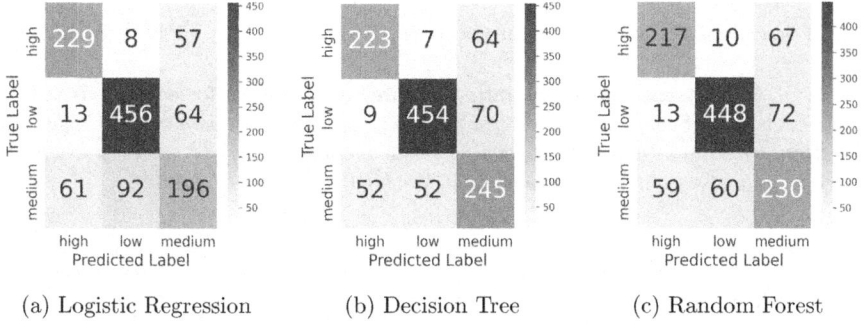

(a) Logistic Regression  (b) Decision Tree  (c) Random Forest

**Fig. 6.** Confusion matrices for the three models (Random Split).

Table 4 summarizes the mean accuracy and F1-scores (Macro) across 5 cross validation folds with the Decision Tree outperforming in the random split (highest accuracy/F1 of ≈ 0.78/0.77) but being more sensitive to new scenarios (dropping to ≈ 0.70/0.68). Logistic Regression and Random Forest demonstrate comparable performance, around 0.75–0.76 accuracy, and they also more robust when tested for new, previously unseen explanations.

**Table 4.** Comparison of classification model performances in predicting satisfaction classes using 5-fold cross-validation for two data-splitting strategies: random split and scenario-based split. Mean ± standard deviation are shown for both Accuracy and Macro F1.

| Model | Random Split | | Scenario-Based Split | |
|---|---|---|---|---|
| | Accuracy | F1-score | Accuracy | F1-score |
| Logistic Regression | 0.757 ± 0.008 | 0.742 ± 0.006 | 0.754 ± 0.043 | 0.734 ± 0.029 |
| Decision Tree | 0.781 ± 0.009 | 0.769 ± 0.009 | 0.704 ± 0.047 | 0.680 ± 0.036 |
| Random Forest | 0.756 ± 0.006 | 0.739 ± 0.004 | 0.756 ± 0.046 | 0.735 ± 0.034 |

Similarly, we conducted SHAP analysis of local feature contributions for different satisfaction classes (low, medium, high) for Scenario 1 using the Random

Forest classification model (Fig. 7). Consistent with previous findings, Feasibility and Trust are the dominant predictors across all classes. However, other metrics such as Completeness, Fairness and Consistency are decisive factors differentiating between low and medium satisfaction classes.

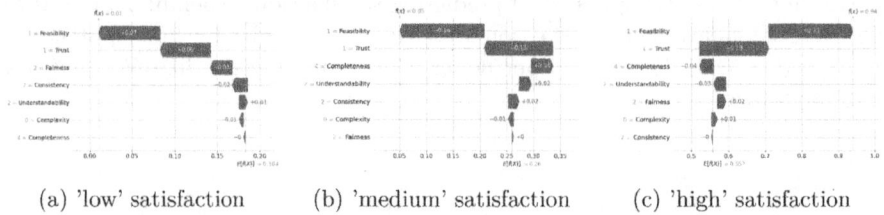

(a) 'low' satisfaction     (b) 'medium' satisfaction     (c) 'high' satisfaction

**Fig. 7.** SHAP waterfall plots illustrating feature contributions for each predicted satisfaction class for Scenario 1: *"You are a 31-year-old divorced woman with high-school education, working 20 h per week, earning below average salary. To earn above average, you must increase your education from high-school to Bachelor's degree."*.

Of particular note, the scenario-based split shows higher variation during cross-validation, reflecting the diverse complexity of different counterfactual scenarios. Because certain scenarios target specific biases and present greater predictive challenges than others, some scenario subsets are inherently easier or harder to model, resulting in more variable performance. This performance drop highlights the challenge of generalizing predictions to entirely new scenarios, underscoring the importance of robust scenario diversity in training data.

## 5 Discussion

This study set out to model overall satisfaction with counterfactual explanations by examining user ratings on multiple explanatory metrics (Feasibility, Consistency, Completeness, Trust, Fairness, Complexity, and Understandability). The results consistently highlight Feasibility and Trust as the most influential factors in predicting user satisfaction. *Feasibility*, defined as the degree to which recommended changes are realistic and actionable, and *Trust*, understood as the belief that the suggested changes would bring about the intended outcome, both stood out through large coefficients in linear regression and prominent splits in decision trees. Their dominance confirms longstanding user-centric observations in explainable AI research: participants place high value on seeing counterfactuals that they can readily implement and that they can credibly believe will lead to the desired effect. Importantly, *Completeness* also emerged as a contributor in some of our analyses, though it did not overshadow the two primary drivers of satisfaction, suggesting that in certain domains users favor more detailed explanations if those explanations are simultaneously feasible and trustworthy. At the same time, our analyses show that even when Feasibility and Trust are omitted, the remaining metrics (Completeness, Consistency, Fairness, Complexity,

Understandability) still capture around 58% of the variance in satisfaction. This suggests that *other explanatory qualities also remain relevant in shaping overall satisfaction, though Feasibility and Trust are clearly the most influential.*

One central methodological insight is that *asking users about multiple explanatory metrics, rather than only about overall satisfaction, brings more nuanced understanding of why an explanation succeeds or fails.* Our correlation and factor analyses revealed strong overlap among many of these metrics–Feasibility, Trust, Completeness, Consistency, and Fairness loaded together on a primary factor, while Complexity appeared partly independent. It indicates that participants generally perceive a holistic notion of a "good" or "poor" explanation. This pattern implies that, for many users, evaluating a counterfactual is not a matter of distinctly disentangling fairness, consistency, or completeness, but rather forming a more integrated sense of overall quality. At the same time, Complexity appears to be at least partly independent, which aligns with the idea that *an explanation can be somewhat complex yet still garner high satisfaction, provided it remains actionable and believable.*

By comparison, Fairness did not emerge as driver of satisfaction in this dataset. Still, every scenario with low fairness also ranked with low Satisfaction, suggesting that fairness's impact may have been absorbed by correlated metrics. In real applications, fairness can be critical for decisions involving potential discrimination (e.g., loan approvals, medical treatments), while understandability might become vital if the system outputs specialized or highly technical explanations [13]. Future studies should examine user groups that are more sensitive to these specific metrics. One of the findings was that human evaluation is significantly influenced by user backgrounds (medical professionals and machine learning experts). Individuals with a strong clinical focus might value feasibility and clarity differently than those trained in algorithmic reasoning, while ML experts could emphasize completeness or consistency more strongly [2,10,12].

In practical terms, these findings underscore several implications for counterfactual explanation algorithms design. First, the emphasis on Feasibility suggests that XAI systems should ensure their generated counterfactuals appear realistic to end users, for instance by embedding domain constraints or avoiding implausible feature changes. Second, the prominence of Trust implies that systems should provide evidence of the proposed modifications' effects (e.g., model confidence or analogy to past successes). Third, while Completeness is secondary, there may be domains where users do want more detailed explanations covering multiple angles of the model's logic.

**Limitations and Future Work.** The 30 scenarios in our dataset, while varied, do not represent the full spectrum of real-world counterfactuals, especially regarding fairness or domain-specific constraints. Nevertheless, it is important to note that average time of evaluating those scenarios is 42 min. Future work should aim at gathering similar dataset but for specialized application and with different levels of expert knowledge to generalize modeling satisfaction question. The participant group of roughly 200 respondents is fairly large for a user study, yet it may not reflect domain experts or culturally varied perspectives, more specialized user group might value fairness or completeness more strongly [13]. There are inherent limitations in online studies, such as the inability to ensure that participants completed the questionnaire without distractions. Also, we did not systematically vary fairness or clarity, their roles might be underrepresented here. Future work should examine more diverse or extreme variations in these factors to see if they become decisive under particular conditions.

Despite these limitations, our findings provide a tangible contribution to understanding overall satisfaction through the lens of key explanatory qualities. We show that focusing on a handful of core metrics, especially feasibility, trustworthiness, and completeness, goes a long way toward predicting user contentment with counterfactual explanations. At the same time, complexity appears relatively independent, suggesting that adding details or allowing higher complexity does not need to undermine satisfaction if the explanation remains realistically implementable and fosters confidence in its correctness. This insight can guide the dilemma of explaining 'less is more' versus 'fully detailed is better'. Future research could validate these findings in other domains (e.g., medical, financial) and with specialized user cohorts (e.g., clinicians, ML engineers). By refining how we measure and optimize these explanatory metrics for diverse audiences, we can further advance the practical and ethical utility of explainable AI systems.

**Acknowledgments.** This research was supported by Estonian Research Council Grants PRG1604 and PUTJD1252, the European Union's Horizon 2020 Research and Innovation Programme under Grant Agreement No. 952060 (Trust AI), Foundations of Secure Digital Solutions and Artificial Intelligence TEM-TA119, the Estonian Centre of Excellence in Artificial Intelligence (EXAI), funded by the Estonian Ministry of Education and Research grant TK213.

**Disclosure of Interests.** The authors have no competing interests to declare that are relevant to the content of this article.

**Code Availability.** The implementation of the models and analyses presented in this paper is publicly available at CounterEval GitHub repository.

# A Appendix

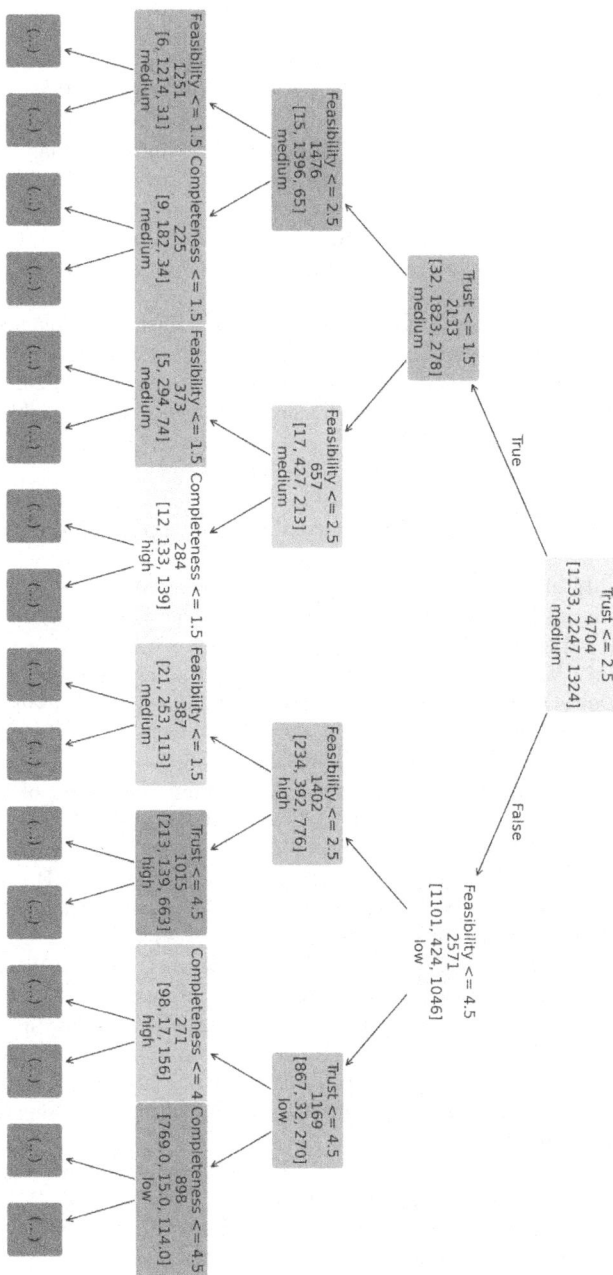

**Fig. 8. Decision Tree Trained on Scenario-Based Split.** This tree classifies user satisfaction (low, medium, high) with seven explanation metrics. Node colors indicate the predicted class, and thresholds (e.g., Trust ≤ 2.5) reflect how the model discriminates different satisfaction levels.

# References

1. Adadi, A., Berrada, M.: Peeking inside the black-box: a survey on explainable artificial intelligence (XAI). IEEE Access **6**, 52138–52160 (2018)
2. Bansal, G., Nushi, B., Kamar, E., Lasecki, W.S., Weld, D.S., Horvitz, E.: Beyond accuracy: the role of mental models in human-AI team performance. In: Proceedings of the AAAI Con Human Computation and Crowdsourcing, vol. 7, pp. 2–11 (2019)
3. Barbu, E., Domnich, M., Vicente, R., Sakkas, N., Morim, A.: Exploring commonalities in explanation frameworks: a multi-domain survey analysis. arXiv preprint arXiv:2405.11958 (2024)
4. Byrne, R.M.J.: Counterfactuals in explainable artificial intelligence (XAI): evidence from human reasoning. In: Proceedings of the Twenty-Eighth International Joint Conference on Artificial Intelligence, IJCAI-19, pp. 6276–6282. International Joint Conferences on Artificial Intelligence Organization (2019). https://doi.org/10.24963/ijcai.2019/876
5. Byrne, R.M.: The rational imagination (2005)
6. De Bona, F.B., Dominici, G., Miller, T., Langheinrich, M., Gjoreski, M.: Evaluating explanations through LLMs: beyond traditional user studies. arXiv preprint arXiv:2410.17781 (2024)
7. Domnich, M., et al.: Towards unifying evaluation of counterfactual explanations: leveraging large language models for human-centric assessments. arXiv preprint arXiv:2410.21131 (2024)
8. Domnich, M., Vicente, R.: Enhancing counterfactual explanation search with diffusion distance and directional coherence. In: Longo, L., Lapuschkin, S., Seifert, C. (eds.) Explainable Artif. Intell., pp. 60–84. Springer Nature Switzerland, Cham (2024). https://doi.org/10.1007/978-3-031-63800-8_4
9. Domnich, M., et al.: Countereval: towards unifying evaluation of counterfactual explanations (2024). https://doi.org/10.57967/hf/3824
10. Ehsan, U., et al.: The who in XAI: how ai background shapes perceptions of AI explanations. In: Proceedings of the 2024 CHI Conference on Human Factors in Computing Systems. CHI '24, Association for Computing Machinery, New York, NY, USA (2024). https://doi.org/10.1145/3613904.3642474
11. Förster, M., Hühn, P., Klier, M., Kluge, K.: Capturing users' reality: a novel approach to generate coherent counterfactual explanations. In: 54th Hawaii International Conference on System Sciences, HICSS 2021, Kauai, Hawaii, USA, January 5, 2021, pp. 1–10. ScholarSpace (2021). http://hdl.handle.net/10125/70767
12. Ghassemi, M., Oakden-Rayner, L., Beam, A.L.: The false hope of current approaches to explainable artificial intelligence in health care. Lancet Digit. Health **3**(11), e745–e750 (2021)
13. Goethals, S., Martens, D., Calders, T.: PreCoF: counterfactual explanations for fairness. Mach. Learn. **113**(5), 3111–3142 (2024)
14. Guidotti, R.: Counterfactual explanations and how to find them: literature review and benchmarking. Data Min. Knowl. Disc. (2022)
15. Karimi, A.H., Barthe, G., Schölkopf, B., Valera, I.: A survey of algorithmic recourse: contrastive explanations and consequential recommendations. ACM Comput. Surv. **55**(5), 1–29 (2022)
16. Keane, M.T., Kenny, E.M., Delaney, E., Smyth, B.: If only we had better counterfactual explanations: five key deficits to rectify in the evaluation of counterfactual XAI techniques (2021). https://arxiv.org/abs/2103.01035

17. Miller, T.: Explanation in artificial intelligence: insights from the social sciences. Artif. Intell. **267**, 1–38 (2019)
18. Mothilal, R.K., Sharma, A., Tan, C.: Explaining machine learning classifiers through diverse counterfactual explanations. In: Proceedings of the 2020 Conference on Fairness, Accountability, and Transparency, pp. 607–617. FAT* '20, Association for Computing Machinery (2020). https://doi.org/10.1145/3351095.3372850, event-place: Barcelona, Spain
19. Rasouli, P., Chieh, Yu., I.: Care: Coherent actionable recourse based on sound counterfactual explanations. Int. J. Data Sci. Anal. **17**(1), 13–38 (2024)
20. Van Looveren, A., Klaise, J.: Interpretable counterfactual explanations guided by prototypes. In: Joint European Conference on Machine Learning and Knowledge Discovery in Databases, pp. 650–665. Springer (2021)
21. VanNostrand, P.M., Hofmann, D.M., Ma, L., Rundensteiner, E.A.: Actionable recourse for automated decisions: examining the effects of counterfactual explanation type and presentation on lay user understanding. In: Proceedings of the 2024 ACM Conference on Fairness, Accountability, and Transparency, pp. 1682–1700 (2024)
22. Wachter, S., Mittelstadt, B., Russell, C.: Counterfactual explanations without opening the black box: automated decisions and the GDPR. Harv. JL Tech. **31**, 841 (2017)
23. Wang, X., Yin, M.: Are explanations helpful? A comparative study of the effects of explanations in AI-assisted decision-making. In: Proceedings of the 26th International Conference on Intelligent User Interfaces, pp. 318–328 (2021)
24. Warren, G., Byrne, R.M.J., Keane, M.T.: Categorical and continuous features in counterfactual explanations of ai systems. In: Proceedings of the 28th International Conference on Intelligent User Interfaces, pp. 171–187. IUI '23, Association for Computing Machinery, New York, NY, USA (2023). https://doi.org/10.1145/3581641.3584090
25. Zemla, J.C., Sloman, S., Bechlivanidis, C., Lagnado, D.A.: Evaluating everyday explanations. Psychon. Bull. Rev. **24**, 1488–1500 (2017)

**Open Access** This chapter is licensed under the terms of the Creative Commons Attribution 4.0 International License (http://creativecommons.org/licenses/by/4.0/), which permits use, sharing, adaptation, distribution and reproduction in any medium or format, as long as you give appropriate credit to the original author(s) and the source, provide a link to the Creative Commons license and indicate if changes were made.

The images or other third party material in this chapter are included in the chapter's Creative Commons license, unless indicated otherwise in a credit line to the material. If material is not included in the chapter's Creative Commons license and your intended use is not permitted by statutory regulation or exceeds the permitted use, you will need to obtain permission directly from the copyright holder.

# Explainability, Privacy, and Fairness in Trustworthy AI

# Too Sure for Trust. The Paradoxical Effect of Calibrated Confidence in Case of Uncalibrated Trust in Hybrid Decision Making

Federico Cabitza[1,2](✉) , Caterina Fregosi[1] , and Lucia Vicente[1]

[1] Università degli Studi di Milano-Bicocca, Milan, Italy
federico.cabitza@unimib.it
[2] IRCCS Ospedale Galeazzi-Sant'Ambrogio, Milan, Italy

**Abstract.** Advances in artificial intelligence (AI) have shown significant potential in supporting decision-making in high-stakes domains such as medical diagnostics, where accuracy and reliability are crucial. In this context, presenting AI-generated confidence levels has been proposed as a strategy to promote appropriate reliance on AI systems, assuming both perfect confidence calibration of the AI and optimally calibrated trust of human decision-makers. However, the impact of providing users with indications of AI confidence on decision-making remains underexplored when these ideal conditions are not met. This study examines how different ways of presenting AI support—through recommendations alone, recommendations with calibrated confidence scores, and recommendations with explicit correctness feedback (as an ideally extreme baseline condition)—influence diagnostic accuracy, reliance, and cognitive biases in medical students. A total of 222 participants completed an image-based diagnostic task with a misaligned mental model of AI behavior (a kind of 'theory of mind'), reflecting a knowledge mismatch induced by instructing the participants to consider two diagnostic criteria while ignoring a third one that the AI system correctly applied. Results showed that, unsurprisingly, providing correctness feedback led to the most significant improvement in appropriate reliance, outperforming both the confidence and advice-only conditions, and proving to be an optimal strategy to reduce knowledge mismatches between humans and machines. More interestingly, we found that providing confidence levels can result in significantly worse reliance and more conservatism bias than not providing them when such a knowledge mismatch exists. Therefore, when human and AI knowledge cannot be assumed to be aligned, confidence levels should be presented with caution, even if their calibration is assured. This study provides insights into the design of hybrid intelligence systems that enhance diagnostic decision-making and supports the integration of AI into critical domains such as healthcare.

**Keywords:** Human-AI Collaboration · Appropriate Reliance · Hybrid Intelligence · Medical Decision-Making

## 1 Introduction

It is evident, though rarely discussed, that for AI systems to fulfill the promise of enhancing the efficiency and accuracy of decision-making, they must influence human decisions. In a hybrid, human-AI collaborative approach, this means that the AI-based decision support system should confirm correct human decisions and help users prevent incorrect ones. However, this also requires decision-makers to distinguish between useful and misleading AI support ensuring appropriate reliance [4,8,26]. That is, appropriate reliance refers to the human behavior of rejecting incorrect AI advice while adopting what is correct.

For reliance to be appropriate—recognizing that neither humans nor machines are infallible—it is crucial that users can discern when AI is accurate and when it is not. This fundamental requirement underlies the popularity of eXplainable AI (XAI) methods: these, rather than merely making AI systems more explainable (if possible), should be aimed at enhancing transparency and interpretability [5], enabling users to assess their reliability and trustworthiness. Among XAI methods, displaying confidence levels is widely considered a simple yet effective means of calibrating trust [1,13,33] and fostering appropriate reliance [2]. Recent findings suggest that individuals' self-confidence in a given task is influenced by and aligns with the AI's previously observed confidence levels during collaboration [17].

For confidence levels to positively influence decision-making, two conditions must be met. First, the AI's confidence estimates must be well-calibrated. For instance, Bansal et al. [3] showed that providing well-calibrated confidence information allows people to discern when the AI system is likely making an error, thus improving decision outcomes. Second, users must have a well-calibrated trust in the AI [20][1]. The first condition is often unverified [21], despite substantial research indicating that machine learning models - particularly artificial neural networks [12] - are frequently miscalibrated [22,29]. Even if we assume that a model's confidence estimates are calibrated (an assumption that is rarely tested and often false [29]), users may still misplace their trust in the system.

Our research question is: What is the effect of providing confidence levels (compared to not providing them) and feedback about AI accuracy on i) reliance behaviors [4]—; ii) on the associated cognitive biases - operationalized in terms of odds ratios [4]—, and iii) on overall decision accuracy, *when human and AI knowledge are misaligned*? In addressing this question, we will demonstrate that providing confidence levels, even calibrated ones, can result in low appropriate reliance and higher cognitive biases, whenever a knowledge mismatch exists between humans and AI systems.

---

[1] Trust calibration can be easily operationalized in terms of correspondence between the AI-based decision support system reliability and user trust in the system, that is in terms of the extent they follow the AI advice when it is correct and disregard it when it is wrong: this is also the definition of appropriate reliance we adopt [4,26].

## 2 Methods

As mentioned earlier, our goal was to investigate how AI advice, AI confidence levels, and corrective feedback differentially influence the reliance behaviors of medical students and their performance in image-based diagnosis. To this end, participants were asked to detect the presence of what we told them was a newly discovered, virus-acquired rare immunodeficiency in simulated blood smears, classifying each smear as either positive or negative for the disease. For ethical reasons and to minimize biases related to prior knowledge, we used a dataset of synthetic blood smear images depicting this (fictitious) immunodeficiency.

Our research group developed a custom Python script to generate simulated blood smear images with random variability. The script defined characteristics for erythrocytes, lymphocytes, and platelets, focusing on parameters such as ellipticity, size, and brightness (including both the nucleus and cytoplasm for lymphocytes). Each cell type could exist in one of two states: normal (negative) or pathological (positive). By randomly combining different numbers of pathological features within plausible ranges for each cell type, the script produced blood smear images with varying levels of complexity.

Based on the three types of cells present in the blood smear, we established three main criteria for determining whether a sample was pathogenic: (1) more than one-third of erythrocytes exhibit an elliptical shape, (2) more than half of the platelets are larger than normal, and (3) lymphocytes have a smaller-than-normal nucleus and a very lightly colored cytoplasm. A smear was classified as positive if at least two of these criteria were met, while cases meeting none or only one criterion were classified as negative. This systematic approach allowed us to generate a dataset of images with well-defined diagnostic features. Figure 1 illustrates examples of both negative and positive cases.

Participants completed the study by responding to an online questionnaire developed on the LimeSurvey platform[2]. Blood smear images were embedded in the questionnaire, which presented cases to participants and recorded their diagnostic classifications. As said above, to enhance ecological validity, participants were informed that a recent scientific study had identified a newly discovered immunodeficiency and that an AI system had been developed to assist in its diagnosis from blood smears. They were also told that we had developed another AI system that created simulated (but realistic) blood smears to augment available smear datasets for both machine training and diagnostic simulations, as in their case. Additionally, they were informed that the AI that they would use in the following simulation exhibited high classification accuracy, potentially surpassing traditional diagnostic methods.

The study followed a structured learning and testing sequence (see Fig. 2). After an introduction to the experimental setting, participants were trained to classify blood smear images based on predefined pathogenicity criteria. However, they were only taught two of the three criteria used to determine the presence of the disease. Specifically, they learned that the disease could be identified if (1)

---

[2] https://www.limesurvey.org/.

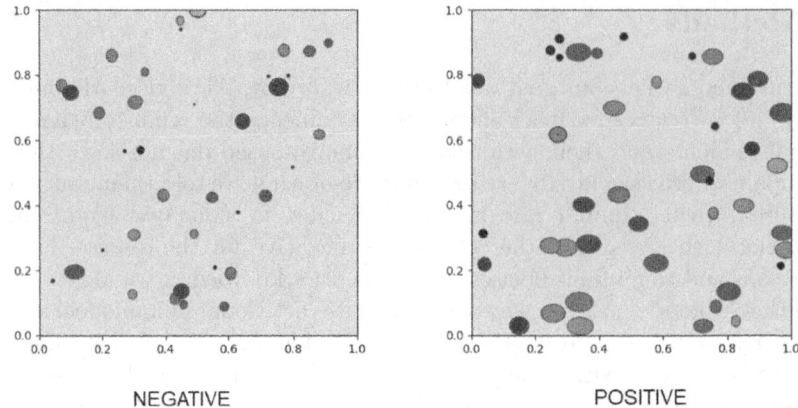

**Fig. 1.** Example of the synthetic blood smears used in the study. The sample on the left is classified as negative, as none of the specified criteria are met. The sample on the right is classified as positive, meeting two of the three criteria: more than one-third of erythrocytes (red cells) exhibit an elliptical shape, and more than half of the platelets (purple cells) are larger than normal. (Color figure online)

more than one-third of the erythrocytes were elliptical and (2) more than half of the platelets were larger than normal.

However, the third criterion—lymphocytes with a smaller-than-normal nucleus and a very light-colored cytoplasm—was intentionally withheld from participants to create a knowledge mismatch. While participants were unaware of this criterion, the simulated AI assisting them in the diagnostic task "knew" it. The rationale for this manipulation will be further elaborated later in this section.

During the Practice Phase (see Fig. 2), participants reviewed an initial set of 12 blood smear images, one at a time. This phase aimed to ensure that they understood and could accurately apply the classification criteria outlined in the instructions at the beginning of the task. For each image, participants classified it and then received feedback on the correct classification, along with a detailed explanation of the specific criteria detected in that case. Only images containing the two explicit criteria were presented during this phase, so the explanations focused solely on the criteria that participants had been instructed to use.

After completing this feedback-based task, participants classified an additional 10 images without receiving feedback in a self-administered test (see Fig. 2). This test phase provided them with insight into their diagnostic performance and allowed us to assess whether baseline classification accuracy differed between groups.

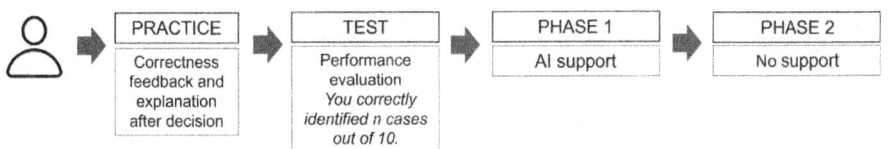

**Fig. 2.** Sequence of diagnostic task phases: First, participants completed a training phase in which they received corrective feedback along with an explanation of the correct choice. Next, after a test phase, they were provided with information about their own performance. In Phase 1, all participants performed the diagnostic task with AI support, followed by Phase 2, in which they completed the task without AI support (not covered in this study).

Upon completing the practice phase, participants were randomly assigned to one of three experimental groups based on their birth date[3] to enter Phase 1 of our experiment.

In Phase 1[4] (see Fig. 2 and Fig. 4), all participants classified 100 blood smear images as either positive or negative based on the two diagnostic criteria they had learned during the practice phase. To ensure clarity, these classification criteria were reiterated at the start of Phase 1.

During this phase (see Fig. 4 for an overview of our experimental design), we followed a human-first decision protocol [7]. For each of the 100 cases, we recorded both the initial decisions made by participants, which we refer to as the pre-AI or human first decision (HD1), and their final decisions, for which we use the terms post-AI or final human decision (FHD). In each trial, participants were first shown a blood smear image along with the patient's sex (female or male) and made an initial, unaided decision regarding the presence of pathogenicity criteria–classifying the smear as either positive or negative.

After submitting their initial response, a second page displayed the same blood smear image and patient sex information, now accompanied by a recommendation from the simulated AI system, presented as: "The AI classification for this blood smear is: *positive/negative*."

All groups viewed the same sequence of images under identical conditions, with the following key differences: in the Advice-only Group, participants received only the AI's categorical suggestion (*Positive/Negative*); in the Confidence Group, participants also saw a confidence level associated with the AI's recommendation (*High/Low*); and in the Feedback Group, participants received the categorical AI suggestion, but after submitting their final response they were provided with feedback on both (1) the correctness of the AI's recommendation and (2) the correctness of their final response. This feedback explicitly indicated whether the AI's classification matched the correct diagnosis and whether the

---

[3] This method was chosen because LimeSurvey's randomization did not allow for groups of similar sizes. Additionally, it ensured that the control group (advice-only) was the smallest, though only slightly, to optimize the statistical power of the study.

[4] Phase 2 will be the subject of another study.

participant's final decision was correct, allowing them to assess both the AI's reliability and their own performance over time.

As previously mentioned, a key aspect of the study design was that the simulated AI applied a diagnostic criterion unknown to participants. As a result, in 40 cases (see Fig. 3), the AI's predictions appeared inconsistent with human expectations. In these cases, an unknown criterion - because it had not been disclosed during the instruction and training phase - was applicable alongside one of the two known criteria. Figure 5 illustrates an example of a case with both explicit criteria applicable and another where the unknown criterion can also apply alongside an explicit one.

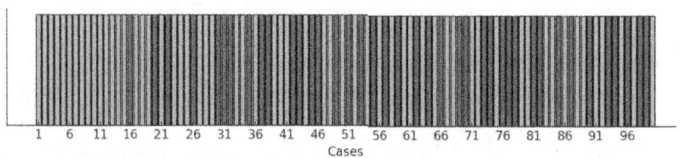

**Fig. 3.** The sequence of 100 cases presented to participants for diagnosis with AI support in Phase 1 of the experiment. Cases highlighted in red indicate those that triggered a knowledge mismatch (KM) between humans and AI, as they were classified as positive based on two diagnostic criteria–one known only to the AI and not to the participants. (Color figure online)

As a result, participants were likely to classify these cases as negative, as they could identify only one pathogenic criterion, whereas a positive classification required the presence of two criteria. In contrast, the AI recognized that lymphocytes with abnormally small nuclei and brightly colored cytoplasm - the criterion unknown to humans because left undisclosed - indicated pathogenicity. Consequently, the AI correctly identified two applicable criteria in these blood smears and recommended a positive classification. However, participants could not understand the reasoning behind the AI's decisions, unless they learned it through direct interaction with the AI.

Our experimental manipulation enabled us to examine how participants responded to AI-generated recommendations and how confidence level reporting and performance feedback influenced their reliance behavior, particularly when the AI's rationale was opaque or appeared misaligned with the learned diagnostic criteria.

Due to the introduced knowledge mismatch, participants might have perceived that the AI had access to additional information unavailable to them or, alternatively, that it was providing incorrect recommendations in cases involving the unknown criterion. Despite these perceptions, the AI's overall accuracy was high (96%) across all cases (see Fig. 3), with 100% accuracy in cases involving the unknown criterion (red cases in Fig. 3).

To ensure consistency across groups, all participants encountered cases with the unknown criterion in the same order. These cases were excluded from the first ten trials, and their frequency gradually increased as the classification task progressed (see Fig. 3). This design aimed to prevent an early negative impression and loss of trust in the AI while allowing participants to adjust their mental models of the system through experience.

Reliance behaviors were assessed along the dimensions of decision accuracy, deference, appropriate reliance, automation bias and conservatism bias. Deference, appropriate reliance and their associated cognitive biases are defined adopting the metric framework proposed in Cabitza et al.'s work [4]. *Deference* is defined as the ratio of AI-induced changes leading to an agreement to the total number of advice bits provided. *Appropriate reliance* is the ratio of the sum of beneficial trust and distrust pattern occurrences to the total number of advice bits provided. These two concepts are described respectively in Eqs. 1 and 2. *Automation bias* and *conservatism bias* are odd ratios as described in the formulae, 3, and 4, respectively. In the formulae, correct decisions are indicated as 1s, errors as 0s, the figure triplets (such as $N_{001}$ and $N_{100}$) indicate the number of times an outcome occurs in terms of concurrent first or pre-AI human decision (HD1), AI advice (AI) and final or post-AI human decision (FHD), ↑ (resp., ↓) denote an increase (resp., decrease) in confidence between HD1 and FHD, and $N$ is the total number of advice bits given.

Cases where users changed their decisions to align with the AI's advices

$$Deference = \frac{N_{011} + N_{100}}{N}$$

Total number of advice provided by the AI

(1)

Beneficial trust and distrust pattern · Confidence Decrease

$$AppropriateReliance = \frac{N_{011} + N_{101} + N_{001} + N_{111}\uparrow + N_{000}\downarrow}{N}$$

Total number of advice provided by the AI · Confidence Increase

(2)

Inverse of odds of users rejecting incorrect AI advice compared to all other cases

$$AutomationBias = \frac{N_{100}}{N - N_{100}} \cdot \frac{N - N_{101}}{N_{101}}$$

Odds of users following incorrect AI advice

(3)

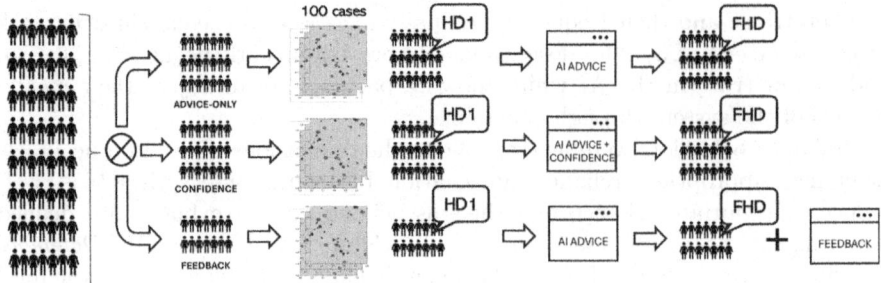

**Fig. 4.** Experimental design conditions for the response collection in phase 1. Each panel represents one of the three experimental groups: Advice-only, Confidence and Feedback. Participants classified 100 blood smear images while receiving AI-generated recommendations. The AI-only (traditional) group received only a categorical suggestion indicating whether the smear was 'Positive' or 'Negative'. The Confidence group received the same suggestion along with a confidence level (High/Low). The Feedback group initially received the categorical suggestion and later feedback on the correctness of the AI's recommendation. HD1 stands for the initial unaided decision while FHD is the final human decision.

$$ConservatismBias = \frac{\overbrace{N_{010}}^{} }{\underbrace{N - N_{010}}_{\text{Odds of users rejecting correct AI advice}}} \cdot \frac{\overbrace{N - N_{011}}^{\text{Inverse of odds of users following correct AI advice}}}{N_{011}} \tag{4}$$

## 3 Results

In this section, we report the results regarding the effects of the three experimental conditions described above on human performance: advice only (advice-only group), advice complemented with calibrated confidence level (confidence group), and advice complemented with correctness feedback (feedback group), on decision accuracy (See Tables 1 and 2), and in Table 3 deference (defined as the ratio of AI-induced changes leading to agreement to the total number of advice bits provided, see Eq. 1), reliance behaviors (see Eq. 2) and the related cognitive biases (see Eqs. 3 and 4) [7].

In our statistical analysis, we employed the two-proportion z-test with pooled variance to determine whether there were significant differences between the groups' performance on several measures: accuracy, deference, appropriate reliance, automation bias, and conservatism bias. Ninety-five percent confidence intervals were computed based on a binomial approximation to the sampling distribution.

**Table 1.** The accuracy rates and 95% confidence interval of participants' initial decisions (pre-AI advice, HD1) were analyzed both for all cases combined and separately for cases involving knowledge mismatch (unknown criterion) and those based solely on known criteria.

|  | All cases | Unknown criterion | Known criteria |
| --- | --- | --- | --- |
| Advice-only | 0.65[0.63-0.67] | 0.46[0.41-0.51] | 0.78[0.75-0.81] |
| Confidence | 0.66[0.65-0.68] | 0.45[0.42-0.50] | 0.80[0.79-0.82] |
| Feedback | 0.65[0.63-0.67] | 0.48[0.44-0.53] | 0.75[0.72-0.79] |

In our study, we recruited a total of 222 medical students (mean age = 19.6, SD = 1.40, range: 18–30). Among them, 72% self-identified as female, 24.9% as male, 1.4% as non-binary, and 0.9% preferred not to respond. Upon completing the practice phase, participants were randomly assigned to one of three experimental groups on the basis of their birth date: the Advice-only involved 70 participants, the Confidence Group 94 and the Feedback Group 58 (the unbalance was intended for power considerations). The groups were not significantly different with respect to age and gender balance. Additionally, no between-group differences were found in basal classification skill, which was assessed both at the end of the test step (see Fig. 4) (test accuracy = 63%, 64%, 61% respectively, p-value = 0.91, $\chi^2 = 0.19$) and at the pre-AI step of phase 1 (HD1 accuracy = 65.4%, 66.7%, 65.1% respectively, p-value=0.12, $\chi^2 = 4.3$).

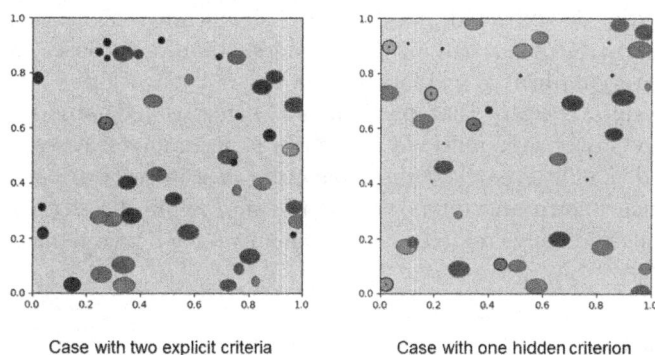

Case with two explicit criteria    Case with one hidden criterion

**Fig. 5.** Example of blood smears with explicit (left) and unknown (right) criteria. The sample on the left is positive and meets two criteria, specifically (1) more than one-third of the erythrocytes (red cells) are elliptical in shape and (2) more than half of the platelets (purple cells) are larger than normal. The sample on the right is positive and meets one explicit criterion, (1) more than one-third or erythrocytes (red cells) are elliptical in shape, as well as the third criterion, unknown to the participants and known only to the AI: (3) the nucleus of the lymphocytes (blue cells) is smaller than normal and the cytoplasm of the lymphocytes is very light in color. (Color figure online)

**Table 2.** The accuracy rates and 95% confidence interval of participants' final decisions (post-AI advice, FHD) were analyzed both for all cases combined and separately for cases involving knowledge mismatch (unknown criterion) and those based solely on explicit criteria. Since the AI was always correct in cases with an unknown criterion, the corresponding accuracy rate also reflects the agreement rate between humans and the machine.

|  | All cases | Unknown criterion | Known criteria |
| --- | --- | --- | --- |
| Advice-only | 0.74[0.71-0.77] | 0.58[0.51-0.65] | 0.84[0.83-0.87] |
| Confidence | 0.75[0.72-0.77] | 0.57[0.52-0.62] | 0.86[0.84-0.88] |
| Feedback | 0.78[0.75-0.81] | 0.70[0.64-0.75] | 0.84[0.80-0.87] |

**Table 3.** Results of the statistical analyses of the reliance related metrics.

|  | Advice-only | Confidence | Feedback |
| --- | --- | --- | --- |
| Deference | 0.13 [0.12, 0.14] | 0.11 [0.10, 0.12] | 0.17 [0.16, 0.18] |
| Appropriate Reliance | 0.146 [0.14, 0.15] | 0.129 [0.12, 0.14] | 0.181 [0.17, 0.19] |
| Automation Bias | 0.36 [0.27, 0.49] | 0.23 [0.17, 0.31] | 0.68 [0.50, 0.93] |
| Conservatism Bias | 1.98 [1.81, 2.17] | 2.45 [2.26, 2.66] | 1.10 [1.00, 1.21] |

As a manipulation check, we first examined whether participants' initial classification accuracy differed between cases involving the unknown criterion—incorporated by the AI but undisclosed to participants—and cases with known, explicit criteria. As expected, accuracy was significantly higher for cases with explicit criteria (78% across all participants) than for those involving the unknown criterion (46%; $Z = 48.93$, $p < .001$).

These results indicate that participants correctly understood and applied the instructed criteria, as reflected in their high accuracy for cases with explicit criteria. Additionally, the clear discrepancy in classification accuracy between cases to which known and unknown criteria were applicable confirms that our manipulation effectively created a knowledge mismatch between participants and the AI.

### 3.1 Accuracy

To examine whether the presence of confidence cues and feedback influenced diagnostic accuracy, we compared the three experimental conditions: advice-only, confidence, and feedback. The advice-only group ($\Delta = 8.79\%$, 95% CI: [8.13, 9.45]) demonstrated slightly higher improvement in accuracy than the confidence condition ($\Delta = 8.18\%$, 95% CI: [7.63, 8.73]), but this difference was not statistically significant ($Z = 1.3764$, $p = 0.1687$). However, the feedback group ($\Delta = 13.22\%$, 95% CI: [12.35, 14.09]) exhibited significantly higher accuracy improvement than both the confidence and advice-only groups. The statistical tests confirmed these differences, with a $Z$-statistic of $-9.56$ ($p < .001$)

for confidence vs. feedback and $-7.93$ ($p < .001$) for advice-only vs. feedback. These results confirmed the conjecture that providing feedback has a substantial and statistically significant positive impact on accuracy compared to both the confidence and advice-only conditions.

### 3.2 Deference

Deference is the ratio of AI-induced changes leading to human-AI agreement to the total number of advice bits provided (see Eq. 1). The confidence group showed the lowest deference ($D = 0.11$, 95% CI: [0.103, 0.115]), followed by the advice-only group ($D = 0.13$, 95% CI: [0.122, 0.138]), while the feedback condition exhibited the highest deference ($D = 0.17$, 95% CI: [0.164, 0.184]). Statistical comparisons revealed a significant difference between the three groups ($\chi^2 = 132.39$, $p < .001$), indicating that deference was significantly higher in the feedback group also with respect to the confidence group ($Z = -11.44$, $p < .001$) and the advice-only group ($Z = -6.94$, $p < .001$) (Fig. 6).

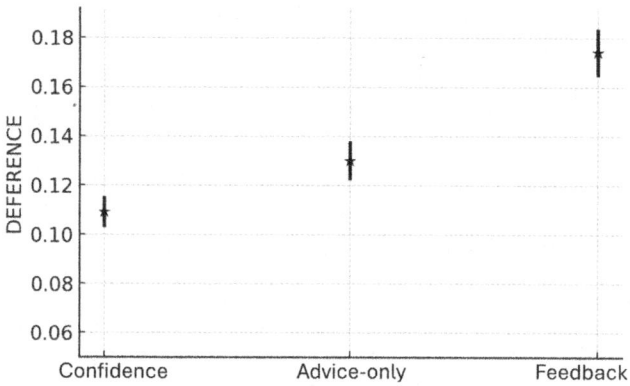

**Fig. 6.** Deference rates across conditions (the higher the value, the higher the bias). The confidence group exhibited the lowest deference, followed by the advice-only group. The feedback group showed a significant increase in deference.

### 3.3 Appropriate Reliance

The key analysis of this study focuses on appropriate reliance, operationalized as proposed in [4], as the ratio of beneficial trust (following correct advice) and distrust (discarding incorrect advice) to the total number of advice instances provided (see Eq. 2).

The confidence group ($AR = 0.129$, 95% CI: [0.122, 0.136]) exhibited slightly lower appropriate reliance than the advice-only group ($AR = 0.146$, 95% CI: [0.138, 0.154]), with a significant difference ($Z = -3.12$, $p = 0.0018$). However, the feedback condition ($AR = 0.181$, 95% CI: [0.171, 0.191]) resulted in significantly higher appropriate reliance than both the confidence ($Z = -8.49$, $p < .001$) and advice-only groups ($Z = -5.31$, $p < .001$) (Fig. 7).

These findings suggest that, as expected, feedback on AI accuracy enhances participants' ability to rely appropriately on AI recommendations. More interestingly, they also indicate that providing confidence levels is associated with lower appropriate reliance compared to presenting AI advice without confidence information. To further analyze appropriate reliance, we examine the behavioral patterns associated with its lower levels–specifically, automation bias and conservatism bias in the following sections.

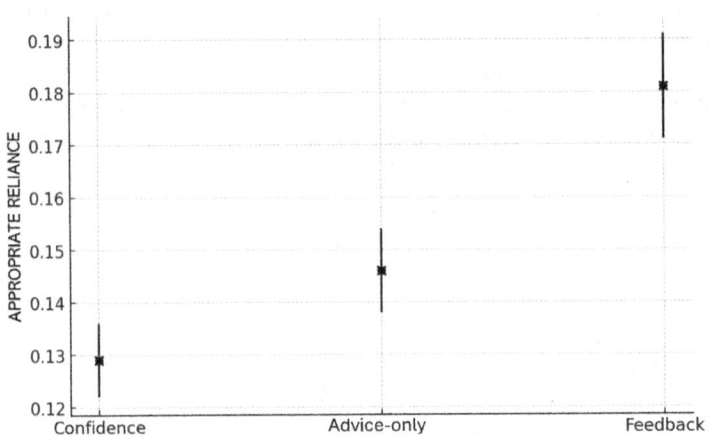

**Fig. 7.** Appropriate Reliance across conditions.

### 3.4 Automation Bias

Automation bias (AB) was evaluated as the tendency to over-rely on incorrect AI-generated recommendations (see Eq. 3). The confidence group showed the lowest odds of automation bias ($OR = 0.23$, 95% CI: [0.17, 0.31]), followed by the advice-only group ($OR = 0.36$, 95% CI: [0.27, 0.49]), while the feedback condition exhibited the highest odds ($OR = 0.68$, 95% CI: [0.50, 0.93]). Statistical comparisons revealed a significant difference between the confidence and advice-only groups ($Z = -2.08$, $p = 0.038$), indicating that automation bias was significantly higher in the advice-only group (Fig. 8). Moreover, the feedback group led to a significant increase in automation bias compared to both the confidence ($Z = -4.92$, $p < .001$) and advice-only groups ($Z = -2.90$, $p = 0.0038$). Since lower levels of automation bias can be interpreted as a sign of distrust, these results suggest that, in cases of human-AI knowledge mismatch, providing calibrated confidence levels increases distrust compared to not providing them.

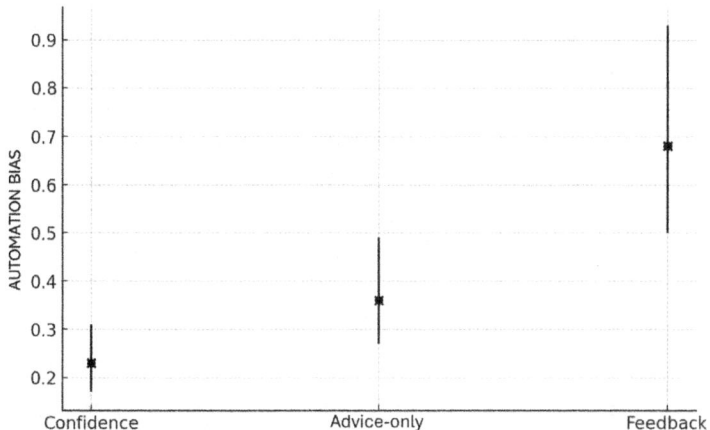

**Fig. 8.** Automation bias odds ratios across conditions (the higher the value, the higher the bias). The confidence group showed the lowest odds of automation bias, followed by the advice-only group, while the feedback condition exhibited the highest odds. Notably, even if the CI of the confidence and advice-only conditions slightly overlap, the difference is still statistically significant.

### 3.5 Conservatism Bias

Conservatism bias is the opposite of automation bias—it reflects users' tendency to reject correct AI advice (see Eq. 4), demonstrating overconfidence in their initial faulty judgments. To this regard, the confidence group resulted in the highest odds of conservatism bias ($OR = 2.45$, 95% CI: $[2.26, 2.66]$), followed by the advice-only group ($OR = 1.98$, 95% CI: $[1.81, 2.17]$), while the feedback group exhibited a substantial lower conservatism bias ($OR = 1.10$, 95% CI: $[1.00, 1.21]$) (Fig. 9). Comparisons between conditions revealed statistically significant differences: confidence vs. advice-only ($Z = 3.42$, $p < .001$), confidence vs. feedback ($Z = 12.52$, $p < .001$), and advice-only vs. feedback ($Z = 8.76$, $p < .001$). These findings suggest that providing confidence levels is associated with conservatism bias, and then higher distrust, than the other conditions, confirming the results related to automation bias reported above.

## 4 Discussion

Our study examined how presenting AI confidence levels alongside AI recommendations influenced medical students' diagnostic performance, compared to providing AI recommendations alone and AI recommendations followed by corrective feedback after students' final decisions. The latter condition represents a deliberately extreme scenario with limited practical application in real-world settings that, in this study, served as an ideal case where users can recognize that the AI possesses knowledge they lack and thus learn from its recommendations. We will come back to this later in this discussion.

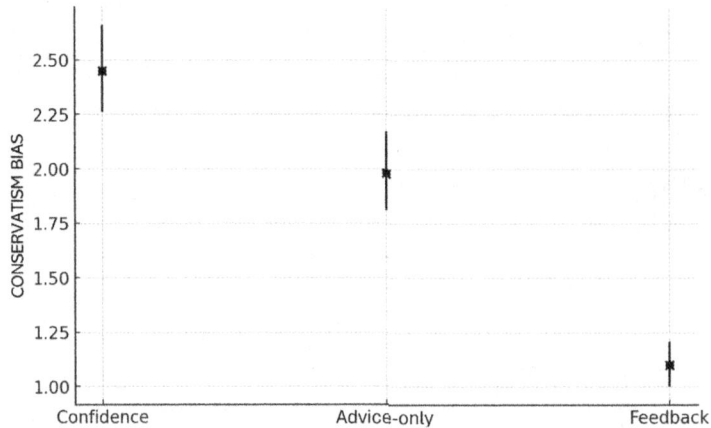

**Fig. 9.** Conservatism bias odds ratios across conditions (the higher the value, the higher the bias). The confidence group exhibited the highest conservatism bias, followed by the advice-only group.

Our main finding is that simply displaying AI confidence levels, even when calibrated, did not significantly enhance appropriate reliance or accuracy compared to omitting them when a knowledge mismatch occurs between human experts and AI. That is, when humans and AI do not share perfectly aligned classification criteria, discrepancies arise, leading to misunderstandings of the uncertainty estimations conveyed by the AI. This finding aligns with recent reports in the specialist literature. For instance, a systematic review and meta-analysis by Vaccaro et al. [28] concluded that the presence or absence of confidence cues alongside AI recommendations had no clear impact on the effectiveness of human-AI collaboration. Our study offers an empirical explanation for this lack of effect.

Moreover, our findings challenge the common assumption that confidence cues help users appropriately calibrate their trust and reliance on AI [23,24,32]. This is particularly relevant given that AI confidence or uncertainty communication is often regarded as a key strategy for improving AI interpretability and trustworthiness. The considerable attention these techniques have received in recent literature further underscores their perceived importance [2,17,28,33].

In fact, in cases of knowledge mismatch, we found that confidence cues can even be detrimental to the appropriateness of reliance–i.e., users' ability to distinguish helpful AI advice from misleading recommendations and to benefit from the former. In this regard, our study provides initial evidence that a phenomenon similar to the "white-box paradox" observed in explanations [6] may also occur when AI provides calibrated confidence cues. This paradox arises when a feature designed to help users assess the trustworthiness of AI instead undermines their interpretation, particularly in the presence of a knowledge mismatch. Specifically, users may misinterpret high AI confidence as unwarranted boasting, leading to skepticism and ultimately influencing how they weigh AI recommendations.

A similar conclusion was drawn in [3], which found that AI confidence does not necessarily improve human trust calibration when users have incomplete or erroneous mental models of the AI's capabilities.

Our results align with recent research highlighting the interplay of multiple factors in how people interpret AI confidence levels. For instance, the impact of AI confidence is strongly influenced by users' perceptions of the AI's actual accuracy [16]. Similar to human-human interactions, individuals are not blind to discrepancies between an advisor's perceived accuracy and the confidence they express. An advisor is considered a reliable trustee only when high confidence is justified by high accuracy [25].

Moreover, the relationship between users' self-confidence in a decision task and the AI's expressed confidence remains complex and underexplored [9,17,19]. Our findings suggest that users often struggle to integrate AI confidence or uncertainty into their decision-making. Some researchers have even argued that, due to users' biased interpretations of AI confidence, uncalibrated information can sometimes be beneficial [30].

For instance, Vodrahalli et al. [30] found that an overconfident AI helped participants better calibrate their reliance on the model, improving both accuracy and self-confidence, particularly when the AI's advice was more accurate. The authors suggested that an overconfident AI could enhance users' ability to utilize AI-generated information effectively. However, our results indicate that this strategy is effective only when users perceive the AI as highly accurate. If there is a mismatch between users' perceptions of the AI's accuracy and its expressed confidence, reliance on the model may decrease.

Our findings highlight the importance of a well-calibrated *theory of machine* when deploying confidence-calibrated explainable AI (XAI) to mitigate cognitive biases and promote appropriate reliance. The term *theory of machine* (ToM) [18] refers to the mental model users develop regarding a machine's internal functioning (its "mind," so to speak) through interaction, which informs their assessments of its reliability and trustworthiness. These mental models of AI can be refined and updated through mechanisms extensively studied in the "theory of mind" literature [31] and applied to human-AI collaboration. Such mechanisms include information about the machine's reputation—how others perceive its accuracy and usefulness—and more specifically, its prestige, that is its status or reputation based on technical capabilities and intended function[5]. Additional sources include past interactions and, as in our study, the AI's confidence in its recommendations—both in current and analogous cases—as well as the extent to which these confidence estimates are well-calibrated [27].

A possible explanation for our findings is that confidence cues fail to encourage appropriate reliance on AI when users cannot fully grasp their rationale, meaning their ToM is imperfect. In our study, participants were unaware that the AI employed an additional diagnostic criterion unknown to them. As a

---

[5] Following anthropology (e.g., [14,15]), we distinguish reputation, a broader concept encompassing moral judgment, temperament, and attitudes, from prestige, which refers specifically to status earned through demonstrated skill and achievement.

result, they could not fully comprehend the AI's decision-making strategy. Our results suggest that when AI confidence levels deviated from participants' expectations, they were perceived as unjustified overconfidence rather than reliable indicators of uncertainty. This misinterpretation led to reduced reliance on AI recommendations—even when they were correct—ultimately decreasing automation bias but increasing conservatism bias, a reluctance to revise initial incorrect judgments when AI advice is correct.

### 4.1 Limitations

We acknowledge two main limitations in our study. First, while using a synthetic dataset allowed for controlled experimentation, real-world diagnostic tasks involve additional complexities such as contextual information, prior medical knowledge, and patient history. Future research should explore whether similar patterns emerge in real-world clinical settings.

Second, in real-world contexts, providing immediate and continuous feedback on AI performance is not always feasible. This challenge is particularly evident in high-stakes domains such as clinical decision support, where outcomes may not be immediately available. Nevertheless, we believe this experimental manipulation remains valuable. In our setting, the feedback condition served as a useful baseline for comparing the influence of AI confidence on users' reliance. Moreover, although immediate feedback on decision outcomes is typically unavailable in practice, this approach could serve as an effective training method for users before the actual implementation of the AI [11]. By helping users better understand the reliability and accuracy of the machine learning tool they will be working with, such training with corrective feedback can support the development of an adequate mental model of the AI's capabilities in collaborative decision-making.

Despite the limitations mentioned, we believe that our study makes an interesting contribution by opening avenues for further investigation. For instance, the long-term effects of different trust calibration strategies are still unclear. Future studies could explore whether repeated exposure to AI confidence cues or feedback mechanisms leads to more stable trust calibration over time.

### 4.2 Interaction as Solution to Knowledge Mismatch

Let us revisit the rationale for designing a feedback group as a reference condition, aimed at helping users recognize that the AI was correct in critical cases involving the unknown criterion (see Fig. 3) and, consequently, that they could learn from it. Evidence of learning can indeed be observed in Tables 1 and 2. While initial pre-AI accuracy (HD1) did not differ significantly (see Table 1), even in cases of knowledge mismatch (see Fig. 3), final post-AI accuracy (FHD) showed significant improvement specifically in those cases.

To further examine this phenomenon, we conducted a temporal analysis of average accuracy across respondents. As shown in Fig. 10, this analysis reinforces our findings. Despite the even distribution of case complexity over time—due to the randomness of the generating script—and the potential impact of fatigue bias in a 100-case task, which typically hinders improvement, accuracy in difficult cases significantly increased across all conditions. In particular, a linear regression analysis of the time series, based on average accuracy and human-AI agreement rates, revealed a significant positive trend in initial accuracy (HD1) and final agreement rates (AI = FHD) for the feedback group ($\beta = 0.0071$ and $\beta = 0.0086$, respectively, $p < .001$). This was followed by the AI-Only group ($\beta = 0.0039$, $\beta = 0.0018$, $p = .02$) and the Confidence group ($\beta = 0.0035$, $\beta = 0.0030$, $p = .02$). These results indicate that accuracy and agreement rates increased over time, demonstrating a clear learning effect, with the feedback method leading to the most pronounced improvement, as expected.

Notably, learning progressed slightly slower in the Confidence group than in the AI-Only group, yet final agreement with AI decisions was higher. This suggests that confidence levels may have had a hampering effect on learning the implicit criterion used by the AI in its recommendations. This finding further supports the white-box paradox, in which confidence cues, in the presence of a knowledge mismatch, contribute to uncalibrated trust. Additionally, participants in the feedback group showed a tendency to more readily accept highly confident AI recommendations in cases of knowledge mismatch, potentially leading to less critical evaluation and increased deference (Fig. 11).

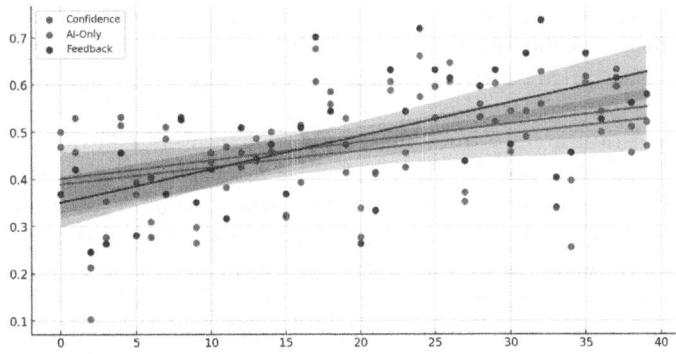

**Fig. 10.** The improvement of accuracy in pre-AI decision in the cases with a knowledge mismatch between humans and AI.

### 4.3 Implications for XAI Design

This finding suggests a constructive, design-oriented approach to addressing the paradox we identified regarding the presentation of AI confidence. On the one hand, given that human and AI knowledge cannot be assumed to be perfectly aligned—particularly in the case of expert practitioners with extensive tacit knowledge and black-box models such as artificial neural networks and other deep learning architectures (e.g., LLMs)—confidence levels should be presented with caution, even when well-calibrated, or perhaps avoided altogether.

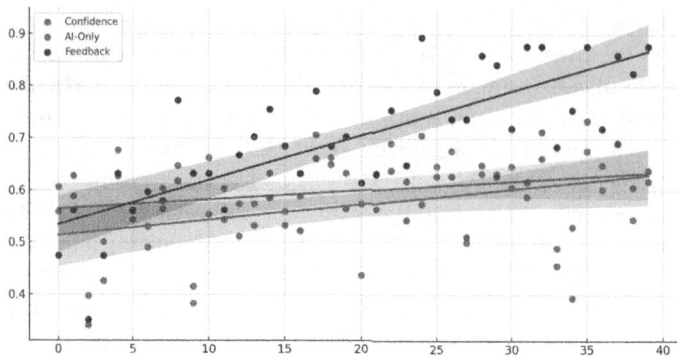

**Fig. 11.** The increase in FHD-AI agreement rates in the cases with a knowledge mismatch between humans and AI.

On the other hand, humans continuously learn from any knowledge source they perceive as authoritative, even in the absence of explicit correctness feedback (as in our feedback condition). This suggests that XAI solutions should focus on enhancing users' ability to recognize AI outputs as reliable, thereby supporting the refinement of their mental models and *theories of machine*. If users do not fully understand how AI arrives at its conclusions, even well-calibrated confidence levels may be misinterpreted, reinforcing a flawed theory of machine— that is, an incorrect mental model of how the AI applies its knowledge. This, in turn, can lead to inappropriate reliance on AI outputs and exacerbate cognitive biases such as conservatism bias.

A key question arising from this study is how users can develop an accurate understanding of an AI system's decision-making process. Based on our study's findings, we propose a general design recommendation along with specific examples: interfaces should go beyond simply presenting confidence levels and incorporate additional transparency mechanisms to help users better understand the AI's decision-making process or at least assess its reliability. For instance, confidence scores could be presented across different bins to reflect case-specific model uncertainty [10]. Variance scores, such as those derived from Monte Carlo Dropout for deep learning models or Deep Ensembles for machine learning models, could help users quantify epistemic uncertainty and evaluate how much the AI's predictions vary across multiple requests or independently trained models. Additionally, alerts and Out-of-Distribution (OOD) warnings could be issued when a given case significantly deviates from any instance in the training set; another useful approach would be referencing past cases where similar recommendations were either validated or later found to be incorrect. The common element of these solutions is the requirement that any design effort should focus on actively assisting users in developing a sufficiently accurate and functional mental model of the AI's capabilities.

## 5 Conclusion

This study highlights a fundamental paradox in AI-assisted decision-making: even when AI confidence is perfectly calibrated, it may fail to foster appropriate reliance if users' trust is uncalibrated due to a knowledge mismatch between humans and AI. Our findings suggest that while displaying AI confidence levels is often assumed to enhance trust calibration and reliance, its effectiveness is significantly limited when users possess incomplete or incorrect mental models of the AI's reasoning. In such cases, confidence cues may be misinterpreted, leading to increased skepticism, conservatism bias, and lower reliance on correct AI recommendations.

Through our experimental design, we demonstrated that when human and AI knowledge are misaligned, confidence cues can inadvertently undermine trust rather than enhance it. Specifically, participants exposed to confidence levels exhibited lower appropriate reliance compared to those who received only categorical AI recommendations. Interestingly, while the provision of feedback on AI correctness significantly improved appropriate reliance and accuracy, confidence cues alone did not yield similar benefits. These findings challenge the conventional wisdom that calibrated confidence always improves human-AI collaboration and underscore the critical role of mental model alignment in decision support systems.

Our results have direct implications for the design of hybrid intelligence systems, particularly in high-stakes domains such as medical decision-making. Rather than focusing solely on presenting AI confidence scores, designers should consider integrating additional transparency mechanisms such as reliability indicators and periodic feedback. These strategies can help users refine their mental models of AI behavior, what we called *theories of machine*, ultimately leading to better-calibrated trust and improved decision accuracy. Furthermore, given the challenges of real-world implementation, future research should explore adaptive approaches that dynamically adjust AI explanations and confidence presentations based on user expertise and evolving trust levels.

In conclusion, our study calls for a more nuanced approach to designing AI-human collaboration frameworks. Rather than assuming that calibrated confidence inherently leads to improved trust and reliance, researchers and practitioners must carefully consider how users interpret and act upon confidence cues. Ultimately, the goal should not be merely to make AI more confident but to ensure that its confidence is correctly understood and integrated into human decision-making. By fostering better-aligned mental models, we can pave the way for AI systems that genuinely enhance human judgment rather than inadvertently hinder it in hybrid decision making settings.

**Acknowledgments.** F. Cabitza, C. Fregosi and L. Vicente acknowledge funding support provided by the Italian project PRIN PNRR 2022 InXAID - Interaction with eXplainable Artificial Intelligence in (medical) Decision making. CUP: H53D23008090001 funded by the European Union - Next Generation EU.

# References

1. Antifakos, S., Kern, N., Schiele, B., Schwaninger, A.: Towards improving trust in context-aware systems by displaying system confidence. In: Proceedings of the 7th International Conference on Human Computer Iteraction with Mobile Devices & Services, pp. 9–14 (2005). https://doi.org/10.1145/1085777.1085780
2. Banerji, C.R., Chakraborti, T., Harbron, C., MacArthur, B.D.: Clinical ai tools must convey predictive uncertainty for each individual patient. Nat. Med. **29**(12), 2996–2998 (2023). https://doi.org/10.1038/s41591-023-02562-7
3. Bansal, G., Nushi, B., Kamar, E., Lasecki, W.S., Weld, D.S., Horvitz, E.: Beyond accuracy: The role of mental models in human-ai team performance. In: Proceedings of the AAAI Conference on Human Computation and Crowdsourcing, vol. 7, pp. 2–11 (2019). https://doi.org/10.1609/hcomp.v7i1.5285
4. Cabitza, F., Campagner, A., Angius, R., Natali, C., Reverberi, C.: Ai shall have no dominion: on how to measure technology dominance in ai-supported human decision-making. In: Proceedings of the 2023 CHI Conference on Human Factors in Computing Systems, pp. 1–20 (2023). https://doi.org/10.1145/3544548.3581095
5. Cabitza, F., Campagner, A., Malgieri, G., Natali, C., Schneeberger, D., Stoeger, K., Holzinger, A.: Quod erat demonstrandum?-towards a typology of the concept of explanation for the design of explainable ai. Expert Syst. Appl. **213**, 118888 (2023). https://doi.org/10.1016/j.eswa.2022.118888
6. Cabitza, F., Campagner, A., Natali, C., Parimbelli, E., Ronzio, L., Cameli, M.: Painting the black box white: Experimental findings from applying xai to an ecg reading setting. Mach. Learn. Knowl. Extraction **5**(1), 269–286 (2023). https://doi.org/10.3390/make5010017
7. Cabitza, F., et al.: Rams, hounds and white boxes: investigating human-ai collaboration protocols in medical diagnosis. Artif. Intell. Med. **138**, 102506 (2023). https://doi.org/10.1016/j.artmed.2023.102506
8. Cao, S., Liu, A., Huang, C.M.: Designing for appropriate reliance: The roles of ai uncertainty presentation, initial user decision, and user demographics in ai-assisted decision-making. Proceedings of the ACM on Human-Computer Interaction 8(CSCW1), pp. 1–32 (2024). https://doi.org/10.1145/3637318
9. Chong, L., Zhang, G., Goucher-Lambert, K., Kotovsky, K., Cagan, J.: Human confidence in artificial intelligence and in themselves: the evolution and impact of confidence on adoption of ai advice. Comput. Hum. Behav. **127**, 107018 (2022). https://doi.org/10.1016/j.chb.2021.107018
10. Famiglini, L., Campagner, A., Cabitza, F.: Towards a rigorous calibration assessment framework: advancements in metrics, methods, and use. In: ECAI 2023, pp. 645–652. IOS Press (2023). https://doi.org/10.3233/FAIA230327
11. Green, B., Chen, Y.: The principles and limits of algorithm-in-the-loop decision making. Proc. ACM Hum.-Comput. Interact. **3**(CSCW) (Nov 2019). https://doi.org/10.1145/3359152
12. Guo, C., Pleiss, G., Sun, Y., Weinberger, K.Q.: On calibration of modern neural networks. In: Proceedings of the 34th International Conference on Machine Learning - Volume 70, pp. 1321–1330. ICML'17 (2017)
13. Helldin, T., Falkman, G., Riveiro, M., Davidsson, S.: Presenting system uncertainty in automotive uis for supporting trust calibration in autonomous driving. In: Proceedings of the 5th International Conference on Automotive User Interfaces and Interactive Vehicular Applications, pp. 210–217. AutomotiveUI '13. Association for Computing Machinery, New York (2013). https://doi.org/10.1145/2516540.2516554

14. Henrich, J., Chudek, M., Boyd, R.: The big man mechanism: how prestige fosters cooperation and creates prosocial leaders. Philosophical Trans. Roy. Soc. B: Biological Sci. **370**(1683), 20150013 (2015)
15. Henrich, J., Gil-White, F.J.: The evolution of prestige: Freely conferred deference as a mechanism for enhancing the benefits of cultural transmission. Evol. Hum. Behav. **22**(3), 165–196 (2001)
16. Ishizu, N., Yeoh, W.L., Okumura, H., Fukuda, O.: The effect of communicating ai confidence on human decision making when performing a binary decision task. Appl. Sci. **14**(16) (2024). https://doi.org/10.3390/app14167192
17. Li, J., Yang, Y., Liao, Q.V., Zhang, J., Lee, Y.C.: As confidence aligns: Exploring the effect of ai confidence on human self-confidence in human-ai decision making. arXiv preprint (2025). https://doi.org/10.48550/arXiv.2501.12868
18. Logg, J.: Theory of machine: When do people rely on algorithms. Harvard Business School working paper series (17-086) (2017)
19. Ma, S., Wang, X., Lei, Y., Shi, C., Yin, M., Ma, X.: "are you really sure?" understanding the effects of human self-confidence calibration in ai-assisted decision making. In: Proceedings of the 2024 CHI Conference on Human Factors in Computing Systems. CHI '24. Association for Computing Machinery, New York (2024). https://doi.org/10.1145/3613904.3642671
20. Merritt, S.M., Lee, D., Unnerstall, J.L., Huber, K.: Are well-calibrated users effective users? associations between calibration of trust and performance on an automation-aided task. Hum. Factors **57**(1), 34–47 (2015). https://doi.org/10.1177/0018720814561675
21. Navarro, C.L.A., et al.: Systematic review identifies the design and methodological conduct of studies on machine learning-based prediction models. J. Clin. Epidemiol. **154**, 8–22 (2023). https://doi.org/10.1016/j.jclinepi.2022.11.015
22. Niculescu-Mizil, A., Caruana, R.: Predicting good probabilities with supervised learning. In: Proceedings of the 22nd International Conference on Machine Learning, pp. 625–632. ICML '05. Association for Computing Machinery, New York (2005). https://doi.org/10.1145/1102351.1102430
23. Okamura, K., Yamada, S.: Adaptive trust calibration for human-ai collaboration. PLOS ONE **15**(2), 1–20 (2020). https://doi.org/10.1371/journal.pone.0229132
24. Rezaeian, O., Bayrak, A.E., Asan, O.: Explainability and ai confidence in clinical decision support systems: Effects on trust, diagnostic performance, and cognitive load in breast cancer care (2025). https://arxiv.org/abs/2501.16693
25. Sah, S., Moore, D.A., MacCoun, R.J.: Cheap talk and credibility: the consequences of confidence and accuracy on advisor credibility and persuasiveness. Organ. Behav. Hum. Decis. Process. **121**(2), 246–255 (2013). https://doi.org/10.1016/j.obhdp.2013.02.001
26. Schemmer, M., Kuehl, N., Benz, C., Bartos, A., Satzger, G.: Appropriate reliance on ai advice: Conceptualization and the effect of explanations. In: IUI: Proceedings of the 28th International Conference on Intelligent User Interfaces, pp. 410–422 (2023). https://doi.org/10.1145/3581641.3584066
27. Tejeda, H., Kumar, A., Smyth, P., Steyvers, M.: Ai-assisted decision-making: a cognitive modeling approach to infer latent reliance strategies. Comput. Brain Behav. **5**(4), 491–508 (2022). https://doi.org/10.1007/s42113-022-00157-y
28. Vaccaro, M., Almaatouq, A., Malone, T.: When combinations of humans and ai are useful: a systematic review and meta-analysis. Nature Human Behaviour, pp. 1–11 (2024). https://doi.org/10.1038/s41562-024-02024-1

29. Van Calster, B., McLernon, D.J., Van Smeden, M., Wynants, L., Steyerberg, E.W., diagnostic tests, T.G. prediction models' of the STRATOS initiative: Calibration: the achilles heel of predictive analytics. BMC Med. **17**(1), 230 (2019). https://doi.org/10.1186/s12916-019-1466-7
30. Vodrahalli, K., Gerstenberg, T., Zou, J.: Uncalibrated Models Can Improve Human-AI Collaboration. Advances in Neural Information Processing Systems **35**(NeurIPS) (2022)
31. Wellman, H.M.: Making minds: How theory of mind develops. Oxford University Press (2014)
32. Zhang, Q.s., Zhu, S.C.: Visual interpretability for deep learning: a survey. Front. Inf. Technol. Electron. Eng. **19**(1), 27–39 (2018). https://doi.org/10.1631/FITEE.1700808
33. Zhang, Y., Liao, Q.V., Bellamy, R.K.: Effect of confidence and explanation on accuracy and trust calibration in ai-assisted decision making. In: Proceedings of the 2020 Conference on Fairness, Accountability, and Transparency, pp. 295–305 (2020). https://doi.org/10.1145/3351095.3372852

**Open Access** This chapter is licensed under the terms of the Creative Commons Attribution 4.0 International License (http://creativecommons.org/licenses/by/4.0/), which permits use, sharing, adaptation, distribution and reproduction in any medium or format, as long as you give appropriate credit to the original author(s) and the source, provide a link to the Creative Commons license and indicate if changes were made.

The images or other third party material in this chapter are included in the chapter's Creative Commons license, unless indicated otherwise in a credit line to the material. If material is not included in the chapter's Creative Commons license and your intended use is not permitted by statutory regulation or exceeds the permitted use, you will need to obtain permission directly from the copyright holder.

# The Impact of Concept Explanations and Interventions on Human-Machine Collaboration

Jack Furby[1](✉)[iD], Dan Cunnington[2][iD], Dave Braines[3][iD], and Alun Preece[1][iD]

[1] Cardiff University, Cardiff, UK
furbyjl@cardiff.ac.uk
[2] Imperial College London, London, UK
[3] IBM Research Europe, Hursley, UK

**Abstract.** Deep Neural Networks (DNNs) are often considered black boxes due to their opaque decision-making processes. To reduce their opacity Concept Models (CMs), such as Concept Bottleneck Models (CBMs), were introduced to predict human-defined concepts as an intermediate step before predicting task labels. This enhances the interpretability of DNNs. In a human-machine setting greater interpretability enables humans to improve their understanding and build trust in a DNN. In the introduction of CBMs, the models demonstrated increased task accuracy as incorrect concept predictions were replaced with their ground truth values, known as intervening on the concept predictions. In a collaborative setting, if the model task accuracy improves from interventions, trust in a model and the human-machine task accuracy may increase. However, the result showing an increase in model task accuracy was produced without human evaluation and thus it remains unknown if the findings can be applied in a collaborative setting. In this paper, we ran the first human studies using CBMs to evaluate their human interaction in collaborative task settings. Our findings show that CBMs improve interpretability compared to standard DNNs, leading to increased human-machine alignment. However, this increased alignment did not translate to a significant increase in task accuracy. Understanding the model's decision-making process required multiple interactions, and misalignment between the model's and human decision-making processes could undermine interpretability and model effectiveness.

**Keywords:** Concept Models · Human study · Alignment · Interpretability · XAI

## 1 Introduction

Concept Model (CMs), such as Concept Bottleneck Model (CBMs) [13], is a class of Deep Neural Network (DNN) which aims to improve the interpretability of model predictions by structuring predictions around human-understandable components, called concepts. These concepts often correspond to intermediate attributes of tasks, effectively "splitting" the prediction process into sub-tasks. For instance, a CM that predicts types of birds, might predict concepts for the wing colour and beak shape.

After a CM makes a prediction a human collaborating with the model will be able to inspect concept predictions, known as *concept explanations*, to help understand the model's decision-making process. In domains such as healthcare this may be used to answer why a downstream task was predicted. With some CM architectures, such as CBMs, the concept explanations also introduce the capability for a human to intervene in the concept predictions. As CBMs predict concepts in the range of 0 to 1 (not present to present) with a 0.5 threshold, concept outputs can be replaced with new values within this range. Interventions may be made to correct mistakes the model made when predicting concepts, or otherwise query the model to see what task prediction would be made with a different set of concept predictions. In these scenarios the model's concept vector provides counterfactual explanations [13]. In a collaborative setting, we may consider interventions as a way to increase trust in a model as interventions may reveal the sensitivity a model has to concept values, and thus any bias the model has to concepts.

The authors of CBMs [13] presented results using automated metrics demonstrating improved model accuracy as incorrect concept predictions were intervened and replace with their ground truth values. In addition, model predictions have been shown as a preferred method to identify bias [1]. As the intervention metric was automated it remains unknown if the findings can be applied in a collaborative setting.

The authors of CBMs also made claims of improved human-machine collaboration [13], but human studies to show this are limited and instead compare CBMs to other model architectures [6,12], or complete tasks such as selecting the concepts participants believe the model detected [28]. Only a few studies analyse the class of CMs with collaborative tasks [21,22].

This paper presents two human studies where we analysed CBMs in a collaborative setting. We answer the research question: *Do Concept Models improve task accuracy and model interpretability in a human-machine setting?* We have broken this question down into the following sub-questions:

1. Do test-time interventions improve human-machine task and concept accuracy?
2. Do interventions increase the interpretability of CBMs?
3. Are CBMs trusted?

The main contributions of this paper are as follows:

- We perform the first human studies using CBMs in a joint human-machine task setting which analyses the interaction between humans and the CBM. We find interventions often increased trust in a model but this trust was sometimes misplaced. In addition, the CBM decision-making process is not aligned with that of the humans.

– We show the initial promise of interpretability from high-level concepts is upheld. However, understanding the model's decision-making process requires participants to actively interact with the model. Additionally, providing concept predictions without the capability to intervene has a similar effect on task accuracy.

Although we used CBMs, our findings also apply to other CMs with intervention capabilities and that predict task labels in the same feed-forward fashion from input to concepts, to task label. Namely these are Concept Embedding Models [31], Sidecar CBMs [18], and hybrid CBMs [19].

## 2 Related Work

Several studies have analysed CMs with human participants. These can be placed into several categories; human concept preference [2,23], concept explanations [6,11,12,27], human-in-the-loop [21,22] and bias discovery [20,30].

In studies on concept preference, one study found that concepts humans identified in samples varied widely and performed worse when used by a CM on downstream tasks compared to those identified by the model [2]. Separately, Participants have also been found to prefer to see 32 or fewer concepts [23] instead of all concepts a model uses for task predictions, if greater than 32. This is consistent with balancing a models completeness [15] to keep participants engaged [14].

Next, studies exploring concept explanations preference have demonstrated a mixed response where concept explanations are favoured in some studies [11], while not in others [6,12,27]. Out of these studies [6,27] evaluated explanation types for bias discovery and model task prediction. As concept explanations underperformed in this area it raises the question of whether CM's concept explanations improve the interpretability of models such that they can aid in human-machine collaboration.

Some studies have investigated human-machine collaboration with CMs. A CBM inspired recommender system was introduced that combined user-provided and automatically generated concepts to suggest relevant text documents [21]. Participants could intervene in the concepts by editing a concept value, leading to improvements of 20–47% in recommendation accuracy compared to initial concept values. A separate study asked participants to label images [22]. Participants either had fixed model predictions to help them or could select parts of the input image for the model to focus on, finding little difference in performance (73.57% vs. 72.68% respectively). Additionally, participants often agreed with the model's predictions regardless of whether the model was correct or incorrect. Both of these studies look at humans updating a model's prediction, similar to interventions with CBMs. As the recommender system [21] is explicitly based on CBMs, their findings suggest similarities could be observed in an image modality.

For bias discovery, [30] (and repeated in the study [20]) used CBM-like architectures to study human-guided pruning on a model where input samples had shifted (e.g. the correlation of concepts co-occurring is changed after training). Participants selected concepts to prune based on input samples and model predictions, outperforming random pruning and only slightly less effective than fine-tuning or greedy performance. This demonstrates that the concept explanations are effective at aiding a human-in-the-loop understanding of bias in a model.

From these studies, we have identified no papers which look at CBMs or similar model architectures that evaluate the capabilities of CBMs in real-world tasks. Most importantly it has not been shown if human performed interventions improve joint task performance, and whether these models are more interpretable than standard DNNs.

**Table 1.** Participants in the expert study were split into two groups, both with access to the same model. Participants in the lay-person study were split into eight groups where the model used and explanations provided were varied.

| Expert study | Lay-person study | |
|---|---|---|
| Participant groups | Participant groups | |
| | Accurate model | Inaccurate model |
| CExp+Int | NoExp | NoExp |
| CExp+Int+SMap | CExp | CExp |
| | CExp+Int | CExp+Int |
| | CExp+Int+SMap | CExp+Int+SMap |

## 3 Methods

We ran two human studies: (1) An expert study where participants had extensive knowledge about the task domain (skin disease diagnosis) where the model acted as a second opinion. (2) A lay-person study with a general task (Playing games of Blackjack), involving participants with experience levels ranging from novices to skilled individuals, but none being professionals. The model also acted as a second opinion, but could also serve as a guide for participants with less experience. Both studies received favourable ethical opinion from the School of Computer Science and Informatics at Cardiff University.

By running two studies we were able to compare results in similar, but distinct settings where participants can interact with an AI agent to assist them. Following the taxonomy by [5], our lay-person study is human-grounded as we do not use expert participants and use a simulated task, while the expert study is application-grounded as we use both expert participants and a real-world task.

We split participants into two groups in the expert study, and eight groups in the lay-person study, detailed in Table 1, and example explanations are shown in Fig. 1. As our sub-questions required us to analyse the use of interventions, interpretability, and trust of CBMs, both groups for the expert study included participant access to interventions. As we did not have the same limitation in the lay-person study we also included groups that had access to a different model and included groups with no model explanations and just concept explanations. 12 participants took part in the expert study who were either doctors, consultants or trainees with expertise in dermatology. 104 participants took part in the lay-person study where most were either university staff or students.

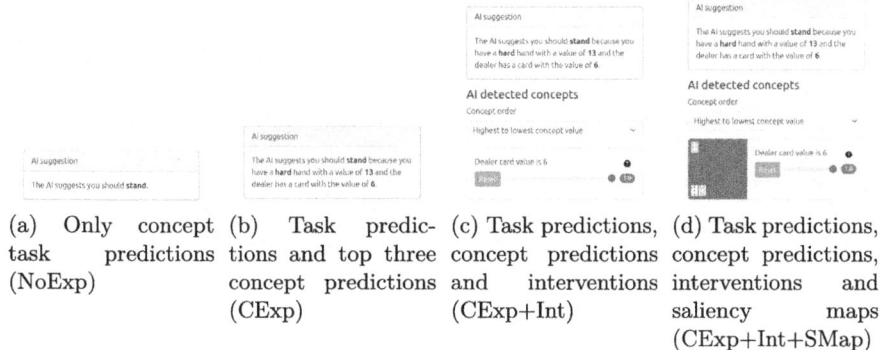

(a) Only concept task predictions (NoExp)  (b) Task predictions and top three concept predictions (CExp)  (c) Task predictions, concept predictions and interventions (CExp+Int)  (d) Task predictions, concept predictions, interventions and saliency maps (CExp+Int+SMap)

**Fig. 1.** Model output variations.

We use the following acronyms to separate each participant group:

Accurate model (Acc) Accurate model (lay-person study only).
Inaccurate model (Inacc) Inaccurate model (lay-person study only).
NoExp No explanations (lay-person study only).
CExp Predicted task label and concept explanations (lay-person study only).
CExp+Int CExp plus Intervention capability.
CExp+Int+SMap CExp+Int plus Saliency maps.
With Interventions (WithInt) Participants who not perform interventions or samples where interventions were performed.
No Interventions (NoInt) Participants who did not perform interventions or samples where no interventions were performed.

Acc and Inacc are placed before the model output and feature capabilities. WithInt and NoInt are placed after model output and feature capabilities. For example, participants using the accurate Blackjack model with concept explanations and interventions, and who performed interventions would be referred to as Acc-CExp+Int-WithInt.

## 3.1 Human Study Design

Expert study participants were asked to diagnose skin conditions in 10 images from the Skincon dataset [4]. We excluded images that were out of focus and limited images to those with the label "malignant melanoma" and "seborrhoeic keratosis" as a dermatologist would typically look to diagnose a patient. The images were shown in a random order.

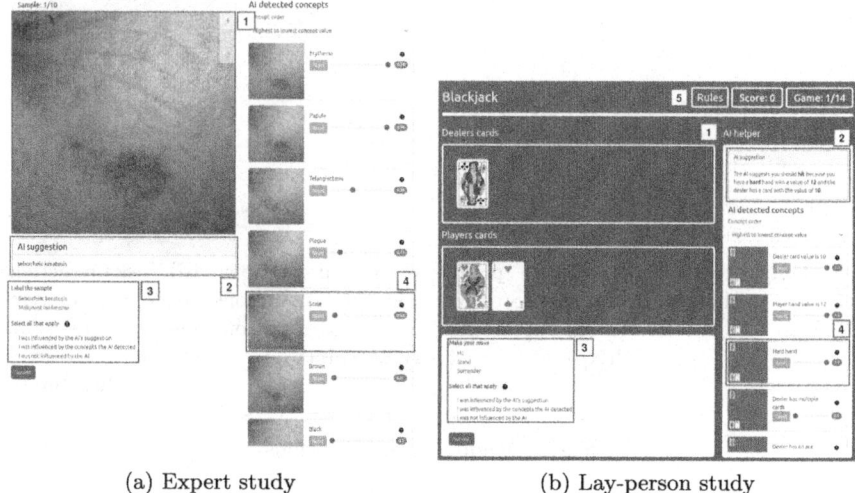

(a) Expert study     (b) Lay-person study

1: Sample image
2: AI agent output class and concept labels
3: Label selection and AI use options for the participant to select
4: Concept outputs, salience map, and intervention slider
5: Game rules, participant score, and game counter (lay-person study)

**Fig. 2.** Study interfaces with key components labeled.

For the lay-person study, each participant played 15 games of Blackjack, where the first game was without the model enabled while the other 14 included model predictions. Like with the expert study, the model suggested actions for participants to take. Each game had a maximum between 1 and 7 moves (depending on the cards dealt) with cards drawn from a single deck of cards. We removed betting and added a score which increased or decreased based on the number of wins and losses. Participants could select one of three moves: hit, stand, or surrender.

For each sample labelled/move made participants selected how they used the model. These options were: (1) I was influenced by the AI's suggestion, (2) I was influenced by the concepts the AI detected, and (3) I was not influenced by the

AI. These were designed to capture whether participants selected labels based on the model's outputs or disregarded them.

Depending on the explanation group, participants were provided with the model's task and concept predictions, saliency maps, and an intervention slider for each concept. Adjusting any intervention slider automatically updated the model's predicted task label. An example of the interfaces is shown in Fig. 2.

At the end of the study, participants completed a closing survey where they were asked to complete questions asking about the model explanations.

## 4 Experiment Set-Up

The studies share a number of similarities including interfaces and model capabilities. The studies also apply findings from [23] by reducing the number of concepts initially shown to participants by placing them into a scrollable list.

Both studies start with a short demographic survey asking participants for their age, gender, computer science experience and skin disease identification/blackjack experience. Computer science experience and skin disease identification/blackjack experience are recorded using a Likert scale [17]. Next, participants were briefed on how the model works at a high level and followed a tutorial so they know how to participate in the study and interact with the model. Following this participants compete the study, and finally complete a closing survey.

### 4.1 Datasets and Models

**Expert Study**[1]: The expert study uses a model trained on the Skincon dataset [4], a combination of Fitzpatrick 17k [8] and DDI [3]. This is a real-world dataset with 48 clinical concepts, of which we have kept 22 that occur 50 or more times. Concepts were selected by two dermatologists using standard descriptive terms such as "plaque" and "scale". We have provided an example sample with concept annotation in Fig. 3a . For task labels, we used the malignant label. We kept the original dataset splits with 10 samples removed from the training and validation splits for the study. In total, we used 2574 train samples, 644 validation samples and 656 test samples.

The Skincon model used a Densenet121 architecture [10] for the concept encoder which was initialised with pre-trained weights from ImageNet, and two linear layers with a ReLU activation function for the task predictor which was not pre-trained. The concept encoder was trained to maximise the AUC of concept predictions, while the task predictor was trained to minimise task loss. The concept encoder was trained with a learning rate of 0.00053, a SGD optimiser and trained for 100 epochs. The task predictor was trained with a learning rate of 0.0593, an Adam optimiser and trained for 100 epochs. The resulting model had a concept accuracy of 91.235% and a task accuracy of 88.474%. For the samples included in the study, the model was 70% accurate.

---

[1] Expert Study: https://github.com/JackFurby/skin-cbm-study.

**Lay-Person Study**[2]: For the lay-person study we created the dataset Blackjack[3] which is similar to Playing cards [7]. Concepts represent the sum of card values in the player's hand, whether the player has an "Ace" card with the value 11, the dealer's first card, and if the dealer has multiple cards. Task labels represent the best move available to the player according to the single deck strategy guide [25]. These labels are *hit* (player gets another card), *stand* (player ends the game with their current cards), *surrender* (player forfeits their hand for a smaller loss), and *bust* (player's cards sums to over 21).

We created two versions *standard Blackjack*, and *mixed Blackjack*. Standard Blackjack uses one style of playing cards, whereas mixed Blackjack uses a different style for all "Ace" and "Seven" cards. This allowed us to artificially reduce the accuracy of a model trained on mixed Blackjack if tested on standard Blackjack samples. Each dataset variation has 10,000 samples which are split into training samples and test samples with a 70%-30% split respectively. Example samples can be seen in Figs. 3b and 3c.

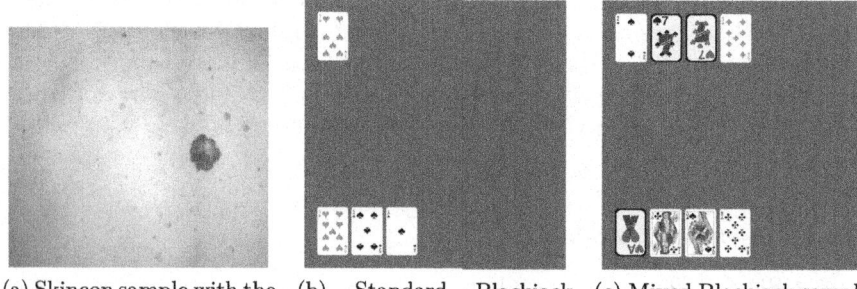

(a) Skincon sample with the present concepts "Plaque" and "Patch"
(b) Standard Blackjack sample
(c) Mixed Blackjack sample

**Fig. 3.** Example samples from the datasets.

Blackjack models used a VGG-11 architecture with batch normalisation [26] for the concept encoder and two linear layers with a ReLU activation function for the task predictor. Blackjack models were trained to minimise the concept and task loss. The concept encoder was trained with a learning rate of 0.02 using a SGD optimiser. The task predictors had a learning rate of 0.01, used used an Adam optimiser. The models were trained for 200 epochs. The standard Blackjack model achieved a concept accuracy of 99.818% and a task accuracy of 98.874%. The mixed Blackjack model achieved a concept accuracy of 96.434% and a task accuracy of 81.306%.

---

[2] Lay-person study: https://github.com/JackFurby/blackjack-cbm-study.
[3] Blackjack dataset: https://huggingface.co/datasets/JackFurby/blackjack.

## 4.2 Evaluation Methodology

In our studies, we analysed interventions, trust, interpretability, and human-machine performance. To understand when interventions are made we have classified them into two categories: *error correction* and *feature adjustment*. Error correction interventions are concepts that are intervened a maximum of once per sample where the intervened concept value $\bar{c}$ is in the range $0 \leq \bar{c} \leq 0.1$ or $0.9 \leq \bar{c} \leq 1$. Feature adjustments are all other interventions, including concepts that are intervened more than once in a sample, or where the intervened concept value is in the range $0.1 < \bar{c} < 0.9$. Feature adjustment interventions are when the participant is not certain the model has incorrectly predicted the presence of a concept, or where they are inspecting how concepts change task label predictions.

We have also assigned the following labels to understand how the concept value changes with interventions:

- Binary change: A concept changes from present to not present, or vice versa.
- Changed model task label: An intervention changes the predicted task label.
- Magnitude: How much interventions changes concept values by.
- Cumulative Change: The total difference between model predicted concept values to the final intervened concept values.
- Reversal: Whether final intervened concept values are close to initial concept values.

We also tracked interventions over time to evaluate if the rate of interventions increased or decreased. For trust, we evaluated participant and model task label alignment. If the model and human task labels are the same for a large proportion of samples we can argue the human participants trust the model [16,29]. We also analysed team performance in comparison to ground truth labels from the dataset.

We repeated the test-time intervention metric [13] to measure the change in task accuracy and concepts after interventions. This metric measures the change in model task accuracy when concepts are intervened on. Unlike the original evaluation with CBM [13], our results used human-performed interventions.

At the end of the study participants answered SCS [9] questions to measure quality for AI explanations. Specifically these questions use a Likert scale and ask participants how they perceived the models ability to answer "why" it made task and concept predictions.

## 5 Results

The expert study demographic survey showed participants either agreed or strongly agreed that they can diagnose skin diseases from images. Computer experience was evenly distributed between strongly disagree and agree. In the lay-person study participant demographic showed computer experience increased with blackjack experience.

In the expert study, 120 samples were labelled with 93 interventions performed by 7 out of the 12 participants. Meanwhile, in the lay-person study, 1,456 games of blackjack were played with model move suggestions, and 104 games were played without a model output. 243 interventions were performed by 23 participants out of 52 who had the capability to do so. 65.4% of interventions were performed on the inaccurate model, and 34.6% of interventions performed on the accurate model.

### 5.1 Intervention Classification

Table 2. Breakdown of interventions performed in the studies.

| Data subset | Total interventions (count) | Error correction (count) | Feature adjustment (count) | Interventions per sample (count) | Concept intervened per sample (count) | Binary (count) | Changed model task label (count) | Reversal (count) | Mean intervention magnitude (normalized value) | Mean cumulative magnitude (normalized value) |
|---|---|---|---|---|---|---|---|---|---|---|
| **Expert study** | | | | | | | | | | |
| All | 93 | 48 | 45 | 2.91 | 2.50 | 44 | 14 | 11 | 0.48 | 0.5 |
| CExp+Int | 82 | 48 | 34 | 3.04 | 2.78 | 41 | 12 | 6 | 0.49 | 0.52 |
| CExp+Int+SMap | 11 | 0 | 11 | 2.20 | 1 | 3 | 2 | 5 | 0.39 | 0.11 |
| **Lay-person study** | | | | | | | | | | |
| All | 243 | 83 | 160 | 4.05 | 2.42 | 152 | 29 | 60 | 0.58 | 0.53 |
| Acc-CExp+Int | 55 | 11 | 44 | 3.93 | 2.71 | 38 | 8 | 7 | 0.59 | 0.57 |
| Inacc-CExp+Int | 73 | 47 | 26 | 3.48 | 2.57 | 41 | 8 | 20 | 0.56 | 0.52 |
| Acc-CExp+Int+SMap | 29 | 0 | 29 | 4.83 | 1.50 | 17 | 5 | 8 | 0.52 | 0.11 |
| Inacc-CExp+Int+SMap | 86 | 25 | 61 | 4.53 | 2.32 | 56 | 8 | 25 | 0.62 | 0.58 |

Table 2 summarises interventions. Expert study CExp+Int participants performed 58.5% error correction interventions and 41.5% feature adjustment interventions. 17.6% of interventions were reversed. 2.78 concepts were intervened per sample with at least one intervention with each intervention changing a concept value by approximately 0.5. Half of all interventions change a concept's presence. 12 interventions changed the model's task prediction, suggesting the model is not sensitive to the concepts participants intervened on.

CExp+Int+SMap participants performed fewer interventions with all being feature adjustments and almost all interventions reversed. This indicates all interventions were performed to explore a model's concept sensitivity.

Lay-person study participants demonstrated similar trends with CExp+Int+SMap participants performing more feature adjustment interventions while CExp+Int participants performed a mix of both intervention types. Those with an accurate model primarily performed feature adjustments, aligning with model sensitivity exploration, while those with an inaccurate model split interventions nearly evenly between error correction (47.2%) and feature adjustments (52.7%).

CExp+Int+SMap participants increased intervention frequency (4.53–4.83 vs. 3.48–3.93 concept intervened), though reduced the number of interventions per sample (1–2 vs. 2–3). Binary interventions were common with inaccurate models, likely due to increased error corrections (47 vs. 11 concepts intervened). High reversal rates for inaccurate models suggest participants required additional interventions to refine their mental model, possibly indicating a misalignment between participants and the model's decision processes. E.g. if the participant plays with a different strategy.

## 5.2 Human-Machine Task Alignment

We measured the alignment between participant-selected task labels and model predicted task labels to determine if participants trusted the model or not. To further reinforce if alignment is helping the human-machine team, we also compare team accuracy to determine if trust is justified.

Table 3 shows expert study alignment. As there is no guarantee the final model task prediction is the model prediction that a participant aligns with, the overall alignment includes agreement with initial and post-intervention task labels. Alignment for this ranges from 60% to 81.8%. Initial alignment reflects the model's original label and is consistently higher for participants without interventions, final alignment only includes the model's last task label after interventions, and intermediate alignment includes model labels between the initial model task prediction and final task prediction.

A slight decline in alignment is observed with WithInt participants (78.1% vs. 81.8%) and CExp+Int+SMap participants (80% vs. 81.7%). These findings suggest interventions influence participants' labelling decisions, reducing agreement with the model. In fact, initial alignment with interventions (65.6%) is closer to the model's actual accuracy (70%). This indicates interventions help participants calibrate trust to align with the model's true accuracy. Meanwhile, NoInt participants appear to over-trust the model. A one-tailed t-test reveals statistical significance with a p-value of 0.03, below the 0.05 threshold, confirming that the absence of interventions led to increased alignment in this study.

**Table 3.** Expert study human-machine task alignment.

| Data subset | Overall (%) | Initial model task prediction (%) | Intermediate model task prediction (%) | Final model task prediction (%) |
|---|---|---|---|---|
| All | 80.8 (±3.6) | 77.5 (±3.8) | 77.8 (±8.2) | 65.6 (±8.5) |
| CExp+Int | **81.7 (±5.0)** | 76.7 (±5.5) | 81.8 (±8.4) | 70.4 (±9.0) |
| CExp+Int+SMap | 80.0 (±5.2) | 78.3 (±5.4) | 60.0 (±24.5) | 40.0 (±24.5) |
| NoInt | **81.8 (±4.1)** | 81.8 (±4.1) | – | – |
| WithInt | 78.1 (±7.4) | 65.6 (±8.5) | 77.8 (±8.2) | 65.6 (±8.5) |
| CExp+Int-NoInt | **81.8 (±6.8)** | 81.8 (±6.8) | – | – |
| CExp+Int-WithInt | 81.5 (±7.6) | 70.4 (±9.0) | 81.8 (±8.4) | 70.4 (±9.0) |
| CExp+Int+SMap-NoInt | **81.8 (±5.2)** | 81.8 (±5.2) | – | – |
| CExp+Int+SMap-WithInt | 60.0 (±24.5) | 40.0 (±24.5) | 60.0 (±24.5) | 40.0 (±24.5) |

However, the difference in alignment between CExp+Int and CExp+Int+SMap participants was not statistically significant (p-value of 0.59), suggesting that saliency maps had no meaningful impact on alignment. However, a larger study may confirm otherwise.

Alignment for the lay-person study is shown in Table 4 averages to 77.3%, which is lower than the model task accuracy (99.8% for the accurate model and 96.4% for the inaccurate model). However, participants may have playing strategies misaligned with the training data. Alignment in this study differs from the expert study as interventions increase alignment (86.7% vs. 77.1%). Further, participants using the accurate model consistently had a higher alignment than the inaccurate model.

Across all participant groups, interventions improve human-machine alignment. Alignment also increases from the initial model prediction to the final model prediction for most participant subsets. A one-tailed t-test supports this by rejecting the null hypothesis (no alignment increase) and accepting the alternative (interventions improve alignment), with p-values of 0.041 for all participants and 0.04 for those capable of performing interventions, both below the 0.05

**Table 4.** Lay-person study human-machine task alignment.

| Data subset | Overall (%) | Initial model task prediction (%) | Intermediate model task prediction (%) | Final model task prediction (%) |
|---|---|---|---|---|
| All | 77.3 (±0.8) | 77.1 (±0.8) | 81.5 (±5.3) | 83.3 (±4.9) |
| NoInt | 77.1 (±0.8) | 77.1 (±0.8) | – | – |
| WithInt | **86.7 (±4.4)** | 76.7 (±5.5) | 81.5 (±5.3) | 83.3 (±4.9) |
| Acc | **80.1 (±1.1)** | 80.0 (±1.1) | 93.8 (±6.2) | 90.0 (±6.9) |
| Inacc | 74.6 (±1.2) | 74.3 (±1.2) | 76.3 (±7.0) | 80.0 (±6.4) |
| Acc-NoExp | **79.8 (±2.2)** | 79.8 (±2.2) | – | – |
| Inacc-NoExp | 70.4 (±2.6) | 70.4 (±2.6) | – | – |
| Acc-CExp | **84.5 (±2.0)** | 84.5 (±2.0) | – | – |
| Inacc-CExp | 73.9 (±2.5) | 73.9 (±2.5) | – | – |
| Acc-CExp+Int-NoInt | 78.8 (±2.4) | 78.8 (±2.4) | – | – |
| Acc-CExp+Int-WithInt | **92.9 (±7.1)** | 78.6 (±11.4) | 90.0 (±10.0) | 92.9 (±7.1) |
| Inacc-CExp+Int-NoInt | 74.8 (±2.5) | 74.8 (±2.5) | – | – |
| Inacc-CExp+Int-WithInt | **76.2 (±9.5)** | 66.7 (±10.5) | 73.7 (±10.4) | 71.4 (±10.1) |
| Acc-CExp+Int+SMap-NoInt | 76.0 (±2.5) | 76.0 (±2.5) | – | – |
| Acc-CExp+Int+SMap-WithInt | **100 (±0.0)** | 100 (±0.0) | 100 (±0.0) | 83.3 (±16.7) |
| Inacc-CExp+Int+SMap-NoInt | 78.5 (±2.4) | 78.5 (±2.4) | – | – |
| Inacc-CExp+Int+SMap-WithInt | **89.5 (±7.2)** | 78.9 (±9.6) | 78.9 (±9.6) | 89.5 (±7.2) |

significance threshold. Additionally, comparing CExp participants to NoExp participants resulted in a p-value of 0.036, showing concept explanations also result in a higher human-machine alignment. These results show both interventions and concept explanations increase human-machine task alignment.

If appropriate trust is given to the model, we should expect the human-machine accuracy to be higher than the model alone. Table 5 shows human-machine accuracy for the expert study. Accuracy is averaged by participants, assuming that they build a mental model of the model over time. Even if an indi-

**Table 5.** Expert study human-machine task accuracy.

| Data Subset | Overall Accuracy (%) | Malignant Melanoma(%) | Seborrheic Keratosis (%) |
|---|---|---|---|
| All | 78.3 (±2.4) | 88.3 (±4.6) | 68.3 (±3.9) |
| CExp+Int | 75.0 (±3.4) | 83.3 (±8.0) | 66.7 (±4.2) |
| CExp+Int+SMap | **81.7 (±3.1)** | 93.3 (±4.2) | 70.0 (±6.8) |
| NoInt | 78.0 (±3.7) | 88.0 (±8.0) | 68.0 (±8.0) |
| WithInt | **78.6 (±3.4)** | 88.6 (±5.9) | 68.6 (±4.0) |
| CExp+Int-NoInt | 75.0 (±5.0) | 80.0 (±20.0) | 70.0 (±10.0) |
| CExp+Int-WithInt | 75.0 (±5.0) | 85.0 (±9.6) | 65.0 (±5.0) |
| CExp+Int+SMap-NoInt | 80.0 (±5.8) | 93.3 (±6.7) | 66.7 (±13.3) |
| CExp+Int+SMap-WithInt | **83.3 (±3.3)** | 93.3 (±6.7) | 73.3 (±6.7) |

vidual prediction is ignored, they may still influence participants. For instance, participants may recognise when the model is incorrect without the need to perform interventions.

In the expert study CExp+Int participants achieved an accuracy of 75% and CExp+Int+SMap participants achieved an accuracy of 81.7%, indicating that the additional information provided by saliency maps aids decision-making. WithInt Participants had a slightly higher accuracy than NoInt participants (78.6% vs. 78%), suggesting interventions either match or slightly enhance participant performance. However, the expert study lacks the sample size to show statistical significance. A one-tailed t-test resulted in a p-value of 0.09 for accuracy being higher if participants had saliency maps, and a p-value of 0.46 if participants performed interventions.

In the lay-person study (Table 6) the largest increase in task accuracy came from participants using the accurate model compared to the inaccurate model. Interventions only increased human-machine accuracy for participants using the inaccurate model. This suggests participants are over-trusting the model, expectedly considering interventions increased alignment as just discussed in Table 4. Despite this, the lowest task accuracy was achieved by Inacc-CExp and Inacc-NoExp participants and participants with the AI disabled. Therefore interventions are still showing signs of increasing human-machine accuracy.

A one-tailed t-test resulted in a p-value of 0.042 showed CExp improved task accuracy compared to NoExp. In contrast, participants who performed inter-

**Table 6.** lay-person study human-machine task accuracy averaged by participant.

| Data Subset | Accuracy (%) |
|---|---|
| AI disabled | 74.4 (±3.9) |
| All | 83.6 (±0.9) |
| WithInt | 83.3 (±1.1) |
| NoInt | **84.7 (±1.8)** |
| Acc | **84.6 (±2.7)** |
| Inacc | 78.1 (±3.2) |
| Acc-NoExp | **84.6 (±2.7)** |
| Inacc-NoExp | 78.1 (±3.2) |
| Acc-CExp | **91.0 (±2.4)** |
| Inacc-CExp | 81.4 (±1.6) |
| Acc-CExp+Int-NoInt | **86.6 (±3.3)** |
| Acc-CExp+Int-WithInt | 83.8 (±2.9) |
| Inacc-CExp+Int-NoInt | 75.7 (±4.6) |
| Inacc-CExp+Int-WithInt | **84.3 (±1.8)** |
| Acc-CExp+Int+SMap-NoInt | 83.4 (±2.4) |
| Acc-CExp+Int+SMap-WithInt | 83.4 (±6.4) |
| Inacc-CExp+Int+SMap-NoInt | 83.5 (±2.9) |
| Inacc-CExp+Int+SMap-WithInt | **86.6 (±3.6)** |

ventions did not achieve a statistically significant improvement in task accuracy compared to those who did not, achieving a p-value of 0.27 when compared to all NoExp and CExp participant groups and 0.195 when compared to participants who did not perform interventions but had the capability to do so. While we observed a trend of higher accuracy among participants using interventions, we cannot conclude that interventions directly improve task accuracy.

Overall, our findings indicate that concepts are beneficial for improving human-machine alignment and human-machine task accuracy. Interventions are beneficial for increasing human-machine task alignment but do not result in a statistically significant increase in task accuracy and can result in over-trust.

### 5.3 Interventions Over Time

We may expect the number of interventions to decrease over time as participants learn about a model's sensitivity to concepts. We found this is the case in both the expert study (Fig. 4a) where we show we show the average number of interventions per sample with the standard error, and the layperson study when the model correctly predicts concepts (Fig. 4b) where we show the decline with a rolling average. An exception to the decline is seen with Acc-CExp+Int participants in the lay-person study where there is a spike of interventions performed on game 13 with an average of 7 and a standard error of ±2. As this occurs once, this spike is not representative of all participants.

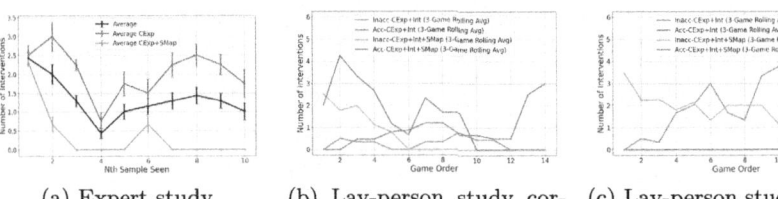

(a) Expert study   (b) Lay-person study correctly predicted concepts   (c) Lay-person study incorrectly predicted concepts

**Fig. 4.** Interventions performed declined over time except for incorrectly predicted concepts in the lay-person study where the number of interventions performed remains constant.

In the expert study, CExp+Int+SMap participants see a sharp decline in interventions, while CExp+Int participants see an initial decline which recovers for later samples. This suggests saliency map explanations provide additional insights into the model's concept predictions. CExp+Int participants appear to be incentivised to use interventions as a means of understanding the model's decision-making process.

For incorrect concept predictions in the lay-person study, participants consistently performed around 2 interventions per sample. These results demonstrate participants identify concepts that need to be intervened on while ignoring the concepts that are correctly predicted by the models.

Overall, these results show that participants initially explore the model's capabilities and sensitivity to concept values before developing a mental model and reducing the number of interventions performed to where it is required.

### 5.4 Test-Time Intervention and Concept Accuracy

The authors of CBMs showed results using the metric test-time intervention where interventions updating concept predictions with ground truth concept values improved model task performance [13]. However, it remains unknown how interventions improve model task performance when interventions are made by humans.

In the related work section, we discussed [2] where they found CBMs may not apply the same weight to concepts for task labels as humans would. Therefore we hypothesise interventions performed by humans may not see an improvement in task accuracy which would show a misalignment between humans and the model's sensitivity to concepts.

Test-time intervention results are shown in Fig. 5a for the expert study and Figs. 5d and 5g for the lay-person study. Task accuracy is averaged by participant and explanation groups. We only included the same samples between with interventions and without. For example, if participants intervened on concepts for samples 1 and 3 but not 2, we only work out the task accuracy for samples 1 and 3. As participants performed 2–3 interventions on average in each study conclusions for concept and task accuracy past these intervention counts cannot always be made.

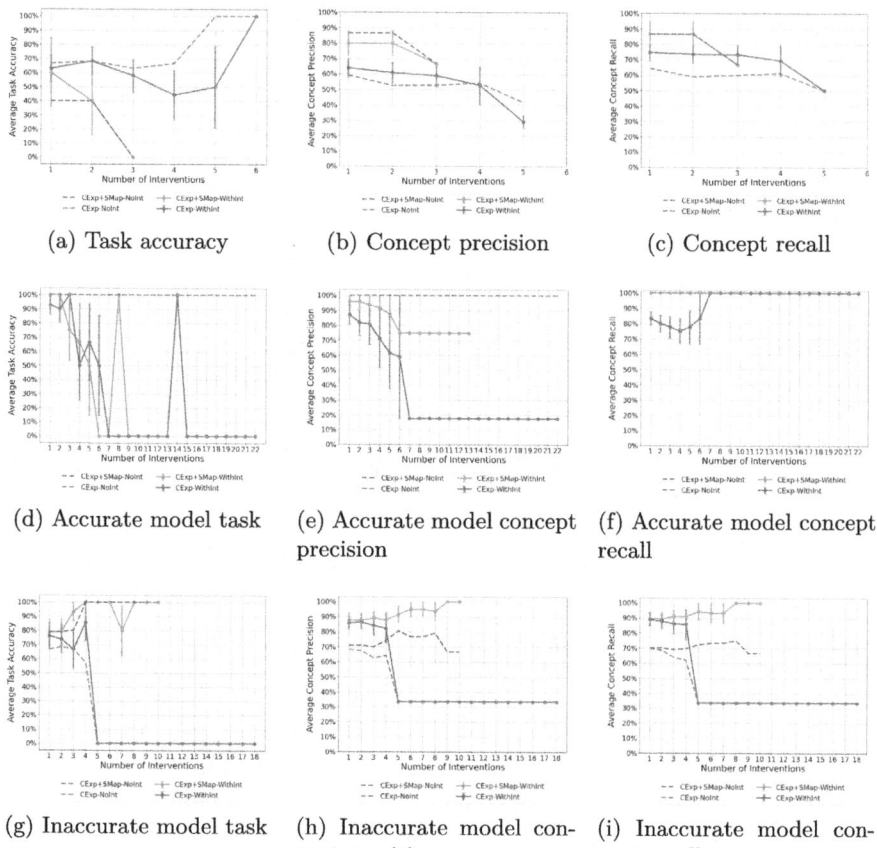

**Fig. 5.** Interventions decrease model task accuracy in the expert study and the layperson study accurate model while increasing model task accuracy with the lay-person study inaccurate model. Concept precision and recall increase with interventions in most cases.

Task accuracy, for the most part, does not improve with interventions compared to no interventions. In the expert study between 1–3 interventions task accuracy is close to matching the accuracy of the model with no interventions, and outperforms the model with 1 intervention for CExp+Int+SMap participants. In the lay-person study task accuracy initially declines slightly for the accurate model before sharply declining, although with large error bars. The exception to declining task accuracy is observed for the lay-person study inaccurate model where interventions increase or match the model's initial task accuracy.

In addition to task accuracy, we have also measured the change in concept accuracy. Figure 5b and Fig. 5c shows the precision and recall for the expert study, Fig. 5e and Fig. 5f for the lay-person study accurate model, and Fig. 5h and Fig. 5i for the inaccurate model. Notably, in the expert study and lay-person study with the inaccurate model, interventions lead to an increase or matching the precision and recall. In the lay-person study with the accurate model, precision is lower than the model concept prediction, while recall initially declines before rising the match the model. Most of these results also have no overlapping error bars between the model-predicated concepts and intervened concepts.

Table 7. Likert Scores for SCS questions.

| Question | All | CExp+Int | CExp+Int+SMap | WithInt | NoInt | Skin Experience Agree | Skin Experience Strongly Agree |
|---|---|---|---|---|---|---|---|
| Factors in data | 3.09 | 3.00 | 3.20 | 3.00 | 3.20 | 2.80 | **3.33** |
| Understood | 3.73 | 3.33 | 4.20 | 3.67 | 3.80 | 3.60 | **3.83** |
| Change detail level | 3.18 | **3.67** | 2.60 | 3.50 | 2.80 | 2.80 | 3.50 |
| Need support | 3.64 | 3.33 | **4.00** | 3.50 | 3.80 | **4.00** | 3.33 |
| Understanding causality | 3.00 | 3.17 | 2.80 | **3.33** | 2.60 | 2.80 | 3.17 |
| Use with knowledge | 3.45 | 3.50 | 3.40 | 3.50 | 3.40 | 3.00 | **3.83** |
| No inconsistencies | 3.00 | 3.17 | 2.80 | 3.00 | 3.00 | 2.60 | **3.33** |
| Learn to understand | 3.55 | 3.50 | 3.60 | 3.50 | 3.60 | 3.20 | **3.83** |
| Needs references | 3.73 | 3.67 | 3.80 | 3.50 | 4.00 | 3.60 | **3.83** |
| Efficient | 3.45 | **3.67** | 3.20 | **3.67** | 3.20 | 3.40 | 3.50 |
| **Overall score** | 0.68 | 0.68 | 0.67 | 0.68 | 0.67 | 0.64 | **0.71** |

As previously discussed. We expect participants to explore a model's sensitivity to concept values. In the lay-person study accurate model we observe the clearest sign of this. In particular with concept recall where recall initially falls before increasing from 4 interventions. This shows participants appear to be exploring the concept speck before correcting concept values and making a move.

When combining all test-time intervention results, it becomes clear that CBMs are mostly not aligned to the concepts participants are adjusting. Although interventions often make concept vectors more accurate, task accuracy does not reflect this improvement. This aligns with the findings in [2].

### 5.5 System Causability Scale

We used the SCS [9] to get a subjective rating of explanation suitability with expert study results presented in Table 7. The overall score, computed as the average of participants' summed responses normalised by the maximum possible score. This score is between 0 and 1 where 0.68 indicates an average response [9]. Almost all overall scores are either 0.68 or slightly below. The sub-section of participants who's overall score exceeded this are participants who selected "strongly agree" as their experience at classifying skin diseases in the demographic survey, with a score of 0.71.

For individual questions, most averaged to be between high 2 and high 3 (Likart options "disagree" and "neutral"). A few questions stand out. Starting with *change detail level* (*I could change the level of detail on demand*) was rated higher for CExp+Int participants, WithInt participants, and participants who self-rated their experience at skin disease identification as "strongly agree" (of which 57% performed interventions). This suggests that if participants perform interventions they understand the information it provides.

*Need support* (*I did not need support to understand the explanations*) averaged to 4 for both CExp+Int+SMap participants and participants who answered their skin disease identification experience as "agree". For CExp+Int+SMap participants these results indicates the potential benefit saliency maps provide to help participants interpret the model's concept predictions. For skin experience agree participants, 60% of which used interventions (with two of these participants performing almost 60 interventions), suggests their increased interaction with the model improved their understanding of the model.

Finally, *efficient* (*I received the explanations in a timely and efficient manner*) was also consistently rated slightly over 3. WithIntParticipants answered this question with a slightly higher score than NoInt participants.

Responses from the SCS questions for the lay-person study are shown in Table 8. All overall scores are 0.70 or above. The highest score was 0.78 for Acc-CExp participants. Surprisingly, Acc-NoExp participants score was 0.74 which matches some participant groups who had access to concepts and interventions. As each participant only answered questions for one version of the explanations instead of ranking each, this may be attributed to the similar scores.

The SCS results suggest that incorporating concepts improves participants' understanding of causality as shown by the questions *Understanding causality* (*I found the explanations helped me to understand causality*) scoring higher with the inclusion of explanation techniques, although the differences between participant groups was small. Additionally, These results varied between studies where the

**Table 8.** Lay-person study Likert scores for SCS questions.

| Question | All Participants | Acc-NoExp | Inacc-NoExp | Acc-CExp | Inacc-CExp | Acc-CExp+Int | Inacc-CExp+Int | Acc-CExp+Int+SMap | Inacc-CExp+Int+SMap | CExp+Int-WithInt and CExp+Int+SMap-WithInt | CExp+Int-NoInt and CExp+Int+SMap-NoInt |
|---|---|---|---|---|---|---|---|---|---|---|---|
| Factors in data | 3.39 | 3.08 | 2.85 | **3.92** | 3.69 | 3.62 | 3.50 | 3.23 | 3.25 | 2.87 | 3.25 |
| Understood | 4.18 | 4.08 | 4.15 | **4.31** | **4.31** | 4.23 | 4.17 | 4.08 | 4.08 | 4.13 | 4.08 |
| Change detail level | 2.91 | 2.69 | 2.31 | 2.77 | 2.38 | 3.38 | **3.50** | 3.31 | 3.00 | 3.13 | 3.00 |
| Need support | 3.77 | 3.92 | 3.92 | 3.77 | 3.62 | 3.54 | **4.17** | 3.54 | 3.75 | 3.61 | 3.75 |
| Understanding causality | 3.51 | 3.15 | 3.38 | 3.62 | 3.46 | 3.31 | 3.75 | 3.46 | **4.00** | 3.43 | **4.00** |
| Use with knowledge | 3.99 | 4.15 | 3.92 | 4.23 | 3.62 | 3.92 | 3.92 | 3.85 | **4.33** | 3.91 | **4.33** |
| No inconsistencies | 3.59 | 3.77 | 3.38 | **4.15** | 3.54 | 3.54 | 3.08 | 3.77 | 3.42 | 2.96 | 3.42 |
| Learn to understand | 4.06 | **4.31** | 4.15 | 4.00 | 4.15 | 3.92 | 4.00 | 3.92 | 4.00 | 3.74 | 4.00 |
| Needs references | 3.64 | **4.00** | 3.77 | 3.85 | 3.46 | 3.54 | 3.33 | 3.54 | 3.58 | 3.13 | 3.58 |
| Efficient | 4.24 | 4.08 | 3.85 | 4.15 | **4.62** | 4.15 | 4.42 | 4.08 | 4.58 | 4.26 | 4.58 |
| **Overall score** | 0.75 | 0.74 | 0.71 | **0.78** | 0.74 | 0.74 | 0.76 | 0.74 | 0.76 | 0.70 | 0.76 |

expert study answered this question inline with the lay-person study with no model explanations. Model outputs were generally well understood as shown by the results for *Understood* (*I understood the explanations within the context of my work.*), and *learn to understand* (*I think that most people would learn to understand the explanations very quickly*).

Overall, while model outputs were generally well understood, reflected in the scores for Understood ("I understood the explanations within the context of my work") and Learn to understand ("I think that most people would learn to understand the explanations very quickly"), there are indications of a possible mismatch between human and machine decision-making. *Understood, Learn to understand, Use with knowledge, No inconsistencies* ("I did not find inconsistencies between explanations"), and *Need references* ("I did not need more references in the explanations: e.g., medical guidelines, regulations") were all scored lower if participants made interventions. Although *no inconsistencies* was also low for the inaccurate model it also shows interventions may be causing confusion over how they relate to task predictions or how they are used instead of aiding in completing the task.

## 6 Discussion

Before beginning the discussion, we have detailed several limitations in our studies. The expert study had a small sample size, which may limit the generalisability of our findings. To address this, we conducted a larger lay-person study and drew parallels between the two to provide additional context. Additionally, participants in the expert study lacked access to patient history, high-quality diagnostic images, and multiple images of each sample, which may be expected in clinical settings. To mitigate this, we simplified the task to distinguish between "malignant melanoma" and "seborrhoeic keratosis" which have clear visual differences. Finally, in the lay-person study, participants played Blackjack, meaning game success depended partly on luck, though our evaluation focused on optimal moves rather than overall game outcomes.

From our human studies evaluating CBMs, we observed mixed results regarding interpretability and task performance. While our findings reinforce CBMs interpretability with participants who utilised concepts and interventions to explore the concept space and inspect task predictions, task accuracy improvements were inconsistent. Notably, while concept accuracy increased, task accuracy mostly decreased.

### 6.1 Do Test-Time Interventions Improve Human-Machine Task and Concept Accuracy?

Test-time interventions found mixed results across models. In most cases, task accuracy with interventions matched or underperformed the model's accuracy with no interventions, with further declines in task accuracy as the number of interventions increased. The only notable increases in model task accuracy was seen in the lay-person study with the inaccurate model. Following our test-time intervention results, it suggests interventions have the risk of leading to decreased task accuracy if humans follow model task predictions after interventions are performed.

For concept accuracy, interventions increased accuracy. Despite this not being consistent across all models, decreases in some situations (e.g. accurate blackjack model) were expected to account for participants learning the model's sensitivity to concepts.

Similar to [2], our findings suggest that CBMs task predictions may use different concepts than humans use. Future research should explore methods to align CBM decision-making with human decision-making.

## 6.2 Do Interventions Increase the Interpretability of Concept Bottleneck Models?

In the expert study, interventions were almost evenly split between error correction and feature adjustments. Further, intervention decreased over time, suggesting that participants relied on interventions less as they developed a mental model of the model's behaviour. This aligns with the idea that CBMs improve interpretability.

Saliency maps decreased the number of interventions performed suggesting they provide sufficient insight into the model's behaviour. However, participants also reported they placed little weight on the model's predictions, implying that participants preferred their own intuition than relying on the model.

Regarding the lay-person study, participants using the accurate models primarily performed feature adjustments, with nearly 75% of interventions involving changes to concept presence. Combined with the eventual increase in concept recall, this indicates participants used the interpretability of concepts to improve their understanding of the model. More interventions, including reversals, were performed with the inaccurate model.

While we observe a decline in interventions over time in both studies, part of this decline may be attributed to the novelty of interventions, with engagement naturally decreasing as participants became more familiar with the task. Although we cannot entirely rule out this effect, the fact that the decline is not uniform, particularly in the lay-person study, where interventions remained higher when concepts were incorrectly predicted suggests that participants were not merely losing interest but actively leveraging interventions to improve their understanding of the model.

Our findings support the claim that CBMs improve interpretability by allowing users to interactively query and adjust concept predictions. However, we have identified this process is limiting as humans are required to seek explanations and iteratively probe the model's concept sensitivity, which may not be practical or obvious for all users or applications. Further, our study does not look at the role of the interface in engaging participants to interact with the model. We suggest future research should look at the delivery of concept explanations to ensure they are efficiently delivered.

## 6.3 Are Concept Bottleneck Models Trusted?

We chose to use alignment as a proxy for trust [24]. In the expert study, NoInt participants aligned to the model's predictions 81% of the time, which is 11% higher than the model's accuracy on the samples in the study suggesting overtrust. In contrast, WithInt participants were aligned to the model's initial task prediction 66% of the time, 4% lower than the model's accuracy. Alignment then increased by almost 13% after interventions. In addition, accuracy was higher for WithInt participants compared to NoInt participants. This shows interventions increased trust, which itself was better justified compared to participants who did not use interventions.

For the lay-person study, alignment was lower than the model's accuracy before interventions. When participants used interventions, alignment increased significantly across all participant groups. However, this increase in alignment only increased task accuracy for participants using the inaccurate model. This shows the potential for interventions to lead to over-trust. In addition, providing just concept explanations lead to an increase in alignment while also increasing task accuracy.

The trends of alignment and joint task accuracy are conflicting between the studies. We hypothesis this is because in the expert study the model outputs were used purely as a second opinion as the participants would have sufficient expertise in the task domain. As this is not guaranteed in the lay-person study we believe participants may follow the model if they are unsure themselves. This is a concerning point if these models are deployed in situations where humans are not domain experts.

## 7 Conclusion

In this paper, we ran the first studies to evaluate how humans use CBMs in a collaborative setting. We focused on how concepts are interacted with and the interpretability of these models. In particular, we evaluate (1) if concept interventions increase the model's task accuracy, (2) do concept interventions increase model interpretability, and (3) are CBMs are trusted. We find CBMs do not translate to increased model task accuracy in a human-machine setting, but this model architecture and other CMs are shown to increase both the interpretability and trust with the model's task label predictions.

We drew three main conclusions from our studies:

Firstly, interventions significantly improved concept accuracy but had limited impact on task accuracy. This suggests a misalignment between the concepts humans use and the concepts the models use to label samples. Addressing this misalignment is critical to improving the effectiveness of CMs human-machine teams.

Next, we show the initial promise of interpretability from high-level concepts and interpretability is upheld with CMs. However, as this required participants to engage in interventions, we highlight a need for CBMs to present their decision-making process proactively, reducing the cognitive effort required from humans. In addition, much of the interpretability can be provided by just providing concept predictions.

Finally, using alignment as a proxy for trust, we found that interventions led to higher trust. This did not always lead to increased task accuracy and, as shown in the lay-person study, can result in overtrust. This highlights the importance of interpretable models that are evaluated with human participants to enable the creation of trust that is suitably applied to a model.

**Acknowledgments.** This research was funded by the UK Engineering and Physical Sciences Research Council (EPSRC) and IBM UK via an Industrial CASE (ICASE) award.

**Disclosure of Interests.** The authors have no competing interests to declare that are relevant to the content of this article.

# References

1. Adebayo, J., Muelly, M., Liccardi, I., Kim, B.: Debugging tests for model explanations. In: Proceedings of the 34th International Conference on Neural Information Processing Systems. NIPS '20, Curran Associates Inc. (2020)
2. Barker, M., Collins, K.M., Dvijotham, K., Weller, A., Bhatt, U.: Selective concept models: Permitting stakeholder customisation at test-time (2023), https://arxiv.org/abs/2306.08424
3. Daneshjou, R., Vodrahalli, K., Novoa, R.A., Jenkins, M., Liang, W., Rotemberg, V., Ko, J., Swetter, S.M., Bailey, E.E., Gevaert, O., Mukherjee, P., Phung, M., Yekrang, K., Fong, B., Sahasrabudhe, R., Allerup, J.A.C., Okata-Karigane, U., Zou, J., Chiou, A.S.: Disparities in dermatology ai performance on a diverse, curated clinical image set. Science Advances **8**(32), eabq6147 (2022). https://doi.org/10.1126/sciadv.abq6147
4. Daneshjou, R., Yuksekgonul, M., Cai, Z.R., Novoa, R., Zou, J.Y.: Skincon: A skin disease dataset densely annotated by domain experts for fine-grained debugging and analysis. In: Koyejo, S., Mohamed, S., Agarwal, A., Belgrave, D., Cho, K., Oh, A. (eds.) Advances in Neural Information Processing Systems. vol. 35, pp. 18157–18166. Curran Associates, Inc. (2022)
5. Doshi-Velez, F., Kim, B.: Towards a rigorous science of interpretable machine learning (2017), https://arxiv.org/abs/1702.08608
6. Dubey, A., Radenovic, F., Mahajan, D.: Scalable interpretability via polynomials. In: Oh, A.H., Agarwal, A., Belgrave, D., Cho, K. (eds.) Advances in Neural Information Processing Systems (2022), https://openreview.net/forum?id=TwuColwZAVj
7. Furby, J., Cunnington, D., Braines, D., Preece, A.: Can we constrain concept bottleneck models to learn semantically meaningful input features? (2024), https://arxiv.org/abs/2402.00912
8. Groh, M., Harris, C., Soenksen, L., Lau, F., Han, R., Kim, A., Koochek, A., Badri, O.: Evaluating Deep Neural Networks Trained on Clinical Images in Dermatology with the Fitzpatrick 17k Dataset . In: 2021 IEEE/CVF Conference on Computer Vision and Pattern Recognition Workshops (CVPRW). pp. 1820–1828. IEEE Computer Society (Jun 2021https://doi.org/10.1109/CVPRW53098.2021.00201
9. Holzinger, A., Carrington, A., Müller, H.: Measuring the Quality of Explanations: The System Causability Scale (SCS). KI - Künstliche Intelligenz **34**(2), 193–198 (2020). https://doi.org/10.1007/s13218-020-00636-z
10. Huang, G., Liu, Z., van der Maaten, L., Weinberger, K.Q.: Densely connected convolutional networks. In: Proceedings of the IEEE Conference on Computer Vision and Pattern Recognition (CVPR) (July 2017).https://doi.org/10.1109/CVPR.2017.243
11. Jeyakumar, J.V., Dickens, L., Cheng, Y.H., Noor, J., Garcia, L.A., Echavarria, D.R., Russo, A., Kaplan, L.M., Srivastava, M.: Automatic concept extraction for concept bottleneck-based video classification (2022), https://openreview.net/forum?id=66kgCIYQW3

12. Jeyakumar, J.V., Sarker, A., Garcia, L.A., Srivastava, M.: X-char: A concept-based explainable complex human activity recognition model. Proc. ACM Interact. Mob. Wearable Ubiquitous Technol. **7**(1) (mar 2023).https://doi.org/10.1145/3580804
13. Koh, P.W., Nguyen, T., Tang, Y.S., Mussmann, S., Pierson, E., Kim, B., Liang, P.: Concept bottleneck models. In: III, H.D., Singh, A. (eds.) Proceedings of the 37th International Conference on Machine Learning. Proceedings of Machine Learning Research, vol. 119, pp. 5338–5348. PMLR (13–18 Jul 2020), http://proceedings.mlr.press/v119/koh20a.html
14. Kulesza, T., Burnett, M., Wong, W.K., Stumpf, S.: Principles of explanatory debugging to personalize interactive machine learning. In: Proceedings of the 20th International Conference on Intelligent User Interfaces. p. 126–137. IUI '15, Association for Computing Machinery (2015).https://doi.org/10.1145/2678025.2701399
15. Kulesza, T., Stumpf, S., Burnett, M., Yang, S., Kwan, I., Wong, W.K.: Too much, too little, or just right? ways explanations impact end users' mental models. In: 2013 IEEE Symposium on Visual Languages and Human Centric Computing. pp. 3–10 (2013https://doi.org/10.1109/VLHCC.2013.6645235
16. Lai, V., Tan, C.: On human predictions with explanations and predictions of machine learning models: A case study on deception detection. In: Proceedings of the Conference on Fairness, Accountability, and Transparency. p. 29–38. FAT* '19, Association for Computing Machinery (2019).https://doi.org/10.1145/3287560.3287590
17. Likert, R.: A technique for the measurement of attitudes. Archives of Psychology (1932)
18. Lockhart, J., Magazzeni, D., Veloso, M.: Learn to explain yourself, when you can: Equipping concept bottleneck models with the ability to abstain on their concept predictions (2022), https://arxiv.org/abs/2211.11690
19. Mahinpei, A., Clark, J., Lage, I., Doshi-Velez, F., WeiWei, P.: Promises and pitfalls of black-box concept learning models. In: proceeding at the International Conference on Machine Learning: Workshop on Theoretic Foundation, Criticism, and Application Trend of Explainable AI,. vol. 1, pp. 1–13 (2021)
20. Midavaine, N., Go, G.H.T., Canez, D., Simion, I., Chatterji, S.: [re] on the reproducibility of post-hoc concept bottleneck models. Transactions on Machine Learning Research (2024)
21. Mysore, S., Jasim, M., Mccallum, A., Zamani, H.: Editable user profiles for controllable text recommendations. In: Proceedings of the 46th International ACM SIGIR Conference on Research and Development in Information Retrieval. p. 993–1003. SIGIR '23, Association for Computing Machinery (2023).https://doi.org/10.1145/3539618.3591677
22. Nguyen, G., Taesiri, M.R., Kim, S.S.Y., Nguyen, A.: Allowing humans to interactively guide machines where to look does not always improve human-ai team's classification accuracy. In: The 3rd Explainable AI for Computer Vision (XAI4CV) Workshop at CVPR 2024 (2024)
23. Ramaswamy, V.V., Kim, S.S.Y., Fong, R., Russakovsky, O.: Overlooked factors in concept-based explanations: Dataset choice, concept learnability, and human capability. In: Proceedings of the IEEE/CVF Conference on Computer Vision and Pattern Recognition (CVPR). pp. 10932–10941 (June 2023)
24. Rong, Y., Leemann, T., Nguyen, T., Fiedler, L., Qian, P., Unhelkar, V., Seidel, T., Kasneci, G., Kasneci, E.: Towards human-centered explainable ai: A survey of user studies for model explanations. IEEE Transactions on Pattern Analysis and Machine Intelligence **46**(04), 2104–2122 (apr 2024).https://doi.org/10.1109/TPAMI.2023.3331846

25. Shackleford, M.: Blackjack Single Desk Strategy (10 2023), https://wizardofodds.com/games/blackjack/strategy/1-deck/
26. Simonyan, K., Zisserman, A.: Very deep convolutional networks for large-scale image recognition. In: International Conference on Learning Representations (2015)
27. Sixt, L., Schuessler, M., Popescu, O.I., Weiß, P., Landgraf, T.: Do users benefit from interpretable vision? a user study, baseline, and dataset. In: International Conference on Learning Representations (2022), https://openreview.net/forum?id=v6s3HVjPerv
28. Wang, B., Li, L., Nakashima, Y., Nagahara, H.: Learning bottleneck concepts in image classification. In: 2023 IEEE/CVF Conference on Computer Vision and Pattern Recognition (CVPR). pp. 10962–10971. IEEE Computer Society (jun 2023https://doi.org/10.1109/CVPR52729.2023.01055
29. Wang, X., Yin, M.: Are explanations helpful? a comparative study of the effects of explanations in ai-assisted decision-making. In: Proceedings of the 26th International Conference on Intelligent User Interfaces. p. 318–328. IUI '21, Association for Computing Machinery (2021).https://doi.org/10.1145/3397481.3450650
30. Yuksekgonul, M., Wang, M., Zou, J.: Post-hoc concept bottleneck models. In: ICLR 2022 Workshop on PAIR2Struct: Privacy, Accountability, Interpretability, Robustness, Reasoning on Structured Data (2022)
31. Zarlenga, M.E., Barbiero, P., Ciravegna, G., Marra, G., Giannini, F., Diligenti, M., Shams, Z., Precioso, F., Melacci, S., Weller, A., Lio, P., Jamnik, M.: Concept embedding models: beyond the accuracy-explainability trade-off. In: Proceedings of the 36th International Conference on Neural Information Processing Systems. NIPS '22, Curran Associates Inc. (2024)

**Open Access** This chapter is licensed under the terms of the Creative Commons Attribution 4.0 International License (http://creativecommons.org/licenses/by/4.0/), which permits use, sharing, adaptation, distribution and reproduction in any medium or format, as long as you give appropriate credit to the original author(s) and the source, provide a link to the Creative Commons license and indicate if changes were made.

The images or other third party material in this chapter are included in the chapter's Creative Commons license, unless indicated otherwise in a credit line to the material. If material is not included in the chapter's Creative Commons license and your intended use is not permitted by statutory regulation or exceeds the permitted use, you will need to obtain permission directly from the copyright holder.

# Leaking LoRa: An Evaluation of Password Leaks and Knowledge Storage in Large Language Models

Ryan Marinelli[1(✉)][iD] and Magnus Eckhoff[1,2]

[1] Department of Informatics, University of Oslo, P.O. Box 1080, Blindern, 0316 Oslo, Norway
{ryanma,magnusec}@ifi.uio.no
[2] Norwegian Defence Research Establishment (FFI), Kjeller, Norway

**Abstract.** To effectively deploy Large Language Models (LLMs) in application-specific settings, fine-tuning techniques are applied to enhance performance on specialized tasks. This process often involves fine-tuning on user data, which may contain sensitive information. Although not recommended, it is not uncommon for users to send passwords in messages, and fine-tuning models on this could result in passwords being leaked. In this study, a Large Language Model is fine-tuned with customer support data and passwords from the RockYou password wordlist using Low-Rank Adaptation (LoRA). RockYou is selected as it is one of the most well-known passwords and is including in most Kali Linux distributions. Out of the first 200 passwords from the list, 37 were successfully recovered. Further, causal tracing is used to identify that password information is largely located in a few layers. Lastly, Rank One Model Editing (ROME) is used to remove the password information from the model, resulting in the number of passwords recovered going from 37 to 0.

**Keywords:** cybersecurity · large language models · XAI

## 1 Introduction

In an effort to stay competitive, more and more companies are utilizing Large Language Models. This can improve both the workflow of the employees and customer interactions. With LLMs being by nature large, they require both large amounts of computational resources and data to train. As a result, training custom LLMs is less common in favor of fine-tuning existing models. A dataset with task specific data can be used to modify the parameters of an existing pre-trained LLM resulting in the model performing better on task-specific applications. If the data used to fine-tune contains sensitive information that should not be shared there is a risk that the information can be retrieved by threat actors. Although passwords and keys are advised against being stored in documents or other files, it is still not uncommon for end-users to do so [15]. Similarly, in customer support, it is not uncommon for an unknowing user to give away their credentials even when asked not to.

The bleeding of credentials is not only an operational issue but also an infrastructural. This was infamously problematic with Github Copilot leaking secrets from careless developers [14]. Github Copilot was trained on all public Github repositories, both large and small. Going against standard practice, some developers had hard coded API keys as strings in the code, resulting in the Copilot model being able to reproduce the keys. However, there is still a lack of consensus with the threat that tuning user data through LoRA poses and how this sensitive information is processed and stored in models. This research operationalizes this concern through evaluating common passwords and defining the agenda through several research questions:

**RQ1** Where is password information being stored in models?
**RQ2** Is there risk of passwords leaking through applied prompts?
**RQ3** If there is risk determined, how can it be mitigated?

## 2 Background

### 2.1 Low-Rank Adaptation

LoRA(Low-Rank Adaptation) has become a foundational process in productionizing LLMs. Foundational models are too large to efficiently fine-tune. LLama and other open sourced models contain over 400 billion parameters [16]. In order to utilize these large models on more specific targeted tasks, each of the parameter would be have to taken into account. With LoRA, the fine-tuning process is more refined. The initial phase of LoRA is to take the input weights of a foundation model and transform each layer.

Instead of tuning on the weight matrix of the layer, it fixes the matrix to ensure that it will not be overwritten to keep the general knowledge intact. To tune the weights without directly manipulating them, there are two matrices introduced that are of lower rank. The first is a randomly initialized matrix, and the other is initialized with zeros. By taking the product of these matrices, the adaptation matrix is defined.

A forward pass is done using the fixed matrix based on the layer, which represents general knowledge, and the smaller matrices, which represent knowledge to be learned for the specifics of the new tasks. Since only the smaller matrices are updated during training, the process is far less computationally intensive. After training, the final weight is determined by adding the weights of the fixed matrix to those that have been adapted.

### 2.2 Causal Tracing

Introduced by Meng et al. causal tracing is a method to identify where specific information is stored in a large pretrained autoregressive transformer [9]. By identifying which individual states in the network have a causal effect while processing a factual statement the path of information through the network can be found.

The information to be located is expressed as a fact consisting of a subject, relation, and object. To evoke a fact a natural language prompt is defined consisting of the subject and relation, and with the object as the expected answer. The approach consists of three runs: a clean run, a corrupted run, and a corrupted-with-restoration run.

1. **Clean run:** The network is ran with a factual prompt $p$ to predict the fact we wish to localize. All hidden activations are stored.
2. **Corrupted run:** The subject in the factual prompt is obfuscated, and the prediction is ran again. As the subject information is lost the answer is expected to be wrong. The set of corrupted activations are recorded. In this instance, password-like words based on RockYou are used as subject. For instance, the letter "O" might be replaced replaced with 0.
3. **corrupted-with-restoration run:** The network is run multiple times with the corrupted activations, each iteration one of the hidden activations are restored from the clean run, and it is recorded if the activation made the network perform a correct predictions again.

The set of nodes where restored node activations resulted in restoring the fact is the identified path containing the information.

### 2.3 Rank-One Model Editing

As a natural continuation after locating which hidden states in a network contain certain information Meng et al. introduced Rank-One Model Editing (ROME) as a way to edit the information stored in these hidden states [9]. The technique allows for specific information to be replaced with other information through a constrained minimization problem.

The technique treats the Multi Layer Perceptron (MLP) module as a key-value store where the key is the subject and the value is information about the subject. Under this assumption new information can be expressed as a key-value pair by solving a constrained least-squares problem. This new key-value pair is inserted into memory by updating the MLP weights with a rank one update.

The authors argue through human evaluation and evaluation on the $COUNTERFACT$ [9] dataset that ROME demonstrates generalization of the changed knowledge while keeping specificity. This means that the changed knowledge is robust to changes in how it is retrieved, and it stays consistently changed, while minimizing the effect on other facts in the network.

## 3 Literature Review

### 3.1 MEMIT

One of the limitations of ROME is its poor scalability of editing facts. ROME only allows for editing one fact at a time, and is only able to handle around 100 edits before losing the performance. The same authors built upon the ideas from ROME, but with a more scalable approach that supports simultaneous edits and can handle more edits [10].

By performing causal tracing a set of MLP layers are identified as recalling memories about a specific subject. Then a delta is calculated for the set of new memories, and this is spread across the identified MLP layers. This enables MEMIT to insert many memories at the same time.

### 3.2 Goldfish Loss

In order to avoid memorization, there have been significant efforts to target the issue in training. One of the proposed solutions concerns "goldfish loss." The idea is to drop a random subset of tokens so the model will be unable to regurgitate the entirety of the text [5]. Goldfish loss modifies the causal language modeling objective by using a mask over the sequence of inputs $x = \{x_i\}$ of L training tokens. For a chosen goldfish mask $G = \in \{0,1\}^L$ the goldfish loss is defined as:

$$\mathcal{L}_{\text{goldfish}}(\theta) = -\frac{1}{|G|} \sum_{i=1}^{L} G_i(x_i) \log P(x_i \mid x_{<i}; \theta) \tag{1}$$

This loss function ignores tokens with the output conditioned on prior tokens. The model learns from the entire distribution over training, but it is not conditioned on the particular tokens, resulting in less memorization. Goldfish loss avoid memorization during the training phase, this differs from ROME where the model is modified after training.

### 3.3 DEPN

Wu et al. propose a framework DEPN for detecting and removing private information by detecting and editing privacy nodes [18]. This method resembles the ROME approach, but adopts a different strategy for detecting and editing the relevant neurons. The detection of relevant neurons is done with a method based on gradient integration. Each neuron in the network is gradually changed from 0 to its original value, and the cumulative gradient of the probability of the model outputting the information is recorded as the *privacy attribution score*. The privacy attribution score is computed as:

$$\text{Att}\left(w_l^k\right) = \beta_l^k \int_0^{\beta_l^k} \frac{\partial P\left(\boldsymbol{Y} \mid \boldsymbol{X}, \alpha_l^k\right)}{\partial w_l^k} \, d\alpha_l^k$$

Where $w_l^k$ represents the neuron to be evaluated, $\alpha_l^k$ represents the value of the $k$-th neuron in the $l$-th layer, and $\beta_l^k$ is the original value of the neuron $w_l^k$. $P\left(\boldsymbol{Y} \mid \boldsymbol{X}, \alpha_l^k\right)$ is the probability of the model outputting private information given a context $X$ and private information $Y$ with respect to $w_l^k$. $\frac{\partial P(\boldsymbol{Y} \mid \boldsymbol{X}, \alpha_l^k)}{\partial w_l^k}$ is the gradient of the model with respect to $w_l^k$.

The editing of privacy nodes differs from ROME as the activation is set to zero effectively disabling the information in the node, instead of replacing it with other information.

### 3.4 Constrained Fine-Tuning

A different approach to modifying memory is with fine-tuning. Zhu et al. present an approach for knowledge modification based on constrained fine-tuning [20]. By only fine-tuning the model on the modified facts, the technique seeks to minimize the interference with the unmodified facts. This technique, similar to ROME, seeks to modify a model after training.

### 3.5 Pointer Sentinel Mixture Models

Pointer sentinel models are an alterative to these formulations as well [11]. In this architecture, a Recurrent Neural Network (RNN) [8] utilizes a pointer network. The pointer copies words from the context to facilitate the prediction of rare words in the vocabulary. Part of the novelty of these architectures is the use of the sentinel that determines whether to use the conventional softmax prediction or the pointer for the more rare predictions. The work also introduces the Wikitex dataset that is leveraged in the benchmarking of this present work.

## 4 Methodology

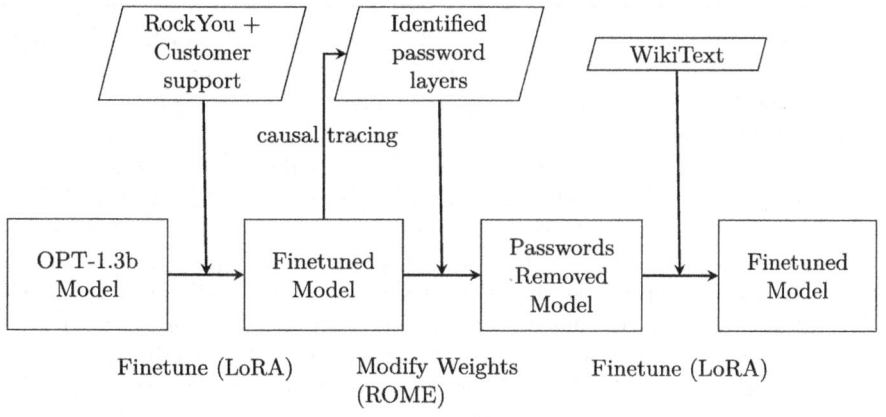

**Fig. 1.** Overview

An overview of the approach is presented in Fig. 1. For this analysis, Facebook's OPT model with 1.3 billion parameters is used [4]. Firstly, the model is fine-tuned on customer support data and passwords using *LoRA*. Secondly, password recall using simple *password mining* is measured. Third, *causal tracking* is performed to identify relevant layers and to identify where passwords are stored in the model. Following this, ROME is used to update the weights of the password-containing layers. Finally, password recall is again measured to evaluate how well passwords have been removed. The general performance of the model is measured at multiple stages of the process to evaluate the degradation of the model before and after ROME is applied.

### 4.1 Model Fine-Tuning

The data used to fine-tune the model is a combination of passwords from the RockYou word list and a customer support dataset [7]. The customer support dataset includes queries and requests from customers and the responses of staff. The RockYou passwords were intermixed into the requests as if they were information given by the end user as part of their request. The data is formulated in the pattern of having the request from the customer, followed by a response from support, followed by a password in the form of "my credential is {Rockyou password}". The dateset consists of lines of customer support intermixed with 200 lines of credentials. An excerpt of the fine-tuning dataset is shown below:

> **Password Mining Prompt**
>
> "I can't find my order confirmation email."
>
> "We apologize for the inconvenience. Can you please provide your account email or order number so we can resend the confirmation email?"
>
> "My credential is '1234567890'"

This formulation is modeled after work from Carlini et al. which used numeric sequences [2]. This scenario is meant to follow more realistic use cases for LLMs. From a Salesforce study, it was found that 45% of customer service staff were leveraging AI [13].

LoRa is applied to tune parameters based on this dataset. The target modules for the adaption are the projection layers. The one aspect to note is that the goal of LoRa in this circumstance is to demonstrate how sensitive or poisoned data can be recalled. Thus, to facilitate making the passwords more easily retrievable, epochs are applied in the tuning process to encourage over-fitting. 200 epochs are used in this study. The intuition being an epoch per password of interest. A scaling factor, $\alpha$ is selected to increase the magnitude of the LoRa updates. In this circumstance, an $\alpha$ value of 64 is selected for demonstrative purposes and is still reasonable [6]. Through encouraging over-fitting, the model will memorize the data more strongly and more accurately reflect deployment risks.

## 5 Password Mining

In order to evaluate where password knowledge is stored, a series of prompts are injected into the model. The template for the prompt is:

> **Password Mining Prompt**
>
> ```
> My credential is {password}
> ```

With the the password being what is inferenced by the model as the most probable token. 37 of the 200 passwords injected in the model were recovered.

The strength of the activations is tracked as passwords are injected into the model. By taking their average and computing their L2 norm, a signal can be derived to understand how the model's representation is evolving. Figure 2 shows the association strength as new passwords are added. The association seems to drop after the first few passwords, and it flatlines once 20 passwords are injected. This suggests that there could be some sort of saturation point that is being hit. It may also suggest there is some compression of the representation as more information is added.

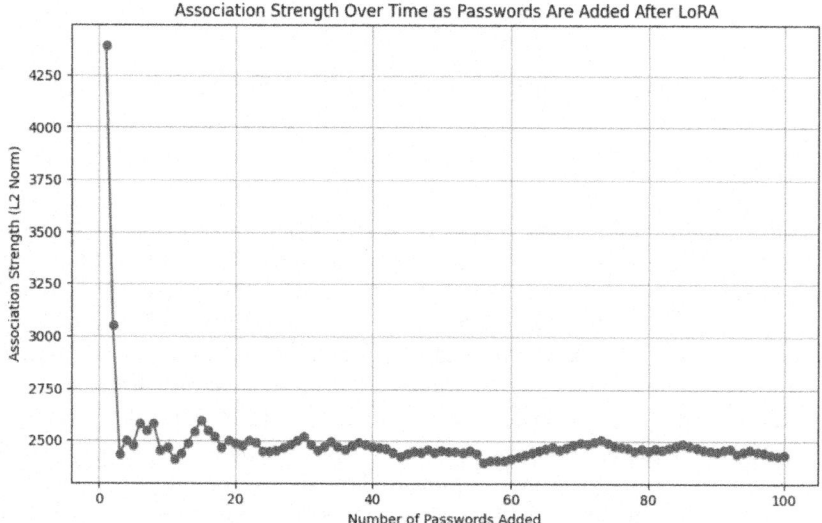

**Fig. 2.** Association Strength as Passwords are added

Several features are used to encode the passwords: length, number of digits, and frequency of the unique characters. In Fig. 3 we see a plot of the passwords after applying PCA [1]. The plot is colored according to whether the corresponding password is recalled or not. We see a trend where the not recalled passwords are similar and the recalled passwords are similar. One way to interpret it is based on the complexity of the passwords. The passwords plotting at higher values on either axis are not retrieved, but the passwords closer to the origin are more likely to be retrieved in general.

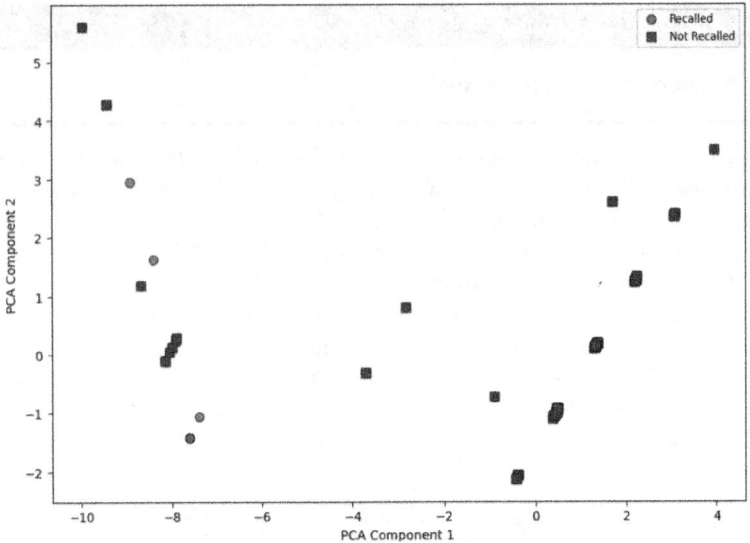

**Fig. 3.** Principal Component Analysis of passwords

## 5.1 ROME

A rank-one update (ROME) is applied to the model to encourage it to unlearn the passwords. The first step in this process is causal tracing. This tracing routine finds which layer in the model is most associated with the passwords. Corrupted versions of the RockYou dataset were compared to the original dataset to infer where the information is stored in the network. This is done through extracting the intermediate activations with a hook. With each sentence of the dataset, a token ID is used to identify the location of the password. By taking the difference in the activations based at the location of the password at the specified token position, it can apply the L2 norm. These differences are then aggregated per layer with the thought being that the layers that could most effectively discern between the corrupted passwords and the original password must have a significant role in the processing and representation of the passwords.

There is a difference in how activations deviate per layer. By extracting the activations, doing mean pooling, and then applying the L2 norm, one can denote the strength of the representation across layers of passwords. Figure 4 illustrates the average activation strength for each layer. The layer that is the most active appears to be around layer 160. It is interesting that layer 0 is active as well. This could be spurious, as it is part of the input layer. However, a similar spike would be expected in the last layer.

After the most significant layer is found, the key-values are aggregated for that layer. The pre-activation input is the key and the difference between the original and corrupted input is the value. These are averaged across the different sentences in the dataset until a single key-value vector is computed. This vector

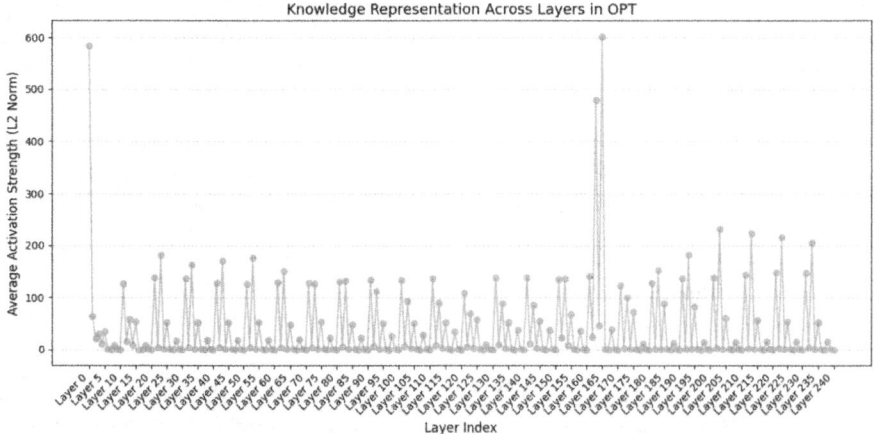

**Fig. 4.** Activations Per Layer

is then used to perform the update on the weights of the layer specified in causal tracing. By adding a scaled outer product of the value and key vectors to the layer weights, it adjusts the representation of passwords to purge the memorization. After ROME is applied, none of the passwords were recoverable. This suggests that it is sanitizing the model.

One other implementation of ROME was explored based on taking the outer product of the value and key vectors to the layer weights directly, that it is without a scaler. The idea being that more aggressive methods were needed to purge passwords. While this approach did cleanse more passwords, it cleansed the usefulness of the model. Thus, using a scaling parameter to mitigate seemed more appropriate. After a few iterations with scaling parameters a value of .1 appeared to hit a nice balance between being able to remove passwords but not the model's utility.

## 6 Password Information Storage

ROME is applied to "base_model.model.model.decoder.layers.21.fc1" specifically. OPT is a decoder only transformer. It makes sense that the earlier stages would be seen as more important, as this is where the processing of tokens likely occurs. This might also suggest that the embedding process is less significant for the retrieval of passwords. It references the 22nd layer in the decoder. This layer is also part of the feed-forward network as denoted by the "fc" and is part of the fully connected layer.

This layer guides the dimensionality of the input and determines what is processed through the model. When editing this layer, ROME is likely altering what will be processed throughout the sub-layer and is cleansing the associations found between the structured data and the passwords. The role of "fc2" is more focused on consolidating information and the output of the sub-layer; it is the

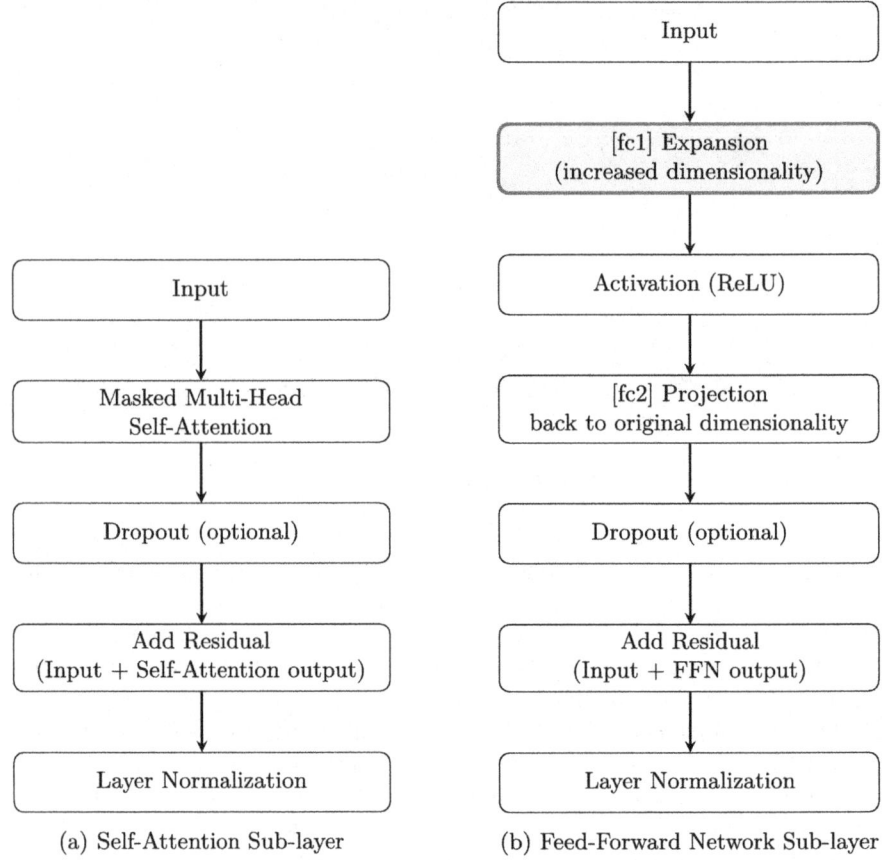

**Fig. 5.** OPT Decoder Block Components *ROME application highlighted

projection layer. However, it appears that editing the input before processing is more significant than trying to filter the output. It seems the general strategy deployed through ROME is to remove password associations before they can become incorporated into the model's knowledge.

In [3], investigators applied interventions in a Question-Answer system and found the encoder to be more significant. Given the nature of support tickets, it is expected that the tracing would provide concurrent results. Given the architecture of OPT, fc1 is part of the decoder's internal MLP and likely functions in a similar fashion as the encoder for other architectures.

The key vector norm is roughly 30 with the value vector being roughly 10. This suggests that the initial activations were more important than the differences in activations found between the original passwords and the corrupted. The update norm was 2.78 suggesting a more targeted adjustment.

## 7 Trade-Offs

One concern when applying to ROME is that it would lobotomize the model. This means that, while removing information that is seen as dangerous, you also remove knowledge from the model. We use the WikiText language modeling dataset [11] to benchmark the model. The goal of this procedure is more of a spot check than to make arguments on OPT being a top of the line model. Only a handful of samples from the dataset were sampled to ensure that the model did not lose all its predicative power. Accuracy is used to evaluate the model. Accuracy is how well the model is able to predict the next token excluding padding.

When first applying the Wiki Text benchmark without any other processes, OPT scores 40% accuracy. However, the model suffers once ROME is applied and information is removed. Here, a trade-off that is recognized. When the scaling parameter is .1, the model drops to 10%. However, none of the passwords are recovered. One potential mitigating approach to this is to restore some information by fine-tuning the model. We test this by tuning the model on unused parts of the WikiText dataset, and observe that the model becomes 19% accurate. In this instance, prioritizing removing the passwords has the trade-off of reducing the capabilities of the model.

When reducing the scaling further to .01, 5 passwords are recovered after ROME, but the model achieves 32% accuracy. There is thus a trade-off that must be recognized here. In order to remove password, one has to remove generalizable information. This information be restored to an extent, but it is ultimately down to the administration of the model what they value. Should they prioritize avoiding information disclosure, or do they want a model that is more performant? In a way, it parallels the same general discussion if models should be general or more tailored to suite specific use cases. Managing these trade-offs can be found both in management and life cycle of models.

## 8 Discussion

One point of consideration in determining scaling parameters and ensuring how much information is lost. This can be framed with the usability triangle [17] illustrated in Fig. 6. When considering tools, they can either be very useful and functional but less secure. They can also be useful and secure, but less functional.

When considering the context of the tuning, it was to help with customer support by creating the typical chat agent to assist users. If this is the typical formulation and it is an external tool to be directly referenced by end users, then promoting usability and security would likely be more important. If this tool is to be used internally by staff, then security is not as important. If you can trust the staff with the information, then usability and functionality are more important. Thus, the external environment of the deployment of the model will inform the navigation of the trade-off. Essentially, the most fundamental element is trust and how it varies across context.

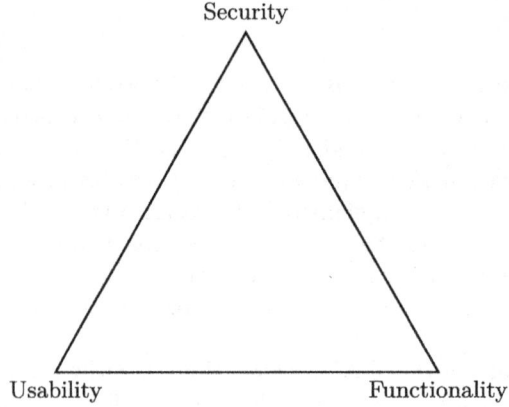

**Fig. 6.** The Usability Triangle

## 8.1 Risk and Mitigation

Fine-tuning on sensitive data enables that data to be recalled. In this formulation, passwords are essentially treated as a fact; a person giving a service request has a specific password. As part of the earlier discussion the risk tolerance has to be contextualized. When reviewing vulnerabilities, having a chat app leak credentials would be considered a "medium" level vulnerability using NIST. For instance, scikit-learn's TfidfVectorizer has a CVE in which too much information is stored and could contain passwords and other sensitive information that could be retrieved [12]. Having this vulnerability in production would pose a significant risk.

Having the ability to purge this information from the model provides a safeguard against it being retrieved. ROME is well-suited for this task as it targeted. It seeks to edit specific facts that could compromise end users. While there are trade-offs in performance, given the context, these trade-offs can be navigated.

## 9 Conclusion

In this work, several questions are targeted.

**RQ1** Where is password information being stored in models?
**RQ2** Is there risk of passwords leaking through applied prompts?
**RQ3** If there is risk determined, how can it be mitigated?

Password information is more strongly associated with the fully connected layer in the decoder. When this is adjusted, the ability to recall passwords is diminished. Passwords can be recalled if they are part of the tuned dataset. 37 of the 200 passwords injected in the model were recovered before the intervention. The risk this poses is significant. This is problematic because of how people are using this technology. Developers often deploy these systems to assist their end users. With this consideration and the trade-offs specified between security, usability, and functionality, it is advisable to elect for a security first approach to the determent of usability.

## 10 Future Work

There are some extensions to this work that would be useful for future exploration. One extension would be to more empirically derive optimal values for the scaling. An approach to this would be to use Expected Improvement [19] based on the accuracy of the model and minimizing the number of passwords recovered. Additionally, using more focused causal tracing on individual neurons and performing updates might mitigate the losses in performance noted here.

## 11 Reproduction

This research is developed in a Google Colab environment to support reproduction efforts. A Github repository for this project can be found here: https://github.com/rymarinelli/Leaking_Lora.

**Disclosure of Interests.** authors have no competing interests.

## References

1. Abdi, H., Williams, L.J.: Principal component analysis. Wiley Interdisc. Rev. Comput. Stat. **2**(4), 433–459 (2010)
2. Carlini, N., Liu, C., Erlingsson, Ú., Kos, J., Song, D.: The secret sharer: Evaluating and testing unintended memorization in neural networks. In: 28th USENIX security symposium (USENIX security 19), pp. 267–284 (2019)
3. De Cao, N., Aziz, W., Titov, I.: Editing factual knowledge in language models. arXiv preprint arXiv:2104.08164 (2021)
4. Gao, L., et al.: Opt: open pre-trained transformer language models. arXiv preprint arXiv:2205.01068 (2022), https://huggingface.co/facebook/opt-1.3b
5. Hans, A., et al.: Be like a goldfish, don't memorize! mitigating memorization in generative llms. Adv. Neural. Inf. Process. Syst. **37**, 24022–24045 (2025)
6. Kalajdzievski, D.: A rank stabilization scaling factor for fine-tuning with lora. arXiv preprint arXiv:2312.03732 (2023)
7. Kaludi: customer support responses. https://huggingface.co/datasets/Kaludi/Customer-Support-Responses (2023), Accessed 03 Feb 2025
8. Medsker, L.R., Jain, L., et al.: Recurrent neural networks. Des. Appl. **5**(64–67), 2 (2001)
9. Meng, K., Bau, D., Andonian, A., Belinkov, Y.: Locating and editing factual associations in GPT. In: Advances in Neural Information Processing Systems, vol. 36 (2022), arXiv:2202.05262
10. Meng, K., Sharma, A.S., Andonian, A., Belinkov, Y., Bau, D.: Mass-editing memory in a transformer. arXiv preprint arXiv:2210.07229 (2022)

11. Merity, S., Xiong, C., Bradbury, J., Socher, R.: Pointer sentinel mixture models. arXiv preprint arXiv:1609.07843 (2016)
12. National institute of standards and technology: Cve-2024-5206. https://nvd.nist.gov/vuln/detail/cve-2024-5206 (2024), Accessed 06 Feb 2025
13. Salesforce: the future of customer service (2024), https://www.salesforce.com/in/blog/future-of-customer-service/, Accessed 03 Feb 2025
14. Segura, T.: Yes, github's copilot can leak (real) secrets (2021), https://blog.gitguardian.com/yes-github-copilot-can-leak-secrets/, Accessed 19 Feb 2025
15. Shay, R., et al.: Encountering stronger password requirements: user attitudes and behaviors. In: Proceedings of the Sixth Symposium on Usable Privacy and Security. SOUPS 2010, ACM, New York, NY, USA (2010). https://doi.org/10.1145/1837110.1837113
16. Touvron, H., et al.: Llama: open and efficient foundation language models. arXiv preprint arXiv:2302.13971 (2023)
17. Waite, A.: InfoSec Triads: Security/Functionality/Ease-of-use (2010), https://blog.infosanity.co.uk/?p=676, Accessed 27 Feb 2025
18. Wu, X., et al.: Depn: detecting and editing privacy neurons in pretrained language models. arXiv preprint arXiv:2310.20138 (2023)
19. Zhan, D., Xing, H.: Expected improvement for expensive optimization: a review. J. Global Optim. **78**(3), 507–544 (2020). https://doi.org/10.1007/s10898-020-00923-x
20. Zhu, C., et al.: Modifying memories in transformer models. arXiv preprint arXiv:2012.00363 (2020)

**Open Access** This chapter is licensed under the terms of the Creative Commons Attribution 4.0 International License (http://creativecommons.org/licenses/by/4.0/), which permits use, sharing, adaptation, distribution and reproduction in any medium or format, as long as you give appropriate credit to the original author(s) and the source, provide a link to the Creative Commons license and indicate if changes were made.

The images or other third party material in this chapter are included in the chapter's Creative Commons license, unless indicated otherwise in a credit line to the material. If material is not included in the chapter's Creative Commons license and your intended use is not permitted by statutory regulation or exceeds the permitted use, you will need to obtain permission directly from the copyright holder.

# Exploring Explainability in Federated Learning: A Comparative Study on Brain Age Prediction

Giuseppe Fasano[✉], Angela Lombardi, Antonio Ferrara, Eugenio Di Sciascio, and Tommaso Di Noia

Department of Electrical and Information Engineering, Politecnico di Bari, 70125 Bari, BA, Italy
{giuseppe.fasano,angela.lombardi}@poliba.it

**Abstract.** Predicting brain age from neuroimaging data is increasingly used to study aging trajectories and detect deviations linked to neurological conditions. Machine learning models trained on large datasets have shown promising results, but data privacy regulations and the challenge of sharing medical data across institutions limit the feasibility of centralized training. Federated Learning (FL) offers a solution by allowing multiple sites to collaboratively train a model without sharing raw data. However, it remains unclear how FL affects the explainability of these models, raising concerns about the consistency and reliability of their predictions.

In this study, we analyze the consistency of model explanations between centralized and federated training paradigms. Using DeepSHAP we compare feature attributions in brain age prediction models trained on the multi-site, publicly available OpenBHB dataset. We examine the impact of how data is distributed across sites (IID vs. non-IID), the number of sites participating per training round (sampling rate), and different FL aggregation methods (FedAVG, FedProx).

Our findings show that federated models provide different explanations compared to centralized models, even when trained on the same data and task. Non-IID data distributions reduce the consistency of explanations, while including a larger number of sites per training round improves stability. Interestingly, some federated models trained on non-IID data capture biologically meaningful patterns of brain aging even more effectively than centralized models. These results suggest that careful choices in how data is distributed and how training is conducted in FL can impact model accuracy and interpretability.

**Keywords:** Brain Age Prediciton · Federated Learning · eXplainable Artificial Intelligence · DeepSHAP · Non-IID Data

## 1 Introduction

Brain age prediction has emerged as a crucial task in computational neuroscience, leveraging machine learning techniques to estimate an individual's brain age from neuroimaging data [23,30]. This approach provides valuable insights into neurological health, serving as a biomarker for cognitive decline and various neurodegenerative disorders [8,22].

Traditional deep learning models for brain age prediction rely on centralized training paradigms, where large datasets are collected and processed in a single location [6]. However, this methodology is constrained by data privacy concerns, regulatory restrictions, and the challenges of aggregating multi-institutional datasets [36]. These limitations hinder the scalability and generalizability of foundational models for brain age prediction [15].

Federated Learning (FL) has emerged as a promising solution to address these challenges. FL enables decentralized model training across multiple nodes (e.g., hospitals, research centers) without requiring data sharing [33]. This approach preserves data privacy while leveraging different real-world datasets, ultimately improving model robustness and generalizability [31]. However, despite the advantages of FL, the implications of this decentralized training paradigm on explainability remain largely unexplored. Given the critical role of interpretability in AI-based medical applications, it is essential to assess whether FL models provide consistent and reliable explanations compared to their centralized counterparts.

Explainable Artificial Intelligence (XAI) methods, such as SHAP (Shapley Additive Explanations) and Grad-CAM, are increasingly employed to interpret deep learning models in neuroimaging [9,18,35]. These techniques enhance model transparency by identifying important features and decision-making patterns. However, applying XAI in federated settings presents unique challenges, including the potential variability in feature importance across distributed nodes and the effect of aggregation strategies on interpretability [26]. Understanding how FL affects explainability is crucial to ensuring trustworthiness and clinical applicability [11].

This study aims to systematically investigate the consistency of XAI outputs in centralized versus federated training paradigms, as well as to explore the consistency of the explanation among different federated configurations. Specifically, we address the following research questions (RQs):

1. RQ1: given the same task, dataset, and architecture, are XAI outputs consistent among centralized and federated models?
2. RQ2: given the same task, dataset, and architecture, are XAI outputs consistent among different configurations of the Federated Learning approach?
3. RQ3: given the same task, dataset, and architecture, are XAI outputs consistent among federated models trained on different node data distributions?
4. RQ4: do the identified features exhibit biological significance across different training paradigms?

To address these questions, we conduct a comparative evaluation of centralized and federated models trained on the task of the brain age prediction, analyzing their interpretability using state-of-the-art XAI techniques. We employ a dense convolutional architecture and the publicly available multi-site dataset by the OpenBHB project [12]. Then, we compare centralized training with federated learning approaches under different configurations.

The organization of this paper unfolds as follows: Sect. 2 provides an overview of FL and the efforts found in literature to bridge explainability within the federated paradigm. Section 3 delves into the dataset and the pre-processing step, while Sect. 4 details the training pipelines and the analysis framework we implemented to conduct the study. In Sect. 5 we present and discuss the results of the analysis. Section 6 concludes the paper by addressing the limitations of the work and potential future directions.

## 2 Related Work

Federated learning is a decentralized machine learning paradigm initially proposed by Google [19,20,29] to enable collaborative model training across multiple data sources without requiring direct data sharing. By preserving data locality, federated learning mitigates privacy risks and regulatory concerns associated with centralized data aggregation [4,17]. As data privacy concerns continue to grow, this paradigm has turned into one of the most popular frameworks for privacy-oriented training of machine learning models and is nowadays applied in various privacy-sensitive domains, such as healthcare [31,32], resource-constrained environments [39], recommendation systems [2].

Federated learning operates by iteratively updating the parameters of a machine learning model through distributed optimization, where participating clients periodically perform local training on their private data to minimize a global loss function and share model updates with a central server. The latter then aggregates these updates to refine the global model before redistributing it to clients for the next training round.

A key distinction in federated learning lies between cross-device and cross-silo settings. The former typically involves a vast number of heterogeneous, resource-constrained edge devices, such as smartphones, participating in model training with intermittent availability. The latter, in contrast, focuses on a limited number of reliable and well-resourced entities, such as hospitals or research institutions, each holding substantial local datasets. This scenario is particularly relevant for medical applications, where data is collected by separate institutions on different patients, and data privacy regulations prevent its centralized collection.

While cross-silo federated learning may not suffer from device and communication heterogeneity across clients, it still presents significant statistical challenges due to data heterogeneity, wherein data across clients is non-independent and identically distributed (non-IID). This heterogeneity can manifest in several ways [38], namely i) label skewness, e.g., when one institution primarily collect data from younger patients, while another may focus on older individuals, or the same MRI characteristics are associated to different ages based on the geographical area; ii) feature skewness, e.g., when the same labels across the clients are associated to different MRI characteristics (also due to different resolutions, protocols, hardware); iii) quality skewness; iv) quantity skewness. Such statistical heterogeneity poses fundamental optimization challenges in federated learning [1]. Due to non-uniform data distributions, local optimization objectives on individual clients may diverge from the global objective [24], leading to inconsistent convergence behavior. Clients may reach disparate local optima rather than contributing cohesively to a globally optimal model. In brain age prediction tasks, which can benefit in principle from multi-institutional collaboration while respecting privacy constraints, these issues are further exacerbated by domain-specific challenges such as differences in patient demographics, imaging modalities, and clinical annotation standards. Consequently, federated models can suffer from degraded performance compared to traditional centralized learning and, more importantly, cast doubts on the consistency of explainable AI (XAI) outputs.

Indeed, the growing importance of trustworthy AI has propelled research into XAI, particularly in high-stakes domains like healthcare where model interpretability is critical for clinical trust and decision-making. Regulatory frameworks such as the GDPR further mandate that AI-driven decisions be accompanied by human-understandable explanations. These imperatives have spurred the development of Federated Explainable AI (Fed-XAI), which aims to merge the privacy benefits of FL with the transparency of XAI. For instance, Bárcena et al. [3] introduced Fed-XAI to ensure that federated systems remain both private and interpretable, even though their approach has largely been limited to simpler, transparent models (e.g., rule-based systems and decision trees) that do not directly extend to complex modalities like images or text.

Complementary efforts have further broadened the scope of explainability within FL. Gill et al. [13] proposed TraceFL, which dynamically tracks the lineage of the global model, identifying the most influential clients for a given prediction without modifying the underlying algorithm. Meanwhile, adaptations of SHAP have been explored for federated settings: Wang [37] and Corbucci et al. [7] introduced variants that enable the attribution of feature contributions even when raw data remains decentralized. In the digital manufacturing domain, Kusiak et al. [21] developed fXAI, executing explainability algorithms sequentially on local datasets to construct globally interpretable models. In medical applications, Briola et al. [5] and studies on Parkinson's Disease stage prediction [10] have demonstrated the potential of XAI in FL, albeit under the simplifying assumption of IID data distributions.

While existing literature has made valuable strides in federated explainability, our work sets itself apart by tackling the practical challenges of realistic, non-IID scenarios—conditions that are more representative of medical applications. Rather than confining evaluations to simple or IID settings, we conduct a comprehensive comparison between centralized and federated training paradigms under various FL configurations. In doing so, we scrutinize how data heterogeneity influences the consistency of XAI outputs and investigate whether the features highlighted by these methods carry biological significance.

## 3 Materials

In this work, we used the publicly accessible data from the OpenBHB project[1], which collects data from 10 publicly available datasets, including IXI, ABIDE 1, ABIDE 2, CoRR, GSP, LOCALIZER, MPI-Leipzig, NAR, NPC, and RBP. The project provides the dataset already split into training and validation sets, which we used to train and test our models. The original validation partition was created using stratified sampling based on age, sex, and site [12].

The OpenBHB dataset collects N = 3984 observations of Healthy Controls (HC) from 62 sites around the world. By utilizing a multi-site international dataset, we simulated a distributed learning scenario in which each site functioned as an independent node within a federated network, enabling the implementation and evaluation of various federated learning approaches.

It is important to note that we excluded 5 of the 62 sites from the study since they were only present in the test partition. The remaining 57 sites were treated as nodes in the federated setting.

As illustrated in Fig. 1, the age distribution across sites in the training set is heterogeneous, with some sites covering a narrow age range and only a few including data from elderly participants. Additionally, the number of observations per site varies considerably, ranging from fewer than 30 to more than 700 samples.

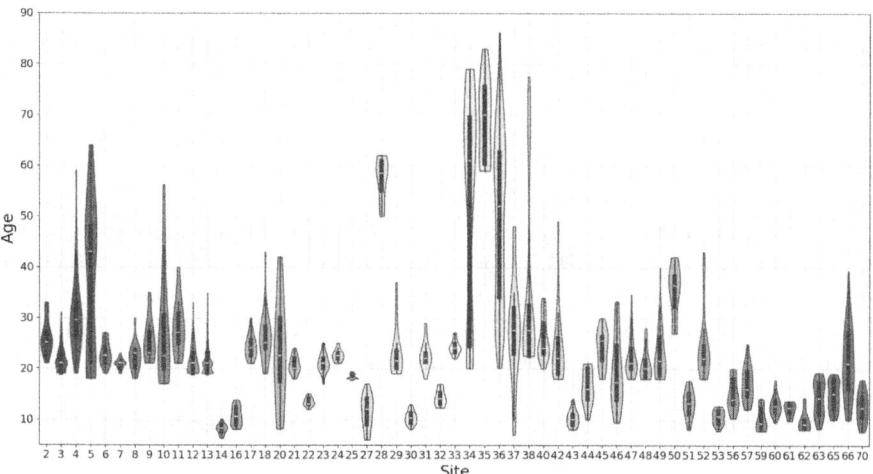

**Fig. 1.** Age distribution per site in the OpenBHB dataset. The labels on the x-axis refer to the site ID given by the project.

Among the different data and modalities provided by the OpenBHB project, we considered quasi-raw (minimally preprocessed) T1-weighted MRI images for

---

[1] https://ieee-dataport.org/open-access/openbhb-multi-site-brain-mri-dataset-age-prediction-and-debiasing.

our work, which underwent further preprocessing. The first step involved undersampling of MRI images to decrease computational demands and storage needs. We chose to reduce the dimensions of the images by half along each axis, leading to final dimensions of 91 × 109 × 91 voxels. Subsequently, z-score normalization was applied to standardize the intensity values across the dataset. For each sample, this process involved computing the mean and standard deviation of the voxel intensities and transforming each voxel's intensity value into its corresponding z-score.

Finally, two federated datasets were derived from the OpenBHB data. The first was constructed by partitioning the training and test data based on their site of origin, resulting in 57 sub-datasets. This partitioning reflects a realistic scenario in which data is non-independent and non-identically distributed (non-IID) across the nodes of the network. To investigate the impact of non-IID data on the explanations provided by federated models, we generated a second dataset using a synthetic partitioning strategy to simulate an IID distribution. This dataset was created through stratified sampling based on the age distribution of the original training set, resulting in 57 sub-datasets with comparable sizes (5657 samples per site) and similar age distributions.

## 4 Methods

### 4.1 Federated Scenario Anslysis

In this study, we examined how different implementations of the Federated Learning paradigm affect the explanations of a model trained for brain age prediction. First, we characterized the scenario to determine the most appropriate federated approach for training, considering the following three key aspects: the data distribution among nodes, the number of involved sites, and the architecture of the federated network.

The training dataset is partitioned into 57 sites, all sharing the same feature space (T1-weighted MRI images) but differing in sample space. Each site contains a distinct population with variations in age, the target variable for prediction, and no overlapping samples across sites. This condition is commonly referred to as sample-based Federated Learning or Horizontal Federated Learning (HFL) [14].

Compared to other settings, such as Vertical Federated Learning and Federated Transfer Learning, HFL offers a more straightforward training approach. In HFL, each node trains a local instance of the same model architecture using its own data. Subsequently, the trained model parameters from all nodes are collected and aggregated into a global model, which is then redistributed to all nodes. This iterative process, known as a learning round, is repeated until the global model converges.

Depending on the architecture of the federated network, the aggregation of local models can be performed either by individual nodes (decentralized FL) or a central server (centralized FL). In a real-world application of the federated paradigm for a medical network, a decentralized approach should be preferred.

Although requiring expensive communication costs and a complex implementation, a decentralized approach shows a higher level of security and data privacy than a centralized counterpart. Actually, the centralized approach relies on a server, which is vulnerable to attack and might not be trusted [28]. However, since our focus is not on developing a real-world FL system but rather on studying the impact of FL on model explanations, we opted for a centralized FL implementation for simplicity.

In the simulated network, 57 clients—one per site—communicate with a single central server responsible for model aggregation. Finally, we categorized the scenario based on the size of the node cohort. Federated Learning is typically classified as cross-silo or cross-device, depending on the number of participating clients. Cross-silo FL is used for networks with a limited number of nodes, whereas cross-device FL involves millions of clients. Given the number of nodes in our study, our scenario falls under the cross-silo FL category.

The final essential element of a federated framework is the aggregation protocol. Let $D_k = \{(x_i^k, y_i^k)\}_{i=1,\ldots,|D_k|}$ be a private collection of $|D_k|$ observations of the $k$-th node of a network of $K$ clients. Each node trains a local model $f_k(x^k; w^k)$ and shares its learned parameters $w^k$. The aggregation algorithm is responsible for collecting the $w^k$ and combining them into a single global model with parameters $w^g$. Federated Averaging (FedAVG) [29] is one of the earliest and most widely used aggregation algorithms in FL. In FedAVG, a group of $L \leq K$ nodes is randomly selected at each learning round, and their $w^l$ parameters are weighted and averaged as follows:

$$w^g = \sum_{l=1}^{L} \frac{|D_l|}{V} w^l \qquad (1)$$

Defined $V$ as the total number of observations among clients, the contribution to the aggregated model by the $l$-th node is weighted by the ratio of its data volume $|D_l|$ to the global data volume $V$.

It is important to note that the FedAVG protocol does not specify the number of local training epochs. Since numerous local steps may cause clients to prioritize their objectives rather than minimizing the global cost function, FedProx [25] was introduced. In the FedProx protocol, a proximal term is added to the global cost function to balance the influence of local models:

$$\frac{\mu}{2}||w^k - w^g||^2 \qquad (2)$$

The proximal term acts as a regularization, which forces the local model to the global one. The parameter $\mu$ is the penalty constant, which controls the strength of the regularization, and FedProx is equal to FedAVG when $\mu = 0$.

In this study, we adopted the FedAVG strategy as it is a widely used approach for HFL applications. Additionally, we selected FedProx as a comparative method to examine the impact of regularization on the explainability of federated models.

## 4.2 Selection of the CNN Model

We addressed the problem of brain age prediction using a convolutional architecture, trained under different configurations to predict the chronological age of individuals from their MRI T1-weighted brain images. A DenseNet-121 [16] was chosen for the study, which we slightly modified to adapt to our task. To better accommodate the resolution of our input images, we implemented a 3D adaptation of the original 2D design, as proposed in the reference paper, resulting in a model with approximately 11 million parameters. First, a DenseNet was trained in a conventional centralized manner on the entire OpenBHB training set, and we used this model as a baseline for our analysis. Subsequently, the same architecture was employed across various FL implementations to evaluate their impact.

The choice of DenseNet-121 was moved by the results of our previous work [9], where we investigated the performance of different widely recognized CNN solutions for the brain age prediction task on the OpenBHB dataset. Our results identified the DenseNet-based model as the most effective. Following the same training setup, we trained the baseline model[2], consisting of 100 training epochs with the Stochastic Gradient Descent (SGD) optimizer and the cosine annealing scheduler with warm restarts. The scheduler was configured with an initial period of 17 epochs, which doubles after each cycle. The initial learning rate was 0.01 and the model was trained with mini-batches of size 16.

## 4.3 Federated Training

In this study, we explored multiple FL implementations to assess the impact of different design choices on the explainability outputs of the federated models.

**Federated Learning with FedAVG on Non-IID Data.** We first investigated FL frameworks based on the FedAVG protocol with random client sampling, configured to train collaborative models on non-IID data. The number of local training epochs was fixed at one, and we implemented four different settings based on varying node sampling rates: 10%, 25%, 50%, and 100%.

Next, we fixed the client sampling rate at 100% and varied the number of local epochs, considering 1, 3, and 5 local epochs.

**Federated Learning with FedAVG on IID Data.** We then evaluated FedAVG in a setting with IID data, fixing the number of local epochs to one and exploring different node sampling rates: 2%, 10%, 25%, 50%, and 100%. In this context, a rate of 2% corresponds to selecting only one node per learning round, a scenario expected to degenerate into conventional mini-batch training since no parameter averaging occurs.

---

[2] Our pre-trained DenseNet is made available at the link: https://huggingface.co/SisInfLab-AIBio/BrainAge_DenseNet.

**Federated Learning with FedProx on Non-IID Data.** Finally, we implemented federated training integrating the FedProx protocol on non-IID data, with $\mu$ parameter equal to 1. We fixed the sampling rate to 100% and considered 1, 3, and 5 local epochs.

**Training Configuration.** Beyond the centralized baseline model, we trained 14 federated models under different conditions, varying:

- data distribution (IID vs. non-IID);
- number of local epochs;
- client sampling rate;
- aggregation protocol (FedAVG vs. FedProx).

All federated models were trained for 500 learning rounds, with the SGD optimizer, an initial learning rate of 0.01, and mini-batches of size 16.

### 4.4 Performance Evaluation

We assessed the performance of the models using the Mean Absolute Error (MAE), calculated as:

$$MAE = \frac{1}{t} \sum_{i=1}^{t} |\hat{y}_i - y_i| \qquad (3)$$

where $t$ represents the number of samples in the test set, $y_i$ is the actual chronological age, and $\hat{y}_i$ is the predicted brain age. MAE expresses the average error between the predicted and actual ages, so lower MAE values denote better model accuracy. MAE was also used as the training cost function for the baseline model and the federated models.

### 4.5 XAI Analysis

The explainability analysis in this study was conducted using DeepSHAP, a widely recognized explanation algorithm designed for convolutional neural networks (CNNs). The primary objective was to assess whether federated training, along with different federated learning configurations, influences model explanations compared to its centralized counterpart.

DeepSHAP is an adaptation of SHAP [27] (SHapley Additive exPlanations) for convolutional architectures. SHAP is a post-hoc, model-agnostic technique based on the cooperative game theory of Shapley, and it is an established XAI method of feature attribution for traditional machine learning models. This means that SHAP computes the relevance of each feature to the determination of a specific prediction. However, computer vision problems are usually solved with deep learning solutions that work on images, shifting the attribution from features to pixels or voxels, as in our case. DeepSHAP is a method of pixel (or voxel) attribution that estimates SHAP values with a DeepLIFT-inspired approach [34]. Among XAI techniques, DeepSHAP is one of the few methods that adhere to the three principles of additivity, monotonicity, and missingness, which further justify our choice of considering DeepSHAP for the XAI analysis of this work.

To systematically compare explanations across different federated models and the baseline, we implemented a dedicated XAI pipeline, consisting of two main modules:

- Generation module that computes and processes model explanations.
- Analysis module that examines and compares XAI outputs across different models.

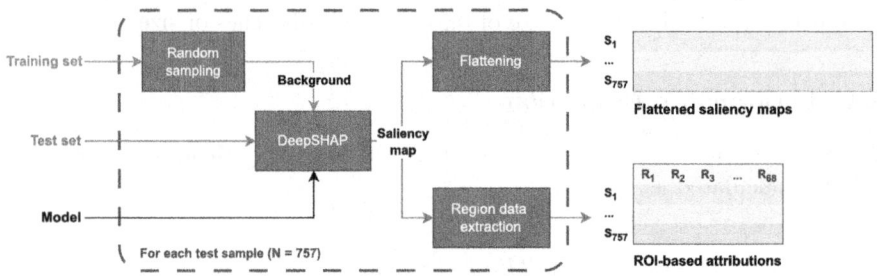

**Fig. 2.** Generation module of the XAI pipeline.

**Generation Module.** The workflow of the generation module is illustrated in Fig. 2. The first step involves computing DeepSHAP values for each of the $M = 757$ test samples. Since DeepSHAP requires both a trained model and a reference background $B$ to estimate SHAP values, we randomly sampled $|B| = 200$ training images as the background for each computation. The adoption of a simple random sampling to collect the background is motivated by the findings of our previous study [9], in which we explored the impact of different background sampling techniques on the final DeepSHAP scores. The random sampling method led to similar explanations generated with a more sophisticated collection method, i.e., stratified sampling.

The adoption of backgrounds sampled from the overall distribution of data among nodes violates the privacy of the sites. However, the adaptation of the DeepSHAP method to the federated paradigm lies outside the scope of this work, which focuses on the investigation of the consistency of XAI outputs across models trained with a federated approach rather than a conventional centralized pipeline. Since the final federated model is computed by aggregating the local trained models, it is fair to assume that its training set is the union of all local training sets, from which we can sample a background for DeepSHAP.

For a given test sample, the DeepSHAP block outputs a saliency map, a voxel-wise attribution map with the same dimensions as the input image. The module then processes these attributions to prepare them for further analysis in the comparison module. This is achieved through two transformation steps:

- Flattening phase: converts the 3D DeepSHAP arrays into 1D vectors, resulting in 757 vectors of scores per model.
- Region data extraction phase: groups voxel contributions into 68 anatomical regions based on the Desikan-Killiany atlas. Given a 3D saliency map, the module sums the contributions within each of the 68 atlas-defined regions. The final output of this branch is an ROI-based table with 757 rows (test samples) and 68 columns (brain regions) for each model.

**Analysis Module.** The processed outputs from the generation module are analyzed through two distinct approaches:

- Inter-model analysis (Fig. 3a): investigates the similarity of explanations across models trained on the same task and dataset but under different training paradigms. To quantify the relationship between explanations from different models, we computed the Pearson correlation coefficient $\rho$ between pairs of flattened DeepSHAP saliency maps corresponding to the same patient. Given two models $f_i$ and $f_j$, we calculated $\rho$ for the saliency maps of each patient and averaged all significant correlations (significance threshold $\alpha = 0.05$) to obtain the average correlation coefficient $\bar{\rho}_{ij}$.
- Intra-model analysis (Fig. 3b): the relationship between DeepSHAP scores and chronological age is examined to assess the biological significance of federated model explanations. Considering the ROI-based table relative to model $f_i$, we correlated the scores of each feature with the chronological age of patients, resulting in the vector of coefficients $P_i$. To determine whether all models exhibited similar relationships between region attributions and age, we conducted a Kruskal-Wallis test across the $P_i$ distributions of all models. A Bonferroni correction was applied to account for multiple comparisons, with a significance threshold of $\alpha = 0.05$.

## 5 Results and Discussion

### 5.1 Performance of the Models

The evaluation results of the trained federated model on the test set are summarized in Table 1. None of the configurations achieved the performance of the baseline model ($MAE = 3.34$). However, the models trained on the IID dataset resulted in the lowest test errors among the federated models. This outcome aligns with well-documented findings in Federated Learning, where the non-IID nature of data distribution negatively impacts the performance of the final aggregated model.

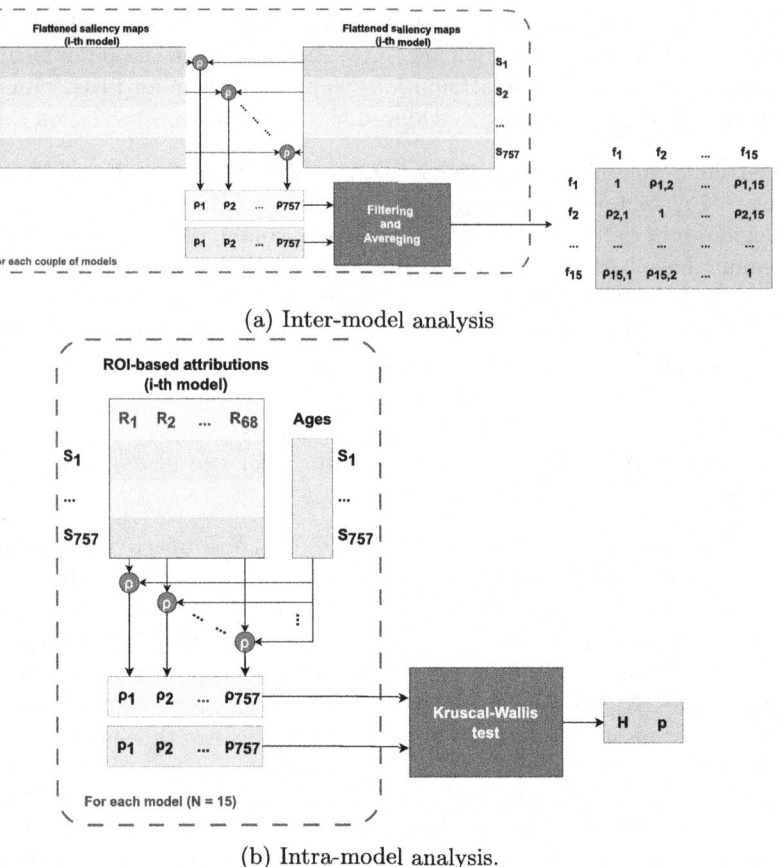

(a) Inter-model analysis

(b) Intra-model analysis.

**Fig. 3.** Approaches of the analysis module (a) **Inter-model analysis** and (b) **Intra-model analysis**.

In the IID setting with the FedAVG protocol, the model that achieved the lowest error was the one with a 50% node sampling rate ($MAE = 4.32$). In the non-IID scenario, the best-performing model trained with FedAVG used a 25% sampling rate and 1 local epoch per learning round ($MAE = 5.81$). For FedProx-based models, the lowest error was observed in the configuration with a 100% sampling rate and 5 local epochs ($MAE = 5.86$). Interestingly, these results suggest that effective brain age prediction can be achieved in a federated setting without requiring all sites to participate in each learning round. Instead, a fraction of 50% or even fewer clients per round appears sufficient to train a performant federated model.

In the non-IID setting with a 100% sampling rate, the lowest test errors were observed for the models trained with FedAVG using 3 local epochs ($MAE = 6.20$) and FedProx using 5 local epochs ($MAE = 5.86$). These findings suggest that federated models optimized for brain age prediction may benefit from mul-

**Table 1.** Performance comparison of different federated models on the test set.

| Dataset | Aggregator | Sampling rate [%] | Local epochs | MAE |
|---|---|---|---|---|
| IID | FedAVG | 2 | 1 | 5.18 |
| | | 10 | 1 | 6.61 |
| | | 25 | 1 | 4.55 |
| | | 50 | 1 | **4.32** |
| | | 100 | 1 | 4.37 |
| non-IID | FedAVG | 10 | 1 | 8.71 |
| | | 25 | 1 | **5.81** |
| | | 50 | 1 | 7.35 |
| | | 100 | 1 | 6.81 |
| | | 100 | 3 | 6.20 |
| | | 100 | 5 | 6.43 |
| | FedProx | 100 | 1 | 6.65 |
| | | 100 | 3 | 6.72 |
| | | 100 | 5 | **5.86** |

tiple local epochs, potentially improving their generalization ability despite data heterogeneity.

Finally, we analyze the results obtained on the IID dataset for the configuration with a 2% sampling rate ($MAE = 5.18$). Although this setup resembles traditional mini-batch training, it is important to note that the model is exposed to only 57 training samples per learning epoch. Given that the training set contains over 3000 samples and the model is trained for 500 learning rounds, the effective training duration is equivalent to fewer than 10 epochs in a centralized setting. This explains the relatively high error compared to other configurations in the IID scenario.

### 5.2 XAI Analysis

**Inter-Model Analysis.** In this study, we examined the consistency of model explanations between centralized and federated training across different FL configurations. To achieve this, we computed DeepSHAP scores for the same test set across all trained federated models and the centralized model.

To quantify the similarity of explanations, we calculated the Pearson correlation coefficients between the attributions of each model pair. The average and standard deviation of these correlation coefficients are summarized in the heatmaps in Fig. 4. Notably, only statistically significant correlations were considered when computing the averages. Across all model pairs, the proportion of significant correlations was consistently high, never falling below 93% of the total number of coefficients.

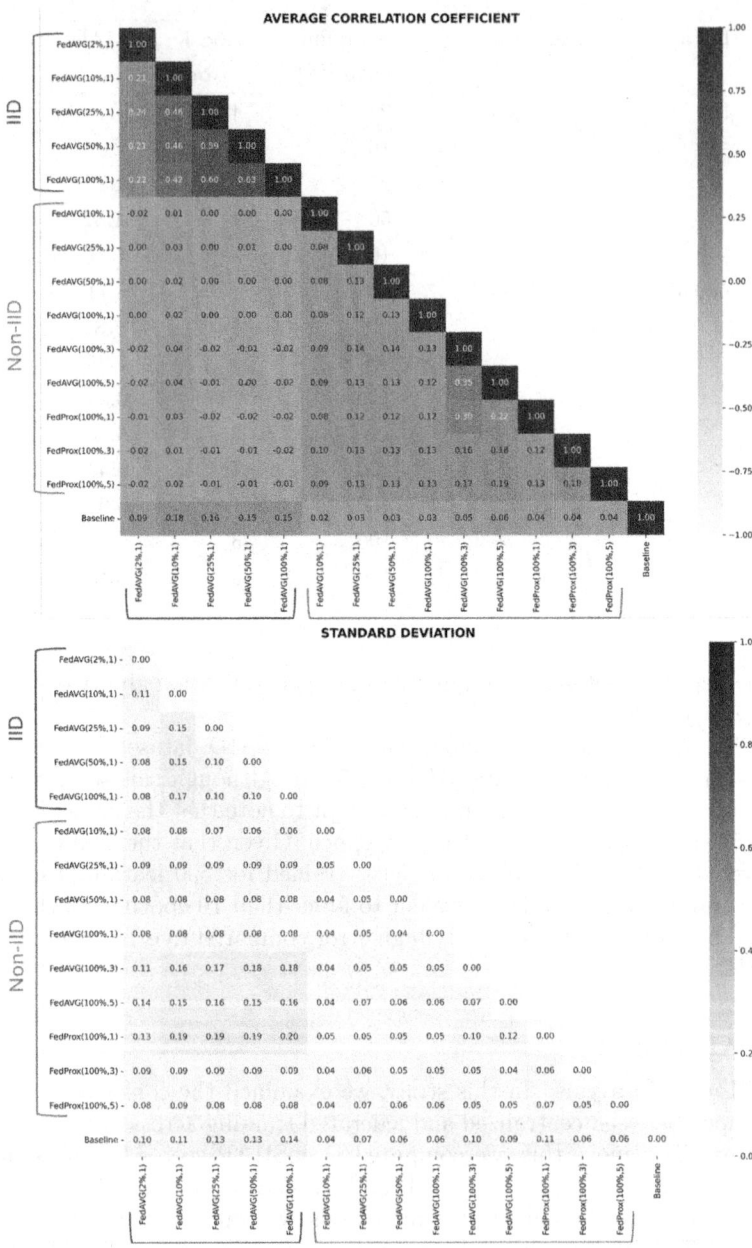

**Fig. 4.** Heatmaps of the average and the standard deviation of significant correlations between explanation distributions per couple of models. For each couple of models, the proportion of significant correlations never falls below 93% of the total number of coefficients.

*RQ1: given the same task, dataset, and architecture, are XAI outputs consistent among centralized and federated models?* The last row of the first heatmap in Fig. 4 represents the average correlation values between the explanations of the baseline model and those of the federated models. The results clearly indicate a lack of strong correlation between the attributions generated by the baseline model and any of the federated models. Despite sharing the same task, dataset, and architecture, the federated models appear to have learned different representational patterns for solving the brain age prediction task compared to the centralized baseline.

A notable difference emerges when considering the nature of the training dataset. While models trained on the non-IID dataset exhibit near-zero correlations with the baseline, those trained on the IID dataset demonstrate small but positive correlations, with values ranging between 0.10 and 0.20. This finding suggests that data distribution plays a significant role in shaping model explanations, as no similar trend is observed for other federated learning parameters, such as the number of local epochs, sampling rate, or aggregation protocol.

Among the IID-trained models, the configuration with a 2% sampling rate exhibits the lowest average correlation with the baseline. Although this setting was expected to resemble traditional mini-batch training, the extremely low sampling rate likely hindered the learning process by limiting the amount of data seen during each federated round. As previously discussed, this configuration can be interpreted as a centralized model trained on a very limited number of epochs, which partially explains the weak correlation with baseline attributions.

These findings highlight a key consideration: explanations generated by federated models are inconsistent with those of the centralized model, despite using the same task and dataset. While most federated learning parameters appear to have minimal influence on this discrepancy, the distribution of training data does exert a slight effect on model explanations.

*RQ2: Given the same task, dataset, and architecture, are XAI outputs consistent among different configurations of the Federated Learning approach?* Among the considered aspects of FL, the sampling rate appears to have a notable influence on explanation consistency, particularly in the IID dataset setting. Specifically, higher sampling rates correspond to higher correlation values among models trained under the IID condition. A similar, albeit weaker, trend is observed in the non-IID setting, where the configuration with a 10% sampling rate exhibits the lowest correlations within this group.

These findings suggest that neither the number of local epochs nor the aggregation protocol significantly impacts the consistency of model explanations across different FL configurations. Instead, a high node sampling rate should be prioritized to enhance explanation consistency in both IID and non-IID scenarios. However, it is important to note that a higher sampling rate does not always correspond to the best-performing model (see Table 1).

Interestingly, the effect of the node sampling rate per learning round is more pronounced in the IID setting, further emphasizing the importance of selecting a high sampling rate to maintain explanation consistency in federated models.

*RQ3: Given the same task, dataset, and architecture, are XAI outputs consistent among federated models trained on different node data distributions?* Regarding the consistency of model explanations across different data distributions among nodes, the heatmap reveals key patterns. First, models exhibit higher correlations with other models trained on the same dataset type rather than with configurations involving a different data distribution. Indeed, the average correlations between models trained on different dataset distributions are effectively null.

Furthermore, models trained with the IID dataset show stronger and higher correlations compared to those trained on the non-IID dataset, with some values exceeding 0.50. These results suggest that IID data distribution leads to more stable and consistent DeepSHAP attributions across different federated learning configurations.

Overall, these findings highlight that ensuring IID data distribution should be a priority when implementing a federated learning framework to enhance explanation stability across configurations. In a real-world scenario, collaborating clinics should establish standardized data acquisition protocols to facilitate IID sample distribution across nodes. This preprocessing step should be integrated into the data collection phase, as it precedes the implementation of any federated framework.

These observations align with the findings from RQ1, further reinforcing that maintaining IIDness in federated datasets is a fundamental prerequisite for ensuring consistency in model explanations.

**Table 2.** Number and percentage of features with a statistically significant correlation with chronological age per federated model.

| Dataset | Aggregator | Sampling rate [%] | Local epochs | Features Number | Percentage |
|---|---|---|---|---|---|
| IID | FedAVG | 2 | 1 | 60 | 88 |
| | | 10 | 1 | 49 | 72 |
| | | 25 | 1 | 57 | 83 |
| | | 50 | 1 | 54 | 79 |
| | | 100 | 1 | 54 | 79 |
| non-IID | FedAVG | 10 | 1 | 62 | 91 |
| | | 25 | 1 | 61 | 89 |
| | | 50 | 1 | 54 | 79 |
| | | 100 | 1 | 61 | 89 |
| | | 100 | 3 | 63 | 92 |
| | | 100 | 5 | 63 | 92 |
| | FedProx | 100 | 1 | 61 | 89 |
| | | 100 | 3 | 61 | 89 |
| | | 100 | 5 | 62 | 91 |

**Intra-model Analysis.** The last aim of this study was to explore the biological significance of ROI-based features across different training paradigms. We extracted region-based attributions by masking each saliency map with the Desikan-Killiany atlas and summing voxel attributions included in the same region. Next, the correlation between ROI-based features and chronological age was considered. The results of the analysis are displayed in Table 2 and Fig. 5.

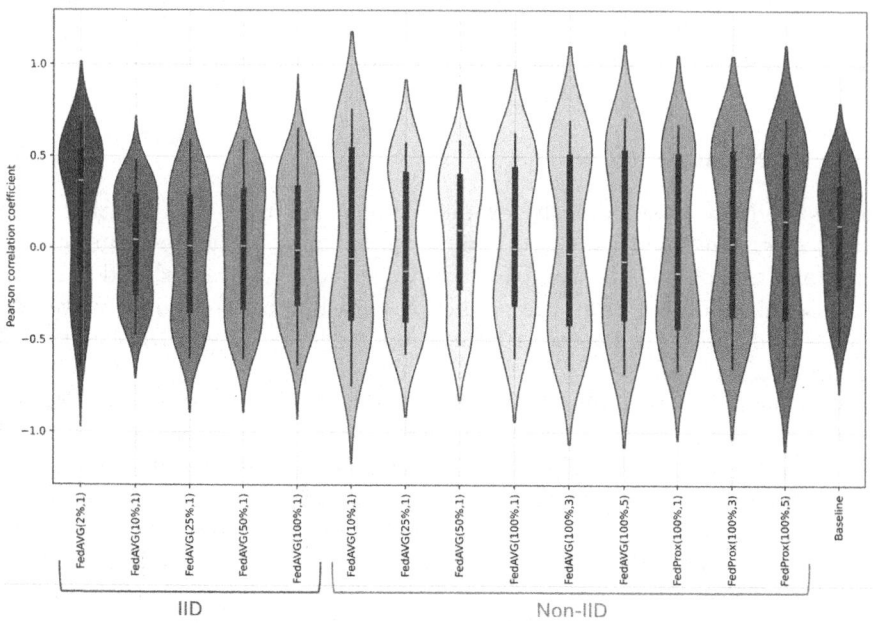

**Fig. 5.** Violin plots of Pearson correlation coefficient distribution between each ROI-based feature and the chronological age of the subjects per model.

*RQ4: Do the identified features exhibit biological significance across different training paradigms?* The number and percentage of ROI-based feature attributions that showed statistically significant correlations with chronological age for each federated model are summarized in Table 2. Most federated configurations identified a greater number of significant features compared to the centralized baseline model, which identified 55 significant features (80%). These results suggest that DeepSHAP effectively captures the influence of age on brain regions across both federated and centralized models.

Interestingly, among federated models trained on non-IID data, only the FedAVG model with a 50% sampling rate and 1 local epoch exhibited a lower percentage of significant features (79%), while all other non-IID configurations exceeded 89%. In contrast, federated models trained on the IID dataset exhibited lower percentages of relevant features, with three out of five configurations identifying fewer than 80% of significant features. These findings suggest that federated models trained on IID datasets may struggle to capture meaningful age-related variations in certain brain regions, whereas non-IID federated models demonstrate an improved ability to detect age-related changes—sometimes even outperforming the centralized model.

To further assess the consistency of age-related attributions, we compared the distributions of Pearson correlation coefficients per model, as depicted in the violin plots in Fig. 5. Except for the 2% sampling rate configuration, all IID-trained models exhibited near-zero median correlations. In contrast, non-IID-trained models displayed medians fluctuating around zero. A Kruskal-Wallis test revealed no significant difference in Pearson correlation coefficients across models ($H = 17.96$, $p = 0.2085$), using a significance level of $\alpha = 0.05$.

## 6 Conclusions

In this study, we systematically examined the consistency of XAI attributions across centralized and federated training paradigms. To address our research questions, we conducted a comparative evaluation of centralized and federated models trained on the brain age prediction task, leveraging a publicly available multi-site dataset. Explanations were computed using DeepSHAP, a state-of-the-art XAI technique.

Our findings reveal that federated models produce substantially different explanations compared to their centralized counterparts, regardless of the specific federated learning configuration. This suggests that federated training alters feature attribution patterns, which could have implications for the interpretability and trustworthiness of federated models in medical applications. Within federated models, the non-IID nature of the dataset strongly reduces the consistency of DeepSHAP attributions, emphasizing the need for careful data distribution strategies in real-world FL applications.

Among the evaluated FL parameters, node sampling rate was the only factor that significantly influenced the consistency of XAI outputs. Our results suggest that high node sampling rates and IID data distributions should be preferred to enhance the reliability of federated explanations. However, it is important to note that a higher sampling rate does not always lead to the best predictive performance, highlighting a potential trade-off between model accuracy and explanation consistency.

A key limitation of this study is that we did not explore aggregation protocols beyond FedAVG and FedProx, nor did we investigate the potential influence of training hyperparameters (e.g., optimizer choice, learning rate) on explanation consistency. Future research will address these limitations by extending the analysis to alternative FL configurations, including different aggregation strategies and common extensions of the FL paradigm, such as differential privacy or secure aggregation. Future studies should also explore whether the observed inconsistencies in explanations affect the usability and trustworthiness of federated models in clinical decision-making. Additionally, the found biological significance of the models should be assessed through human evaluation by domain experts.

**Acknowledgement.** This work was partially supported by the following projects: "LIFE: the itaLian system wIde Frailty nEtwork"; DEMETRA: "Development of an ensemble learning-based, multidimensional sensory impairment score to predict cognitive impairment in an elderly cohort of Southern Italy" (CUP D99J22001970006) Missione 6/componente 2/Investimento: 2.1 "Rafforzamento e potenziamento della ricerca biomedica del SSN", funded by European Commission NextGenerationEU; "IDENTITA - rete Integrata meDiterranea per l'osservazione ed Elaborazione di percorsi di Nutrizione"; GenoCollab: Bando a Cascata - Prima Edizione - progetto PNRR, MISURA 4 - COMPONENTE 2—INVESTIMENTO 1.4 —"Programma di Ricerca del Centro Nazionale Di Ricerca - Sviluppo di Terapia Genica e Farmaci con Tecnologia a Rna" CN00000041, SPOKE 9 "From target to therapy: pharmacology, safety and regulatory competence center", finanziato dall'Unione Europea —NextGenerationEU.

**Disclosure of Interests.** None.

# References

1. Anelli, V.W., Deldjoo, Y., Noia, T.D., Ferrara, A.: Prioritized multi-criteria federated learning. Intelligenza Artificiale **14**(2), 183–200 (2020)
2. Anelli, V.W., Deldjoo, Y., Noia, T.D., Ferrara, A., Narducci, F.: User-controlled federated matrix factorization for recommender systems. J. Intell. Inf. Syst. **58**(2), 287–309 (2022)
3. Bárcena, J.L.C., et al.: Fed-XAI: federated learning of explainable artificial intelligence models. In: Musto, C., Guidotti, R., Monreale, A., Semeraro, G. (eds.) Proceedings of the 3rd Italian Workshop on Explainable Artificial Intelligence co-located with 21th International Conference of the Italian Association for Artificial Intelligence (AIxIA 2022), Udine, Italy, November 28 - December 3, 2022. CEUR Workshop Proceedings, vol. 3277, pp. 104–117. CEUR-WS.org (2022). https://ceur-ws.org/Vol-3277/paper8.pdf
4. Bonawitz, K., et al.: Towards federated learning at scale: System design. CoRR abs/1902.01046 (2019)
5. Briola, E., Nikolaidis, C.C., Perifanis, V., Pavlidis, N., Efraimidis, P.S.: A federated explainable AI model for breast cancer classification. In: Li, S., Coopamootoo, K.P.L., Sirivianos, M. (eds.) European Interdisciplinary Cybersecurity Conference, EICC 2024, Xanthi, Greece, June 5-6, 2024, pp. 194–201. ACM (2024). https://doi.org/10.1145/3655693.3660255
6. Cole, J.H., et al.: Predicting brain age with deep learning from raw imaging data results in a reliable and heritable biomarker. Neuroimage **163**, 115–124 (2017)
7. Corbucci, L., Guidotti, R., Monreale, A.: Explaining black-boxes in federated learning. In: Longo, L. (ed.) Explainable Artificial Intelligence - First World Conference, xAI 2023, Lisbon, Portugal, July 26-28, 2023, Proceedings, Part II. Communications in Computer and Information Science, vol. 1902, pp. 151–163. Springer (2023). https://doi.org/10.1007/978-3-031-44067-0_8
8. Corps, J., Rekik, I.: Morphological brain age prediction using multi-view brain networks derived from cortical morphology in healthy and disordered participants. Sci. Rep. **9**(1), 9676 (2019)
9. Bonis, M.L.N., et al.: Explainable brain age prediction: a comparative evaluation of morphometric and deep learning pipelines. Brain Inf. **11**(1), 33 (2024)

10. Ducange, P., Marcelloni, F., Renda, A., Ruffini, F.: Federated learning of XAI models in healthcare: a case study on Parkinson's disease. Cogn. Comput. **16**(6), 3051–3076 (2024). https://doi.org/10.1007/S12559-024-10332-X
11. Ducange, P., Marcelloni, F., Renda, A., Ruffini, F.: Federated learning of XAI models in healthcare: a case study on Parkinson's disease. Cogn. Comput. **16**(6), 3051–3076 (2024)
12. Dufumier, B., Grigis, A., Victor, J., Ambroise, C., Frouin, V., Duchesnay, E.: OpenBHB: a large-scale multi-site brain MRI data-set for age prediction and debiasing. Neuroimage **263**, 119637 (2022)
13. Gill, W., Anwar, A., Gulzar, M.A.: TraceFL: Interpretability-driven debugging in federated learning via neuron provenance. arXiv preprint arXiv:2312.13632 (2023)
14. Guendouzi, S.B., Ouchani, S., Assaad, H.E., El-Zaher, M.: A systematic review of federated learning: challenges, aggregation methods, and development tools. J. Netw. Comput. Appl. **220**, 103714 (2023). https://doi.org/10.1016/J.JNCA.2023.103714
15. He, Y., et al.: Foundation model for advancing healthcare: challenges, opportunities and future directions. IEEE Reviews in Biomedical Engineering (2024)
16. Huang, G., Liu, Z., Van Der Maaten, L., Weinberger, K.Q.: Densely connected convolutional networks. In: Proceedings of the IEEE Conference on Computer Vision and Pattern Recognition, pp. 4700–4708 (2017)
17. Kairouz, P., et al.: Advances and open problems in federated learning. arXiv preprint arXiv:1912.04977 (2019)
18. Kiani, M., Andreu-Perez, J., Hagras, H., Rigato, S., Filippetti, M.L.: Towards understanding human functional brain development with explainable artificial intelligence: Challenges and perspectives. IEEE Comput. Intell. Mag. **17**(1), 16–33 (2022)
19. Konecný, J., McMahan, B., Ramage, D.: Federated optimization: Distributed optimization beyond the datacenter. CoRR abs/1511.03575 (2015)
20. Konecný, J., McMahan, H.B., Ramage, D., Richtárik, P.: Federated optimization: Distributed machine learning for on-device intelligence. CoRR abs/1610.02527 (2016)
21. Kusiak, A.: Federated explainable artificial intelligence (fXAI): a digital manufacturing perspective. Int. J. Prod. Res. **62**(1-2), 171–182 (2024). https://doi.org/10.1080/00207543.2023.2238083
22. Lee, J., et al.: Deep learning-based brain age prediction in normal aging and dementia. Nat. Aging **2**(5), 412–424 (2022)
23. Leonardsen, E.H., et al.: Deep neural networks learn general and clinically relevant representations of the ageing brain. Neuroimage **256**, 119210 (2022)
24. Li, T., Sahu, A.K., Zaheer, M., Sanjabi, M., Talwalkar, A., Smith, V.: Federated optimization in heterogeneous networks. In: MLSys. mlsys.org (2020)
25. Li, T., Sahu, A.K., Zaheer, M., Sanjabi, M., Talwalkar, A., Smith, V.: Federated optimization in heterogeneous networks. Proc. Mach. Learn. Syst. **2**, 429–450 (2020)
26. López-Blanco, R., Alonso, R.S., González-Arrieta, A., Chamoso, P., Prieto, J.: Federated learning of explainable artificial intelligence (fed-XAI): a review. In: International Symposium on Distributed Computing and Artificial Intelligence, pp. 318–326. Springer (2023)
27. Lundberg, S.M., Lee, S.I.: A unified approach to interpreting model predictions. In: Proceedings of the 31st International Conference on Neural Information Processing Systems, pp. 4768–4777. NIPS'17, Curran Associates Inc., Red Hook, NY, USA (2017)

28. Luzón, M.V., et al.: A tutorial on federated learning from theory to practice: foundations, software frameworks, exemplary use cases, and selected trends. IEEE/CAA J. Automatica Sinica **11**(4), 824–850 (2024)
29. McMahan, B., Moore, E., Ramage, D., Hampson, S., y Arcas, B.A.: Communication-efficient learning of deep networks from decentralized data. In: Proceedings of 20th International Conference on Artificial Intelligence and Statistics, pp. 1273–1282 (2017). http://proceedings.mlr.press/v54/mcmahan17a.html
30. More, S., et al.: Brain-age prediction: a systematic comparison of machine learning workflows. Neuroimage **270**, 119947 (2023)
31. Nguyen, D.C., et al.: Federated learning for smart healthcare: a survey. ACM Comput. Surv. **55**(3), 60:1–60:37 (2023)
32. Pfitzner, B., Steckhan, N., Arnrich, B.: Federated learning in a medical context: a systematic literature review. ACM Trans. Internet Techn. **21**(2), 50:1–50:31 (2021)
33. Rauniyar, A., et al.: Federated learning for medical applications: a taxonomy, current trends, challenges, and future research directions. IEEE Internet Things J. **11**(5), 7374–7398 (2023)
34. Shrikumar, A., Greenside, P., Kundaje, A.: Learning important features through propagating activation differences. ICML **70**, 3145–3153 (2017). https://proceedings.mlr.press/v70/shrikumar17a.html
35. Sihag, S., Mateos, G., McMillan, C., Ribeiro, A.: Explainable brain age prediction using covariance neural networks. Adv. Neural. Inf. Process. Syst. **36**, 46958–46988 (2023)
36. Tafuri, B., et al.: The impact of harmonization on radiomic features in Parkinson's disease and healthy controls: a multicenter study. Front. Neurosci. **16**, 1012287 (2022)
37. Wang, G.: Interpret federated learning with shapley values. CoRR abs/1905.04519 (2019). http://arxiv.org/abs/1905.04519
38. Ye, M., Fang, X., Du, B., Yuen, P.C., Tao, D.: Heterogeneous federated learning: state-of-the-art and research challenges. ACM Comput. Surv. **56**(3), 79:1–79:44 (2024)
39. Yin, H., et al.: On-device recommender systems: A comprehensive survey. CoRR abs/2401.11441 (2024)

**Open Access** This chapter is licensed under the terms of the Creative Commons Attribution 4.0 International License (http://creativecommons.org/licenses/by/4.0/), which permits use, sharing, adaptation, distribution and reproduction in any medium or format, as long as you give appropriate credit to the original author(s) and the source, provide a link to the Creative Commons license and indicate if changes were made.

The images or other third party material in this chapter are included in the chapter's Creative Commons license, unless indicated otherwise in a credit line to the material. If material is not included in the chapter's Creative Commons license and your intended use is not permitted by statutory regulation or exceeds the permitted use, you will need to obtain permission directly from the copyright holder.

# The Dynamics of Trust in XAI: Assessing Perceived and Demonstrated Trust Across Interaction Modes and Risk Treatments

Mohsen Abbaspour Onari[1,2(✉)], Gregor Baer[1,2], Chao Zhang[3], Isel Grau[1,2], Marco S. Nobile[4], and Yingqian Zhang[1,2]

[1] Information Systems, Eindhoven University of Technology, Eindhoven, The Netherlands
{m.abbaspour.onari,i.d.c.grau.garcia,yqzhang}@tue.nl
[2] Eindhoven Artificial Intelligence Systems Institute, Eindhoven University of Technology, Eindhoven, The Netherlands
[3] Human-Technology Interaction, Eindhoven University of Technology, Eindhoven, The Netherlands
c.zhang.5@tue.nl
[4] Computational Biology, Bioinformatics and Biomedicine, Department of Environmental Sciences, Informatics and Statistics, Ca' Foscari University of Venice, Venice, Italy
marco.nobile@unive.it

**Abstract.** The increasing use of artificial intelligence (AI) models across various fields has raised concerns about whether these models can meet user trust expectations. As a result, researchers are focusing on assessing AI models' performance relative to user expectations to determine trust levels. Evidence suggests that effective interaction with eXplainable AI (XAI) techniques can mitigate over-reliance on AI models and better align user expectations with the actual capabilities of these models in decision-making. In this study, we analyze trust from two perspectives: perceived trust, based on user self-reported trust, and demonstrated trust, which evaluates whether users, when given a choice, prefer to rely on AI or make decisions independently. We also explore how different interactions between human subjects and XAI models, along with varying levels of task risk, influence trust. Our findings reveal that these two types of trust are substantially different; human subjects do not always exhibit trust behavior in actual decision-making tasks, even when they perceive themselves as trusting the AI. Furthermore, we show that an AI model's low error rate in making correct decisions can influence human subjects' mental models, leading them to report a higher tendency to trust the AI. Finally, we conclude that human perceptions of trust are fragile and may change based on ongoing interactions with the model.

**Keywords:** Trust · User Study · Explainable AI · Decision Making

# 1 Introduction

The advancement of increasingly complex artificial intelligence (AI) systems has driven the adoption of AI-assisted decision-making. Research in eXplainable AI (XAI) has explored various methods to clarify the complex behavior of machine learning (ML) models. These explainability techniques are essential for justifying the decisions made by black-box models. Enhancing the fairness and trustworthiness of AI systems is frequently cited as a key objective of XAI [10]. However, there are numerous ambiguous aspects of trust that are challenging to formalize using the tools currently available in the AI and human-computer interaction (HCI) literature [12].

The aim of building trust from the user's perspective is to enhance the ability to anticipate behavior in situations involving risk [12]. In this context, XAI serves as a tool that provides users with easier access to the signals that facilitate this anticipation [12]. Prior studies have shown that unintuitive explanations can erode users' trust in an ML model [26]. Therefore, it is essential to design AI-assisted decision-making tools that enable users to interact with the model's explanations, ensuring they can intuitively understand the AI model's logic and ultimately build trust in the system. Another significant challenge is how researchers model and report trust in AI-assisted decision-making. Trust is often conceptualized as a subjective perception of AI, referred to as *perceived trust*, and is typically measured using self-report scales [19]. However, these methods may not accurately capture real trust behavior. The concept of trust reflection within real AI-assisted decision-making tasks, as proposed by Zhang *et al.* [36], is more accurately described as *demonstrated trust* wherein users decide whether to delegate the decision *without* seeing the AI's prediction–thus representing a stricter test of trust. We argue that this approach provides a more reliable measure of trust, as it allows human users to exercise agency in deciding whether to rely on the AI model, rather than merely reporting their perceived trust. Building on this foundation, we aim to take a step further by investigating the role of interaction modes with the XAI model.

In this paper, we aim to investigate the significant disparity between perceived trust and demonstrated trust in AI-assisted decision-making. We will also evaluate how the mode of interaction with the XAI model and the decision-making risk treatment impact human trust. To explore these dynamics, human subjects will be randomly assigned to one of the two XAI modes in the training phase. In the *evaluative AI* mode, participants can manipulate the SHapley Additive exPlanations (SHAP) feature importance plot to observe changes in the AI model's prediction probabilities and feature importance. In contrast, the *non-evaluative AI* mode presents participants with the SHAP feature importance plot and prediction probability for a given sample without any interactive features. At the end of the training phase, participants will report their satisfaction with the efficacy of the explanations and their perceived trust in the XAI modes. During the test phase, participants will be divided into two risk treatment groups: high-risk and low-risk. Each group will be presented with 20 tasks, each involving specific reward and penalty scores. Participants will make decisions either independently or by delegating them to the AI model, thereby reflecting their demonstrated trust. After completing the decision-making task, participants will again report their perceived trust. Based on this setup, our research seeks to address the following questions:

**RQ1:** How does the XAI interaction mode affect participants' satisfaction with the effectiveness of the provided explanations during decision-making?
**RQ2:** Does the evaluative AI mode significantly impact perceived trust during the training phase?
**RQ3:** How do the XAI mode and risk treatment affect both perceived and demonstrated trust?
**RQ4:** Does demonstrated trust influence perceived trust after the test phase?
**RQ5:** Is demonstrated trust significantly different from perceived trust?

The rest of this paper is organized as follows: Sect. 2 reviews the relevant literature. Section 3 introduces our methodology for designing the user study and measuring trust. Section 4 details the conducted user study, while Sect. 5 presents the results of trust measurement. Finally, Sect. 6 concludes the study and highlights directions for future research.

## 2 Related Work

The increasing use of AI-powered decision aids has sparked a series of experimental studies within HCI communities. These studies aim to understand how humans interact with, rely on, and trust AI models in the context of AI-assisted decision-making [15,18,19]. With the emergence of XAI, researchers have focused on integrating explanations into AI-assisted decision-making. This includes examining the impact of explanations on complementary team performance [3], error detection with explanations [9], application-oriented contexts for fraud detection [2], improving objective performance and subjective usability of model [13], and the impact of model and explanation errors on human decision-making [17,22]. As LLMs gain popularity, explanations play a crucial role in guiding Human-AI collaboration [23], generating counterfactual examples for fairer learning models [21], and facilitating Human-LLM collaborative annotation [33].

Ribeiro et al. [28] demonstrated that explanations are valuable across various models for trust-related AI-assisted decision-making tasks. The widespread use of XAI methods has inspired numerous empirical studies examining how humans trust AI models in AI-assisted decision-making. Consequently, researchers have explored various factors influencing trust in XAI models, including example-based explanations for ML classifiers [35], confidence scores and local explanations [36], and the impact of different types of AI assistance [16]. Studies have also examined AI descriptions as algorithmic recommendations [7], dissenting explanations [27], and XAI for skill development in community health workers [24].

Other research has investigated the effects of feature-based explanations on distributive fairness [30], interpretability and outcome feedback [1], and sociotechnical mismatches in AI explainability [6]. Additionally, studies have analyzed the impact of explanations in cases of AI errors [25], unintuitive feature explanations [26], and different treatments such as explanations, model bias disclosure, and proxy correlation disclosure [10]. Unlike previous research, this study examines users' trust behavior across different scenarios–both when they do not interact with an XAI assistant and when they do under two distinct decision-making risk treatments. By assessing both perceived and demonstrated trust, we aim to provide deeper insights into trust behavior in AI-assisted decision-making.

## 3 Methods

In this section, after reviewing the definitions of trust, we introduce our AI-assisted decision-making approach for designing our experiment to evaluate trust.

### 3.1 Perceived Trust vs. Demonstrated Trust

Ueno et al. [31] defines trust as "the willingness of a party to be vulnerable to the actions of another party based on the expectation that the other will perform a particular action important to the trustor, irrespective of the ability to monitor or control that other party." Jacovi et al. [12] extends the Human-AI trust definition as "if H (human) perceives that M (AI model) is trustworthy to contract C, and accepts vulnerability to M's actions, then H trusts M contractually to C. The objective of H in trusting M is to anticipate that M will maintain C in the presence of uncertainty, and consequently, trust does not exist if H does not perceive risk." However, most studies assess perceived trust in AI using self-report scales [19]. Prior research suggests that perceived trust may not reliably reflect actual trusting behaviors [14,29]. Therefore, some scholars have proposed alternative indicators to study trust, such as switch percentage and agreement percentage [36], as well as relying on Cohen's d score [34]. In addition to examining users' perceived trust, this study simulates risky situations to investigate whether participants choose to delegate their decisions to an AI model when they are also capable of making decisions independently (demonstrated trust). We quantify this type of trust as the ratio of the number of decisions delegated to the AI to the total number of decision-making tasks. We believe this approach better aligns with established definitions of Human-AI trust.

### 3.2 Evaluative AI

In cognitive forcing, the decision-maker is actively engaged in evaluating different options and making trade-offs. Providing explanatory information from the start can help the decision-maker focus on relevant details and make more informed decisions [20]. Buçinca et al. [4] and Gajos and Mamykina [8] demonstrated that cognitive forcing significantly decreases over-reliance compared to basic XAI methods. Miller [20] introduced the concept of evaluative AI, a framework for explainable decision support that resembles cognitive forcing. This framework assists decision-makers in accessing the information they need to evaluate a hypothesis as and when required. Unlike traditional approaches, evaluative AI does not automatically provide recommendations. Instead, it helps users filter out unlikely options, generate new hypotheses, or both. The decision-maker then examines a hypothesis and requests the decision aid to present evidence both supporting and challenging it.

In this study, we utilize the evaluative AI framework for AI-assisted decision-making. For each sample, we present the corresponding SHAP feature importance plot alongside the prediction probability instead of direct recommendations for classifying the instance in a binary classification task. In our evaluative AI mode, human subjects can modify feature values and observe how these changes impact both the SHAP feature importance values and the prediction probabilities. This approach helps human subjects filter out less critical features and focus on those with the greatest influence on the prediction. Additionally, observing how the prediction probability shifts with different feature values can provide human subjects with intuitive insights into the likely classification of the instance. After evaluating various hypotheses, SHAP feature importances, and prediction probabilities, human subjects can make an informed final decision.

## 4 Human-Subject Experiment

In this section, we present our proposed human-subject experiment designed to measure perceived and demonstrated trust across two different risk levels and interaction modes with XAI models, providing insights into the underlying trust mechanisms.

### 4.1 Decision Making Task

In our experiment, we ask our human subjects to classify mushroom instances into "Edible" or "Poisonous" classes. The dataset [32] comprises 17 nominal variables and three quantitative variables. It is balanced with respect to the class distribution, with an overall ratio of $e : 0.45$ and $p : 0.55$. During the data preprocessing phase, we first removed variables with more than 50% missing values. Next, we eliminated variables exhibiting high multicollinearity based on the correlation coefficient between features. This process resulted in a final dataset containing 12 variables: nine nominal and three quantitative. We randomly split the dataset into training and test sets using an 80%/20% partition. We tested several ML algorithms, tuning their hyperparameters with GridSearch and assessing performance via 5-fold cross-validation. Among these, AdaBoost emerged as the most suitable model for our study, achieving an accuracy of 0.7989 on the test dataset. Although not perfect, this accuracy is sufficient for our user study. To effectively simulate a risky situation and assess human subjects' trust in the AI model, we need a model that is not perfect and exhibits some prediction errors. This approach will reveal how human subjects behave in various risky scenarios when they are aware that the model might make mistakes. Next, we implemented SHAP to enhance model explainability by highlighting the importance of each local feature for each instance. In the decision-making task, the primary objective is to classify each mushroom instance as either "Poisonous" or "Edible," with the added risk of penalties for incorrect decisions. If participants are uncertain about their decision, they have the option to delegate it to the AI model. Our goal is to investigate whether, in risky situations where participants are capable of making decisions independently, their choice to delegate decision-making to the AI model reflects trust in its decision.

### 4.2 Experimental Treatments

To evaluate how interactions with the XAI model affect both types of trust, we implemented two treatment modes: non-evaluative AI mode and evaluative AI mode in the training phase. In the test phase, human subjects are divided into two groups: high-risk and low-risk treatments. Although the reward for correct decisions is 15 points for both treatments, the high-risk group faces a penalty of 25 points for incorrect decisions, while the low-risk group incurs a 10-point penalty. Consequently, our study includes four treatment conditions to explore how interaction with the XAI model and the level of risk influence participants' trust behavior. The holistic AI-assisted decision-making task in this study is illustrated in Fig. 1.

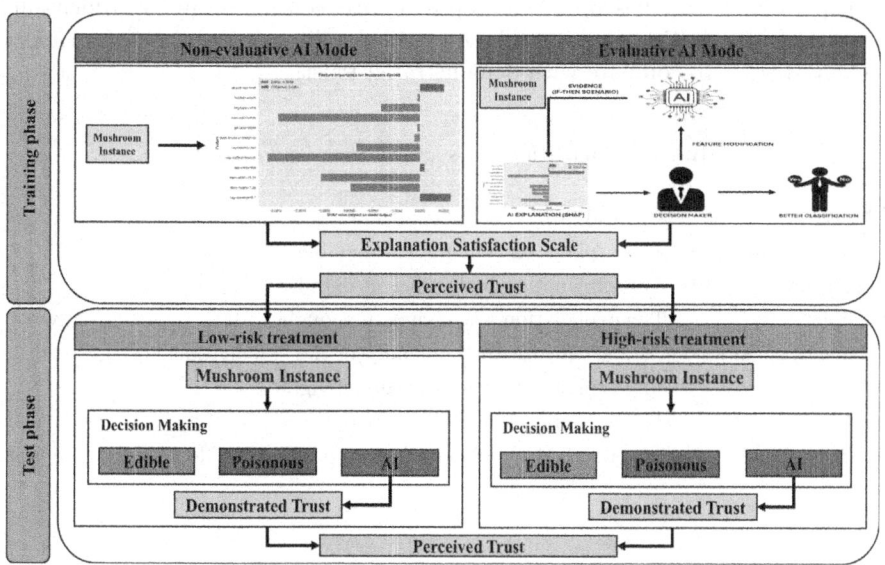

**Fig. 1.** AI-Assisted Decision-Making Experimental Procedure of This Study

## 4.3 Experimental Procedure

We conducted our experiment on Prolific, recruiting highly active participants from the US and UK. To assess the impact of both XAI mode and risk treatment on trust, resulting in four experimental groups, we performed a power analysis using a two-way between-subjects ANOVA. We selected an effect size of 0.2, an alpha level of 0.05, and a desired statistical power of 0.9, with a numerator degrees of freedom of 3. This analysis indicated that a sample size of 360 participants would be required to achieve statistically meaningful results. Among the 360 human subjects, 181 were randomly assigned to the evaluative AI model, with 85 participants in the high-risk group and the remaining 96 in the low-risk group. The non-evaluative AI group included 179 participants, with 92 in the high-risk group and 87 in the low-risk group. At the start of the experiment, they were presented with an ethical consent form, and the experiment was terminated if they did not agree to the terms[1]. Human subjects then provided demographic information, including age, gender, and their level of knowledge about mushroom detection and AI.

Following this, human subjects received a brief tutorial on how mushrooms are typically distinguished between poisonous and edible in the real world. They also received a tutorial on XAI and how to interpret SHAP feature importance plots. The training phase started with the presentation of five mushroom instances. After each decision, participants received immediate feedback, including the AI model's prediction. After completing the training task, human subjects rated their satisfaction with the explanations provided during the decision-making process using Explanation Satisfaction Scale (ESS) [11] (See Table 1) on a 5-point Likert scale from disagree strongly to agree strongly. They also assessed their perceived trust based on the proposed trust continuum by [5], which aims to quantify trust (See Table 2). The quantified value can help us to normalize perceived trust to compare with demonstrated trust.

**Table 1.** Explanation Satisfaction Scale and description

| ESS | Description |
| --- | --- |
| Understandability | The explanation was understandable. |
| Sufficiency of details | The explanation had sufficient details. |
| Completeness | The explanation was complete enough. |
| Feeling of satisfaction | I am satisfied with the quality of the explanation. |
| Accuracy | The explanation was accurate enough. |
| Usability | The explanation was easy to use. |
| Functionality | In general, the explanation helped me in the decision-making task. |

---

[1] This study has been approved by Ethical Board of the university with reference number: ERB2023IEIS10.

**Table 2.** Perceived Trust Scale

| Linguistic terms | Description | Quantified value |
|---|---|---|
| Distrust | I distrust the model. | −1 |
| Undistrust | I have a tendency to distrust the model. | −0.5 |
| Ignorance | I feel ignorant about the model. | 0 |
| Untrust | I have a tendency to trust the model. | 0.5 |
| Trust | I trust the model. | 1 |

The test phase commenced after human subjects completed the training phase. Based on their risk treatment group, they were informed whether they would face a penalty of 10 or 25 points, with their credit starting at 0. Participants were also informed that their performance in the real experiment would affect their base payment by a maximum of 2 GBP. They then evaluated 20 new mushroom instances (not seen during training) without any additional information or model predictions. The distribution of instances was consistent with the AI model's accuracy, including 16 correctly classified and 4 misclassified instances. During the test phase, human subjects had three decision options: classify as "Edible," classify as "Poisonous," or delegate the decision to the AI model. After making a decision, they were immediately informed if their answer was correct, and their credit was updated accordingly.

Upon completing the real experiment, participants were informed that they would receive a base payment of 2.5 GBP regardless of their performance. To simulate a risky situation, they were told their final reward or penalty would be adjusted by up to 2 GBP based on their performance. An additional 1 GBP bonus was awarded to the top 13 participants with the highest credit balance. Finally, participants were asked another question about their perceived trust level to assess any shifts in trust before and after the test phase.

## 5 Evaluations

This section has been divided into different subsections, each addressing one or more research questions defined in this study.

### 5.1 Impact of Evaluative AI on ESS

Addressing RQ1, we evaluated the impact of XAI mode on human subjects' satisfaction with the efficacy of the provided explanations. Given that ESS (the dependent variable) has a meaningful order, we employed the MANOVA test, which is designed to assess whether there are statistically significant differences in multiple dependent variables across different groups. MANOVA is particularly useful when dealing with multiple correlated dependent variables, allowing us to analyze the effect of the independent variable (XAI mode) while accounting for these relationships.

The MANOVA test revealed no significant effect of XAI mode on ESS. The results are summarized in Table 3 and illustrated in Fig. 2. The key observation is that, across both XAI modes, ESS is generally high, with participants somewhat agreeing that the explanations are helpful. However, it is noteworthy that for the evaluative AI mode, there is a higher concentration of responses in the "I agree somewhat" scale. In contrast, for the non-evaluative AI mode, responses are more evenly distributed across different satisfaction scales. Thus, our assumption that evaluative AI would lead to higher satisfaction with explanations is rejected.

**Table 3.** Results of the MANOVA Test for ESS

| Intercept | Value | Num DF | Den DF | F Value | Pr > F |
|---|---|---|---|---|---|
| Wilks' lambda | 0.0570 | 7.0 | 352.0 | 831.5447 | 0.0 |
| Pillai's trace | 0.9430 | 7.0 | 352.0 | 831.5447 | 0.0 |
| Hotelling-Lawley trace | 16.5364 | 7.0 | 352.0 | 831.5447 | 0.0 |
| Roy's greatest root | 16.5364 | 7.0 | 352.0 | 831.5447 | 0.0 |
| **C(XAI Mode)** | **Value** | **Num DF** | **Den DF** | **F Value** | **Pr > F** |
| Wilks' lambda | 0.9803 | 7.0 | 352.0 | 1.0126 | 0.4219 |
| Pillai's trace | 0.0197 | 7.0 | 352.0 | 1.0126 | 0.4219 |
| Hotelling-Lawley trace | 0.0201 | 7.0 | 352.0 | 1.0126 | 0.4219 |
| Roy's greatest root | 0.0201 | 7.0 | 352.0 | 1.0126 | 0.4219 |

## 5.2 Impact of Evaluative AI on Perceived Trust After Training Phase

To address RQ2, at the end of the training phase, human subjects rated their perceived trust in relation to the XAI modes, as shown in Table 2. A one-way ANOVA (see Table 4) reveals no significant differences in perceived trust levels between the XAI modes at this stage. Both groups demonstrated a high tendency to trust the guidance provided by the XAI models (Although it is still not perfect trust). However, as indicated in Fig. 3, the proportion of "Ignorance" responses is lower for the non-evaluative AI mode. Additionally, Cohen's d score

**Table 4.** One-way ANOVA Results with Cohen's d for Perceived Trust After Training Phase

|  | df | sum_sq | mean_sq | F | PR(>F) | Cohen's d |
|---|---|---|---|---|---|---|
| XAI Mode | 1.0 | 1.1148 | 1.1148 | 1.1850 | 0.2770 | -0.1148 |
| Residual | 358.0 | 336.7851 | 0.9407 |  |  |  |

suggests a slight increase in perceived trust for the non-evaluative AI mode, although this difference is not statistically significant. Therefore, our assumption that evaluative AI will lead to higher perceived trust after the training phase is rejected.

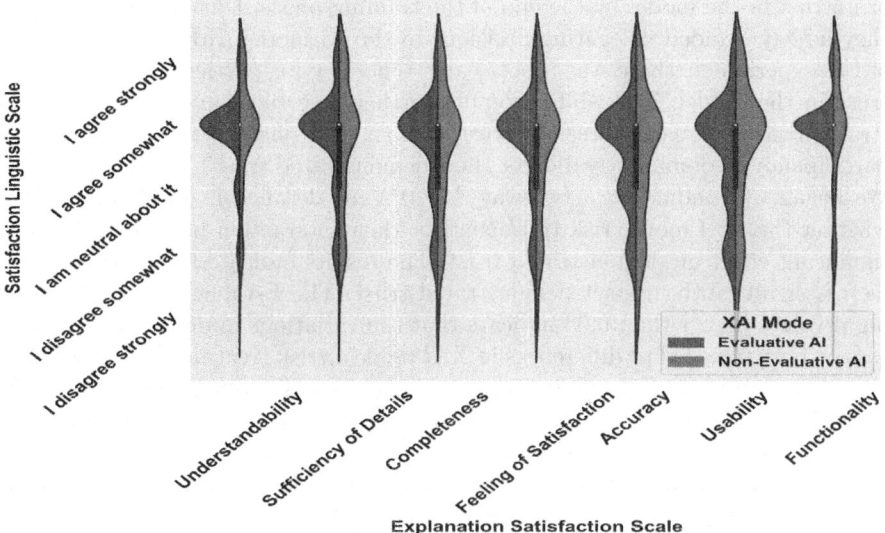

**Fig. 2.** Violin Plot of ESS

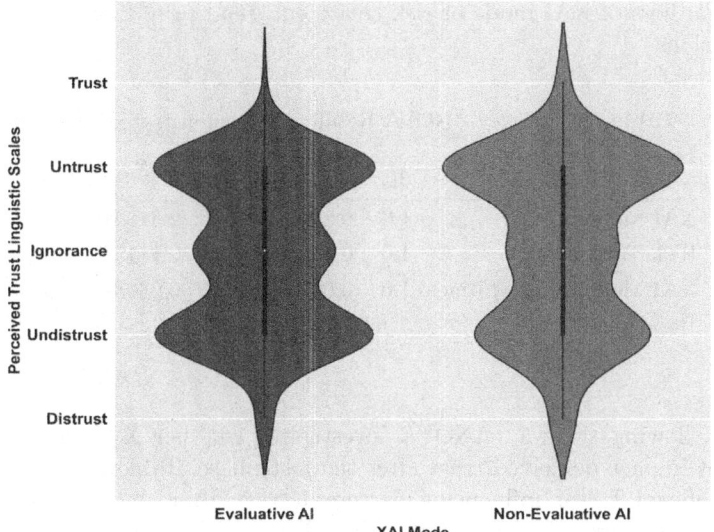

**Fig. 3.** Violin Plot of Perceived Trust after Training Phase

## 5.3 Trust in Test Phase

This section addresses RQ3 and RQ4, focusing on identifying which factors most significantly influence human subjects' trust both in terms of perceived trust and demonstrated trust. Visualizing the three types of trust measured in this experiment, as shown in Fig. 4, reveals that most participants either felt undistrust or untrust in the model by the end of the training phase. During the test phase, they largely avoided delegating decisions to the AI model. However, by the end of the experiment, there was a noticeable tendency for participants to perceive trust in the model. This shift prompts further investigation into how demonstrated trust influences perceived trust after the test phase, despite the fact that participants predominantly did not show demonstrated trust towards the model. We began by conducting a two-way ANOVA, as detailed in Table 5, to assess whether the XAI mode, risk treatment, or their interaction have a statistically significant effect on demonstrated trust. The results indicate that none of these factors significantly impact demonstrated trust. The F-values and corresponding p-values higher than 0.05 indicate that the variations in demonstrated trust cannot be attributed to differences in XAI mode or risk treatment. This suggests that demonstrated trust is relatively stable across different experimental conditions. Further analysis is supported by the interaction plot presented in Fig. 5. The plot visually confirms the lack of significant interaction effects between XAI mode and risk treatment on demonstrated trust. The parallel lines across the XAI modes suggest that the combined influence of XAI mode and risk treatment does not lead to meaningful differences in demonstrated trust. Therefore, we cannot support the hypothesis that different XAI modes or risk treatments have a significant impact on demonstrated trust. Our findings indicate that human subjects, regardless of XAI mode or risk treatment, tend to rely primarily on their own decisions.

Table 5. Two-way ANOVA Results for Demonstrated Trust

|  | df | sum_sq | mean_sq | F | PR(>F) |
|---|---|---|---|---|---|
| XAI Mode | 1.0 | 0.2150 | 0.2150 | 2.3164 | 0.1289 |
| Risk Treatment | 1.0 | 0.1960 | 0.1960 | 2.1115 | 0.1470 |
| XAI Mode:Risk Treatment | 1.0 | 0.0028 | 0.0028 | 0.0308 | 0.8606 |
| Residual | 356.0 | 33.0559 | 0.0928 | | |

The following two-way ANOVA investigates whether XAI mode and risk treatment impact perceived trust after the test phase. Table 6 reveals that the only significant factor influencing perceived trust after the test phase is the interaction between XAI mode and risk treatment (p-value=0.0472<0.05). This finding is further supported by the interaction plot presented in Fig. 6, which illustrates how different combinations of XAI modes and risk treatments influence perceived trust. The plot shows that the impact of XAI mode on trust is

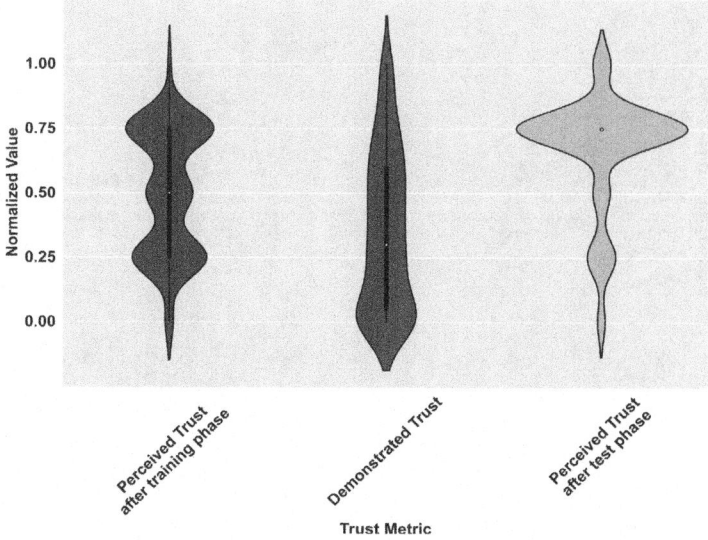

**Fig. 4.** Violin Plot for All Measured Trust

modulated by the level of risk treatment, suggesting that the effectiveness of AI explanations varies depending on the contextual risk factors.

**Table 6.** Two-way ANOVA Results for Perceived Trust

|  | df | sum_sq | mean_sq | F | PR(>F) |
|---|---|---|---|---|---|
| XAI Mode | 1.0 | 0.0277 | 0.0277 | 0.5748 | 0.4488 |
| Risk Treatment | 1.0 | 0.1303 | 0.1303 | 2.7000 | 0.1012 |
| XAI Mode:Risk Treatment | 1.0 | 0.1913 | 0.1913 | 3.9635 | 0.0472 |
| Residual | 356.0 | 17.1893 | 0.0482 | | |

To investigate the significant interaction effect observed in the two-way ANOVA, we conducted post-hoc Tukey HSD analysis for both XAI modes and risk treatments. The results, presented in Table 7, indicate that despite the significant interaction effect identified by the ANOVA, the Tukey HSD comparisons do not show significant differences between the specific groups, as the p-values for all comparisons exceed 0.05. This suggests that while there is a significant interaction, the pairwise comparisons alone do not capture the underlying complexities or additional factors influencing the results. To further explore and understand the nature of this interaction effect, we proceeded with additional ANCOVA analysis.

Analyzing the ANCOVA results shown in Table 8 highlights several important points regarding the influence of XAI modes and risk treatments on perceived

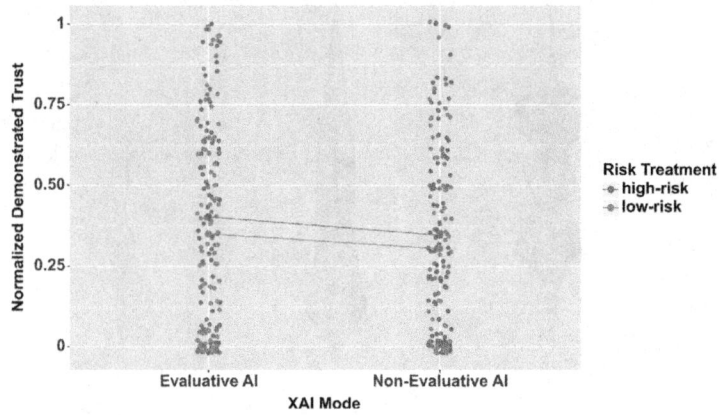

**Fig. 5.** Interaction Plot of Demonstrated Trust

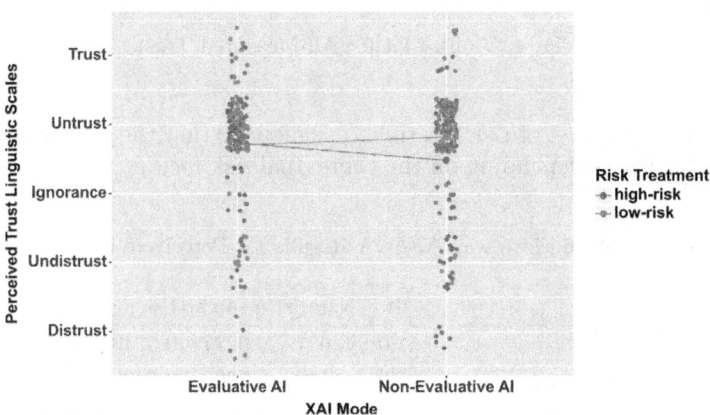

**Fig. 6.** Interaction Plot of Perceived Trust

**Table 7.** Post-Hoc Analysis: Tukey HSD Results

|  | XAI Modes | Risk Treatment |
| --- | --- | --- |
| Group 1 | Evaluative AI | High-risk |
| Group 2 | Non-evaluative AI | Low-risk |
| Mean Diff. | −0.0176 | 0.0388 |
| Adj. p-value | 0.4518 | 0.0959 |
| Lower CI | −0.0634 | −0.0069 |
| Upper CI | 0.0283 | 0.0845 |
| Reject | False | False |

trust after the test phase. Although the effect of risk treatment is not statistically significant, it approaches significance, suggesting it may have a subtle impact on perceived trust. The most noteworthy finding is the significant effect of demonstrated trust on perceived trust after the test phase (RQ4).

Table 8. ANCOVA Test Results

|  | sum_sq | df | F | PR(>F) |
|---|---|---|---|---|
| XAI Mode | 0.0123 | 1.0 | 0.2572 | 0.6123 |
| Risk Treatment | 0.1566 | 1.0 | 3.2754 | 0.0711 |
| XAI Mode:Risk Treatment | 0.1876 | 1.0 | 3.9234 | 0.0483 |
| Demonstrated Trust | 0.2132 | 1.0 | 4.4584 | 0.0354 |
| Residual | 16.9761 | 355.0 |  |  |

## 5.4 Impact of Demonstrated Trust on Perceived Trust

To address the unusual observation that perceived trust increased even when demonstrated trust by the human subject was not significant, we conducted further analysis. First, we examined the impact of credit balance on trust. A T-test revealed a significant p-value of 0.0037, indicating a strong relationship between credit balance and demonstrated trust. The Pearson correlation coefficient of 0.3488 suggests a moderate positive correlation between these two variables. Figure 7 is another piece of evidence that shows human subjects with higher demonstrated trust end up with higher credit balances at the end of the experiment, though there is some variability at certain balance levels. In the same way, the p-value and Pearson correlation coefficient between credit balance and perceived trust after the test phase were 0.0750 and 0.1772, respectively. This confirms that the main reason for the increased perceived trust after the test is not the credit balance, which could otherwise serve as a motivating factor to enhance trust.

The reason behind these results largely stems from the AI model's role in decision-making. As depicted in Fig. 8, human participants relied on their own knowledge to classify mushrooms in 65% of the decision-making tasks. This aligns with earlier conclusions that the XAI mode and risk treatment did not significantly impact demonstrated trust, and this plot further supports that finding. There is no significant difference between the correct decisions made by participants influenced by the XAI mode, suggesting that evaluative AI did not substantially help participants gain more knowledge in mushroom classification. However, evaluative AI did reduce the number of incorrect decisions. Notably, the error rate among human participants in correctly classifying mushrooms is quite high at 44.8%. This increased reliance on their own decision-making correlates with a higher error rate in mushroom classification. This is particularly striking given that 88.8% of participants reported having little to no prior knowledge of

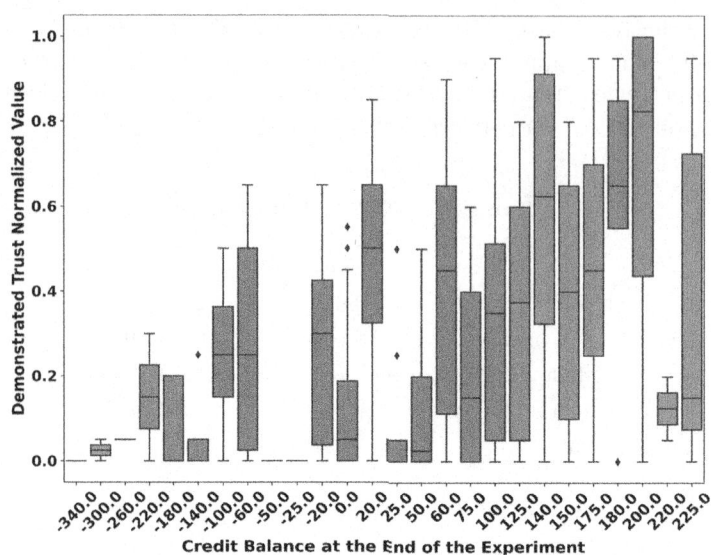

**Fig. 7.** Relationship Between Credit Balance and Demonstrated Trust

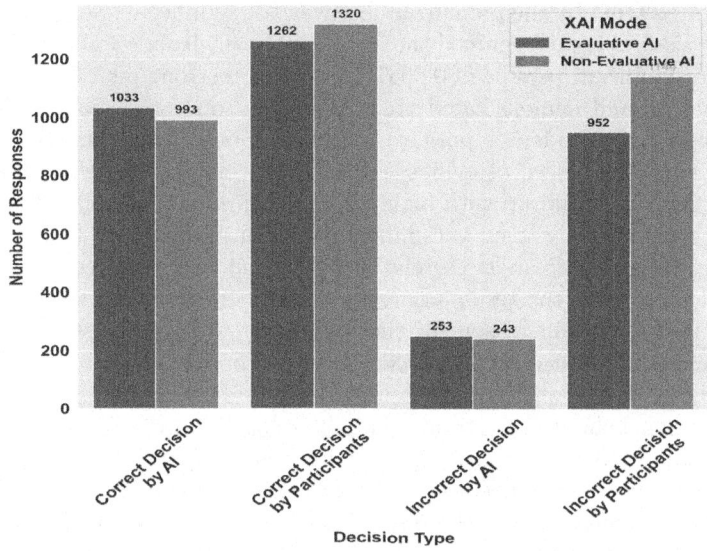

**Fig. 8.** Number and Type of Responses in Risk Treatment

mushroom identification, indicating a generally low demonstrated trust rate in the decision-making tasks. Conversely, in 35% of the decision-making tasks, participants chose to delegate the decision to the AI model. The AI model, with an error rate of 19.67% and a performance close to its expected prediction accuracy of 80%, was able to correctly identify the mushroom instances. This suggests that, within the context of the experiment, the AI model was more accurate than the human participants. In conclusion, the lower rate of incorrect decisions made by the AI likely influences participants' mental models of perceived trust, leading them to report higher levels of trust after the decision-making task. The most significant finding of this study is the clear distinction between demonstrated trust and perceived trust–two fundamentally different aspects of trust that should be studied independently (RQ5). According to the proposed trust definitions, demonstrated trust aligns more closely with a human's practical understanding of trust. On the other hand, perceived trust is not only fragile and easily swayed, but it also fails to accurately reflect real-world behavior, where trust is demonstrated by the actual delegation of decisions to AI models.

## 6 Conclusion and Discussion

In this study, we highlighted the substantial difference between demonstrated trust and perceived trust in AI-assisted decision-making. Our results indicate that there is no significant difference in human subjects' satisfaction with the efficacy of explanations provided by different XAI modes; satisfaction rates are relatively high in both cases. We also found that perceived trust during the training phase does not significantly differ across XAI modes, with human subjects generally displaying mostly undistrust and untrust toward XAI. Another key finding is the lack of a significant effect of XAI modes and risk treatment on both demonstrated and perceived trust. However, despite human users largely not delegating decisions to the AI model during the test phase, this interaction significantly impacts perceived trust, leading most subjects to develop a tendency to trust the model. It turns out that, beyond satisfaction with credit balance at the end of the experiment, the higher accuracy of the AI model leads to increased perceived trust. This finding shows that perceived trust is fragile and that human mental models can be influenced by the noticeable performance of an AI model, even when they do not delegate their decisions to it.

This paper has some limitations that we plan to address in future studies. First, we intend to include an additional control group without the risk of penalization to better understand how risk influences human subjects' tendency to rely on their own decisions rather than the AI's. Second, we plan to design a novel experiment that improves human subjects' decision-making accuracy to align more closely with that of the AI. This will enable us to study how such a setup impacts decision delegation to AI and overall trust. Third, we aim to compare human reliance on AI with perceived trust and demonstrated trust. Unlike perceived trust, which is based on subjective self-reports, reliance reflects objective behavior in response to AI system's recommendations. This study could be highly insightful for modeling human mental models during interactions with AI. It aims to distinguish differences in behavior based on subjective perceptions, objective actions, and demonstrated trust.

**Acknowledgements.** G. Baer, C. Zhang, and I. Grau are supported by the European Union's HORIZON Research and Innovation Program under grant agreement

No. 101120657, project ENFIELD (European Lighthouse to Manifest Trustworthy and Green AI). Disclosure of Interests All authors declare that they have no conflicts of interest.

# References

1. Ahn, D., Almaatouq, A., Gulabani, M., Hosanagar, K.: Impact of model interpretability and outcome feedback on trust in AI. In: Proceedings of the CHI Conference on Human Factors in Computing Systems, pp. 1–25 (2024)
2. Amarasinghe, K., et al.: On the importance of application-grounded experimental design for evaluating explainable ML methods. In: Proceedings of the AAAI Conference on Artificial Intelligence. vol. 38, pp. 20921–20929 (2024)
3. Bansal, G., et al.: Does the whole exceed its parts? The effect of AI explanations on complementary team performance. In: Proceedings of the 2021 CHI Conference on Human Factors in Computing Systems, pp. 1–16 (2021)
4. Buçinca, Z., Malaya, M.B., Gajos, K.Z.: To trust or to think: cognitive forcing functions can reduce overreliance on AI in AI-assisted decision-making. Proc. ACM Hum. Comput. Interact. **5**(CSCW1), 1–21 (2021)
5. Cho, J.H., Chan, K., Adali, S.: A survey on trust modeling. ACM Comput. Surv. (CSUR) **48**(2), 1–40 (2015)
6. Ehsan, U., Liao, Q.V., Passi, S., Riedl, M.O., Daumé, H.: Seamful XAI: operationalizing Seamful design in explainable AI. Proc. ACM Hum. Comput. Interact. **8**(CSCW1), 1–29 (2024)
7. Figueiredo, M.C., Ankrah, E., Powell, J.E., Epstein, D.A., Chen, Y.: Powered by AI: examining how AI descriptions influence perceptions of fertility tracking applications. Proc. ACM Interact. Mobile Wearable Ubiquitous Technol. **7**(4), 1–24 (2024)
8. Gajos, K.Z., Mamykina, L.: Do people engage cognitively with AI? Impact of AI assistance on incidental learning. In: Proceedings of the 27th International Conference on Intelligent User Interfaces, pp. 794–806 (2022)
9. González, A.V., et al.: Do explanations help users detect errors in open-domain QA? An evaluation of spoken vs. visual explanations. In: Findings of the Association for Computational Linguistics: ACL-IJCNLP 2021, pp. 1103–1116 (2021)
10. Goyal, N., Baumler, C., Nguyen, T., Daumé III, H.: The impact of explanations on fairness in human-AI decision-making: protected vs proxy features. In: Proceedings of the 29th International Conference on Intelligent User Interfaces, pp. 155–180 (2024)
11. Hoffman, R.R., Mueller, S.T., Klein, G., Litman, J.: Measures for explainable AI: explanation goodness, user satisfaction, mental models, curiosity, trust, and human-AI performance. Front. Comput. Sci. **5**, 1096257 (2023)
12. Jacovi, A., Marasović, A., Miller, T., Goldberg, Y.: Formalizing trust in artificial intelligence: prerequisites, causes and goals of human trust in AI. In: Proceedings of the 2021 ACM Conference on Fairness, Accountability, and Transparency, pp. 624–635 (2021)
13. Kuhl, U., Artelt, A., Hammer, B.: Let's go to the alien zoo: introducing an experimental framework to study usability of counterfactual explanations for machine learning. Front. Comput. Sci. **5**, 1087929 (2023)

14. Kunkel, J., Donkers, T., Michael, L., Barbu, C.M., Ziegler, J.: Let me explain: impact of personal and impersonal explanations on trust in recommender systems. In: Proceedings of the 2019 CHI Conference on Human Factors in Computing Systems, pp. 1–12 (2019)
15. Li, Z., Lu, Z., Yin, M.: Modeling human trust and reliance in AI-assisted decision making: a Markovian approach. In: Proceedings of the AAAI Conference on Artificial Intelligence. vol. 37, pp. 6056–6064 (2023)
16. Li, Z., Lu, Z., Yin, M.: Decoding AI'S nudge: a unified framework to predict human behavior in AI-assisted decision making. In: Proceedings of the AAAI Conference on Artificial Intelligence. vol. 38, pp. 10083–10091 (2024)
17. Liu, F., Lv, J., Cui, S., Luan, Z., Wu, K., Zhou, T.: Smart "error"! Exploring imperfect AI to support creative ideation. Proc. ACM Hum. Comput. Interact. 8(CSCW1), 1–28 (2024)
18. Lu, Z., Li, Z., Chiang, C.W., Yin, M.: Strategic adversarial attacks in AI-assisted decision making to reduce human trust and reliance. In: IJCAI, pp. 3020–3028 (2023)
19. Ma, S., Wang, X., Lei, Y., Shi, C., Yin, M., Ma, X.: are you really sure? Understanding the effects of human self-confidence calibration in AI-assisted decision making. In: Proceedings of the CHI Conference on Human Factors in Computing Systems, pp. 1–20 (2024)
20. Miller, T.: Explainable AI is dead, long live explainable AI! Hypothesis-driven decision support using evaluative AI. In: Proceedings of the 2023 ACM Conference on Fairness, Accountability, and Transparency, pp. 333–342 (2023)
21. Mishra, A., Nayak, G., Bhattacharya, S., Kumar, T., Shah, A., Foltin, M.: LLM-guided counterfactual data generation for fairer AI. In: Companion Proceedings of the ACM on Web Conference 2024, pp. 1538–1545 (2024)
22. Morrison, K., Spitzer, P., Turri, V., Feng, M., Kühl, N., Perer, A.: The impact of imperfect XAI on human-AI decision-making. Proc. ACM Hum. Comput. Interact. 8(CSCW1), 1–39 (2024)
23. Mozannar, H., Lee, J., Wei, D., Sattigeri, P., Das, S., Sontag, D.: Effective human-AI teams via learned natural language rules and onboarding. Adv. Neural Inf. Process. Syst. **36** (2024)
24. Okolo, C.T., Agarwal, D., Dell, N., Vashistha, A.: "if it is easy to understand then it will have value": examining perceptions of explainable AI with community health workers in rural India. Proc. ACM Hum. Comput. Interact. 8(CSCW1), 1–28 (2024)
25. Pafla, M., Larson, K., Hancock, M.: Unraveling the dilemma of AI errors: exploring the effectiveness of human and machine explanations for large language models. In: Proceedings of the CHI Conference on Human Factors in Computing Systems, pp. 1–20 (2024)
26. Qu, J., Arguello, J., Wang, Y.: Why is "problems" predictive of positive sentiment? A case study of explaining unintuitive features in sentiment classification. In: The 2024 ACM Conference on Fairness, Accountability, and Transparency, pp. 161–172 (2024)
27. Reingold, O., Shen, J.H., Talati, A.: Dissenting explanations: leveraging disagreement to reduce model overreliance. In: Proceedings of the AAAI Conference on Artificial Intelligence. vol. 38, pp. 21537–21544 (2024)
28. Ribeiro, M.T., Singh, S., Guestrin, C.: "why should i trust you?" Explaining the predictions of any classifier. In: Proceedings of the 22nd ACM SIGKDD International Conference on Knowledge Discovery and Data Mining, pp. 1135–1144 (2016)

29. Schaffer, J., O'Donovan, J., Michaelis, J., Raglin, A., Höllerer, T.: I can do better than your AI: expertise and explanations. In: Proceedings of the 24th International Conference on Intelligent User Interfaces, pp. 240–251 (2019)
30. Schoeffer, J., De-Arteaga, M., Kuehl, N.: Explanations, fairness, and appropriate reliance in human-AI decision-making. In: Proceedings of the CHI Conference on Human Factors in Computing Systems, pp. 1–18 (2024)
31. Ueno, T., Sawa, Y., Kim, Y., Urakami, J., Oura, H., Seaborn, K.: Trust in human-AI interaction: scoping out models, measures, and methods. In: CHI Conference on Human Factors in Computing Systems Extended Abstracts, pp. 1–7 (2022)
32. Wagner, D., Heider, D., Hattab, G.: Mushroom data creation, curation, and simulation to support classification tasks. Sci. Rep. **11**(1), 8134 (2021)
33. Wang, X., Kim, H., Rahman, S., Mitra, K., Miao, Z.: Human-LLM collaborative annotation through effective verification of LLM labels. In: Proceedings of the CHI Conference on Human Factors in Computing Systems, pp. 1–21 (2024)
34. Wang, X., Yin, M.: Are explanations helpful? A comparative study of the effects of explanations in AI-assisted decision-making. In: Proceedings of the 26th International Conference on Intelligent User Interfaces, pp. 318–328 (2021)
35. Yang, F., Huang, Z., Scholtz, J., Arendt, D.L.: How do visual explanations foster end users' appropriate trust in machine learning? In: Proceedings of the 25th International Conference on Intelligent User Interfaces, pp. 189–201 (2020)
36. Zhang, Y., Liao, Q.V., Bellamy, R.K.: Effect of confidence and explanation on accuracy and trust calibration in AI-assisted decision making. In: Proceedings of the 2020 Conference on Fairness, Accountability, and Transparency, pp. 295–305 (2020)

**Open Access** This chapter is licensed under the terms of the Creative Commons Attribution 4.0 International License (http://creativecommons.org/licenses/by/4.0/), which permits use, sharing, adaptation, distribution and reproduction in any medium or format, as long as you give appropriate credit to the original author(s) and the source, provide a link to the Creative Commons license and indicate if changes were made.

The images or other third party material in this chapter are included in the chapter's Creative Commons license, unless indicated otherwise in a credit line to the material. If material is not included in the chapter's Creative Commons license and your intended use is not permitted by statutory regulation or exceeds the permitted use, you will need to obtain permission directly from the copyright holder.

# XAI in Healthcare

# Systematic Benchmarking of Local and Global Explainable AI Methods for Tabular Healthcare Data

Gizem Karagoz(✉)[📷], Tanir Ozcelebi, and Nirvana Meratnia

Eindhoven University of Technology, Eindhoven 5612, AZ, Netherlands
{g.karagoz,t.ozcelebi,n.meratnia}@tue.nl

**Abstract.** Explainable Artificial Intelligence (XAI) is essential for ensuring transparency and trust in healthcare. However, a systematic evaluation of XAI methods for tabular healthcare data is lacking. In this paper, we present a comprehensive benchmarking framework designed to evaluate the quality of explanations produced by local and global explainable AI (XAI) methods applied to tabular healthcare data. The framework integrates predictive model-centered evaluation, which assesses how well explanations capture model behavior, and human-centered evaluation, which measures alignment between explanations and expert-defined clinical reasoning. We apply this framework to a stroke prediction dataset and evaluate it with six predictive models (i.e., interpretable models, tree-based ensemble algorithms, and kernel-based methods) representing a wide range from interpretable to black-box models. These models are explained using nine different local and global XAI methods covering both model-agnostic and model-specific techniques to provide diverse methodological coverage. The benchmark results provide practical insights into the strengths and limitations of different XAI methods across model types and explanation scopes, offering a structured guide for selecting reliable and clinically meaningful XAI methodpredictive model combinations for healthcare decision support systems.

**Keywords:** Explainable AI · Tabular Healthcare Data · XAI Evaluation · XAI Benchmark · Local Explanation · Global Explanation · User Study

## 1 Introduction

Artificial intelligence (AI) has demonstrated significant potential in healthcare, particularly in disease prediction and diagnosis. However, the black-box nature of many AI models remains a major obstacle to their adoption in real-world clinical settings. The lack of transparency of these models makes it difficult for medical professionals to trust or validate their outputs. This raises concerns about reliability, ethics, and accountability of AI-based decision making, specifically for the high stake domains such as healthcare [8,31]. Explainable AI (XAI) has emerged as a solution to this challenge by providing insights into model's decision-making ability through feature attributions, rule-based logic, or example-based explanations [1]. These explanations aim to enhance transparency and trust to ensure that AI-driven decisions align with medical knowledge and clinical reasoning for utilization of their benefit in healthcare decision making.

Despite increasing research efforts in XAI, evaluating the quality and reliability of explanations remains a critical challenge. Unlike standard performance metrics used for predictive models such as accuracy or F1-score, which are objective and well-established, measuring the quality, reliability, and usefulness of explanations is subjective and as such far more complex. Many XAI studies rely on visual explanations or qualitative case studies, which leaves significant gaps in systematic and reproducible evaluation methodologies [21]. However, for AI to be effectively integrated into medical workflows, explanations must not only faithfully reflect the predictive model's reasoning but also align with expert knowledge [11,18]. This dual requirement is especially crucial in healthcare, where decisions based on misleading or clinically irrelevant explanations could directly threaten patient safety.

Existing works on XAI Evaluation largely focus on one of two perspectives: predictive model-centered evaluation which assess whether explanations accurately capture the internal logic of the predictive model [4,14,21], or human-centered evaluation which assess whether explanations are coherent and useful from the perspective of domain experts [31]. These two perspectives, however, are often studied mutually-exclusive which leads to incomplete evaluations. Furthermore, most benchmarking studies focus on XAI methods applied to medical image data whereas structured tabular healthcare data, the primary format of patient records in electronic health records(EHRs), remains relatively unexplored [15,22,28]. Since that tabular data captures a wide spectrum of critical medical information, including diagnoses, treatment histories, laboratory results, and demographics, the explainability of predictive models trained on such data is becoming more essential for building trustworthy and practically usable clinical decision support systems(CDSS) [6,26].

To address these gaps, this paper presents a comprehensive benchmarking framework designed to evaluate local and global XAI methods applied to tabular healthcare data. Our framework explicitly integrates both predictive model-centered and human-centered evaluation, ensuring that the evaluated XAI methods are not only technically faithful to the predictive model's decision process but also clinically meaningful for medical experts. Specifically, we contribute the following:

- A systematic benchmarking framework that evaluates local and global XAI methods applied to six machine learning models including interpretable models, ensemble learners, and kernel-based classifiers. As part of this framework, we introduce a structured transformation process that normalizes the diverse outputs of these XAI methods into a unified, feature importance-based explanation format to ensure comparisons across methods are consistent, quantitatively meaningful, and directly comparable.
- A predictive model-centered evaluation captures both input-based evaluation to assess whether explanations reflect the model's internal decision logic, and

output-based evaluation to assess whether explanations adapt appropriately
to changes in predicted class.
- A human-centered evaluation, involving a user study with medical experts,
in which XAI-generated explanations are directly compared to expert-defined
feature important rankings in a stroke prediction task. Therefore, clinical
coherence of different XAI methods are enlightened.

The remainder of this paper is structured as follows: Sect. 2 reviews previous research for XAI on tabular data and evaluation methodologies.Section 3 introduces the selected XAI methods, predictive models, evaluation metrics, their specific implementations used in the study and the reasoning behind the selection of them with design details of the proposed benchmarking framework. Section 4 presents the findings of the experiments. Finally, Sect. 5 discusses key takeaways and future research directions.

## 2 Related Works

Several recent studies have focused on benchmarking XAI methods for tabular healthcare data by aiming to evaluate the reliability, faithfulness, and usefulness of different explanation techniques in clinical prediction tasks.

Brankovic et al. [7] benchmarked SHAP and Deep Taylor Decomposition on two EHR datasets, aiming at deterioration and patient readmission prediction. This study primarily conducted an explanation-level comparison across methods, using Union, Spearman Correlation, and sign agreement metrics which is identified by the authors to compare the predictive probabilities of XAI methods. Therefore, evaluation is completed without applying predictive model centered or human centered approaches.

Metsch et al. [17] applied LIME, Kernel SHAP, Integrated Gradients, and DeepLIFT to breast cancer and heart disease tabular datasets. This benchmarking study similarly compared explanations across statistical methods using Bonferroni corrected p-values, without including predictive model centered or human centered evaluation. Similarly Duell et al. [12] focused on comparing SHAP, LIME, Anchors, and Explainable Boosting Machine (EBM) on lung cancer prediction from tabular data. Their evaluation centered exclusively on comparing shared features across explanation methods, without deeper model or human centered evaluation.

In contrast, Panigutti et al. [23] conducted a human centered evaluation by involving 31 medical experts including medical experts who assessed explanations generated by an ontology-based method applied to myocardial infarction prediction using EHR data. This study measured Explicit Trust, Weight of Advice, Confidence, and Behavioral Intention to assess the usability and relevance of the explanations from a clinical perspective.

Agarwal et al. [2] introduced OpenXAI, a benchmarking framework that evaluated LIME, SHAP, Vanilla Gradients, SmoothGrad, GradientxInput, and Integrated Gradients across multiple datasets but as healthcare related; diabetes and heart disease prediction tasks using tabular data. Notably, this study included a predictive model-centered evaluation, using 22 diverse metrics to assess faithfulness, stability, and fairness, highlighting the importance of covering multiple dimensions of explainability evaluation.

Moreira et al. [20] benchmarked counterfactual explanation methods (DiCE, Prototype, GrowingSpheresCF, WatcherCF) applied to tabular breast cancer and diabetes prediction datasets. This study conducted predictive model-centered evaluations while also comparing explanation characteristics across methods using metrics such as Proximity, Sparsity, Plausibility, Diversity, Feasibility, Coverage, Stability, and Efficiency.

Finally, Dimitsaki et al. [10] benchmarked SHAP across multiple machine learning models (KNN, Decision Tree, Random Forest, SVM, Extra Trees, XGBoost, MLP) for COVID-19 severity prediction from tabular plasma proteomic data. This work combined predictive model-centered evaluation (SHAP importance ranking) with biological pathway enrichment analysis to connect explanations with clinically relevant pathways, effectively bridging algorithmic transparency and biomedical interpretability.

As revealed in the literature review, most benchmarking studies focus solely on predictive model-centered evaluations (e.g., faithfulness checks or feature importance comparisons) or exclusively on human-centered assessments (e.g., medical expert studies). Only a few works attempt to combine both perspectives within a unified evaluation framework, which highlights a critical gap in the holistic evaluation of explanations in healthcare.

Despite significant advancements in XAI for tabular healthcare data, none of these studies offer a truly integrated benchmarking framework that concurrently assesses the faithfulness of explanations to the predictive model and their alignment with domain knowledge through expert validation. This missing comprehensive evaluation pipeline is crucial for ensuring that XAI methods used in clinical decision support are not only technically sound but also practically useful for medical professionals.

## 3 Methodology

We propose a benchmarking framework to evaluate the correctness, contrastivity and coherence of XAI methods applied to various predictive models for tabular healthcare data, and these characteristics of XAI are based on the taxonomy provided by Nauta et al. [21]. Our primary objective is to systematically evaluate local and global feature importance explanations across multiple dimensions such as the ability to reflect changes on input/output data and the inner decision making mechanism of the predictive model. Additionally, since without human-centered evaluation, the XAI evaluation in healthcare would be incomplete, we also perform a user study.

### 3.1 Predictive Models

In this study, we include a set of six machine learning models categorized based on their interpretability and algorithmic properties. These models include interpretable models (i.e., decision tree classifier and logistic regression), ensemble learning models (i.e., random forest, XGBoost and CatBoost), and kernel-based support vector machines to have a balanced comparison between performance-driven and explainability-focused approaches. The selection of these models is based on their widespread use in healthcare applications, their various simple and complex decision-making mechanisms, their built-in feature importance approaches, and their intrinsic interpretability levels to analyze their explanations using post hoc XAI methods.

Table 1 summarizes the selected predictive models including algorithm type, built-in feature importance approach, interpretability level [19], and regularization strategy. The built-in feature importance column refers to the model's inherent ability to provide insights into feature contributions, which is primarily used for global explainability. Additionally, the regularization column provides information on how each model mitigates over-fitting, with techniques ranging from pruning in decision trees to L1/L2 penalties in logistic regression and boosting models, and soft margin tuning in SVMs.

**Table 1.** Summary of the selected predictive models

| Model | Built-in Feature Importance | Interpretability | Algorithm Type | Regularization |
|---|---|---|---|---|
| Decision Tree | Gini Importance | High | Interpretable Tree | Pruning |
| Logistic Regression | Coefficient Weights | High | Interpretable Linear | L1/L2 (Ridge, Lasso) |
| XGBoost | Gain, Weight, Cover | Moderate | Ensemble-Boosting | L1/L2 Regularization |
| Random Forest | Gini Importance | Moderate | Ensemble-Bagging | Implicit via Ensembles |
| CatBoost | Loss-based Importance | Moderate | Ensemble-Boosting | L2 Regularization |
| SVM | Model Coefficients (Linear Kernel) | Moderate | Kernel-Based | Soft Margin (C Parameter) |

### 3.2 XAI Methods

In general, XAI methods can be categorized in two main groups: *local* and *global* [29]. Local XAI methods focus on explaining individual predictions by identifying the most influential features for specific instances. These methods are particularly useful for checking whether model behavior is reflected on the explanation for case-specific decision-making. In contrast, global XAI methods provide insights into how the model makes predictions across the entire dataset. They help to identify key features driving model behavior and assist in ensuring transparency in high-stakes decision-making.

To ensure a diverse evaluation, we incorporate both local and global methods, including model-agnostic and model-specific approaches, which generate feature importance as explanations. The selected methods cover a wide range of explainability approaches including perturbation-based techniques such as Shapley value-based methods [16], LIME [24] and anchors [25]. Additionally, we include intrinsically interpretable models such as built-in feature importance for both tree based with the light of tree-structures and linear coefficients from logistic regression and SVM. Additionally, Acumulated Local Effects (ALE) which captures global feature attributions by aggregating local modal behaviour across the feature space has extended the XAI methods [5]. Finally, surrogate models, such as decision trees fitted on black-box predictions are also included as a model-agnostic global explanation approach.

As shown in Fig. 1, each predictive model is paired with all applicable XAI methods. For instance, tree-based models have access to both built-in feature importance and Tree SHAP, while models like logistic regression and SVM rely on Linear SHAP for Shapley-based explanations. The figure also highlights the distinction between local and global explanations for each method, emphasizing that some methods, such as Kernel SHAP and surrogate trees, can be applied in both settings, while others, like ALE and permutation importance, focus exclusively on global explanations. This comprehensive mapping summarizes the used XAI model-predictive model combinations with different levels of model transparency and explanation scope.

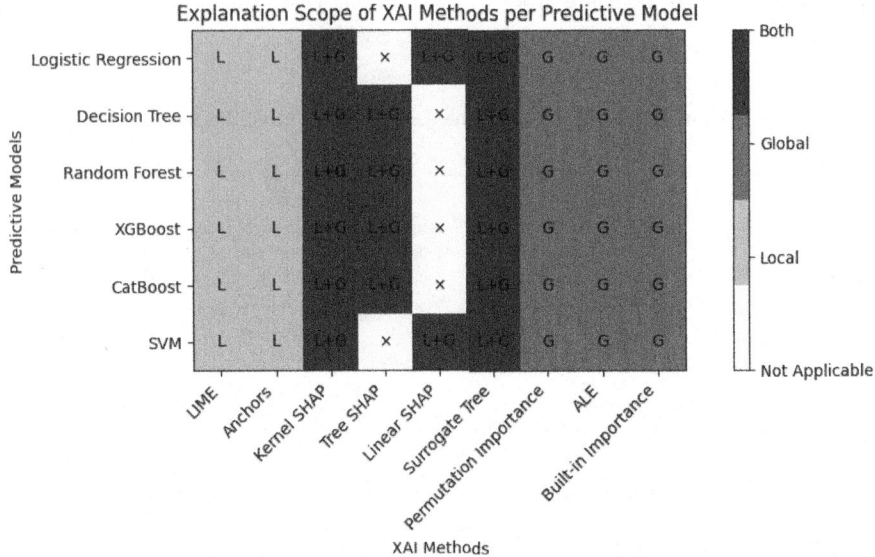

**Fig. 1.** Explanation scope of the selected XAI methods applied to each predictive model. "L" denotes local explanations, "G" global explanations, and "L+G" indicates methods that can generate both. "X" denotes XAI Methods that do not apply to specific predictive models because of the model-specific approach of the XAI method.

The majority of used XAI methods in this study, generate feature importance explanations where each feature is assigned a numerical score reflecting its contribution to the model's prediction. However, the explanation formats of Anchors and ALE are different from this format. Anchors generates rule-based explanations, where individual features appear as conditions within the rule [25], and ALE provides plots that visualize how the model's prediction changes when a given feature varies across its range [5].

To propose a fair and consistent evaluation across all methods, this benchmark focuses specifically on feature importance-based explanations, ensuring that explanations from all methods are directly comparable under the same evaluation criteria. To achieve this, Anchors explanations are transformed into feature importance scores by assigning each feature a score ($\phi_j$) equal to the coverage-precision product of the rule in which the feature appears:

$$\phi_j = \sum_{r \in R_j} \text{Coverage}(r) \cdot \text{Precision}(r) \tag{1}$$

where $R_j$ denotes the set of rules that include feature $j$.

For ALE, which originally provides plots rather than numerical scores, feature importance is calculated by measuring the range of the ALE curve as proposed by Greenwell et al. [13]. This approach is formally given by:

$$I(X_j) = max(ALE(X_j)) - min(ALE(X_j)) \tag{2}$$

Therefore, the overall influence of feature $X_j$ on the prediction is captured by quantifying the total effect span observed across the feature's value range.

### 3.3 Similarity Metrics

To measure the similarity between explanations generated by different methods, we apply three complementary metrics, each capturing a different aspect of similarity:

**Spearman's Rank Correlation Coefficient** [30] : measures how consistently two methods rank the importance of features by capturing ranking similarity even if the actual importance magnitudes are different. Lower values (closer to 0 or negative) indicate that feature rankings change significantly, Higher values (closer to 1) suggest that the feature rankings remain mostly unchanged.

**Euclidean Distance:** calculates the straight-line distance between two points, or in other words, two feature importance vectors, in a multidimensional space. Higher values indicate a greater magnitude shift in feature importance scores while lower values suggesting minimal change.

**Wasserstein Distance (Earth Mover's Distance)** [27,32]: measures the minimum cost of transforming one distribution into another. Higher values reflect larger changes in both rank and magnitude and lower values suggest that feature importance rankings and magnitudes remain mostly the same. Therefore, it considers both the ranks and magnitudes of feature importance.

By combining these complementary metrics, the evaluation captures not only ranking agreement but also magnitude-based similarity and distributional consistency which provides a multi-dimensional view of explanation similarity across methods.

### 3.4 Evaluation Framework

The evaluation is structured into two key components: (1) *Predictive Model-Centered Evaluation*, which examines explanation reliability through input and output data-based techniques, and (2) *Human-Centered Evaluation*, which assesses how well explanations align with expert-defined medical insights. By integrating both predictive model-centered and expert-aligned evaluation strategies, this framework provides a comprehensive evaluation of XAI methods by ensuring that explanations are both technically reliable and practically useful in a healthcare setting.

**Predictive Model-Centered Evaluation.** Within the *Predictive Model-Centered Evaluation*, two major evaluation approaches are used to check the ability of XAI method to reflect the inner behavior of the predictive model from both an input-based and an output-based perspectives to assess how accurately explanations capture the decision-making process of the predictive model.

**Input-Based: Incremental Deletion Check (IDC).** The *input-based evaluation* examines to what extent the XAI method can accurately identify the most influential features affecting the ability of the predictive model's decision-making. This is addressed through *IDC*, where top-ranked features, identified by the XAI method, are progressively removed from the dataset to observe their impact on model performance.

Algorithm 1 provides details about the IDC procedure. Given a predictive model $M$, a subset of test instances $X$ with corresponding labels $y$, and a set of local XAI methods $\mathcal{X}$, IDC computes the model's predicted probability for the predicted class before and after sequentially masking the most important features. Masking is performed by getting the mean value of the specified feature if the feature is numeric, otherwise masking with the mode of the categorical value. The process involves the following steps:

---

**Algorithm 1.** Incremental Deletion Check for Local Explanations
---
1: **procedure** IDC-LOCAL($M, X, y, \mathcal{X}$)
2:     Initialize results matrix $\mathcal{P} \leftarrow$ zeros($|X|, d+1$)     ▷ $\mathcal{P}[i, 0]$ stores the baseline probability
3:     **for all** $x_i \in X$ **do**     ▷ Iterate over instances
4:       $P_0 \leftarrow P(y_i | x_i)$     ▷ baseline probability
5:       $\mathcal{P}[i, 0] \leftarrow P_0$
6:       **for all** $\mathcal{X}_k \in \mathcal{X}$ **do**     ▷ For each XAI method
7:         $\phi_k(x_i) = \mathcal{X}_k(M, x_i)$     ▷ Calculate feature importances
8:         $\mathcal{F}_i = \text{Sort}(\phi_k(x_i), \text{descending})$     ▷ Sort features
9:         $\hat{x}_i \leftarrow x_i$     ▷ Initialize modified instance
10:         **for** $j = 1$ to $|\mathcal{F}_i|$ **do**     ▷ Iterate over features
11:           $\hat{x}_i[f_j] \leftarrow \mathbb{E}[x_i]$     ▷ Mask top feature $f_j$ with feature mean
12:           $P_j \leftarrow P(y_i | \hat{x}_i)$     ▷ Calculate new probability
13:           $\mathcal{P}[i, j] \leftarrow P_j$
14:         **end for**
15:       **end for**
16:     **end for**
17:     **return** $\bar{\mathcal{P}} \leftarrow \frac{1}{n} \sum_{i=1}^{n} \mathcal{P}[i, j]$     ▷ Return avg probabilities across instances
18: **end procedure**

Similarly, IDC for global explanations follows a similar fundamental principle as its local counterpart but operates at the dataset level rather than on individual instances. The goal remains to assess whether the globally identified important features meaningfully contribute to the predictive model's decision-making process. Unlike local IDC, where feature importance is computed for each instance separately, global IDC evaluates feature significance based on a dataset-wide ranking such that $X[:, f_j] \leftarrow \mathbb{E}[X[:, f_j]]$ where $f_j$ is the selected feature to be masked and it is calculated via the mean value of the feature in the entire dataset. Therefore, the feature is grayed out for the predictive model.

**Output-Based: Target Sensitivity Check (TSC).** The *output-based evaluation* examines whether XAI methods generate explanations that appropriately adapt to variations in the predictive model's outputs. This is addressed through TSC, which evaluates whether feature attributions meaningfully change in between different targets.

For local explanations, given an instance $x_i$, feature attributions are computed for its predicted class (by predictive model) as well as for an alternative class. The resulting feature importance rankings are then compared using multiple ranking similarity metrics.

For global explanations, target sensitivity is checked by computing separate global feature importance scores for each class across all instances in the dataset. The aggregated feature attributions for class 0 and class 1 are then compared to examine whether global explanations appropriately differentiate between the two prediction groups.

By comparing explanations across different target outputs, this analysis verifies whether an XAI method remains sensitive to the decision boundary shifts of the predictive model. If an XAI method provides identical explanations regardless of the output class, it may indicate a lack of responsiveness to model behavior, raising concerns about its reliability in capturing the underlying decision-making process.

**Human-Centered Evaluation.** In addition to predictive model-centered evaluation, this study incorporates a human-centered evaluation to assess the clinical coherence of XAI explanations. The primary goal is to evaluate whether the explanations generated by XAI methods align with the reasoning process of medical experts, rather than solely capturing the internal logic of the predictive models. This step is particularly important in healthcare, where the practical usefulness of explanations depends heavily on their ability to reflect clinically meaningful reasoning.

**User Study Setup.** The human-centered evaluation considers both local and global perspectives on feature importance to align with the explanation scope of evaluated XAI methods in the study. In the local perspective, the objective is to assess whether explanations correctly highlight the most relevant patient features for individual cases, simulating the reasoning process that clinicians apply when reviewing specific patient histories. In contrast, the global perspective aims to evaluate whether the methods correctly capture the general importance of features across the patient population, reflecting broader medical knowledge about stroke risk factors.

For case-specific (local) feature importance, multiple patient cases are incorporated rather than a single case study, to enhance the robustness of the findings even though the number of participating experts is limited. In each case, patient factors along with the ground truth label (whether the patient experienced a stroke or not) are provided to the participants. The medical experts are then asked to rank the presented features based on their perceived importance in supporting the given ground truth for that specific case. For global feature importance evaluation, the participants are asked to rank the features independently of any individual case, focusing instead on the general contribution of each feature to stroke prediction. This global ranking reflects population-level domain knowledge, complementing the case-specific (local) reasoning. (For details of dataset and user study, See Sect. 4.2)

To enable quantitative comparison between expert-defined and model-generated explanations, the collected expert rankings are subsequently evaluated against the feature importance scores produced by the selected XAI methods using multiple similarity metrics. These similarity metrics are further detailed in Sect. 3.3 and form the basis for assessing clinical alignment within the benchmark. However, while previous tests aimed to detect differences in explanations, the goal in this case is the opposite: explanations should be as similar as possible to expert knowledge.

## 4 Experimental Results

This section presents the experimental setup and results obtained from evaluating XAI methods across multiple perspectives. The evaluation is conducted using a binary classification task on a stroke prediction dataset. The assessment includes both *Predictive Model-Centered Evaluation*, covering *Incremental Deletion* and *Target Sensitivity*, and *Alignment with Domain Knowledge* to analyze the reliability of XAI methods in real-world medical decision-making.

The experiments were conducted on the publicly available Stroke Prediction Dataset[1], which contains clinical features related to stroke occurrence. The dataset consists of 5,110 instances, with 10 features which are detailed in Table 2.

The target variable represents stroke occurrence (binary classification, i.e., stroke vs. no stroke). Due to class imbalance, SMOTE (Synthetic Minority Oversampling Technique) [9] was applied to balance the dataset before model training. To ensure robust and consistent model evaluation, the experiments implemented via PyCaret [3] for predictive model training and hyperparameter tuning. The dataset is split into 80%-20% training and test sets, and models are evaluated using 10-fold cross-validation.

---

[1] https://www.kaggle.com/datasets/fedesoriano/stroke-prediction-dataset.

**Table 2.** Features in the Stroke Prediction Dataset including their types and value ranges or possible categories.

| Feature | Type | Possible Values/Range |
|---|---|---|
| Gender | Categorical | Male, Female, Other |
| Hypertension | Categorical | Yes, No |
| Heart Disease | Categorical | Yes, No |
| Ever Married | Categorical | Yes, No |
| Work Type | Categorical | Private, Self-employed, Governmental Job, Children, Never worked |
| Residence Type | Categorical | Urban, Rural |
| Smoking Status | Categorical | Formerly Smoked, Never Smoked, Smokes, Unknown |
| Age | Numeric | Continuous [0 - 82] |
| Avg. Glucose Level | Numeric | Continuous [55.12 - 271.74] |
| BMI | Numeric | Continuous [10.1 - 97.6] |
| Class | Categorical | Stroke, Non-Stroke |

Machine learning models, which are used for the experiments are provided in Table 1 and the reasoning behind the selection of the predivtive models with the XAI models are provided in Sect. 3.3.

### 4.1 Predictive Model Centered Evaluation

To ensure robustness in the predictive model-centered evaluation process, local explanation tests are performed over 20 randomly selected instances, and their average is taken to reduce variability. Global explanations are generated once for the entire dataset to obtain a stable feature importance ranking.

**Input-Based Evaluation: Incremental Deletion Check(IDC).** One of the key aspects of IDC is the masking strategy which ensures that the removal of a feature does not introduce unrealistic distortions. The purpose of feature removal is graying-out the feature from the decision making mechanism. For numerical features, the applied masking approach was mean imputation which is based on the mean value of the masked feature in the entire dataset. On the other hand, for categorical data, the most frequent category (mode) is used as a masking value.

Local IDC results are presented in Fig. 2. Across most models, the predicted probability drops significantly as the first few top-ranked features are removed. Therefore, XAI methods correctly identify features that strongly influence predictions. Tree-based models (i.e., Decision Tree, Random Forest, XGBoost, CatBoost) show decent declines, particularly in the first few removed features which indicates strong reliance on top-ranked features. SVM and Logistic Regression show a gradual decrease, meaning feature importance is more evenly distributed across multiple variables.

Linear SHAP, Tree SHAP and Kernel SHAP tend to produce the steepest declines, suggesting a strong alignment with the model's feature importance. LIME and Anchors exhibit more fluctuating behavior, which could indicate instability in their feature rankings. Surrogate Tree behaves similarly to tree-based methods but shows slight inconsistencies in some models such as random forest.

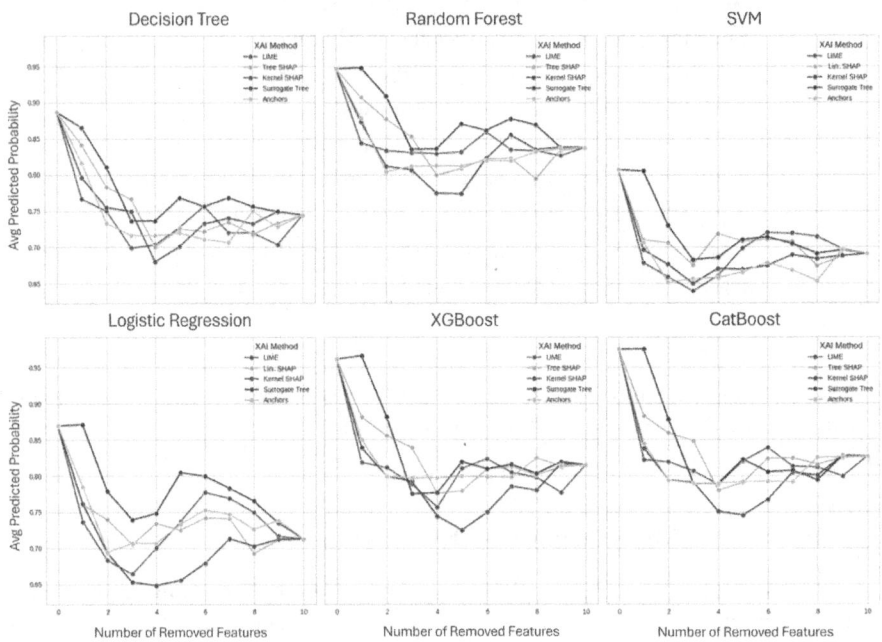

**Fig. 2.** Incremental Deletion Check for Local Explanations

Evaluation of global XAI methods over incremental deletion check is shown in Fig. 3. While some models show a clear downward trend, others fluctuate significantly, suggesting that some XAI methods may not rank global feature importance optimally.

Tree-based models (i.e., Decision Tree, Random Forest, XGBoost, CatBoost) show more stable degradation with Tree SHAP, Kernel SHAP, and Surrogate Tree. SVM and Logistic Regression have fluctuations, which indicates that XAI methods may struggle to rank global features effectively in these models.

Surrogate Tree and Tree SHAP consistently lead to expected AUC drop especially for the first 5 feature removal. However, the random forest explanations does not show that the degradation starts just after the removal of the features. Since, Random Forest is an ensemble of decision trees, when a highly ranked feature is removed, some trees in the ensemble may not have relied heavily on that feature and that might keep fluctuations on it. Additionally, Permutation Importance and ALE struggle with ranking consistency, possibly due to its dependency on feature distributions rather than direct model impact.

Built-in Feature Importance (red) exhibits unexpected behavior, particularly in Logistic Regression and SVM. Since both of them are based on linear combinations of features, removing a feature forces the model to redistribute importance across the remaining ones. This can cause certain feature importance values to increase artificially, as the model compensates for missing information. On the other hand, some features may have high correlation and when one of these correlated features is removed, its importance is often absorbed by another feature that was already contributing similar information. For example, in XGBoost, Built-in Feature Importance is decreased gradually for the first 5 features which might highlight the XGBoost has found highly correlated top-features.

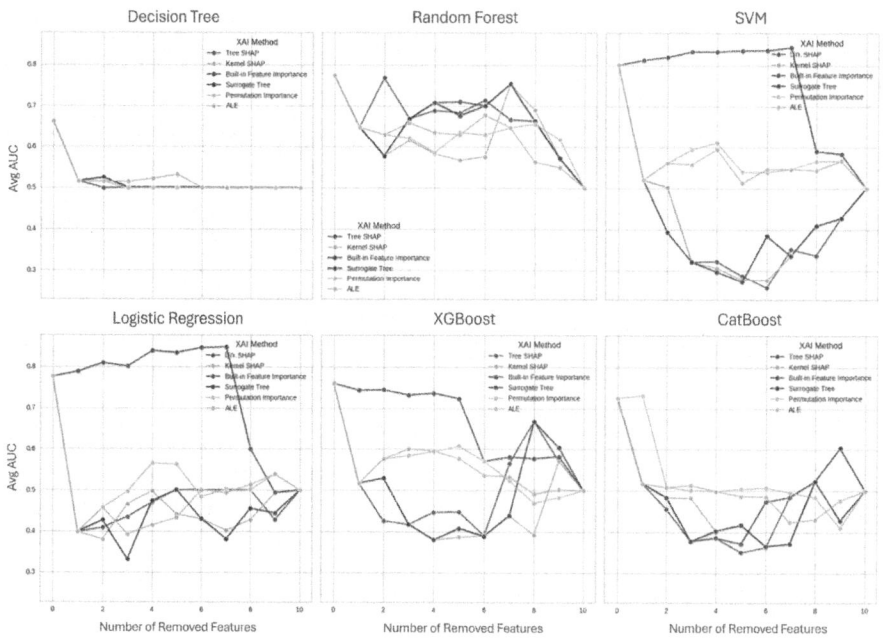

**Fig. 3.** Incremental Deletion Check Global Explanation

**Output-Based Evaluation: Target Sensitivity Check.** Target Sensitivity Check results for local XAI methods that support target-specific explanations are illustrated via radar charts in Fig. 4. In all predictive models, Linear SHAP, Tree SHAP and Kernel SHAP exhibit low Spearman correlation and high Euclidean/Wasserstein distances. Therefore, when distance metrics are checked, they are the best performers with respect to the target sensitivity. However, both methods tend to generate the opposite signed feature values for each value on the opposite target for the binary classification. LIME provides distinct feature values for different classes while keeping distance metric results to SHAP implementation. It can also be identified by the higher euclidean distance measurements.

For Anchors, because of the high Spearman correlation values, the ability to generate different rankings on the features for distinct targets is lower than the others.

Extremely high Euclidean distance values on Tree SHAP and Linear SHAP indicate that the magnitudes of features that are important for opposite classes are quite distant. Therefore, the SVM and Tree SHAP combination recorded the highest ranked-based distance between explanations of different targets.

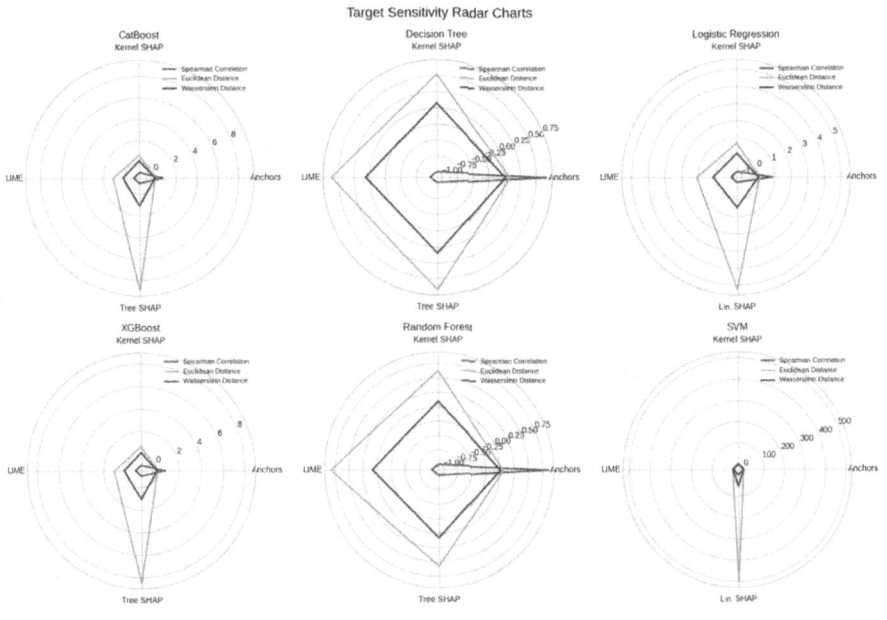

**Fig. 4.** Target Sensitivity Check Local Explanation

Figure 5 represents the global explanation perspective of the target sensitivity check. In the decision tree classifier and the random forest, for all XAI methods, high target sensitivity is recorded with low Spearman correlation and high Euclidean and Wasserstein distances, so that these tree-based predictive models can effectively adjust feature importance rankings across different target predictions. Especially, ALE results for magnitude-based similarity is higher than the other XAI methods. For boosting algorithms (XGBoost and CatBoost), quite similar results are recorded especially the feature values are distinct from one class to another since Euclidean Distances are much higher than other combinations.

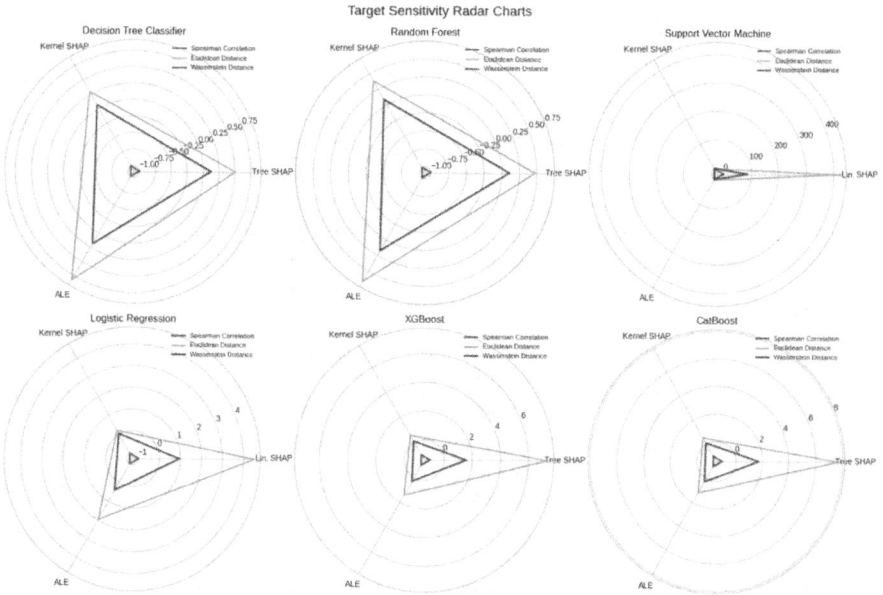

**Fig. 5.** Target Sensitivity Check Global Explanation

### 4.2 Human-Centered Evaluation: User Study

Within the human-centered part of this study, three medical doctors from different specializations, including neurology, manually ranked the most critical features influencing stroke prediction.For each participant, 10 different patient cases were provided for local feature ranking including all of the patient features with their case-specific values (See Table 2).

Table 3 presents the results of the local explanation alignment which details how closely each XAI method's feature importance rankings align with expert knowledge. Surrogate Tree consistently achieves the highest alignment across all predictive models.It has the highest Spearman correlation across models ( 0.62 to 0.63) that indicates its feature ranking order closely matches expert knowledge. Euclidean and Wasserstein distance values of it are relatively higher than other methods, so that while feature ranking is correct, the magnitude of importance values is exaggerated.

**Table 3.** User Study Results: Local Feature Importance Alignment with Medical Knowledge. **Bold values** indicate the best expert alignment, while underlined values highlight the highest Euclidean/Wasserstein distances representing the largest deviations from expert-defined feature importance magnitudes. Spearman Correlation: Higher values indicate better alignment with expert rankings. Euclidean Distance and Wasserstein Distance: Lower values indicate better alignment.

| Predictive Model | XAI Method | Spearman Correlation | Euclidean Distance | Wasserstein Distance |
|---|---|---|---|---|
| CatBoost | Anchors | −0.093306 | 18.556164 | 5.483784 |
| | **Kernel SHAP** | −0.083329 | **18.486377** | **5.4598** |
| | LIME | −0.023377 | 18.591605 | 5.496133 |
| | **Surrogate Tree** | **0.619413** | <u>36.368494</u> | <u>6.890837</u> |
| | Tree SHAP | −0.111198 | 20.384983 | 5.902354 |
| Decision Tree Classifier | Anchors | 0.11709 | 18.557907 | 5.485391 |
| | **Kernel SHAP** | −0.054198 | **18.494593** | **5.460009** |
| | LIME | −0.010852 | 18.575695 | 5.489662 |
| | **Surrogate Tree** | **0.619245** | <u>31.870778</u> | <u>6.365867</u> |
| | Tree SHAP | 0.093511 | 18.668226 | 5.52 |
| Logistic Regression | Anchors | 0.152576 | 18.521522 | 5.474277 |
| | Kernel SHAP | 0.026674 | 18.496959 | 5.467036 |
| | **LIME** | 0.109823 | **18.47603** | **5.461475** |
| | **Surrogate Tree** | **0.587217** | <u>52.777981</u> | <u>9.013644</u> |
| | Linear SHAP | 0.003268 | 19.214157 | 5.599617 |
| XGBoost | Anchors | 0.108057 | 18.556931 | 5.48476 |
| | **Kernel SHAP** | −0.089631 | **18.495081** | **5.460322** |
| | LIME | 0.006188 | 18.506681 | 5.469774 |
| | **Surrogate Tree** | **0.62847** | <u>36.561092</u> | <u>6.926036</u> |
| | Tree SHAP | −0.061024 | 20.145428 | 5.85802 |
| Random Forest | Anchors | 0.100234 | 18.543023 | 5.481394 |
| | **Kernel SHAP** | −0.068966 | **18.489039** | **5.458599** |
| | LIME | −0.082791 | 18.603537 | 5.498021 |
| | **Surrogate Tree** | **0.619245** | <u>31.870778</u> | <u>6.365867</u> |
| | Tree SHAP | 0.030984 | 18.667713 | 5.51825 |
| SVM | Anchors | 0.218531 | 18.514754 | 5.474007 |
| | Kernel SHAP | 0.03905 | 18.506228 | 5.470062 |
| | **LIME** | 0.095777 | **18.478855** | **5.462431** |
| | **Surrogate Tree** | **0.629715** | 75.439197 | 11.279291 |
| | Linear SHAP | 0.043867 | <u>256.952729</u> | <u>45.881625</u> |

For XGBoost, CatBoost, and Decision Tree models, Tree SHAP and Kernel SHAP produce negative Spearman correlations so that their rankings contradict expert rankings. However, the other metric values similar with the average. Therefore, SHAP based models are better on magnitude assignment for the features rather than ranking.

SVM and Logistic Regression both show high Euclidean distances (SVM: 256.95, Logistic Regression: 52.77) which suggests that feature importance values deviate significantly from expert rankings. In medical data, features often

**Table 4.** User Study Results: Global Feature Importance Alignment with Medical Knowledge. **Bold values** indicate the high(est) expert alignment, while underlined values highlight the high(est) Euclidean/Wasserstein distances representing the largest deviations from expert-defined feature importance magnitudes. Spearman Correlation: Higher values indicate better alignment with expert rankings. Euclidean Distance and Wasserstein Distance: Lower values indicate better alignment.

| Predictive Model | XAI Method | Spearman Correlation | Euclidean Distance | Wasserstein Distance |
|---|---|---|---|---|
| CatBoost | Tree SHAP | 0.030395 | 16.270090 | 4.644914 |
| | Kernel SHAP | 0.121581 | 18.948943 | 5.544033 |
| | Built-in Feature Importance | −0.243162 | <u>39.786214</u> | 5.483673 |
| | Surrogate Tree | −0.352585 | 18.488254 | 5.400000 |
| | **Permutation Importance** | **0.772040** | **15.907927** | **4.497637** |
| | ALE | −0.310032 | 18.631494 | 5.441334 |
| Decision Tree | Tree SHAP | −0.060791 | 18.607033 | 5.439168 |
| | Kernel SHAP | 0.048632 | 18.902153 | 5.533281 |
| | Built-in Feature Importance | −0.316111 | 18.487838 | 5.400000 |
| | Surrogate Tree | −0.364743 | 18.489969 | 5.400000 |
| | **Permutation Importance** | **0.565352** | **15.892142** | **4.492722** |
| | ALE | −0.346506 | 18.670642 | 5.447982 |
| Logistic Regression | Linear SHAP | 0.346506 | 17.225489 | 5.025674 |
| | Kernel SHAP | −0.547115 | 18.870522 | 5.517963 |
| | **Built-in Feature Importance** | **0.449850** | 16.606233 | **4.830169** |
| | Surrogate Tree | 0.024316 | 18.441794 | 5.400000 |
| | **Permutation Importance** | −0.024316 | **15.844304** | **4.479823** |
| | ALE | 0.498483 | 18.491903 | 5.415543 |
| XGBoost | Tree SHAP | 0.036474 | 16.437420 | 4.718632 |
| | Kernel SHAP | −0.072949 | 18.952627 | 5.544523 |
| | Built-in Feature Importance | **0.474166** | 18.480868 | 5.400000 |
| | Surrogate Tree | −0.352585 | 18.489172 | 5.400000 |
| | **Permutation Importance** | **0.571431** | **15.903203** | **4.495522** |
| | ALE | −0.279637 | 18.603739 | 5.430617 |
| Random Forest | Tree SHAP | -0.091186 | 18.625671 | 5.445911 |
| | Kernel SHAP | −0.030395 | 18.936005 | 5.543108 |
| | Built-in Feature Importance | −0.267478 | 18.497988 | 5.400000 |
| | Surrogate Tree | −0.364743 | 18.489243 | 5.400000 |
| | **Permutation Importance** | **0.680854** | **15.896064** | **4.493767** |
| | ALE | −0.346506 | 18.600722 | 5.428584 |
| SVM | Linear SHAP | 0.048632 | <u>199.522515</u> | <u>37.143950</u> |
| | Kernel SHAP | −0.358664 | 18.855627 | 5.514980 |
| | **Built-in Feature Importance** | **0.510641** | <u>150.861548</u> | <u>35.258489</u> |
| | Surrogate Tree | 0.206688 | 18.430826 | 5.400000 |
| | **Permutation Importance** | **0.668696** | **15.880183** | **4.492084** |
| | ALE | 0.291795 | 18.561809 | 5.427584 |

have strong correlations (e.g., age, blood pressure, and BMI). When features are correlated, linear models may distribute importance inconsistently which leads fluctuating rankings with numerically large coefficients.

LIME and Anchors consistently have near-zero Spearman correlation values and their Euclidean and Wasserstein distances remain relatively stable. This average non-extreme behavior indicates that their feature importance, on both ranks and magnitudes, do not significantly contradict expert-defined rankings but also do not strongly align with them.

Similarly, Table 4 represents the global explanation alignment with the medical knowledge. Permutation Importance consistently outperforms other methods by achieving the highest expert alignment across almost all predictive models. Tree SHAP and Kernel SHAP show instability, with some models producing strong positive correlations and others yielding negative correlations (e.g., Logistic Regression and Decision Tree). This suggests that SHAP explanations are more susceptible to model-specific behavior when generating global attributions. Built-in Feature Importance works well for linear models (Logistic Regression and SVM) but shows inconsistency for tree-based and ensemble models. Surrogate Tree consistently underperforms, so that globally fitting a decision tree to approximate feature attributions fails to align well with expert rankings which was the opposite in local explanations.

## 5 Conclusion and Future Work

This paper introduced a comprehensive benchmarking framework for evaluating explainable AI (XAI) methods in tabular healthcare data. By integrating both predictive model-centered and human-centered perspectives, we assessed the correctness, completeness, and coherence(clinical alignment) of various XAI techniques. Our findings highlight key strengths and limitations of different methods that offer insights into their suitability for medical decision-making.

In local explanation evaluations, Tree SHAP and Kernel SHAP demonstrated the most reliable feature rankings, while LIME and Anchors exhibited greater variability, suggesting potential instability. Tree-based models were found to be more sensitive to incremental deletion, whereas SVM and Logistic Regression displayed more evenly distributed feature importance scores. In global evaluations, Permutation Importance and Tree SHAP provided the most consistent and meaningful explanations, while built-in feature importance measures proved unreliable due to inconsistencies across models. Surrogate Trees were highly effective for global interpretability but struggled with medical alignment.

From a target sensitivity perspective, Tree SHAP and Kernel SHAP excelled at distinguishing feature importance rankings across predicted classes, while Anchors performed poorly. On the global level, ALE surpassed SHAP-based methods for tree-based models, demonstrating stronger adaptability in target sensitivity.

Regarding alignment with medical knowledge, Surrogate Trees proved most reliable for local feature ranking but tended to overestimate importance values. Tree SHAP and Kernel SHAP performed well in model-centered evaluations but struggled to align with expert-defined clinical importance, particularly for tree-based models. In contrast, Linear Explainers for SVM and Logistic Regression exhibited large numerical deviations, suggesting a lack of interpretability for medical professionals. For global alignment, Permutation Importance emerged as the most reliable method, whereas Tree SHAP and Kernel SHAP showed inconsistencies due to feature dependencies. Notably, Surrogate Tree explanations failed to align with medical expertise in global evaluations, reinforcing concerns over their general applicability.

Overall, our results indicate that while Tree SHAP and Kernel SHAP offer strong model fidelity, their alignment with clinical knowledge remains an open challenge. Permutation Importance stands out as a promising approach for global medical interpretability, while Surrogate Trees, despite their ranking reliability, require careful consideration in real-world applications. These findings emphasize the need for further research on harmonizing model-centered and expert-driven evaluations to ensure trustworthy and actionable AI explanations in healthcare.

While this study provides a comprehensive benchmarking framework for XAI methods in tabular healthcare data, several avenues for future research remain. One key direction is expanding the benchmark to include a broader range of medical datasets, such as those related to neurological disorders, diabetes, cardiovascular diseases, oncology and so on. This would allow for a more detailed comparison of explainability methods across different medical contexts. It would allow that insights derived from one dataset are not overly specific to a particular condition but extendable. Additionally, improving the user study by involving a larger and more diverse group of medical experts would be a crucial next step. Expanding the user study to include professionals from different specialties, backgrounds, and experience levels would improve the robustness of medical knowledge alignment evaluation.

**Acknowledgement.** This work has been done in the context of the ITEA 3, Privacy preserving cross-organizational data analysis in the healthcare sector (Secure-Health) project. We sincerely thank Medical Dr. Busra Alkis for her invaluable support in participant recruitment and active involvement in conducting the user study. We also thank all medical experts who participated in the user study; this study would not have been possible without their contributions and insights.

# Appendix

In the user study, three medical experts independently ranked features based on their perceived importance in explaining the absence of stroke. The question asked to participants was:

*Based on your expertise, which features do you consider the most important in determining stroke risk?*
*Rank 1 = The most important feature.*
*Rank 10 = The least relevant feature.*

These rankings provided in Fig. 6 reflect clinical expert judgment regarding stroke risk factors and provide a baseline for comparing XAI method explanations.

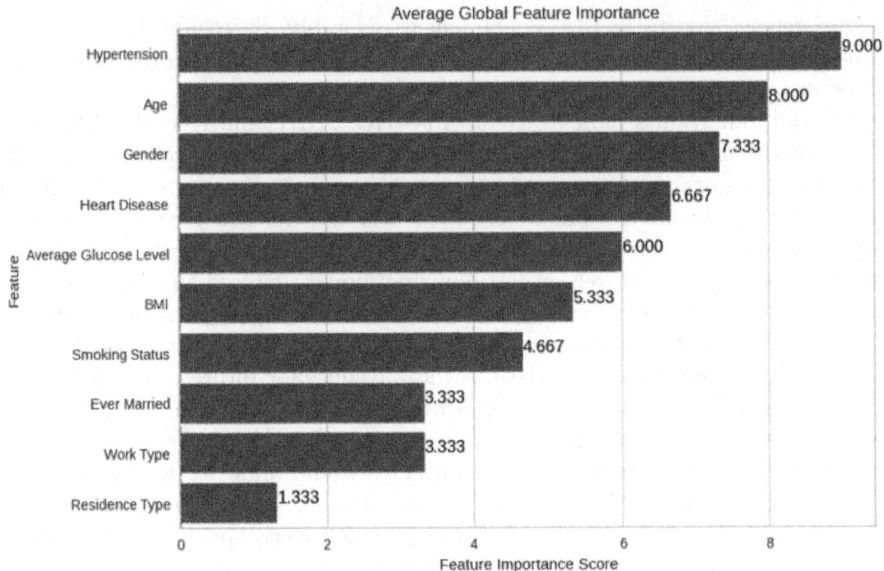

**Fig. 6.** The global feature rankings for having a stroke collected from the medical experts.

# References

1. Adadi, A., Berrada, M.: Peeking inside the black-box: a survey on explainable artificial intelligence (XAI). IEEE Access **6**, 52138–52160 (2018)
2. Agarwal, C., et al.: OpenXAI: towards a transparent evaluation of model explanations. Adv. Neural. Inf. Process. Syst. **35**, 15784–15799 (2022)
3. Ali, M.: PyCaret: An open source, low-code machine learning library in Python (2020). https://www.pycaret.org, pyCaret version 1.0.0
4. Alvarez-Melis, D., Jaakkola, T.S.: On the robustness of interpretability methods. arXiv preprint arXiv:1806.08049 (2018)
5. Apley, D.W., Zhu, J.: Visualizing the effects of predictor variables in black box supervised learning models. arXiv preprint arXiv:1612.08468 (2016). https://arxiv.org/abs/1612.08468
6. Batko, K., Ślzak, A.: The use of big data analytics in healthcare. J. Big Data **9**(1), 3 (2022)
7. Brankovic, A., Cook, D., Rahman, J., Khanna, S., Huang, W.: Benchmarking the most popular XAI used for explaining clinical predictive models: untrustworthy but could be useful. Health Inf. J. **30**(4), 14604582241304730 (2024)
8. Carvalho, D.V., Pereira, E.M., Cardoso, J.S.: Machine learning interpretability: a survey on methods and metrics. Electronics **8**(8), 832 (2019)
9. Chawla, N.V., Bowyer, K.W., Hall, L.O., Kegelmeyer, W.P.: SMOTE: synthetic minority over-sampling technique. J. Artif. Intell. Res. **16**, 321–357 (2002)
10. Dimitsaki, S., Gavriilidis, G.I., Dimitriadis, V.K., Natsiavas, P.: Benchmarking of machine learning classifiers on plasma proteomic for COVID-19 severity prediction through interpretable artificial intelligence. Artif. Intell. Med. **137**, 102490 (2023)

11. Doshi-Velez, F., Kim, B.: Towards a rigorous science of interpretable machine learning. arXiv preprint arXiv:1702.08608 (2017)
12. Duell, J.A.: A comparative approach to explainable artificial intelligence methods in application to high-dimensional electronic health records: Examining the usability of XAI. arXiv preprint arXiv:2103.04951 (2021)
13. Greenwell, B.M., Boehmke, B.C., McCarthy, A.J.: A simple and effective model-based variable importance measure. arXiv preprint arXiv:1805.04755 (2018). https://arxiv.org/abs/1805.04755
14. Hooker, S., Erhan, D., Kindermans, P.J., Kim, B.: A benchmark for interpretability methods in deep neural networks. In: NeurIPS (2019)
15. Jin, W., Li, X., Hamarneh, G.: Evaluating explainable AI on a multi-modal medical imaging task: Can existing algorithms fulfill clinical requirements? In: Proceedings of the AAAI Conference on Artificial Intelligence. vol. 36, pp. 11945–11953 (2022)
16. Lundberg, S.M., Lee, S.I.: A unified approach to interpreting model predictions. In: Guyon, I., Luxburg, U.V., Bengio, S., Wallach, H., Fergus, R., Vishwanathan, S., Garnett, R. (eds.) Advances in Neural Information Processing Systems 30, pp. 4765–4774. Curran Associates, Inc. (2017). http://papers.nips.cc/paper/7062-a-unified-approach-to-interpreting-model-predictions.pdf
17. Metsch, J.M., Hauschild, A.C.: BenchXAI: Comprehensive benchmarking of post-hoc explainable AI methods on multi-modal biomedical data. bioRxiv, pp. 2024–12 (2024)
18. Mohseni, S., Zarei, N., Ragan, E.D.: A multidisciplinary survey and framework for design and evaluation of explainable AI systems. ACM Trans. Interact. Intell. Syst. **11**(3–4), 1–45 (2021)
19. Molnar, C.: Interpretable Machine Learning. 3 edn. (2025). https://christophm.github.io/interpretable-ml-book
20. Moreira, C., Chou, Y.L., Hsieh, C., Ouyang, C., Pereira, J., Jorge, J.: Benchmarking instance-centric counterfactual algorithms for XAI: from white box to black box. ACM Comput. Surv. **57**(6), 1–37 (2025)
21. Nauta, M., et al.: From anecdotal evidence to quantitative evaluation methods: a systematic review on evaluating explainable AI. ACM Comput. Surv. **55**(13s), 1–42 (2023)
22. Oliveira, M., et al.: Benchmarking the influence of pre-training on explanation performance in MR image classification. Front. Artif. Intell. **7**, 1330919 (2024)
23. Panigutti, C., Beretta, A., Giannotti, F., Pedreschi, D.: Understanding the impact of explanations on advice-taking: a user study for AI-based clinical decision support systems. In: Proceedings of the 2022 CHI Conference on Human Factors in Computing Systems, pp. 1–9 (2022)
24. Ribeiro, M.T., Singh, S., Guestrin, C.: "why should i trust you?" Explaining the predictions of any classifier. In: Proceedings of the 22nd ACM SIGKDD International Conference on Knowledge Discovery and Data Mining, pp. 1135–1144 (2016)
25. Ribeiro, M.T., Singh, S., Guestrin, C.: Anchors: high-precision model-agnostic explanations. In: Proceedings of the AAAI Conference on Artificial Intelligence. vol. 32 (2018)
26. Richesson, R.L., Horvath, M.M., Rusincovitch, S.A.: Clinical research informatics and electronic health record data. Yearb. Med. Inform. **23**(01), 215–223 (2014)
27. Rubner, Y., Tomasi, C., Guibas, L.J.: A metric for distributions with applications to image databases. In: Sixth International Conference on Computer Vision (IEEE Cat. No. 98CH36271), pp. 59–66. IEEE (1998)
28. Saporta, A., et al.: Benchmarking saliency methods for chest X-ray interpretation. Nat. Mach. Intell. **4**(10), 867–878 (2022)

29. Schwalbe, G., Finzel, B.: A comprehensive taxonomy for explainable artificial intelligence: a systematic survey of surveys on methods and concepts. Data Min. Knowl. Disc. **38**(5), 3043–3101 (2024)
30. Spearman, C.: The proof and measurement of association between two things. Am. J. Psychol. **15**(1), 72–101 (1904)
31. Tjoa, E., Guan, C.: A survey on explainable artificial intelligence (XAI): toward medical AI transparency, interpretability, and explainability. Comput. Sci. Rev. **39**, 100422 (2021)
32. Vaserstein, L.N.: Markov processes over denumerable products of spaces, describing large systems of automata. Problemy Peredachi Informatsii **5**(3), 64–72 (1969)

**Open Access** This chapter is licensed under the terms of the Creative Commons Attribution 4.0 International License (http://creativecommons.org/licenses/by/4.0/), which permits use, sharing, adaptation, distribution and reproduction in any medium or format, as long as you give appropriate credit to the original author(s) and the source, provide a link to the Creative Commons license and indicate if changes were made.

The images or other third party material in this chapter are included in the chapter's Creative Commons license, unless indicated otherwise in a credit line to the material. If material is not included in the chapter's Creative Commons license and your intended use is not permitted by statutory regulation or exceeds the permitted use, you will need to obtain permission directly from the copyright holder.

# A Combination of Integrated Gradients and SRFAMap for Explaining Neural Networks Trained with High-Order Statistical Radiomic Features

Oleksandr Davydko[1(✉)], Vladimir Pavlov[2], and Luca Longo[1]

[1] Artificial Intelligence and Cognitive Load Researfch Lab, The Centre of Explainable Artificial Intelligence, Technological University Dublin, Dublin, Republic of Ireland
d22125337@mytudublin.ie
[2] The National Technical University of Ukraine Igor Sikorsky Kyiv Polytechnic Institute, Kyiv, Ukraine

**Abstract.** This research tackles the problem of high-order statistical radiomic features' visual explainability. While methods like Radiomic Features Activation Maps exist to solve this problem, they have important limitations. This includes the inability to produce a single explanation for all features and a lack of direct connection between classification results and generated explanations. This study contributes to the body of knowledge with a new explanatory saliency map generation approach for models trained with high-order statistical radiomic features. It extends the existing SRFAMap method using the Integrated Gradients method from Explainable AI. In detail, it exploits the integrated gradients of high-order statistical radiomic feature functions. Results with the tuberculosis classification dataset demonstrated better insertion and deletion correlation faithfulness metrics for saliency maps generated with the proposed approach than Radiomic Features Activation Maps.

**Keywords:** Explainable artificial intelligence · Radiomics · Texture analysis · Medical image processing · Saliency map · Integrated Gradients · Neura Networks · Interpretable Machine Learning

## 1 Introduction

Imaging plays a significant role in biomedical applications nowadays. Modern medical image acquisition techniques allow the noninvasive diagnosis of a living human or animal body, allowing the diagnosis to be determined with minimal harm to the patient. Medical image acquisition techniques are critical in modern healthcare, enabling accurate diagnosis and treatment planning. With the development of imaging techniques, various AI/ML methods emerged and became a valuable tool in medical image processing. One such technique is called radiomics – a quantitative approach to medical imaging which aims to enhance the existing data available to clinicians, offering richer analysis [47]. Radiomic features were used to solve many different medical diagnostic tasks. Among them there are neuroimaging processing [7,8,36], pneumonia diagnostic [17,25,35] and oncology diagnostics [20,27,30,42,54]. At the same time, the medical field requires machine learning models to be interpretable to allow end-users to make an informed decision after examining their outputs. Explainable Artificial Intelligence (XAI) [28], an interdisciplinary active research discipline, is devoted to supporting the development of trustworthy AI solutions [4,14]. In the specific healthcare sector, XAI methods are useful, particularly AI-based systems, for supporting and enhancing the effectiveness of collaborative decision support systems. Thanks to XAI techniques, inferential black-boxes, such as models trained with neural networks, can be globally interpreted [3] or converted to explainable rules [49], along with visual saliency maps, with impact on decision-making and human performance [32].

The research problem tackled in this study is the insufficiency of current XAI methods to generate explanatory saliency maps for models trained with statistical radiomic features. While these features are valuable for capturing texture-level information, current xAI methods do not allow the construction of a saliency map that reflects all feature contributions simultaneously. This study aims to develop a method for transforming the attributions of features calculated with non-differentiable functions—meaning it is not possible to compute the derivative of such functions, which makes using gradient-based methods impossible—into saliency maps that will not suffer from the limitations of the current techniques while maintaining the same or better level of faithfulness. The goal is to improve the visual interpretability of such classification models, allowing end users to analyse a single saliency map instead of multiple ones. The solution includes using the Integrated Gradients XAI attribution method with SRFAMap additive mapping to convert texture statistics matrices attributions to saliency maps. The specific question tackled is:

> To what extent can the application of additive mapping to convert statistical radiomic feature attributions into an interpretable saliency map achieve the same explanation faithfulness as a radiomic feature activation map?

The remainder of this article is structured as follows: Sect. 2 synthesises the current advances in radiomic features explainability and methods to generate image saliency maps for models trained with high-order statistical radiomic features. Section 3 describes how Integrated Gradients and SRFAMap method are combined to achieve the proposed aim and describes the design of an empirical work. Section 4 introduces the results of such work, followed by a critical discussion, while Sect. 5 summarises the study and presents possible future work.

## 2 Related Work

The current literature describes two primary approaches for generating radiomic features. The first approach is data-driven and provides a methodology for extracting features automatically for an exact learning task. The second relies on theoretical knowledge and uses theoretically justified operators to convert an image into a set of features. Theoretically justified image feature extraction relies on various mathematical methods to form representations of different image aspects. The review conducted in [24] mentions 18 different methods and their modifications for image feature extraction. Statistical texture features are a subset of theoretically justified radiomics methods designed to analyse medical image texture statistical properties. These methods extract features that correspond to the frequencies of texture substructures. The most basic statistical feature extraction method is the first-order histogram [9], which reflects the distribution of pixel intensities in the image and properties of this distribution. Other methods extract texture features by analysing spatial relations between pixels:

- Grey-level co-occurrence matrix (GLCM) [19],
- Grey-level run length matrix (GLRLM) [16],
- Grey-level size zone matrix (GLSZM) [46]
- Grey-level dependency matrix (GLDM) [44]
- Neighbouring grey-tone difference matrix (NGTDM) [6].

They produce matrices that are now referred to as texture statistics matrices. Such matrices are formed by computing the frequency of some texture substructure appearing in an underlying image (Fig. 5). Some examples of such substructures are:

- Pair of pixels with intensities $i, j$
- Run-length of pixels with the same intensity $i$
- Cluster of connected pixels with same intensity $i$

Features derived from these matrices are called second-order statistical radiomic features according to [38]. Works also define a set of formulas for second-order statistical radiomic features computation [6,16,19,44,46]. The list of such features is provided in Table 2 (Appendix). In many cases, using high-order radiomic features allowed for near-state-of-the-art classification performance. Several authors have attempted to fuse grey-level co-occurrence matrix (GLCM), grey-level run length matrix (GLRLM), and segmentation-based fractal texture analysis (SFTA) features to detect the presence of COVID-19 lesions on the chest X-ray images and reported the F1-score at a 0.98 rate [35]. In [54], the authors report 0.975 accuracy while classifying brain tumours with GLCM features on magnetic resonance images (MRI). The saliency maps were established as the commonly accepted way to explain image classification models [21]. The examples of saliency maps are shown in Fig. 1.

Commonly, researchers utilise saliency map methods such as Integrated Gradients [45], layer-wise relevance propagation (LRP) [31], DeepLIFT [43], Grad-CAM [40] for interpreting image classification models. Works [5,10] show an example of saliency maps application to explain the output of a classification model in medical image classification. The work presented in [52] describes an application of SHAP-based saliency maps to explain the output of the Vision Transformer model [15], showing a sufficient saliency map quality. Saliency maps were used in a study even for burn lesion segmentation, reaching the 91% segmentation accuracy level [1]. However, explaining the classification models whose inputs are built upon some theory-driven radiomic features or their derivatives may be challenging. Here, theory-driven means a feature is built following an ad-hoc method inspired by specific theories. For example, the mathematical nature of statistical texture features (non-differentiability) prevents conventional gradient-based saliency map generation methods as they rely heavily upon the ability to compute the function derivative. Current advances in the interpretability of classification models trained with non-differentiable theory-driven radiomic features mainly involve interpreting their importance. For example, the authors of the work in [53] use SHAP [29] to identify the most influential features. In another research work [34], authors interpret radiomic feature groups' importance by analysing logistic regression coefficients. Similarly, the study in [7] uses SHAP to reveal the most influential features to diagnose schizophrenia by brain magnetic resonance images (MRI). The research in [8] employed the same technique to find the connection between particular features and panic disorder signs.

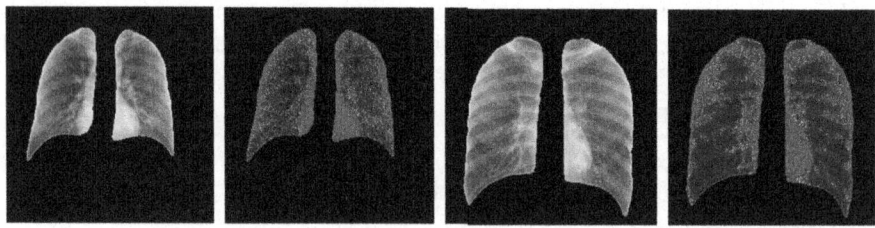

**Fig. 1.** Example of explanatory saliency maps for classification models. The zones that an underlying model pays greatest attention to are highlighted in red. (Color figure online)

A fusion of deep learning and theory-driven radiomics is described in work [37]. The main contribution of this work is developing the RadX4CNN method to associate deep radiomic features, generated with a CNN Vision Transformer, with theory-driven features via their global explanations. Other work includes building activation maps by calculating statistical radiomic features for each pixel using a sliding window (local statistical radiomic features) for each feature that is chosen as valuable by a feature selection algorithm [26,41,50]. Still, the classification models in such works used global statistical radiomic features (calculated for the whole region of interest), while attributions/importances were calculated using local features, meaning these approaches do not establish an exact connection between feature attribution and the resulting activation map. Another weakness of this approach is the inability to produce a single explanatory map that will simultaneously include all features' contributions. These problems were initially addressed in [13], where the SRFAMap method was introduced. Such a method was preliminarily tested only for the case when texture statistics matrix elements are used as the individual classification features, in contrast to studies [26,41,50] that operate with high-order statistical radiomic features. The SRFAMap method introduces ad-hoc rules to convert texture statistics matrices attributions into an image saliency map. Such ad-hoc rules operate at the pixel level and assign to each one the sum of the attributions of the texture statistics matrix elements that were affected by this pixel. For each texture statistics method, an individual set of rules is defined. However, there is no defined approach to transition from attributions of high-order statistical features to attributions of texture statistics matrix elements, which SRFAMap needs to work. The current study aims to fill this gap and extend the SRFAMap method to higher-order features.

## 3 Design and Methodology

While a previous SRFAMap study discusses saliency maps for classification models trained with texture statistic matrices [13], this research extends it with an approach that exploits high-order radiomic features. The hypothesis is:

> IF deep neural network classification models, implementing high-order features calculation automatically via a dedicated layer, are trained with texture statistics matrices extracted from X-ray images to fit classes of lesions AND the Integrated Gradients feature attribution XAI method is run on the output of these models to identify the most salient texture statistics matrices elements AND such attributions are converted into visual saliency maps with SRFAMap
> THEN the insertion and deletion correlation metrics associated with such saliency maps will be equal or statistically significantly higher than those derived from the Radiomic Feature Activation Maps method [51].

To test such a hypothesis, an experiment is designed and described in the following sections, as outlined in the Fig. 2.

### 3.1 Data Understanding

The Schenzen tuberculosis pulmonary disease dataset was selected, containing 662 x-ray scans [23]. The data were collected from Shenzhen No. 3 People's Hospital in China. All patient data were anonymised before the dataset was approved for public release. Data is balanced: 326 x-ray scans of lungs from healthy subjects and 336 from subjects with signs of tuberculosis. Patients' ages ranged from 1 to 89 years. There are 460 male and 202 female patients.

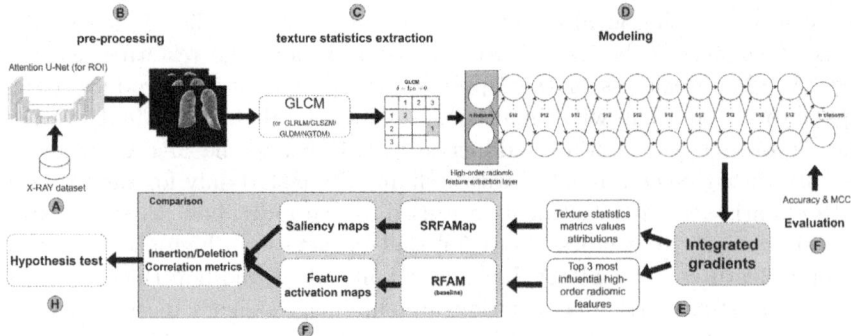

**Fig. 2.** A detailed illustration of the experiment's flow. An input chest X-ray dataset (A) is used for high-order statistical radiomic features extraction (B). Resulting features (C) are used as input to a neural network classifier (D). Texture static matrices are attributed with the Integrated Gradients methods (E) and converted into saliency maps with SRFAMap (F). Also, the three most influential features (extracted in C) are determined by analysing the integrated gradients, and the Radiomic Feature Activation Maps method is run to produce their feature activation maps. Subsequently, insertion and deletion correlation metrics are calculated from such maps (F), and the research hypothesis is tested from such metrics (H).

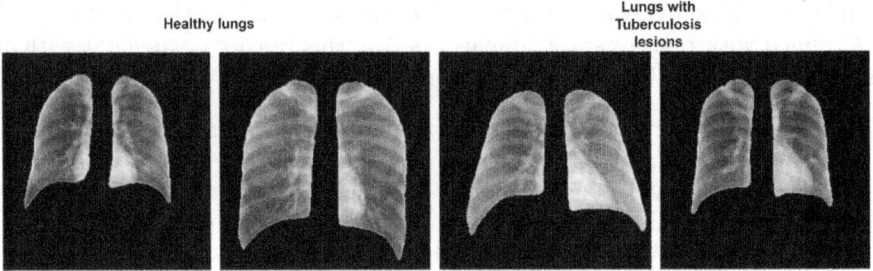

**Fig. 3.** Examples of healthy lungs X-ray scans and those containing tuberculosis lesions after data pre-processing.

## 3.2 Data Preprocessing

All the X-ray scans were resized to 256 × 256 pixels before usage to ensure a constant input size for the subsequent neural network model training. The resulting X-ray scans have an aspect ratio close to 1:1 regarding width to height compared to the originals. Examples of images after cropping can be found in Fig. 3. Regions of interest (ROI) were extracted from chest X-ray scans; such extraction is illustrated in Fig. 4. All pixels not belonging to the ROI were assigned a zero value. Attention U-Net [33], a fully convolutional neural network, was used to extract ROIs, as the U-Net family of networks shows acceptable Intersection-over-Union (IoU) rates (greater than 0.8) in biomedical segmentation tasks [2,22,39]. The network was trained to segment lung tissues with the

Darwin chest X-ray dataset [48], which contains 6106 chest X-ray images with corresponding lung masks done by radiologists. This dataset was chosen to train a segmentation model because the primary Schenzen dataset does not contain lung segmentation masks. It was split into train, validation, and test sets in $70\% - 15\% - 15\%$ proportion. Adam was the optimisation strategy to train such a network with a constant learning rate of $1e-4$. The Focal-Tversky loss was used as the optimisation criterion since it was proven to be a better loss function in highly imbalanced classification tasks, such as pixel-wise segmentation [2]. The network was trained until the IoU stopped improving on the validation set. The early stopping strategy was used with five epochs of patience. After training, the model reached 0.958 IoU rate on the validation set and 0.944 IoU on the test set.

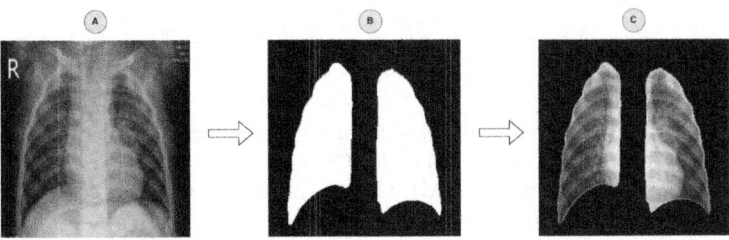

**Fig. 4.** An example of ROI segmentation process. A raw image (A) is processed with the Attention U-Net network. The binary segmentation mask (B) produces the cropped image (C) by setting a zero value to all pixels that do not belong to the segmentation mask.

### 3.3 Texture Statistics Matrices Extraction

Five types of texture statistics matrices are extracted during the experiment: GLCM, GLRLM, GLSZM, GLDM, and NGTDM. Zero pixels were not included in the statistics (Fig. 5). The parameters of such statistics are: GLCM ($\alpha = 0, \delta = 1$), GLRLM ($\alpha = 0$), GLSZM (no additional parameters), GLDM ($\alpha = 1, \delta = 1$), NGTDM ($\delta = 1$).

### 3.4 Modelling

As outlined before, higher-order radiomic features are derived from applying methods producing texture statistic matrices (as described in Sect. 2). The SRFAMap method can compute the attributions of such texture statistic matrices. However, applying the SRFAMap requires a technique that transitions from high-order statistical radiomic feature attributions to texture statistic matrix elements' attributions. In this study, this adapter is implemented with a specific neural network layer, which implements high-order feature calculation and allows the backpropagation from these back to first-order, enabling researchers

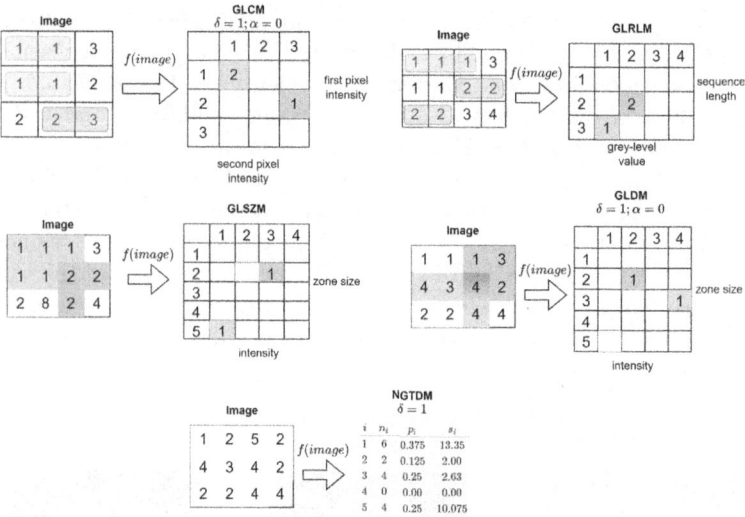

**Fig. 5.** A visual illustration of the methods for texture statistics matrices computation: Grey-level co-occurrence matrix (GLCM), Grey-level run length matrix (GLRLM), Grey-level size zone matrix (GLSZM), Grey-level dependency matrix (GLDM), and Neighbouring grey-tone difference matrix (NGTDM).

to use the gradient-based Integrated Gradients method to obtain attributions. Such a layer accepts texture matrices and returns a vector of radiomic features, the higher-order radiomic features. It has no learnable parameters but allows for a consistent gradient flow while backpropagating. Such a layer is implemented with the PyTorch framework as a Python class inherited from torch.nn.Module. A separate class was created for each of the five texture statistics extraction methods (GLCM, GLRLM, GLSZM, GLDM, NGTDM). The formulas for all high-order statistical radiomic features can be found in the documentation of the *pyradiomics* library[1]. More details on such features implemented in this research are provided in Table 2 (Appendix). The output size for such a layer equals the count of higher-order features defined for each specific extraction method. The subsequent part of the neural network contains 10 hidden dense layers, each containing 512 neurons. Each layer is followed by ReLU activation and a dropout layer with a probability of 0.5 for regularisation purposes. The output layer consists of $n$ neurons, where $n$ is the number of classes to distinguish between, followed by the Softmax activation function. In this research, $n$ equals 2, as the classification task is to differentiate between inputs containing lesions or not.

---

[1] https://pyradiomics.readthedocs.io/en/latest/features.html.

**Neural Network Training Process** - An individual neural network instance is trained for each texture feature extraction method (GLCM, GLRLM, GLSZM, GLDM, NGTDM). The PyTorch framework is used for model implementation. All networks are trained from scratch without using any pre-trained weights. For the proposed 10-layer models, no hyperparameter optimisation is performed. Adam optimiser with a constant learning rate of $1e-4$ is selected as the optimisation technique. The repeated Monte-Carlo sampling technique was used. Twenty splits of train, validation, and test sets in $70\% - 15\% - 15\%$ proportion were performed. Each network was trained to prevent overfitting until the Matthews Correlation Coefficient (MCC) between predicted and actual chest X-ray labels stopped improving on the validation dataset. The early stopping strategy was used with 20 epochs of patience.

### 3.5 Integrated Gradients Computation

Attributions to input into SRFAMap are calculated over the neural network using the Integrated Gradients method. Formally, the integrated gradients are calculated in the following way:

$$\text{IG}_i(x) = (x_i - x_i') \int_{\alpha=0}^{1} \frac{\partial F(x' + \alpha(x - x'))}{\partial x_i} d\alpha \quad (1)$$

with $x$ as an element of the texture statistics matrix, $x'$ as the baseline value, and $F$ as the neural network function, which means the trained model. Taking into account the structure of the designed neural network with an ad-hoc first layer, this formula transforms to Eq. 2

$$\text{IG}_i(x) = (x_i - x_i') \int_{\alpha=0}^{1} \frac{\partial F(R(x' + \alpha(x - x')))}{\partial x_i} d\alpha \quad (2)$$

with the additional $R$ term being the high-order radiomic feature function. According to such an updated formula, Integrated Gradients are calculated with respect to each high-order radiomic feature function $R$. Integrated Gradients are used in this research to identify the most influential high-order radiomic features and generate baseline explanatory maps. The output of the specific radiomic features calculation layer is attributed to Integrated Gradients, allowing for sorting features in descending order of their attributions. Three features with the highest attribution value are picked for further processing out of all those computed. While more than three top features could be selected, the rationale is to compare only a limited number of generated saliency maps to those produced by the baseline method (RFMAM), as described in the following section.

### 3.6 Baseline Comparison and Hypothesis Testing

The lung lesion trained classification models are evaluated using the Accuracy and Matthews Correlation Coefficient (MCC) score (as formally described in

Eqs. 3 and 4). The MCC metric was chosen in addition to Accuracy as it produces a high score in binary classification problems where false positives and negatives matter, as shown in [12].

$$\text{Accuracy} = \frac{TP + TN}{TP + TN + FP + FN} \quad (3)$$

$$\text{MCC} = \frac{TP \cdot TN - FP \cdot FN}{\sqrt{(TP + FP)(TP + FN)(TN + FP)(TN + FN)}} \quad (4)$$

with $TP$ and $TN$ respectively the true positives and true negatives (true classified lung lesions and true classified non-lung lesions), the $FP$ and $FN$ respectively the false positives and false negatives (false classified lung lesions and false classified non-lung lesions).

On the one hand, saliency maps are generated with the SFRAMap and extended using the proposed approach. On the other hand, the Radiomic Features Activation Map (RFAM) is used as a baseline to generate saliency maps. However, RFAM can only build a map for one feature at a time. Therefore, as mentioned before, only the saliency maps of the top three are selected for comparison (as depicted in Fig. 9 in the appendix).

The faithfulness of the generated saliency map is tested with Insertion Correlation and Deletion Correlation metrics (Eqs. 5 and 6) as described in [18]. Insertion Correlation is calculated by sequentially adding pixels to a black 'zero' image and computing the correlation between pixel saliency score and target class score change after the pixel was added. The Deletion Correlation computation is the same, but pixels are sequentially removed from the image.

$$\text{IC} = \rho(\boldsymbol{S}, \Delta P_i) \quad (5)$$

$$\text{DC} = \rho(\boldsymbol{S}, \Delta P_d) \quad (6)$$

with $\rho$ is a correlation function, $\Delta P_i$ is a vector of target class score changes after a pixel, or multiple is/are inserted, and $\Delta P_d$ is a vector of target class score changes after a pixel or multiple pixels is/are deleted, and $\boldsymbol{S}$ is a vector of saliency values correponding to the inserted/deleted pixel/s.

The insertion and deletion correlation distributions are presumed to be non-conforming to the normal distribution. The Wilcoxon statistics test the research hypothesis, comparing the mentioned distributions and taking their equality as the null hypothesis. The magnitudes of such resulting values are also compared, and those that are further from zero are considered superior.

## 4 Results and Discussion

As mentioned, repeated Monte Carlo sampling was used, and 20 dataset splits were performed to train different models. The averaged Accuracy and MCC classification scores along with their standard deviations are provided in Table 1. The distributions of such scores are provided in Fig. 6. Instead, the distributions of the Insertion Correlation (IC) and Deletion Correlation (DC) metrics are provided in Fig. 7. As mentioned before, only the 3 top features are gauged by analysing the results of the Integrated Gradients method. This is because it is impractical to showcase all radiomic feature activation maps for each input x-ray scan. According to the Wilcoxon test results, the IC and DC metrics distributions for SRFAMap have statistically significant differences against the same metrics for the selected baseline, RFAMs, with $p = 0.05$.

**Table 1.** Accuracy and Matthews Correlation Coefficient (MCC) scores for the trained MLP neural network classification models with repeated Monte Carlo sampling (20 times)

| Method | Accuracy | | MCC | |
|---|---|---|---|---|
| | Dev | Test | Dev | Test |
| MLP + GLCM | 0.7571 ± 0.0689 | 0.7440 ± 0.0641 | 0.5162 ± 0.1405 | 0.4903 ± 0.1328 |
| MLP + GLRLM | 0.7576 ± 0.0701 | 0.7400 ± 0.0621 | 0.5171 ± 0.1432 | 0.4822 ± 0.1289 |
| MLP + GLSZM | 0.7606 ± 0.0427 | 0.7505 ± 0.0379 | 0.5229 ± 0.0857 | 0.5035 ± 0.0763 |
| MLP + GLDM | 0.7530 ± 0.0675 | 0.7380 ± 0.0655 | 0.5070 ± 0.1373 | 0.4775 ± 0.1354 |
| MLP + NGTDM | 0.7621 ± 0.0372 | 0.7250 ± 0.0475 | 0.5332 ± 0.0750 | 0.4628 ± 0.1004 |

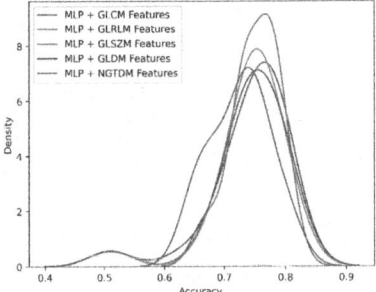
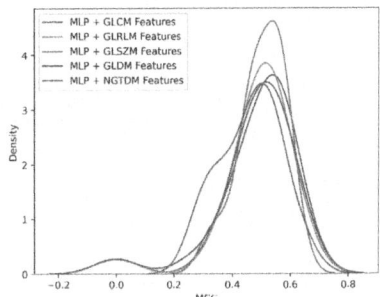

**Fig. 6.** Distribution of the Accuracy and MCC scores for radiomic-features-based MLP neural network models while distinguishing between healthy lungs and the signs of tuberculosis lesions.

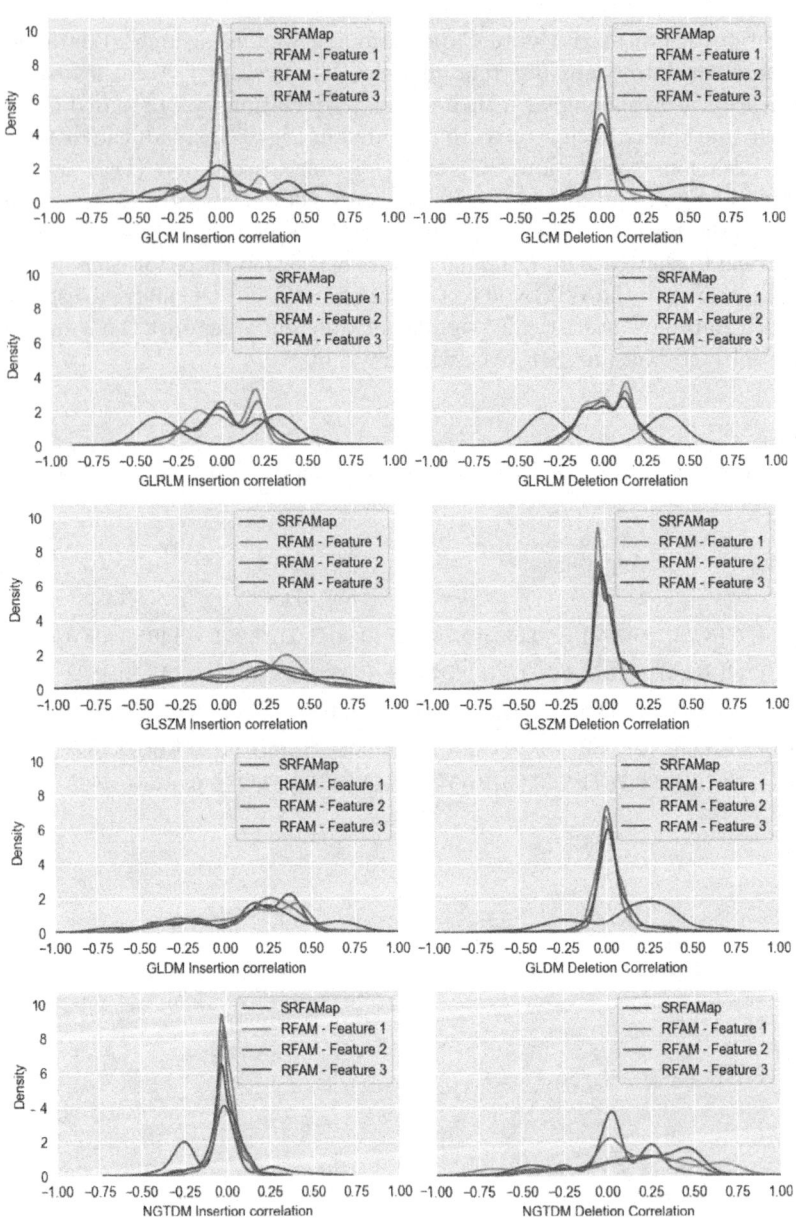

**Fig. 7.** Distributions of the Insertion and Deletion Correlation scores for saliency maps generated with SRFAMap + Integrated Gradients compared with those generated by the baseline Radiomic Feature Activation Maps method, for the five texture statistical methods (GLCM, GLRLM, GLSZM, GLDM, NGTDM).

The classification results are mostly the same for all models (using the different texture statistics), and the Wilcoxon test identified no statistically significant differences between metric distributions. This means that the models built with the five different texture statistics matrices lead to similar results across accuracy and MCC, and are consistent, demonstrating stability (Table 1, accuracy on average 0.75 and MCC on average 0.5). These results may indicate an equal discriminatory power for all presented texture statistics in this classification task and are aligned with those observed in [25], only excluding the GLRLM features.

The findings concerning the faithfulness of the saliency maps, the insertion and deletion scores (Fig. 7), are interesting. They show that in most cases, the explanatory maps generated by the Radiomic Feature Activation Maps method do not correlate with a change in classification score when corresponding pixels are added or removed, since they are often around zero (for insertion and deletion correlations). In other words, the distributions in Fig. 7 show that IC and DC consistently score around zero for the Radiomic Feature Activation Maps method. In contrast, the saliency maps generated with the proposed approach yield more spread values around zero, demonstrating a higher faithfulness in principle. In some cases, SRFAMap and RFAM generate a saliency map with a negative Insertion or Deletion correlation score. A deeper investigation showed that a positive target class score was produced when the classification model processed the zero matrix (the extreme starting point for the insertion and deletion operations) in such cases. Subsequently, this score drastically dropped after some pixels were revealed (added or removed), leading to a negative correlation between score change and saliency map magnitudes (Fig. 8). Another critical effect observed in Fig. 8 was the most significant positive score change achieved only after all pixels were removed. This happens when presenting out-of-distribution images to the model, a known weakness of existing saliency map faithfulness metrics, which can lead to unexpected model behaviour [18]. This effect is observed in the first iteration, where the score change has a large negative value, while it has a large positive value on the last iteration. At the same time, saliency scores monotonically decrease. Results show that the greater importance of a high-order radiomic feature does not lead to a higher Insertion and Deletion correlation of its corresponding generated activation map (Fig. 7). In other words, the abnormal behaviour is that the maps generated by RFAM (baseline) do not contain high saliency scores in the pixels that had the highest influence on the target class predicted by the classification model.

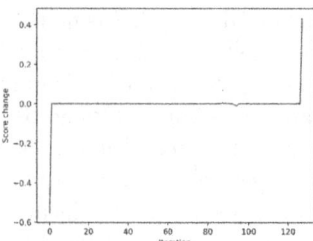 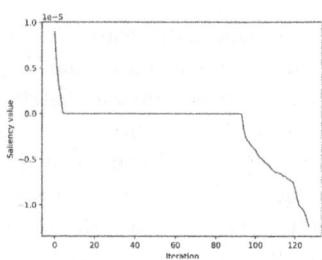

**Fig. 8.** Target class score change across consecutive iterations, in the insertion procedure and the saliency map scores, computed by SRFAMap, corresponding to inserted pixels.

Another critical aspect to discuss is the choice of the faithfulness metrics. Insertion and Deletion correlation methods are appropriate for establishing a connection between actual saliency values and classification score change. Other metrics, such as Increase-In-Confidence, Average Drop, Insertion Area Under Curve, and Deletion Area Under Curve, do not consider the magnitudes of the saliency map values [11]. Consequently, such metrics are vulnerable because they might erroneously consider some attribution faithful enough to explain the classification output, even if they are not, because the relative differences in magnitude of saliency map values are not considered. At the same time, the Insertion and Deletion correlation methods perform an input image modification by removing or inserting pixels. Such modified images differ significantly from those used for training the neural network, thus becoming out-of-distribution. Therefore, when inserted in a trained model, they may lead to unpredictable outputs. Developing a saliency map evaluation method for this issue remains an open research problem.

A visual examination of some of the generated saliency maps by SRFAMap (examples in Fig. 9) shows denser and less scattered patterns than the maps produced by RFAM. Moreover, some RFAM-generated maps demonstrate no quantifiable pattern (RFAM 1 for GLSZM in Fig. 9) with no sign of relevant attribution, since they seem to have the same magnitude (right lung, bottom left region). In summary, visually, SRFAMap seems to produce less scattered attributions and more densely localised compared to the RFAM method. Despite the promising findings, the proposed approach can only be used with models learnt by training a neural network, not other architectures such as Decision trees or Support Vector Machines. This is because it relies on the Integrated Gradients attribution method, which requires differentiable models and access to their gradients.

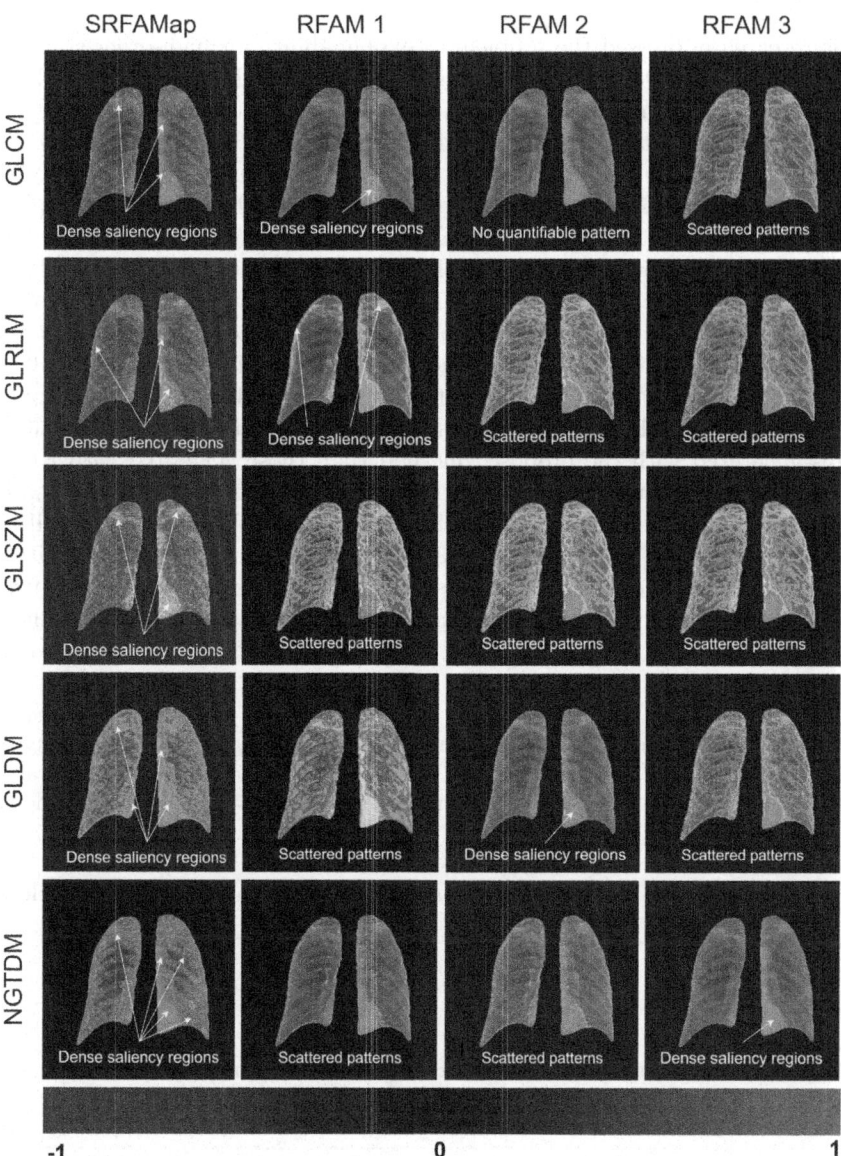

**Fig. 9.** Examples of generated saliency maps. The first column shows maps generated with SRFAMap + Integrated Gradients of high-order statistical radiomic features; other columns show maps produced by the Radiomic Feature Activation Maps for the three most influential radiomic features. Maps contain both positive and negative values. Positive values indicate zones that increase the probability of the class under explanation, and negative values indicate the opposite (in binary classification tasks).

## 5 Conclusions and Future Work

This research addressed the problem of explainability for high-order statistical radiomic features. Despite their importance, current XAI methods for producing visual explanations of classification models built with such features suffer from an important limitation. Specifically, this is the inability of such XAI methods to provide a single explanation (saliency map) for all features simultaneously and not for each one. This research proposed a novel approach to generating explanatory saliency maps for black-box models trained with neural networks from high-order statistical radiomic features in the context of medical X-ray scans classification. This approach simultaneously utilizes additive mapping (SFRAMap) and the Integrated Gradients method to produce importance attributions. Its main advantage is the ability to explain the contributions of all features simultaneously compared to the Radiomic Feature Activation Maps method. Empirical work demonstrated higher insertion and deletion correlation metrics for saliency maps generated with the proposed method than those generated with RFAM. Future research will evaluate the proposed approach with different datasets, considering other medical image modalities like MRI and Ultrasound. It will also focus on developing a new metric to assess saliency maps' faithfulness without using model predictions on input that significantly differs from the data on which the model was trained. Extending the additivity mechanism to form saliency scores for individual pixels with other properties, such as multiplicativity, could improve SRFAmap.

**Acknowledgements.** We want to thank IBM for granting us access to computing resources and the access to powerful IBM Power stations on which models were trained, and the Technological University Dublin for funding and support, which made this research possible.

**Disclosure of Interests.** The authors have no competing interests to declare relevant to this article's content.

## Appendix

**Table 2.** The second-order statistical radiomic features employed in this research

| Method | Features | Total | Ref. |
|---|---|---|---|
| GLCM | Autocorrelation, Joint Average, Cluster Prominence, Cluster Shade, Cluster Tendency, Contrast, Correlation, Difference Average, Difference Entropy, Difference Variance, Joint Energy, Joint Entropy, Informational Measure of Correlation (IMC) 1, Informational Measure of Correlation (IMC) 2, Inverse Difference Moment (IDM), Maximal Correlation Coefficient (MCC), Inverse Difference Moment Normalized (IDMN), Inverse Difference (ID), Inverse Difference Normalized (IDN), Inverse Variance, Maximum Probability, Sum Average, Sum Entropy, Sum of Squares | 24 | [19] |

(*continued*)

**Table 2.** (*continued*)

| Method | Features | Total | Ref. |
|---|---|---|---|
| GLRLM | Short Run Emphasis, Long Run Emphasis, Grey Level Non-Uniformity, Gray Level Non-Uniformity, Run Length Non-Uniformity, Run Length Non-Uniformity Normalized, Run Percentage, Grey Level Variance, Run Variance, Run Entropy, Low Gray Level Run Emphasis, High Gray Level Run Emphasis, Short Run Low Gray Level Emphasis, Short Run High Gray Level Emphasis, Long Run Low Gray Level Emphasis, Long Run High Gray Level Emphasis | 16 | [16] |
| GLSZM | Small Area Emphasis, Large Area Emphasis, Gray Level Non-Uniformity, Gray Level Non-Uniformity Normalized, Size-Zone Non-Uniformity, Size-Zone Non-Uniformity Normalized, Zone Percentage, Gray Level Variance, Zone Variance, Zone Entropy, Low Gray Level Zone Emphasis, High Gray Level Zone Emphasis, Small Area Low Gray Level Emphasis, Small Area High Gray Level Emphasis, Large Area Low Gray Level Emphasis, Large Area High Gray Level Emphasis | 16 | [46] |
| GLDM | Small Dependence Emphasis, Large Dependence Emphasis, Gray Level Non-Uniformity, Dependence Non-Uniformity, Dependence Non-Uniformity Normalized, Gray Level Variance, Dependence Variance, Dependence Entropy, Low Gray Level Emphasis, High Gray Level Emphasis, Small Dependence Low Gray Level Emphasis, Small Dependence High Gray Level Emphasis, Large Dependence Low Gray Level Emphasis, Large Dependence High Gray Level Emphasis | 14 | [44] |
| NGTDM | Coarseness, Contrast, Busyness, Complexity, Strength | 5 | [6] |

# References

1. Abdolahnejad, M., et al.: Novel CNN-based approach for burn severity assessment and fine-grained boundary segmentation in burn images. IEEE Trans. Instrum. Meas. **74**, 1–10 (2025)
2. Abraham, N., Khan, N.M.: A Novel Focal Tversky loss function with improved attention U-Net for lesion segmentation. In: 2019 IEEE 16th International Symposium on Biomedical Imaging (ISBI 2019), Venice, Italy, pp. 683–687. IEEE (2019)
3. Ahmed, T., Longo, L.: Examining the size of the latent space of convolutional variational autoencoders trained with spectral topographic maps of EEG frequency bands. IEEE Access **10**, 107575–107586 (2022)
4. Albahri, A., et al.: A systematic review of trustworthy and explainable artificial intelligence in healthcare: assessment of quality, bias risk, and data fusion. Inf. Fusion **96**, 156–191 (2023)
5. AlZoubi, A., Eskandari, A., Yu, H., Du, H.: Explainable DCNN decision framework for breast lesion classification from ultrasound images based on cancer characteristics. Bioengineering **11**(5), 453 (2024)
6. Amadasun, M., King, R.: Textural features corresponding to textural properties. IEEE Trans. Syst. Man Cybern. **19**(5), 1264–1274 (1989)

7. Bang, M., et al.: An interpretable multiparametric radiomics model for the diagnosis of schizophrenia using magnetic resonance imaging of the corpus callosum. Transl. Psychiatry **11**(1) (2021)
8. Bang, M., et al.: An interpretable radiomics model for the diagnosis of panic disorder with or without agoraphobia using magnetic resonance imaging. J. Affect. Disord. **305**, 47–54 (2022)
9. Bevk, M., Kononenko, I.: A statistical approach to texture description of medical images: a preliminary study. In: Proceedings of 15th IEEE Symposium on Computer-Based Medical Systems (CBMS 2002), Maribor, Slovenia, pp. 239–244. IEEE Computer. Soc (2002)
10. Byra, M., Dobruch-Sobczak, K., Piotrzkowska-Wroblewska, H., Klimonda, Z., Litniewski, J.: Explaining a deep learning based breast ultrasound image classifier with saliency maps. J. Ultrasonography **22**(89), 70–75 (2022)
11. Chattopadhay, A., Sarkar, A., Howlader, P., Balasubramanian, V.N.: Grad-CAM++: generalized gradient-based visual explanations for deep convolutional networks. In: 2018 IEEE Winter Conference on Applications of Computer Vision (WACV), pp. 839–847 (2018)
12. Chicco, D., Jurman, G.: The advantages of the Matthews correlation coefficient (MCC) over F1 score and accuracy in binary classification evaluation. BMC Genom. **21**(1), 6 (2020)
13. Davydko, O., Pavlov, V., Biecek, P., Longo, L.: SRFAMap: a method for mapping integrated gradients of a CNN trained with statistical radiomic features to medical image saliency maps, pp. 3–23. Springer, Cham (2024)
14. Dondio, P., Longo, L.: Trust-based techniques for collective intelligence in social search systems. In: Next Generation Data Technologies for Collective Computational Intelligence, pp. 113–135. Springer (2011)
15. Dosovitskiy, A., et al.: An image is worth 16x16 words: transformers for image recognition at scale (2020). Version Number: 2
16. Galloway, M.M.: Texture analysis using gray level run lengths. Comput. Graphics Image Process. **4**(2), 172–179 (1975)
17. Gaudêncio, A.S.: Evaluation of COVID-19 chest computed tomography: a texture analysis based on three-dimensional entropy. Biomed. Signal Process. Control **68**, 102582 (2021)
18. Gomez, T., Fréour, T., Mouchére, H.: Metrics for saliency map evaluation of deep learning explanation methods. In: El Yacoubi, M., Granger, E., Yuen, P.C., Pal, U., Vincent, N. (eds.) Pattern Recognition and Artificial Intelligence. LNCS, vol. 13363, pp. 84–95. Springer, Cham (2022)
19. Haralick, R.M., Shanmugam, K., Dinstein, I.: Textural features for image classification. IEEE Trans. Syst. Man Cybernet. **SMC-3**(6), 610–621 (1973)
20. Hectors, S.J., et al.: Radiomics features measured with multiparametric magnetic resonance imaging predict prostate cancer aggressiveness. J. Urol. **202**(3), 498–505 (2019)
21. Hu, B., Tunison, P., RichardWebster, B., Hoogs, A.: XAITK-saliency: an open source explainable AI toolkit for saliency. In: Proceedings of the AAAI Conference on Artificial Intelligence, vol. 37, no. 13, pp. 15760–15766 (2023)
22. Huang, H., et al.: UNet 3+: a full-scale connected UNet for medical image segmentation. In: ICASSP 2020–2020 IEEE International Conference on Acoustics. Speech and Signal Processing (ICASSP), pp. 1055–1059. IEEE (2020)
23. Jaeger, S., Candemir, S., Antani, S., Wáng, Y.X.J., Lu, P.X., Thoma, G.: Two public chest X-ray datasets for computer-aided screening of pulmonary diseases. Quant. Imaging Med. Surg. **4**(6), 475–477 (2014)

24. Josphineleela, R., Preethi, S., Ashwin, M., Srikanth, M., Ramesh, E., Kolluru, V.A.: Feature extraction techniques in medical imaging: a systematic review. Int. J. Recent Innov. Trends Comput. Commun **11**(5), 23–29 (2023)
25. Koyuncu, H., Barstuğan, M.: COVID-19 discrimination framework for X-ray images by considering radiomics, selective information, feature ranking, and a novel hybrid classifier. Signal Process. Image Commun. **97**, 116359 (2021)
26. Lavrova, E., et al.: Exploratory radiomic analysis of conventional vs. quantitative brain MRI: toward automatic diagnosis of early multiple sclerosis. Front. Neurosci. **15**, 679941 (2021)
27. Li, Y., Chen, C., Li, W., Shao, M., Dong, Y., Zhang, Q.: Radiomic features based on pyradiomics predict cd276 expression associated with breast cancer prognosis. Heliyon **10**(17), e37345 (2024)
28. Longo, L., et al.: Explainable artificial intelligence (XAI) 2.0: a manifesto of open challenges and interdisciplinary research directions. Inf. Fusion **106**, 102301 (2024)
29. Lundberg, S.M., Lee, S.I.: A unified approach to interpreting model predictions. In: Guyon, I., et al. (eds.) Advances in Neural Information Processing Systems, vol. 30, pp. 4765–4774. Curran Associates, Inc. (2017)
30. Luo, W., Huang, Q., Huang, X., Hu, H., Zeng, F., Wang, W.: Predicting breast cancer in breast imaging reporting and data system (BI-RADS) ultrasound category 4 or 5 lesions: a nomogram combining radiomics and BI-RADS. Sci. Rep. **9**(1) (2019)
31. Montavon, G., Binder, A., Lapuschkin, S., Samek, W., Müller, K.R.: Layer-wise relevance propagation: an overview. In: Samek, W., Montavon, G., Vedaldi, A., Hansen, L.K., Müller, K.R. (eds.) Explainable AI: Interpreting, Explaining and Visualizing Deep Learning. LNCS, vol. 11700, pp. 193–209. Springer, Cham (2019)
32. Müller, R.: How explainable AI affects human performance: a systematic review of the behavioural consequences of saliency maps. Int. J. Hum.-Comput. Interact. **41**(4), 2020–2051 (2025)
33. Oktay, O., et al.: Attention U-net: learning where to look for the pancreas (2018). arXiv:1804.03999 [cs]
34. Orton, M.R., et al.: Interpretability of radiomics models is improved when using feature group selection strategies for predicting molecular and clinical targets in clear-cell renal cell carcinoma: insights from the tracerx renal study. Cancer Imaging **23**(1) (2023)
35. Öztürk, Ş, Özkaya, U., Barstuğan, M.: Classification of coronavirus (COVID-19) from X-ray and CT images using shrunken features. Int. J. Imaging Syst. Technol. **31**(1), 5–15 (2020)
36. Park, Y.W.: Differentiating patients with schizophrenia from healthy controls by hippocampal subfields using radiomics. Schizophr. Res. **223**, 337–344 (2020)
37. Prinzi, F., Militello, C., Zarcaro, C., Bartolotta, T.V., Gaglio, S., Vitabile, S.: Rad4XCNN: a new agnostic method for post-hoc global explanation of CNN-derived features by means of Radiomics. Comput. Methods Programs Biomed. **260**, 108576 (2025)
38. Rizzo, S., et al.: Radiomics: the facts and the challenges of image analysis. Eur. Radiol. Exp. **2**(1) (2018)
39. Ronneberger, O., Fischer, P., Brox, T.: U-Net: convolutional networks for biomedical image segmentation. In: Navab, N., Hornegger, J., Wells, W.M., Frangi, A.F. (eds.) Medical Image Computing and Computer-Assisted Intervention – MICCAI 2015. LNCS, vol. 9351, pp. 234–241. Springer, Cham (2015)

40. Selvaraju, R.R., Cogswell, M., Das, A., Vedantam, R., Parikh, D., Batra, D.: Grad-CAM: visual explanations from deep networks via gradient-based localization. In: 2017 IEEE International Conference on Computer Vision (ICCV), pp. 618–626 (2017)
41. Severn, C., Suresh, K., Görg, C., Choi, Y.S., Jain, R., Ghosh, D.: A pipeline for the implementation and visualization of explainable machine learning for medical imaging using radiomics features. Sensors **22**(14) (2022)
42. Shi, L., et al.: Application of computed tomography-based radiomics combined with clinical factors in the diagnosis of malignant degree of lung adenocarcinoma. J. Thorac. Dis. **14**(11), 4435–4448 (2022)
43. Shrikumar, A., Greenside, P., Kundaje, A.: Learning important features through propagating activation differences (2019). arXiv:1704.02685 [cs]
44. Sun, C., Wee, W.G.: Neighboring gray level dependence matrix for texture classification. Comput. Vis. Graph. Image Process. **23**(3), 341–352 (1983)
45. Sundararajan, M., Taly, A., Yan, Q.: Axiomatic attribution for deep networks. In: Proceedings of the 34th International Conference on Machine Learning, ICML 2017, vol. 70, pp. 3319–3328. JMLR.org (2017)
46. Thibault, G., et al.: Texture indexes and gray level size zone matrix application to cell nuclei classification. In: 10th International Conference on Pattern Recognition and Information Processing (2009)
47. Timmeren, J.E., Cester, D., Tanadini-Lang, S., Alkadhi, H., Baessler, B.: Radiomics in medical imaging–"how-to" guide and critical reflection. Insights Imaging **11**(1), 91 (2020)
48. Danilov, V.: Chest X-ray dataset for lung segmentation (2022)
49. Vilone, G., Rizzo, L., Longo, L.: A comparative analysis of rule-based, model-agnostic methods for explainable artificial intelligence. In: Longo, L., Rizzo, L., Hunter, E., Pakrashi, A. (eds.) Proceedings of The 28th Irish Conference on Artificial Intelligence and Cognitive Science, Dublin, Republic of Ireland, 7–8 December 2020. CEUR Workshop Proceedings, vol. 2771, pp. 85–96. CEUR-WS.org (2020)
50. Vuong, D., et al.: Radiomics feature activation maps as a new tool for signature interpretability. Front. Oncol. **10** (2020)
51. Vuong, D., et al.: Radiomics feature activation maps as a new tool for signature interpretability. Front. Oncol. **10**, 578895 (2020)
52. Xia, L., Zhang, J., Liang, Z., Tang, J., Xia, J., Liu, Y.: Shapley-based saliency maps improve interpretability of vertebral compression fractures classification: multicenter study. Radiol. Med. (Torino) **130**(3), 412–421 (2025)
53. Ye, J.Y., Fang, P., Peng, Z.P., Huang, X.T., Xie, J.Z., Yin, X.Y.: A radiomics-based interpretable model to predict the pathological grade of pancreatic neuroendocrine tumors. Eur. Radiol. **34**(3), 1994–2005 (2023)
54. Zulpe, N., Pawar, V.: GLCM textural features for brain tumor classification. IJCSI **9**, 354–359 (2012)

**Open Access** This chapter is licensed under the terms of the Creative Commons Attribution 4.0 International License (http://creativecommons.org/licenses/by/4.0/), which permits use, sharing, adaptation, distribution and reproduction in any medium or format, as long as you give appropriate credit to the original author(s) and the source, provide a link to the Creative Commons license and indicate if changes were made.

The images or other third party material in this chapter are included in the chapter's Creative Commons license, unless indicated otherwise in a credit line to the material. If material is not included in the chapter's Creative Commons license and your intended use is not permitted by statutory regulation or exceeds the permitted use, you will need to obtain permission directly from the copyright holder.

# FAIR-MED: Bias Detection and Fairness Evaluation in Healthcare Focused XAI

Katsiaryna Bahamazava[1] and Ruairi O'Reilly[2(✉)]

[1] Department of Mathematical Sciences G.L. Lagrange, Politecnico di Torino, Turin, Italy
`katsiaryna.bahamazava@polito.it`
[2] Department of Computer Science, Munster Technological University, Tralee, Ireland
`ruairi.oreilly@mtu.ie`

**Abstract.** Artificial Intelligence models are increasingly used for classification tasks in healthcare. However, many healthcare professionals and machine learning engineers are still unaware of how these models contribute to and amplify biases. This work introduces a new framework (FAIR-MED) for bias detection and fairness evaluation in healthcare AI models, with a particular emphasis on intersectional fairness, which accounts for the compounded effects of multiple demographic attributes rather than assessing bias in isolation. Current methods often focus solely on data biases and overlook the compounded impact of multiple demographic attributes (e.g., age, gender, socioeconomic status) leading to unequal outcomes across diverse patient populations. To bridge this gap, a comprehensive, model-agnostic framework that incorporates a *Compound Fairness Score* is proposed. This approach to fairness goes beyond traditional methods by providing insights into the compounded impact of biases across different groups. Additionally, entropy-based weighting is introduced to quantify and aggregate bias metrics in a data-driven manner, ensuring that fairness evaluations prioritize the most impactful sources of bias. The proposed framework is evaluated on widely adopted families of AI models (linear, non-linear and neural network-based approaches) against open-source breast cancer dataset. The results suggest that Neural Networks may be more prone to amplifying existing biases, while Random Forest models tend to exhibit a better fairness balance in this evaluation. Logistic Regression, the most interpretable among the evaluated models, demonstrated overall stability but exhibited noticeable accuracy disparities across age groups. By aligning with transparency and accountability principles outlined in the EU AI Act, FAIR-MED offers a systematic, interpretable, and reproducible approach to bias analysis and fairness assessment, contributing to the development of ethical, equitable, and trustworthy AI-driven healthcare solutions.

**Keywords:** Artificial Intelligence · Bias · Discrimination · Fairness · Breast cancer

# 1 Introduction

Breast cancer is one of the most prevalent oncological diseases, affecting approximately 36% of all cancer patients worldwide. Early diagnosis is critical for improving survival rates, and Artificial Intelligence (AI) models have demonstrated remarkable potential in enhancing diagnostic accuracy for breast cancer classification [2,15]. The increasing adoption of AI in medical decision-making is evident in regulatory approvals, with 951 AI/ML-enabled medical devices approved for clinical use in the U.S. as of September 2024 [14]. However, as AI adoption in healthcare expands, so does the risk of exacerbating biases that disproportionately impact underrepresented demographic groups.

While existing research on AI fairness has made strides in detecting biases related to single demographic attributes (e.g., gender or race) [1], most studies fail to address intersectional biases–disparities that emerge from the interplay of multiple demographic attributes. These compounded biases can lead to systematically worse outcomes for marginalized subgroups. For example, a breast cancer classification algorithm trained predominantly on a homogenous patient population (e.g., 88.6% white patients in a German study [11]) may demonstrate significantly reduced accuracy when applied to patients from different racial backgrounds. Such disparities highlight the urgent need for fairness-aware AI evaluation frameworks that go beyond traditional single-attribute bias assessments.

This paper presents FAIR-MED, a model-agnostic framework designed to systematically detect and quantify biases in AI-driven healthcare applications. Unlike conventional fairness evaluations that focus primarily on either dataset imbalances or model fairness, FAIR-MED integrates both into a Compound Fairness Score (CFS)–a novel metric that holistically captures fairness across data and model dimensions. The key contributions of this work are:

i) Introduction of the Compound Fairness Score (CFS). Unlike traditional fairness metrics, which separately assess data and model biases, the CFS provides an integrated, interpretable measure of fairness by combining Data Fairness Score (DF) and Algorithmic & Model Fairness Score (AMF). Additionally, the framework is model-agnostic, ensuring that fairness assessments are applicable across diverse machine learning models–including linear (Logistic Regression), non-linear (Random Forest), and deep learning (Neural Networks).

ii) Intersectional Bias Analysis. FAIR-MED explicitly accounts for biases that emerge when multiple demographic attributes interact, ensuring that fairness assessments reflect real-world disparities rather than isolated statistical measures.

iii) Entropy-Based Weighting for Fairness Evaluation. The framework employs entropy-based weighting to quantify and aggregate fairness metrics in a data-driven manner, ensuring that fairness evaluations prioritize the most impactful sources of bias.

iv) Benchmarking Fairness in AI-driven Breast Cancer Classification. Using the SEER Breast Cancer dataset, FAIR-MED identifies critical fairness disparities, demonstrating how Neural Networks amplify existing biases while Random

Forest models exhibit the most balanced fairness performance. The empirical evaluation highlights that Neural Networks amplify existing biases, while Random Forest models exhibit the most balanced fairness performance.

The findings indicate that dataset imbalances remain the dominant driver of fairness disparities in AI-driven healthcare models. By integrating FAIR-MED into AI development pipelines, researchers, clinicians, and policymakers can systematically assess and mitigate biases, ensuring that AI-driven healthcare solutions are ethical, equitable, and transparent.

## 2 Related Work

Bias and fairness in AI models have been extensively studied, particularly in healthcare applications. Much of the prior work focuses on either data fairness or algorithmic bias mitigation, but relatively few approaches adopt a comprehensive, model-agnostic framework that systematically integrates both.

Agarwal et al. [1] introduce fairness quantification techniques like the Bias Index and Fairness Score. While useful, these rely heavily on data-centric mitigation and do not account for algorithmic or intersectional disparities. Similarly, Ferrara et al. [6] examine bias sources in data and algorithm design but lack a systematic evaluation framework applicable across models and datasets.

In diagnostics, Chen et al. [4] highlight fairness challenges and propose mitigation via Federated Learning and Fair Representation Learning. However, they do not offer a standardized way to compare fairness across model types, making it hard to determine which models are most robust in clinical settings.

Several works have focused on fairness for underrepresented demographic groups. Park et al. [10] tailor survival models for Hispanic and Black women, while Hu et al. [7] apply distributionally robust optimization (DRO) to ensure subgroup fairness. However, these focus on single attributes (e.g., race), and do not capture intersectional biases, disparities that arise from the interaction of multiple demographic factors like age, race, and marital status.

Large-scale healthcare datasets such as SEER and Duke-Breast-Cancer-MR are increasingly used for fairness analysis. Studies using SEER, such as Li et al. [9], have shown age-related biases and proposed fairness-aware classifiers. Yet, these approaches typically evaluate fairness within a single model and fail to provide comparative insights across different ML architectures. Moreover, they overlook intersectional fairness and lack a unified metric for integrating data and model biases.

Recent efforts have begun exploring intersectionality in fairness evaluations. For example, D'Aloisio et al. [5] propose a model-driven analysis of compounded demographic effects. However, most of these works still lack a unified metric that incorporates both dataset bias and algorithmic disparities, limiting their broader applicability.

There is also a growing ecosystem of fairness auditing tools, such as Aequitas [12] and Fairlearn [16]. While these offer valuable technical capabilities for developers, they are often not designed for clinical interpretability or practical usability by healthcare professionals. Conversely, clinical tools focus on usability but may lack algorithmic granularity.

Despite significant progress in fairness evaluation, current approaches face three main limitations: i) Lack of intersectional fairness analysis that captures compounded disparities across multiple attributes. ii) Absence of a unified metric that integrates data-related and model-induced biases. iii) Limited model-agnostic frameworks that are accessible to both AI practitioners and clinicians.

These limitations motivate the development of a general-purpose, interpretable, and systematic fairness evaluation framework for healthcare AI, capable of handling both dataset and model-level biases in a unified manner.

## 3 Methodology

### 3.1 Overview and Motivation

To address the limitations identified in prior research, FAIR-MED is positioned at the intersection of technical rigor and clinical usability. It is designed to be accessible and actionable for both AI engineers and clinicians, fostering collaborative fairness evaluation.

The framework introduces a Compound Fairness Score (CFS), a unified, interpretable metric that integrates both data-related and algorithmic biases. This model-agnostic score enables AI practitioners to identify and mitigate disparities, while providing clinicians with transparent insights into how model predictions may differentially impact patient subgroups.

FAIR-MED thus serves not only as a technical contribution but also as a bridge for interdisciplinary collaboration. It addresses a critical research gap by offering a framework that is both statistically rigorous and clinically interpretable, empowering diverse stakeholders to jointly audit, interpret, and improve fairness in AI-driven healthcare. This joint accountability and transparency are essential for deploying trustworthy, ethical, and equitable AI systems in sensitive medical settings.

Key advantages of FAIR-MED over existing methods include:

- A Unified Metric for Fairness: The Compound Fairness Score (CFS) combines dataset bias and model bias into a single interpretable metric.
- Intersectional Fairness Evaluation: FAIR-MED captures compounded impacts of multiple demographic attributes, moving beyond single-attribute assessments.
- Model-Agnostic Fairness Assessment: The framework supports diverse models, including Logistic Regression, Random Forest, and Neural Networks, enabling broad applicability.
- Explainability and Transparency: Entropy-based weighting highlights the most influential fairness factors, ensuring an interpretable, data-driven evaluation.

The methodology is organized into four key components: Data Fairness Score (DF), Entropy-Based Weights, Algorithmic & Model Fairness Score (AMF), and the final Compound Fairness Score (CFS). These components together provide a structured and reproducible approach to bias detection and fairness evaluation in AI-driven breast cancer classification models.

The SEER Breast Cancer Dataset [13] serves as the primary dataset for evaluation, offering diverse demographic information critical for bias detection.

The demographic features used in this study (age, race, and marital status) were selected based on their availability in the SEER dataset and their known clinical relevance to breast cancer outcomes. However, the FAIR-MED framework is fully model-agnostic and data-agnostic: users can apply the same methodology to any dataset with different sensitive attributes depending on the context. The intersectional fairness evaluation is thus not limited to these features, and FAIR-MED can accommodate other combinations of demographic or clinical attributes as appropriate for the domain.

### 3.2 Data Fairness Score

To quantify dataset fairness, the Data Fairness Score (DF) is derived as a weighted sum of key fairness metrics. For each individual fairness metric, a smaller value indicates lower bias in the dataset. Consequently, a lower overall DF score reflects a dataset with fewer biases.

A critical aspect of fairness in AI-driven healthcare models is demographic balance. Underrepresentation of certain demographic groups in the training dataset can lead to biased predictions and poor generalization. To measure representation disparities, the Representation Ratio (RR) (see Table 1) was employed where an ideal $RR = 1$ indicating perfect demographic representation. Since raw RR values may vary significantly, we introduce the *Standard Deviation of RR Values* ($NRR_{std}$), which quantifies the extent of demographic imbalance by measuring the spread of RR values. $NRR_{std}$ highlights variations in demographic representation more effectively. A higher $NRR_{std}$ value indicates significant disparities between overrepresented and underrepresented groups, whereas a value close to zero suggests a well-balanced dataset.

To ensure that significant correlations are not masked, we compute the *Maximum Absolute Correlation Score* ($CS_{max}$) (See Table 1). This approach highlights the strongest demographic influence rather than averaging all correlations, providing a more sensitive measure of potential biases. This step serves as a checkpoint in the fairness evaluation roadmap, identifying whether demographic variables alone drive disparities or if more complex interactions must be considered. If correlations are high, models might unfairly rely on certain attributes, justifying further fairness adjustments. If correlations are low, fairness concerns might stem from intersectional biases rather than individual demographic features, requiring deeper model evaluation.

Fairness in AI models extends beyond demographic representation and direct relationships. *Feature Distribution Weighted* ($FD_{weighted}$) helps detect hidden biases by comparing how key clinical variables are distributed across demographic groups. Even if a group appears well-represented ($RR \approx 1$), differences in feature distributions may introduce unintended biases, affecting prediction reliability. To detect potential biases in the distribution of clinical features across different demographic groups, a Kolmogorov-Smirnov (K-S) test was applied. The K-S test is a non-parametric statistical test that compares the cumulative distribution functions (CDFs) of two independent samples to determine whether they originate from the same distribution. A significant K-S statistic (low p-value) indicates that the two groups have statistically different distributions, suggesting potential fairness concerns. If FD (See Table 1) is high (close to 1) it indicates that no major distributional bias is present. Otherwise, ML models may result in systematically biased predictions for certain groups. If FD reveals disparities, further investigation is required to discover whether this bias comes from data collection or real-world disparities.

*Intersectional Imbalance Score (IIS).* (See Table 1) quantifies class imbalance at an intersectional level, capturing disparities arising from intersecting demographic attributes. For each intersectional subgroup $g$, the majority class and minority class counts are computed as $N_{\text{majority}}$ and $N_{\text{minority}}$, respectively. To prevent division errors, Laplace smoothing is applied: $N_{\text{minority}} = \max(N_{\text{minority}}, \epsilon)$ where $\epsilon = 10^{-6}$. A higher Imbalance Ratio (IR) indicates greater underrepresentation of the minority class. To normalize IIS values, a log-sigmoid transformation is applied. The final IIS score is a weighted combination of the worst-case bias ($\max(IS_{\text{normalized},g})$) and the overall weighted mean IS.

The DF score is computed as $DF = w_1 \cdot NRR_{std} + w_2 \cdot CS_{\max} + w_3 \cdot FD_{weighted} + w_4 \cdot IIS$, where $w_1, w_2, w_3, w_4$ are the respective entropy-based weights assigned to each fairness metric. The DF score quantifies the overall bias present in the dataset, where higher values indicate greater bias, and lower values indicate a fairer, more balanced dataset.

## 3.3 Entropy-Based Weights Definition

The entropy-based weighting approach is employed to assign weights to fairness metrics based on their informativeness (uncertainty). Shannon entropy quantifies the unpredictability of each fairness metric, ensuring that metrics with greater variability receive higher weights as they contribute more to overall fairness disparities. This ensures a data-driven, unbiased approach to fairness evaluation, preventing arbitrary weight selection.

To compute entropy, we first normalize the fairness metric values into a probability distribution by converting each fairness metric $x_i$ into probabilities as $P(x_i) = \frac{x_i}{\sum x_i}$, ensuring that $0 \leq P(x_i) \leq 1$ and $\sum P(x_i) = 1$. This transformation guarantees that fairness metrics are on a comparable scale, preventing larger absolute values from dominating the entropy calculation and ensuring that entropy captures relative uncertainty across fairness metrics.

The entropy for each metric $X$ is computed as $H(X) = -\sum_i P(x_i) \log_2 P(x_i)$, where $P(x_i)$ represents the normalized probability of each fair-

**Table 1.** Data Fairness Score Calculation Methods

| Method | Details |
|---|---|
| $NRR_{std}$ | $RR = \dfrac{\text{Proportion in sample}}{\text{Proportion in population}}$ <br> $NRR_{std} = \sqrt{\frac{1}{n}\sum_{i=1}^{n}(RR_i - 1)^2}$, where $RR_i$ is the representation ratio for each group and $n$ is the number of groups. |
| $CS_{max}$ | $CS_{max} = \max(|\rho_i|)$, $\rho_i$ is a Spearman Correlation |
| $FD_{weighted}$ | FD Score $= \min\left(1, \frac{\text{p-value}}{0.05}\right)$. <br> $FD_{weighted} = \dfrac{\sum_{i=1}^{N}(1-FD_i)\cdot(1-p_i)}{\sum_{i=1}^{N}(1-p_i)}$, where $p_i$ is the p-value from the Kolmogorov-Smirnov test for that comparison. |
| IIS | $IR_g = \dfrac{N_{\text{majority}}}{N_{\text{minority}}}$. $IS_g = |1 - IR_g|$. $IIS_{\text{normalized},g} = \dfrac{\log(1+IS_g)}{\log(1+IS_{max})}$, where $IS_{max}$ is the highest IS value in the dataset. <br> $IIS = 0.7 \times \max(IS_{\text{normalized},g}) + 0.3 \times \dfrac{\sum w_g \cdot IS_{\text{normalized},g}}{\sum w_g}$ where $w_g = N_{\text{majority}} + N_{\text{minority}}$ ensures that subgroup frequencies are proportionally represented. |

ness metric value. The final weights are derived by normalizing the entropy values as $W_i = \frac{H(X_i)}{\sum H(X)}$, ensuring that the sum of all weights equals 1.

This method prioritizes fairness metrics with higher uncertainty, making the evaluation transparent, interpretable, and mathematically justified.

### 3.4 Algorithmic & Model Fairness Score

Interpretable (Logistic Regression), minimally interpretable (Random Forest), and non-interpretable (Neural Network) models are trained and evaluated for fairness. Random Forest, as described by Breiman, falls within the class of algorithmic methods, offering limited interpretability (primarily through variable importance and ensemble aggregation) compared to more traditional linear statistical methods like Logistic Regression [3]. Algorithmic & Model Fairness Score (AMF) is proposed to quantify model disparities.

To assess fairness, the *Performance Score (PS)* (Table 2) is introduced, which quantifies model performance across different demographic subgroups. In this study, the max difference in accuracy is used as the default performance metric. However, depending on the application, alternative measures such as precision, recall, F1-score, or AUC can be employed to better align with the model's objectives. The models were trained on the complete dataset, ensuring that they learned from the entire distribution of patient data. To evaluate fairness, predictions were subsequently analyzed for distinct demographic groups. By comparing the max difference model performance across these groups, potential disparities in predictive accuracy were identified. This approach enables a systematic assessment of whether certain subgroups experience disproportionate misclassification rates due to model bias.

*Perturbation Score (PrS).* (Table 2) assesses whether AI models exhibit excessive sensitivity to minor changes in sensitive attributes such as age, race, or marital status. A fair model should maintain stable predictions when such attributes are slightly modified. Higher Perturbation Score reflects the instability of the model potentially reflecting the biased model. To evaluate Perturbation Score, the controlled random shifts in the Age attribute, a key factor in breast cancer diagnosis, was introduced. This method helps identify whether small variations in input data significantly alter model predictions, which may indicate bias in feature interactions. In real-world clinical applications, minor age misrecordings should not drastically change AI predictions. If they do, this suggests potential fairness concerns that could lead to inconsistent or inequitable treatment.

*Residual Score (RS).* (Table 2) enables an evaluation of how different ML models perform across demographic subgroups in terms of predictive errors. Higher Residual Score indicates greater prediction error for a specific group, meaning the AI model may systematically underperform for those individuals. Disparities in residuals across groups indicate potential fairness concerns, as some groups receive less reliable predictions than others.

AMF is computed as $AMF = w_1 \cdot PS + w_2 \cdot PrS + w_3 \cdot RS$, where $w_1, w_2, w_3$ are the respective entropy-based weights assigned to each fairness metric.

**Table 2.** Methods for Evaluating Fairness Metrics in AI Models.

| Metric | Calculation |
|---|---|
| PS | Compute performance metrics (e.g., accuracy, precision, recall) for each group: Max Difference = $\max(X_i) - \min(X_i)$ where $X_i$ is the metric for a group. |
| PrS | Slightly alter sensitive features and observe prediction changes: Absolute Change = |Original Prediction − Perturbed Prediction|, Average Change = $\frac{1}{N}\sum_{i=1}^{N}$ |Absolute Change| |
| RS | Analyze residuals across groups: |Residual| = |Actual Outcome − Predicted Outcome|, Residual Difference = $\max(\text{Average Residual}_{\text{group}}) - \min(\text{Average Residual}_{\text{group}})$ |

### 3.5 Compound Fairness Score

The Compound Fairness Score (CFS) integrates both DF (See Sect. 3.2) and AMF (See Sect. 3.4) into a single interpretable metric, computed as $CFS = \frac{2 \cdot DF \cdot AMF}{DF + AMF}$. This harmonic mean formulation ensures that if either DF or AMF is high (indicating significant bias), the overall CFS remains high. Thus, a low fairness in either component cannot be masked by good performance in the other, ensuring balanced fairness assessment.

Consequently, a lower CFS indicates better fairness (low bias), while higher values highlight fairness imbalances that necessitate targeted mitigation strategies.mitigation.

Unlike existing fairness toolkits that analyze model or dataset bias in isolation, CFS offers a single interpretable score integrating both, minimizing the risk of compensating for bias in one dimension while overlooking the other.

### 3.6 Computational Environment

The experiments were conducted using Google Colab, a cloud-based platform providing a Python environment for machine learning experiments. No GPU-specific configurations were used, and the primary libraries utilised were based on the default Python environment in Colab. The experimental analysis notebook is publicly available here.

## 4 Evaluating Data Fairness

Ensuring fairness in AI-driven healthcare requires a systematic assessment of dataset biases. This section evaluates the *Data Fairness Score (DF)* via the quantification of four key metrics: i) Standard Deviation of RR Values (NRR$_{std}$) – demographic balance, ii) Maximum Absolute Correlation Score ($CS_{\max}$) – demographic influence on outcomes, iii) Feature Distribution Score (FD) – disparities in clinical variable distributions, and iv) Intersectional Imbalance Score (IIS) – outcome class imbalances. The DF is computed as a weighted sum of these metrics, with the respective entropy-based weights. By identifying and mitigating biases before model training, DF ensures more equitable AI predictions and enhances transparency in medical decision-making.

### 4.1 Standard Deviation of RR Values

To illustrate the utility fairness evaluation framework NRR$_{std}$ are computed for the SEER Breast Cancer Dataset by comparing its demographic distribution to the Italian female population as of 01.01.2025. It is acknowledged that referencing population statistics may exhibit structural biases. To mitigate this, the Italian National Statistics [8] were used, which, while imperfect, offer the best available demographic baseline for fairness comparison.

The results of this step indicate a notable underrepresentation of younger patients (RR < 1) (See Table 3), particularly the 30–34 (RR = 0.157) and 35–39 (RR = 0.411) age groups. This suggests a potential data gap that could impair model generalization for these subgroups. Conversely, middle-aged and older groups are overrepresented, particularly 45–49 (RR = 1.338), 55–59, and 65–69, which could lead to models that favor older patients.

Similarly, marital status representation is examined. Single individuals are underrepresented (RR = 0.6193), meaning ML models may lack sufficient exposure to their clinical characteristics, potentially reducing predictive accuracy for

**Table 3.** Representation Ratios (RR) for Age Groups and Marital Status

| Group | Seer | Real | RR |
|---|---|---|---|
| 30–34 | 0.0152 | 0.0964 | 0.1573 |
| 35–39 | 0.0420 | 0.1021 | 0.4113 |
| 40–44 | 0.0984 | 0.1128 | 0.8724 |
| 45–49 | 0.1809 | 0.1352 | 1.3381 |
| 50–54 | 0.1722 | 0.1481 | 1.1628 |
| 55–59 | 0.1732 | 0.1515 | 1.1433 |
| 60–64 | 0.1742 | 0.1359 | 1.2819 |
| 65–69 | 0.1439 | 0.1180 | 1.2194 |
| Married | 0.6568 | 0.6443 | 1.0194 |
| Single | 0.1528 | 0.2468 | 0.6193 |
| Divorced | 0.1320 | 0.0651 | 2.0286 |
| Widowed | 0.0584 | 0.0439 | 1.3313 |

this group. Conversely, divorced (RR = 2.0286) and widowed (RR = 1.3313) patients are overrepresented, leading to potential overfitting to these groups.

The computed $NRR_{std}$ of 0.4721 indicates substantial demographic imbalance within the dataset. A higher $NRR_{std}$ suggests significant disparities between overrepresented and underrepresented groups. In this case, younger patients (30–39 years) and single individuals exhibit notable underrepresentation, potentially leading to biased AI predictions that generalize poorly for these subgroups. Conversely, middle-aged patients and divorced individuals are overrepresented, raising concerns of model overfitting to these demographics.

### 4.2 Maximum Absolute Correlation

Results in Table 4 indicate that the Spearman correlation coefficients between demographic variables and key clinical outcomes are negligible.

**Table 4.** Spearman Correlation Between Demographic Variables and Target Candidates. The low $CS_{\max} = 0.0827$ suggests that no single demographic variable exhibits a strong linear correlation with these clinical outcomes

| Group | Status | Tumor Size | Survival Months |
|---|---|---|---|
| Age | 0.0625 | −0.0827 | −0.0193 |
| Race | −0.0304 | −0.0137 | 0.0202 |
| Marital Status | 0.0214 | 0.0114 | −0.0160 |

The $CS_{\max}$ is 0.0827, indicating an almost negligible linear monotonic relationship between any single demographic variable and clinical outcomes. This aligns with the understanding that breast cancer is a multifactorial disease influenced by genetic, environmental, and clinical factors beyond basic demographics.

However, single-variable correlations may fail to capture more complex patterns of bias. Intersectional effects, where multiple demographic attributes interact, can introduce disparities that are not evident when analyzing variables in isolation. To address this, we extend our fairness evaluation by assessing intersectional fairness, examining how combined demographic subgroups influence clinical outcomes.

### 4.3 Feature Distribution Weighted

Feature Distribution Weighted ($FD_{weighted}$) analysis is crucial in evaluating fairness in AI-driven healthcare models. In the SEER dataset, the Tumor Size variable was found to be similarly distributed across racial groups, as evidenced by an FDA Score of 1 across all race-based comparisons. This suggests that racial bias is not a significant factor in this particular feature.

However, disparities emerge when considering marital status. A moderate bias was detected in Tumor Size between married and single patients (FDA Score $= 0.5006, p = 0.025$) (See Table 5), indicating that single individuals may exhibit different tumor size distributions compared to their married counterparts. This could reflect disparities in healthcare access, diagnosis timing, or underlying demographic differences.

For Survival Months, notable biases were observed across racial groups. The distribution of survival duration significantly differed between the "Other" and Black racial categories (FDA Score $= 0.0013, p = 6.28 \times 10^{-5}$) and between White and Black patients (FDA Score $= 0.0660, p = 0.0033$). These disparities suggest potential structural inequities in treatment outcomes or survival rates across racial demographics, which could introduce biases in AI model predictions if left unaddressed.

Despite the absence of severe bias in some comparisons, the overall $FD_{weighted}$ score of 0.7556 indicates that feature distribution disparities exist in the dataset, particularly concerning marital status and survival duration across racial groups. These imbalances highlight the importance of a comprehensive fairness evaluation to ensure AI models do not propagate or exacerbate existing inequities. Addressing these biases may require data rebalancing strategies or fairness-aware learning techniques to improve model reliability across demographic subgroups.

### 4.4 Intersectional Imbalance Score

Intersectional groups in this study were constructed by combining the available demographic variables in the SEER dataset, specifically age, race, and marital status. Importantly, the construction of intersectional groups is not fixed within FAIR-MED; it is adaptable and guided by the available data and specific research goals. The framework is both data-agnostic and model-agnostic, meaning users can define relevant intersectional attributes according to the context of their healthcare application and the characteristics of their dataset.

**Table 5.** Feature Distribution Results for Tumor Size and Survival Months Across Racial Groups

| Feature | Group Comparison | K-S Statistic | p-value | FD Score |
|---|---|---|---|---|
| Tumor Size | Other vs White | 0.0501 | 0.4386 | 1 |
| | Other vs Black | 0.0606 | 0.6008 | 1 |
| | White vs Black | 0.0340 | 0.9045 | 1 |
| | Married vs Divorced/Separated | 0.0621 | 0.0807 | 1 |
| | Married vs Single | 0.0659 | 0.0250 | 0.5006 |
| | Married vs Widowed | 0.0467 | 0.7143 | 1 |
| | Divorced/Separated vs Single | 0.0918 | 0.8461 | 1 |
| | Divorced/Separated vs Widowed | 0.0446 | 0.8927 | 1 |
| | Single vs Widowed | 0.0454 | 0.8552 | 1 |
| Survival Months | Other vs White | 0.0741 | 0.0764 | 1 |
| | Other vs Black | 0.1826 | $6.28 \times 10^{-5}$ | 0.0013 |
| | White vs Black | 0.1086 | 0.0033 | 0.0660 |
| | Married vs Divorced/Separated | 0.1547 | 0.2499 | 1 |
| | Married vs Single | 0.0423 | 0.3246 | 1 |
| | Married vs Widowed | 0.0580 | 0.4452 | 1 |
| | Divorced/Separated vs Single | 0.1453 | 0.3088 | 1 |
| | Divorced/Separated vs Widowed | 0.0679 | 0.4324 | 1 |
| | Single vs Widowed | 0.0417 | 0.9137 | 1 |

Intersectional Imbalance Score (IIS) provides a more granular measure of dataset imbalances by evaluating class distributions across multiple demographic attributes simultaneously. Unlike traditional single-variable class imbalance metrics, which assess the overrepresentation of majority groups in isolation, IIS highlights how intersecting demographic characteristics contribute to disparities in model learning.

Applying this approach to the dataset reveals a general Imbalance Ratio (IR) of 5.532, indicating that the Alive class is significantly overrepresented compared to the Dead class. This suggests that an AI model trained on this dataset may struggle to accurately predict mortality cases due to the limited number of instances in the minority class.

Further disaggregation by intersectional subgroups reveals critical disparities:

i) Age Bias: Middle-aged groups (40–49 years old) exhibit the highest IR values (>7), suggesting that survival predictions may be biased in favor of these age groups.

ii) Marital Status Bias: Married individuals have a higher IR (6.38), indicating a potential bias in mortality risk assessment for this group.

iii) Racial Bias: The "Other" racial category experiences an extreme IR (8.70), suggesting that models trained on this dataset may underperform for this subgroup due to limited training data.

To investigate how demographic attributes compound imbalance effects, the IIS at the intersectional level is computed. The results are visualized using a heatmap (Fig. 1), where white spaces indicate the absence of mortality data in specific subgroups. Table 6 presents the Top 10 most imbalanced intersectional groups, where certain subpopulations experience extreme IR values, reaching up to 37.00.

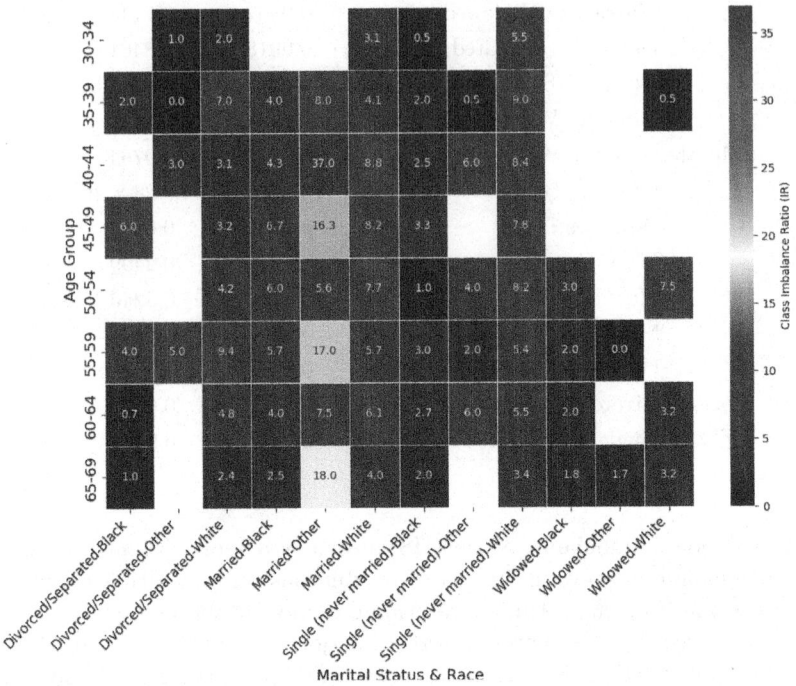

**Fig. 1.** IIS across different demographic subgroups, combining age, marital status, and race. The color scale represents class imbalance ratios (IR), with higher values (red) indicating severe underrepresentation of the Dead class within specific subgroups. White spaces indicate the absence of mortality data in those categories. (Color figure online)

To ensure a fairness-aware evaluation, we employed a log-sigmoid transformation (See Sect. 3.2) to normalize IIS values. The final computed IIS is 0.7365. The high IIS value for specific intersectional groups confirm the presence of structural imbalances in the dataset, which can negatively impact model generalization and fairness. AI models trained on this dataset may disproportionately favor well-represented groups while exhibiting high error rates for underrepresented subgroups.

**Table 6.** Top 10 Most Imbalanced Intersectional Groups

| Age Group | Marital Status | Race | Alive | Dead | IR | IS |
|---|---|---|---|---|---|---|
| 40–44 | Married | Other | 37 | 1 | 37.00 | 36.00 |
| 65–69 | Married | Other | 18 | 1 | 18.00 | 17.00 |
| 55–59 | Married | Other | 34 | 2 | 17.00 | 16.00 |
| 45–49 | Married | Other | 49 | 3 | 16.33 | 15.33 |
| 55–59 | Divorced | White | 85 | 9 | 9.44 | 8.44 |
| 35–39 | Single (never married) | White | 27 | 3 | 9.00 | 8.00 |
| 40–44 | Married | White | 203 | 23 | 8.83 | 7.83 |
| 40–44 | Single (never married) | White | 42 | 5 | 8.40 | 7.40 |
| 45–49 | Married | White | 377 | 46 | 8.20 | 7.20 |
| 50–54 | Single (never married) | White | 90 | 11 | 8.18 | 7.18 |

### 4.5 Deriving the Data Fairness Score

To quantify dataset fairness, the Data Fairness Score (DF) is derived as a weighted sum of key fairness metrics. Since different fairness metrics capture distinct biases within the dataset, their contributions are weighted based on their entropy, ensuring that more informative metrics receive higher importance.

The entropy-based weighting approach assigns importance to fairness metrics based on their unpredictability (Shannon entropy). A metric with greater variability carries more information about dataset fairness and is thus assigned a higher weight. This ensures a data-driven, unbiased weighting process instead of arbitrary selection.

The computed entropy-based weights for the fairness metrics are: i) $w_{\text{NRR}_{std}} = 0.3113$, ii) $w_{\text{CS}_{\max}} = 0.1351$, iii) $w_{\text{FD}_{\text{weighted}}} = 0.2511$, iv) $w_{\text{IIS}} = 0.3025$. These weights indicate that $\text{NRR}_{std}$ and IIS contribute most to the dataset's fairness evaluation. The computed DF = 0.4423, indicating a moderate level of fairness within the dataset. A higher DF (closer to 1) suggests significant disparities in demographic representation, feature distributions, or class imbalances.

Since $\text{NRR}_{std}$ and IIS contribute the most to fairness disparities, future efforts should prioritize strategies aimed at enhancing demographic representation to better match real-world populations and implement class rebalancing techniques to mitigate intersectional biases.

## 5 Assessing Algorithmic and Model-Specific Fairness

This section evaluates how model-specific factors contribute to disparities in ML-based classification. Three fairness assessment criteria are employed: i) Performance Score (PS) – measuring differences in accuracy across demographic groups. ii) Perturbation Score (PrS) – Evaluating model sensitivity to changes in sensitive attributes and iii) Residual Score (RS) – Identifying variations in prediction errors across groups. Each of these criteria provides insight into potential biases, enabling the assessment of models' capacity to deliver fair and equitable healthcare predictions.

### 5.1 Performance Score

Three widely adopted machine learning models were selected to provide an overview of breast cancer classifiers' performance: Logistic Regression, a Random Forest Classifier, and a Neural Network (Fully Connected Feed-forward Neural Network). If a model achieves significantly different accuracies for different subgroups, it suggests disparities in predictive performance that may disadvantage certain populations. Table 7 provides a comparative analysis of maximum accuracy differences across race, age, and marital status. A model exhibiting significant differences in accuracy across demographic groups may introduce algorithmic bias, which could lead to disparities in real-world clinical applications.

**Table 7.** Differences in Model Accuracy Across Demographic Groups

| Model | Category | Max Accuracy Difference | Highest Accuracy | Lowest Accuracy |
|---|---|---|---|---|
| Logistic Regression | Racial | 0.045 | 0.911 (Black) | 0.865 (Other) |
| | Age | 0.120 | 0.940 (55–59) | 0.821 (35–39) |
| | Marital Status | 0.014 | 0.903 (Single) | 0.889 (Married) |
| | **Average** | **0.060** | | |
| Random Forest | Racial | 0.065 | 0.911 (Black) | 0.846 (Other) |
| | Age | 0.127 | 0.948 (55–59) | 0.821 (35–39) |
| | Marital Status | 0.022 | 0.918 (Widowed) | 0.897 (Married) |
| | **Average** | **0.071** | | |
| Neural Network | Racial | 0.020 | 0.885 (White) | 0.865 (Other) |
| | Age | 0.220 | 0.938 (30–34) | 0.718 (35–39) |
| | Marital Status | 0.141 | 0.856 (Married) | 0.714 (Widowed) |
| | **Average** | **0.127** | | |

Each model struggles with accuracy for age group, having the lower accuracy for younger patients (35–39), indicating potential bias in early breast cancer detection. The Neural Networks show the highest accuracy disparity (22.0%). Random Forest and Logistic Regression exhibit higher racial disparities, suggesting performance variations across ethnic groups. Marital Status bias is highest in Neural Networks, where predictions for widowed individuals show the lowest accuracy. The analysis of PS indicates that while all models exhibit biases, Neural Networks demonstrate the highest disparities, particularly for younger and widowed patients. Logistic Regression emerges as the most stable model, with the least overall bias, while Random Forest exhibits the highest racial disparities. These findings underscore the importance of intersectional fairness analysis and bias mitigation techniques to improve AI-driven breast cancer detection models.

## 5.2 Perturbation Score

The Perturbation Score (PrS) (See Sect. 3.4) measures the sensitivity of model predictions to small changes in demographic attributes. Higher PrS values indicate greater instability, which can lead to unfair decision-making in real-world applications. The Neural Network exhibits the highest PrS for race (0.014), suggesting it is more sensitive to racial attributes compared to Logistic Regression (0.001). This could indicate that Neural Network-based models rely more heavily on racial characteristics, leading to higher prediction variability (Table 8).

**Table 8.** Perturbation Scores (PrS) Across Demographic Groups for Different Models

| Demographic Group | LR | RF | NN |
|---|---|---|---|
| Age Group | 0.008 | 0.011 | 0.010 |
| Marital Status | 0.003 | 0.006 | 0.004 |
| Race | 0.001 | 0.002 | 0.014 |
| Overall PrS | **0.004** | **0.006** | **0.009** |

Since the SEER dataset already exhibits underrepresentation of younger patients (30–39) (See Sect. 4.1), it was investigated whether perturbations exacerbate these imbalances and impact model predictions across different demographic groups.

**Table 9.** Comparison of Accuracy Differences Before and After Perturbation Across Models

| Model | Group | Original | | Perturbed | | Diff. |
|---|---|---|---|---|---|---|
| | | High Acc. | Low Acc. | High Acc. | Low Acc. | Max |
| LR | Age | 0.940 (55–59) | 0.821 (35–39) | 0.926 (55–59) | 0.718 (35–39) | **+0.088** |
| | Marital | 0.903 (S) | 0.889 (M) | 0.898 (W) | 0.881 (D) | **+0.003** |
| | Race | 0.911 (B) | 0.865 (O) | 0.894 (W) | 0.857 (B) | **−0.008** |
| RF | Age | 0.948 (55–59) | 0.821 (35–39) | 0.925 (65–69) | 0.795 (35–39) | **+0.003** |
| | Marital | 0.918 (W) | 0.897 (M) | 0.918 (W) | 0.899 (M) | **−0.002** |
| | Race | 0.911 (B) | 0.846 (O) | 0.911 (B) | 0.827 (O) | **+0.019** |
| NN | Age | 0.938 (30–34) | 0.718 (35–39) | 0.919 (55–59) | 0.718 (35–39) | **−0.019** |
| | Marital | 0.856 (M) | 0.714 (W) | 0.918 (W) | 0.873 (S) | **−0.096** |
| | Race | 0.846 (W) | 0.696 (B) | 0.895 (W) | 0.804 (B) | **−0.058** |

**Legend:** LR: Logistic Regression, RF: Random Forest, NN: Neural Network. S: Single, M: Married, W: Widowed, D: Divorced, B: Black, O: Other, W: White. Diff.: Difference, Acc.: Accuracy.

The Logistic Regression model exhibits the highest accuracy drop (−0.103) for the 35–39 age group, which suggests that minor variations in age significantly alter predictions. This is likely due to the underrepresentation of younger patients in the SEER dataset, causing the model to learn less reliable decision boundaries for this subgroup. While the Neural Network exhibited improved fairness for age groups, it remained biased against Black patients, maintaining the lowest accuracy among racial subgroups even after perturbation. This suggests that the model learns complex non-linear representations that may amplify dataset biases, particularly when racial attributes correlate with other clinical factors. The Random Forest model demonstrated the highest stability, exhibiting minimal sensitivity to perturbations across all demographic groups. This robustness is likely due to its ensemble learning approach, which reduces the effect of single-feature variations by aggregating multiple decision trees.

### 5.3 Residual Analysis

The residual analysis enables the evaluation of how different AI models perform across demographic subgroups in terms of predictive errors. The results provide key insights into fairness, bias, and explainability (See Table 10). Higher residuals indicate greater prediction error for a specific group, meaning the AI model may systematically underperform for those individuals. Disparities in residuals across groups indicate potential fairness concerns, as some groups receive less reliable predictions than others (Table 9).

**Table 10.** Residual Scores (RS) Across Demographic Groups for Different Models

| Demographic Group | LR | RF | NN |
|---|---|---|---|
| Age Group | 0.1044 | 0.0602 | 0.0812 |
| Marital Status | 0.0365 | 0.0280 | 0.0313 |
| Race | 0.0720 | 0.0310 | 0.0500 |
| Overall RS | **0.0703** | **0.0397** | **0.0542** |

Since the goal of the FAIR-MED framework is also to **explain** why some models perform better than others, further analysis of AI model performance is undertaken

Across all demographic groups (age, race, marital status), we observe that the Random Forest model consistently has the lowest residuals, while Logistic Regression has the highest residuals. This suggests that Random Forest is the most stable model in terms of predictive performance. Random Forest is an ensemble learning algorithm that combines multiple decision trees, allowing it to capture non-linear relationships in the data.

As confirmed by Correlation Analysis (Sect. 4.2), the relationships between demographic variables and clinical outcomes in the dataset are non-linear. Since Logistic Regression assumes a linear decision boundary, it struggles to capture these complex interactions, resulting in higher residuals. Even though Neural

Networks generally excel at learning non-linear data, they require a large amount of training examples per subgroup to generalize well. This is due to the high-dimensional parameter space and non-convex optimization involved in training. As confirmed by Intersectional Class Imbalance Analysis (Sect. 4.4), many subgroups in the dataset have blank spaces, indicating missing data. This suggests that some groups have insufficient training samples, making it difficult for the Neural Network to generalize well across all subgroups. In contrast, Random Forest does not require a large dataset to generalize well, as it is composed of multiple decision trees, where each tree samples a subset of data. This ensures that even underrepresented groups contribute proportionally to the final prediction, reducing bias and maintaining lower residuals.

The residual analysis findings validate the initial fairness assessment, confirming that bias in model predictions is influenced by dataset imbalances. Moreover, algorithmic choices impact fairness (Logistic Regression struggles, Random Forest performs best). And the data sparsity affects explainability (Neural Networks require more balanced data for fairness).

## 5.4 Calculation of Algorithmic and Model-Specific Fairness Score

The AMF Score is computed as $\text{AMF} = w_1 \times \text{PS} + w_2 \times \text{PrS} + w_3 \times \text{RS}$, where $w_1 = 0.329$ (Performance Score (PS), measuring accuracy disparities), $w_2 = 0.33$ (Perturbation Score (PrS), accounting for model sensitivity), and $w_3 = 0.34$ (Residual Score (RS), capturing prediction errors). These entropy-based weights ensure that the most informative fairness metrics contribute more significantly to the final AMF score. Applying these weights to the computed fairness component scores, we derive the AMF Score for each model, as presented in Table 11.

**Table 11.** Comparison of AMF and CFS across different models. A lower AMF score indicates better fairness performance. The CFS score integrates both DF and AMF, providing an overall fairness assessment. RF exhibits the lowest AMF score and the best overall fairness (CFS = 0.072), while NN demonstrate the highest fairness disparities (CFS = 0.110), particularly due to higher accuracy disparities and sensitivity to perturbations. LR remains stable but has higher residuals, affecting fairness. These findings suggest that model selection plays a crucial role in mitigating fairness disparities, but data biases remain the dominant fairness challenge.

| Fairness Component | LR | RF | NN |
|---|---|---|---|
| *AMF Score Components* | | | |
| Performance Score (PS) | 0.06 | 0.071 | 0.127 |
| Perturbation Score (PrS) | 0.004 | 0.006 | 0.009 |
| Residual Score (RS) | 0.0703 | 0.0397 | 0.0542 |
| AMF Score | 0.045 | 0.039 | 0.063 |
| *Compound Fairness Score (CFS)* | | | |
| CFS Score | **0.082** | **0.072** | **0.110** |

Random Forest (AMF = 0.039) demonstrates the lowest fairness disparity across demographic groups. It has the second least sensitivity to perturbations and maintains the lowest residual errors, indicating greater fairness compared to the other models. While Logistic Regression (AMF = 0.045) performs well in terms of stability, it exhibits the greatest prediction error disparities, particularly in age-based subgroup accuracy differences. Neural Networks (AMF = 0.063) has the highest overall fairness disparity, primarily due to its increased sensitivity to demographic shifts and greater accuracy discrepancies among different subgroups. This suggests that the model struggles to maintain equitable performance across demographic groups.

### 5.5 The Compound Fairness Score Calculation

The Compound Fairness Score Calculation (CFS) serves as a unified metric for assessing fairness by integrating both DF and AMF within AI-driven healthcare models (See Table 11).

Random Forest achieves the best fairness balance. It minimizes algorithmic disparities while not amplifying dataset biases as much as other models. Its ensemble nature may help mitigate biases that affect single classifiers more strongly. Neural Networks introduce the highest fairness disparities. While it can learn complex patterns, Neural Networks are more prone to reinforcing existing dataset biases, possibly due to the underrepresentation of key demographic groups. This suggests a need for fairness-aware training techniques for NN models.

Since all models share the same DF score (0.4423), dataset imbalances remain the primary driver of fairness issues. Addressing fairness solely through model selection is insufficient, data balancing and bias mitigation at the dataset level are crucial. However, the CFS evaluation is influenced by the choice of machine learning models (Logistic Regression, Random Forest, and Neural Networks). Different models may exhibit varying fairness characteristics depending on their decision-making processes.

Additionally, the scalability of CFS to other medical applications requires further investigation. This study focuses on breast cancer classification. However, fairness challenges may differ significantly in other healthcare applications, such as emergency care triage or disease prognosis, where disparities arise from different patient pathways, time-sensitive decision-making, or access to care.

While the experimental evaluation presented in this study focused on the SEER Breast Cancer dataset, the FAIR-MED framework itself is both model-agnostic and data-agnostic. The demographic attributes (age, race, marital status) used in the analysis were selected based on their availability and clinical relevance in the SEER dataset. However, the methodology is not limited to these features. FAIR-MED enables users to flexibly define sensitive or relevant attributes depending on their specific dataset and healthcare context. For instance, additional attributes such as gender, socioeconomic status, or geographic region can be seamlessly integrated into the fairness evaluation pipeline. All the components of the CFS would apply similarly to these groups. This adaptability ensures that FAIR-MED can be generalized to a wide range of fairness-sensitive healthcare applications beyond breast cancer classification. Future work will include validation across diverse datasets and feature sets to further demonstrate this generalizability.

## 6 Conclusion

This paper introduced FAIR-MED, a structured and interpretable framework for bias detection and fairness evaluation in AI-driven healthcare models, with a particular emphasis on intersectional fairness. Unlike conventional fairness evaluations that primarily address single-attribute biases, FAIR-MED systematically integrates demographic representation analysis, feature distribution disparities, and intersectional class imbalance assessments to capture the compounded effects of multiple demographic attributes.

A key contribution of this work is the introduction of the Compound Fairness Score (CFS)–a holistic metric that quantifies fairness by combining data fairness (DF) and algorithmic fairness (AMF). By providing an integrated fairness assessment, CFS enables AI practitioners and policymakers to move beyond isolated bias mitigation strategies and adopt a comprehensive, data-driven approach to fairness evaluation.

The application of FAIR-MED on real-world breast cancer datasets revealed critical insights: i) The Intersectional Imbalance Score uncovered demographic subgroups with extreme imbalance ratios (IR up to 37.00)–disparities that conventional fairness metrics would have failed to detect. ii) Among the evaluated models, Neural Networks exhibited the highest fairness disparities (CFS = 0.114), particularly for underrepresented subgroups, due to their greater sensitivity to data biases. iii) With a lower AMF score (0.039) and a more stable performance across demographic groups, Random Forest exhibited the most equitable model behavior, making it a favorable candidate for fairness-aware AI applications in healthcare. iv) Dataset imbalances are the primary source of fairness disparities. With DF = 0.4423, the findings confirm that data-related biases exert a stronger influence on fairness than model-specific biases, reinforcing the necessity of data rebalancing strategies before training AI models.

While FAIR-MED is primarily a fairness evaluation tool, it also contributes to the broader goals of explainable and trustworthy AI. The inclusion of residual and perturbation-based analyses enhances interpretability by revealing model sensitivities to demographic attributes, insights that are directly actionable by developers and healthcare practitioners. The entropy-based weighting further strengthens this explainability by highlighting the most impactful sources of bias in a transparent and interpretable way. Importantly, while this work does not include a direct user evaluation, FAIR-MED is designed with clinical usability in mind. It complements traditional model explainers like SHAP or LIME by adding a fairness perspective to the explainability pipeline. For example, if a model systematically underperforms for a specific demographic subgroup, this can be flagged for attention during model validation, audit, or deployment. This aligns with the transparency requirements of the EU AI Act and helps ensure that AI systems do not unintentionally disadvantage vulnerable populations.

To extend FAIR-MED's applicability, future research will focus on three key areas: expanding model diversity, conducting large-scale empirical assessments, and enhancing automation for wider adoption. The choice of model can influence the CFS score derived, as different models exhibit varying fairness characteristics due to differences in decision-making processes. Future work will expand the evaluation to include additional AI models and architectures. A large-scale empirical assessment of commonly used datasets for healthcare-focused AI models will be undertaken. This will systematically evaluate fairness disparities across different datasets, helping identify common biases that persist in medical AI applications. To facilitate wider adoption, a Python library will be developed to automate the computation of CFS, making it accessible to researchers and practitioners.

# References

1. Agarwal, A., Agarwal, H., Agarwal, N.: Fairness score and process standardization: framework for fairness certification in artificial intelligence systems. AI Ethics **3**(1), 267–279 (2023)
2. Alhussan, A.A., Eid, M.M., Towfek, S., Khafaga, D.S.: Breast cancer classification depends on the dynamic dipper throated optimization algorithm. Biomimetics **8**(2), 163 (2023)
3. Breiman, L.: Random forests. Mach. Learn. **45**, 5–32 (2001)
4. Chen, R.J., et al.: Algorithm fairness in AI for medicine and healthcare. arXiv preprint arXiv:2110.00603 (2021)
5. d'Aloisio, G., Lisi, F.A., Lenzerini, M., Giacomo, G.D., Calvanese, D.: How fair are we? from conceptualization to automated assessment of fairness definitions. Softw. Syst. Model., 1–27 (2025). https://doi.org/10.1007/s10270-025-01277-2
6. Ferrara, E.: Fairness and bias in artificial intelligence: a brief survey of sources, impacts, and mitigation strategies. Science **6**(1), 3 (2023)
7. Hu, S., Chen, G.H.: Fairness in survival analysis with distributionally robust optimization. J. Mach. Learn. Res. **25**(246), 1–85 (2024)
8. Istituto Nazionale di Statistica: Popolazione residente al 1 gennaio (2025). https://esploradati.istat.it/databrowser/#/it/dw/categories/IT1,POP,1.0/POP_POPULATION/DCIS_POPRES1. Accessed 28 Mar 2025
9. Li, Y., Chen, H., Zhang, L., Zhang, Y.: Fairness in survival outcome prediction for medical treatments. In: 2024 58th Annual Conference on Information Sciences and Systems (CISS), pp. 1–6. IEEE (2024)
10. Park, J.I., Bozkurt, S., Park, J.W., Lee, S.: Evaluation of race/ethnicity-specific survival machine learning models for hispanic and black patients with breast cancer. BMJ Health Care Inform. **30**(1) (2023)
11. Pfob, A., et al.: 147p racial bias in pretreatment MRI radiomics features to predict response to neoadjuvant systemic treatment in breast cancer: a multicenter study in China, Germany, and the US. ESMO Open **9** (2024)
12. Saleiro, P., et al.: Aequitas: a bias and fairness audit toolkit. arXiv preprint arXiv:1811.05577 (2018)
13. Teng, J.: Seer breast cancer data (2019). https://doi.org/10.21227/a9qy-ph35. https://dx.doi.org/10.21227/a9qy-ph35

14. U.S. Food & Drug Administration: Artificial Intelligence and Machine Learning (AI/ML)-Enabled Medical Devices (2024). https://www.fda.gov/medical-devices/software-medical-device-samd/artificial-intelligence-and-machine-learning-aiml-enabled-medical-devices
15. Walshe, D., O'Reilly, R.: Fair skin lesion classification workflows using transfer learning. In: 2022 33rd Irish Signals and Systems Conference (ISSC), pp. 1–6. IEEE (2022)
16. Weerts, H., Dudík, M., Edgar, R., Jalali, A., Lutz, R., Madaio, M.: FairLearn: assessing and improving fairness of AI systems (2023). http://jmlr.org/papers/v24/23-0389.html

**Open Access** This chapter is licensed under the terms of the Creative Commons Attribution 4.0 International License (http://creativecommons.org/licenses/by/4.0/), which permits use, sharing, adaptation, distribution and reproduction in any medium or format, as long as you give appropriate credit to the original author(s) and the source, provide a link to the Creative Commons license and indicate if changes were made.

The images or other third party material in this chapter are included in the chapter's Creative Commons license, unless indicated otherwise in a credit line to the material. If material is not included in the chapter's Creative Commons license and your intended use is not permitted by statutory regulation or exceeds the permitted use, you will need to obtain permission directly from the copyright holder.

# Weakly Supervised Pixel-Level Annotation with Visual Interpretability

Basma Nasir[1(✉)], Tehseen Zia[1], Muhammad Nawaz[2], and Catarina Moreira[2]

[1] Department of Computer Science, COMSATS University Islamabad, Islamabad, Pakistan
sp22-rcs-004@isbstudent.comsats.edu.pk, tehseen.zia@comsats.edu.pk
[2] Data Science Institute, University of Technology Sydney, Sydney, Australia
muhammad.nawaz@student.uts.edu.au, catarina.pintomoreira@uts.edu.au

**Abstract.** Medical image annotation is essential for diagnosing diseases, yet manual annotation is time-consuming, costly, and prone to variability among experts. To address these challenges, we propose an automated explainable annotation system that integrates ensemble learning, visual explainability, and uncertainty quantification. Our approach combines three pre-trained deep learning models–ResNet50, EfficientNet, and DenseNet–enhanced with XGrad-CAM for visual explanations and Monte Carlo Dropout for uncertainty quantification. This ensemble mimics the consensus of multiple radiologists by intersecting saliency maps from models that agree on the diagnosis while uncertain predictions are flagged for human review. We evaluated our system using the TBX11K medical imaging dataset and a Fire segmentation dataset, demonstrating its robustness across different domains. Experimental results show that our method outperforms baseline models, achieving 93.04% accuracy on TBX11K and 96.4% accuracy on the Fire dataset. Moreover, our model produces precise pixel-level annotations despite being trained with only image-level labels, achieving Intersection over Union IoU scores of 36.07% and 64.7%, respectively. By enhancing the accuracy and interpretability of image annotations, our approach offers a reliable and transparent solution for medical diagnostics and other image analysis tasks.

**Keywords:** Medical Image Annotation · Image Segmentation · Uncertainty Quantification · Ensemble Learning · Explainable Artificial Intelligence

## 1 Introduction

Medical image annotation, also referred to as data tagging or labeling, is essential for identifying pathological conditions and guiding clinical decision-making. This process involves adding descriptive labels to medical images from modalities such as Magnetic Resonance Imaging (MRI) and Computed Tomography (CT) scans, enabling accurate detection of anatomical structures, tumors, and other abnormalities. Traditionally, this task is performed manually by radiologists, whose expertise ensures diagnostic precision. However, manual annotation is both time-consuming and resource-intensive, especially for large datasets, and is susceptible to inter-observer variability due to differences in expert judgment [35]. These limitations can delay diagnosis and compromise the consistency of medical image analysis, particularly in regions with a shortage of skilled professionals, such as Pakistan [16].

Recent advancements in Artificial Intelligence (AI), particularly deep learning, have transformed medical image analysis by enabling automated annotation systems [5,12,15,45]. These systems can significantly reduce the time and cost associated with manual labeling while improving the accuracy and consistency of annotations [26]. Despite their promise, AI models often function as "black boxes," offering limited insight into their decision-making processes [4]. This lack of transparency limits their acceptance in clinical practice, where understanding the reasoning behind predictions is essential for building trust among healthcare professionals [11,44]. To address this, the field of Explainable Artificial Intelligence (XAI) has emerged, focusing on developing interpretable models that provide visual and conceptual explanations for their outputs [27,29,51].

However, existing explainable models primarily rely on datasets annotated with pixel-level masks, which are costly and labor-intensive to produce [39]. Furthermore, most AI systems struggle with the open-set problem, where they encounter previously unseen data that falls outside the scope of their training set [30]. The ability to detect and flag such cases is critical for ensuring diagnostic reliability. Therefore, there is a need for an automated annotation system that can generate accurate pixel-level masks using only image-level labels while also estimating prediction uncertainty to identify novel data.

To bridge this gap, we propose an automated explainable annotation system that integrates ensemble learning, visual explainability, and uncertainty quantification. Our method combines three pre-trained deep learning models, ResNet50, EfficientNet, and DenseNet, augmented with XGrad-CAM to generate saliency maps that highlight class-specific image regions. Monte Carlo Dropout is incorporated into each model to quantify prediction uncertainty, allowing the system to flag ambiguous cases for human review. By intersecting the saliency maps of models that agree on the classification, the system produces pixel-level annotations that closely align with expert-labeled ground truth masks. This approach eliminates the need for pixel-level annotations during training, significantly reducing the time and resources required for model development.

The main contributions of this paper are as follows:

- **Ensemble Learning for Robust Predictions:** We introduce an ensemble framework combining ResNet50, EfficientNet, and DenseNet to enhance the accuracy, reliability, and consistency of medical image annotations.
- **Weakly Supervised Pixel-Level Annotations:** We extend XGrad-CAM beyond standard visual explanations, enabling pixel-level mask generation using only image-level labels, significantly reducing the need for manual annotations.

- **Uncertainty Quantification for Open-Set Detection:** By integrating Monte Carlo Dropout, our system estimates prediction uncertainty, allowing it to flag ambiguous and novel data, improving reliability in real-world scenarios.

By addressing the limitations of traditional AI models and introducing an interpretable, reliable, and resource-efficient annotation system, our work advances medical image analysis and the broader field of Explainable Artificial Intelligence.

## 2 Literature Review

Recent advancements in computer vision and explainable AI have significantly improved object segmentation and interpretation in medical and general imaging. However, many state-of-the-art methods still rely on pixel-level annotations, which are costly and time-consuming [35]. Additionally, neural networks often lack transparency, limiting their applicability in high-stakes domains like healthcare [4]. This section reviews key developments in semantic segmentation, weakly supervised learning, generative adversarial networks, and uncertainty quantification, highlighting their strengths and limitations. The identified research gaps provide the foundation for our proposed approach, which integrates ensemble learning, XGrad-CAM explainability, and Monte Carlo Dropout-based uncertainty estimation to generate reliable pixel-level annotations using only image-level labels.

### 2.1 Semantic Segmentation

Recent advances in semantic segmentation have improved the accuracy of object localization in medical imaging. For example, GroupViT [49] employs a Hierarchical Grouping Vision Transformer that segments image regions using text supervision. While effective, its reliance on pre-trained object detectors with bounding box annotations limits its applicability in scenarios where pixel-level annotations are unavailable. In medical imaging, SMR-UNet [14] uses self-attention mechanisms, multi-scale feature integration, and residual structures to improve the segmentation of lung nodules. Although it captures both local and global contextual information, its performance depends on detailed pixel-level annotations, which are costly to obtain.

USegTransformer-P and USegTransformer-S [10] combine transformers with CNNs to improve segmentation accuracy. However, both models require large, annotated datasets and high computational resources, making them less practical in data-limited or resource-constrained environments. Similarly, the hybrid attention-based residual UNet [48] enhances brain tumor segmentation but relies on resized inputs, which may omit diagnostic information critical for clinical applications.

While these methods have advanced pixel-level segmentation, they rely heavily on pixel-level annotations and are sensitive to data quality and computational constraints. In contrast, our approach addresses these limitations by using a weakly supervised learning framework that requires only image-level labels. By integrating XGrad-CAM within an ensemble of ResNet50, EfficientNet, and DenseNet, our method produces pixel-level masks without manual annotations, reducing data preparation costs while maintaining interpretability and reliability.

### 2.2 Weakly Supervised Semantic Segmentation

Weakly supervised semantic segmentation (WSSS) aims to segment objects or regions of interest without relying on detailed pixel-level annotations. This is particularly important in medical imaging, where obtaining pixel-level labels is time-consuming and resource-intensive.

The Multi-class Token Transformer (MCTformer) [50] enhances object localization using class-specific attention mechanisms, improving segmentation precision. However, it still requires class labels and struggles with complex boundaries, limiting its applicability in medical contexts. Causal Class Activation Maps (C-CAM) [9] address WSSS challenges in medical imaging by leveraging anatomy and co-occurrence causalities, generating pseudo-segmentation masks with clearer boundaries. Yet, C-CAM's reliance on heatmap thresholding can reduce accuracy for small or overlapping regions.

ReFit [33] integrates unsupervised segmentation and saliency methods to create edge maps that refine object boundaries using Grad-CAM. Despite improved boundary delineation, its effectiveness depends on the quality of edge maps, which can be inconsistent in noisy medical images. For brain tumour segmentation, [7] proposes classifiers trained with only image-level labels, producing heatmaps that guide ROI segmentation. However, its performance is limited by the thresholding process, which may exclude subtle features. A 3D segmentation technique [31] combines semi-supervised and self-supervised learning to generate pseudo-labels, but its reliance on ground truth labels for central slices restricts its use in datasets with specific annotations.

Although these methods reduce annotation requirements, they still depend on partial pixel-level labels or struggle with accurate segmentation from image-level annotations. Our approach overcomes these limitations by generating pixel-level masks using only image-level labels. By integrating XGrad-CAM within an ensemble of ResNet50, EfficientNet, and DenseNet, we produce accurate annotations without manual pixel-level labeling. Additionally, using Monte Carlo Dropout quantifies uncertainty, ensuring reliable segmentation even in open-set scenarios where unseen data may occur.

### 2.3 Generative Adversarial Networks and Interpretability

Generative Adversarial Networks (GANs) [3] consists of two components: a generator that creates synthetic data and a discriminator that distinguishes between real and generated data. GANs have been applied across various domains, including realistic image synthesis [47], domain translation, and medical image generation [8]. However, their limited explainability hinders their use in critical applications like medical imaging. Existing explainability methods for GANs, such as image-to-image translation [6,41], struggle to generate accurate pixel-level masks, reducing their effectiveness in visualizing decision-making processes.

CycleGAN [54], designed for unpaired image-to-image translation, has improved tissue segmentation and disease detection in cardiac, liver, and retinal imaging [52]. Although it enhances visual interpretability by revealing disease impacts, it does not produce binary masks, limiting its use for precise annotations. Class Activation Maps (CAM) [53] provide visual explanations by highlighting class-specific image regions using the final convolutional layer. Grad-CAM [38] extends this approach by leveraging gradient information to generate coarse localization maps. However, CAM and Grad-CAM only offer heatmaps and cannot produce binary masks, limiting their utility for pixel-level annotation.

MDVA-GAN [28] addresses this limitation by integrating CycleGAN with Grad-CAM to visualize multi-class features and generate binary masks. Despite this improvement, MDVA-GAN often misclassifies images from unseen classes, reducing its reliability in open-set scenarios. Additionally, its reliance on adversarial training can lead to unstable results, especially when training data is limited.

These limitations highlight the need for an approach to generate pixel-level annotations from image-level labels while maintaining reliability in open-set scenarios. Our method addresses these challenges by integrating XGrad-CAM within an ensemble of ResNet50, EfficientNet, and DenseNet to generate pixel-level masks without adversarial training. Unlike MDVA-GAN, our approach quantifies prediction uncertainty using Monte Carlo Dropout, enabling it to flag ambiguous or novel data, ensuring more reliable annotations even when encountering unseen classes.

### 2.4 Uncertainty Quantification

Deep learning has advanced diagnostic evaluations in medical imaging, including CT, MRI, ultrasound, and histopathology [34]. Despite these advancements, neural networks often function as "black boxes," offering limited insight into their decision-making processes [13]. This opacity raises safety and reliability concerns, as models can overestimate their confidence when processing anomalous data [30] and are vulnerable to adversarial attacks [25]. Identifying these limitations is critical for ensuring the reliable integration of DL models into clinical workflows.

Uncertainty Quantification (UQ) techniques address these challenges by estimating the confidence of model predictions, enabling the identification of ambiguous cases that require human review [1]. This is especially important in healthcare, where undetected errors can lead to misdiagnoses and inappropriate treatments [20]. Traditional neural networks use the Softmax function to output probability distributions across classes, but these probabilities often do not reflect true uncertainty, particularly in open-set scenarios where the input data differs from the training distribution.

The Uncertainty-Inspired Open Set (UIOS) model [46] improves the detection and classification of retinal anomalies by using evidential uncertainty estimation. While UIOS is trainable and computationally efficient, its reliance on specific annotations, such as central slice labels, and the need for manual threshold tuning limit its applicability to datasets with predefined reference points. This dependency restricts its generalizability to broader medical imaging tasks.

Our approach overcomes these limitations by integrating Monte Carlo Dropout into an ensemble of ResNet50, EfficientNet, and DenseNet models. Unlike UIOS, our method does not require specific annotations or manual thresholding. By performing multiple stochastic forward passes during inference, Monte Carlo Dropout estimates the variance of predictions, providing a measure of uncertainty. This uncertainty flags ambiguous cases for human review, improving reliability when the system encounters novel data outside its training distribution. Additionally, integrating UQ within an ensemble framework enhances interpretability, as uncertainty estimates can be analyzed alongside visual explanations generated by XGrad-CAM, ensuring that both the confidence and rationale behind predictions are transparent to clinicians.

### 2.5 Research Gaps

Existing segmentation methods rely heavily on pixel-level annotations or bounding boxes, increasing the time, cost, and expertise required for data preparation. Explainability techniques like CAM and Grad-CAM generate heatmaps but cannot produce pixel-level binary masks. At the same time, MDVA-GAN, despite addressing this limitation, suffers from instability and misclassification of unseen data. Open-set detection remains challenging, as models often fail to identify novel inputs outside the training distribution. Although UIOS estimates uncertainty for open-set scenarios, its dependence on specific annotations and manual thresholding limits its generalizability. Moreover, few methods integrate uncertainty quantification and visual explainability within the same framework, reducing reliability and transparency. This study addresses these gaps by developing a weakly supervised approach that uses only image-level labels to generate pixel-level annotations. By integrating Monte Carlo Dropout within an ensemble of ResNet50, EfficientNet, and DenseNet models, the system estimates prediction uncertainty to improve reliability in open-set scenarios. Additionally, XGrad-CAM enhances interpretability by providing visual explanations, ensuring both confidence and reasoning behind predictions are transparent and accessible.

## 3 Auto Annotation eXplainable (AXX) Model

The Auto Annotation eXplainable (AAX) Model integrates three pre-trained deep learning models (ResNet50, DenseNet, and EfficientNet) enhanced with

Monte Carlo Dropout for uncertainty estimation and XGrad-CAM for visual explainability. This ensemble framework is designed to classify chest X-ray images as "Diseased" or "Healthy" while providing robust prediction confidence and pixel-level annotations using only image-level labels. Combining these models ensures complementary feature extraction: ResNet50 captures low-level patterns, EfficientNet balances efficiency and accuracy, and DenseNet leverages dense connections to improve feature propagation.

The methodology is structured into three phases: the Training Phase, Inference and Output, and Decision Protocol, each aligning with one of the three main contributions: (1) ensemble learning for robust predictions, (2) weakly supervised pixel-level annotations using XGrad-CAM, and (3) uncertainty quantification for open-set detection.

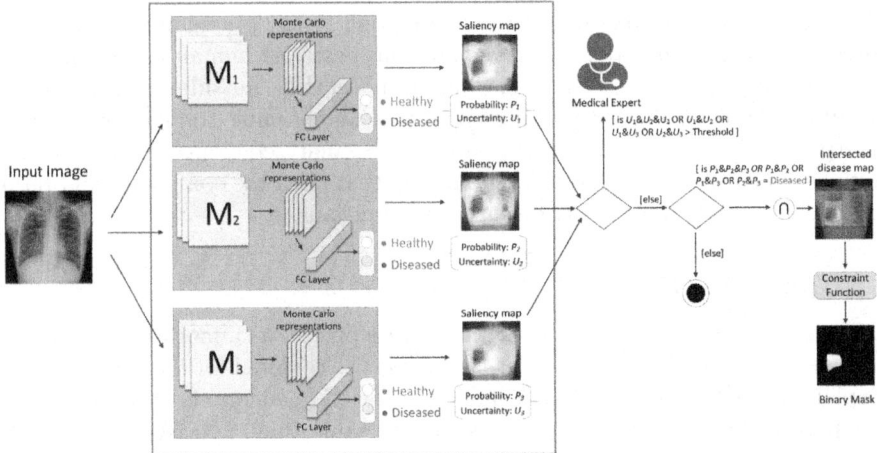

**Fig. 1. Architecture of the Auto Annotation eXplainable (AAX) Model.** The pipeline integrates ResNet50, EfficientNet, and DenseNet with Monte Carlo Dropout and XGrad-CAM. Images with high uncertainty in at least two models are flagged for expert review, while confident predictions are classified as "Healthy" or "Diseased." For diseased cases, intersected saliency maps generate a binary mask highlighting disease-specific regions.

Figure 1 provides a visual representation of the AAX architecture, illustrating the flow from input image analysis to final classification and annotation. This diagram highlights the role of each model, the generation of saliency maps, and the integration of uncertainty scores into the decision-making process.

### 3.1 Training Phase

Each model $M_i$ in the ensemble is independently trained on a dataset $D = \{(x_j, y_j)\}$, where $x_j$ is an input image and $y_j$ is the corresponding image-level label. The objective is to minimize a composite loss function $L$ that balances classification accuracy and prediction uncertainty, with Monte Carlo Dropout encouraging diverse predictions across stochastic forward passes. Formally, the loss function is:

$$L(M_i, D) = L_{\text{cls}}(M_i, D) + \lambda L_{\text{dropout}}(M_i, D)$$

where $L_{\text{cls}}$ is the cross-entropy classification loss, $L_{\text{dropout}}$ is the variance of predictions across stochastic passes, and $\lambda$ controls the balance between these components. This formulation enables each model to not only classify input images but also quantify the uncertainty associated with its predictions.

### 3.2 Inference and Output

During inference, an input image $x$ is processed concurrently through all three models. Each model $M_i$ performs multiple stochastic forward passes using Monte Carlo Dropout to produce three outputs:

- $p_i(x)$: The probability of the image being "Diseased" (derived from the softmax layer).
- $u_i(x)$: The uncertainty score is calculated as the standard deviation of the predictive distribution.
- $S_i(x)$: The saliency map generated using XGrad-CAM, highlighting regions that most influence the model's prediction.

These outputs are then aggregated to form the final prediction and pixel-level annotation, ensuring that the ensemble's collective judgment is both robust and interpretable.

### 3.3 Decision Protocol

The decision-making process integrates both consensus among models and uncertainty thresholding to improve reliability, particularly in open-set scenarios. The protocol is as follows:

**(a) Uncertainty Thresholding:**

- An uncertainty threshold $\theta$ is defined to identify ambiguous or novel cases. If at least two models produce uncertainty scores $u_i(x)$ above $\theta$, the image is flagged for expert review:

$$\sum_{i=1}^{3} \mathbb{I}[u_i(x) > \theta] \geq 2$$

**(b) Consensus-Based Prediction:**

- If uncertainty scores are below $\theta$, the ensemble classifies the image based on consensus. For a "Diseased" classification, at least two models must output probabilities $p_i(x) > 0.5$ with low uncertainty:

$$\sum_{i=1}^{3} \mathbb{I}[p_{\text{Diseased},i}(x) > 0.5 \wedge u_i(x) < \theta] \geq 2$$

- The saliency maps of the agreeing models are then intersected to generate a binary mask highlighting disease-specific features:

$$S_{\text{int}}(x) = \bigcap_{\{i|p_{\text{Diseased},i}(x)>0.5 \wedge u_i(x)<\theta\}} S_i(x)$$

- If at least two models classify the image as "Healthy" with low uncertainty, the image is labeled as "Healthy" without generating a saliency map:

$$\sum_{i=1}^{3} \mathbb{I}[p_{\text{Healthy},i}(x) > 0.5 \wedge u_i(x) < \theta] \geq 2$$

This protocol ensures that the system only provides pixel-level annotations when predictions are confident and consistent across multiple models, reducing the risk of erroneous annotations while maintaining interpretability.

### 3.4 Pseudocode

The operational framework of the AAX model is summarized in Algorithm 1, which outlines the process from input image analysis to final classification and annotation. The pseudocode ensures reproducibility and provides a clear reference for implementing the model.

---

**Algorithm 1. AXX Model**

---

**Require:** $X$: Set of input images, $\theta$: Uncertainty threshold, $M = M_1, M_2, M_3$: Set of pre-trained models
**Ensure:** Class predictions, uncertainty values, saliency maps, binary masks
1: **for** each image $x \in X$ **do**
2:    **for** each model $M_i \in M$ **do**
3:       Perform $K$ stochastic forward passes using MC Dropout
4:       Calculate mean probability $p_i(x)$ and uncertainty $u_i(x)$
5:       Generate saliency map $S_i(x)$ using XGrad-CAM
6:    **end for**
7:    **if** $\sum_{i=1}^{3} \mathbb{1}_{u_i(x)>\theta} \geq 2$ **then**
8:       Flag $x$ for expert review
9:    **else**
10:      **if** $\sum_{i=1}^{3} \mathbb{1}_{p_{\text{Diseased},i}(x)>0.5 \wedge u_i(x)<\theta} \geq 2$ **then**
11:         Classify $x$ as "Diseased"
12:         $S_{\text{int}}(x) \leftarrow \bigcap_{\{i|p_i(x)>0.5 \wedge u_i(x)<\theta\}} S_i(x)$
13:         Convert $S_{\text{int}}(x)$ to a binary mask
14:      **else**
15:         Classify $x$ as "Healthy"
16:      **end if**
17:    **end if**
18: **end for**

## 3.5 Summary

The AAX Model integrates ResNet50, DenseNet, and EfficientNet within an ensemble framework to reduce model variability and enhance classification accuracy. Each model, equipped with Monte Carlo Dropout and XGrad-CAM, processes input images to generate class probabilities, uncertainty scores, and saliency maps. This design enables weakly supervised pixel-level annotations using only image-level labels, eliminating the need for manual pixel annotations. By intersecting saliency maps from models that classify an image as "Diseased" with low uncertainty, the system produces a binary mask highlighting disease-specific regions. In cases where at least two models exhibit high uncertainty, the image is flagged for expert review, ensuring reliable performance in open-set scenarios. This approach directly addresses the identified research gaps, combining ensemble learning for robust predictions, weakly supervised annotation with XGrad-CAM, and uncertainty quantification through Monte Carlo Dropout to enhance reliability and interoperability.

## 4 Experiments

To evaluate the performance, reliability, and generalizability of the AXX Model, we conducted experiments on both medical and general image segmentation datasets. These experiments assess the model's ability to generate accurate pixel-level annotations using only image-level labels, as well as its capacity to quantify uncertainty and flag ambiguous cases. Using two distinct datasets we aim to highlight the model's versatility and robustness across different application domains.

### 4.1 Experimental Setup

The AXX Model was evaluated using two datasets:

- **TBX11K dataset for tuberculosis detection** [24]. It is a key resource for tuberculosis (TB) detection, comprising 11,200 high-resolution chest X-ray images (512 × 512 pixels) across four categories: healthy, active TB, latent TB, and non-TB unhealthy. Its diverse cases support robust diagnostic model development. Training primarily focuses on distinguishing 'healthy' from 'TB' using weakly supervised learning, eliminating the need for bounding boxes and allowing models to learn from global image features.
- **Fire Segmentation dataset for general image segmentation** [19]. It comprises video frames from YouTube, categorized into $Fire$ (27,460 images with visible fire pixels of varying intensities and spreads) and $Not_{Fire}$ (11,392 images without fire). All images are standardized to 256 × 256 pixels, ensuring consistency for training and evaluating fire detection models.

Each model (ResNet50, DenseNet, and EfficientNet) was trained using the Adam optimizer with a learning rate of 0.0001, a batch size of 16, and a maximum of 50 epochs. Early stopping was applied, terminating training if validation loss did not improve for five consecutive epochs. Monte Carlo Dropout was implemented during both training and inference, with 50 stochastic forward passes performed per image to estimate prediction uncertainty. The uncertainty threshold $\theta = 0.1$ was determined empirically using validation data to balance sensitivity and specificity in detecting ambiguous cases. Values lower than 0.1 led to increased misclassification of true positives as false positives, whereas values above 0.1 incorrectly classified false positives as true positives.

## 5 Results

### 5.1 Quantitative Results

The quantitative performance of the AAX Model is evaluated on two datasets: Fire and TBX11K. Results are presented separately for each dataset, with tables summarizing model accuracy and pixel-level annotation performance using IoU.

**Fire Dataset.** Table 1 shows the classification accuracy of the AAX model compared to baseline methods, while Table 2 reports IoU scores, reflecting pixel-level annotation performance. The AAX model achieved the highest accuracy and IoU, demonstrating the benefits of ensemble learning and weakly supervised pixel-level annotations. The low uncertainty flag rate indicates that the model maintained high confidence across most predictions while effectively identifying ambiguous cases.

**Table 1. Fire Dataset. Comparison of the AAX Model with State-of-the-Art Methods.** The table presents the average accuracy of the proposed AAX model compared to baseline and state-of-the-art methods. The AAX model achieves the highest accuracy, demonstrating the effectiveness of ensemble learning and weakly supervised annotations.

| Methodology | Average Accuracy (%) |
|---|---|
| SGD [36] | 92.27 |
| AlexNet [21] | 94.8 |
| DBN [17] | 95.0 |
| Inceptionv3 [40] | 93.6 |
| ForestResNet [42] | 92.0 |
| VGG19 [18] | 94.0 |
| ResNet50 | 93.7 |
| EfficientNet | 95.1 |
| DenseNet | 92.6 |
| **Proposed AAX** | **96.4** |

**Table 2. Fire Dataset. IoU Scores.** The table compares the IoU scores of individual models using XGrad-CAM and Monte Carlo Dropout with the proposed AAX model. The AAX model achieves the highest IoU, demonstrating improved pixel-level annotation accuracy through ensemble learning.

| Methodology | IoU (%) |
| --- | --- |
| ResNet50 with XGrad-CAM and Monte Carlo | 51.2 |
| DenseNet with XGrad-CAM and Monte Carlo | 49.6 |
| EfficientNet with XGrad-CAM and Monte Carlo | 55.1 |
| Proposed AAX Model | 64.7 |

**TBX11K Dataset.** Table 3 presents the classification accuracy for the TBX11K dataset, and Table 4 reports IoU scores, evaluating the model's ability to localize tuberculosis-related abnormalities. Despite the complexity of medical image annotation, the AAX model outperformed baseline methods, highlighting the effectiveness of using XGrad-CAM for weakly supervised pixel-level annotations. The uncertainty flag rate was higher than the Fire dataset, indicating that the model correctly identified more ambiguous or novel cases, which is essential in healthcare applications.

**Table 3. TBX11K. Comparison of the AAX Model with State-of-the-Art Methods.** The table presents the average accuracy of the proposed AAX model compared to baseline and state-of-the-art methods. The AAX model achieves the highest accuracy, demonstrating the effectiveness of ensemble learning and uncertainty quantification in medical image classification.

| Methodology | Average Accuracy (%) |
| --- | --- |
| ResNet50 without Monte Carlo Dropout [2] | 92.61 |
| CNN and Grad-CAM [32] | 92.5 |
| UIOS with Dirichlet distribution [46] | 88.27 |
| SSD [23] | 84.7 |
| RetinaNet [22] | 87.45 |
| Faster R-CNN [37] | 89.7 |
| FCOS [43] | 88.9 |
| ResNet50 with Monte Carlo Dropout | 89.1 |
| EfficientNet with Monte Carlo Dropout | 90.3 |
| DenseNet with Monte Carlo Dropout | 88.7 |
| **Proposed AAX** | **93.04** |

**Summary.** Across both datasets, the AAX model consistently achieved higher accuracy and IoU than individual models and MDVA-GAN. Combining ensem-

**Table 4. TBX11K. IoU Scores.** The table compares the IoU scores of the proposed AAX model with baseline and state-of-the-art methods. The AAX model achieves the highest IoU, demonstrating improved pixel-level annotation accuracy using ensemble learning and weakly supervised segmentation.

| Methodology | IoU (%) |
|---|---|
| MDVA-GAN [28] | 25.40 |
| VA-GAN [6] | 29.15 |
| Pre-trained ResNet50 (with XGrad-CAM) | 16.1 |
| DenseNet (with XGrad-CAM) | 15.0 |
| EfficientNet (with XGrad-CAM) | 23.3 |
| **Proposed AAX** | **36.07** |

ble learning, weakly supervised annotations, and uncertainty quantification contributed to this performance, validating the model's generalizability and reliability. Further interpretation of these results and their implications is provided in the Discussion section.

### 5.2 Qualitative Results

The qualitative performance of the AXX Model is illustrated using visual comparisons from both the TBX11K and Fire datasets. Each example shows the input image, ground truth mask, predictions from baseline methods, and the AAX model's pixel-level annotations. Saliency maps generated using XGrad-CAM highlight regions most influential to the model's predictions, demonstrating the interpretability of the annotations.

**(a) Fire Dataset**

The Fire Segmentation dataset was selected for its visually interpretable data, making it accessible to both experts and non-experts. This dataset tests the AAX model's ability to focus on class-specific features, such as fire pixels, demonstrating its versatility beyond medical imaging.

Figure 2 compares the AAX model with ResNet50, EfficientNet, and DenseNet, respectively. Each figure shows the input image, ground truth mask, saliency maps generated using XGrad-CAM, and binary masks derived from each model's predictions. The AAX model's binary masks consistently align more closely with the ground truth, demonstrating superior pixel-level annotation accuracy.

**(b) TBX11K Dataset**

The TBX11K dataset, designed for tuberculosis detection in chest X-rays, includes bounding-box annotations but lacks pixel-level labels. Despite being trained using only image-level labels, the AAX model successfully generates pixel-level masks, enhancing the dataset's utility for segmentation tasks and disease localization.

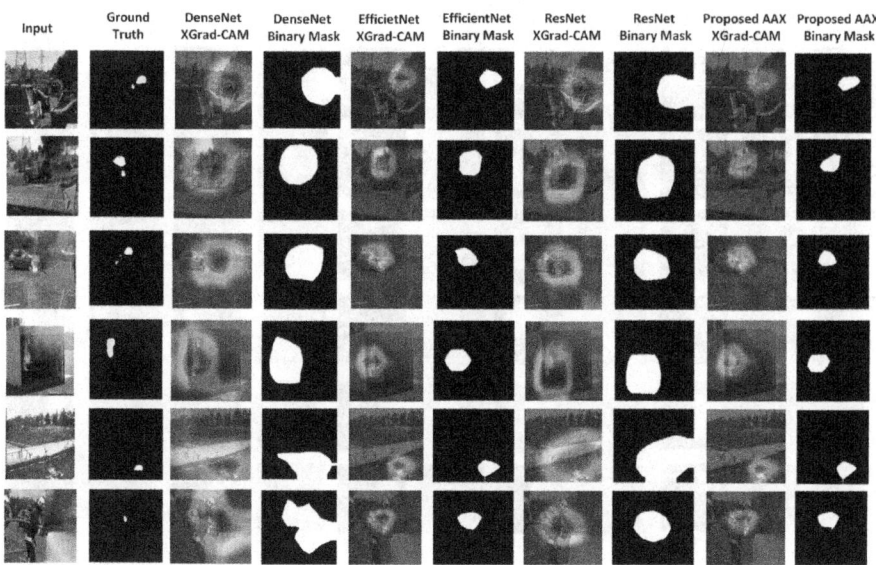

**Fig. 2.** Comparative Results of AAX Model and Baseline Methods on Fire Dataset. Visual comparison of input images, ground truth masks, and model outputs from DenseNet, EfficientNet, ResNet50, and the proposed AAX model. Columns show XGrad-CAM saliency maps and binary masks for each model. The AAX model's binary masks align more closely with ground truth annotations, demonstrating improved feature localization and pixel-level annotation accuracy.

Figure 3 compares the proposed AXX model with ResNet50, EfficientNet, and DenseNet, respectively. Each figure includes input images, ground truth bounding boxes, binary masks derived from these boxes, and saliency maps from each model. The AAX model's binary masks demonstrate greater alignment with the ground truth, accurately localizing tuberculosis regions despite the lack of pixel-level training data.

**Summary.** The qualitative results demonstrate that the AAX model produces more accurate pixel-level annotations compared to baseline methods, aligning closely with ground truth masks despite being trained using only image-level labels. The ensemble approach enhances feature localization, while uncertainty quantification ensures that ambiguous cases are flagged for expert review. These visual comparisons validate the model's three main contributions, showcasing its effectiveness in medical and general image segmentation tasks.

## 6 Discussion

(1) **Ensemble Learning Improves Prediction Accuracy:** The AAX model outperformed individual ResNet50, DenseNet, and EfficientNet models, confirming that ensemble learning reduces model variability and enhances classification

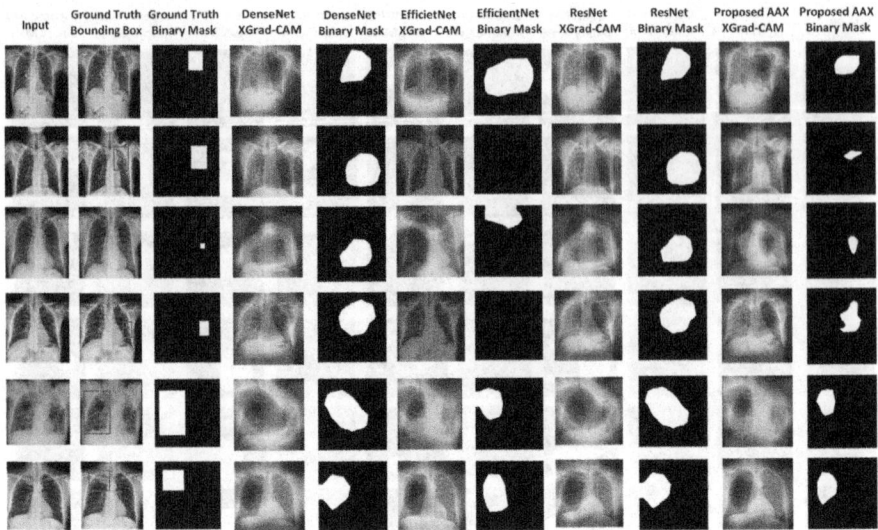

**Fig. 3. Comparative Results of AAX Model and Baseline Methods on TBX11K Dataset.** Visual comparison of chest X-ray inputs, ground truth annotations (bounding boxes and binary masks), and model outputs from DenseNet, EfficientNet, ResNet50, and the proposed AAX model. The AAX model's binary masks align more closely with ground truth annotations, demonstrating improved pixel-level localization despite being trained using only image-level labels.

accuracy. By combining the diverse feature extraction capabilities of the three models, the ensemble achieved higher accuracy and IoU scores, demonstrating the benefit of aggregating predictions from complementary architectures. This improvement was consistent across both medical (TBX11K) and general (Fire) image segmentation tasks, highlighting the robustness of the ensemble approach.

(2) **Weakly Supervised Annotations Align with Ground Truth:** Despite being trained using only image-level labels, the AAX model produced pixel-level masks that closely matched ground truth annotations. By leveraging XGrad-CAM to generate saliency maps and intersecting these maps across models with consistent predictions, the system effectively localized disease-specific regions. This weakly supervised approach eliminates the need for manual pixel-level annotations, reducing data preparation costs and making the model more scalable for real-world applications.

(3) **Uncertainty Quantification Enhances Open-Set Detection:** Monte Carlo Dropout enabled the model to estimate prediction uncertainty, improving reliability in open-set scenarios. By flagging highly uncertain images for expert review, the system reduced the risk of misclassification for novel or ambiguous cases. The relatively low uncertainty flag rates of 8.2% for TBX11K and 6.5% for Fire indicate that the model maintained high confidence in most predictions while still identifying challenging cases. This balance ensures both diagnostic

efficiency and safety, aligning with clinical requirements for reliable AI-assisted decision-making.

(4) **Generalizability Across Domains Demonstrates Model Robustness:** The AAX model's high performance on TBX11K and Fire datasets demonstrates its generalizability beyond medical imaging. The consistent improvement in accuracy and IoU across different domains validates the effectiveness of the ensemble approach and highlights the potential for broader applications, including industrial inspection, environmental monitoring, and object detection. This versatility positions the AAX model as a reliable solution for diverse segmentation tasks where pixel-level annotations are unavailable.

(5) **Visual Interpretability Builds Trust in Automated Predictions:** The saliency maps generated using XGrad-CAM provided visual explanations aligned with clinically relevant regions, enhancing the interpretability of model predictions. By intersecting saliency maps from models with consistent classifications, the system highlighted critical features with greater precision, reducing false positives and improving diagnostic clarity. The visual alignment between predicted masks and ground truth annotations reinforces the model's reliability, supporting its integration into healthcare workflows where explainability is essential for clinical trust.

(6) **Open-Set Detection Reduces the Risk of Misdiagnosis:** The model's ability to flag uncertain cases for expert review is crucial for ensuring reliability in real-world applications. By setting an uncertainty threshold of $\theta = 0.1$, the system effectively identified edge cases with subtle abnormalities or overlapping features. This mechanism prevents the model from making overconfident predictions on novel or ambiguous inputs, reducing the risk of misdiagnosis and supporting a collaborative workflow where AI assists rather than replaces human expertise.

(7) **Experimental Results Validate Key Contributions:** The experimental results directly support the three main contributions of this study. Ensemble learning improved prediction accuracy and consistency, weakly supervised pixel-level annotations generated interpretable masks without manual labels, and uncertainty quantification enabled reliable open-set detection. Together, these contributions address critical challenges in medical image analysis and demonstrate the potential of explainable AI to enhance diagnostic accuracy and efficiency.

# 7 Limitation and Challenges

While the proposed framework demonstrates strong performance in single-label classification tasks, several challenges remain, particularly in more complex scenarios. The system's performance in multi-label classification is limited, especially when known and unknown classes coexist. Although the uncertainty module effectively identifies novel patterns, the simultaneous presence of multiple labels can cause classification ambiguity, reducing prediction accuracy.

Additionally, the ensemble-based decision-making relies on the collective performance of ResNet50, EfficientNet, and DenseNet. If two out of the three models fail to converge adequately during training, the system's consensus mechanism is compromised, leading to decreased stability and predictive accuracy. This dependency highlights the need for robust training processes to ensure consistent performance across all ensemble members.

Addressing these limitations in future work will involve enhancing the model's multi-label classification capabilities, refining the uncertainty module to better differentiate between known and unknown classes, and optimizing the ensemble framework to reduce reliance on individual model performance.

## 8 Ethical Considerations

The development and deployment of the AAX Model are guided by principles of transparency, accountability, and fairness, particularly in high-stakes domains like medical imaging. By integrating XGrad-CAM for visual explanations, the model enhances interpretability, allowing users to understand and validate its predictions, thus fostering trust in AI-assisted decision-making. Monte Carlo Dropout for uncertainty quantification ensures that ambiguous cases are flagged for expert review, promoting human oversight and reducing the risk of misdiagnosis.

To mitigate bias, future work will focus on training and validating the model using diverse datasets to ensure consistent performance across different populations. Additionally, the system's reliance on image-level labels reduces the need for detailed annotations, minimizing the risk of exposing sensitive information during data labeling. The AAX model is intended *to support, not replace, human expertise, ensuring that AI serves as an assistive tool that enhances diagnostic accuracy and efficiency while maintaining ethical standards in healthcare and beyond.*

## 9 Conclusions and Future Work

This study introduced an automated data annotation system that improves classification accuracy, pixel-level annotations, and prediction reliability. *(1) Ensemble learning enhances accuracy and consistency:* Combining ResNet50, EfficientNet, and DenseNet reduced variability, achieving higher accuracy and IoU scores on both TBX11K and Fire datasets; *(2) Weakly supervised learning enables pixel-level annotations using only image-level labels:* By intersecting XGrad-CAM saliency maps, the system generated masks closely aligned with ground truth annotations, reducing annotation costs. *(3) Uncertainty quantification improves reliability in open-set scenarios:* Monte Carlo Dropout flagged ambiguous cases for expert review, maintaining high confidence while detecting novel inputs. Future work will focus on incremental learning to adapt to new data and advanced open-set detection methods to identify unseen classes, enhancing scalability and robustness across diverse applications.

## 10 Source Code

The source code for all experiments and the implementation of the Auto Annotation eXplainable Model is available at https://github.com/basmakhan11/Auto-Annotation-eXplainable-AAX-Model).

**Acknowledgments.** The work reported in this article was partially supported under the auspices of the UNESCO Chair on AI & VR by national funds through Fundação para a Ciência e a Tecnologia with references DOI:10.54499/UIDB/50021/2020, DOI:10.54499/DL57/2016/CP1368/CT0002 and 2022.09212.PTDC (XAVIER project).

## References

1. Abdar, M., et al.: A review of uncertainty quantification in deep learning: techniques, applications and challenges. Inf. Fusion **76**, 243–297 (2021)
2. Acharya, V., et al.: Ai-assisted tuberculosis detection and classification from chest x-rays using a deep learning normalization-free network model. Comput. Intell. Neurosci. **2022**(1), 2399428 (2022)
3. Aggarwal, A., Mittal, M., Battineni, G.: Generative adversarial network: an overview of theory and applications. Int. J. Inf. Manage. Data Insights **1**(1), 100004 (2021)
4. Alzubaidi, L., et al.: Towards risk-free trustworthy artificial intelligence: significance and requirements. Int. J. Intell. Syst. **2023**(1), 4459198 (2023)
5. Balasamy, K., Seethalakshmi, V., Suganyadevi, S.: Medical image analysis through deep learning techniques: a comprehensive survey. Wireless Pers. Commun. **137**(3), 1685–1714 (2024)
6. Baumgartner, C.F., Koch, L.M., Tezcan, K.C., Ang, J.X., Konukoglu, E.: Visual feature attribution using wasserstein gans. In: Proceedings of the IEEE Conference on Computer Vision and Pattern Recognition, pp. 8309–8319 (2018)
7. Chatterjee, S., Yassin, H., Dubost, F., Nürnberger, A., Speck, O.: Weakly-supervised segmentation using inherently-explainable classification models and their application to brain tumour classification. arXiv preprint arXiv:2206.05148 (2022)
8. Chen, Y., et al.: Generative adversarial networks in medical image augmentation: a review. Comput. Biol. Med. **144**, 105382 (2022)
9. Chen, Z., Tian, Z., Zhu, J., Li, C., Du, S.: C-cam: causal cam for weakly supervised semantic segmentation on medical image. In: Proceedings of the IEEE/CVF Conference on Computer Vision and Pattern Recognition, pp. 11676–11685 (2022)
10. Dhamija, T., Gupta, A., Gupta, S., Anjum, Katarya, R., Singh, G.: Semantic segmentation in medical images through transfused convolution and transformer networks. Appl. Intell. **53**(1), 1132–1148 (2023)
11. Duell, J., Fan, X., Burnett, B., Aarts, G., Zhou, S.M.: A comparison of explanations given by explainable artificial intelligence methods on analysing electronic health records. In: 2021 IEEE EMBS International Conference on Biomedical and Health Informatics (BHI), pp. 1–4. IEEE (2021)
12. Galbusera, F., Cina, A.: Image annotation and curation in radiology: an overview for machine learning practitioners. Europ. Radiol. Exp. **8**(1), 11 (2024)

13. Guo, C., Pleiss, G., Sun, Y., Weinberger, K.Q.: On calibration of modern neural networks. In: International Conference on Machine Learning, pp. 1321–1330. PMLR (2017)
14. Hou, J., Yan, C., Li, R., Huang, Q., Fan, X., Lin, F.: Lung nodule segmentation algorithm with smr-unet. IEEE Access **11**, 34319–34331 (2023)
15. Hsieh, C., et al.: Mdf-net for abnormality detection by fusing x-rays with clinical data. Sci. Rep. **13**(1), 15873 (2023)
16. Javed, H., Imran, M., Nazir, Q.u.A., Fatima, I., Humayun, A.: Increased trend of unnecessary use of radiological diagnostic modalities in Pakistan: radiologists perspective. Int. J. Quality Health Care **31**(9), 712–716 (2019)
17. Kaabi, R., Sayadi, M., Bouchouicha, M., Fnaiech, F., Moreau, E., Ginoux, J.M.: Early smoke detection of forest wildfire video using deep belief network. In: 2018 4th International Conference on Advanced Technologies for Signal and Image Processing (ATSIP), pp. 1–6. IEEE (2018)
18. Khan, A., Hassan, B., Khan, S., Ahmed, R., Abuassba, A.: Deepfire: a novel dataset and deep transfer learning benchmark for forest fire detection. Mob. Inf. Syst. **2022**(1), 5358359 (2022)
19. Kumoro, R.N., Anandaputra, L.W., Nugraha, R.F.D., Wahyono, W.: Efficient wildfire detection framework based on artificial intelligence using convolutional neural network and multi-color filtering. In: 2024 IEEE Conference on Artificial Intelligence (CAI), pp. 470–475. IEEE (2024)
20. Lambert, B., Forbes, F., Doyle, S., Dehaene, H., Dojat, M.: Trustworthy clinical ai solutions: a unified review of uncertainty quantification in deep learning models for medical image analysis. Artif. Intell. Med., 102830 (2024)
21. Lee, W., Kim, S., Lee, Y.T., Lee, H.W., Choi, M.: Deep neural networks for wild fire detection with unmanned aerial vehicle. In: 2017 IEEE International Conference on Consumer Electronics (ICCE), pp. 252–253. IEEE (2017)
22. Lin, T.Y., Goyal, P., Girshick, R., He, K., Dollár, P.: Focal loss for dense object detection. In: Proceedings of the IEEE International Conference on Computer Vision, pp. 2980–2988 (2017)
23. Liu, W., Anguelov, D., Erhan, D., Szegedy, C., Reed, S., Fu, C.Y., Berg, A.C.: Ssd: single shot multibox detector. In: Computer Vision–ECCV 2016: 14th European Conference, Amsterdam, The Netherlands, October 11–14, 2016, Proceedings, Part I 14, pp. 21–37. Springer (2016)
24. Liu, Y., Wu, Y.H., Ban, Y., Wang, H., Cheng, M.M.: Rethinking computer-aided tuberculosis diagnosis. In: Proceedings of the IEEE/CVF Conference on Computer Vision and Pattern Recognition, pp. 2646–2655 (2020)
25. Ma, X., Niu, Y., Gu, L., Wang, Y., Zhao, Y., Bailey, J., Lu, F.: Understanding adversarial attacks on deep learning based medical image analysis systems. Pattern Recogn. **110**, 107332 (2021)
26. Monshi, M.M.A., Poon, J., Chung, V.: Deep learning in generating radiology reports: a survey. Artif. Intell. Med. **106**, 101878 (2020)
27. Moreira, C., Chou, Y.L., Hsieh, C., Ouyang, C., Pereira, J., Jorge, J.: Benchmarking instance-centric counterfactual algorithms for xai: from white box to black box. ACM Comput. Surv. **57**(6), 1–37 (2025)
28. Nawaz, M., Al-Obeidat, F., Tubaishat, A., Zia, T., Maqbool, F., Rocha, A.: Mdvagan: multi-domain visual attribution generative adversarial networks. Neural Comput. Appl. **35**(11), 8035–8050 (2023)
29. Neves, J., et al.: Shedding light on ai in radiology: a systematic review and taxonomy of eye gaze-driven interpretability in deep learning. Eur. J. Radiol. **172**, 111341 (2024)

30. Nguyen, A., Yosinski, J., Clune, J.: Deep neural networks are easily fooled: High confidence predictions for unrecognizable images. In: Proceedings of the IEEE Conference on Computer Vision and Pattern Recognition, pp. 427–436 (2015)
31. Osman, Y.B.M., Li, C., Huang, W., Elsayed, N., Ying, L., Zheng, H., Wang, S.: Semi-supervised and self-supervised collaborative learning for prostate 3d mr image segmentation. In: 2023 IEEE 20th International Symposium on Biomedical Imaging (ISBI), pp. 1–4. IEEE (2023)
32. Pasa, F., Golkov, V., Pfeiffer, F., Cremers, D., Pfeiffer, D.: Efficient deep network architectures for fast chest x-ray tuberculosis screening and visualization. Sci. Rep. **9**(1), 6268 (2019)
33. Prabakaran, B.S., Ostrowski, E., Shafique, M.: Refit: a framework for refinement of weakly supervised semantic segmentation using object border fitting for medical images. In: International Symposium on Visual Computing, pp. 44–55. Springer (2023)
34. Puttagunta, M., Ravi, S.: Medical image analysis based on deep learning approach. Multimed. Tools Appl. **80**(16), 24365–24398 (2021)
35. Rahimi, S., Oktay, O., Alvarez-Valle, J., Bharadwaj, S.: Addressing the exorbitant cost of labeling medical images with active learning. In: International Conference on Machine Learning in Medical Imaging and Analysis (2021)
36. Rahul, M., Saketh, K.S., Sanjeet, A., Naik, N.S.: Early detection of forest fire using deep learning. In: 2020 IEEE region 10 conference (TENCON), pp. 1136–1140. IEEE (2020)
37. Ren, S., He, K., Girshick, R., Sun, J.: Faster r-cnn: towards real-time object detection with region proposal networks. IEEE Trans. Pattern Anal. Mach. Intell. **39**(6), 1137–1149 (2016)
38. Selvaraju, R.R., Cogswell, M., Das, A., Vedantam, R., Parikh, D., Batra, D.: Gradcam: visual explanations from deep networks via gradient-based localization. Int. J. Comput. Vision **128**, 336–359 (2020)
39. Singh, P., et al.: Shifting to machine supervision: annotation-efficient semi and self-supervised learning for automatic medical image segmentation and classification. Sci. Rep. **14**(1), 10820 (2024)
40. Sousa, M.J., Moutinho, A., Almeida, M.: Wildfire detection using transfer learning on augmented datasets. Expert Syst. Appl. **142**, 112975 (2020)
41. Sun, L., Wang, J., Huang, Y., Ding, X., Greenspan, H., Paisley, J.: An adversarial learning approach to medical image synthesis for lesion detection. IEEE J. Biomed. Health Inform. **24**(8), 2303–2314 (2020)
42. Tang, Y., Feng, H., Chen, J., Chen, Y.: Forestresnet: A deep learning algorithm for forest image classification. In: Journal of Physics: Conference Series, vol. 2024, p. 012053. IOP Publishing (2021)
43. Tian, Z., Shen, C., Chen, H., He, T.: Fcos: fully convolutional one-stage object detection. In: Proceedings of the IEEE/CVF International Conference on Computer Vision, pp. 9627–9636 (2019)
44. Velmurugan, M., Ouyang, C., Moreira, C., Sindhgatta, R.: Developing a fidelity evaluation approach for interpretable machine learning. arXiv preprint arXiv:2106.08492 (2021)
45. Wang, H., Jin, Q., Li, S., Liu, S., Wang, M., Song, Z.: A comprehensive survey on deep active learning in medical image analysis. Medical Image Analysis, p. 103201 (2024)
46. Wang, M., Lin, T., Wang, L., Lin, A., Zou, K., Xu, X., Zhou, Y., Peng, Y., Meng, Q., Qian, Y., et al.: Uncertainty-inspired open set learning for retinal anomaly identification. Nat. Commun. **14**(1), 6757 (2023)

47. Wei, Y., Gan, Z., Li, W., Lyu, S., Chang, M.C., Zhang, L., Gao, J., Zhang, P.: Maggan: High-resolution face attribute editing with mask-guided generative adversarial network. In: Proceedings of the Asian Conference on Computer Vision (2020)
48. Worden, K., Tsialiamanis, G., Cross, E., Rogers, T.: Artificial neural networks. In: Machine Learning in Modeling and Simulation: Methods and Applications, pp. 85–119. Springer (2023)
49. Xu, J., De Mello, S., Liu, S., Byeon, W., Breuel, T., Kautz, J., Wang, X.: Groupvit: semantic segmentation emerges from text supervision. In: Proceedings of the IEEE/CVF Conference on Computer Vision and Pattern Recognition, pp. 18134–18144 (2022)
50. Xu, L., Ouyang, W., Bennamoun, M., Boussaid, F., Xu, D.: Multi-class token transformer for weakly supervised semantic segmentation. In: Proceedings of the IEEE/CVF Conference on Computer Vision and Pattern Recognition, pp. 4310–4319 (2022)
51. Yang, C.C.: Explainable artificial intelligence for predictive modeling in healthcare. J. Healthcare Inform. Res. **6**(2), 228–239 (2022)
52. Yi, X., Walia, E., Babyn, P.: Generative adversarial network in medical imaging: a review. Med. Image Anal. **58**, 101552 (2019)
53. Zhou, B., Khosla, A., Lapedriza, A., Oliva, A., Torralba, A.: Learning deep features for discriminative localization. In: Proceedings of the IEEE Conference on Computer Vision and Pattern Recognition, pp. 2921–2929 (2016)
54. Zhu, J.Y., Park, T., Isola, P., Efros, A.A.: Unpaired image-to-image translation using cycle-consistent adversarial networks. In: Proceedings of the IEEE International Conference on Computer Vision, pp. 2223–2232 (2017)

**Open Access** This chapter is licensed under the terms of the Creative Commons Attribution 4.0 International License (http://creativecommons.org/licenses/by/4.0/), which permits use, sharing, adaptation, distribution and reproduction in any medium or format, as long as you give appropriate credit to the original author(s) and the source, provide a link to the Creative Commons license and indicate if changes were made.

The images or other third party material in this chapter are included in the chapter's Creative Commons license, unless indicated otherwise in a credit line to the material. If material is not included in the chapter's Creative Commons license and your intended use is not permitted by statutory regulation or exceeds the permitted use, you will need to obtain permission directly from the copyright holder.

# Assessing the Value of Explainable Artificial Intelligence for Magnetic Resonance Imaging

Giada Frasson[1], Matteo Rizzo[1]($\boxtimes$), Marco Salvatore Nobile[1], Amalia Lupi[2], and Emilio Quaia[2]

[1] Ca' Foscari University of Venice, Venice, Italy
869359@stud.unive.it, {matteo.rizzo,marco.nobile}@unive.it
[2] University of Padua, Padua, Italy
{amalia.lupi,emilio.quaia}@unipd.it

**Abstract.** Recent advancements in Artificial Intelligence (AI) have often improved the accuracy of medical diagnostics in several fields, such as cancer detection and diagnosing cardiovascular or neuromuscular diseases. However, the opaque nature of AI decision-making can limit its adoption in the clinical setting, as physicians require clear and interpretable explanations to trust these tools. To address this issue, the field of eXplainable Artificial Intelligence (XAI) aims to clarify the rationale behind AI predictions while ensuring compliance with ethical standards and advanced regulations such as the GDPR and the AI Act. This study applies multiple explainability methods to a diagnostic support model for Distal Myopathies (DMs), a rare neuromuscular disorder marked by subtle, early-stage tissue alterations. Beyond classification, our approach generates detailed explanations for the model's predictions. We propose novel techniques, including a hierarchical occlusion method and an ensemble framework that combines individual explanations to produce refined, interpretable visualizations. Feedback from expert radiologists is used to assess the effectiveness of these methods, highlighting their potential to enhance trust and usability in clinical practice. Our results show that pretrained convolutional networks achieve high classification accuracy, exceeding 88%, with perfect recall in identifying affected cases, while underscoring the need for adaptive and user-centric approaches to explainability in AI-driven diagnostic tools.

**Keywords:** Deep learning (DL) · eXplainable Artificial Intelligence (XAI) · Magnetic Resonance Imaging (MRI) · Neuromuscular Disorders (NMD) · Distal Myopathies

## 1 Introduction

Artificial Intelligence (AI) has revolutionized medicine in recent years, driving significant advancements across various domains, from drug design and discovery [14,26] to clinical decision support [6,23]. In particular, AI has demonstrated

---

G. Frasson and M. Rizzo—Equal contribution.

remarkable potential as a decision-support tool in medical diagnostics [15,16]. A study by McKinney et al. [11] revealed that an AI system for breast cancer diagnosis used to interpret mammograms reduced false positives and false negatives by 5.7% and 9.4%, respectively. Multiple studies observed that AI systems can outperform human experts in some specific diagnostic tasks, enhancing physicians' capabilities through AI-assisted analysis. For instance, Kim et al. [7] showed an AI system with higher sensitivity in diagnosing breast cancer compared to radiologists, effectively identifying early-stage cases. Similarly, Haenssle et al. [5] showed that their AI model achieved superior diagnostic performance for melanoma cases, outperforming most, though not all, dermatologists involved in the study.

Despite these promising results, widespread adoption of AI in clinical practice is hindered by a critical challenge: physicians are unlikely to trust an algorithm's decision without a clear understanding of its reasoning process. To address this issue, the field of eXplainable Artificial Intelligence (XAI) has emerged, aiming to enhance the interpretability of AI models. XAI provides insights into AI decision-making, making models more transparent and comprehensible to human users. This topic is particularly sensitive in medicine, where ethical considerations and regulatory frameworks necessitate accountability and fairness. For example, the European Union's General Data Protection Regulation (GDPR, Article 15) and AI Act grant patients the right to understand how and why decisions affecting them are made. A comprehensive review by Van der Velden et al. [24] discusses various explainability methods applied to medical imaging across different anatomical regions, emphasizing the growing importance of XAI in healthcare. Our study focuses on deep-learning-based analysis of Magnetic Resonance Imaging (MRI) scans to diagnose Distal Myopathies (DMs), a rare Neuromuscular Disease (NMD). Radiological diagnosis of this condition requires significant expertise, as early-stage cases often exhibit subtle tissue alterations that can be challenging for less experienced observers to detect. AI systems can assist radiologists by identifying these patterns and providing supporting evidence for their predictions. Our objective is to move beyond classification and generate explanations that clarify the rationale behind the model's decisions and investigate the effectiveness of such explanations. However, the existing literature presents several gaps: (1) current explainability methods for MRI-based diagnosis have primarily focused on common diseases with large datasets, with limited attention given to rare conditions such as DMs; (2) existing saliency-based methods often generate noisy, low-resolution explanations that are difficult for clinicians to interpret; and (3) few studies have evaluated the practical clinical relevance of XAI outputs through direct user studies with radiologists. To fill these gaps, we introduce two novel explainability techniques tailored for MRI-based diagnosis of rare neuromuscular disorders: a hierarchical occlusion method and an ensemble explainability strategy. The hierarchical occlusion provides a multiscale view of regional importance by systematically masking image patches at various resolutions to improve the localization and clarity of the model's attention. The ensemble explainability strategy aggregates multiple explanation maps (e.g.,

GradCAM methods) to produce more robust and stable outputs that reduce artifacts and enhance interpretability. We benchmark these approaches against state-of-the-art methods and conduct a user study with expert radiologists to validate the clinical utility of the resulting explanations. Their feedback assesses the AI-generated explanations' trustworthiness, interpretability, and usability, providing critical insights into their potential adoption in real-world medical practice. The following research questions drive our study:

- **RQ1:** How accurately can Deep Learning (DL) models classify MRI scans for DMs, and what factors influence their misclassification?
- **RQ2:** How do expert radiologists perceive AI-generated explanations' interpretability and clinical relevance?
- **RQ3:** How does the radiologist's experience impact the interpretation and trust in explainability techniques?
- **RQ4:** What improvements are needed to enhance AI explainability for clinical adoption?

Our code is publicly available: https://github.com/matteo-rizzo/xai-for-mri.

## 2 Related Work

NMDs comprise a vast and heterogeneous group of pathologies affecting muscles and the nerves that control them [12]. These conditions manifest in childhood and adulthood and present significant diagnostic challenges due to their variable clinical features. Diagnosis involves an evaluation of patient history and symptoms, supplemented by instrumental examinations such as electromyography, muscle imaging, genetic analyses, and muscle biopsy.

Recent research has explored the potential of AI to improve diagnostic accuracy for NMDs. Pineros et al. [17] and related work on muscle MRI [19] underscore the utility of AI in this domain. Verdù-Dìaz et al. [25] analyzed patterns of muscle fatty replacement in T1-weighted MRIs of 976 pelvic and lower limb scans quantifying fatty infiltration with the Mercuri score and applying a Random Forest classifier to achieve an accuracy of 95.7% compared to experts. Yang et al. [27] developed a model for differentiating dystrophinopathies from other muscular diseases using 432 thigh-focused MRI cases, with the ResNet50 architecture achieving 91% accuracy, surpassing expert diagnoses ranging between 80% and 84%. Complementary studies include Felisaz et al. [4], who compared multiple Machine Learning (ML) models for predicting fat fraction and muscle water T2 from MRI texture analysis, and Fabry et al. [3], who employed a 1-Lipschitz neural network on whole-body MRI examinations to distinguish facioscapulohumeral dystrophy from myositis with accuracies between 69% and 77%. While these studies demonstrate the promise of AI in diagnosing NMDs, they also highlight a critical gap: the explainability of model predictions. Only a few works, notably Yang et al. [27], have integrated explainability techniques into their models. This gap motivates the need to explore XAI methods in rare conditions such as DM systematically. XAI comprises a range of techniques and methodologies to interpret complex models' decision-making processes, particularly deep neural networks that are often regarded as opaque *black boxes*. Despite their impressive predictive performance, these models lack transparency, hindering clinical adoption. The field of XAI remains underdeveloped, lacking a universally accepted taxonomy a situation partly attributed to divergent definitions of *interpretability* and *explainability* [20,21,28]. In this work, we adopt the taxonomy proposed by Linardatos et al. [9], which categorizes methods based on dimensions such as model specificity (model-specific vs model-agnostic) and explanation scope (local vs global).

Among the well-established approaches for XAI, Class Activation Maps (CAMs) and their extensions have received significant attention. CAMs, introduced by Zhou et al. [30], are post-hoc, local, and model-specific techniques that visualize the discriminative regions used by a CNN for prediction. By performing global average pooling on the final convolutional feature maps and projecting the resulting weights back onto these maps, CAM highlights the regions most influential to the final decision. However, this method is limited to specific network architectures and only provides explanations from the last convolutional layer. To address these limitations, GradCAM [22] was developed. GradCAM extends CAM by incorporating the gradients of the class score concerning feature maps from any convolutional layer, thereby generating a class-discriminative localization map via global averaging of these gradients. Nonetheless, GradCAM may struggle to localize multiple instances of an object within an image accurately. GradCAM++ [1] refines this approach by computing a weighted average of the pixel gradients, while HiResCAM [2] further improves explanation fidelity by highlighting only the regions actively contributing to the class score. Comparative analyses indicate that GradCAM tends to produce broader explanations, whereas GradCAM++ and HiResCAM, mainly when applied to architectures such as ResNet50v, may occasionally highlight extraneous background regions though HiResCAM consistently yields more focused and detailed explanations.

In a contrasting paradigm, SHapley Additive Explanations (SHAP) [10] adopts a game-theoretic perspective to assign an importance value to each input feature based on its marginal contribution to a prediction. As a post-hoc, model-agnostic method, SHAP approximates complex models with an additive explanation model that satisfies properties such as local accuracy, missingness, and consistency. Despite the computational challenges inherent in exact Shapley value computation, practical approximations have rendered SHAP a powerful tool for both local and global interpretability.

Another noteworthy approach within XAI is occlusion, a sensitivity analysis methodology that evaluates the impact of masking specific input regions on model predictions. Initially introduced by Zeiler et al. [29], occlusion systematically masks parts of an input image using a sliding window, thereby identifying regions whose absence leads to a significant decrease in prediction confidence or a change in classification outcome. Although conceptually straightforward, occlusion is computationally intensive, requiring multiple forward passes through the network. Thus, careful selection of parameters such as window size, stride, and occlusion value is crucial; larger windows reduce computational cost at the expense of granularity, while smaller windows offer finer resolution but require more computations. Occlusion is particularly relevant to our work as we propose a novel occlusion algorithm that works at multiple levels of granularity.

Collectively, these approaches from CAM-based visualizations to SHAP and occlusion methods provide a robust foundation for interpreting the decisions of complex DL models. These particular strategies are the base for our ensemble method.

## 3 The Use Case: Distal Myopathies

In the context of NMDs, the utility of muscle MRI has already been assessed in the diagnostic work-up and in monitoring the progression of muscle involvement. In fact, given the rarity of these disorders, a thorough clinical, histological, and imaging investigation should be carried out since the clinical heterogeneity and broad genetic spectrum of these conditions often make it difficult to reach a defined molecular diagnosis. In this scenario, muscle MRI proves helpful in identifying different patterns of muscle involvement. Nonetheless, such clinically and genetically heterogeneous conditions require knowledge about radiological characteristics based on distinct genetic mutations to improve diagnostic accuracy. Specific patterns are most recognizable in patients presenting mild phenotypes, with individual muscles selectively affected. In contrast, extensive and severe muscle involvement and very mild and initial involvement do not allow for clear pattern detection, even if an expert radiologist can identify them. For this purpose, different AI approaches could be implemented to improve diagnostic performance, and their explainability will be discussed in this work.

### 3.1 Dataset

Our proprietary dataset comprises 529 T1-weighted MR images of the lower limbs, capturing each patient's right and left sides. It contains seven patients affected by DM and six healthy controls. To augment the dataset, each image is divided into two separate images corresponding to the left and right lower limbs. Although this division could introduce bias, mainly when the disease affects only one side, consultation with an experienced radiologist confirmed that the benefits of a larger dataset outweigh this risk. An example of an affected lower limb is shown in Fig. 1a, while an example of a healthy lower limb is presented in Fig. 1b. A side-by-side comparison of both cases can be seen in Fig. 1.

### 3.2 Preprocessing

Our preprocessing pipeline is illustrated in Fig. 2. Central to the pipeline is a cropping algorithm designed to extract the minor crop that encloses the patient's body from each MRI. Initially, the algorithm enhances the image contrast using Contrast Limited Adaptive Histogram Equalization (CLAHE) [18] to address

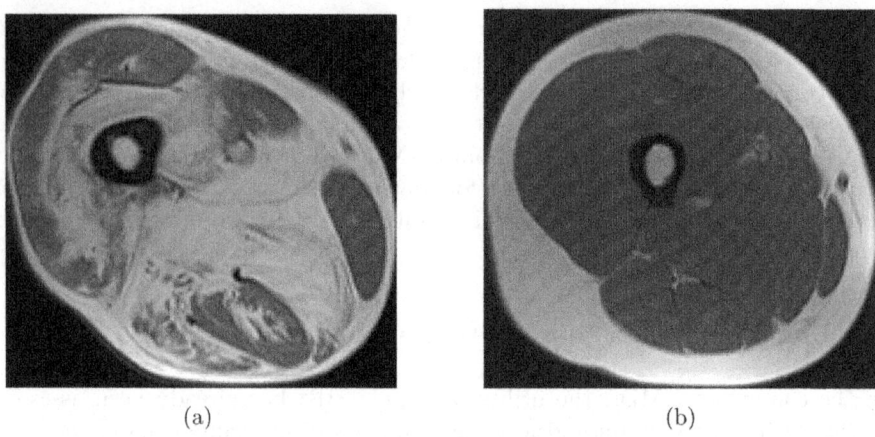

**Fig. 1.** Comparison of affected (a) and healthy (b) lower limb MRIs.

the uneven brightness and contrast inherent in the original MRIs. The enhanced image is then binarized by applying a threshold set at the mean intensity, isolating the image's significant regions. Despite producing a clear binary outline of the patient's body, this process can introduce internal holes and noise. To resolve these issues, the outer boundaries of the white regions are detected, with smaller contours filtered out in favor of retaining the two largest contours, which typically correspond to the pelvis and the legs. Subsequently, the rough contours are refined by computing their convex hulls, yielding smoother and more accurate boundaries. The background, which in MRIs often appears as shades of dark gray rather than pure black, is removed by multiplying the original image by its binary mask, thus preventing any confusion between background and anatomical structures. Finally, the smallest bounding box enclosing the refined contours is determined using OpenCV's `boundingRect`, and the image is cropped accordingly. Another significant challenge is the heterogeneity in image dimensions, as the scans range from pelvises to calves. Since the model requires fixed-size inputs of 224 × 224 pixels, directly resizing the images is not viable because it could introduce artifacts and distort anatomical proportions. To address this, expert guidance was followed in splitting pelvis images into left and right sections, given that the central pelvis area primarily contains organs rather than muscles. Images smaller than 224 × 224 pixels are padded to achieve the desired dimensions, while those larger than 224 × 224 pixels are segmented into 224 × 224 tiles. If an image exceeds the required size in one dimension only, it is divided into two tiles; if it exceeds in both dimensions, it is partitioned into four tiles. This approach minimizes the number of generated tiles, thereby reducing the risk of bias from mislabeling healthy regions in patients with the disease. The significant overlap between the tiles further ensures that critical border features are preserved. Table 1 displays the dataset structure after completing these preprocessing operations.

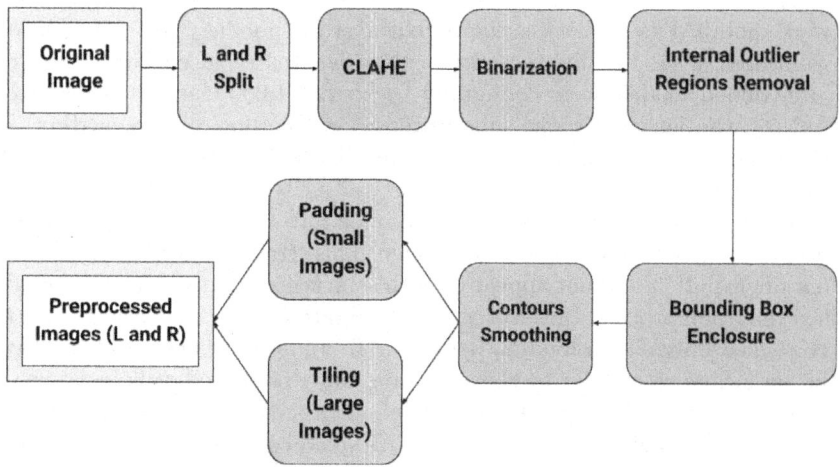

**Fig. 2.** Workflow of the preprocessing pipeline.

**Table 1.** Dataset structure after preprocessing.

|          | Before preprocessing | After preprocessing | Number of tiles |
|----------|----------------------|---------------------|-----------------|
| Healthy  | 202                  | 404                 | 438             |
| Affected | 327                  | 654                 | 969             |
| **Total**| **529**              | **1058**            | **1407**        |

## 4  Deep Learning Models

Due to the limited size of the dataset, a transfer learning approach was adopted. ResNet50 was chosen based on its strong performance in a similar application reported in [27]. Although both studies address a binary classification task, the previous work focused on differentiating between two diseases, whereas our objective is to distinguish between healthy and affected individuals. ResNet18 the lightest Residual network available in PyTorch was also experimented with. Given the dataset's size, this choice maintained consistency within the model family while reducing complexity and mitigating the risk of overfitting.

Several modifications were made to adapt the pre-trained models to our specific task. First, the input layer was adjusted because the PyTorch pre-trained models are designed for 3-channel images, while our MRI images are in grayscale (1-channel). To incorporate the pre-trained weights appropriately, they were summed across the channels, following the intuition that for an RGB image with equal channel values, $R \cdot w_0 + G \cdot w_1 + B \cdot w_2$ simplifies to $R \cdot (w_0 + w_1 + w_2)$. Next, the global average pooling layer was removed from the network architecture. This change was necessary because techniques such as GradCAM and HiResCAM converge to CAM when applied to networks without global average pooling on the last convolutional feature maps. Accordingly, the architectures described in

[2] were modified by replacing the global average pooling with an additional convolutional layer. Finally, the output classifier was replaced. Since the original pre-trained models were configured to predict 1,000 classes (as trained on ImageNet), the final layer was substituted to enable binary classification. The resulting modified models are ResNet18v and ResNet50v, with "v" denoting the variant.

Before training, the dataset was partitioned into training and test sets using a patient-based split to prevent data leakage. This strategy ensured that the data from a single patient did not appear in both sets, thereby preserving the integrity of the evaluation process. However, given the limited number of patients, the test set contained only one individual per class. To address the potential sensitivity of the performance metrics to this selection, an experienced radiologist recommended including a healthy patient with a higher body fat percentage in the test set, thereby challenging the model and providing a conservative lower bound for evaluation.

Due to the dataset imbalance, ROSE oversampling was applied to the training set to equalize the class instances [13]. Furthermore, the feature extraction layers were frozen, and only the network's classifier layer was trained using a cross-validation framework with early stopping to reduce the risk of overfitting. Since the number of patients was limited, it was not feasible to reserve a separate validation set with one healthy and one affected individual; instead, each patient was treated as a separate fold in the cross-validation process. During training, data augmentation techniques provided by PyTorch such as random brightness and contrast modifications were applied to artificially increase the size and diversity of the training dataset. These augmentations, chosen in consultation with a domain expert, were designed to reflect the natural variations typically encountered in MRI images, thereby improving the model's generalization capability.

## 5 Novel XAI Methods

### 5.1 Hierarchical Occlusion

As previously described, Occlusion is a practical yet computationally intensive sensitivity analysis technique, particularly when a high level of detail is desired. Moreover, selecting appropriate parameters such as window size, stride, and occlusion value is nontrivial, as these parameters may require extensive tuning and may not be universally optimal for all inputs. To address these challenges, a hierarchical occlusion algorithm was developed. The central idea is to start with relatively large occlusion windows and progressively reduce their size, thereby achieving a balance between computational cost and the desired granularity of the analysis. The initial concept involved leveraging an existing occlusion function, such as the `Occlusion` class provided by Captum [8]. However, this implementation exhibited two significant limitations. First, it does not permit the selection of an alternative metric, as it defaults to using the difference in the model's output. Second, it lacks the flexibility to perform occlusion on a designated subarea of the image, which is a requirement for the hierarchical approach. Consequently, a custom design and implementation were pursued.

The proposed hierarchical occlusion algorithm performs occlusion at multiple levels of granularity. Still, it restricts the refinement process to those windows that, at a coarser level, induce a change in the network's output. Several strategies were explored in the development process. Inspired by Captum, an initial approach employed the difference in the model's raw output before and after occlusion as the metric. However, combining results across different levels proved problematic, as each level inherently possesses a distinct value range; larger windows tend to produce more pronounced differences than smaller windows, thereby complicating direct comparisons. Using the difference in probability bound in the interval $[0, 1]$ appeared to be a more interpretable alternative, similar issues in merging results across varying granularities persisted. Smaller windows naturally yield more minor differences and may erroneously be interpreted as less significant. Furthermore, establishing a universal threshold for further refinement is challenging, given that each image exhibits its own range of output differences. To overcome these issues, an alternative metric focused on identifying windows that cause actual change in the network's classification. This approach is more stringent, as it disregards minor variations in output and concentrates solely on those occlusion windows that result in a class switch. By assigning a binary value (1 for windows that induce a change in the predicted class and 0 for those that do not), the results from different levels of granularity can be aggregated by summation. The outcome is a composite map that indicates, at various levels of detail, the regions whose occlusion induces a change in the network's prediction.

The algorithm initially computes occlusions using larger windows across the entire image to contain the computational cost. It then refines the analysis by applying occlusion with progressively smaller windows exclusively on those regions where the initial occlusions resulted in a change in the network's output. Algorithm 1 provides a high-level algorithm description. Several parameters are critical in our implementation. We provide the model used for classification, the input image, and the target class for occlusion. The initial window size and stride are chosen based on the input dimensions (in our case, $224 \times 224$ pixels), and they are halved at each successive level of granularity until a predefined minimum window size is reached. The occlusion window is filled with a specified value (zero in our implementation).

Selecting optimal parameters is challenging due to the heterogeneous nature of the dataset, which contains images of body parts with varying sizes, and the necessity of balancing computational efficiency with the quality of the resulting occlusion maps. For instance, given that the network input is $224 \times 224$ pixels, the initial parameters were set to a window size of 56 and a stride of 28, with a minimum window size of 7. These settings are intended to capture relevant details without being excessively small, which might fail to cover more extensive regions of interest. In practice, the hierarchical algorithm frequently yielded void outputs, meaning that none of the occlusion windows produced a change in the network's prediction. This phenomenon was particularly notable for images of pelves and thighs and, to a lesser extent, calves and knees. In response, the window size was increased for images that initially produced void outputs, thereby reducing computational overhead by avoiding unnecessary recalculations across all images while preserving finer occlusion maps when available.

---

**Algorithm 1.** Hierarchical Occlusion

---
1: **Input:** Model, image, target class, initial window size, stride, minimum window size, occlusion value
2: $hierarchical\_map, areas \leftarrow$ compute occlusion at level $n$ over the entire image
3: **while** $areas \neq \emptyset$ **do**
4: $\quad single\_map, areas \leftarrow$ compute occlusion at level $n-1$ restricted to the regions in **areas**
5: $\quad hierarchical\_map \leftarrow hierarchical\_map + single\_map$
6: $\quad n \leftarrow n - 1$
7: **end while**
8: **return** $hierarchical\_map$

---

Table 2 summarizes the results obtained using the hierarchical occlusion methods. As expected, increasing the window size generally reduces the occurrence of void outputs. However, an increase in window size does not necessarily correlate with increased importance, as many new activations may result from occluding a large portion of the patient's body. An additional experiment was conducted with an exaggeratedly large window size of 200. Although a larger window is more likely to affect network predictions, Table 2 indicates that, particularly for the *affected* class, many images still do not exhibit a response to occlusion. This observation is counterintuitive since it would be expected that occluding regions in an affected image would more readily switch the prediction to *healthy*, whereas the converse should be more difficult.

A classical, non-hierarchical occlusion method was implemented to investigate this phenomenon further using the difference in probability as the metric. Figures 3a and 3b display the results of the initial occlusion windows for images classified as *affected* and *healthy*, respectively, using ResNet18. The numerical values annotated on the images represent the percentage difference between the original and occluded probabilities. A positive difference signifies a decrease in the network's confidence, whereas a negative value indicates an increase. Notably, the initial occlusions in Fig. 3a remained classified as *affected* with high confidence despite the occluded regions corresponding to healthy fat. A similar pattern was observed for the *healthy* images in Fig. 3b. This suggests that the network may misinterpret subcutaneous fat as infiltrated fat when analyzed in isolation, potentially indicating an inherent bias toward predicting the *affected* class.

Table 2. Occlusion results across different occlusion window sizes.

| Model | Prediction | Occlusion Window Size | | | | | | | |
|---|---|---|---|---|---|---|---|---|---|
| | | 56 | | 86 | | 112 | | 200 | |
| | | Void | Not Void | Void | Not Void | Void | Not Void | Void | Not Void |
| Resnet18v | Affected | 109 | 62 | 93 | 78 | 84 | 87 | 81 | 90 |
| | Healthy | 17 | 39 | 7 | 49 | 0 | 56 | 0 | 56 |
| Resnet50v | Affected | 102 | 67 | 88 | 81 | 88 | 81 | 55 | 114 |
| | Healthy | 22 | 36 | 12 | 46 | 6 | 52 | 0 | 58 |

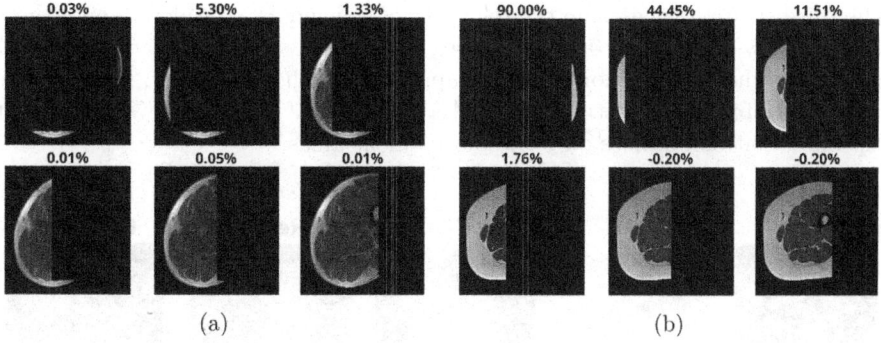

**Fig. 3.** Occlusion windows comparison for affected (a) and healthy (b) MRIs.

### 5.2 Ensemble of Explainability Methods

Given that no single XAI technique consistently outperforms the others, an ensemble approach is adopted to integrate multiple explainability methods. By aggregating the outputs of diverse models, the ensemble capitalizes on the strengths of each technique while compensating for their limitations, yielding more robust and reliable explanations. In this work, the ensemble is constructed by combining the non-zero heat maps produced by the various explainability methods with void occlusion maps excluded from the aggregation. Preliminary experiments combined outputs from all the explainability techniques; however, GradCAM was ultimately excluded from the final ensemble because its tendency to produce wider activation regions was found to dilute the more focused insights provided by the other methods. The proposed ensemble strategy therefore involves GradCAM++, HiResCAM, SHAP, and Hierarchical Occlusion. Before integration, a preprocessing step is applied to the heatmaps to reduce noise and enhance interpretability. Rather than operating at the pixel level, the heatmaps are partitioned into $7 \times 7$ square blocks, with each block assigned a value equal to the average of its constituent pixels. Negative values are removed to focus exclusively on areas that contribute positively to the model's prediction. Finally, the data are normalized to the interval $[0, 1]$, ensuring that the outputs from different techniques are on a comparable scale. Three ensemble strategies were investigated, each with a different degree of restrictiveness. Figure 4 compares the base explainability methods and our three proposed ensemble strategies. The first strategy computes the average of the heatmaps and selects regions where the average exceeds 0.5, a procedure analogous to majority voting; this approach tends to yield broader areas of evidence. The second strategy is based on an intersection approach: heatmaps are first filtered to retain only activation values above 0.2, and the ensemble is then defined as the common regions across all methods. While emphasizing regions with unanimous support, this intersection approach may exclude significant areas according to all but one method. The third strategy focuses on the relevance of saliency by considering only those pixels with values above 0.7 and aggregating pixels selected by at least $n - 1$ of the $n$ methods. This more selective approach highlights smaller, more precise regions of interest. This study adopted a threshold of 0.7 to achieve a stringent ensemble that emphasizes only the most salient areas.

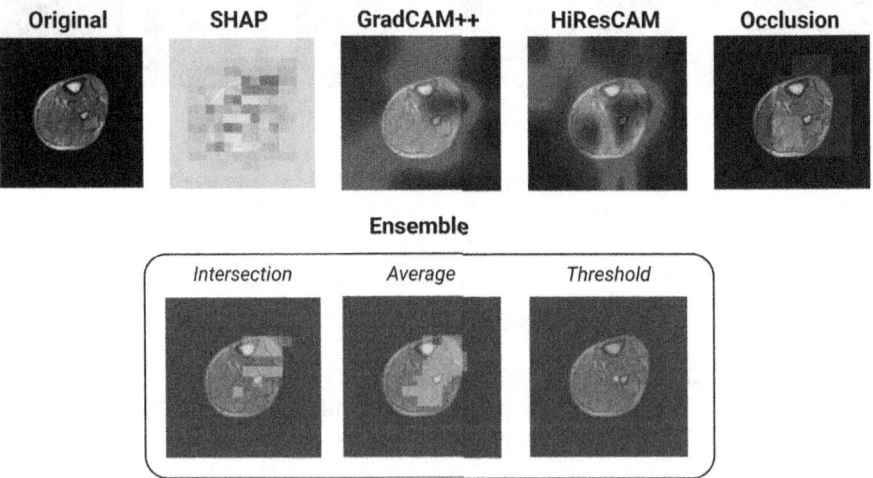

**Fig. 4.** Comparison of base explainability methods and proposed ensemble strategies.

## 6 Results

### 6.1 Model Accuracy

The performance of the AI models was quantified using standard classification metrics, including accuracy, precision, recall, and F1-score. As summarized in Table 3, both ResNet18v and ResNet50v demonstrated strong classification performance, achieving accuracies close to 90%. The high recall scores indicate that both models reliably identified all positive class instances while precision remained competitive, leading to robust F1 scores.

**Table 3.** Performance metrics for the final models evaluated on the test set.

| Model | Accuracy | Precision | Recall | F1-score |
|---|---|---|---|---|
| ResNet18v | 88.55% | 84.80% | 100% | 91.77% |
| ResNet50v | 89.43% | 85.80% | 100% | 92.36% |

Analysis of the confusion matrices (Fig. 5) reveals that both networks consistently identified all instances of the positive class, while misclassifications predominantly occurred within the *healthy* class. A closer inspection suggests that images misclassified as *affected* often exhibited prominent subcutaneous fat, which may have contributed to the incorrect classification. This indicates that the model may rely on fat distribution patterns as a proxy for pathology. This unintended bias could be addressed through refined preprocessing techniques such as explicit muscle segmentation or feature calibration.

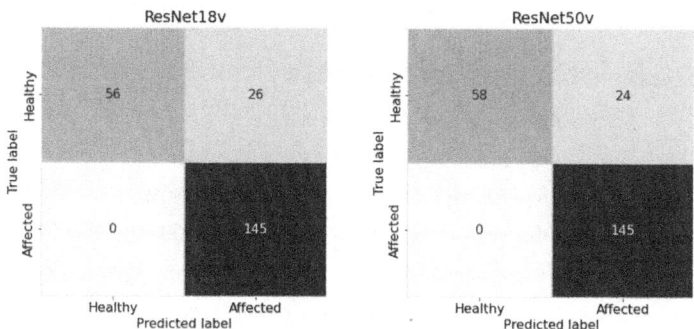

**Fig. 5.** Confusion matrices for ResNet18v and ResNet50v.

## 6.2 Explainability Methods

Beyond quantitative performance, this study investigated the interpretability and clinical relevance of AI-generated explanations through a structured evaluation involving seven radiologists, six residents, and one experienced specialist. The assessment required participants to classify the original MRIs and rate the explainability outputs on a five-point Likert scale. The key aspects assessed were diagnostic usefulness, appropriateness of highlighted regions, ease of interpretation, and overall reliability.

**Diagnostic Accuracy and Observer Performance.** Table 4 summarizes the accuracy of the radiologists compared to the most experienced observer (Observer G). The average diagnostic accuracy was 80%, with notable variability among residents. While some observers closely aligned with the network's predictions, others misclassified most cases. This variability suggests that some instances are inherently ambiguous, even for human experts, highlighting the potential for AI assistance in diagnostic workflows. Despite the high recall of the AI models, misclassified instances occurred among the network and human observers. Analysis of confusion matrices (Fig. 6) reveals that ambiguous cases lacked conclusive explainability outputs, which may explain neutral or negative ratings regarding their reliability. This finding underscores the subjectivity inherent in XAI techniques and the challenge of ensuring trust in AI-generated explanations.

**Table 4.** Diagnostic accuracy of radiologists on the test subset.

| Physician  | Experience (years) | Accuracy |
|------------|--------------------|----------|
| Observer A | 1                  | 60%      |
| Observer B | 1                  | 90%      |
| Observer C | 2                  | 60%      |
| Observer D | 2                  | 80%      |
| Observer E | 2                  | 100%     |
| Observer F | 3                  | 90%      |
| Observer G | 9                  | 100%     |

**Perception and Evaluation of Explainability Methods.** Figure 7 illustrates the votes for different explainability techniques. No method emerged as the clear favorite, as all received at least three votes. GradCAM and SHAP were among the most frequently selected methods. However, a deeper examination of individual preferences shows that Observer F strongly favored SHAP, while GradCAM was chosen by only three out of seven observers. Notably, experienced

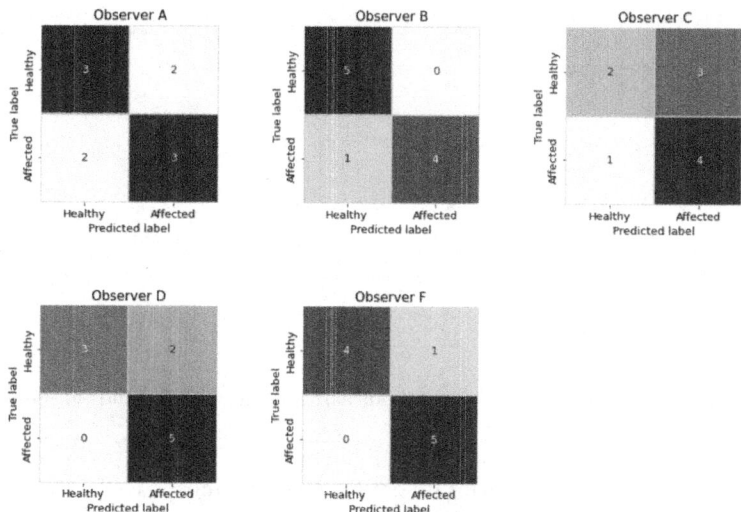

**Fig. 6.** Confusion matrices for the observers who committed classification errors.

radiologists did not favor these methods but slightly preferred GradCAM++. This discrepancy suggests that experience influences how explainability methods are interpreted, with expert users valuing refined and localized attributions over broader attention-spanning visualizations. The evaluations highlight significant variability in how different explainability techniques were perceived. Some observers consistently selected GradCAM, while those preferring ensemble methods tended to exclude it. Ensemble-based approaches, though receiving fewer overall votes, were regarded as producing more diagnostically relevant explanations by the experienced radiologist. This preference divergence underscores the importance of tailoring XAI methods to different user expertise levels. Further analysis of the explainability evaluations is presented in Fig. 8, illustrating the distribution of observer votes for each image. The chart highlights the high variability in observer preferences, ranging from a maximum agreement of 42% (three out of seven observers) for images 1, 9, and 10, to complete disagreement for image 3, where each radiologist selected a different explainability method. This lack of consensus underscores the subjective nature of explainability assessments and the need for more tailored, adaptable XAI techniques.

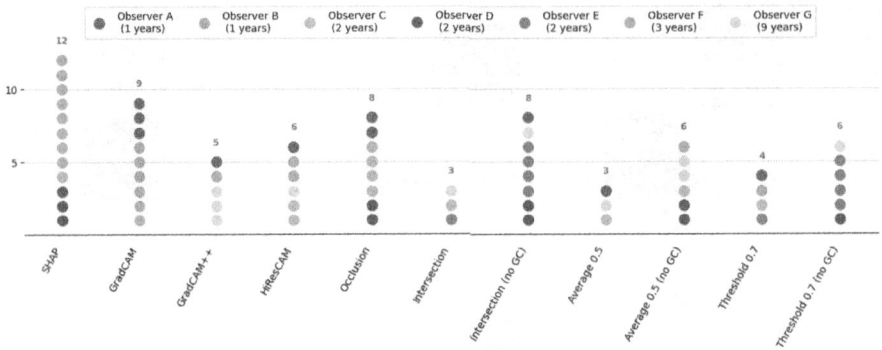

**Fig. 7.** Preferences for explainability methods across dataset. GC stands for GradCAM.

**Explainability Ratings and Observer Preferences.** To further analyze the perceptions of explainability techniques, we examined the distribution of scores across four evaluation criteria: (i) *Usefulness of the highlighted area for diagnosis*, (ii) *Appropriateness of the highlighted region size*, (iii) *Ease of interpretation*, and (iv) *Perceived diagnostic reliability*. Figure 9 presents the score distributions. The median ratings were predominantly neutral or low, indicating limited confidence in the AI-generated explanations. Notably, SHAP and the "Average 0.5" ensemble received the highest median ratings (4) for diagnostic usefulness. In contrast, occlusion-based methods received lower scores, likely due to their occasional failure to generate clear explanations. For perceived diagnostic reliability, most methods received scores concentrated in the lower range, except for the SHAP and "Average 0.5" ensemble, which exhibited symmetric distributions around neutral values. This suggests an overall hesitation in fully trusting the AI-generated explanations. During the evaluation, there were five cases where the AI correctly suggested a diagnosis to an observer who initially misclassified the input. However, in none of these cases did the observer change their decision after reviewing the AI explanations, reinforcing the challenge of aligning AI interpretability with clinical reasoning.

**Comparison of Individual vs. Ensemble Methods.** We grouped the evaluations into Individual and Ensemble methods to assess the effectiveness of ensemble approaches. Figure 10 shows the proportion of observer preferences for each category. Although Individual methods received slightly more votes overall, experienced radiologists slightly preferred ensemble techniques. Figure 11 displays score distributions for the two groups. Individual methods exhibited higher variability, with a skew towards lower values, while Ensemble methods had a more stable and neutral distribution. Interestingly, despite observers showing a preference for Individual methods, they rated Ensemble methods higher for perceived reliability, suggesting that while ensemble techniques are less familiar, they may provide more clinically meaningful insights.

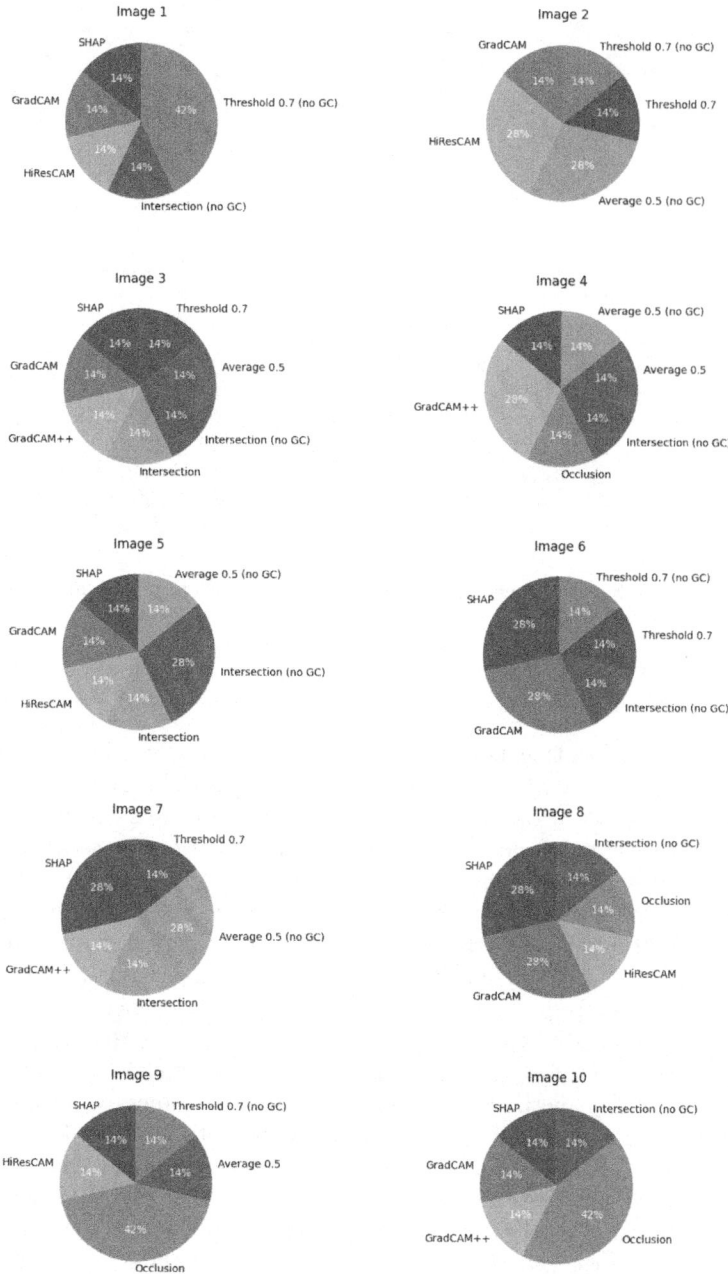

**Fig. 8.** Observer preferences for explainability methods across different images.

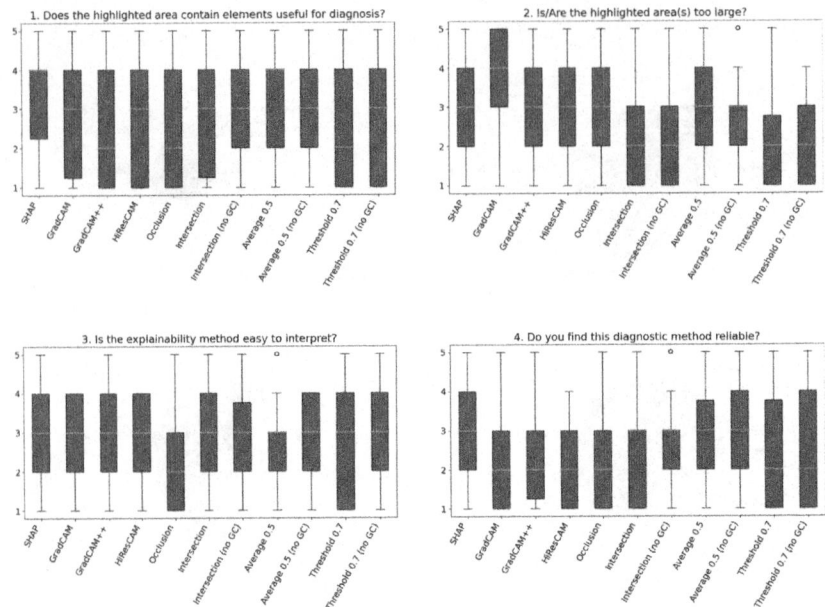

**Fig. 9.** Distributions of observer ratings (1 to 5) across different explainability methods. GC stands for GradCAM.

### 6.3 Discussion

Our evaluation shows that both ResNet18v and ResNet50v achieve strong classification performance, with accuracies exceeding 88% and perfect recall in identifying affected cases. However, a closer examination of misclassified instances reveals that these models occasionally base their predictions on secondary visual cues such as fat distribution that do not directly correspond to pathological markers. This reliance on non-specific features suggests the presence of unintended biases. It underscores the potential value of incorporating refined preprocessing techniques, such as explicit muscle segmentation or domain-aware feature extraction, to enhance model robustness and medical relevance.

We conducted a structured user study involving seven radiologists to assess the practical utility of AI-generated explanations. Participants evaluated different explainability methods regarding diagnostic usefulness, appropriateness, and reliability. Results indicate substantial variability in how different techniques were perceived. While methods like GradCAM and SHAP were found to be helpful in some instances, their effectiveness was highly dependent on both the observer's experience and the specific image context. Despite receiving fewer total votes, experienced radiologists consistently saw ensemble-based approaches producing more focused and diagnostically relevant explanations. A key insight from the study is the divergence in preferences between radiology residents and experienced practitioners. Less experienced users tended to favor broad and visually prominent explanation maps, which offered a general sense

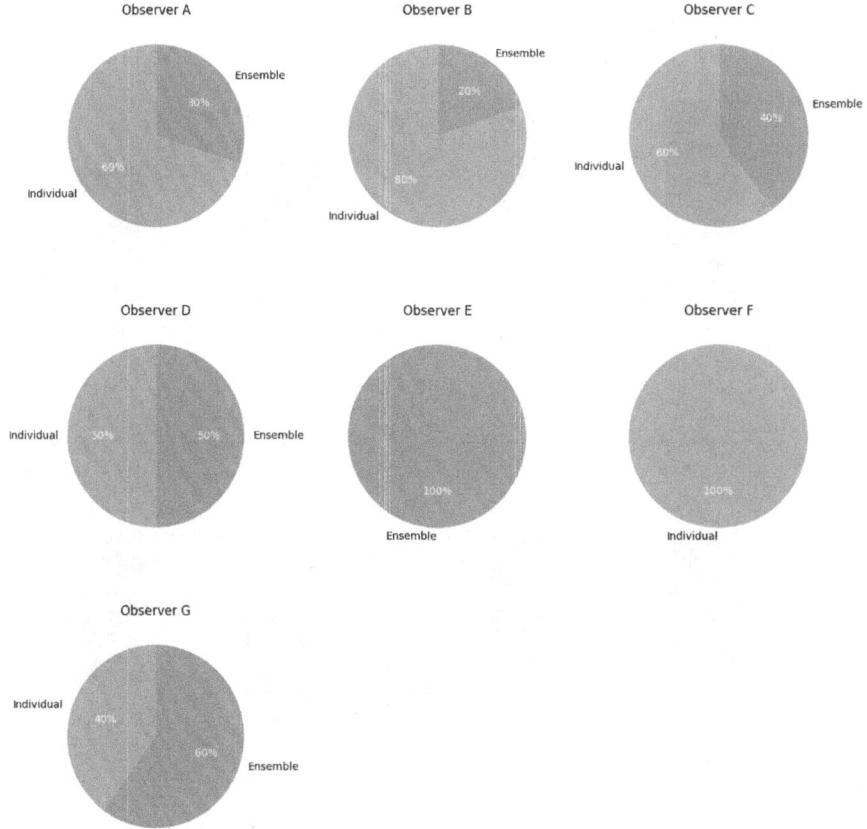

**Fig. 10.** Proportional distribution of observer preferences.

of model focus. In contrast, senior radiologists preferred precise and localized attributions that aligned more closely with clinically relevant structures. This distinction highlights the critical role of domain expertise in interpreting explainability outputs and suggests the need for adaptable visualization strategies that cater to different levels of clinical experience. Our findings suggest that no single explainability method can universally satisfy all users. Instead, there is a clear need for adaptive, user-centric approaches that balance clarity, precision, and flexibility. Potential improvements include: (i) integrating anatomical priors to reduce model reliance on irrelevant features, (ii) refining saliency techniques to reflect clinical reasoning patterns better, and (iii) developing interactive, customizable explainability tools that allow clinicians to tailor outputs to their diagnostic preferences.

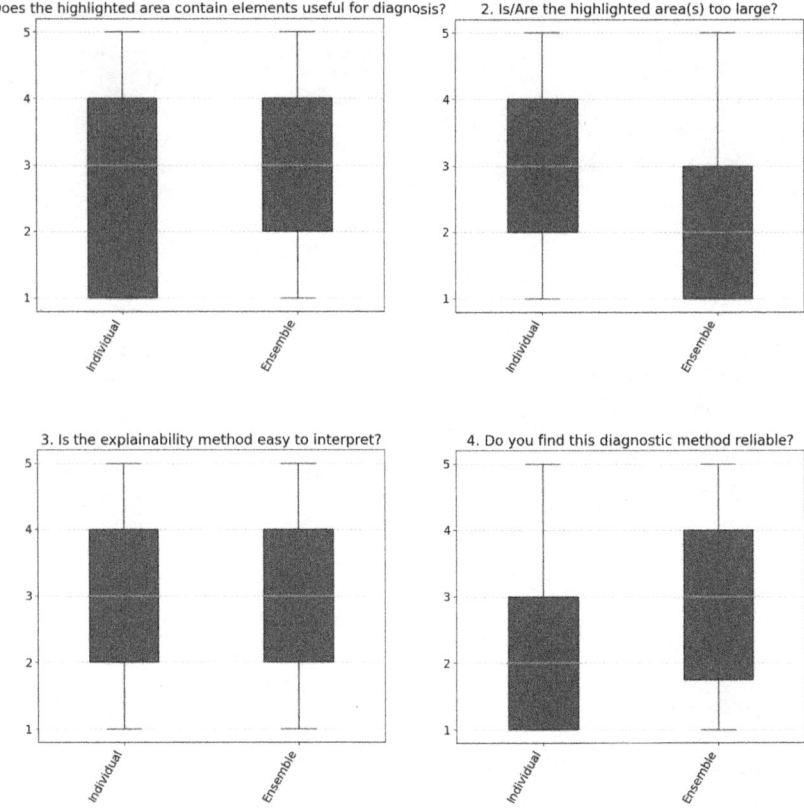

**Fig. 11.** Score distributions for Individual and Ensemble explainability methods.

## 7 Limitations

While this study provides valuable insights into AI models' diagnostic performance and explainability for DMs, several limitations must be acknowledged. First, though representative, the dataset used for training and evaluation may not fully capture the diversity of real-world MRI scans. Variability in imaging protocols, scanner models, and patient demographics could influence model generalizability. Future studies should validate these findings on larger, more heterogeneous datasets to ensure robustness across clinical settings. Second, the structured evaluation of explainability methods involved a limited number of radiologists, with only one experienced specialist. While this provided valuable perspectives on how expertise influences the interpretation of AI explanations, a broader sample of radiologists with varying experience levels would be necessary to derive more generalizable conclusions. Additionally, inter-observer variability suggests that user preferences for explainability methods may be highly individualized, emphasizing the need for adaptive and customizable XAI frameworks. Another limitation relates to the reliance on retrospective image assessments rather than real-time clinical workflows. The physicians reviewed AI-generated explanations in a controlled experimental setting, which may not fully reflect how these methods would be used in actual diagnostic practice. Future studies should investigate the impact of AI explanations in prospective settings where radiologists integrate them into routine clinical decision-making. Furthermore, while the study examined various explainability techniques, it did not explore the full spectrum of available XAI methods or assess how combinations of techniques could enhance interpretability. Given the variability in observer preferences, future research should investigate hybrid approaches that dynamically combine multiple explanation strategies to better align with radiologists' diagnostic reasoning. Finally, the study primarily focused on interpretability and diagnostic performance without considering the proposed methods' computational efficiency and real-time feasibility. Some explainability techniques, particularly ensemble approaches, may be computationally expensive, potentially limiting their practical deployment in clinical environments. Future work should explore optimization strategies to balance explainability quality with computational constraints to ensure seamless integration into medical imaging workflows.

## 8 Conclusion and Future Work

In this work, we applied a DL approach to diagnose DM, a rare NMD. We investigated the feasibility of AI-based diagnostic support coupled to explainability methods to give physicians a rationale for predictions. Due to the limited size of the dataset, we exploited transfer learning. According to our results, two variants of the ResNet neural network achieved high classification performance, with nearly 90% accuracy on the test set, despite the inherent challenges posed by heterogeneous imaging data. Notably, misclassifications were often associated with increased subcutaneous fat, suggesting that the models may rely on secondary visual cues rather than strictly pathological features. The evaluation of explainability techniques including SHAP, GradCAM, occlusion-based methods, and ensemble approaches revealed no universally superior method. Instead, effectiveness varied significantly across different images and observers, underscoring the subjective nature of AI interpretability. Less experienced radiologists often favored broader visualizations, while more experienced specialists preferred refined, localized explanations, as observed in their inclination toward ensemble methods. This discrepancy highlights the importance of tailoring explainability frameworks to different expertise levels, reinforcing the need for adaptive, user-centric AI interfaces. Moreover, the study reveals an essential gap in trust between radiologists and AI-generated explanations. Even when AI models correctly identified cases misclassified by human observers, physicians rarely adjusted their diagnoses based on the provided explanations. This finding suggests that increasing the transparency and clinical alignment of explainability techniques is crucial for fostering trust in AI-assisted diagnostics.

While our findings demonstrate the potential of AI-based diagnostic support for DMs, several challenges warrant further investigation. A key priority is refining explainability techniques to better align with radiologists' diagnostic reasoning. This includes improving saliency methods to highlight pathologically relevant regions more precisely and exploring multimodal feature attributions that combine spatial, textual, and temporal information for enhanced interpretability. Additionally, the reliance of AI models on secondary visual cues, such as fat distribution, suggests the need for more sophisticated preprocessing strategies, such as anatomical priors and domain-aware feature extraction, to ensure that model predictions are based on clinically meaningful features. Another critical direction is the development of adaptive explainability frameworks that account for varying levels of radiological expertise. Our study indicates that radiology residents and experienced specialists interpret AI explanations differently, suggesting that a one-size-fits-all approach may not be optimal. Future research should focus on designing interactive diagnostic tools that allow users to customize explainability outputs based on their preferences and expertise. Such tools could include user-adjustable explanation granularity, interactive overlays, and AI-guided annotation support to bridge the gap between automated analysis and human decision-making. Furthermore, improving trust in AI-generated explanations remains an essential challenge. Even when AI models correctly identified cases misclassified by human observers, radiologists did not modify their decisions based on the provided explanations. This underscores the need for human-centered AI design that fosters interpretability, transparency, and trust. Future studies should investigate how to optimize the presentation of AI explanations to encourage meaningful engagement and integration into clinical workflows. This may involve usability testing with radiologists in real-world diagnostic settings and iterative refinement of explanation delivery mechanisms. Finally, the clinical deployment of AI-driven diagnostic tools necessitates robust validation across diverse patient populations and imaging protocols. While our study provides insights into using DL models for DM diagnosis, further validation on larger and more heterogeneous datasets is needed to ensure generalizability. Future research should also explore prospective clinical trials where AI-assisted diagnostic recommendations are evaluated in real-time clinical decision-making scenarios. Establishing standardized evaluation metrics and regulatory frameworks for AI explainability in medical imaging will be crucial for facilitating safe and effective adoption in practice. While DL models show strong potential for supporting DM diagnosis, their successful clinical integration depends on performance improvements and refining interpretability methods to meet medical professionals' expectations. Bridging this gap will require a multidisciplinary effort involving advances in XAI, domain-specific feature extraction, and targeted user training to ensure that AI-driven diagnostic tools are accurate and clinically reliable.

# References

1. Chattopadhay, A., Sarkar, A., Howlader, P., Balasubramanian, V.N.: Gradcam++: generalized gradient-based visual explanations for deep convolutional networks. In: 2018 IEEE Winter Conference on Applications of Computer Vision (WACV), pp. 839–847. IEEE (2018)
2. Draelos, R.L., Carin, L.: Use hirescam instead of grad-cam for faithful explanations of convolutional neural networks. arXiv preprint arXiv:2011.08891 (2020)
3. Fabry, V., et al.: A deep learning tool without muscle-by-muscle grading to differentiate myositis from Facio-Scapulo-Humeral dystrophy using MRI. Diagn. Interv. Imag. **103**(7–8), 353–359 (2022)
4. Felisaz, P.F., et al.: Texture analysis and machine learning to predict water t2 and fat fraction from non-quantitative MRI of thigh muscles in facioscapulohumeral muscular dystrophy. Eur. J. Radiol. **134**, 109460 (2021)
5. Haenssle, H.A., et al.: Man against machine: diagnostic performance of a deep learning convolutional neural network for dermoscopic melanoma recognition in comparison to 58 dermatologists. Ann. Oncol. **29**(8), 1836–1842 (2018)
6. Jang, H., et al.: Classification of Alzheimer's disease leveraging multi-task machine learning analysis of speech and eye-movement data. Front. Hum. Neurosci. **15** (2021). https://doi.org/10.3389/fnhum.2021.716670
7. Kim, H.E., et al.: Changes in cancer detection and false-positive recall in mammography using artificial intelligence: a retrospective, multireader study. Lancet Digital Health **2**(3), e138–e148 (2020)
8. Kokhlikyan, N., et al.: Captum: a unified and generic model interpretability library for PyTorch. arXiv preprint arXiv:2009.07896 (2020)
9. Linardatos, P., Papastefanopoulos, V., Kotsiantis, S.: Explainable AI: a review of machine learning interpretability methods. Entropy **23**(1), 18 (2020)
10. Lundberg, S.: A unified approach to interpreting model predictions. arXiv preprint arXiv:1705.07874 (2017)
11. McKinney, S.M., et al.: International evaluation of an AI system for breast cancer screening. Nature **577**(7788), 89–94 (2020)
12. MedlinePlus: Neuromuscular disorders. https://medlineplus.gov/neuromusculardisorders.html
13. Menardi, G., Torelli, N.: Training and assessing classification rules with imbalanced data. Data Min. Knowl. Disc. **28**, 92–122 (2014)
14. Multari, S., Özçelik, R., Mazzolari, A., Nobile, M.S., Grisoni, F.: Predicting metabolic reactions with a molecular transformer for drug design optimization. In: 2024 IEEE Conference on Computational Intelligence in Bioinformatics and Computational Biology (CIBCB), pp. 1–8. IEEE (2024)
15. Nobile, M.S., et al.: Unsupervised neural networks as a support tool for pathology diagnosis in MALDI-MSI experiments: a case study on thyroid biopsies. Expert Syst. Appl. **215**, 119296 (2023)
16. Papetti, D.M.: An accurate and time-efficient deep learning-based system for automated segmentation and reporting of cardiac magnetic resonance-detected ischemic scar. Comput. Methods Programs Biomed. **229**, 107321 (2023)
17. Piñeros-Fernández, M.C.: Artificial intelligence applications in the diagnosis of neuromuscular diseases: a narrative review. Cureus **15**(11) (2023)
18. Pizer, S.M., et al.: Adaptive histogram equalization and its variations. Comput. Vis. Graph. Image Process. **39**(3), 355–368 (1987). https://doi.org/10.1016/S0734-189X(87)80186-X

19. Radiopaedia: MRI sequences (overview). https://radiopaedia.org/articles/mri-sequences-overview
20. Rizzo, M., Marcuzzo, M., Zangari, A., Schiavinato, M., Albarelli, A., Gasparetto, A.: Stop overkilling simple tasks with black-box models, use more transparent models instead. In: Wallraven, C., Liu, C.L., Ross, A. (eds.) Pattern Recognition and Artificial Intelligence, pp. 279–293. Springer, Singapore (2025)
21. Rizzo, M., Veneri, A., Albarelli, A., Lucchese, C., Nobile, M., Conati, C.: A theoretical framework for AI models explainability with application in biomedicine. In: 2023 IEEE Conference on Computational Intelligence in Bioinformatics and Computational Biology (CIBCB), pp. 1–9 (2023). https://doi.org/10.1109/CIBCB56990.2023.10264877
22. Selvaraju, R.R., Cogswell, M., Das, A., Vedantam, R., Parikh, D., Batra, D.: Grad-cam: visual explanations from deep networks via gradient-based localization. In: Proceedings of the IEEE International Conference on Computer Vision, pp. 618–626 (2017)
23. Soroski, T., et al.: Differentiating memory clinic patients and healthy volunteers using machine-learning analysis of speech and eye movements during a reading task. Alzheimer's Dementia **17**(S6), e055717 (2021). https://doi.org/10.1002/alz.055717
24. Velden, B.H., Kuijf, H.J., Gilhuijs, K.G., Viergever, M.A.: Explainable artificial intelligence (XAI) in deep learning-based medical image analysis. Med. Image Anal. **79**, 102470 (2022)
25. Verdú-Díaz, J., et al.: Accuracy of a machine learning muscle MRI-based tool for the diagnosis of muscular dystrophies. Neurology **94**(10), e1094–e1102 (2020)
26. Vora, L.K., Gholap, A.D., Jetha, K., Thakur, R.R.S., Solanki, H.K., Chavda, V.P.: Artificial intelligence in pharmaceutical technology and drug delivery design. Pharmaceutics **15**(7), 1916 (2023)
27. Yang, M., et al.: A deep learning model for diagnosing dystrophinopathies on thigh muscle MRI images. BMC Neurol. **21**, 1–9 (2021)
28. Zangari, A., Marcuzzo, M., Rizzo, M., Albarelli, A., Gasparetto, A.: Crossing the divide: designing layers of explainability. In: Rutkowski, L., Scherer, R., Korytkowski, M., Pedrycz, W., Tadeusiewicz, R., Zurada, J.M. (eds.) Artificial Intelligence and Soft Computing, pp. 253–265. Springer, Cham (2025)
29. Zeiler, M.D., Fergus, R.: Visualizing and understanding convolutional networks. In: Computer Vision–ECCV 2014: 13th European Conference, Zurich, Switzerland, September 6–12, 2014, Proceedings, Part I 13, pp. 818–833. Springer (2014)
30. Zhou, B., Khosla, A., Lapedriza, A., Oliva, A., Torralba, A.: Learning deep features for discriminative localization. In: Proceedings of the IEEE Conference on Computer Vision and Pattern Recognition, pp. 2921–2929 (2016)

**Open Access** This chapter is licensed under the terms of the Creative Commons Attribution 4.0 International License (http://creativecommons.org/licenses/by/4.0/), which permits use, sharing, adaptation, distribution and reproduction in any medium or format, as long as you give appropriate credit to the original author(s) and the source, provide a link to the Creative Commons license and indicate if changes were made.

The images or other third party material in this chapter are included in the chapter's Creative Commons license, unless indicated otherwise in a credit line to the material. If material is not included in the chapter's Creative Commons license and your intended use is not permitted by statutory regulation or exceeds the permitted use, you will need to obtain permission directly from the copyright holder.

# Author Index

**A**
Abbaspour Onari, Mohsen  316
Akila, Maram  3

**B**
Baer, Gregor  316
Bahamazava, Katsiaryna  380
Bich, Philippe  48
Braines, Dave  255

**C**
Cabitza, Federico  233
Cerquitelli, Tania  48
Chakraborty, Tanmay  139
Ciravegna, Gabriele  48
Cunnington, Dan  255

**D**
Davydko, Oleksandr  359
De Santis, Francesco  48
Di Noia, Tommaso  295
Di Sciascio, Eugenio  295
Domnich, Marharyta  210
Dorszewski, Teresa  28

**E**
Eckhoff, Magnus  281
Erogullari, Eren  68

**F**
Fasano, Giuseppe  295
Ferrara, Antonio  295
Frasson, Giada  423
Fregosi, Caterina  233
Furby, Jack  255

**G**
Giordano, Danilo  48
Grau, Isel  316

**H**
Haedecke, Elena  3
Hansen, Lars Kai  28
Holzapfel, Antonia  90

**I**
Ibs, Inga  162

**J**
Jenssen, Robert  28

**K**
Kackovic, Monika  115
Karagoz, Gizem  337

**L**
Lapuschkin, Sebastian  68
Lombardi, Angela  295
Longo, Luca  359
Lupi, Amalia  423

**M**
Marinelli, Ryan  281
Meratnia, Nirvana  337
Moreira, Catarina  402

**N**
Nasir, Basma  402
Nawaz, Muhammad  402
Nobile, Marco S.  316
Nobile, Marco Salvatore  423

© The Editor(s) (if applicable) and The Author(s), under exclusive license to Springer Nature Switzerland AG 2026
R. Guidotti et al. (Eds.): xAI 2025, CCIS 2576, pp. 449–450, 2026.
https://doi.org/10.1007/978-3-032-08317-3

**O**
O'Reilly, Ruairi   380
Ozcelebi, Tanir   337

**P**
Pahde, Frederik   68
Palmirani, Monica   185
Pavlov, Vladimir   359
Posada Moreno, Andres Felipe   90
Preece, Alun   255

**Q**
Quaia, Emilio   423

**R**
Rizzo, Matteo   423
Rothkopf, Constantin A.   162

**S**
Samek, Wojciech   68
Saou, Youssef   115
Sapienza, Salvatore   185
Sauka, Kudzai   115
Seifert, Christin   139
Situmeang, Frederik B. I.   115

**T**
Tětková, Lenka   28
Trimpe, Sebastian   90
Tulver, Kadi   210

**V**
Välja, Julius   210
Veski, Rasmus Moorits   210
Vicente, Lucia   233
Vicente, Raul   210
von Rueden, Laura   3

**W**
Wickstrøm, Kristoffer Knutsen   28
Wirth, Christian   139

**Z**
Zhang, Chao   316
Zhang, Yingqian   316
Zia, Tehseen   402

Made in the USA
Monee, IL
04 May 2026

49490776R00260